Arts & Crafts Style

Arts & Crafts Style

Isabelle Anscombe

Φ

Phaidon Press Limited
Regent's Wharf
All Saints Street
London N1 9PA

First published 1991
First paperback edition 1996
© 1991 Phaidon Press Limited
Text © 1991 Isabelle Anscombe

ISBN
0 7148 2614 6 (hardback)
0 7148 3469 6 (paperback)

A CIP catalogue record for this book is available
from the British Library

Printed in Hong Kong

Jacket illustrations: Front cover from left to
right, details of *La Dame aux Camelias*, poster by
Alphonse Mucha, Historisches Museum der Stadt,
Vienna (p. 160); 'Cockatoo and Pomegranate',
hand-printed wallpaper designed in 1899 by
Walter Crane and manufactured by Jeffrey and
Co., Whitworth Art Gallery, Manchester (p. 57);
Pomona, tapestry designed in *c.* 1890 by William
Morris with figures by Edward Burne-Jones,
made by Morris and Co., Whitworth Art Gallery,
Manchester; *Emilie Flöge*, painted in 1902 by
Gustav Klimt, Historisches Museum der Stadt,
Vienna (p. 159): Back cover from left to right,
details of *La Belle Iseult*, painted in 1858 by
William Morris, Tate Gallery, London (p. 148);
Flora, tapestry designed in *c.* 1890 by William
Morris with figures by Edward Burne-Jones,
made by Morris and Co., Whitworth Art Gallery,
Manchester; woven silk 'Butterfly' brocade,
designed in *c.* 1874 by E. W. Godwin, Victoria
& Albert Museum, London (p. 78); 'Blue Fruit',
wallpaper designed in the late nineteenth
century by William Morris, Victoria & Albert
Museum, London (p. 117): Spine, detail of
woven silk, wool and cotton double cloth,
designed in 1898 by Lindsay P. Butterfield for
Alexander Morton and Co., Victoria & Albert
Museum, London (p. 185).

Frontispiece: Watercolour copy of an original
painting by Edward Burne-Jones's studio
assistant, Thomas Mathews Rooke, of *The Dining
Room at The Grange* (Burne-Jones's house), 1904,
furnished with a table by Philip Webb made at the
time of Burne-Jones's marriage in 1860, a Morris
and Co. 'Sussex' chair, a painted sideboard and two
stained glass panels of minstrel figures.

Part openers: Wallpapers designed by Archibald
Knox, hand-printed by Alexander Beauchamp ©.

Contents

Introduction

'The devotees of this creed,' wrote the art critic and painter Roger Fry of the Arts and Crafts movement in 1926, 'cultivated the exotic and precious with all the energy and determination of a dominant class. With the admirable self-assurance which this position gave them they defied ribaldry and flouted common sense. They had the courage of their affectations; they openly admitted to being "intense".' The products of the Arts and Crafts movement were indeed deliberately and selfconsciously artistic – a vital expression of the individuality of the craftsmen and women who made them – yet, for many of its devotees (such as A. H. Mackmurdo, who saw the movement 'not as an aesthetic excursion; but as a mighty upheaval of man's spiritual nature'), it was far more than a mere style: it was a way of life.

The Arts and Crafts movement had its beginnings in the mid-Victorian reaction to the squalor, ugliness and inequalities caused by industrialization. It was a search, at times almost a sacred quest, for a supposed return to quiet beauty, simplicity and honesty, to 'olde English' hospitality and a sense of nationality, that found expression initially through a revival of the style and 'manners' of the medieval period, and then through the day-to-day experience of a craft workshop. As the young Pre-Raphaelite painter Edward Burne-Jones once said, it was a matter of venturing 'all on the unseen', as in some Arthurian romance.

Architecture and the decorative arts were seen as a reflection of the health of a society: no wonder, so the argument went, that a people who can tolerate furnishings and public buildings created out of a mishmash of half-understood past styles, using materials totally unsuited to their purposes, have to endure working-class agitation, riots and other such signs of misery and confusion. Many shared A. H. Mackmurdo's view on the relationship between industrialization and class relations: 'All interest and joy in the work having gone, the man's interest gravitates to his wage. These working men become known . . . not as individuals, but as a class . . . with somewhat disturbing results to the community.'

In the 1880s the designers who allied themselves to the Arts and Crafts movement set out to subvert the contemporary tendency to use art as a means of signifying grandeur and power, and to propagandize a visual democracy of humble, plain, honest furniture. What had once been considered minor household arts became the decorative arts, which, together with architecture,

Left: Liberty and Co. ebonized chair similar to their 'Thebes' stool

Above: Silver kettle on a stand and a lidded cup designed by C.R. Ashbee for the Guild of Handicraft

now took their place beside painting and sculpture. Just as John Ruskin had perceived the work of the masons who carved the gargoyles and stonework of the medieval cathedrals to be an expression of their individual humanity, so the guildsmen of the Arts and Crafts movement saw craft practice as a celebration of the expressive potential that lay within even the most humble worker.

It was but a short step from self-expression to the recognition of the legitimate rights of the workers, and many designers followed William Morris along the path of socialism. In setting up the Guild of Handicraft, C. R. Ashbee's avowed aim was no less than 'the destruction of the commercial system, to discredit it, undermine it, overthrow it'. Followers of the Arts and Crafts movement passionately believed that the only way to quell working-class unrest was to create working conditions that would restore the worker's dignity and give him satisfaction in his labour. These conditions were

to be found by looking back to the medieval guild system which had existed in harmony with traditional, largely rural communities. The new socialist Utopia was to be established on the basis of the craft guild. As C. R. Ashbee wrote in 1908, even after the failure of his own Guild: 'Industrial machinery is now finding its limitation, and therefore a new political era is beginning.'

Although not all Arts and Crafts designers rejected the use of the machine, few believed in the Victorian doctrine of progress, of a future made increasingly perfect by technological advance. Within the workshop, the machine must not dictate to the craftsman, nor limit his expressive freedom: the true purpose of the craft workshop was, according to Gustav Stickley, 'not the work itself, so much as the making of the man; the soul-stuff of a man is the product of work, and it is good, indifferent or bad, as is his work.' This led some craftsmen to adopt an almost artificial crudeness in the style of their work, and some writers to adopt an

anti-intellectual stance in their critical appreciation of Arts and Crafts products. As the American writer and architect Charles Fletcher Lummis put it: 'Any fool can write a book but it takes a man to dovetail a door.'

But the Arts and Crafts movement remained a middle-class revolution. It affected the taste and buying habits of middle-class consumers, who were taught to display their taste and sensibility by redecorating their houses with 'Art' furnishings. And, by making art respectable and even worthy, it allowed many young gentlemen to reject careers in law or banking in favour of architecture or workshop experience, and hundreds of ladies to earn money from their handiwork.

The movement was predominantly British; only in America was it directly copied, adapted and continued into parallel traditions. On the Continent, designers were inspired by the movement's ideals but did not necessarily follow its style. Indeed, there is no single recognizable style that was Arts and Crafts. An interior could be exotic and precious, with rich colours and patterns, or whimsical and self-consciously artistic, or downright plain and homely. Proportion, simplicity of form, fitness for purpose, honesty to materials, the revival of 'lost' craft techniques and the enhancement of natural textures are all elements which, added to hand-craftsmanship, combined to create the Arts and Crafts style. To the Victorian generation, brought up on cabriole legs, cut glass and ormolu decoration, however, such simple, honest furniture must have seemed daringly innovative; and the social aims of the movement, too, were almost frighteningly liberal.

Part One

COHERENCE OUT OF CHAOS

The Search for a New Style

The Great Exhibition – the world's first-ever international exhibition – was held in Joseph Paxton's Crystal Palace in Hyde Park, London, in 1851. There were thousands of exhibitors, and the event was an unabashed celebration of British wealth, power and know-how, designed as a showcase for the artistic prowess of a great imperial and industrial nation: 'a marvellous, stirring, bewildering sight – a mixture of a genii palace, and a mighty bazaar', thus Charlotte Brontë described her impressions. It made a vast profit, and successfully distracted the British people from the political and industrial unrest of the previous decade; yet not everyone agreed on its splendour. Edward Burne-Jones, for example, described the 'gigantic weariness' of the Crystal Palace, and John Ruskin saw it merely as 'a greenhouse larger than had ever been built before'.

Certainly, in their desire to outdo one another in luxury and ingenuity, manufacturers of furniture, ceramics, textiles and other decorative artefacts attained new heights of vulgarity, imitating every conceivable period and style, and often combining several in one object: the majority of exhibits were met with cries of outraged good taste.

Revivals of past styles had been popular since the beginning of the century – for example, Horace Walpole's Strawberry Hill Gothick, Sir Walter Scott's great hall at Abbotsford, Sir Charles Barry's Gothic designs for the Houses of Parliament or Anthony Salvin's Elizabethan revival houses – but these had usually tended to be carefree, with little attempt to puzzle out the original grammar of a period. Gradually, however, the spirit of the age was brought to bear on such levity, and greater knowledge and understanding were insisted upon.

In *The Grammar of Ornament*, published in 1856, Owen Jones, one of the critics of the Great Exhibition, attempted an overview of the principles that underlay different national and historical styles. The notion of principles of design caught the imagination of a public sold on the doctrine of progress based on discoverable scientific laws. Even the official Government Schools of Design were reformed according to these new ideas by Henry Cole, who had assisted Prince Albert in the organization of the 1851 Exhibition. Design, said Cole and his followers, was like science, and the job of designing a carpet or table-cloth well should be a matter merely of discovering the correct principles and applying them. In 1857 Cole established a new Museum of Manufactures,

The gallery overlooking the entrance hall at 8 Addison Road, Holland Park, London, designed by Halsey Ricardo in 1907 for Ernest Debenham

Frederic E. Church's
Moorish-style Court Hall at
'Olana', built in the 1880s
above the Hudson River,
New York State

renamed the Victoria and Albert Museum in 1899, to provide a study collection of both historical and approved contemporary artefacts for commercial designers.

As the century progressed, designers and manufacturers made greater efforts to be exact in their imitations. Owen Jones had popularized Moorish architecture in his *Plans, Elevations, Sections and Details of the Alhambra*, (1836-45), and his designs for furniture for Jackson and Graham, and for wallpapers, silks and carpets, were based on Renaissance or Moorish styles. In the 1870s in New York, cabinet-makers such as Anthony Roux or Kimbel and Cabus made Renaissance revival furniture, and the Renaissance revival style of the architectural firm McKim, Mead and White remained popular.

A desire for novelty or the exotic ensured that revivalism remained a potent force, especially in public rooms and buildings such as hotels. Louis Comfort Tiffany created rooms in the Moorish style; the slightly erotic classicism of Lawrence Alma-Tadema's paintings received popular acclaim; the 'archaeological' jewellery of Castellani or Carlo Giuliano created a new fashion; while the craze for Japonisme swept both America and Europe. Certain individuals were drawn to specific cultures: William Morris collected Islamic arts from Persia, Turkey and Spain, William de Morgan drew heavily on Persian originals in his ceramics, Christopher Dresser often employed Egyptian motifs in his furniture, while the Manx artist Archibald Knox led a revival of interest in Celtic forms.

Artists especially appreciated the bohemian aspect of romantic foreign cultures –

Frederic, Lord Leighton, created his Moorish hall in Holland Park in the 1860s, while in the 1870s the American painter Frederic E. Church built himself a Persian palace, named Olana, on a hilltop overlooking the Hudson River. Revivalism remained a vital element in architecture and design well into the twentieth century.

But while critics of design reacted to the lavish vulgarity of the Great Exhibition with demands that designers become more scholarly in their approach to historical sources, social critics insisted that they adopt one coherent, national style, to suit the age and, moreover, symbolically unify and heal a fragmented nation 'at once destitute of faith and terrified at scepticism', as Thomas Carlyle had written in 1836.

One suggestion for a fitting national style had already been forcefully put forward in the 1830s by a young draughtsman, still only in his mid-twenties, who had recently converted to Catholicism – Augustus Welby Northmore Pugin. The Catholic Emancipation of 1829 and the Oxford Movement of the 1830s had fostered interest in the ceremonial and ritual practices of pre-Reformation days and encouraged nostalgia for the Middle Ages. To Pugin, the medieval cathedral symbolized a sense of community lacking in modern times: 'Catholic England was merry England,' he wrote in 1841, 'at least for the humbler classes; and the architecture was in keeping with the faith and manners of the times – at once strong and hospitable.' In 1836 he published *Contrasts; or a Parallel between the Noble Edifices of the Middle Ages and the corresponding Buildings of the Present Day: showing the Present Decay of Taste*, a frankly

Illustration from A.W.N. Pugin's *Contrasts*, 1836, showing the 'Present Decay in Taste'

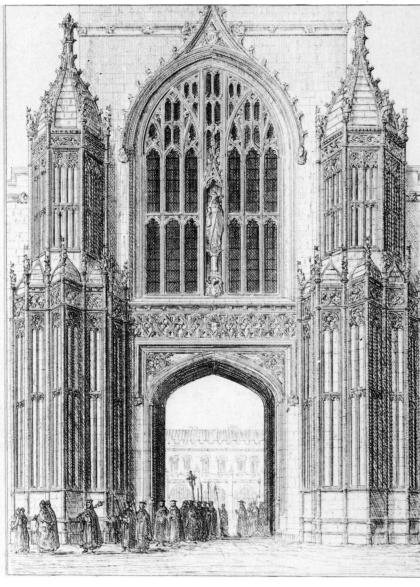

propagandist pamphlet which advocated Gothic as the most apt symbol of both national and spiritual cohesion.

In the flurry of articles which appeared in the wake of the Great Exhibition, Gothic emerged as the front-runner for a national style. It was now also championed by a Protestant, John Ruskin, who saw Gothic as expressive of the craftsman's freedom within an earlier benign, but now lost, social order; its regeneration would restore social harmony in a country riddled with class conflict. His influential books, *The Seven Lamps of Architecture* (1849) and *The Stones of Venice* (1851 and 1853), described how moral regeneration was to be brought about through craftsmanship, which he saw as a form of labour based on nature not the machine. Not surprisingly, he and others, including such redoubtable figures as Charles Dickens, exploded in anger at the principles of design put forward by Henry Cole or Owen Jones, seeing them as allied to those very products of science – the mills and factories – that had produced social unrest.

The most important of Cole and Jones's principles was conventionalization, and its greatest champion was the botanist-turned-designer, Dr Christopher Dresser. His motto was 'Knowledge is Power', and he believed that the more knowledge – whether of botany or historical sources – a designer brought to his work, the more truthful, and therefore uplifting, the finished design would be. At only twenty-two, he had contributed a plate to Owen Jones's *Grammar of Ornament* showing 'several varieties of flowers, in plan and elevation, from which it will be seen that the basis of all form is geometry'. He lectured in the Schools of Design, teaching that conventionalized design should be based on the underlying geometry of strict botanical truth.

But Ruskin passionately denied that such a regimented set of rules could ever be mistaken for art. Conventionalization, he said, cut the designer or craftsman off from 'natural delight' and that all-important freedom of expression which Ruskin found most potently in the medieval cathedrals. 'In all things that live there are certain irregularities and deficiencies which are not only signs of life, but sources of beauty,' he wrote in 1853 in his famous essay on *The Nature of Gothic*. 'No human face is exactly the same in its lines on each side, no leaf perfect in its lines, no branch in its symmetry. All admit irregularity as they imply change; and to banish imperfection is to destroy perfection, to check exertion, to paralyze vitality.'

In many key respects, such as an acceptance of two-dimensional pattern or the absence of applied, non-structural ornament, the end-products created by the followers of conventionalization differed little from work later produced by the Arts and Crafts designers who took Pugin and Ruskin's oratory to heart. But the principles championed by Cole, Jones or Dresser were anathema to Morris and his followers. Conventionalization supported the belief in scientific progress, which was also used to vindicate the economic doctrine of *laissez-faire* that had led to unrestrained industrialization, squalor and working-class unrest – the very ills that the adoption of Gothic as a national style had set out to defeat. With the writings of Pugin and Ruskin, revivalism became no longer simply a matter of style, but a burning question of moral regeneration.

Drawing by John Ruskin from his book *The Seven Lamps of Architecture*, published in 1849

The Choice of Gothic

The Gothic Revival swiftly took hold of the popular imagination, fuelled not only by the writings of Pugin and Ruskin, but also by the stirring tales of chivalry recounted by Sir Walter Scott in novels such as *Ivanhoe* or *Redgauntlet*, by the publicity given to the Eglinton Tournament of 1839 (an aristocratic re-enactment of jousting), and by the romantic images of the Pre-Raphaelites who painted Tennysonian heroines and Arthurian knights with gem-like intensity. Indeed, the notion of the creation of a contemporary Camelot remained current until the First World War, with medieval chivalry being allied first to a concern for the poor and oppressed, then, more poignantly, to an officer's responsibility for his men in the trenches. Philanthropy of this nature, allied to Ruskin's argument that it was vital for society that workers should be craftsmen, finding self-expression in their daily toil, and ultimately linked by Morris to socialism, became a central facet of the Arts and Crafts movement: good design should benefit both those who made an object and those who used it.

For Pugin, the Gothic Revival meant literally that — the accurate re-creation of a medieval England infused with the awe-inspiring mysteries of early religious practice. The interest of Catholics such as he in medieval ceremony and ritual led to a demand for furniture and equipment such as chalices, monstrances, pastoral staffs, crosses and candlesticks to replace those lost during the Reformation, and Pugin set about reviving 'lost' craft techniques for ecclesiastical metalwork, stained glass, tiles and embroidery. He had in fact made his first designs for metalwork when he was only fifteen; his earliest designs for furniture, working-drawings for Gothic furniture for Windsor Castle, had been made for his father, Augustus Charles Pugin, an architectural draughtsman. These first efforts were based on his father's work in the Regency Gothic style, and were largely fanciful, but, after a study of medieval originals, his ideas became radically more simple, following as closely as possible the structure and grammar of the original style.

In 1837, two years after his conversion to Catholicism, the twenty-five-year-old Pugin received his first major architectural commission, the remodelling of Scarisbrick Hall in Lancashire as 'a standing illustration of good old English hospitality', for the wealthy landowner, Charles Scarisbrick. Pugin, himself a great collector of antiquities, also furnished the house with 'ancient'

The Royal Gallery in the Palace of Westminster, London, with interior decoration and furnishings by A.W.N. Pugin

furniture and carvings which he imported from Europe. Like many of his major commissions, including Alton Towers, Staffordshire, and Abney Hall, Cheshire, that for Scarisbrick Hall came from a Catholic patron. But his most famous work was for the Palace of Westminster, rebuilt by Sir Charles Barry after the fire of 1834. Pugin had first been commissioned by Barry in 1836 to execute his drawings for the competition to rebuild the Palace, and later to make estimate drawings. By June 1844, when Barry employed him to design the interiors, Pugin was acknowledged as the foremost expert in Gothic.

A recent inventory of his surviving furniture in the House of Lords has revealed Pugin's astonishing creativity. Between 1844 and his death in 1852, he designed over one thousand pieces, including forty-nine different types of armchair and one hundred different tables. Many of the differences between pieces were intended to signify rank and dignity, a vital element in Pugin's medieval world. He believed that all decoration should be meaningful, and further, that 'all ornament should consist of enrichment of the essential construction'. He also held that nature should provide the basis of ornament, but rejected Ruskin's naturalism in favour of an architectural interpretation of structure. In his furniture designs, made by Gillow's of Lancaster and J. G. Crace and Son, Pugin relied upon the strong outlines of revealed construction, such as curved cross braces, enhanced simply by chamfered decoration, revealed tenons or geometric inlays.

After a period of insanity, possibly brought on by overwork, Pugin died aged forty in 1852. He had worked without assistants, and had produced nine major books and endless sketches of medieval buildings, as well as thousands of drawings for furniture, mouldings, brass door furniture, fireplaces, stained glass, tiles, curtains, jewellery, even inkpots. The richness and vision of Pugin's designs, allied to his belief that society itself would be healed by such architecture and interiors, cemented Gothic powerfully in the popular imagination, and many younger architects emulated the visual coherence of his style and were influenced by his ideas on the relationship between nature, religious symbolism and aesthetics.

In the mid-nineteenth century there were no full-time schools of architecture, and pupils learnt from their masters and by studying historical models. Gothic was now interpreted in a variety of ways, from Alfred Waterhouse's 'municipal palaces', such as Manchester Town Hall or the Natural History Museum in South Kensington, to the Venetian Gothic of Sir George Gilbert Scott's St Pancras Station; from William Butterfield's stately church furnishings to the more eclectic church silver and metalwork of Henry Wilson and John Paul Cooper at the turn of the century.

The writings of the celebrated French architectural historian, Eugène Viollet-le-Duc, who had been responsible for the restoration of several important sites in France, including Notre Dame in Paris and the ramparts of Carcassonne, regenerated interest in medieval French architecture. Like Ruskin and Pugin, he believed that design began with interior spaces, not exterior style. In 1853 Ruskin wrote in *The*

The Natural History Museum in South Kensington by Alfred Waterhouse, built between 1873 and 1881

Nature of Gothic: 'It is one of the chief virtues of Gothic builders, that they never suffered ideas of outside symmetries and consistencies to interfere with the real use and value of what they did. If they wanted a window, they opened one; a room, they added one; a buttress, they built one; utterly regardless of any established conventionalities of external appearance. . . .'

For architects such as Philip Webb or Frank Lloyd Wright, this teaching, allied to a belief in the primacy of nature as a source for ornament, supplied the basis of their 'organic' style of building; for Hector Guimard and Emile Gallé in France or Victor Horta in Belgium, this interpretation of Gothic directly inspired Art Nouveau.

But in the 1850s and 1860s perhaps the most important offshoot of the Gothic Revival was the regeneration of medieval craft techniques, which thrived as the study of medieval originals became more detailed and scholarly. With the development of the Arts and Crafts movement, this revival of traditional methods was allied to the Ruskinian ideal of a craftsman's way of life, that of living simply, close to the land, and in harmony with the raw materials of his trade, far from industrial machinery or the artificial bustle of the city. It began, however, in the desire to re-create the lost richness and beauty of the ancient cathedrals.

In 1837 Pugin had persuaded John Hardman, a fellow Catholic who ran his family's button-making business in Birmingham, to set up a firm of church furnishers and 'Medieval Metalworkers' producing jewellery, ecclesiastical metalwork, stained glass, embroidery and also painted decoration to Pugin's designs. With Hardman, Pugin pioneered the rediscovery of the medieval methods employed in making ecclesiastical stained glass. With another friend, Herbert Minton, he also contributed to the revival of the Cistercian technique of making encaustic floor tiles; from 1840 thousands of tiles, based on medieval originals, were made to Pugin's designs by Minton and Co. of Stoke-on-Trent and used in churches, country houses, town halls and other public buildings.

The man most closely associated with the revival of ecclesiastical embroidery was the architect George Edmund Street. Street had trained in the office of Gilbert Scott, and was associated with the powerful Anglican Ecclesiological Society. He became Professor of Architecture at the Royal Academy, and many influential architects trained in his office, including J. D. Sedding, Philip Webb and Richard Norman Shaw. Street's early embroidery designs for altar frontals, sedilia hangings, copes and other vestments used appliquéd motifs, including monograms, crosses and floral designs copied from fifteenth-century models and were executed by Jones and Willis of Birmingham. When exhibited in 1851 they received much attention and were often imitated. William Morris and Philip Webb, whom Morris met during the nine months he spent in Street's office in 1856, both became embroidery enthusiasts. In the mid-1850s Street's sister was a founding member of the Ladies' Ecclesiastical Embroidery Society, which undertook many of her brother's commissions, as did the Leek Embroidery Society, founded in 1879 by Elizabeth Wardle, the wife of

Oak cabinet designed by J.P. Seddon for Morris and Co., 1861, inlaid with various woods and painted by Ford Madox Brown, Edward Burne-Jones, William Morris and Dante Gabriel Rossetti with scenes based on the honeymoon of King René of Anjou. Victoria & Albert Museum, London

Oak table designed by Philip Webb, c.1868, for Major Gillum, one of Webb's earliest patrons, showing the influence of Japanese furniture

depicted in their paintings, and their interest in medieval furnishings led directly to the foundation of Morris, Marshall, Faulkner and Co. at 8 Red Lion Square in April 1861 (the firm was renamed Morris and Co. in 1875 when it was reorganized with Morris as sole proprietor). Several of their early pieces of painted furniture were exhibited in 1862 at the 'Medieval Court' laid out by William Burges for the Ecclesiological Society at the International Exhibition at South Kensington.

There had been a Medieval Court at the 1851 Exhibition, almost exclusively designed by Pugin and executed by Hardman's. In 1862, however, furniture by many different architects and painters was included. Burges himself showed six pieces; there were many examples of church furnishings by G. E. Street and others, Norman Shaw contributed a carved and painted bookcase, and J. P. Seddon exhibited an inlaid roll-top desk and the 'King René's Honeymoon' cabinet, with panels painted by Dante Gabriel Rossetti, Ford Madox Brown, Burne-Jones and Morris after Walter Scott's account of the honeymoon of King René of Anjou.

Morris, Marshall, Faulkner and Co., exhibiting for the first time, showed a variety of pieces of furniture, designed by Philip Webb, Rossetti and Madox Brown and decorated by Burne-Jones, Rossetti, Madox Brown and Morris, as well as embroidery, tiles and metalwork. The firm's contribution won them two gold medals and was commended by the jury for the 'exactness of the imitation' of the medieval manner. Seven stained-glass panels designed by Rossetti to illustrate 'The Parable of the

William Morris's associate Thomas Wardle, who owned silk mills at Leek in Staffordshire. Wardle, who had helped Morris with his early experiments in dyeing, also printed silks and cottons especially for embroidery.

In 1872, when the Royal School of Art Needlework was founded in London, the revival of embroidery as an art, not just a ladylike pastime, was complete. Many leading Arts and Crafts designers – Edward Burne-Jones, William Morris, Walter Crane, Selwyn Image – supplied embroidery designs for a wide variety of domestic purposes to be worked by the ladies associated with the School, and the high standards of their work, which was exhibited in Europe and America, inspired many followers.

The painted furniture and interiors of the Middle Ages were also revived, although often fancifully. The Pre-Raphaelite painters, for instance, were tempted to construct the romantic painted chests and cabinets

Vineyard' and made by James Powell and Sons of Whitefriars caught the attention of the ecclesiastical architect George Frederick Bodley, and led to the firm's most important early commissions.

Bodley, like Street, was a pupil of Gilbert Scott, and also a friend of Philip Webb. He belonged to the new generation that believed an architect should be concerned with every detail of a building, providing a complete scheme of decoration. Bodley in particular used painted decoration for interior walls and roofs, employing bright primary colours to add richness and harmony: '. . . imbue your building to your utmost with refined beauty and restrained power,' he said in an address to the students of the Royal Academy in 1885. 'Little and infrequent touches of beauty, if they must be few, grafted, as it were, on to a well-proportioned fabric, will give a building a tender grace, and it will be a delight to all passers-by. Be not afraid of beauty and richness when you can get it.'

Morris, Marshall, Faulkner and Co. were only too happy to provide such touches of beauty and richness. One of the firm's earliest commissions was from Bodley for a tiled fireplace in the hall of Queens' College, Cambridge, which Bodley was restoring, and two other commissions from Cambridge followed: stained glass for All Saints' Church in Jesus Lane and painted ceiling decoration for Jesus College Chapel.

In the 1860s Morris's firm was probably best known for its ecclesiastical stained glass, and supplied windows for many of the churches Bodley was building or restoring. Rossetti and the young and inexperienced Burne-Jones had first been introduced to Powell's in 1857 as designers of cartoons for stained glass by Charles Winston, a lawyer and amateur archaeologist, who, with William Warrington, had published *An Inquiry into the Difference of Style observable in Ancient Glass Paintings, especially in England: with Hints on Glass Painting* in 1847. Winston was an adviser to Powell's, and had experimented with them in re-creating the original, rough and uneven medieval 'pot metal' glass. Morris and his colleagues continued to research traditional methods with glass supplied by Powell's, using strong colours and simple construction. Initially Rossetti, Burne-Jones, Madox Brown and Morris all designed cartoons for windows, with Morris in charge of colouring and Webb responsible for their arrangement. In the 1870s, when Burne-Jones took over sole charge of the firm's glass design, they began to produce domestic, secular designs, often based on tales from Chaucer or Malory.

Bodley later broke completely with Morris and Co. after the Society for the Protection of Ancient Buildings (known as 'Anti-Scrape'), of which Morris and Webb were founding members, criticized some of his church restorations. However, he had already established his own 'Art' decorating firm, Watts and Co. in Baker Street, in 1874, with fellow architects Thomas Garner and G. G. Scott, junior, to produce wallpapers, embroidery and church silver.

By the late 1870s Morris and Co.'s commercial success had come to rest mainly on the wallpapers and textiles designed by Morris himself, and the earlier, Gothic mood of their productions was dissipated in the light mists of the Queen Anne revival. Nevertheless, both Morris and Webb's ideas

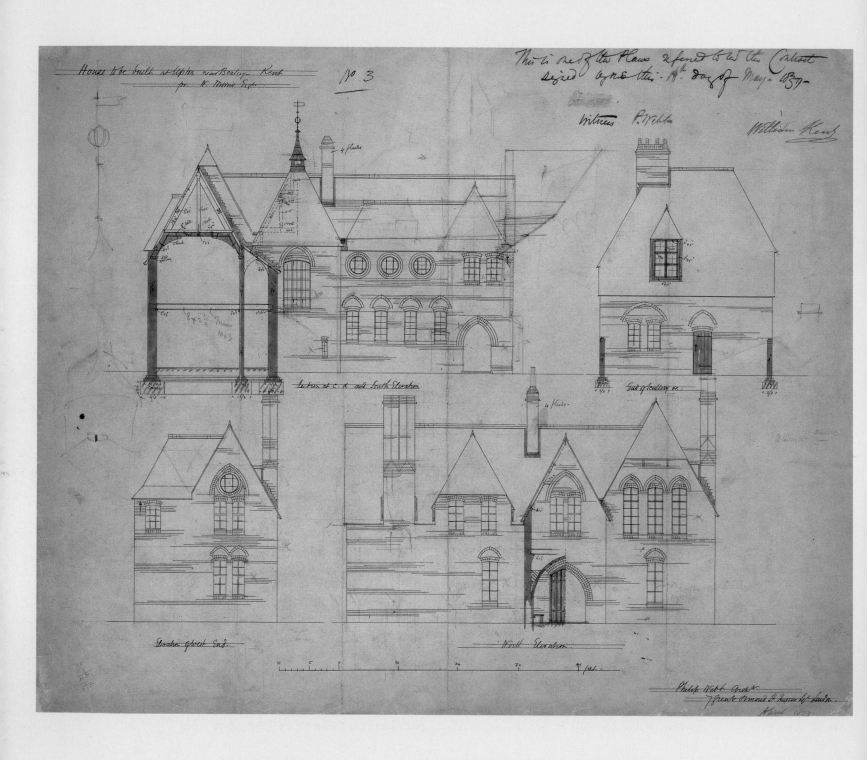

House to be built at Upton near Bexley — Kent
for W. Morris Esqr.

N° 3

This is one of the Plans refered to let the Contract
signed by me this 14th day of May 1859

Witness P. Webb

William Morris

Section at c. d. and South Elevation.

End of Scullery &c.

Elevation of West End.

North Elevation.

Philip Webb Archt.
7 Great Ormond St Queen Sq. London.
April 1859

about interiors and furniture had their beginnings in the romantic medieval dreams of their youth, and especially in Morris and Burne-Jones's youthful veneration for Malory's *Morte d'Arthur* – on which Morris's first book, *The Defence of Guenevere*, and his paintings in the Oxford Union, had been based. Morris and Webb's journeys in France together in the late 1850s, when they had visited French cathedrals and especially admired the great French tapestries, had inspired the ideas put into practice in the Red House, built by Webb for Morris's marriage in 1859. As Lewis F. Day later wrote of Morris: 'he did all he could to forget six centuries or so and make believe we were living in the Middle Ages – a feat impossible for most of us, but all of a piece with the childlike simple-mindedness of the man.'

Webb believed that architecture should be both 'barbaric' and 'commonplace', possessed of rude strength yet not over-artistic. Morris, too, in his ideas for furniture, appreciated both grandeur and simplicity, and later wrote, in a lecture entitled 'The Lesser Arts of Life', that there should be both 'work-a-day' tables and chairs and 'what I should call state furniture ... sideboards, cabinets and the like, which we have quite as much for beauty's sake as for use: we need not spare ornament on these, but may make them as elegant and as elaborate as we can with carving, inlaying or painting; these are the blossoms of the art of furniture.' After his first, early experiments with painted furniture, Morris left Webb in charge of the firm's furniture production, but Webb's early designs, in their simplicity and proportion, show a sophisticated understand-

Opposite: One of Philip Webb's plans for the Red House, built for William Morris at Upton near Bexley Heath, Kent in 1859–60. Victoria & Albert Museum, London

Bedroom suite in American black walnut with bird's eye maple veneer, by Daniel Pabst of Philadelphia, *c.*1875. Philadelphia Museum of Art

ing of the essential qualities of Gothic as first demonstrated by Pugin.

By the end of the 1860s the Gothic Revival, in both architecture and design, was being gradually absorbed into a less frankly imitative idiom of greater elegance and coherence, and some of the original emotional content of medieval romance was lost. In the designs of Bruce Talbert, for example, the revealed construction, the use of plain, unstained oak, and the added enrichment of mouldings and inset panels of the Gothic style were combined with the simplicity of strong horizontal and vertical forms and flat, naturalistic designs favoured by the new Anglo-Japanese taste of the early 1870s. Talbert, regarded in the 1860s as a leader in the field, designed textiles, carpets, metalwork, tapestries and wallpapers, as well as furniture for such firms as Jackson and Graham, Gillow's of Lancaster, J. G.

Illustration of a library bookcase designed by Charles L. Eastlake and executed by Jackson and Graham, from Eastlake's *Hints on Household Taste*

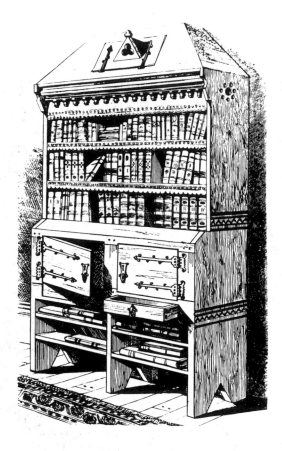

Crace of London, Marsh and Jones of Leeds, and Lamb's of Manchester. Some of his later pieces were in mahogany or satinwood, or ebonized, with stencilled or incised and gilded decoration in the prevailing Aesthetic style, but his earlier, often massive, furniture made of fumed oak, with tongue and groove planking, relief carving or prominent metal hinges, created a smart new secular style of Gothic. The intensity of the Gothic Revival as a national mission thus ebbed away, only to be replaced in the 1880s by the more overtly socialist aims of the Arts and Crafts movement.

Talbert published two influential design books, *Gothic Forms Applied to Furniture, Metal Work and Decoration for Domestic Purposes* in 1868, and *Examples of Ancient & Modern Furniture, Metalwork, Tapestries, Decoration & Etc.* in 1876. These books helped to export this new, modern form of Gothic to America, where it proved to be enormously popular. The prestigious New York cabinet-makers, Kimbel and Cabus, for example, began to make pieces similar to those illustrated in Talbert's books, with elaborate metal strap-hinges and incised gilded decoration, carved panels or inset tiles, while still producing grand Renaissance-style furniture.

Although few Americans espoused the medieval ideal with the intensity of Pugin or the romance of Rossetti or Morris, there were many who admired Ruskin's writings and who adopted Gothic as a symbol of reform, in rejection of the over-lavish vulgarity of the mid-century. In Philadelphia, for example, the architect Frank Furness and the furniture designer with whom he collaborated, Daniel Pabst, were both influenced by Owen Jones's books and by Christopher Dresser, who lectured in the city in 1876, and Pabst began to make furniture of modern Gothic form. In Boston, the architect Ralph Adams Cram, a founder member of the Boston Society of Arts and Crafts, worked in the Gothic style, as did Isaac Scott in Chicago. Whatever the beliefs and ideals of individual men, however, there was no Gothic Revival in America; Gothic never became a movement, evincing the passions it had in England, but remained merely a style.

Further, as this more refined form of Gothic became popular in the mid-1870s in

Opposite: 'The Pet' sideboard designed by Bruce Talbert and made by Gillow's, shown at the International Exhibition, London in 1873. Victoria & Albert Museum, London

both England and America, it melded with the new vogue for ebonized furniture, which derived from the Anglo-Japanese taste of the Aesthetic movement. In England, a commercial firm such as Collinson and Lock, in their catalogue of 'Artistic Furniture' for 1871, illustrated pieces (possibly designed by the architect T. E. Collcutt), in both the modern Gothic style and in ebonized cherry with incised gilt decoration. The prolific designer Charles Bevan also designed for various commercial firms from about 1865, and in 1872 he set up his own company, C. Bevan and Son, Designers, Wood Carvers and Manufacturers of Art Furniture. He employed distinctive conventionalized designs, not unlike those published by Christopher Dresser, in dark-coloured inlays against lighter woods, as well as producing ebonized pieces.

In America, the greatest popularizer of secular Gothic was Charles Locke Eastlake, nephew of the Royal Academy painter. In 1872 his book, *Hints on Household Taste*, originally serialized in *The Queen* magazine in 1865–6, first appeared in Boston (and over the next decade there were seven American editions). Here Eastlake gave advice on the choice of tiles, curtains, door furniture and other furnishings, rejecting the false principles of naturalistic patterning or ornate carving in favour of the honesty of designs 'based on the sound artistic principles of early tradition', by which he meant Gothic. The illustrations of his own designs for furniture show side-tables and bookcases in the modern Gothic style which were eagerly copied in America and further popularized by the Philadelphia Centennial Exposition in 1876.

By 1870 furniture manufacture in America had moved away from the eastern seaboard to the river and railway towns of the Midwest, such as Cincinnati, Ohio or Grand Rapids, Michigan, where newly equipped factories, with native ash, cherry and walnut, could respond to the changes in taste led by Eastlake's book. Charles Tisch in New York, the Cincinnati firm of Mitchell and Rammelsburg, and, in Chicago, the Tobey Furniture Company, all produced furniture in the modern Gothic style during the 1870s and 1880s, although, in later editions of *Hints on Household Taste*, Eastlake was at pains to deny authorship of such furniture.

The accurate re-creation of the medieval world desired by Pugin or Ruskin had been side-stepped, but images of Arthurian legend or noble chivalry remained current well into the present century, demonstrating the power that the Gothic ideal held in popular imagination as a symbol of all that was worthy and true in British institutions. In America, while elements of Pugin or Talbert lingered on in 'reform' furniture, revealing Europe's continuing influence upon American taste, Gothic held a somewhat distant appeal, overlaid as it was by the more local call of Henry David Thoreau, Ralph Waldo Emerson or Walt Whitman and the equally romantic values of the wild frontier spirit. In a country that had so recently fought a bitter civil war, the notion of a mere 'national style' providing a social panacea was a little far-fetched. It was only in England, at once so anxious to deny social unrest and so fearful of it, that such a complex and subtle ideology as Arts and Crafts could develop and flourish.

Ecclesiastical window designed by Edward Burne-Jones for Morris and Co.

maria soror aaron

STAINED GLASS

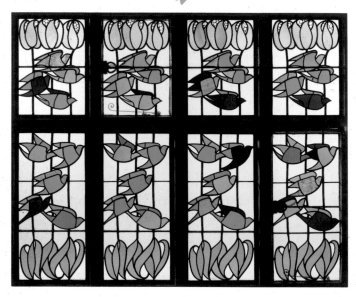

Leaded and stained glass window designed by M.H. Baillie Scott for a private house in Douglas, Isle of Man and (*opposite*) a window designed by L. C. Tiffany

Stained glass underwent a revolution in the nineteenth century in both technique and design. Initially, firms such as Hardman's, Clayton and Bell, Heaton, Butler and Bayne or Lavers, Barraud and Westlake, and individual designers such as William Wailes, of Newcastle, and Charles Eamer Kempe, made painted glass in the Gothic Revival style for the hundreds of churches being built or restored in the 1850s and 1860s, but with Morris and Co. the idea of using clear glass with painted detail in paler tones as part of a scheme of interior decoration was introduced.

Designers such as Henry Holiday, who supplied to Powell's, Christopher Whall, who lectured on stained glass at the Central School of Arts and Crafts and pioneered the use of 'slab' glass, or Harry Clarke in Ireland, brought more painterly qualities to their figure painting, but leaded glass came gradually to rely more on colour and texture than on painted decoration and, by the 1890s, was used not only in windows but also inset into doors and furniture.

In America, John La Farge and Louis Comfort Tiffany used layers of opalescent glass to create sumptuous, richly coloured windows with designs of flowers, exotic birds or shimmering skies which could not have been more different from the medieval-style windows made in England only thirty or forty years before.

M. H. Baillie Scott, Selwyn Image and Frank Brangwyn in England, E. A. Taylor and C. R. Mackintosh in Scotland, and Frank Lloyd Wright in America all designed leaded glass; in Europe, the Austrians Koloman Moser and Josef Hoffmann, the Belgian Victor Horta, the Frenchman Eugène Grasset and the Dutchman Jan Thorn Prikker also used coloured glass, generally with no painted detail whatsoever, or in strictly geometric designs, as part of their decorative schemes.

WILLIAM MORRIS

In his own lifetime William Morris (1834–96) was enormously influential: a busy, gregarious man, with wide-ranging interests, he was involved in many different causes, from the preservation of ancient buildings to revolutionary socialism. He is best known today for his textiles and wallpaper designs, but he also pioneered the revival of numerous techniques in crafts as diverse as the use of natural dyes and the design of typefaces, as well as being a prolific poet and writer, a tireless lecturer and a passionate Icelandic scholar.

He was born into a prosperous Walthamstow family in 1834 and educated at Marlborough and at Exeter College, Oxford. He intended at first to become a clergyman, but was already in love with the Middle Ages, through his avid reading of Sir Walter Scott and his wanderings among old churches, when he met Edward Burne-Jones and began to read Ruskin and Carlyle.

In 1856, following a trip to France with Burne-Jones when the two undergraduates decided to devote their lives to art, Morris entered the Oxford architectural office of G. E. Street, where he met Philip Webb. When Street moved to London later that year, Morris went too; he took rooms in Red Lion Square with Burne-Jones and they made their own heavy, painted furniture. Morris soon gave up architecture, and, inspired by a new friend, D. G. Rossetti, decided to become a painter.

It was in 1857, while they were working on the decorations for the Oxford Union based on Malory's *Morte d'Arthur* that Rossetti introduced Morris to a seventeen-year-old model he had discovered, Janey Burden, the daughter of a local stableman. She became Morris's 'glorious lady fair' and they were married in April 1859. They had two daughters, Jenny and May, but the relationship was not a happy one – she had a long affair with Rossetti – and this unaccustomed failure perplexed and saddened Morris throughout his life.

Edward Burne-Jones with William Morris at the Grange, Fulham, from an original photograph taken in the 1890s and (*opposite*) a page from an illuminated book of verse, *Lapse of the Year*, 1870, by William Morris

In 1877 Morris began his extensive programme of lectures on the decorative arts. He won over many young men to the cause of Arts and Crafts, and gradually came himself to see that the improvement of the decorative arts could not stop at romantic notions of re-creating the Middle Ages, but must lead on to real social change. In 1883, during his most prolific period as a designer, he became a socialist: he was a founding member of the Socialist League and first editor of *The Commonweal*.

In 1878 Morris had moved to a house overlooking the Thames at Hammersmith where, in 1890, he established his Kelmscott Press, the last great enterprise of his life.

THE LAPSE OF THE YEAR

SPRING am I, too soft of heart
Much to speak ere I depart:
Ask the summer-tide to prove
The abundance of my love

SUMMER looked for long am I,
Much shall change or ere I die
Prithee take it not amiss
Though I weary thee with bliss!

Laden AUTUMN here I stand,
Weak of heart and worn of hand;
Speak the word that sets me free
Nought but rest seems good to me

Ah, shall WINTER mend your case?
Set your teeth the wind to face,
Beat the snow down, tread the frost,
All is gained when all is lost.

MORRIS AND COMPANY

William Morris's drawing room at Hammersmith House in 1896,
showing various Morris and Co. products, including Morris's woven
'Bird' tapestry, pottery by William de Morgan, and an adjustable
armchair and a settle, both based on designs by Philip Webb

In addition to their ecclesiastical work, Morris, Marshall, Faulkner and Co. experimented with painted earthenware tiles, tapestries, embroideries, gesso decoration and wallpaper as well as furniture and stained glass during the 1860s, creating furnishings for medieval-style interiors. The work executed for such early commissions as the Green Dining-Room at the South Kensington Museum, the Armoury and Tapestry Rooms at St James's Palace or the interiors at 1 Palace Green, built in 1868–70 by Philip Webb for George Howard, later 9th Earl of Carlisle, was expensive but of very high quality.

Morris welcomed the artistic involvement of anyone associated with the firm: his wife Janey and her sister Elizabeth Burden both executed embroidery, as did Burne-Jones's wife Georgiana, while Kate and Lucy Faulkner, sisters of the firm's bookkeeper, Charles Faulkner, designed or executed tiles, gesso and china decoration, and wallpapers. Morris's friend William de Morgan, set up a kiln in the basement of his home in Fitzroy Square, producing tiles and stained glass for the firm. In 1872 he moved to Cheyne Row, Chelsea, where he 'rediscovered' the lost art of lustre decoration for pottery after observing accidental iridescence on stained glass. The rich 'moonlight' and 'sunset' effects of the copper, silver and gold lustres, and the gorgeous blues and turquoises of his Islamic-influenced 'Persian' wares (used for a wide range of tiles, bowls, chargers and vases) added a note of sumptuous luxury to the more subdued colours of Webb's early decorative schemes.

In 1877 a retail outlet was opened by Morris and Co. at 449 Oxford Street. Morris's own designs for wallpapers and textiles, including embroideries, tapestries, printed cottons, damasks, brocaded velvets, silks and wools, as well as machine-made carpets and hand-knotted 'Hammersmith' rugs, provided regular sales of repeat orders and gave the company financial security. But they also took in stock from outside sources – items such as light fittings by W. A. S. Benson, who also designed furniture for the firm, and metalwork by John Pearson, who had worked with C. R. Ashbee's Guild of Handicraft.

Morris had produced his first wallpaper design, 'Daisy', in 1862 and began his textile experiments in the 1870s. Influenced by his extensive collection and study of historic textiles, he realized that any improvement in design required a return to basic techniques. He first experimented with vegetable dyes at the firm's premises at 26 Queen Square; then, from 1875, with Thomas Wardle, brother of the firm's manager, he not only developed a durable alternative to the 'crude, livid and cheap' chemical aniline dyes produced from coal-tar that he found so hideous, but also experimented with discharge block-printing as an alternative to engraved roller-printing. Wardle dyed all Morris's silks and wools and printed his chintzes from 1876 until Merton Abbey, the site of a disused silk weaving shed on the river Wandle, only seven miles from London and ideal for workshops, was purchased by the firm in June 1881.

In 1890 George Jack, who had worked in Philip Webb's architectural office for ten years, took over as chief designer. He added a lightness and sophistication to the firm's style, which was evident in such later interiors as Clouds, Wiltshire, built by Webb for the Hon. Percy Wyndham, and Standen, Sussex, also built by Webb for a London solicitor, James Beale.

On William Morris's death in 1896, W. A. S. Benson took over the direction of the company, which continued to sell Morris chintzes, wallpapers, carpets and furniture until it went into voluntary liquidation in 1940.

Above: Design by William Morris for a wallpaper, in pencil and
watercolour

Left: Interior of the Green Dining Room at the South Kensington
Museum (now the Victoria & Albert Museum), decorated by Morris
and Co. in 1866. Victoria & Albert Museum, London

The Victorian Fear of Chaos

While Gothic seemed to refer back to a lost golden age of craftsmanship and social harmony, it also excited a *frisson* of medieval fearfulness which very much appealed to the dark underside of nineteenth-century Britain. The Victorians were terrified of chaos, especially the chaos threatened by working-class unrest and agitation. Memories of the Luddites had not entirely faded, and the European revolutions of 1848, mirrored in Britain by the Chartist risings, seemed uncomfortably close. There was, too, in this age of science and education, a deep-rooted fear of all those newfangled, satanic mills: few people really understood just how such miracles of gas and steam actually worked, and many secretly felt that the progress they represented could somehow run amok, just as the workers – ignorant, brutish, fearsome – had threatened to do. And it was an ugly age. Life was full of dismal and brutal incidents: young children deformed by industrial accidents, famine in Ireland, cholera outbreaks due to bad sanitation, insanity caused by venereal diseases, and domestic drunkenness and violence. The truly grotesque was ever present. How better to disarm it than by a disowning laugh?

Charles Dickens used the grotesque as a literary style, employing distortion and exaggeration to provoke indignation and even revulsion over social evils, hypocrisy and greed, and his creations were immensely popular. The unpleasant characters in his novels were deformed, but had once been human, and so retained a point of contact with the reader, who must nervously and reluctantly have recognized something of himself in such debased creatures. The grotesque is distinguished by just this moment of recognition, and by that element of nervous humour which renders the familiar evil bearable.

Edward Lear's *Book of Nonsense*, published in 1846, and Lewis Carroll's *Alice's Adventures in Wonderland* (1865), followed six years later by *Alice Through the Looking Glass*, in which the *Punch* cartoonist John Tenniel's illustration of the Jabberwocky made its first appearance, all proved the popular appeal of the weird and distorted. The Jabberwocky, whatever its actual meaning for Carroll himself, remains a potent symbol of the Victorian fear of Darwinism gone wrong, of progress taking a wrong turn and allowing natural selection to evolve some hairless, clawed, two-headed, unimaginable creature. The rational principles taught in the Schools of Design were constantly shadowed by this

John Tenniel's illustration of 'The Jabberwocky' from Lewis Carroll's *Through the Looking Glass*, published in 1872

Illustration by Hablot K. Browne ('Phiz') depicting Mrs Sarah Gamp and a friend from Charles Dickens's novel *The Life and Adventures of Martin Chuzzlewit*, first published in 1843–4

taste for the strange and grotesque which reflected a hidden current of fearfulness in Victorian society.

The most popular form of expression for this taste for the grotesque was the portrayal of animals and birds in realistic human situations. The architect and designer William Burges employed such devices on his painted furniture, often executed by Henry Stacy Marks, who worked as a muralist and decorator for him (and also for other architects such as E. W. Godwin and Alfred Waterhouse); Stacy Marks's own favourite

subject-matter was tropical birds. William de Morgan, an admirer of Lear and Lewis Carroll, also developed an interest in grotesque forms of birds, animals and fishes while working at Merton Abbey in the 1880s, and J. Moyr Smith, who worked in Christopher Dresser's design studio, used a sometimes grotesque humour in his pseudo-medieval illustrations for tiles and Christmas cards.

But the ultimate in this combination of humour, caricature and outright unpleasantness were the birds, faces and nameless creatures created by Robert Wallace Martin and his brothers in Southall in the 1880s. The Martin brothers themselves were no strangers to the grotesque in real life, for their family was dogged by accidents and disasters. Their sister Olive was bitten by a monkey on her twenty-first birthday and subsequently died of the infected bite; Robert Wallace's daughter Amy had an illegitimate child, a sin which obsessed her over-religious father; a fire at their Brownlow Street premises in 1903 in which three people were asphyxiated so haunted Charles Martin, who managed the shop, that he eventually had to be confined to an asylum, where he died. Yet in 1882 one reviewer wrote of Robert Wallace's disturbingly vicious pieces: 'There is something so whimsically human in these fancies, they are so impossible and absurd yet so funny and attractive, that they remind us of nothing so much as the good old nursery rhymes. They are nonsense indeed, but good nonsense. . . .'

Another form of the grotesque echoed the ongoing debate about nature: was nature, as Ruskin upheld, beautiful only in

Panel of tiles by William de Morgan

its divine imperfection, or did truth lie, as Christopher Dresser believed, in its underlying structure and geometry? The Ruskinian school culminated in the sinuous tendrils and exuberant curves of European Art Nouveau, but there were also artists who gloried in a more obvious distortion of natural forms. Christopher Dresser, for example, designed some tortured ceramic shapes for the Linthorpe Pottery, and echoed the twisted forms of Art Nouveau in his 'Clutha' glass. In America, the master of naturalistic distortion was the 'Mad Biloxi Potter', George E. Ohr. Ohr tended to portray himself as an untutored showman, a kind of circus act, but in fact had been apprenticed in 1875 to the ceramist Joseph Meyer in New Orleans before returning to Biloxi, Mississippi, to set up his own pottery in 1893.

Ohr used local materials; the clay was thrown with superb skill to almost paper thinness, and then twisted, folded, pinched, dented and crushed into bizarre, ornate forms. This bravura was followed up with equal mastery of glaze techniques, and he often combined different mottled or speckled glazes, including metallic and crystalline effects, in a single piece. His claim was 'No Two Alike', and when he closed his pottery in 1906 there were several thousand pieces left in his warehouse. Contemporary critics did not know what to make of him, but he was undoubtedly unique.

THE MARTIN BROTHERS

From left to right: Walter, Wallace and Edwin Martin in their Southall studio, 1912.
Opposite: two earthenware vases and a bowl, with various glazes, by George E. Ohr

The Martin Brothers – Robert Wallace, Charles, Walter and Edwin – founded their own pottery in 1873, moving from Fulham in 1877 to a disused soap factory on the banks of a canal in Southall. Walter was responsible for throwing and firing the salt-glazed stonewares, achieving a wide and subtle variety of blues, browns and greens; Edwin, who, like Walter had been apprenticed at Doulton's Art Pottery in Lambeth, did much of the painting and the raised and etched decoration of the vases and decorative pieces that they initially produced; Charles was manager of their Dickensian 'curiosity shop' in Brownlow Street, near Holborn; and the fiercely independent Robert Wallace produced the grotesque and strange sculptural pieces that were portrayed, even at the time, as quaint, old-fashioned and mysterious.

In the 1850s Robert Wallace had been assistant to one of the stone-carvers working on the vast building site of Sir Charles Barry's Palace of Westminster. In 1860 he enrolled in evening classes at Lambeth School of Art and the following year joined the studio of the sculptor Alexander Munro. The sly 'bird jars', as he called them, gaping spoon warmers and leering, two-faced Janus jugs which he produced during the 1880s prove him to have been a brilliant sculptor and an inspired caricaturist. By the late 1890s his creations had become pure sculptural fantasies, expressive of his obsessive sense of worldly sin and impending doom, for he was a fervent member of the fundamentalist sect, the Plymouth Brethren.

Collecting Martinware, and visiting the dusty Brownlow Street shop, full of its 'quaint grotesque creatures, hobgoblins, fish and uncanny beasts', fresh from the latest firing, became a kind of hobby for City bankers, lawyers and such patrons as the wealthy ironmonger, Frederick Nettlefold. Many of the 'bird jars' – ostensibly tobacco jars with detachable heads which could be moved to alter the creature's expression – are caricatures of barristers or judges, portraying a rogue's gallery of preening lasciviousness, disobliging spite and malicious hypocrisy.

By the First World War, when Robert Wallace finally ceased production, his three brothers had died. He himself died in 1923.

WILLIAM BURGES

'Ugly Burges who designs lovely things. Isn't he a duck!' wrote Lady Bute in her epitaph of the architect 'Billy' Burges, who died in 1881 while still in his mid-fifties. Burges, a bohemian, an enthusiastic Freemason, and a man with a taste for alcohol and opium, had many friends among the Pre-Raphaelites – Rossetti, Burne-Jones, Simeon Solomon, Henry Holiday and Edward Poynter all painted panels for his idiosyncratic Gothic furniture.

His principal patron was the 3rd Marquess of Bute, reputedly the richest man in the world, whom Burges first met in 1865 when the Marquess was only eighteen. Like Burges himself, Bute, a Catholic, was well-travelled, and an antiquarian with a passion for the Middle Ages. Burges, who collected medieval manuscripts, armour, embroideries, ivories, enamels, jades and gems, particularly admired early French architecture. As soon as Bute attained his majority, they began work rebuilding Cardiff Castle as a medieval treasury. Work was still unfinished when Burges died, but he had been closely involved with every detail of the castle, designing tiles, stained glass, carvings, painted decoration and furniture; even the basins for Lord Bute's bedroom were enhanced by Burges with monsters swimming about a stone arcade and a mermaid combing her hair, all in the style of Italian majolica.

In 1875 he began work on a second major commission for Bute, Castell Coch, and in 1878 moved into his own Tower House in Melbury Road, London – a daring make-believe castle with turrets and gargoyles on the outside, moons, mermaids and fairies painted in gold, silver and heraldic colours on the inside. It was the most complete expression of his private fantasies and provided an Aladdin's cave for his own collection. Each room was given a colourful theme connected with some legend, dream or joke. His bedroom was decorated with 'The Sea and its Inhabitants', while the library has an imposing chimneypiece showing 'The Dispersion of the Parts of Speech at the Time of the Tower of Babel', flanked by bookcases decorated with letters of the alphabet. The letter *H* is painted as having fallen

down from the cornice of the chimney-piece – a joke that Burges, in fact the son of a wealthy marine engineer, had 'dropped his aitches'.

Burges had a far greater understanding of the original medieval French models that inspired his painted furniture than had Morris and the Pre-Raphaelite painters, who merely added painted panels to a wooden carcass. Burges designed his furniture specifically for the decoration he had in mind, and linked the theme of the painting to the function of the piece – the letters of the alphabet in his library, for instance, Sleeping Beauty on a bed, mermaids in a bathroom or Narcissus on a washstand.

Burges was not only responsible for furniture and painted mural decoration; he also designed tiles, stained glass, mosaic, jewellery, and metalwork set with the antique coins, enamels, intaglio gems and semi-precious stones (lapis lazuli, jade, rock crystal) that he collected. A popular, gregarious man, he loved ceremony and enjoyed designing vessels or pieces of furniture for special uses; he was also very short-sighted, which perhaps accounts for the detailed, jewel-like appearance of his work.

Opposite: The drawing-room at Tower House, William Burges's Kensington house, photographed in 1885

Chest on a stand made by Burges for Tower House, 1875. Fred Weeks was probably the designer of the pseudo-medieval figures depicting Adam expelled from Paradise and reclothed, and of the images relating to male toiletry items.

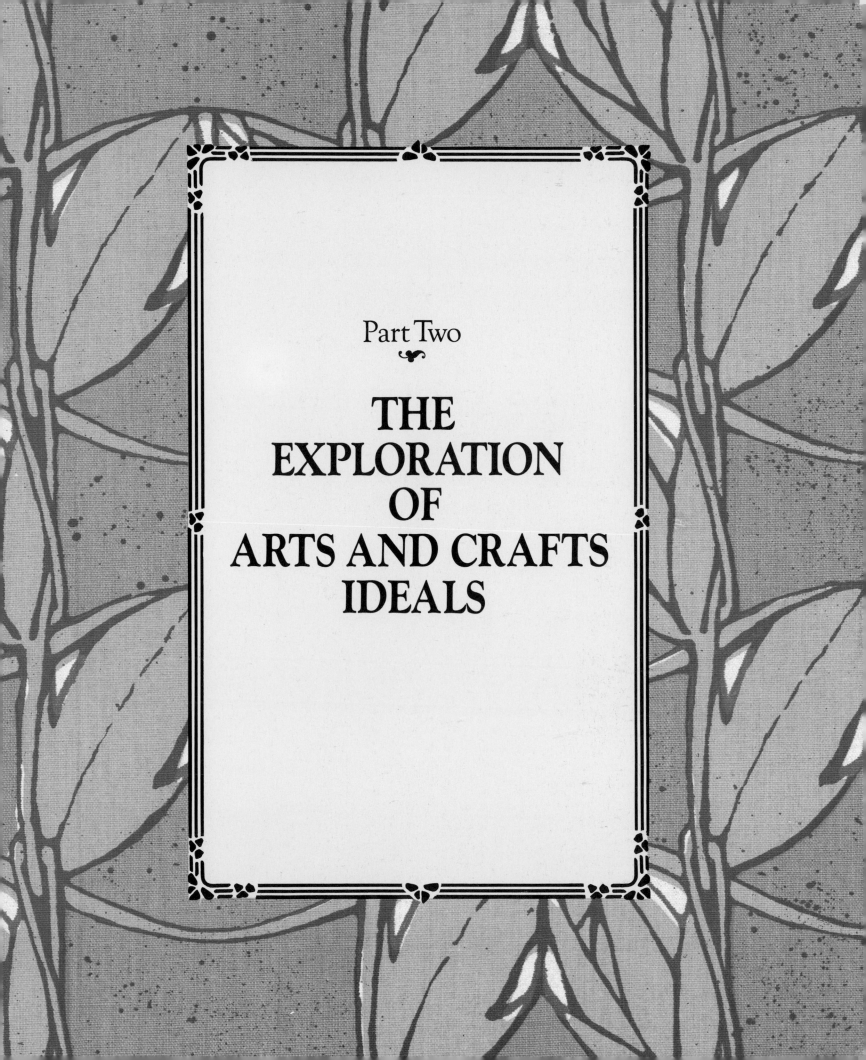

Part Two

THE EXPLORATION OF ARTS AND CRAFTS IDEALS

A New Gospel is Spread

By the 1880s the popularity of Gothic as a decorative style had waned, but the ideals behind the Gothic Revival continued to be felt just as forcefully; as J. D. Sedding said in 1893, the Gothic Revival had been 'the health-giving spark'. The new movement (the term 'Arts and Crafts' was not commonly used until late in the decade) latched on to the ideal of a society regenerated by the values and skills of craftsmanship – an ideal espoused, in different ways, by Ruskin and Morris. The medieval craft workshop seemed to them to be clearly a more humane place than the modern factory or mill, and, further, they believed that the organization of labour, of masters and apprentices, within the workshop benefited the individual and provided a harmonious pattern for society as a whole. The consumer, freed from an environment of shoddy, machine-made imitations of unsuitably grand styles, would also be released into a world where his eye and mind would be rested and calmed by the presence of beautiful things made with love and pride.

The writings of Ruskin, and later Morris, were enormously influential not only in Britain but all over Europe and America, and during the last twenty years of the nineteenth century, craft guilds and artists' col-

onies inspired by their ideas were founded in many countries.

In 1871 Ruskin himself attempted to turn his beliefs to practical account, and founded the Guild of St George, but his somewhat paternalistic enterprise achieved little other than a small museum near Sheffield and some workmen's dwellings in Wales. In 1882, however, his friend and disciple, Arthur Heygate Mackmurdo, founded the Century Guild together with the designer and former curate Selwyn Image. Mackmurdo, an architect, had heard Ruskin lecture at Oxford, and in 1874 had travelled with him in Italy. A few years later, he had met William Morris and had become interested in the decorative arts. The Guild, which produced designs by Herbert P. Horne, Clement Heaton, Heywood Sumner and others, flourished for six years, and carried out decorative work of all kinds, including furniture, metalwork, textiles and wallpapers; everything was presented as a co-operative effort, though much was designed by Mackmurdo himself. His furniture was generally of mahogany and owed more to the eighteenth-century simplicity of the 'Queen Anne' style than to medieval Gothic; his flat designs were masterly, introducing a totally fresh, sinuous elegance into pattern design, prefiguring the whiplash curves of Art Nouveau.

The success of the Century Guild inspired other like-minded designers to band together. In 1883 a group of young architects from Richard Norman Shaw's office set up the St George's Art Society to include 'craftsmen in architecture, painting, sculpture and the kindred arts'. Following in the footsteps of Shaw's own master, G. E. Street, who had encouraged his pupils to practise traditional crafts, they wanted a wider definition of the arts than the official line allowed by the Royal Academy or the Institute of British Architects.

In May 1884 the St George's Art Society joined forces with The Fifteen, a discussion group founded a year or two before under the secretaryship of the successful freelance designer, Lewis F. Day. (The Fifteen also included designers such as Walter Crane and Henry Holiday and the architect J. D. Sedding, another of Street's pupils.) The new society was named the Art Workers' Guild, and is still in existence today. It established common aims, provided a meeting place for discussion and a platform for lectures on techniques and styles; Morris, Norman Shaw, Mackmurdo, Ashbee, Voysey and Lutyens were among its many distinguished members (it did not admit women until 1964); all, despite their individual differences in style, swore allegiance to the Arts and Crafts movement.

The new idiom of Arts and Crafts was strong and simple in form, rich and intricate in craftsmanship, with a fresh morality based on fitness for purpose. While leaving Gothic motifs behind, the style had absorbed the architectural principles of furniture construction championed by Pugin, as well as the return to basics via the study of ancient, traditional techniques that (along with Street and Morris) he pioneered; Pugin and Bodley's love of colour and bold effect also continued unabated. These elements were combined in a new, eclectic style that stressed simplicity and an honesty of construction based on first-hand understanding of the materials employed, while encouraging richness, colour and the use of such precious materials as silver, enamel, mother-of-pearl or iridescent glass.

The architect and metalworker Henry Wilson, a master of the Art Workers' Guild, once described it as 'a club for artists', explaining that, 'as everybody knows, artists are unpractical cranks'. The pride that many of this first generation of Arts and Crafts designers took in being cranks – bohemian, anti-establishment, steeped in the lore of the studio or craft workshop – characterized the movement and the manner in which it presented itself for many years to come.

Arts and Crafts artefacts were honest, sturdy, and, by the standards of their day, decidedly eccentric, yet by the 1880s the style had established itself as the idiom of the liberal middle classes. A. H. Mackmurdo described his aim as being to make 'beautiful things for the homes of simple and gentle folk', which was just how those folk wished to see themselves. Although Morris and Co.'s early commissions had been for grand, indeed palatial, schemes of interior decoration, by the 1880s most Arts and Crafts designers had accepted Morris's own urgent desire to create not 'art for the few', but goods affordable by all. To some degree,

Morris and Co. had achieved this with their 'Sussex' chairs, upholstered armchairs and chintzes, but Morris wallpapers, for example, were always more expensive than most. However, as M. H. Baillie Scott pointed out in *The Studio* in 1897: 'The necessary restrictions imposed by a limited purse often prove to be the best safeguard against over-extravagance; and so to those who can appreciate the beauty of simplicity and restraint, necessity in this case may become a virtue indeed, and instead of trying to emulate the splendours of the palace, so often vulgar, so seldom comfortable and homely, we may accept gladly the limitations which suggest a more cottage-like home.' Simplicity, restraint and the supposed values of cottage life were indeed almost passionately adopted as virtues by those who rejected the ostentation of wealth derived from industrial muscle and from an unjust economic system.

In 1888 a splinter group from the Art Workers' Guild founded the Arts and Crafts Exhibition Society, which, until the First World War provided a showcase for both commercial and amateur designs. Walter Crane was its first president and Lewis F. Day its treasurer. Over five hundred objects selected by committee were shown at its first membership exhibition, held at the New Gallery, which had been set up in Regent Street by two former directors of the influential Grosvenor Gallery. To enhance the occasion, William Morris gave a demonstration of weaving to a selected audience and Isadora Duncan danced. From the start, the society's exhibitions included products from commercial firms, so long as both designer and executant were credited,

Mahogany settle with cane panels designed by A.H. Mackmurdo for the Century Guild, *c.*1886, with hangings and upholstery of Mackmurdo's 'Tulip' chintz, 1875

and in the 1890s retailers from all over Europe, including such notables as Samuel Bing from Paris, visited the triennial exhibitions in search of new talent.

The model provided by both the Art Workers' Guild and the Exhibition Society was quickly copied elsewhere: in 1897 the Boston Society of Arts and Crafts was founded, followed by similar organizations in Chicago, Detroit, New York and Minneapolis. For many, however, the new movement remained not simply a matter of style, but also a search for 'truth' and a solace for social ills. Thus A. H. Mackmurdo later wrote in his unpublished 'History of the Arts and Crafts Movement', it was important to '. . . see this movement not as an aesthetic excursion; but as a mighty upheaval of man's spiritual nature.'

The Arts and Crafts movement, which encompassed the notion that honest craftsmanship was good for both the craftsman and the inhabitant of a 'reformed' home, became increasingly allied to socialism. Many artists and designers, including Rossetti and Morris, had lectured at the Working Mens' Clubs in London's East End, and had seen for themselves the appalling conditions in which the poor lived and worked. 'Apart from my desire to produce beautiful things,' Morris later said, 'the leading passion of my life is hatred of modern civilisation.' If, as he fervently believed, the decorative arts were a standard against which the health of society could be measured, then his Ruskinian ideal of improving the decorative arts could not stop at romantic notions of re-creating the Middle Ages, but must lead on to real social change. For Morris, his cherished chivalric ideal that the strong should look after the weak developed into full-blooded political action, and in 1883 he became a socialist. The possibility of revolution was not remote. There had been working-class riots in London's West End in 1866 and again in February 1886, after a particularly severe winter, a meeting of the unemployed ended in rioting in Hyde Park and St James's. Morris, who spoke for the Socialist League at many open-air meetings at this time, thought these disturbances were indeed 'the first skirmish of the revolution'. He was not alone; several Arts and Crafts designers joined the socialist cause, including Philip Webb, W. R. Lethaby, C. R. Ashbee and, not least, Walter Crane, who painted pictures with socialist themes, designed union banners and contributed covers to *The Practical Socialist*.

But, as he outlined in his *News From Nowhere*, a description of life after the imagined revolution, Morris's socialist Utopia in fact harked back to a rural, medieval idyll based on craftsmanship. Support for this supposed remedy for social injustice came from Ruskin's absolute rejection of the machine, which he saw as having destroyed the vital irregularity and freedom of expression that symbolized man's closeness to nature. The machine had not only spawned the degradation of most factory conditions, but also created a false perfection which mirrored a vacuity within the society that consumed machine-made goods. Only hand-craftsmanship could be free, beautiful and creative. In much the same vein, C. R. Ashbee on a brief visit to Elverhoj, a Danish craft colony overlooking the Hudson River in New York State, wrote in 1915: 'The real thing is the life; and it doesn't matter so very much if their metalwork is second rate. Give them their liberty of production and they'll do it better.'

Ashbee had established his own democratic, profit-sharing Guild of Handicraft in the East End of London in 1888. By the end of the 1890s, when, the Guild became a limited company, it was doing very well, and Ashbee began to work towards his real dream, the establishment of his own Utopia, his 'city of the sun', a guild of craftsmen living and working in the countryside. In 1902 the Guild settled in Chipping Campden, and it survived for nearly five happy years before logistical and administrative difficulties got the better of it. As an experiment in true Arts and Crafts living, however, the Guild's brief rural retreat was of vital importance. Visitors came from all over the world, and the Guild's activities

'Cockatoo and Pomegranate', hand-printed wallpaper designed in 1899 by Walter Crane and manufactured by Jeffrey and Co.. Whitworth Art Gallery, Manchester

and products were much discussed and illustrated in magazines in Europe and America. In England, the Birmingham Guild of Handicraft, established in 1890, was closely modelled on Ashbee's Guild; in Munich, the Vereinigte Werkstätten für Kunst in Handwerk (meaning 'united workshops for art and craft') were founded in 1897; in Vienna, the Wiener Werkstätte was inspired by the Guild of Handicraft; and in 1901 Gustav Stickley in Syracuse, New York State, attempted a similar experiment in profit-sharing with United Crafts. However, none of these European or American guilds shared the largely British abhorrence of the machine, and, as a result, were successfully able to compete commercially in the market-place.

Nevertheless, after the failure of the Guild, Ashbee was more certain than ever that it was the way of life that counted, and that this could not include mechanization. In his book, *Craftsmanship in Competitive Industry*, he argued for legislation to protect craftsmen from industrial competition, and bitterly imagined the comment of the financier: 'If you cannot sell your things . . . your things are worth nothing, if you cannot sell your skill, your skill is worth nothing. . . . As for your workmen and their traditions, and their standard of life – that is not a question of practical finance and is no concern of mine.'

But the desire for a new way, for something better than the teeming squalor and degradation of the large industrial cities, for a style more modern and rational than the excesses of the mid-century, had caught hold. All over the world, art, architecture and design were discussed with as much passion as ecology and the environment are today. Art schools were revolutionized; in England, the Central School of Arts and Crafts was founded in London in 1896 with the architect W. R. Lethaby, a friend of Philip Webb's and a founder member of the St George's Art Society, as its first principal. Its teachers were drawn from the front ranks of the Arts and Crafts movement. In Birmingham, Liverpool and Glasgow, the art schools gave as much emphasis to ceramics, metalwork, furniture making or embroidery as to painting or sculpture; in Europe, too, the Secession movement called for architecture and the decorative arts to be given their proper place. In the 1880s a School of Applied Art was founded in Budapest and a journal of applied arts launched. Many new magazines were founded, using innovative printing techniques such as chromolithography. *The Studio* in England, *Pan, Jugend, Deutsche Kunst und Dekoration* and *Dekorative Kunst* in Germany, *Ver Sacrum* in Austria, *La Casa* in Italy, and *House Beautiful, House and Garden, Ladies' Home Journal* and *The Craftsman* in America all helped to spread the exciting new ideas about design and its connection with social well-being.

Perhaps the closest that anyone came to realizing Ruskin's personal and paternalistic vision was in Russia, where several craft colonies were established by aristocratic patrons to bring artist-designers and peasant craftsmen together. After Tzar Alexander II had freed the serfs in 1861, there had been renewed interest in the education and emancipation of the peasantry and in estate management. Among the liberal middle classes, there was also a fresh artistic awareness of Russian landscape and of traditional

Design for a carved and painted wooden cradle, with embroidered hanging, from the Talashkino workshops near Smolensk, 1906

Russian crafts, especially those associated with the Orthodox Church. Peasant culture, folklore, myth, and the colours, mosaics and icons of the Russian Church were adopted by many artists as the means of fusing together art, a sense of national identity and the spirituality of everyday life.

In 1875 the wealthy Moscow merchant, Savva Mamontov, and his wife Elizaveta founded an artists' colony at Abramtsevo, their estate near Moscow. Mamontov later also founded the Moscow Theatre, which inspired his cousin, Stanislavsky, to establish the Moscow Art Theatre in 1898. The artists associated with the Abramtsevo colony included the portraitist and landscape painter Valentin Serov, Mikhail Vroubel, who painted murals, undertook church restoration and made marvellous ceramics, and Vassily Polenov, who decorated the church at Abramtsevo. In 1885 the latter's sister, Elena Polenova, and her sister-in-law, Maria Yakunchikova, a cousin of Mamontov's, helped Elizaveta Mamontova to set up a wood-carving school to give the peasants a winter occupation. They introduced other crafts, including embroidery, painted decoration and, in 1890, ceramics. Yakunchikova, a painter who had made a study of the decorative motifs of peasant art and also collected fairy-tales and legends, later founded a carpet and dye factory on her own estate.

Polenova, formerly a student of drawing and ceramics in St Petersburg and an illustrator of Russian folk stories, ran the woodwork shop at Abramtsevo. She, too, founded her own workshops, the Trocadero, which produced furniture, pottery and embroidery and undertook bookbinding and illustration; she also accumulated an extensive collection of traditional Russian crafts. Her work inspired the foundation of another workshop in 1893 at Talashkino, near Smolensk, on the estate of the Princess Maria Tenisheva, a painter and a fine enamellist.

At Talashkino, the princess's retainers wore traditional white tunics and black boots; she revived interest in the balalaika; founded a school for peasant children where music, embroidery and design were taught; and established workshops where peasants produced richly carved and painted furniture, enamelwork, embroidery and ceramics which were sold in Moscow at a shop called Rodnik. Drawing on the folk traditions researched by Polenova, the Talashkino artefacts were decorated with stylized fish, flowers, birds and religious motifs.

In 1897 Princess Tenisheva met Sergei Diaghilev through Alexander Benois, whom she had employed to catalogue and organize an exhibition of her collections of folk art and Art Nouveau for her museum in Smolensk. Diaghilev visited her several times, hoping to obtain her financial support for the magazine he wished to start, *Mir Iskoustva* ('World of Art'). She and Mamontov both agreed to finance the periodical, and the first issue appeared in October 1898. It was highly influential and did much to introduce Art Nouveau to Russia and to promote Russian arts and crafts. One issue was devoted to the products of the Talashkino workshops, and in 1899 the second 'World of Art' exhibition featured embroidery designs by Polenova and pottery from Abramtsevo.

Elsewhere, young artists and architects in Europe were abandoning the fine arts to design furniture, textiles or metalwork. In Munich, the Secession was founded in 1892 by artists dissatisfied with the official Neo-classical style of the Bavarian government. It met with official disapproval, but for several years Munich became a centre of new ideas about design. The style set by designers such as Otto Eckmann, Hermann Obrist, Peter Behrens and August Endell, who among them designed furniture, light fittings, wallpapers, carpets, tapestries, embroideries, jewellery, ceramics, glass and woodcut illustrations, became known as *Jugendstil*, being named after *Jugend*, the innovative periodical founded in Munich in 1896 to which Eckmann contributed covers and illustrations

In 1897 Eckmann, Obrist, Behrens, Endell, Bernhard Pankok, Richard Riemerschmid, Bruno Paul and Paul Schultze-Naumburg broke away from the fine craftsmanship and self-conscious style of *Jugendstil* in order to design for industry. They founded the Vereinigte Werkstätten für Kunst in Handwerk, a community of craftsmen producing everyday objects with some common artistic unity. The name was derived from Morris's 'banded workshops' in *News From Nowhere*, but, although they shared the British aims of simplicity and fitness for purpose, the Germans did not support Morris's rural workshop ideal. The artists of the Vereinigte Werkstätten did not execute their own designs, which were made for them by skilled craftsmen using modern machinery. As a result, the Munich guild was commercially extremely successful. In 1902, in *Dekorative Kunst*, Hermann Muthesius described '. . . the peculiar

Right: Silver presentation pitcher by Robert R. Jarvie, 1911. Jarvie exhibited with the Chicago Arts and Crafts Society as an amateur metalworker and went on to found the Jarvie Shop, specializing in commemorative bowls and trophies. The Art Institute of Chicago

Far right: 'Orange Lilies', silk embroidery on silk and cotton brocade designed by Hermann Obrist and made by Berthe Ruchet in 1898 for Obrist's own villa in Munich. Stadtmuseum, Munich

cultural image that William Morris and the English artist-socialists have given us of an "art of the people for the people" which, in the end, produced such expensive things that at the very most only the upper ten thousand could consider buying them.' Muthesius was a Prussian architect, civil servant and critic who had been attached to the German Embassy in London from 1896 to 1903. He had travelled all over Britain and in 1904 published *Das Englische Haus*, a book praising the architecture of the British Arts and Crafts movement and publicizing it in Europe, but at the same time casting a realistic eye over its Utopian dreams.

In 1899 the Vereinigte Werkstätten exhibited four rooms in Dresden at the *Deutsche Kunst-Ausstellung*. Their designs for furnishings showed a burgeoning awareness of the needs of serial, industrial production. As yet, there was no 'machine aesthetic'; the forms were curved, organic, unadorned and still based on methods of hand-craftsmanship, but the move towards the absolute refinement of form required by mass production was there.

In Vienna, the Secession, founded in 1897 in opposition to the established Academy painters with the painter Gustav Klimt as its first president, welcomed foreign inspiration and declared that 'We recognize no distinction between "high art" and "minor arts", between art for the rich and art for the poor. Art is public property.' It was the architects of the Secession, trained in the offices of Otto Wagner, who did most to champion the cause of Arts and Crafts. In his book *Moderne Architektur*, published in 1895, Wagner had provided the inspiration for the concept of the *Gesamtkunstwerk*, the

total work of art, which began with the building and included every detail of decoration and furnishing. Wagner's student, Joseph Maria Olbrich, designed the Secession Building in Vienna, while another student from his architectural office, Josef Hoffmann, and the painter Koloman Moser were given responsibility for the arrangement and display of the first Secession Exhibition, held in 1898 in Olbrich's magnificent and richly adorned exhibition hall. By the time of the eighth Secession Exhibition, held in 1900, not only paintings but also decorative arts, including work by Ashbee, de Morgan and Charles Rennie Mackintosh, were included. Secessionist ideas were spread more rapidly among the next generation after the appointment of Hoffmann and Moser as teachers at the Vienna Kunstgewerbeschule (School of Arts and Crafts).

In 1899 architects, artists and designers from all over Europe were called together in the most ambitious Arts-and-Crafts-inspired programme of regeneration yet undertaken, when Ernst Ludwig, a grandson of Queen Victoria who had succeeded to the Grand Duchy of Hesse in 1892 at the age of twenty-three, established an artists' colony on the Mathildenhöhe, a small hill he owned to the north-east of the old town of Darmstadt. Ludwig had travelled in England and seen the work of Arts and Crafts architects and designers. He had invited Otto Eckmann to furnish his private study in the Neue Palais in Darmstadt and the young English architect M. H. Baillie Scott to contribute furniture and decorations for the drawing-room and dining room. Baillie Scott's designs were made by

'Spring', maple cabinet with fruitwood inlays designed by J.M. Olbrich c.1899, and exhibited in the *Darmstadter Zimmer* in Paris, 1900

Ashbee's Guild of Handicraft, and Ashbee had provided the light fittings.

Ludwig believed that he could stimulate the economy of his little country by bringing about a revival of arts and crafts, and so he set about enticing internationally renowned artists to come to Darmstadt. The artists' colony was formally established on 1 July 1899. Olbrich came from Vienna, and Behrens from Munich, together with six other German painters, sculptors and designers, all aged under thirty-three. Ludwig's plans had the useful support of the publisher Alexander Koch, who gave the colony welcome coverage in his magazines, *Zeitschrift für Innen-Dekoration* and *Deutsche Kunst und Dekoration*.

The artists' first scheme was to devise an interior to be shown at the Exposition Universelle in Paris in 1900 for which Olbrich, who emerged as the unelected leader, contributed the overall design. The colony, which ended in 1914, showed its work at various international exhibitions, including Turin in 1902 and St Louis in 1904, but the most important statement of its aims was *Ein Dokument Deutscher Kunst*, staged in 1901, when, in addition to an exhibition held in a special hall designed by Olbrich, the houses and studios designed and furnished by the various colonists were thrown open to the public. The model homes on the Mathildenhöhe made actual the dream of turning daily life into an aesthetic experience. Olbrich's was like a south German farmhouse, with an open entrance porch, carved wooden flower galleries, a tiled roof and a decorative frieze of blue and white tiles across the side of the building. Inside, carved and plain wood was enhanced by

J.M. Olbrich's house,
built in 1901 on the
Mathildenhöhe, Darmstadt

patterned curtains and decorative friezes.

Peter Behrens built a house where every facet of its design, right down to the cutlery, was integrated in terms of an overall coherence of design. It was hailed as introducing a new age of beauty and was a realization of the *Gesamtkunstwerk*, the 'total design work', which united the material skill of the craftsman with the spiritual content of the artist.

In America, too, Ruskin and Morris were influential figures, though their medieval dreams meant little in a country in the throes of post-Civil War reconstruction, a vast land which had its own potent images in the extension of railroads, the exploration of new territories and the taming the wild frontier. The unpeopled landscapes of the Hudson River painters, the romance of the American Indians, the simplicity of religious sects such as the Shakers were far more compelling to an American public than the Arthurian poetry of Tennyson or Pre-Raphaelite images of 'medieval damozels'. Writers and poets such as Washington Irving, Henry Longfellow or Mark Twain supplied the vocabulary of a primitive, outdoor, pioneer life of simple values and closeness to nature. From the 1880s log-cabins and bungalows began to be popular as weekend or summer retreats for city-dwelling woodsmen and their families, and became to the American Arts and Crafts movement what the country cottage with hollyhocks growing at the gate was in England – a symbol of harmony and spiritual well-being.

In the Yellowstone National Park the Old Faithful Inn was built in 1902 as a log-cabin a mere six storeys high! And hundreds of more modest summer resorts, country clubs and sanatoriums from Florida to Maine, from California to the Adirondacks, were furnished with 'woodsy' tables, settees, chairs and rockers made by firms such as the Old Hickory Furniture Co. in Indiana which used the wood, cane and bark of the region's plentiful hickory trees for porch and garden furniture.

Log-cabins and bungalows, complete

with porches and simple, life-affirming mottoes over the fireplace, were among the designs for 'Craftsman Homes' which Gustav Stickley sold by mail in addition to the plans he published in *The Craftsman* magazine; in 1904 he founded the Craftsman Home-Builders Club which offered complete sets of plans to subscribers. The designs, many of which were by the architect Harvey Ellis, were inexpensive and well suited to the suburbs, where they were seen as being in keeping with the landscape as well as being redolent of a masculine, backwoodsy life lived close to nature. In 1909 Henry L. Wilson founded the *Bungalow Magazine* in Los Angeles; this regularly featured complete plans and drawings for a 'bungalow of the month'.

It was Gustav Stickley more than anyone who married the aims of the British Arts and Crafts movement to the frontier style of the log-cabin and produced what was known in America as 'reform' or 'Mission' furniture. In October 1900 the Tobey Furniture Co. of Chicago launched a range of 'New Furniture' designed by Stickley in plain, solid oak and similar to a range of so-called 'Mission' furniture the firm had introduced earlier that year. The term 'Mission', first coined at that time, was never used by Stickley himself, and it is not known whether it was derived from the Franciscan missions of California or from the notion of 'furniture with a mission'. Whatever name it went by, the new style, tagged as 'an unconventional style for unconventional people', proved to be very popular with the public and in 1901, in addition to a new Art Nouveau line, Tobey's catalogue offered 'New Furniture in Weathered Oak'; in 1902, after Stickley set

up his own Craftsman workshops, they introduced the name 'Russmore' for their Mission-style furniture.

The plain, broad oak planks of Stickley's Craftsman furniture, with its leather upholstery and beaten-copper hinges, went well with leaded glass and stencilled decoration – and with the Navajo rugs, patchwork quilts from Appalachian mountain folk, and distinctive blue and white bedspreads from Deerfield, Massachusetts which were sold with Stickley furniture. Stickley's style was widely copied, not least by L. and J. G. Stickley of Fayetteville, New York, the firm founded in 1902 by his younger brothers, Leopold and John George, and Stickley's own Craftsman enterprises reached from coast to coast.

However, despite the handmade, pioneer spirit of his furniture, and the articles he published in *The Craftsman* advocating the values he saw enshrined in the life of the craft workshop, most of the thousands of pieces of furniture produced in the Craftsman workshops were machine-made. Stickley saw his furniture as expressive of a rugged simplicity quite different from the joy in execution treasured by Ashbee or the furniture maker Sidney Barnsley, and he valued its lack of refinement, which he saw as redolent of the American spirit: 'we have no monarchs and no aristocracy,' he wrote, 'the life of the plain people is the life of the nation'. As he explained in 1904: 'the very crudity of my structural plan . . . was to me proof of its vital power . . . decadence is the natural sequence of over-refinement.' And in 1909 he wrote of his Craftsman furniture: 'Like the Arts and Crafts furniture in England, it represented a revolt from the

Living room of the 'nobly barbaric' log house at Gustav Stickley's Craftsman Farms in Morris Plains, New Jersey, illustrated in *The Craftsman*, November 1911. Stickley's plans for a Utopian community in Morris Plains never materialized

machine-made thing. But there is this difference: the Arts and Crafts furniture was primarily intended to be an expression of individuality, and the Craftsman furniture was founded on a return to sturdy and primitive forms that were meant for usefulness alone.'

In 1908 Stickley bought land near Morris Plains in New Jersey, hoping to found a co-operative community to be called the Craftsman Farms, but the plan came to nothing. Other experiments in Arts and Crafts living met with varied success. The Philadelphia architect William L. Price was, with Wilson Eyre (an architect and founder-editor of *House and Garden*), a member of the T-Square Club, which provided a forum for the discussion of Arts and Crafts topics. Their deliberations led Price to found the Rose Valley Community near Philadelphia in 1901 with financial assistance from several prominent Philadelphians, including Edward Bok, founder of the *Ladies' Home Journal*. Price hired immigrant wood-

carvers to make oak furniture to his designs with carved Gothic decoration, using only hand tools. The community also produced bookbindings and pottery. But after five years the woodwork shop closed amid complaints of poor working conditions and Rose Valley degenerated into little more than a cultural centre.

Ralph Radcliffe Whitehead was a wealthy amateur craftsman who had known Ruskin at Oxford and travelled with him in Italy. In 1902 he founded Byrdcliffe on a wooded mountainside near Woodstock, New York, and used his inherited fortune to keep the colony going until his death in 1926. Although Byrdcliffe produced some simple oak furniture, made by professionally trained artists and craftsmen, as well as picture frames, pottery and weaving, it never really prospered, and soon become more or less Whitehead's private estate, 'the shell of a great life', as Ashbee described it on a visit in 1915. Byrdcliffe was to have been devoted to preserving pre-industrial skills, but the mountain streams proved not to be forceful enough to power machinery. Whitehead also believed that living close to nature would enhance the lives of his workers, but, like his mentor Ruskin, he had attempted, in Ashbee's opinion, 'to solve the problem of the Arts and Crafts in the manner of the Grand Seigneur'.

The most successful of the American craft communities was Roycroft, founded in East Aurora, New York, by Elbert Hubbard, a flamboyant and successful salesman who in his mid-thirties retired from his brother-in-law's Buffalo soap business to establish the Roycroft Press in 1895. Hubbard claimed to have been inspired by a visit to

William Morris's Kelmscott Press the previous year, but that may only have been astute salesmanship. Certainly he shared none of Morris' socialist sympathies and was, from the start, outrageously commercial, an 'Anarkist with a K', as Janet Ashbee described him. Roycroft began with a small press, then a bindery and a leatherwork shop were added, and slowly a guild-like community began to take shape. In 1909 a metalwork shop, run by a former banker, Karl Kipp, was opened. The Roycroft Press also published *The Philistine*, a journal which achieved a circulation of over one hundred thousand copies a month.

In 1896 the Roycroft Shops had begun to make furniture for the Roycroft Inn, a place where visitors curious to see the community could stay, and the woodwork shop expanded to produce souvenirs for them to take home. 'They made it as good as they could – folks came along and bought it', was how Hubbard accounted for its existence. By 1901 furniture was offered in the firm's mail-order catalogue. Simple, square, oak pieces, with little ornament, but slightly more Gothic in style than Craftsman furniture, were constructed with pegs, pins and mortise-and-tenon joints and marked with either the orb and cross, the symbol Hubbard had adopted for the Roycroft Press, or an incised 'Roycroft'. In 1908 the Roycroft designer Dard Hunter, already an avid reader of German publications, visited Vienna and subsequently incorporated Wiener Werkstätte motifs into Roycroft products.

Hubbard said that each piece was made to order by individual craftsmen, a highly unlikely claim given the size of the workshops

– by 1906 over four hundred people worked there – and the machinery he invested in. Nevertheless, he obviously saw that exclusivity was a good marketing ploy, and constantly alerted his customers to the investment potential of his goods. In 1915, following the death of Elbert Hubbard and his wife aboard the *Lusitania*, their son Bert took over the firm, successfully establishing Roycroft 'departments' in several hundred stores; the Roycroft Shops were finally sold in 1938.

For several years before his death, Hubbard's successful commercialization of the original high ideals of the Arts and Crafts movement had been mirrored in thousands of inferior products made throughout Europe and America, although few firms went to the lengths of establishing both a community and a company magazine to reinforce the apparent 'message' they sold with their wares. For most, a passing visual reference to the style was sufficient to market their products.

Painted oak settee with two drawers, carved with 'Roycroft' and the company's orb mark, c.1910

THE ART CHAIR

From left to right: Morris and Co. 'Sussex' armchair, an ebonized chair
with cane seat by E. W. Godwin, 1880s, an ebonized beech side chair by
Bruce Talbert *c.*1880, a ladderback chair in beech by Ernest Gimson
*c.*1890, and a side chair, also of beech, with holly and ebony stringing
by Gimson's chief cabinetmaker, Peter Waals, *c.*1910. Private
collection, Birkenhead and The Fine Art Society

As the rage for 'Art' furniture spread, manufacturers produced rival versions of the cheap and popular Art chair.
The archetypal Art chair was the rush-seated, turned and
spindled, stained 'Sussex' chair produced by Morris and
Co. from 1865, and still part of their standard stock when
the firm was liquidated in 1940. Ford Madox Brown, who
discovered its rural prototype, is traditionally credited with
its design, but there is also a variation named the 'Rossetti'
chair. A light chair, useful in the dining-room or bedroom,
it was also relatively inexpensive – at the turn of the century, for example, it cost only seven shillings (35p) – and
could be bought with or without arms, with square or round
seat, and with matching settee.

E. W. Godwin's very Japanese-looking ebonized chair
design was, he claimed, also based on 'an old English example' and was described in the manufacturer William
Watt's catalogue as 'Jacobean', yet it made itself at home in
the Aesthetic interiors of Tite Street, Chelsea, or Bedford
Park, Chiswick.

Liberty's, of course, also jumped on the bandwagon with
an ebonized chair similar to their 'Thebes' stool, which had
been designed by Leonard F. Wyburd, based on one by the
artist Holman Hunt which had been inspired by an Egyptian original. On the whole, however, it continued to be
the English vernacular that inspired these sophisticated
items of self-consciously simple furniture. In *Hints on Household Taste*, C. L. Eastlake, recommending the traditional
Windsor chair, went so far as to add that, 'We have at the
present time no more artistic workman in his way than the
country cartwright' – a message very much taken to heart by
the furniture designer Ernest Gimson, by Sidney Barnsley
and, in the early years of this century, by Ambrose Heal.

C. R. ASHBEE

Above: Silverwares designed by C.R. Ashbee: a silver teapot of 1901; a
silver-plated muffin dish; a silver-plated clock with chased decoration;
and a cigarette box, c.1904; *(below right)* an embossed copper dish made
in 1891 by John Pearson, who had previously worked for the Guild of
Handicraft; *(below left)* Ashbee photographed by Frank Lloyd Wright,
c.1900

Charles Robert Ashbee (1863–1942) was a fairly typical
middle-class undergraduate at Cambridge until he began to
read Ruskin and to visit the socialist writer Edward Carpenter at his small farm near Sheffield in the early 1880s. In
1886, the year Ashbee went on from Cambridge to train as
an architect in the offices of G. F. Bodley, he went to hear
Carpenter lecture to the Hammersmith branch of the
Socialist League, and there met William Morris. At this
time Ashbee was living at Toynbee Hall in Whitechapel,
opened two years earlier to bring undergraduates into contact with people of the East End, and was lecturing there,
and at Working Men's Clubs, on Ruskin.

Ashbee's lectures led to his class undertaking the decoration of the dining-room in the new Toynbee Hall buildings, and by the end of 1887 he was planning a craft school
and guild. Despite the fact that, when consulted, Morris
poured 'a great deal of cold water' on his ideas, the School
and Guild of Handicraft were established at Toynbee Hall
in June 1888. Ashbee was only twenty-five, and early
members included former office clerks and barrow-boys,
with only one metalworker, John Pearson, and a cabinet-
maker (and active trade unionist) C. V. Adams.

In 1891 the Guild moved to Essex House, an elegant
Queen Anne building in the Mile End Road. Ashbee lived
there until his marriage, although the regular suppers, out-
ings and entertainments with Guild members continued.

Over the next ten years the Guild grew and acquired new
skills, and in 1899 a shop was opened just off Bond Street.
Jewellery, inspired by Ashbee's admiration for Italian
Renaissance originals, and silver tablewares were always
the most popular items. Ashbee used several favourite
design motifs; the peacock, the ship, the sun, the tree of

life, and the pink, which grew in the garden at Essex House
and was adopted as a Guild emblem.

Ashbee worked closely with his silversmiths: craftsman
and designer learned new techniques together, finishing
silver pieces by planishing with a small round hammer to
give a beautiful texture to the surface. The Guild's furniture, too, was remarkable for the quality of the metalwork,
and Ashbee's collaboration with Baillie Scott on the furnishings for the Grand Duke of Hesse's palace in Darmstadt
did much to refine his style.

In 1896 Ashbee made the first of several visits to America;
over the years he met many American designers and architects, including Elbert Hubbard, Charles Sumner Greene
and Frank Lloyd Wright, who became a good friend.

Despite the commercial success of the Guild, Ashbee
wanted something more from his dream, and in 1902 a
democratic decision was taken to remove the Guild and the
members' families to Chipping Campden in Gloucestershire where these Londoners could come 'home' to the
land. They took over a disused silk mill in the village as
workshops, and renovated local houses to live in; they built
a swimming-pool in the river, grew their own vegetables
and sang folk-songs. But in 1907 the Guild, which at one
time numbered 150 working men, women and boys, went
into voluntary liquidation, defeated not only by the costs of
removal to the country and the difficulty of sending goods
to London for sale (for there was no railway nearby), but
also by the impossibility of laying men off when orders were
thin, as they had been able to do in the city.

Ashbee returned to London, to his architectural practice, more convinced than ever of the need for radical social
change in order to allow guilds of the future to survive.

ENTERTAINMENT

Maypole dancing on the village green, an English custom fondly
'remembered' by Arts and Crafts supporters

Nowhere was the Arts and Crafts nostalgia for a lost rural idyll, for 'olde English' hospitality and for a quondam English identity more evident than in the ways in which people enjoyed themselves. Country dances, maypole dancing, morris dancing, ballads, madrigals, Christmas mummers' plays, medieval revels and pageants were all revived, not only in reality but as a source of illustration and decorative motif.

In 1881 Ruskin devised a May Queen ceremony for Whitelands teacher-training college in Chelsea, commissioning gold 'Queen of the May' brooches of hawthorn entwined about a cross from his friends Arthur Severn and Edward Burne-Jones.

In 1885 Walter Crane was involved with a series of tableaux vivants put on by the Royal Society of Painters in Watercolours and entitled 'The Masque of Painters'; twelve years later, another tableau vivant, 'Beauty's Awakening: A Masque of Winter and of Spring', combined his talents with those of C. R. Ashbee, Henry Wilson and other members of the Art Workers' Guild, which had held a meeting on masques and pageants earlier in the year. In Glasgow, too, Fra (Francis) Newbery, principal of the

School of Art, organized masques with his students.

Ernest Gimson and his wife Emily were both interested in traditional English music, and were friendly with both Cecil Sharp, the collector of English folk-songs, and Arnold Dolmetsch, who revived appreciation of early English music, particularly of the recorder. Through the Century Guild in 1892, A. H. Mackmurdo, also a friend of Dolmetsch, organized three concerts of sixteenth- and seventeenth-century music, performed on the viol, lute and harpsichord; Janet Ashbee edited a collection of English folk-songs, the *Essex House Song Book*, published in 1903; Harry Peach, the founder of Dryad Handicrafts, was a prominent member of the Folk Dancing Society.

Ashbee was also a member of the Elizabethan Stage Society, which produced Elizabethan and Jacobean plays according to their original conventions. The contemporary London stage underwent its own revolution, with dramatists such as Oscar Wilde and Arthur Pinero, designers such as Edward Gordon Craig (son of the actress Ellen Terry and E. W. Godwin), and actresses such as Sarah Bernhardt and Eleonora Duse, and Gordon Craig's one-time lover, the dancer Isadora Duncan.

Interior of the Tabard Inn, Bedford Park, Chiswick, as it is today

The Apotheosis of Italian Art, by Walter Crane, 1885, from the tableau vivant 'The Masque of Painters'. City Art Gallery, Manchester

PRIVATE PRESSES

Since his undergraduate days, William Morris had been interested in medieval illumination and book production, and he collected illuminated manuscripts and early printed books throughout his life. In January 1891 he installed a second-hand Albion hand-press in his house at Hammersmith, intending to return to first principles, with authentic papers, inks, and typefaces. He was helped in his researches by his friend Emery Walker, who had advised the Century Guild on the printing of their magazine *The Hobby Horse* in 1884, and who went on to found the Doves Press with T. J. Cobden-Sanderson in 1900. Walker had lectured at the Arts and Crafts Exhibition Society in 1888 on the importance of book design: 'Type and paper may be said to be to a printed book, what stone or bricks and mortar are to architecture,' he declared. 'They are the essentials, without which there can be no book.'

Morris's first volume from the Kelmscott Press, *The Glittering Plain*, was published in May 1891; the initial edition of two hundred copies sold out, and on the basis of his success he moved to bigger premises and installed a second press. He published over fifty titles before his death in 1896, including his own works, those of Ruskin and Chaucer, and his own translations of Icelandic sagas and *The Tale of Beowulf*. He designed typefaces, such as Golden, Troy and Chaucer, decorative borders and initials; Burne-Jones contributed most of the woodblock illustrations.

The success of the Kelmscott Press inspired many other private presses, such as Charles Ricketts's Vale Press, Lucien Pissarro's Eragny Press and C. R. Ashbee's Essex House Press. Like Morris, Ashbee wrote many didactic pamphlets as well as books, and saw the opportunity of acquiring Morris's old presses, which he bought in 1898, as a means of publishing his own views in an Arts and Crafts manner. In 1907 Ananda Coomaraswamy, Ashbee's neighbour in Chipping Campden, took over the Essex House Press to publish his own book, *Medieval Sinhalese Art*. By 1910, when Coomaraswamy left for India, the Essex House Press had printed more than ninety titles.

In America, more than fifty private presses were estab-

The frontispiece of *News From Nowhere* by William Morris, Kelmscott Press, 1892, with an illustration of Kelmscott Manor by Charles March Gere

lished between 1895 and 1910. Daniel Berkeley Updike's Merrymount Press, founded in Boston in 1893, was one of the first. Like the Doves Press, Updike introduced a plainer, more sober style. Other American presses included Elbert Hubbard's Roycroft Press, Will Bradley's Wayside Press, the Blue Sky Press in Chicago, the Alwil Press in New Jersey and Frederic W. Goudy's Village Press, founded in Chicago in 1903 and moved to Massachusetts the following year.

In Europe, the Kelmscott Press inspired new interest in typography and printing, for books, magazines and posters, mainly in the new *Jugendstil* or Art Nouveau style.

Above: Opening pages of Morris's *Notes* on founding the Kelmscott Press, with illustration by Burne-Jones and 'Golden' type, initial and borders by Morris

Below: Title page from *The Book of Common Prayer*, the Merrymount Press, 1928

Right: Pages from the *Song Book of the Guild of Handicraft*, Essex House Press

THE BOOK OF
COMMON PRAYER

and Administration of the Sacraments
and Other Rites and Ceremonies
of the Church

ACCORDING TO THE USE OF THE
PROTESTANT EPISCOPAL CHURCH
IN THE UNITED STATES OF AMERICA

Together with The Psalter
or Psalms of David

PRINTED FOR THE COMMISSION
A. D. MDCCCCXXVIII

ISCELLANY OF SONG, IN WHICH ARE INCLUDED SONGS OF THE UNIVERSITIES AND SONGS OF PURE NONSENSE, BEING THE TENTH PART OF THE SONG BOOK OF THE GUILD OF HANDICRAFT.

THE LEATHER BOTTÈL.

16th or 17th Century.

When I survey the world around
The wondrous things that do abound,
The ships that on the sea do swim
To keep our foes that none come in,
Ay! let them all say what they can,
'Twas for one end the use of man,
So I wish him joy where'er he dwell,
That first found out the leather bottèl.

Now what do you say to those cans of wood?
Oh, no, in faith they cannot be good!
For if the bearer fall by the way
Why on the ground your liquor doth lay:
But had it been in a leather bottèl,
Although he had fallen, all had been well:
So I wish him joy where'er he dwell,
That first found out the leather bottèl.

Then what do you say to these glasses fine?
Oh, they shall have no praise of mine!
For if you chance to touch the brim,
Down falls the liquor and all therein.
But had it been in a leather bottèl,
And the stopper in, all had been well:
So I wish him joy where'er he dwell,
That first found out the leather bottèl.
VII.—2

GUSTAV STICKLEY

Above left: Oak reclining chair made in Gustav Stickley's Craftsman Workshops c.1905, and based on Morris and Co.'s earlier, successful version; oak bookcase (*below left*), with wrought iron lock plate and handle, designed by Gustav Stickley; and (*far right*) a chest of drawers in oak designed by Harvey Ellis and produced by the Craftsman workshops, c.1907

Gustav Stickley (1857–1942) learned his craft from an uncle in Pennsylvania who made wooden and cane-seated chairs, and, during the 1880s, in partnership with his brother, he made and sold reproduction furniture in various styles. However, he came under the influence of a teacher from Syracuse University who admired the writings of Ruskin and Morris, and in 1898 he visited England and saw work by Mackmurdo, Baillie Scott, Voysey and other Arts and Crafts movement designers whose work he knew from the pages of *The Studio* magazine.

On his return to Syracuse, Stickley founded his own company, and in 1901 established United Crafts, intended to be a profit-sharing guild, 'the beginning of a new and unique labor association, a guild of cabinet makers, metal and leather workers, formed for the production of household furnishings', as he described it. In October he launched *The Craftsman* magazine. In its first issue, devoted to William Morris, he wrote that he wanted 'to promote and to extend the principles established by Morris, in both the artistic and the socialistic sense'. Although, as the firm grew, the workers no longer received stock options, and the United Crafts Guild was reorganized and renamed the Craftsman Workshops, Stickley continued for several years to print overtly socialist articles in the *The Craftsman*.

The Craftsman Workshops produced strong, simple, comfortable, plain oak furniture 'in the endeavor', so Stickley wrote in 1901, 'to substitute the luxury of taste for the luxury of costliness'. Some of his early designs owed much to Baillie Scott, and the adjustable reclining chair, produced around 1902, was surely based on a Morris and Co. original. In May 1902 a metalwork shop was opened, making copper handles and strap-hinges for furniture as well as hand-wrought copper vases, jardinières and plaques.

In 1903 Stickley was joined by the architect Harvey Ellis, who refined and lightened the Craftsman style, adding a more subtle and sophisticated sense of mass and line, perhaps partly derived from the work of the Glasgow School designers whose furniture he saw illustrated in *The Studio*. He used less applied metalwork, but introduced conventionalized floral motifs inlaid in pewter, copper and stained and exotic woods. Harvey Ellis died prematurely in January 1904, but his brief influence immensely benefited the furniture made over the next half-dozen years. After 1910 few new designs were introduced.

The Craftsman style struck a chord with the American public and was immensely popular: the mail-order catalogues went all over the United States, and Craftsman furniture could be seen in showrooms from Boston to Los Angeles. But, after a move to New York in 1913, Stickley overextended his growing financial empire and in 1915 went bankrupt: the Craftsman Workshops were amalgamated with his brothers' firm, L. and J. G. Stickley. The last issue of *The Craftsman* was published in December 1916.

An Eclectic Style

A vital influence that tempered the appeal of Gothic just as the Arts and Crafts movement gathered pace was the Aesthetic movement, which brought a lighter, more whimsical, touch to the new style. The Aesthetic movement combined the growing cult for all things Japanese with the developing interest in a revival of the so-called 'Queen Anne' style of architecture, and added its own element of wit, of cultivated artificiality and of decadence. Such an element of modern sophistication was vital: as Richard Norman Shaw, G. E. Street's pupil and the greatest proponent of the 'Queen Anne' revival style, said of Gothic in 1902: 'I am personally devoted to it, admire it in the abstract, and think it superb; but it is totally unsuited to modern requirements. . . .' The influence of the Aesthetic movement prevented the Arts and Crafts from losing themselves in medieval nostalgia.

Japanese arts and crafts were first widely seen in England in 1862 when Sir Rutherford Alcock, Britain's first official representative in Japan, exhibited his personal collection of Japanese lacquer, bronze and porcelain at the International Exhibition in London, for Japan had been closed to the West for many years. Japanese attitudes to design were very much in harmony with the prevailing Western ideas of the time, especially in that oriental art tended to blur the distinctions between the fine and applied arts. Those British artists struggling to escape from the strict demarcations set by the Royal Academy found in Japanese arts not only a welcome simplicity and new forms of representation but also an ancient respect for other media.

One of the first serious collectors of Japanese prints was William Burges, who found in Japanese arts the same freedom of expression and lack of regularity that he most admired in Gothic. His friends D. G. Rossetti and E. W. Godwin were also early collectors. The ebonized couch that Rossetti exhibited in 1862 in the Medieval Court was Japanese-inspired, and Godwin, then living in Bristol, was one of the very first to decorate his home in the Japanese taste, with *tatami* mats on the floor, Japanese fans and prints (bought in the early 1860s) on the walls, and blue and white vases. Nevertheless, Godwin, like Burges and Rossetti, managed to combine all manner of influences, from Gothic to Greek. In 1867, for example, he incorporated Japanese peacock and sun motifs in a Gothic castle built in Ireland for the Earl of Limerick.

Woven silk 'Butterfly' brocade, designed by E. W. Godwin, c. 1874. Victoria & Albert Museum, London

Wallpaper, frieze, filling and dado designed by Bruce Talbert for Jeffrey and Co. in 1887. Victoria & Albert Museum, London

In the 1870s Godwin designed furniture and interiors for his friends, Oscar Wilde and James McNeill Whistler, both of whom lived in Tite Street, Chelsea, and also for the actresses Ellen Terry (by whom he had two children) and Lillie Langtry. The White House at 35 Tite Street was designed for Whistler in 1877; in its lightness and simplicity, it was a far cry from the designs for town halls and Gothic castles he had worked on in the previous decade. The red brick and white woodwork of other similar houses in Tite Street were typical of the new 'Queen Anne' style, not only in their tall, irregular windows, either leaded or enhanced with white glazing bars, but also in their gables, dormers and ornate chimneys. Norman Shaw, the most famous practitioner of this comfortable, light and supposedly hygienic middle-class style, set up his own architectural office in London in 1862, and his clients, too, included such luminaries of the Aesthetic movement as Kate Greenaway, for whom he built a house in Hampstead in 1885; in 1877 he had succeeded Godwin as estate architect at Bedford Park, London's first 'garden suburb'.

Perfection was an essential ingredient of the Aesthetic style, and Godwin oversaw the decoration of Oscar Wilde's house himself. One room was painted in different shades of white and the palest grey, and the dramatist described the dining-room chairs as 'sonnets in ivory', the table as a 'masterpiece in pearl'. In 1874, when decorating the house he shared in Harpenden with Ellen Terry, Godwin had even mixed his own paints – a dark-toned yellow and a pale grey-green, which he described as 'that green sometimes seen at the stem end of a pineapple leaf when the other end has faded – indeed I may as well confess that most of the colours in the rooms have been gathered from the pineapple'. Another room, 'almost entirely furnished with Japanese things', was done in shades of blue, and, in the hall, the floorboards were waxed and left bare, the walls were of creamy vellum and the paintwork light red – a stunningly modern combination.

While it was probably Whistler who inspired Godwin's colour sense, it was Oscar Wilde who did most to ally the Aesthetic movement to new developments in literature and poetry. In France, Baudelaire had translated the works of Edgar Allan Poe, while Proust translated Ruskin; Wilde in turn took works by Huysmans and de Montesquieu and popularized them, in 1891, in *The Picture of Dorian Gray*. The notion common to all these writers, and also, earlier, to Walter Pater and, subsequently, to Henry James, was that beautiful objects had the power to evoke moods and feelings in the beholder. The French theory of *correspondances* held that objects of specially heightened significance – Wilde claimed that, for him, it was blue and white china, but for other aesthetes it might have been a Japanese fan, a sunflower or a lily – were beautiful only in that they reflected and enhanced the passion of the spectator. According to Wilde, 'It is the spectator, and not life, that art really mirrors.'

In self-conscious England, such aesthetic philosophies were doomed to be short-lived. People who worshipped blue and white porcelain, or peacock feathers and used Japanese parasols as summer firescreens were lampooned by W. S. Gilbert in

Stoneware pot with incised decoration of lilies and a dragonfly, made by the Martin Brothers in 1884

Patience, first produced in 1881, and, as the Cimabue Browns, in George du Maurier's *Punch* cartoons. In England, too, the much vaunted admiration of the Aesthetes for decadence and unnaturalness was seen to degenerate into a series of rows and scandals: an attack by Ruskin on Whistler's paintings led to a celebrated libel case, Rossetti retreated into drug abuse, and Oscar Wilde was imprisoned for homosexuality. In France, on the other hand, Baudelaire's poems inspired a series of magnificent vases by the glass designer Emile Gallé, who also greatly admired Japanese art, and Art Nouveau designers such as Louis Majorelle and Hector Guimard thrived upon the intensity of such decadent ideas.

The English Aesthetic movement, perhaps typified by the work of Lewis F. Day, Walter Crane and Thomas Jekyll, remained essentially light, pretty and elegant. Jekyll, who went insane in 1877 and died four years later, executed woodwork for the Liverpool

Sideboard made by Kimbel and Cabus, New York, in their Modern Gothic style, c.1876–82. Cooper-Hewitt Museum, New York

shipping magnate Frederick Leyland; this formed part of the original scheme for the room in Leyland's house at 49 Princes Gate, hung with priceless embossed Spanish leather – a wallcovering that Whistler then obliterated, unasked, with turquoise and gold peacocks. Jekyll was best known for his cast-iron fire grates, often set with blue and white tiles, and enhanced with Japanese-inspired swirls or butterflies.

Japanese design led to the simplification of line and colour in textile design as well as to the adoption of oriental motifs; Godwin, Bruce Talbert and Christopher Dresser all created Aesthetic-style fabrics. In ceramics, too, the influence of Japan was strong, and Wedgwood, Worcester, and Minton all produced porcelains in the Aesthetic taste. In 1871 Minton's Art-Pottery Studio was established in Kensington Gore under the directorship of W. S. Coleman, whose own simpering ceramic portraits of Aesthetic nymphs highlight the gulf between English prettiness and the brooding intensity of French Art Nouveau. However, the Martin Brothers, at their pottery in Southall, turned out stoneware decorated with naturalistic Japanese-inspired plants, birds, fish and insects which showed a true understanding of the basis of Japanese motifs. Edwin Martin also produced abstract vases in the strong, muted colours of stoneware that, by their shape and texture, suggested natural vegetable or marine forms. And at Farmer and Rogers Emporium, which sold all manner of exotic imported items, the oriental manager, Arthur Lasenby Liberty, realized that there was a healthy market for furnishings in the new style; after twelve years' service, he left in 1875 to set up his own store, Liberty and Co.

In the winter of 1881 Oscar Wilde, the 'ultra poetical, super-aesthetical, soul-eyed young man', arrived, lilies in hand, on the shores of America. His lecture tour was greeted with delight, for the Americans had already begun their own Aesthetic movement after both Japanese and modern European arts and crafts had been widely seen at the 1876 Centennial Exposition in Philadelphia. Japanese pottery, porcelain and prints, displayed in the Japanese pavilion, were shown at the Philadelphia Exposition, as were such Anglo-Japanese-style pieces as Godwin's furniture designs for Collinson and Lock. American manufacturers such as Mitchell and Rammelsberg of Cincinnati or Kimbel and Cabus of New York had themselves begun to adopt some of the visual idioms of the Anglo-Japanese style, and

Opposite left: Ebonized cherry wardrobe with inlaid woods, made for the actress Lillian Russell by Herter Brothers, New York in 1880–5. Metropolitan Museum of Art, New York

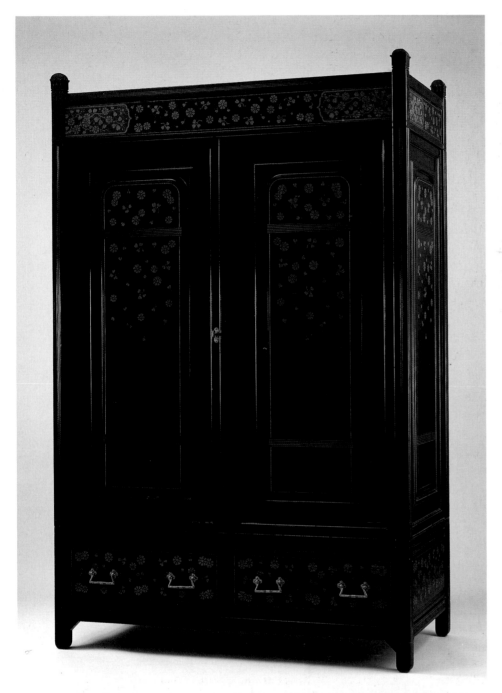

Japanese-inspired white-and-gilt Worcester vase, 1884, photographed on a silk textile by Bruce Talbert, designed for the 1876 Philadelphia Exhibition

ebonized furniture enhanced with gilt was exhibited alongside the plain oak of the American 'Eastlake' or 'Modern Gothic' manner. Kimbel and Cabus, for example, displayed an entire drawing room furnished in ebonized cherry at the exhibition.

The best American Aesthetic movement furniture was made by Herter Brothers of New York. In 1860 Christian Herter, who was born in Stuttgart, joined the cabinet-making firm that his older brother, Gustave, had founded three years earlier in New York. In the mid-1860s Christian returned to Paris, where he had earlier studied, and also visited England in the early 1870s. Gustave retired in 1870, and over the next few years the younger Herter, aided by William B. Bigelow, the architect in charge of the design department, produced furniture to a high standard of craftsmanship in a variety of revival styles, including Modern Gothic. By the time that Christian retired to Paris in 1880, Herter Brothers were producing their finest Anglo-Japanese pieces with incised and gilded carving and inlaid woods and metals, as well as supplying furnishing fabrics, mosaic, light fittings and imported wallpapers and decorative objects.

Herter Brothers' clients in these years included the American financial magnates William H. Vanderbilt, J. Pierpont Morgan and Jay Gould, as well as Broadway stars such as Lillian Russell who played in Gilbert and Sullivan's comic operas. Their furniture, in cherry or rosewood, inlaid with asymmetrical marquetry designs in lighter woods, used Japanese-style flowers and other motifs to elegant and beautiful effect. Christian Herter died in 1883, but the firm continued in business until the turn of the century, working in a variety of styles.

The range of influences introduced by the Centennial Exposition varied from the Gothic Revival and Arts and Crafts to Japanese design or French Art Nouveau, and by the 1890s Americans could choose happily between a wide diversity of home-produced furnishings. Ties with France during the earlier part of the century had been strong in many branches of the arts, most especially in architecture, but the Centennial celebrations encouraged a revival of interest in the American 'old colonial' furnishings of the previous century. In combination with the 'Shingle' style of the architectural firm McKim, Mead and White and the work of the Boston architect H. H. Richardson, which broke with the prevailing taste for ornate Renaissance revival buildings, the Americans now introduced a simplicity and lightness into domestic architecture, similar to the English 'Queen Anne' revival.

In 1876 Dr Christopher Dresser visited America *en route* for Japan, where he was to advise the Japanese Ministry of the Interior on the display of European artefacts in the Imperial Museum, and on adapting crafts to machine production. He had already been commissioned by a merchant in London to make a collection of Japanese goods, and, in New York, Tiffany and Co. requested a similar collection. Following his visit, some of Dresser's own metalwork designs incorporated added Japanese decoration, but it was Tiffany's chief silversmith and silver designer, Edward C. Moore, who most fully exploited the Japanese use of hand-crafted textural effects and their combinations of precious and coloured base metals, where silver and gold contrasted with brass and

Far right: Coffee set in silver, decorated in other metals, by Tiffany and Co., New York

Right: Vase decorated by Matthew Daly at the Rookwood Pottery, Cincinnati, Ohio in 1899

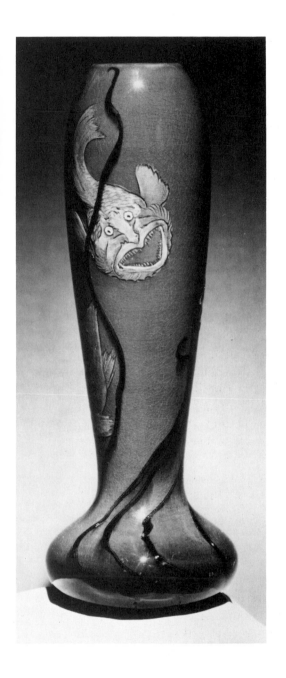

copper. Moore, who before Dresser's visit to Japan had already amassed an extensive reference library and collection, first began using Japanese motifs in the late 1860s; in the 1870s he established a distinctive Aesthetic style, using oriental flowers, vines, gourds, fish and dragonflies made of contrasting metals, and sometimes combining such effects with restrained forms of Art Nouveau.

In 1869 Tiffany's rival, the Gorham Co. of Providence, Rhode Island, also began to produce silver in the Anglo-Japanese style, as did the Whiting Manufacturing Co. of North Attleboro, Massachusetts. In 1897 Gorham launched their 'Martelé' (meaning 'hammered') range under the direction of an Englishman, William Codman. The tea- and coffee-services, fruit dishes and vases in the Martelé range used undulating, natural forms inspired by Art Nouveau.

In ceramics, too, the range of inspiration was diverse. Such visitors to the 1876 Centennial Exposition as Maria Longworth Nichols and M. Louise McLaughlin learned of new methods and techniques from the work of Taxile Doat at Sèvres and Ernest Chaplet at Limoges, from Royal Doulton and Minton's Art-Pottery and from the porcelains in the Japanese pavilion. It was not until 1887, however, seven years after she had founded the Rookwood Pottery, that Nichols employed her first non-American craftsman, the young Kataro Shirayamadani. In 1893, at Rookwood's request, he returned to Japan to study local glazing techniques, and his decorative motifs — carp, wading birds, and chrysanthemum- and peony-like flowers — remained popular long after Oscar Wilde's trail-blazing tour of the early 1880s had been forgotten.

'Peony' stained glass window by John La Farge, c.1893–1908

The American Aesthetic movement produced one unique art form – the leaded glass designed by John La Farge and Louis Comfort Tiffany. Morris and Co. glass had first been introduced to America by an associate of Bruce Talbert, Daniel Cottier, who opened a shop in New York in 1873 selling Morris and Co. furnishings and ecclesiastical glass. Cottier went on to work with H. H. Richardson, contributing windows to his Trinity Church in Boston, where he was also technical adviser to John La Farge.

La Farge was a lawyer who wanted to become a painter. He visited Europe in the late 1850s, when he also began to collect Japanese prints, and again in the early 1870s, when he met several of the Pre-Raphaelite painters and saw the work of Morris and Co. In 1875 he carried out his first experiments with stained glass, and the following year met Daniel Cottier in Boston. In 1878 he began to design sumptuous windows for private clients, including Cornelius Vanderbilt II in New York and Sir Lawrence Alma-Tadema in London, and by the time of his death in 1906 had produced several thousand windows. Influenced by Japanese prints (he published his impressions of a visit to Japan in *An Artist's Letters from Japan* in 1886), he designed flat, asymmetrical flowers with no painted detail, using instead layered or plated glass, including white opalescent glass, to add subtleties of colour and richness of texture. The shimmering irregularities of the glass alone give a suggestion of depth to the bold blossoms and ornate backgrounds of his designs.

La Farge's technical achievements inspired his more famous successor, L. C. Tiffany, in his experiments with both leaded and blown glass. Tiffany started in business in 1879 as an interior decorator in a partnership named L. C. Tiffany and Associated Artists. The other members of the firm were Candace Wheeler, who was responsible for textiles, George Coleman, an expert in oriental textiles, and Lockwood de Forest, who specialized in carved and ornamental woodwork. Clients included Samuel Clemens ('Mark Twain'), an old friend of Mrs Wheeler's, the English actress, Lillie Langtry, for whose bed they made a silken canopy 'with loops of full-blown, sunset-coloured roses' and a coverlet of 'the delicatest shade of rose-pink satin, sprinkled plentifully with rose petals fallen from the wreaths above', and President Arthur, for whom they revamped the White House.

Candace Wheeler was a woman in her early fifties, a friend of many artists and writers, including John La Farge, F. E. Church and Frederick Law Olmstead, who designed New York's Central Park and pioneered the establishment of the National Parks. Impressed by the work of London's Royal School of Art Needlework exhibited at the 1876 Centennial Exposition, she had founded both the New York Society of Decorative Art to sell needlework, painting, wood-carving and china-painting executed by women, and the Women's Exchange, which sold anything women could produce. She developed the 'needleweaving' technique, patented in 1882, to obtain the naturalistic, painterly effects sought by Tiffany for *portières*, curtains and other hangings.

Tiffany himself was strongly influenced at this time by Moorish architecture, and he contributed the pierced metalwork screens and staircases that added an air of the *Arabian Nights* to Associated Artists' early interiors. Work on the Veterans' Room and Library for the Seventh Regiment Armory on Park Avenue, for example, carried out in 1879–80, combined carved oak panelling, scrolling ironwork, turquoise tiles in the fireplace, a frieze of silver, stencilled silver arabesques, five stained-glass panels and embroidered *portières* to create a rich, textured, sumptuous effect that made real the intense, artistic interiors described by Poe, Wilde or Huysmans.

Despite the success of Associated Artists, in 1883 the four partners went their separate ways; Candace Wheeler continued to run the decorating business until her retirement in 1900. Tiffany became increasingly involved in his experiments with glass. So successful were the productions of Tiffany Studios – windows, lamps, vases – and, like the glass of Gallé or Daum Frères in France, so in keeping with the style of the *fin de siècle*, that they were widely copied: in 1901 two former employees started their own firm, the Quezal Art Glass and Decorating Co. of Brooklyn, and in 1904 the Steuben Glass Works in New York first produced their 'Aurene' range in direct imitation of Tiffany's 'Favrile' glass.

By 1900, in both painting and design, the lessons absorbed from Japanese art had been transmuted into new forms and ideas, but it is worth remembering how revolutionary the use of flat perspectives seemed at the time, not to mention the lack of detail and the asymmetrical arrangements, and how great a challenge the new work of those painters who admired Japanese forms, such as Whistler, Van Gogh or Toulouse-Lautrec, was to the established art world.

Opposite: Silver presentation vase with engraved decoration made by the Gorham Company of Providence, Rhode Island in 1881

E. W. GODWIN

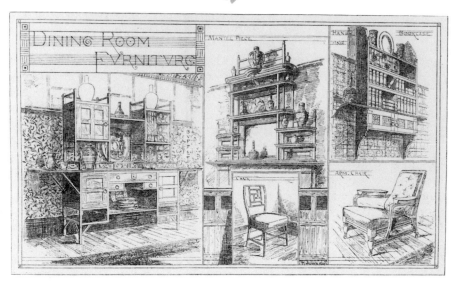

Art furniture for the dining room designed by E. W. Godwin and illustrated in William Watt's
catalogue in 1877

The architect Edwin William Godwin (1833–86) designed his first pieces of furniture when he moved his architectural practice from Bristol to London in the mid-1860s and required inexpensive furniture for his new chambers. By looking at Japanese prints, Godwin had studied the way in which Japanese furniture was constructed, and the fine struts in his designs were inspired by these woodcuts and by *shoji* or *fusama* screens. 'There were to be no mouldings,' he wrote later in 1876, 'no ornamental metal work, no carving. Such effect as I wanted I endeavoured to gain, as in economical building, by the mere grouping of solid and void and by more or less broken outline.'

These early pieces of Anglo-Japanese furniture – a sideboard, side-table and chair, made in ebonized deal – remain his most famous designs, and were later manufactured by William Watt and by Collinson and Lock, and pirated by many other manufacturers. Later, searching for lightness and strength, he used mahogany rather than deal.

In July 1872 he entered into an exclusive three-year contract with Collinson and Lock, Art furnishers, to provide designs not only for furniture but also for fireplaces, gas brackets, lock plates, iron bedsteads and carpets. They parted company before the end of three years, although Collinson and Lock produced rosewood furniture to his designs long afterwards. And in 1877 Watt produced a catalogue of inexpensive Art furniture designed by Godwin.

Sometimes Godwin incorporated in his furniture actual fragments of Japanese ivory, leather-like embossed paper or wooden carved panels (some of them bought at Arthur Lasenby Liberty's new emporium), as well as painted panels by such friends as Whistler, Burne-Jones, Albert Moore and Burne-Jones's pupil Charles Fairfax Murray. At the Paris Exposition Universelle in 1878 he exhibited a group of furniture decorated by Whistler with abstract Japanese-inspired cloud forms.

Godwin's designs for textiles and wallpapers, too, were often based on motifs from Japanese silks, such as a peacock, or the flowering bamboo used for a wallpaper for Jeffrey and Co., and he also designed tiles for Burmantoft and for Minton and Hollins in the new Anglo-Japanese taste.

CHRISTOPHER DRESSER

Dr Christopher Dresser (1834–1904) was every inch the Victorian self-made man, hard-working, talkative and opportunistic. He had entered the Government School of Design when he was thirteen, by the age of twenty-one was lecturing on botany in the provincial Schools, and in the 1860s held professorships in botany both at the South Kensington Museum and at St Mary's School of Medicine. He believed that design should be based upon scientific evidence and principle, and his first books, *Unity in Variety*, 1859, and *The Art of Decorative Design*, 1862, championed the doctrine of conventionalization.

He was a prolific designer, contributing his first freelance designs for textiles, carpets, ceramics and wallpapers to manufacturers such as Brinton and Lewis, Minton, and Wedgwood in the late 1860s. He employed several students and designers in his studio, but all the work went out under his name.

In the 1870s he began designing silver and electroplate for Elkington's, Hukin and Heath and, in 1879, for James Dixon and Son of Sheffield. His sparse, severe designs were quite radical; refusing to compromise with traditional tastes, he had written in 1873: 'In order to its existence [*sic*] a vessel must be constructed but when formed it need not of necessity be ornamented'. His revolutionary metalwork designs are among the earliest celebrations of an industrial aesthetic.

In June 1879, following his trip to America and Japan, Dresser opened a warehouse for Japanese goods in Farringdon Road with Charles Holme (who later founded *The Studio*), and in 1880 he set up the Art Furnishers' Alliance in New Bond Street, with himself as principal designer and 'Art Manager', but despite the craze for all things Aesthetic, both projects were short-lived. However, his time with the Art Furnishers' Alliance did afford Dresser the opportunity to make his début in designing furniture, some of it in the Egyptian style. He also designed cast-iron garden and hall furniture, such as umbrella stands, tables and coat stands, for the Shropshire iron-founders, Coalbrookdale. In 1882 he published a book on his Japanese visit: *Japan: its Architecture, Art and Art Manufactures*.

The energetic Dr Dresser had also been instrumental in setting up the Linthorpe Pottery, established in Yorkshire in 1879, and he remained responsible for design until 1882, when Linthorpe's manager, Henry Tooth, who had also developed most of the glazes, left to go into partnership with William Ault. When Ault founded his own pottery in 1887, Dresser was once again involved.

In the mid-1890s, when he was nearing retirement, Dresser mastered yet another medium when the Glasgow firm of James Couper and Sons began a new venture with the introduction of their 'Clutha' glass. George Walton also designed Clutha glass, but the most distinctive designs were by Dresser and show a rare, romantic sensitivity to natural forms and rhythms. Like L. C. Tiffany, he was influenced by Roman and Middle-Eastern glass, and the blown pieces of opaque green glass, in sinuous, twisted shapes, are often shot with translucent streaks of gold or cream.

'Clutha' glass vase; a silver-plated crow's foot Hukin and Heath claret jug of Egyptian inspiration, 1881; a Wedgwood pottery vase, c. 1885; a three-legged copper kettle made by Benham and Froud, c. 1885; and a Linthorpe pot, all designed by Christopher Dresser. Private collection, Birkenhead

Overleaf, left: 'Lava' glass vases, L.C. Tiffany's expressionistic simulation of the effects of volcanic forces on glass. The black surface, enhanced with gold lustre, was created by the addition of basalt or talc to the molten glass. Howarth Art Gallery, Accrington

Overleaf, right: The Veterans' Room and Library of the Seventh Regiment Armoury on Park Avenue, New York, decorated by L.C. Tiffany and Associated Artists in 1879–80

LOUIS COMFORT TIFFANY

Anyone who was anybody in America at the turn of the century had a Tiffany window, lamp or mosaic in their home, or donated one to their local church, bank or college. Edgar Allan Poe could almost have been thinking of a Tiffany lamp which 'throws a tranquil but magical radiance over all', when he wrote his essay 'The Philosophy of Furniture', and Tiffany himself certainly believed in the value of stained glass which could fill otherwise drab interiors with warmth and light.

Louis Comfort Tiffany (1848–1933) was the son and heir of the founder of the famous American jewellery store, with his own exotic studio on the top floor of his father's New York mansion. He had studied painting under George Inness and travelled widely in Europe and North Africa. After the break with Associated Artists in 1883, he set up the Tiffany Glass Company, making stained-glass windows and also mosaic, tiles, glass plaques and lustred pieces for such architectural details as doorways, fireplaces and decorative friezes. In 1900, when Tiffany Studios reached their peak, the company also began to produce metalwork, enamelling and bronzes and, from 1904, pottery.

In 1892 he had bought his own glass furnaces at Corona, near New York, and began his experiments with the chemistry of glass-making. In 1895 the first leaded-glass lamps on bronze bases were sold to the public. However, not all the lamps – with names like Wisteria, Acorn, Dragonfly – were designed by Tiffany himself, and the firm continued to make them well into the 1930s after Tiffany had retired.

In 1896, the first 'Favrile' (meaning 'handmade') glass vases went on sale. Tiffany employed many different glass-making techniques, influenced not only by the carved cameo and intaglio decoration of the work of Emile Gallé, which he had seen at the Paris Exposition Universelle in 1889, but also by the ancient examples from his own extensive collection of Roman and Middle-Eastern glass, such as millefiori and lustre. He also perfected his own unique finishes, such as 'Cypriote', which imitated the pitted, corroded surface of excavated Roman glass, and 'Lava', with thick runs of gold dripping down a black body. His Favrile vases glow with colour, from the delicate green and white tracery of vine leaves on the intaglio glass, to bright turquoise, from vivid orange and iridescent gold, to sombre browns, blues and blacks; his forms, too, reflect his rather dream-like sensibility, both gentle and extravagant.

Part Three

THE POPULARIZATION OF THE MOVEMENT

The Refinement of the Style

As the Arts and Crafts movement reached maturity, it attained greater domestic elegance and coherence, concentrating far more on the middle-class home than on the grand interiors of the early Morris and Co. commissions. Gothic, too, was left behind, as the romance of chivalry and medieval hospitality gave way to a more manageable conception of domestic pleasures. The Arts and Crafts house symbolized warmth and shelter, informality and welcome, and was inspired no longer by Gothic cathedrals but by the cottage and the farmhouse.

Rural traditions, vernacular architecture, local materials – these were the elements employed by architects such as Philip Webb, C. F. A. Voysey and Edwin Lutyens in England, by Frank Lloyd Wright, and Greene and Greene in America, or Eliel Saarinen in Finland. Rough-cast stucco, tile-hanging, shingles, half-timbering, patterned brickwork, mullioned and leaded windows were all used to place a building within its particular landscape and to enhance the ornamental role of structural elements. At this time, too, architects began to take greater interest in landscaping their sites, thus provoking a fierce debate in England over the proper role of the architect in garden design.

The first house to break with the imitative historicism of the nineteenth century and create an environment for a modern family had been Philip Webb's Red House, built in 1859 for William Morris. Morris required none of the formality demanded by mid-Victorian social conventions, and passionately desired a home that was beautiful, practical and redolent of his dreams and ideals. The embroideries and furniture that he, Janey and their friends made for the house led to the setting up of Morris, Marshall, Faulkner and Co., and set a precedent that was followed by every Arts and Crafts architect. Morris later had plans to extend the house, to provide workshops for the firm and living quarters for Burne-Jones and his family, although this never happened.

By 1891, when Webb came to design Standen, in Sussex, for the London solicitor, James Beale, his ideas had refined even further. It was said that Webb was never satisfied with a building until it began to look commonplace. The exterior of Standen gives the impression almost of a collection of buildings that have grown together over time, linked by different shapes and textures – brick, stone, tile-hanging, weather-boarding and pebble-dash. Inside, the decorative elements are reticent and

The dining-room at Standen, Sussex, built by Philip Webb and originally furnished by Morris and Co.

MVSICA·DONVM·DEI

M.H. Baillie Scott's prize-winning design for the Music Room for a 'House for an Art Lover', a competition held by the *Zeitschrift für Innendekoration* in 1901. Victoria & Albert Museum, London

understated, with many built-in cupboards, sideboards and benches: Webb even specified the colour of much of the paintwork, such as the distinctive blue-green in the dining-room. He commissioned metalwork from John Pearson, who had been associated with Ashbee's Guild, and light fittings from W. A. S. Benson (Standen was one of the first private houses to be completely electrified from its inception); the decoration of the house was carried out by Morris and Co.

Gradually the Arts and Crafts house came to be increasingly characterized by its internal features such as staircases or fireplaces. Sometimes the work was commissioned from individual or specialist firms – for example, the house that Halsey Ricardo designed at 8 Addison Road, Holland Park, for the department store owner Sir Ernest Debenham incorporated tiles by his former partner, William de Morgan, decorative plasterwork by Ernest Gimson and exterior tiles by Doulton's – but with growing frequency architects themselves were designing more of the details of decoration, from door furniture or stained glass to carpets and curtains.

In 1892 the foundation stone was laid for another Red House, this one built for himself by the architect M. H. Baillie Scott on the outskirts of Douglas, Isle of Man. Baillie Scott had come from Kent to the Isle of Man in 1889, and once there won several commissions for private houses. He had already designed a summer residence for the young Crown Princess Marie of Romania, sister-in-law of the Grand Duke Ernst Ludwig of Hesse, and, through the drawings and watercolour schemes for interiors that he later regularly sent to *The Studio*, his work became well known and much admired in Europe.

Baillie Scott's compact Red House bears little resemblance to Webb's radical building. On the outside, its traditional half-timbered and tile-hung brickwork is enlived by decorated eaves and by gargoyles squatting on the drainpipes. It is the interior, however, that most clearly shows not only the architect's attention to detail (for example in the fireplace, plasterwork and stained-glass panels), but also his imaginative and informal use of space with, downstairs, panelled walls between the hall, dining-room and drawing-room which slide open to give one large area for entertaining, and, upstairs, a top-lit, panelled gallery from which the bedrooms open out, the whole scheme making a modest house seem airy and roomy.

His later buildings, while still making use of gabled roofs, casement windows or ingle-nooks, are less self-consciously quaint. Baillie Scott described the home as an 'enchanted realm' and his colourful interiors retain a story-book quality about them. He designed somewhat box-like furniture, decorated with broad, simple patterns and motifs that appear to have their basis in folk traditions, and he often echoed his chosen motifs in stained glass or metalwork. In describing his work, but mistaking his origins, Hermann Muthesius wrote: 'We seem . . . to have stepped into the world of fantasy and romance of the ancient bardic poetry. . . . With Baillie Scott we are among the purely northern poets among British architects.'

It was C. F. A. Voysey who left behind the story-book content of decoration and

Lithograph of Newton Grove, Bedford Park in 1882, by J. Nash, who lived at 36 The Avenue

refined the middle-class house to a basic but easeful simplicity by taking control of every element of an interior. Like Pugin, whose work he greatly admired, he thought that decoration should have meaning. He was particularly interested in the evocative power of symbols, but he integrated the use of such favourite decorative motifs as the stylized heart with strong architectural features. He believed that a house had to provide both physical and spiritual shelter, and the qualities possessed by a home should, he wrote, include 'Repose, Cheerfulness, Simplicity ... Quietness in a storm ... Evidence of Protection ... and making the house a frame to its inmates.'

Voysey specialized in building individual houses set in their own grounds, and could make full use of local materials and traditions; however, in the years after the First World War, his distinctive low-slung roofs and dormer windows were widely copied in suburban housing, which also imitated Baillie Scott's use of black and white timberwork. Just as Ashbee had spoken of his East End Guild workers going 'home' to the land, so increasing numbers of city-dwellers dreamt of a nobler life lived in a cottage with roses round the door, much as Morris had depicted in 1890 in his Utopian romance, News From Nowhere, where the socialist future was exclusively rural. By 1900, indeed, the Arts and Crafts movement had come to symbolize a new Utopianism, based on the 'rediscovery' of a supposedly lost rural past. In fact, the rural areas of Britain had been in decline for decades, and by 1900 more than half the population had left the often bleak conditions of the land to live in cities, but the

notion persisted that an earlier rural golden age had been somehow decayed by industrialization and must now be restored.

The Arts and Crafts movement which had championed the rediscovery of lost arts now turned its attention to other manifestations of traditional rural culture (from cider-making to maypole dancing, from folk music to corn dollies), an interest reflected in the writings of Thomas Hardy or John Masefield and in the music of Vaughan Williams and Elgar. As the First World War approached, the 'Englishness' of this revival of folk culture was increasingly allied to patriotism.

One reflection of this dissatisfaction with city life came in 1898 when Ebenezer Howard published Tomorrow: A Peaceful Path to Social Reform, revised in 1902 as Garden Cities of Tomorrow. In 1899 Howard founded the Garden City Association, which led to the planning and building of the original garden city, at Letchworth, Hertfordshire, in 1903–4.

The first experiment in the creation of an 'aesthetic Eden', with five hundred houses, a kindergarten, other day schools, an art school, co-operative stores, a church and a club was not a garden city but an artistic suburb – Bedford Park in west London. In the 1870s Jonathan T. Carr, a cloth merchant, bought twenty-four acres of land with the intention of building a middle-class Aesthetic estate. His brother, J. W. Comyns Carr, was an art critic and a director of the influential Grosvenor Gallery, and may well have advised on the choice of E. W. Godwin as estate architect. Godwin began designing houses for Bedford Park in 1875 but resigned after criticism of his designs –

the kitchens were said to be poorly planned and the stairs and passageways narrow – and was replaced in 1877 by Norman Shaw. He, too, resigned two years later, although it is thought that he continued as consultant on the project. His successor was E. J. May.

Artists were encouraged to settle in Bedford Park by the provision of studios. Shaw had built several houses for artists, and, to some extent, the irregular disposition of windows in some of his plans was determined by an artist's need of light; certainly his airy, informal interiors suited their modern outlook on life. The Bedford Park houses were advertised as being light, practical and, above all, healthy. The poet W. B. Yeats, the playwright Arthur Pinero, the actor 'Squire' Bancroft, the wallpaper and textile designer C. J. Haité, and even a genuine Russian anarchist were all early residents; Voysey, too, lived there briefly.

Many different designers and manufacturers were involved on the project. The 'old-fashioned' Tabard Inn, designed by Shaw, had tiles by Walter Crane and William de Morgan. The club, by E. J. May, had furniture by Morris and Godwin, with de Morgan tiles and Japanese wallpaper. It not only provided tennis courts but also arranged theatricals, balls and masquerades. Women could also be members, and debates were held there on women's suffrage. Bedford Park received a great deal of publicity – and satiric comment – and other suburbs were quickly built in emulation, such as the Telford Avenue estate in Streatham, south London.

Appalled by the grim conditions of city slums, some industrialists built estate villages for their workers: for example, Port Sunlight in Lancashire or the Bourneville village near Birmingham, developed by the chocolate manufacturer George Cadbury in the 1890s. In 1902 the architects Barry Parker and Raymond Unwin were involved in the Rowntree model village at New Earswick near York, built by the Liberal chocolate manufacturer B. Seebohm Rowntree.

Parker and Unwin had set up in practice in Buxton in 1896. Unwin was Parker's second cousin and in 1893 had married Parker's sister. Both were committed socialists who had been strongly influenced by the writings and example of Edward Carpenter, the original proponent of the 'Simple Life', who lived on his own smallholding near Sheffield. Unwin and his family, like Carpenter, wore specially made sandals, homespun tweeds and 'Ruskin' flannels from the Isle of Man.

Unwin's desire to establish a socialist Utopia led him to become increasingly concerned with town planning and working-class housing. He found himself in tune with Ebenezer Howard's writings on social reform, and with the MP Jesse Collings's 'Back to the Land' movement, which aimed to re-create an ancient yeomanry by encouraging smallholdings. In 1904 Unwin and Parker developed the plans for Letchworth, the first garden city, and went themselves to live there. Their dream was for all classes to live side by side and enjoy the lifestyle of the English country house. Indeed, some of the houses at Letchworth were designed by Baillie Scott, whom Parker greatly admired.

In 1906 Parker and Unwin were involved in the planning of Hampstead Garden Suburb, a community for all classes in north London; however, Edwin Lutyens was

Forest Hills Gardens, Queens in 1914, looking along the arcade towards the inn designed by Grosvenor Atterbury

dens in Queens, New York, planned in 1909 by Frederick Law Olmstead, junior, and Grosvenor Atterbury, while further garden schemes were built in Britain and Europe in the years after the First World War.

But for many, the enduring dream of the Arts and Crafts movement remained the integration of the professional middle classes with village life, ideally through the rural craft guild. Ernest Gimson and Sidney Barnsley moved to Gloucestershire in 1893 because they felt that in the Cotswolds they could not only concentrate on their own ideas but also be inspired by rural life. Gimson later bought land at Sapperton with the intention of founding a community, but the First World War, and afterwards his own failing health, prevented this.

As an architect and designer, it was vital to Gimson not to be limited to the drawing-board, but to find firsthand experience of the materials and practical processes involved in building: this became synonymous with the mastery of disappearing craft techniques. In 1890 he had spent a few weeks learning the basic techniques of chair bodging from Philip Clissett, a traditional bodger from Herefordshire, who made turned, rush-seated chairs. He also spent time with a London firm of plasterworkers, and he continued to execute schemes of decorative plasterwork for ceilings, chimney-pieces, decorative friezes and even furniture, in which he was greatly influenced by examples of Elizabethan work. 'As regards design,' wrote Gimson in an essay on plasterwork, 'the first necessity is that the worker must show in his work something of the pleasure that he takes in natural things. And the second necessity is

appointed consulting architect in 1908. Baillie Scott again contributed to the project, with designs for flats for working women at Waterlow Court, a building of whitewashed brick with tiled roofs and a cloistered walkway around the garden. One of the prime movers in the Hampstead Garden Trust was Henrietta Barnet, wife of Canon S. A. Barnet, the first warden of Toynbee Hall and a founder of the Whitechapel Art Gallery.

The garden suburb idea spread to America, with projects such as Forest Hills Gar-

that he must have knowledge of old work, not that he may reproduce it, but that he may learn from it how to express his ideas. . . .' Gimson also returned to Tudor originals in the metalwork designs executed for him by Alfred Bucknell, the son of a local Cotswold blacksmith.

But it was in Sidney Barnsley's Cotswold work, perhaps more than in that of any other Arts and Crafts designer, that a true rural idiom was successfully re-employed. In his later work especially, Barnsley took the construction of agricultural tools and wagons as a basis; the wagon-back appeared in his designs for stretchers, and he adopted chamfering (used by wheelwrights to reduce the overall weight of a wagon without loss of strength) as a form of decoration. Gimson, too, adopted chamfering both as a reflection of traditional skills and as an attractive means of softening and enhancing the edges of his furniture.

Gimson and Sidney Barnsley were joined by Sidney's brother Ernest, and they and their families all became closely involved in village life, helping to revive the neglected traditions and revelries of the countryside. Their friend Alfred Powell described their rural life: 'It was wonderful [after] old smoky London to find yourself in those fresh clean rooms, furnished with good oak furniture and a trestle table that at seasonable hours surrendered its drawing-boards to a good English meal, in which figured, if I remember right, at least on guest nights, a great stone jar of best ale.' They made their own bread and cider, and cooked in a large brick oven which Philip Webb showed particular interest in. Another friend recalled Ernest Barnsley's search for authentic foods: 'A real

"bon viveur", he enjoyed not only eating a good dinner but buying the ingredients and cooking it himself, with his wife and daughters' assistance. Wherever he went he collected recipes for good dishes or the addresses from whence he could obtain special delicacies. His York hams and Wensleydale cheeses came from farms in Yorkshire direct, Welsh mutton from Brecon and pork pies from Melton Mowbray. . . . His sloe gin he made himself and loved to regale his many visitors on it.'

While the British enjoyed wallpaper and fabric patterns based on hedgerow flowers and foliage, and admired rustic pewter and rural oak, which seemed to symbolize an older, wiser England, other countries throughout the world, from Palestine to Finland, from Ireland to the Austro-Hungarian empire, found their own national symbolism through a revival of native decorative arts allied to folk traditions. In America, for example, a Harvard graduate, Charles F. Lummis, championed the cause of the American Indians, and there was a vogue for such indigenous crafts as Navajo blankets and Appalachian coverlets. In Russia, the Neo-Primitive painters Natalia Goncharova and her lifelong companion Mikhail Larionov, who turned their backs on Western art and embraced the culture and Byzantine religion of the East, were inspired by icons and the peasant woodcuts known as *lubki*.

In Norway, which was striving for independence from Sweden (the union was finally dissolved in 1905), there was a Viking revival: the heroic style and rich carving of such Viking forms as dragon heads appeared in furniture and silver. There was

'The Three Suitors', linen and wool tapestry designed in 1897 by Gerhard Munthe for the 1900 Exposition Universelle in Paris, and woven by Augusta Christensen at the Nordenfjeldske Kunstindustrimuseum Tapestry Studio, Trondheim. Museum für Kunst und Gewerbe, Hamburg

Finnish society. While ordinary people had spoken Finnish for hundreds of years, the educated classes spoke Swedish, and many artists now returned to the Finnish language and to the movement known as Karelianism – the artistic expression of nationalism – named after the remote region in eastern Finland considered to be the source of the ancient dramatic epic, the *Kalevala*.

In 1890 the Finnish painter Akseli Gallen and the Swedish artist Count Louis Sparre went to Karelia in a romantic search for the inspirations of Finnish culture. They built a house there, named Kallela, near Ruovsi, in the style of the sturdy local log dwellings. At the Finnish pavilion at the Paris exhibition in 1900, Akseli Gallen exhibited examples of traditional *ryiji* textiles and Louis Sparre contributed the 'Iris Room', showing pottery, plain wooden furniture and metalwork from his Iris Workshops in Porvoo, Helsinki. Another exhibit was organized by the Friends of Finnish Handicrafts, an association founded in 1879 by Fanny Churberg with Morrisian ideals and the aim of preserving peasant traditions in embroidery and textiles. Similar associations were founded in emulation of the Friends in other Scandinavian countries.

The Finnish pavilion itself was designed by three architects, Eliel Saarinen, Herman Gesellius and Armas Lindgren, who had set up an office together in Helsinki in 1896. The inspiration of Karelianism was evident in an insurance company building they had designed in Helsinki with pine-cones around the windows and bears and squirrels guarding the entrance. In 1902, in emulation of Gallen and Sparre's Kallela, they created Hvitträsk, a group of buildings built

also a revival of weaving techniques. In 1897, the designer Frieda Hansen founded the Norwegian Tapestry Weaving Studio in Oslo producing large woven hangings with stylized flowers and motifs from Norwegian sagas, and the Norwegian Impressionist painter Gerhard Munthe exhibited tapestries based on Nordic legends at the Paris Exposition Universelle in 1900. Munthe also designed furniture painted and decorated with bold carvings of Nordic sagas and legends for a 'Fairy Tale Room' at the Holmenkollen Turisthotell in Oslo.

The Finns, too, turned to their ancient myths and legends as a means of asserting a sense of national identity. Finland had formed part of Sweden until 1809, when it fell under Russian domination as a grand duchy, but Swedish culture still held sway in

Interior of Hvitträsk, Finland, the log dwelling built by Eliel Saarinen, Herman Gesellius and Armas Lindgren in 1902–3

of rough stone and timber on a steep cliff overlooking the clear waters of Lake Hvit-träsk; the place would house all three families and provide office and studio space. The interior had furniture carved with folk motifs, tiled hearths, decorated walls and embossed metalwork made by Erik Ehrström.

In Sweden itself, the expression of folk culture was less rugged and owed more to the elegant simplicity of the Gustavian revival, a style based on the houses built in and around Stockholm during the reign of King Gustav III of Sweden (1771–92). The best-known Swedish Arts and Crafts interiors were those created by the painter Carl Larsson and his wife Karin at their home in the Dalarna. Larsson, who had studied painting in Paris, depicted the interiors of their summer cottage in a series of light, unaffected watercolours published in a series of books: *Ett Hem* (A Home), 1899, *Larssons* (At The Larssons), 1902, and *Åt Solsiden* (On The Sunny Side), 1910. The abundant, clear colours of Karin Larsson's textiles and the painted Gustavian furniture in these unpretentious paintings of gardens and interiors were immensely popular. A German edition of *Åt Solsiden* was subtitled: 'A book about rooms to live in, about children, about you, about flowers, about everything.'

Throughout the countries under the yoke of either Russian or Austro-Hungarian rule – now Romania, Yugoslavia, Hungary, Czechoslovakia and Poland – artists, designers and architects embraced Arts and Crafts ideals, combining the modern forms of Art Nouveau with traditional folk culture in what became known as *Provinzkunst*. In Hungary for example, the 'Magyar' style of architecture of Ödön Lechner and Béla Lajta, which incorporated Transylvanian folk motifs, opposed the official styles of the Austro-Hungarian empire and reasserted both a link with the past and a sense of national identity. Empress Elizabeth, who had been created Queen of Hungary in 1867 in an attempt to placate Magyar nationalism, tactfully commissioned Ödön Faragó to make wooden furniture which combined both Art Nouveau and peasant motifs, and when Hungary celebrated its millennium in 1896, peasant costume and folk motifs were used to create a unifying theme even for official functions and occasions.

By the early years of this century, influenced by Ruskin and Tolstoy, Hungarian artists and architects such as the Young Ones group were using vernacular architecture and folk traditions to symbolize an ideal of closeness to nature, and in 1901 the Gödöllö artists' colony was established near Budapest, producing weaving, sculpture, leatherwork, stained glass and furniture. In 1906 at the Milan International Exposition they exhibited a furnished interior entitled 'The Home of the Artist' which showed a variety of influences from Britain, France and Austria. Walter Crane, whose work had been exhibited in Budapest, visited the colony and admired their work.

By 1900 Arts and Crafts ideals had become identified with political liberalism, with the rejection of the wealth and exploitation of the fast-growing cities and commercial centres, and with an unpretentious lifestyle that espoused a programme of traditional values, closeness to nature and a celebration of the mysticism of ancient myths and legends. It was – and remains – a potent mixture.

Watercolour of his own studio by Carl Larsson, from his book *Ett Hem*, published in Sweden in 1899. National Museum, Stockholm

C. F. A. VOYSEY

Charles Francis Annesley Voysey (1857–1941) was the son of a heretical clergyman from Yorkshire, and himself remained somewhat of a maverick, mistrustful of foreign influences and often difficult and inflexible with clients: like Philip Webb, he was prepared to turn down a commission rather than compromise. He was articled to the architect J. P. Seddon during the 1870s and set up his own practice in 1881, initially concentrating on decorative rather than architectural work. He joined the Art Workers' Guild in 1884 and was elected Master in 1924.

In 1883 his close friend A. H. Mackmurdo introduced him to Jeffrey and Co., for whom he began to design wallpapers; he went on to design for Turnbull and Stockdale and other wallpaper manufacturers, and from 1893 had a regular contract with Essex and Co.; from 1895 he was under contract to Alexander Morton to supply patterns for carpets and textiles. Voysey also designed tiles for Maw and Co., the Pilkington Tile and Pottery Co. and Minton's.

His favourite motifs were birds and trees, which he felt symbolized the joy of unspoilt nature and his own deeply-felt religious convictions. Swans, owls, seagulls, and flowers and foliage were depicted in simple, flat, stylized form.

He began designing furniture in the 1890s, showing a preference for pieces in plain oak decorated only with brass strap-hinges or his favourite pierced heart motif. Voysey felt that the horizontal signified repose, while the vertical represented vigour, and his furniture emphasizes structure and proportion, with tapering legs or supports which often end in a wide, square cap, an element borrowed from Mackmurdo. Between 1901 and 1914 most of his furniture was made by F. C. Nielson, although Liberty and Co. also made and sold his designs.

In 1899 Voysey built a house for himself, The Orchard, Chorleywood, from where he could commute to his architectural office via the newly-built Metropolitan Line – John Betjeman's 'Metro-land'. Nothing in his house, or in

Dining-room designed in 1902 by C.F.A. Voysey for a house in Birkenhead. The walls are panelled in oak and all the furniture was designed by Voysey and made by F.C. Nielson

the other four complete interiors he designed, was too small to win his attention, from the fire-tongs and door furniture to the clocks. The Orchard was plain and simple, with unadorned oak, white woodwork and whitewashed walls, green fireplace tiles, red curtains and green or patterned carpets. The only ornament, apart from the repeated heart motif, was a vase of flowers to leave one 'free as a bird to wander in the sunshine or storm of [one's] own thoughts'.

A home, Voysey believed, should have 'all the qualities of peace and rest and protection and family pride'. Outside, deep gables and long horizontal windows with mullions and leaded lights, porches and doors that were wide in proportion to their height, suggested shelter and welcome; inside, low ceilings and 'light, bright, cheerful rooms' were easy to clean and cheap to maintain. The servants' quarters, too, were bright and airy. His style was much copied here and in Europe.

'Let us Prey', textile design
by C.F.A. Voysey. Victoria
& Albert Museum, London

GIMSON AND THE BARNSLEYS

Ernest Gimson (1864–1919) was born in Leicester, the son of an engineer, and articled to a local architect. In January 1884 William Morris visited Leicester: Gimson and his brother met him at the station 'and, two minutes after his train had come in, we were at home with him and captured by his personality'. After his lecture on 'Art and Socialism', they all sat up talking. Morris later provided letters of introduction for Gimson to London architects, and, as a result, in 1886 he joined J. D. Sedding's office, next door to Morris and Co.'s Oxford Street showrooms, where he remained two years. Influenced by Morris, he joined the Society for the Protection of Ancient Buildings and the Art Workers' Guild.

In London Gimson met the Barnsley brothers, who came from a Nonconformist family of Birmingham builders. Ernest Barnsley (1863–1926) worked in Sedding's office, and Sidney (1865–1926) in Norman Shaw's. In October 1890, inspired by Morris and Co., Gimson and the Barnsleys along with W. R. Lethaby, Reginald Blomfield and Mervyn Macartney, also from Shaw's office and all members of the St George's Art Society, founded Kenton and Co., named after the street around the corner from their rented workshop in Bloomsbury.

They designed furniture for production by professional cabinet-makers. Although Gimson contributed a version of a traditional English dresser in unpolished chamfered oak, most of their pieces were influenced by the eighteenth-century originals admired by Shaw. Kenton and Co. furniture was used by Lethaby in two of his major decorating commissions, and exhibited at the premises of the Art Workers' Guild in 1891, but the firm closed the following year.

In 1893 Gimson and the Barnsleys moved out of London, intending to found a craft community with the aim of revitalizing traditional craftsmanship. They settled first at Ewen, near Circencester, then moved to Pinbury House, a run-down Elizabethan manor house, where they worked in the converted stables. In 1902 they moved again. Gimson and Ernest Barnsley went into partnership at Daneway House, employing cabinet-makers to produce furniture to their designs; Peter Waals, a Dutch cabinet-maker, became their foreman. The partnership foundered in 1905 and Barnsley returned to full-time architecture, but the workshops remained busy and successful, and by 1914 were employing more than a dozen men.

Although Gimson had studied turning and rushing, metalwork and forging, and decorative plasterwork, he made only a few early pieces of furniture himself, preferring to work closely with the craftsmen who executed his designs. He was a versatile designer, and made use of contrasting, geometric veneers as well as the solid woods favoured by Sidney Barnsley. Some of his work, such as the cabinets on stands with floral marquetry inlays, were inspired by Tudor pieces. After Gimson's death, the Daneway workshops closed and Waals opened his own workshop near Stroud.

Sidney Barnsley kept his own separate workshop at Sapperton in Gloucestershire, where he executed his own designs. He was basically self-taught. At first, he used English oak, neither polished nor stained, then other local woods, often obtained from the village wheelwright, such as ash, elm, deal and various fruitwoods, and finally English walnut and some imported woods. As he became more skilled, the heavier pieces such as coffers gave way to lighter, more varied work, constructed with open joinery and little superficial ornamentation, although he often made distinctive use of stringing (inlaid lines of alternate dark and light woods, usually ebony and holly). His work greatly influenced younger designers such as Ambrose Heal, Gordon Russell and A. Romney Green.

Right: Oak sideboard by Sidney Barnsley, 1924. Cheltenham Art Gallery and Museum; (*below left*) the interior of Ernest Barnsley's house, Daneway House, Sapperton in 1905 and (*below right*) a cabinet for storing fishing tackle, made of walnut with brass handles and decorative inlays of various fruitwoods, designed by Ernest Gimson in 1913

WALLPAPERS

'Bees' wallpaper designed by Candace Wheeler in 1881 and produced by
Warren, Fuller and Co., New York in 1882. Metropolitan Museum of
Art, New York
Opposite: 'Blue Fruit' wallpaper design by William Morris

The Victorian love of busy wallpaper patterns of 'cabbage roses and monster lilies' was replaced first by the flat patterns of Owen Jones and Pugin, then by the simple, conventionalized, floral patterns created by William Morris, and later by his assistant J. H. Dearle, or the stylized Anglo-Japanese designs of E. W. Godwin, Bruce Talbert or Christopher Dresser.

From 1864 Morris's wallpapers were produced for him by Jeffrey and Co., to whom Talbert, Walter Crane, Lewis F. Day and C. F. A. Voysey also supplied designs for papers, friezes, nursery papers and figurative panels. Many architects and artists – from A. H. Mackmurdo to Kate Greenaway – designed wallpapers.

Hand-blocked 'Art' papers, however, were expensive, and some people considered Morris's designs too large and palatial for ordinary homes. The order book for Watts and Co., founded in 1874 by the architects G. F. Bodley, Thomas Garner and George Gilbert Scott, junior, to make hand-blocked wallpapers in the Queen Anne revival style, was said to read like *Debrett*. The Silver Studio produced less expensive designs, and stencilling was even cheaper. In the 1890s 'Anaglypta', a lighter version of the embossed 'Lincrusta Walton' paper from the inventor of linoleum, Frederick Walton, was popular for dados.

By the late 1870s Morris and Co. wallpapers were widely available in America, and Christian Herter, L. C. Tiffany and Samuel Coleman all designed Japanese-inspired papers. In 1881, when the New York firm, Warren, Fuller and Co., held a competition for designs, Candace Wheeler, her daughter Dora, and her friends Ida Clark and Caroline Townsend who had become members of Associated Artists, won all four prizes. They continued to supply designs which were increasingly based on American themes.

In Europe, Hector Guimard was among those creating Art Nouveau patterns, but gradually a lighter style prevailed. Otto Eckmann supplied stylized designs for the Mannheim firm, Engelhardt, while in Austria the geometric designs of Josef Hoffmann were gradually replaced by the more baroque, folk-inspired style of Dagobert Peche and Mathilde Flögl. By the 1920s patterned wallpaper was considered positively Victorian and had been replaced in modern homes by whitewashed walls.

Left: Designs for wallpapers
by Alphonse Mucha, 1902.
Victoria & Albert
Museum, London

Opposite: Hand-knotted
'Hammersmith' carpet by
William Morris, *c.* 1880

CARPETS

'Lily', the popular machine-woven wool pile carpet designed by William Morris *c.*1875 and manufactured by the Wilton Royal Carpet Factory; and (*opposite*) a carpet designed by C.F.A. Voysey

The design of carpets, like that of other flat patterns for wallpapers and textiles, rejected the naturalistic, three-dimensional effects that had reigned supreme at the Great Exhibition of 1851 in favour of conventionalized designs that would give no impression of depth or shading. Owen Jones, Digby Wyatt and Pugin all led the change in taste, but, as with so much, it was William Morris who created the most satisfying designs, based on oriental traditions but using larger areas of simple colour.

Morris became interested in Persian carpets in the 1870s, and in 1878 he made his first hand-tufted carpet on a loom in the back attic at Queen Square. The loom was then moved to the coach-house at Hammersmith and, in 1881, to the Merton Abbey works, but these hand-knotted rugs, made with naturally-dyed wools, were always known as Hammersmith carpets. They were extremely expensive, and the larger ones, such as one for George Howard's house, Naworth, took nearly a year to complete.

Influenced by Morris, in 1898 James Morton of the Carlisle carpet and textile firm Alexander Morton and Co., set up the first of three factories in Ireland producing hand-woven Donegal carpets, which were sold through Liberty and Co., Morton's main English agent. (Morton's machine-made carpets included bold, stylized floral designs by C. F. A. Voysey and Lindsay Butterfield.)

Hand-woven Kildare carpets, dyed with natural native dyes, were also produced in Ireland at a firm founded in 1903 with the support of the Countess of Mayo. These rugs were plain with decorative borders.

Morris's designs for machine-woven rugs and carpets, with small motifs in dark, practical colours, were made for the firm by the Wilton Royal Carpet Factory and the Heckmondwike Manufacturing Co. in Yorkshire. In America, old-established manufacturers such as the Bigelow Carpet Co. of Clinton, Massachusetts, produced machine-woven Wiltons in fashionable Arts and Crafts designs.

METALWORK

Metalwork designed by C.F.A. Voysey and made by W. Bainbridge
Reynolds's metalworking firm, c.1896–1903 and (*opposite*) a cast iron
fireplace by Thomas Jekyll

Fireplaces and fire-irons, door and window furniture, decorative hinges and handles for furniture, and larger architectural features all received attention from designers and architects. Items such as doorplates or firedogs with the handmade beaten or hammered appearance, first made popular by the metalworkers of Ashbee's Guild of Handicraft, became an essential component of the Arts and Crafts interior.

During the rage for all things Aesthetic, sunflowers, chrysanthemums and other Japanese motifs appeared on the cast-iron fire grates designed by Thomas Jekyll in the 1870s or on the brass door furniture produced by firms such as the Nashua Lock Co. of New Hampshire, in America.

In 1903 the architect Ernest Gimson established Alfred Bucknell, the son of a local blacksmith, in his own smithy at Sapperton in Gloucestershire: he was eventually assisted by three men, making firedogs, handles, locks, window latches, candlesticks and other items in iron, brass, polished steel and silver to Gimson's designs. Bucknell learned

many of his techniques by copying original Elizabethan examples. In Philadelphia, the Polish immigrant Samuel Yellin based his work on medieval originals.

Voysey designed a wide range of metalwork, including bolts, window catches, letter-boxes, keyhole covers and door handles, which incorporated motifs such as birds or hearts. In 1912 Harry Peach, of Dryad Handicrafts, went into partnership with William Pick, who ran the Leicestershire Art metalwork firm of Collins and Co., to make door furniture, fire-irons and fenders in the Arts and Crafts style, as well as bronze candlesticks, silver tea-sets and even jewellery.

Among the architects who made bold use of decorative ironwork were Antoni Gaudi in Barcelona, Louis Sullivan in Chicago, Hector Guimard in France (his Art Nouveau railings still adorn the Paris Métro), and Charles Rennie Mackintosh, who used cast-iron features to add an heraldic éclat to both the interior and exterior of Glasgow School of Art.

A Middle-Class Enthusiasm

The Arts and Crafts movement provided a new middle-class fashion for interior decoration, and few suburban homes were without their panel of stained glass, their beaten metal vase or carefully displayed piece of 'studio' pottery from Doulton's Art Pottery, Moorcroft, Pilkington's Lancastrian or, in America, Rookwood, Fulper or Grueby. Those who could not afford an architect-designed house could, and did, purchase 'Art' furniture, wallpapers, nursery friezes, rugs or tea-sets in order to display their modernity. The enthusiasm for Art furnishings in England diminished only with the outbreak of war in 1914, and in America continued on into the 1920s.

In America especially, economic expansion and the growth of both manufacturing and service industries in the decades following the Civil War had created a huge middle class: the aspirations of this growing army of salesmen, managers and office workers were chronicled by writers such as Theodore Dreiser who sensed the loss of autonomy experienced by many of the small cogs in the great machine that seemed to benefit only the likes of Carnegie, Morgan or Rockefeller. The chance to participate in an art movement that defied industrialism and upheld the sanctity of individual expression was extremely appealing to the new class of wage-slaves. Enthusiasts for the new style could not only buy work by William Morris or Walter Crane in their local department stores, and read about the latest designs in magazines such as *The Studio* or *Country Life* in England or *The Ladies' Home Journal* or *House & Garden* in America, but could also join Arts and Crafts societies or attend craft classes.

As Walter Crane wrote in 1887, by which time he had become a committed socialist: 'There is room for the highest qualities in the pattern of a carpet, the design of a wallpaper, a bit of repoussé or wrought iron or wood carving. The sincere designer and craftsman . . . with his invention and skill applied to the accessories of everyday life may do more to keep alive the sense of beauty than the greatest painter that ever lived.' Those who flocked to learn embroidery, china-painting or wood-carving could believe that they were joining ranks with the artists they admired.

The leading English designers were well-known in both Europe and America, thanks to the numerous international exhibitions at which British decorative arts took pride of place, and English wallpapers, textiles and ceramics were also successfully

Silk and cotton woven textile, possibly designed by Archibald Knox for the Silver Studios, *c.*1899. Victoria & Albert Museum, London

Bedroom furniture illustrated in a Liberty and Co. catalogue of 1890

Opposite: Moorcroft pottery illustrated in a Liberty and Co. catalogue of 1908. Victoria & Albert Museum, London

several such 'curio' shops selling Indian silks, Chinese porcelain, oriental rugs and 'Arabian' furniture. But gradually Liberty began to see the potential in the craze for Art furnishings, and in 1883 he opened a furnishing and decoration studio under the management of Leonard F. Wyburd. Liberty was astute enough not only to create his own version of Arts and Crafts but to buy designs from most of the leading artists. The Liberty style, however, both popularized and trivialized the movement, turning Ruskin and Morris's ideals of 'honest craftsmanship' and freedom of expression into a mere fad of fashion, albeit an extremely successful one.

Most of Liberty's own furniture, including the 'Thebes' stool, was designed by Wyburd, and in 1887 Liberty's established their own cabinet-making workshops, producing simple chairs and country-style oak furniture with inlaid decoration, inset tiles (sometimes by de Morgan), leaded-glass panels and elaborate strap-hinges and metal handles. In later years, some of their bedroom suites were given Saxon names such as 'Helga', 'Ethelwynn' and 'Athelstan' to reinforce their self-consciously 'quaint' character. 'Athelstan', which was sold from 1902 until 1911, included dressing-tables, chairs, tables, chests of drawers, wardrobes of various sizes with hand-stained panels of landscape designs, and beds in oak with the pierced heart motif beloved by Voysey, but these suites were cumbersome and exaggerated, and lacked the sophistication of the prototypes by Mackmurdo, Baillie Scott or Voysey on which they were modelled.

Liberty's, however, also stocked furniture from outside manufacturers and designers, including a line of eighty-one pieces of

exported. One of the most influential of the European shops was the Maison de l'Art Nouveau, opened in Paris in 1895 by the Hamburg dealer Siegfried (later changed to Samuel) Bing: L. C. Tiffany, John La Farge, Henri van de Velde, W. A. S. Benson and Frank Brangwyn were among some of the artists and designers associated with the gallery.

But the most important retail outlet of all was one which, in Italy, gave its name to the style it inspired – *Stile Liberty*. Liberty and Co. was founded in Regent Street, London, in 1875 by Arthur Lasenby Liberty, a former manager of Farmer and Roger's 'oriental' department, where Godwin, Rossetti and Whistler had purchased their Japanese prints. Several of the new department stores, including Whiteleys and Debenham and Freebody, had opened oriental departments, and Liberty's was at first only one of

Original examples introduced by Liberty & Co. in practical shapes, made and decorated by hand. The surface of this beautiful pottery is enriched with lustrous and scintillating glazes.

No. 1.
6 ins. diameter.
14/6

No. 2.
4 ins. high.
10/6

No. 3.
6 ins. diameter.
9/3

No. 4.
6 ins. high, 6/9
9½ „ 16/6

No. 5.
6 ins. high.
5/-

No. 6.
11 ins. diameter.
18/6

No. 7.
7½ ins. high.
12/9

No. 8.
6 ins. diameter, 6/6
7   „   7/6
8½   „   9/6

No. 9.
9 ins. high.
17/6

No. 10.
8 ins. high.
15/6

No. 11.
11½ ins. high.
£1 2 6

No. 12.
9 ins. high.
9/6

LIBERTY & CO   [Inventors and Makers of Artistic Wares and Fabrics]   **LONDON & PARIS**

Silver mirror frame designed by Archibald Knox in 1902 for Liberty's 'Cymric' range. Virginia Museum of Fine Arts

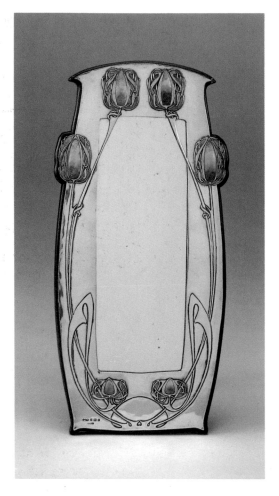

Many of Liberty's fabrics were printed by William Morris's early associate, Thomas Wardle, who also supplied the store with imported Indian silks (which he dyed and printed at his works in Leek), and with printed cottons, and silks for embroidery. The most famous Liberty Art fabrics came from the Silver Studio, even though the majority of the studio's pattern designs were in fact bought by French manufacturers. The Silver Studio was founded in 1880 by the textile designer Arthur Silver, and after his death in 1896 was managed by his son Rex, who designed for Liberty's 'Cymric' and 'Tudric' metalwork ranges. Harry Napper became design manager for a couple of years before leaving to work freelance.

Arthur Liberty was little concerned with the issues that concerned Morris or Ashbee about hand-craftsmanship or the working conditions of the craftsman, and his successful policy of buying designs by good, modern designers and having them made up by established manufacturers seriously undercut the craft workshops. Ashbee bitterly blamed the competition from Liberty metalwork for the failure of his Guild. Nevertheless, many small firms relied on Liberty's success as a retailer: several of the new Art potteries such as Bretby, Brannam, Della Robbia, Moorcroft and Pilkington's Lancastrian, and, later, Doulton and Wedgwood, all sold their wares through the store.

One of Liberty's own most successful ventures was the launch in 1899 of their range of handmade 'Cymric' gold and silverware, mostly made by the Birmingham firm of W. H. Haseler. A second line of pewter wares, named 'Tudric' followed the next year. Several designers were involved in the project,

furniture designed by Baillie Scott and made at John P. White's Pyghtle Works in Bedford; there were also designs by Voysey and by George Walton, whose furniture was made by William Birch and, later, E. G. Punnett, of High Wycombe.

Baillie Scott had begun contributing fabric designs to Liberty and Co. in 1893; Walter Crane, the Scots illustrator Jessie M. King, and Voysey were also among those who sold designs and were prepared to accept Liberty's strict rule on anonymity.

including Jessie M. King, Rex Silver, Arthur Gaskin and Bernard Cuzner, producing designs for a wide range of jewellery, cigarette cases, jewellery boxes, tea-sets, jugs, vases, candlesticks, mirror frames and clocks. Some of it was decorated with elegant turquoise enamelwork. The most distinctive designs, which formed the basis of Liberty's popular and influential 'Celtic Revival', were by Archibald Knox.

The son of a marine engineer, Knox was a Manxman who was deeply interested in the island's Celtic traditions and had made a study of Celtic ornament. He was probably first introduced to Liberty and Co. by Baillie Scott, whom he had met at the Art School in Douglas, and in whose office he had worked for a time. Probably at Baillie Scott's suggestion, he began to send designs for fabrics and wallpapers to Liberty's around 1895 and continued to contribute designs for metalwork, jewellery, carpets and garden ornaments for several years. Knox's distinctive Celtic designs for the 'Cymric' and 'Tudric' lines were widely admired and imitated. He never merely copied existing forms: since his boyhood, he had perfected his own, far from simple versions of Celtic scripts and *entrelac* designs, and much of the superbly controlled delicacy and intricacy of his own Celtic lettering echoed the sinuous, organic style of Art Nouveau.

Among the many other shops and manufacturers that tried to emulate Liberty's success in selling Art furnishings was John Sollie Henry, who produced elegant pieces of Georgian-style furniture inlaid with pretty, stylized motifs of stained wood or metal. In an advertisement of 1896, he

Oak buffet with repoussé copper panel, gilt inlay and gilt wrought iron hinges and lock plates, designed by M.H. Baillie Scott

described himself as a 'Designer of Quaint and Artistic Furniture'. W. A. S. Benson, who had introduced a similar refinement to Morris and Co.'s furnishings after Morris's death, also designed for J. S. Henry, whose delicate chairs, desks and cabinets were well suited to the lighter style of the Queen Anne revival.

In America, perhaps the most quaint and eccentric of the Arts and Crafts designers was Charles Rohlfs. He was the only American cabinet-maker invited to exhibit at the Turin International Exhibition of 1902, and he received commissions from the crowned heads of both Great Britain and Italy as well as from many other wealthy clients. Rohlfs was born in New York, the son of a cabinet-maker, who died when he was only twelve years old. He served his apprenticeship at a foundry, while attending evening classes at the Cooper Union, in the hope of becoming an actor, then found work designing cast-iron stoves and furnaces. He was past his mid-thirties when, around 1889, he began to design and make elaborately pierced and carved oak Gothic furniture in his own workshop in Buffalo. Friends commissioned pieces, and gradually his fame grew. By 1909 he still worked out of the same workshop, but employed eight artisans to execute his designs.

His dark, sturdy chairs, chests and desks are unique: not quite Gothic, not quite Moorish, not quite in the traditions of Scandinavian carved furniture, yet distinctly belonging to the decade that produced Art Nouveau. In 1907 Rohlfs himself described his work as 'strangely suggestive of the days when the world was young, but in spite of that, distinctive of this progressive twentieth century and strictly American. It has the spirit of today blended with the poetry of medieval ages.'

Throughout Britain, Europe and America the desire for beauty in the home led to the foundation of numerous 'studio' potteries and glassworks. Many were founded by individual artist-potters who were searching for some elusive technique, finish or glaze effect. William de Morgan's lustre experiments come to mind in this connection, as do the attractive decorative bowls and plaques made in emulation of Italian originals at Harold Rathbone's Della Robbia Company, founded in Birkenhead in 1894. There were also W. Howson Taylor's attempts to achieve the deep-red Chinese *sang de boeuf* high-fired glazes at the Ruskin Pottery, established in Birmingham in 1898 and the distinctive crackled metallic finishes which Sir Edmund Elton developed around 1900 at the Sunflower Pottery on his family's Somerset estate.

The success of these individual artist-potters led the commercial potteries to set up their own 'studio' departments. Firms such as the Worcester Royal Porcelain Co., Minton's or Wedgwood had responded quickly to the vogue for Japanese-inspired wares. Doulton and Co. then opened a factory for studio pots at Lambeth, where artists such as Hannah Barlow and George Tinworth produced distinctive work, while Wedgwood produced a small number of vases and bowls designed by Lindsay Butterfield and known as 'Lindsay Ware'.

In 1875 Wedgwood had brought Thomas Allen from Minton's to be director of their Fine Art Studios, where he remained until 1904. His portrait plaques and pseudo-historical subjects, such as the 'Ivanhoe' series, were similar to the wide range of quaint illustrated wares later produced by Doulton and Co., and were typical of the Edwardian interpretation of the romantic and chivalric themes featured by Morris in his poetry and by Burne-Jones in his art. Similar subjects were depicted, with greater originality, by Walter Crane, Lewis F. Day and C. F. A. Voysey in their designs for Pilkington's Lancastrian wares. A final flowering of the fey sweetness that came to be associated with Arts and Crafts images was Daisy Makeig-Jones's 'Fairyland Lustre', first produced by Wedgwood in 1915.

In America, too, Art potteries sprang up all over the country. Some individuals, such as Louise McLaughlin or Maria Longworth Nichols, who founded Rookwood, were inspired by the examples of French or Japanese ceramics they had seen at the Philadelphia Centennial Exposition. Some firms, such as the J. and J. G. Low Art Tile Works

Mahogany display cabinet inlaid with various woods and made by J.S. Henry and Co. in 1904

in Chelsea, Massachusetts, began to produce architectural and decorative tiles in imitation of English originals, having recognized the demand that there would be for such products. One of the most distinctive forms of American ceramics was produced by William H. Grueby, who had been employed at the Lows' Art Tile Works before opening his own pottery in Boston in 1894. Grueby produced vases of thick, moulded organic shapes with a heavy matt glaze, usually green, enhanced with yellow or blue, which was widely copied. In Colorado, Artus van Briggle, who had worked at Rookwood, also used matt glazes with sculptural Art Nouveau forms. At the Fulper Pottery, New Jersey, in 1909 the grandson of the founder began producing a range of Art pottery called 'Vase-Kraft' in a variety of matt, flambé, lustre and crystalline glazes. Other individuals who experimented with different glaze effects were Ernest A. Batchelder, Charles Volkmar and Frederick Hurten Rhead.

As early as the 1870s Morris had complained of being tired of 'ministering to the swinish luxury of the rich' and began to long for greater simplicity, but by the time of his death in 1896 the success of the style he had created had taken on a commercial life of its own. Although A. H. Mackmurdo later wrote that the Arts and Crafts movement had been 'a mighty upheaval of man's spiritual nature', many liberal, well-meaning Arts and Crafts designers found themselves unable to do more than produce Art furniture for the newly liberalized middle classes, revolutionizing the middle-class home but not the lives of the working people who produced it.

Opposite: Oak fall-front desk by Charles Rohlfs, decorated with brass nailheads and hammered surface texture, 1898–1901; the whole desk revolves upon its base. Virginia Museum of Fine Arts

Left: Earthenware vase decorated with white jonquils, designed by Wilhelmina Post and produced at the Grueby Faience Co. in Massachusetts

LIGHTING

Thomas Alva Edison developed the first practical model of the incandescent filament bulb in October 1879, and thenceforward designers could dispense with the requirements of bulky oil reservoirs, gas pipes and the hazards of naked flames. In his 'Notes on Electric Wiring and Fittings', written in 1887, W. A. S. Benson, who considered artificial lighting to be a 'fine art', discussed not only the different uses of light in different rooms but also the artistic effects that could be achieved. In 1896 the *Magazine of Art* called his designs 'palpitatingly modern'.

Benson, who interpreted the requirements of electric light in an inventive and technically ingenious way, was a close friend of Burne-Jones and a co-founder of the Art Workers' Guild. As a boy, he had been taught the use of lathes and machinery by his uncle, an amateur scientist and craftsman. He was then articled to the architect Basil Champneys and set up in business as a designer in London in 1880. His catalogue for 1899–1900 lists over eight hundred items, other than electric light fittings, made of copper, brass, iron, polished steel, electroplate and silver, and includes firescreens, trays, teapots, electric kettles and vacuum flasks as well as oil lamps, candlesticks and reflective candle sconces. His wares were often finished with bronzing, lacquer or with dark grey or other coloured films. Veined vaseline, ruby, olive green or opalescent glass shades were provided by Powell's of Whitefriars.

In America and Europe, the development of electric light coincided with the rise of Art Nouveau. Natural forms, especially flowers, were used for lamps, with the stem disguising the wires and the drooping petals forming shades that could now safely enclose the light source. Lights with L. C. Tiffany's leaded-glass shades, or the lamps of carved cameo glass by Emile Gallé or Daum Frères, could glow romantically in dark corners. Tiffany soon had his imitators: the Steuben Glass Works and the Quezal Art Glass and Decorating Co. also made elaborate glass lampshades.

At his San Francisco workshop, Dirk van Erp combined hammered copper bases with shades made of strong, trans-

Green-glazed pottery lamp with inset pink and green glass, made by the Fulper Pottery Company of New Jersey, c.1910 (Virginia Museum of Fine Arts) and (*opposite*) a dining room showing a copper chandelier designed by W.A.S. Benson, with candlesticks possibly designed by Giles Gilbert Scott and wall-mounted lights by Ernest Gimson. Private collection, Birkenhead

lucent mica – clear, yellow or amber – to veil the bright electric light. Gustav Stickley and the Roycroft shops both produced plain wooden lamps in keeping with the Craftsman style; Frank Lloyd Wright also designed wooden lamps as part of his overall decorative schemes. At the Wiener Werkstätte, the simplicity of Josef Hoffmann's designs for electric light fittings began to show a truly modern awareness of the demands of the new technology.

The old forms of lighting did not immediately give way to electricity, however, and candles especially continued to be used, even if only for the beauty of their flames. In Chicago, for example, the Scottish-born Robert Riddle Jarvie, a friend of George Grant Elmslie, made candlesticks and lanterns in brass, copper or patinated bronze.

Right: Hammered copper lamp with mica shade from Dirk van Erp's San Francisco workshop, c.1919

Opposite: 'Lotus' leaded glass table lamp on a bronze base, by Tiffany Studios

THE HOSPITABLE BOARD

Ladies wore high-waisted Aesthetic tea-gowns in pale, muted shades, amber beads around their necks. Seated before an ebonized Godwin table, they poured tea from silver or electroplated tea-sets by Dresser or Benson, or from the fashionable rustic pewter of Liberty's 'Tudric' range, and offered hot scones from a Guild of Handicraft hand-made silver muffin dish.

In Denmark, Georg Jensen, who had been apprenticed to a goldsmith before studying sculpture, opened his own workshop in Copenhagen in 1904, and was assisted from 1906 by Johan Rohde and later by several other goldsmiths and designers. He produced robust, naturalistic tablewares in silver, often decorated with roses or fruit.

Plain, sturdy glasses might be designed by Philip Webb for Powell's of Whitefriars, while, in Europe in the first decade of this century, Richard Riemerschmid and Peter Behrens designed glassware for Benedikt von Poschinger in Oberzweiselau, and the Wiener Werkstätte produced pretty wineglasses and decanters decorated with black or coloured enamels as well as a wide range of metalwork and ceramics.

There was a vast range of ceramics available, from the delicate Japanese-inspired porcelains produced by Royal Worcester to the unpretentious painted and lustre decorations by Alfred Powell for Wedgwood tablewares, first exhibited in 1905. Powell and his wife Louise were friends and neighbours of Gimson and the Barnsleys, and Sidney Barnsley's daughter Grace also worked with them. In Germany, Henri van de Velde and Riemerschmid designed tea-sets and dinner-services for the venerable Meissen factory, while in Sweden around the turn of the century the painter Gunnar Wennerberg introduced simple designs based upon such wild flowers as snowdrops, cowslips and lilies-of-the-valley to the Gustavsberg ceramics factory.

TILES

Tiles by William de Morgan in a bathroom at 8 Addison Road, Holland
Park, and (*opposite*) a collection of tiles by Minton's (the 'Four Seasons'
and the 'Wolf and the Crane'), W.B. Simpson and Sons (central
panel), William de Morgan (flower designs) and Wedgwood (blue and
white tiles)

Hand-made encaustic floor tiles – usually consisting of red-brown clay moulds, filled in with clays of different colours to form designs based on medieval originals – were produced from the 1830s by Minton and Co. of Stoke-on-Trent and Chamberlain's Worcester, a firm, which in the 1850s moved to Shropshire and became Maw and Co.

The Dutch technique of making hand-painted, tin-glazed earthenware Delft tiles, which were too delicate to be used on the floor, gave way to mass production after the development of transfer printing. But the tiles decorated by William de Morgan and those associated with Morris and Co. revived the art of hand-painting. The housing boom of the 1880s and 1890s led to an increased demand for tiles, which, because they were hygienic and easily washable, were popular for dairies, butchers' shops, hospitals, museums, railway stations, pubs and hotels, as well as for the bathrooms, kitchens, fireplaces and entrance halls of suburban houses. Around 1900 the dust-pressing process began to be used to make relief-moulded tiles in fashionable Art Nouveau styles.

Maw and Co., the Pilkington Tile and Pottery Co., and Minton's were the leading British manufacturers, and Walter Crane, Lewis F. Day, Moyr Smith and C. F. A. Voysey were among the many artists who designed for them. Their subject-matter varied from simple animal or floral designs to illustrations from Aesop, Walter Scott or Shakespeare.

In America, at least fifty tile companies were founded between 1875 and 1920; among these were the American Encaustic Tiling Co. of Zanesville, Ohio, who reproduced designs by Crane and other English designers; the J. and J. G. Low Art Tile Works who made moulded, glazed tiles with Japanese-inspired designs of birds, fans and small geometric patterns; the Grueby Faience Co. whose matt glazes came to dominate the market; and the Chelsea Keramik Art Works near Boston which also produced Art tiles that could be inset in furniture or even framed. In 1877 a dozen leading artists including Augustus St Gaudens and Winslow Homer went so far as to found a Tile Club in New York; this was entirely devoted to painting tiles.

THE NURSERY

'Afternoon Tea' by Kate Greenaway, from the *Girl's Own Paper*, 1887

The 1890s ushered in a golden age of childhood. In contrast to the mid-century, it was now believed that a child's sensitivity and intuition were strongly influenced by its environment, and the nursery had to be the brightest, sunniest room in the house. As early as 1874 E. W. Godwin's children had worn tiny kimonos, and their mother, Ellen Terry, later related how '. . . they were allowed no rubbishy picture books, but from the first Japanese prints and fans lined their nursery walls and Walter Crane was their classic. If injudicious friends gave them the wrong sort of present, it was promptly burned! . . . a mechanical mouse . . . was taken away as being realistic and common. Only wooden toys were allowed.'

Fanciful fairy-tales and whimsical folklore were encouraged, and many illustrators of children's books designed decorative nursery friezes, wallpapers, fireside rugs and chintzes for commercial manufacturers, or saw their work widely imitated. Leading architects and designers also produced plans for nurseries, sometimes when their own families were small. In 1912, for example, Jessie M. King designed an elegant and imaginative white-painted nursery complete with stained-glass panels, cupboards decorated with scenes from 'The Frog Prince' and a specially designed doll's house and rocking-horse.

Before the twentieth century was ten years old, stores such as Liberty's, Heal's, and Story and Co. of Kensington were producing entire suites of nursery furniture. The small size of the various items, which were often fancifully decorated, coloured or shaped, showed a new sensitivity to a child's needs and feelings.

Around 1900 the alphabets, maxims, morals and biblical sayings of earlier nursery crockery gave way to more whimsical, less didactic designs, and the Edwardian celebration of Christmas no doubt enlivened the gift-set market. Doulton's earliest wares feature such subjects as mermaids, medieval legends, and games and pastimes such as children tobogganing, all rendered in quite sophisticated styles.

By the 1920s all the major manufacturers – Doulton, Wedgwood, Shelley, Paragon – were producing nursery wares decorated with anthropomorphized animals or scenes from nursery rhymes and contemporary children's books. Mabel Lucie Atwell, for example, designed for Shelley, while Randolph Caldecott had contributed to Doulton's nursery wares as early as 1882.

From 1890, to Burne-Jones's delight, drawing was taught in all elementary schools, and in 1897 the Educational Handwork Association was founded to urge handcraft teaching for older children. The new educational theories put forward by Franz Cizek in Vienna, or Maria Montessori in Rome, endorsed the creative activity and self-expression earlier advocated by J. H. Pestalozzi or Friedrich Froebel. Towards the end of the First World War, Harry Peach developed Dryad Handicrafts, supplying felt, wooden beads and materials for weaving, vegetable dyeing or linoleum printing which were used not only by children but also as occupational therapy for wounded soldiers.

The heyday of Peter Pan, however, was short-lived: ironically, in the 1920s, while manufacturers continued to develop the flourishing market in children's wares, attitudes to childhood and childcare hardened. By 1934 *The Daily Express Book of Home Management* could conclude that 'one of the most important items of nursery furniture is the clock'!

Right: Doll's house of painted wood designed by Jessie M. King as part of a nursery, exhibited *c.*1912. Victoria & Albert Museum, London

Below: Chintz based on the nursery rhyme *The House that Jack Built*, designed by C.F.A. Voysey in 1929 and sold to Morton Sundour

Opposite: Selection of nursery wares from the early 1920s: a duck bowl from the Ashstead Pottery, a cup and saucer painted by Stella Crofts, a mug painted by Jessie M. King and a ship bowl painted by Annie Macbeth, a student from the Glasgow School of Art

ILLUSTRATORS

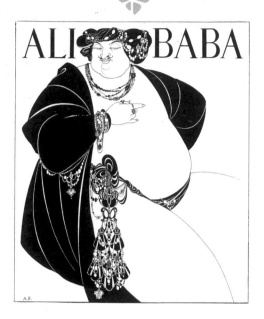

Cover design by Aubrey
Beardsley for a proposed
edition of *The Forty
Thieves*, 1897. Fogg Art
Museum, Massachusetts

The new wave of children's literature was illustrated by a new generation of artists – Beatrix Potter, Edmund Dulac, Arthur Rackham, Jessie M. King, Kate Greenaway and Walter Crane – many of whom, even in their 'adult' work, appealed to the child within.

The young Walter Crane was already working as an illustrator when, in 1867, a naval friend returned from Japan with a collection of Japanese prints. When he subsequently met William Morris, Crane's work went on to combine the simplified colours and flat, stylized manner of Japanese art with the romantic themes of Morris and Burne-Jones. Between 1870 and 1874 he produced more than twenty 'toy' books, including old fairy-tales, rhymes and pictorial ABCs, for Edward Evans of Routledge and Evans, the publisher who first exploited the revolution in colour printing processes. Crane has been described by Maurice Sendak as an 'ornamental illustrator', and many of his illustrations depicted blue and white tiles, sunflowers, peacock feathers and Japanese fans. By 1875 his skills were in demand among architects and manufacturers who wanted decorative designs for wallpapers, friezes, textiles and tiles.

But in 1878 Crane's success was eclipsed by Kate Greenaway's first book for Routledge and Evans, *Under The Window*. She had been designing Christmas cards for ten years, when her father, an engraver, introduced her to Evans. Her demure, Aesthetic children, dressed in their Queen Anne revival outfits proved extremely popular: even Ruskin sent her letters of admiration. She wrote her own poems as well as illustrating well-known rhymes and tales.

Evans's third success was with Randolph Caldecott, who produced fourteen books between 1878 and his early death in 1886. His style was more boisterous and realistic than either Crane's or Greenaway's.

For adults, however, there was a darker side to the new illustrators. Charles Ricketts and Charles Shannon incorporated the sinuous lines of continental Art Nouveau into their work, while in April 1894 the publisher John Lane launched *The Yellow Book* with Aubrey Beardsley as art editor. Both Ricketts and Beardsley illustrated work by Oscar Wilde, making the most of the decadent, erotic language of such plays as *Salomé*.

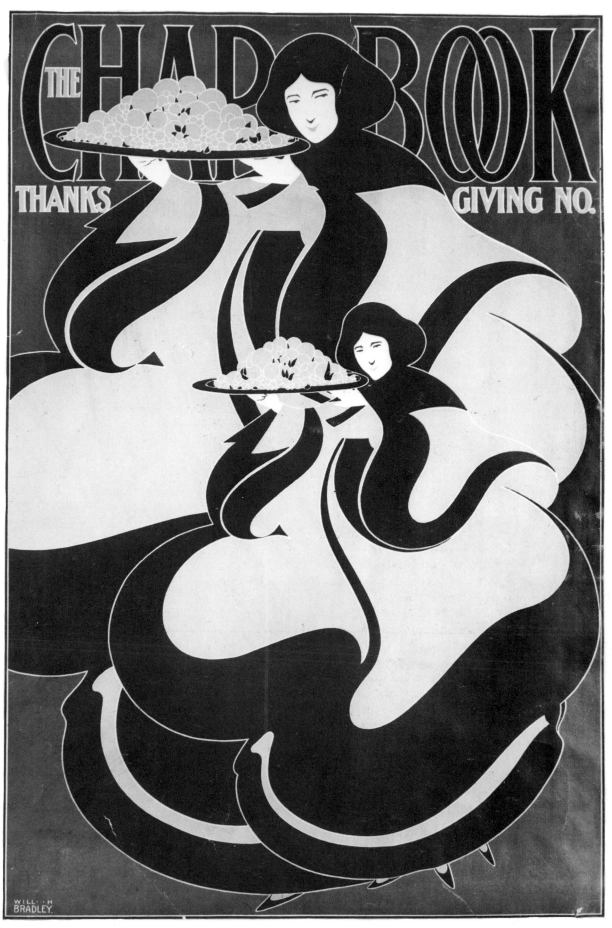

Cover for Stone and
Kimball's *Chap-Book*, 1894,
by Will Bradley, an
American graphic artist
best known for his work for
periodicals and commercial
posters

The Benediction
of Good Taste

Woman's place has never lain more repressively within the home than in the 1860s and 1870s. Women became the guardian angels of the hearth, the upholders of the sacred values of the Victorian home, safely protected from contamination by the outside world. Never had social convention made it more difficult for women to escape the restraints laid upon them in the name of modesty and womanliness.

William Morris, the first to do away with so many conventions, not only married out of his class – Janey Burden was the daughter of an Oxford stableman, Morris financially independent – but also encouraged his wife, sister-in-law and not a few of the other women associated with the firm, such as Kate and Lucy Faulkner, the sisters of his friend Charles Faulkner, to become involved in its work, designing and executing tile-painting, gesso work, wallpaper and, above all, embroidery. Morris himself was not completely without his own ideal of womanhood, and embroidery exemplified his treasured image of the medieval damozel at work upon the hangings for her castle bedchamber. He himself first become interested in embroidery when decorating the Red House, and it subsequently became a vital part of Morris and Co.'s range. Janey

Morris, her sister Elizabeth Burden, Catherine Holiday, wife of the painter and stained glass designer Henry Holiday, Madeleine Wardle, wife of the firm's business manager and, later, Morris's daughter May, all executed designs by Morris, Burne-Jones and others.

The decorative arts were thought to be admirably suited to women, not only because they were associated with the adornment of the home but also because by their very nature – painstaking, delicate, refined – such arts were considered suitably 'feminine'. The Aesthetic movement, which preached that beautiful surroundings promoted spiritual and mental health, made it even more fashionable for women to involve themselves directly in the decoration of their homes; a display of exquisite taste became as important as dressing well and looking beautiful. Both Doulton's and Minton's supplied blank tiles for fashionable young ladies to decorate, and Morris and Co. sold not only finished embroidery work, but also specially dyed silks, wools and marked-out designs. In America, Gustav Stickley also sold embroidery kits.

In the 1870s the publishing house of Macmillan and Co. launched their 'Art at Home' series, which included volumes by

William Morris's portrait of Janey Burden as *La Belle Iseult*, painted in 1858. He is said to have written to his future wife, 'I cannot paint you, but I love you'. Tate Gallery, London

Lucy Faulkner (by then Mrs Orrinsmith), Walter Crane's sister, Lucy, and the ebullient Mrs Haweis who all gave advice on furnishing and decorating the 'Art' home. The tone of these books, however, was not to exhort women merely to take up 'elegant and useful amusements' but rather to emulate the artists and designers they admired. 'Women have only begun to learn that there is no market for unskilled labour,' wrote Mrs M. J. Loftie in Macmillan's *The Dining-Room*. 'In no employment will ladies succeed until they cease to be merely amateurs.' More and more women accordingly enrolled at the new progressive art schools in Birmingham, Liverpool, Glasgow and London. At the Arts and Crafts Exhibition Society exhibitions amateurs, many of them women, could show their work next to that of such accomplished designers as Day, Crane and even Morris himself. *The Studio* gave serious reviews to these exhibits, especially the textiles, which included everything from *portières* and altar frontals to book-covers and cot quilts, and often it illustrated amateur work.

For many women, china-painting or embroidery did remain just another feminine hobby, but for perhaps thousands it supplied an escape into active, practical work, accompanied by the important illusion that they could ally themselves to the great social and spiritual adventure of the century and so feel less marginalized by their own lack of real power over their lives. For some women, Art work, through the benediction of good taste, allowed them an entirely respectable and even laudable means of earning a living. For a very few – such as Kate Greenaway, Phoebe Traquair, Hannah Barlow or Jessie M. King – it meant fame and even fortune.

It was no coincidence that Arts and Crafts became the style of dress and interior decoration associated with forward-looking women. The pioneering Newnham College, Cambridge, for example, a bastion of women's education, was built by Basil Champneys in a romantic Queen Anne revival idiom and furnished and decorated with Morris and Co. 'Sussex' armchairs and wallpapers and simple, medieval-style oak coffers. And Christabel Pankhurst wore a silver brooch that had been designed by Ashbee in the form of a stylized flower-head, set with the suffragette colours – in amethysts, a cabochon emerald and pearls.

The work of amateur craftspeople,

however, highlighted the question that concerned Ashbee after the failure of his Guild: was it enough for people to feel involved in design reform and to enjoy the essential quality of life that he believed accompanied craftsmanship, even if what they produced was without merit or beauty? So many of those who joined Arts and Crafts societies in Europe and America produced work that provoked the belittling description of 'artsy-craftsy'. The question of priorities – aesthetic merit or quality of life – is impossible to resolve: 'Give them their liberty of production and they'll do it better', hoped Ashbee vainly. But the criticism levelled at much of the second-rate amateur work was particularly damaging to the cause of feminism, for poorly conceived or executed designs were seen by some as evidence not of lack of opportunities, training or facilities but of an essential failure in women to meet the challenge of true artistic endeavour.

Agnes Garrett (sister of Elizabeth Garrett Anderson – Kate Greenaway's doctor – and of the feminist Millicent Fawcett) and her cousin Rhoda Garrett found that it took years to discover an architect prepared to take them on and train them as clerks. At last J. M. Brydon, who, in partnership with Bruce Talbert and Daniel Cottier, had run a firm of 'Art Furniture Makers, Glass and Tile Makers', employed them, and eventually they founded their own decorating firm, designing furniture, chimney-pieces and wallpapers in the Queen Anne revival style. They designed furniture (now at Standen) for James Beale's London house in Holland Park. But Rhoda later spoke bitterly of the opposition and prejudice that had faced them. Only in 1907 was a Women's Guild of Arts founded, by May Morris and Mrs Thackeray Turner, wife of a cabinet-maker; it was sponsored by the Art Workers' Guild, which did not itself admit women as members until 1964.

In America, there was not such an ideological force opposed to women making practical use of their skills – skills which had proved essential during the Civil War: the wife of a frontiersman could ill afford to emulate those Society women, described by Edith Wharton, who led 'a temperate life of minor accomplishments . . . child-bearing was their task, needlework their recreation, being respected their privilege'. Many women inspired by the Arts and Crafts movement earned their share of respect not only as artists but as businesswomen, publishers, teachers and innovators.

One of the most influential among American women artists was Candace Wheeler, who had founded Associated Artists with L. C. Tiffany. She was fifty-six years old when her partners left and, with her daughter Dora and her friends Rosina Emmett, Ida Clark and Caroline Townsend, she took over the firm. Not only did they retain such clients as Andrew Carnegie (for whom they created fabric woven with a design of thistles to denote his Scots origin), Cornelius Vanderbilt II and the poet H. W. Longfellow, but they went on to supply designs for wallpapers to the New York manufacturer Warren, Fuller and Co. and for printed and woven textiles to Cheny Brothers of South Manchester, Connecticut. Mrs Wheeler was introduced to Warren, Fuller and Co. after winning a thousand-dollar prize in a design competition they held, but

151

Portrait plaque by W.S. Coleman at Minton's newly-founded Art-Pottery Studio, Kensington Gore, c.1872

the Cheny and Wheeler families were old friends. The Wheelers were well-travelled, and Dora's designs were much influenced by Walter Crane's style; her mother, on the other hand, strove to introduce specifically American themes into her designs. She especially loved the native flowers and plants, described in the poetry of Ralph Waldo Emerson, and she would sketch them at her remote summer retreat in the Catskill Mountains.

Candace Wheeler wrote many articles and books and also taught at the Cooper Union in New York. Her contribution both to the decorative arts and to the cause of women was recognized when she was appointed Director of Color to the Women's Building at the great World's Columbian Exposition in Chicago in 1893. She was given sole responsibility for the decoration of the library in the Women's Building, which she effected with drapery in shades of blue and green to mirror the water that could be seen through the single, large window. She also had the task of collecting exhibits for the Bureau of Applied Arts, where Associated Artists exhibited a vast 'needlewoven' tapestry faithfully copied

from Raphael's cartoon for the *Miraculous Draught of Fishes*.

Mrs Wheeler had first become involved in a life outside the sphere of her family and friends after the death of her eldest daughter, Daisy, in 1876; at that time she had organized the New York Society of Decorative Art and the Women's Exchange to help women who needed some small independent income: the secretary of the New York Society of Decorative Art was Elizabeth Custer, General Custer's widow, and many war widows were grateful for 'the door to honest effort among women' that Mrs Wheeler had opened.

For many women, the ideals of the Arts and Crafts Movement were easily allied to their traditional concern with philanthropic works. In 1889 in Chicago, Jane Addams founded Hull House, a settlement house modelled on London's Toynbee Hall, where immigrants were taught craft skills. In 1900 a Protestant missionary named Sybil Carter went to work among the Ojibway Indians on the White Earth Reservation in Minnesota. And in 1904, in order to give them some skills whereby they could earn a living, she founded the Indian Lace Association, with the successful idea of teaching the Indians lace-making techniques, though mainly based on Italian rather than local originals. The lace sold well, but did little to preserve the traditional craft skills of the Ojibway Indians. The militant socialist Ellen Gates Starr also found that in order to pay its way at all, a craft workshop had to concentrate on making beautiful objects for the rich. She had left Chicago to study bookbinding in England with T. J. Cobden-Sanderson and returned to set up the Hull House bindery, but disillusioned with what she saw as the failure of the Ruskinian ideal, she eventually retired to a Catholic convent.

In England, too, Art for All, the philanthropic aim of bringing beauty into working-class lives became a vital element of the Arts and Crafts movement, and was often allied to the fervent desire of the middle-classes to revive disappearing rural crafts. Small guilds, such as the Keswick School of Industrial Art, the Yattendon Metalworking Class or the Clarion Guild in Leeds were founded all over the country, often by local ladies, and exhibited their work at the Arts and Crafts Exhibition Society shows. Maude King and Mary Blount, with their husbands, helped to found and run the Haslemere Weaving Industry and the Peasant Art Society, also in Haslemere, with the aim of repopulating and regenerating the countryside: local working-class women produced hand-woven silk, cotton and linen textiles, appliqué embroidery, and hand-woven pile and tapestry carpets.

In 1884 the Home Arts and Industries Association was founded by Mrs Jebb; it was dedicated to the revival of village crafts by amateur craftspeople and inspired by the work of an American, Charles Godfrey Leland, who had established a manual training programme for Philadelphia schools. Within two years, schools or classes had been established in over fifty areas, many of which developed into commercial concerns, and in 1904 *Arts and Crafts* began monthly publication. The Association held regular exhibitions at the Albert Hall in London.

Artistic philanthropy took many forms: Selwyn Image and A. H. Mackmurdo, for

example, founded the Fitzroy Picture Society to distribute prints of great paintings to schools; Georgiana Burne-Jones was involved in the establishment of the South London Gallery in Camberwell in 1893, which aimed to exhibit pictures to local poor children without charge; and there were other similar schemes to bring art into tenements and hospitals. Art may not have put bread into hungry mouths or clothed cold, dirty children, but the desire to enfranchise the pleasures of beautiful things did much to alter nineteenth-century attitudes towards the working-class: the 'brutes' and 'dumb animals' of the Chartist risings became the heroes of Morris's socialist Utopia.

'Consider the Lillies of the Field' embroidered and painted *portière*, designed and made by Candace Wheeler in 1879. Mark Twain Memorial, Connecticut

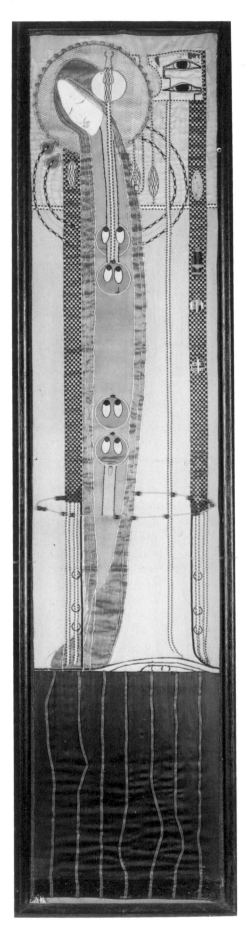

EMBROIDERY

Above left: Embroidered panel designed by May Morris and worked by the Battye family, who commissioned the design; cushion cover (*below left*) designed by Jessie Newbery and embroidered by her mother, Mrs Rowat, *c.*1916; and (*left*) one of a pair of embroidered and appliquéd linen panels, enhanced with glass beads, metal thread, braid and ribbon, designed by Margaret Macdonald Mackintosh and exhibited in the 'Rose Boudoir' at the Turin International Exhibition in 1902

Janey Morris, the medieval chatelaine of Morris's Red House, was taught by her husband how to do simple woollen crewel work, and she became an accomplished embroideress. Her sister, Elizabeth Burden, became chief instructress at the Royal School of Art Needlework, opened in South Kensington in 1872. The women associated with the School were not, however, encouraged to design their own work, but only to execute designs by Morris, Burne-Jones, Crane and others.

May Morris, who took over the Morris and Co. embroidery section in 1885, produced well-spaced, light, floral designs for curtains, table-cloths, cushion covers, cot quilts and work-bags, as well as executing work designed by her father. In 1893 she published *Decorative Needlework*, and in 1910 undertook a lecture tour of America.

Gertrude Jekyll, inspired by a meeting with Morris in the 1860s also became a talented needlewoman and won commissions from Lord Leighton and the Duke of Westminster. She was forced by failing eyesight to abandon close work and concentrate on garden design.

Jessie Newbery, wife of the principal of Glasgow School of Art, established embroidery classes there in 1894. Many of her students intended to become primary- and secondary-school teachers, and Mrs Newbery rejected the highly skilled intricacy of the Royal School of Art Needlework, favouring instead simpler techniques, such as appliqué, and cheaper materials that could be used in local schools. 'I specially aim at beautifully shaped spaces,' she wrote, 'and try to make them as important as the patterns.' It was her assistant, Ann Macbeth, who, in *Educational Needlecraft*,

the book she wrote in 1911 with Margaret Swanson, publicized Jessie Newbery's approach, as well as suggesting new ways of teaching primary-school children to sew and encouraging them to use embroidery as a means of self-expression.

Jessie Newbery's influence can be seen in the work of Frances and Margaret Macdonald, who were students at the School of Art and who opened their studio in Glasgow in 1896, producing not only embroidery but also gesso, book illustrations and metalwork. After her marriage to Charles Rennie Mackintosh in 1900, Margaret used embroidery within schemes he designed for interior decoration at the Turin International Exhibition of 1902, and in the Willow Tea-Rooms and Hill House near Glasgow. Her elongated female figures were strikingly realized through stylized appliqué with added beads, ribbon, braid and metal threads.

In England, there was a resurgence of interest in many traditional rural techniques, such as smocking: in America, too, needlework skills such as quilting were revived. In 1896 Margaret Whiting and Ellen Miller founded the Society of Blue and White Needlework in Deerfield, Massachusetts. Initially they adapted old designs, worked in blue thread on a white ground, but then began to create their own designs, using multi-coloured threads and appliqué on coloured fabric. They exhibited their work at Arts and Crafts Society exhibitions in Boston, New York and Chicago. At the H. Sophie Newcomb College for Women in New Orleans, students used the colours and forms of local flora and fauna in their embroidery designs.

AMERICAN CERAMICS

In Cincinnati, Maria Longworth Nichols turned her hobby of china-painting into a highly successful business – the Rookwood Pottery – when, in 1880, she persuaded her wealthy father to turn an old schoolhouse on the Ohio River into a pottery. The work of the pottery was divided, with different people in charge of throwing, firing and decorating. Laura A. Fry developed the atomizing technique that was used to spray a smooth coloured glaze on to the surface of Rookwood's 'Standard' ware; Matthew A. Daly was responsible for the striking portraits of 'Native Americans'; and many other decorators painted the countless flowers and landscapes that made up the various lines, known as 'Sea Green', 'Iris', 'Aerial Blue', and a series with matt glazes, the most successful of which was 'Vellum'. In 1886 Maria Nichols remarried and thereafter became less involved in the running of Rookwood, which dominated the American pottery market until it closed in 1941.

Louise McLaughlin, also from Cincinnati, returned from the Philadelphia Centennial Exposition inspired by the slip-painted stoneware produced for Limoges by Ernest Chaplet. Already an accomplished china-painter, she now began experimenting herself and in 1878 produced her own 'Cincinnati Limoges'. Ten years later, she went on to experiment with porcelain clays in a kiln in her back yard and in 1898 produced her 'Losanti' ware.

Adelaide Alsop Robineau taught herself china decoration from books, and went on to teach it and, in 1899, to edit *Keramic Studio* magazine, which contained designs and information for china-painters. Longing for more control over the form of her work, she began experimenting with throwing and firing and in 1903 turned to porcelain, fired at extremely high temperatures to achieve distinctive crystalline glaze effects. She also used the time-consuming decorative technique of incising into the clay body. Within two years her work was on sale at Tiffany and Co. in New York. She was involved with the short-lived University City Pottery in Missouri, where she created her prize-winning 'Scarab Vase', which took one thousand hours to complete.

Standard glaze pottery portrait vase of a North American Indian chief decorated by Grace Young at the Rookwood Pottery, Cincinnati, Ohio in 1905; 'Foxes and Grapes' high-glazed earthenware vase (*opposite left*), with incised decoration, made by Adelaide Robineau in Syracuse in 1922; and (*right*) a ceramic pot decorated by Leona Nicholson and fired at Newcomb College, New Orleans, 1910-15

In 1895 a pottery was established at the H. Sophie Newcomb College in New Orleans, where students were encouraged to explore their own visual ideas. They created a distinctive style, using simple, incised decoration combined with bold, bright colours to portray local plants, trees and animals: magnolia, poinsettia, rice, cotton, Cherokee rose or cypress trees appeared in confident, spontaneous forms.

FASHION

Dress reform, especially the lobby against the unhealthy practice of tight-lacing, had been gathering momentum since the 1840s. The American Free Dress League was founded in 1874, and 'reform' garments were displayed at the 1876 Philadelphia Centennial Exposition. In London, Mrs King founded the Rational Dress Society in 1881; its *Gazette* championed the abolition of the corset and the adoption of the divided skirt.

From Janey Morris and Georgiana Burne-Jones onwards, many of the women associated with the Arts and Crafts movement wore loose, uncorseted 'reform' clothes, and Burne-Jones objected when in the 1880s his wife took the reactionary step of wearing a bustle. C. R. Ashbee's wife Janet, who attended meetings of the Healthy and Artistic Dress Union, removed her stays on her honeymoon and never wore them again. She also wore sandals with bare feet, even in London.

Several painters and architects turned their attention to women's fashion and designed loose, flowing 'Art' clothes. E. W. Godwin became director of Liberty's costume department in 1884; Henri van de Velde's 'reform' clothes were unveiled at Krefeld, the centre of the German textile industry, in 1900; Frank Lloyd Wright designed dresses for his wife, Catherine, and even for clients; and, in Vienna, Gustav Klimt designed the wondrous, embroidered dresses that appeared in his paintings, and were made by his lover, Emilie Flöge. The fashion atelier set up at the Wiener Werkstätte in 1910 was directed by Edouard Wimmer, and produced everything from beaded evening bags to pyjamas, evening cloaks to millinery. Couturiers such as Fortuny in Italy or Natalia Lamanova in Moscow all helped to create this new image of women.

In *The Art of Beauty*, Mrs Haweis recommended the ideal background for the modern woman, with oak furniture and dark tapestries in rooms where harmony would replace brilliance and detail would become important; women, she advised, should abandon loud patterns and gaudy colours for loosely draped clothes in soft colours,

worn with delicate jewellery. In the 1870s, various books of this sort paid homage to the influence of such contemporary icons as Janey Morris and the other Pre-Raphaelite models. These images had imbued female beauty with an ethereal spirituality and made it something to be worshipped. They contributed towards the cult of women that flourished in a variety of images, ranging from the medieval damozel, the golden goddesses of Alma-Tadema's paintings or the simpering angels of the portrait plaques painted by W. S. Coleman for Minton's, to the morbid sexuality of the Medusa and Salomé figures of the French Symbolists. Actresses such as Ellen Terry, Lillie Langtry, Eleonora Duse and Sarah Bernhardt were important role-models: Bernhardt, particularly, inspired the jewellery of René Lalique and Georges Fouquet and the posters of Alphonse Mucha.

Three influential women: Janey Morris in 1865 (*opposite*), posed for her photograph by Dante Gabriel Rossetti, who painted her often (Victoria & Albert Museum, London); the Viennese couturier Emilie Flöge (*right*) painted in 1902 by Gustav Klimt who designed dresses made by Emilie and her sister; and (*overleaf*) a poster by Alphonse Mucha of Sarah Bernhardt as *La Dame aux Camelias*. Historisches Museum der Stadt, Vienna

JEWELLERY

Top: Tinted horn tiara set with moonstones in the form of elderberries, made by Fred Partridge and retailed by Liberty and Co., c.1900; *(left)* a breast ornament of gold, set with moonstones, rubies, chrysoprase and abalone shell, designed by John Paul Cooper in 1908 and *(right)* a corsage ornament in silver and gold, set with garnets and pearls, probably designed by C.R. Ashbee for the Guild of Handicraft

Previous page: Brooch and two belt buckles of enamelled silver by Nelson and Edith B. Dawson

Arts and Crafts jewellery, with its use of enamel, semi-precious stones, baroque pearls and inexpensive materials such as horn, provided an alternative to the flashy South African diamonds and sentimental butterflies and flowers, or sporting motifs, beloved by many Victorians. Pugin and Burges both designed Gothic pieces – in gold decorated in bright enamels with such emblems as fleurs-de-lys, roses or doves – and the 'archaeological' jewellery of Carlo Guiliano and Alessandro Castellani was popular among both the Pre-Raphaelites and the aristocratic and artistic group known as The Souls. The Aesthetes also adopted antique jewels, long strings of amber or jade beads, Japanese-style *cloisonné* enamels or the Indian jewellery sold by Liberty's.

But it was Ashbee who totally broke the mould, creating unpretentious, versatile necklaces, pendants, brooches and clasps, often of light silver or gold chain linking his favourite semi-precious materials – moonstones, opals, garnets, amethysts, turquoises and pearls. In later years he also used a shimmering turquoise enamel. His naturalistic forms of flowers, birds and butterflies, although simple, were richly expressive of his ideals.

Ashbee's style was echoed in the work both of Nelson Dawson, who had studied enamelling under Alexander Fisher, and of his wife Edith, a watercolourist. The same influence was evident too in the intricate but delicate and unassuming pieces made in Birmingham by the illustrator Georgina Gaskin and her husband, the wood-engraver Arthur Gaskin, who in 1902 became the head of the Vittoria Street School for Jewellers and Silversmiths.

The Gaskins were among the many artists supplying Liberty's. Fred Partridge, who had been a member of Ashbee's Guild, continued with his wife May Hart to produce carved pieces in coloured horn at their Soho workshop. His work – for example, a tiara in the form of elderberries in purple-tinted horn decorated with moonstones – was perhaps influenced by that of René Lalique. Ella Napper, who worked with Partridge, also supplied Liberty's, as did Murrle Bennett and Co., Arthur Silver, Archibald Knox and Jessie M. King.

The apparent simplicity of much Arts and Crafts jewellery gave way to more sumptuous work, such as the amazing enamelled gold creations of Henry Wilson, which were studded with bizarre jewels, including baroque pearls, opals, rock crystals, star sapphires and mother-of-pearl. John Paul Cooper and Edward Spencer, who designed metalwork and jewellery, were both influenced by his style.

In America, many jewellers and metalworkers were women; for example, Florence Koehler in Chicago, Madeleine Yale Wynne in Deerfield, Massachusetts, and Elizabeth Copeland in Boston. In 1900 Clara Barck, a graduate of the Art Institute of Chicago, founded the Kalo Shops as an all-women workshop producing weaving and leathergoods. The name was derived from the Greek word *kalos*, meaning 'beautiful', and their motto was 'Beautiful, Useful, and Enduring'. In 1905, after her marriage to an amateur metalworker, George Welles, Clara Barck established the Kalo Art-Crafts Community as both a workshop and a school, and began to create simple and elegant jewellery and tablewares with the hammered surface texture inspired by Ashbee.

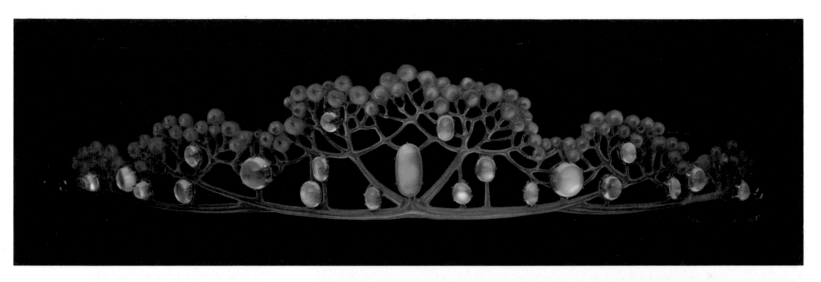

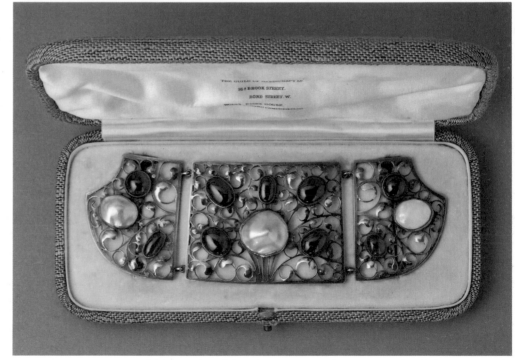

Part Four

INTO THE
TWENTIETH
CENTURY

New Departures

The widespread economic expansion of the 1890s led to a demand for houses, villas and apartment blocks from a new type of client. The European industrialists and financiers who looked forward with such confidence to the new century wanted houses and furnishings that were modern and which reflected the forward-looking outlook that had won them their wealth. In England, the newly-rich patronized Arts and Crafts architects, but the English love of rural traditions led ultimately to the Home Counties style later dubbed 'Stockbroker Tudor'. In Berlin, Vienna and Paris, however, new money wanted an entirely new style.

For the artists and architects of the European Secession movements, the desire to free art and design from sterile historicism was a vital part of their creed. While the English became increasingly concerned with the preservation of rural traditions, in Europe those inspired by the writings of Morris and Ruskin and the designs of Ashbee, Mackmurdo or Crane, developed their own visual imageries. The sinuous curves and tendrils of Art Nouveau – a 'new art' inspired by natural forms – appeared in France in the work of Louis Majorelle, Eugène Grasset, Georges de Feure, Edward Colonna and Eugène Gaillard; in Holland

in the work of the architect Hendrik Berlage and the artist Jan Toorop; and in Belgium in the wrought iron and mosaics of Victor Horta's Maison Tassel and Hôtel Solvay, the town houses of Paul Hankar and the furniture of Gustave Serrurier-Bovy.

One of the most influential figures of this new style was the Belgian painter Henri van de Velde. He was a member of the Société des Vingt, founded in 1884 to promote the work of avant-garde painters, including many of the French Post-Impressionists. Influenced by the Arts and Crafts Exhibition Society show held in Brussels in 1891, van de Velde turned to the decorative arts, and went on to design furniture, interiors, silver, ceramics, textiles, books and typography. In 1896 the four interiors he contributed to Samuel Bing's Maison de l'Art Nouveau in Paris brought him to the attention of French designers, and by the turn of the century he had settled in Berlin. In 1902 he was appointed artistic adviser on arts and industries to the Grand Duke of Saxe-Weimar, and he founded the Weimar Kunstgewerbeschule, which later became the Staatliches Bauhaus. In 1914, as a founder member of the Deutsche Werkbund, he was still adding to the debate on the role of the artist in designing for mass production,

Staircase in the Hotel van Ettvelde, a private mansion in Brussels, designed by Victor Horta in 1897–9

Detail of a carved glass vase by Emile Gallé, 1890s

which, in the decade before war, became the great argument among architects and designers inspired by the Arts and Crafts movement.

In Italy, too, the 'awakening' of the decorative arts in *Stile Floreale* and *Stile Liberty* coincided with the increasing industrialization of the country and so heightened awareness among designers of the need to co-operate with manufacturers and industrialists. Nevertheless, at the International Exhibition held in Turin in 1902, although no reproductions of past styles were allowed, the principal buildings, by Raimonda d'Aronco, were in an ornate Byzantine style, which was echoed in the Moorish tassels and arches of Carlo Bugatti's 'Thousand and One Nights' furniture. It was at Turin that Bugatti unveiled his extraordinary 'Snail Room' – one of four interiors containing almost sculptural furniture decorated with painted vellum, intricate inlaid metals and carved wood; Bugatti also produced sculptural pieces of silverware and jewellery. However, in 1904 he left Milan for Paris, though his furniture continued to be made under licence by the Milan firm of De Vecchi.

The Milanese cabinet-maker Eugenio Quarti, a friend of Bugatti's (who also made luxurious furniture, carved and inlaid with mother-of-pearl and metal), put some elegant pieces, painted white and decorated with stencilled flowers, into the Turin Exhibition. By the time of the Milan International Exposition four years later, however, Pietro Zen, son of the Art Nouveau furniture designer Carlo Zen, was showing furniture designed for industrial production.

In Europe, there was less concern about what would now be termed the 'lifestyle' of the craftsman, and few were concerned with establishing guilds that specifically protected the craftsman's way of life according to medieval ideals. The aspect of Morris's writings that most concerned the Europeans was the vital importance of one's daily environment, and the belief that its simplicity, restraint and fitness for purpose in the home, office or street could influence people for the good. The means by which the economic expansion of the 1890s had been achieved – better communications, faster forms of travel, more powerful industrial machinery, greater numbers of workers employed in factories and offices – had made European cities even busier, more crowded, noisy and dirty. The plain interiors offered by the Arts and Crafts movement, full of calm and integrity, presented a haven of peace and clear thinking.

The luxury of Art Nouveau or *Stile Floreale* was gradually rejected in favour of a new, sophisticated idiom which took as its starting point 'truth to nature' – a truth variously interpreted in the 1860s by Ruskin or Dresser, but which was now reduced to a spatial geometry. This not only provided visual calm and ease, but also had the advantage – for the social aims of the Arts and Crafts movement were still present – that designs based on such a geometry could be made cheaply and in great numbers by machine, and so be available not just to the wealthy who could afford hand-craftsmanship, but to ordinary working people. For many, it was an exciting ideal, but for those who shared Morris's hatred of industrialization, it was anathema.

One of the first architects to move, not in

Opposite: Chair by Carlo Bugatti in wood overlaid with painted parchment, and with inlaid copper; one of a set of four exhibited in his *Salle de Jeu et de Conversation* at the Turin Exposition of 1902. Virginia Museum of Fine Arts

The hall in Hill House, Helensburgh, designed by C.R. Mackintosh

the direction of mass production, but towards a geometric harmony of building and interior, was the Scotsman Charles Rennie Mackintosh. Although the English hated his early work, especially his exaggerated, stylized graphics, he was enormously influential in Europe, where his work was seen in the late 1890s in *The Studio* and in *Deutsche Kunst und Dekoration* and *Dekorative Kunst*, and he had several followers in Glasgow. E. A. Taylor, a former shipyard draughtsman, came under the influence of the 'Glasgow Four' – Mackintosh, his wife Margaret Macdonald, her sister Frances and her husband Herbert MacNair – at the School of Art; John Ednie and George

Logan, whose work was influenced equally by Mackintosh and by Baillie Scott, both designed complete interiors for the large Glasgow firm of Wylie and Lockhead in a watered-down form of the Glasgow style; and George Walton, who worked as a decorator on several houses in the Glasgow area before moving to London (where he designed furniture, fitments and shopfronts for the Kodak Company), also borrowed elements of Mackintosh's style.

In the summer of 1900, a wealthy Viennese banker, Fritz Wärndorfer, visited Glasgow, admired the work of the 'Glasgow Four' and invited them to exhibit with the eighth Secessionist exhibition.

Charles and Margaret Mackintosh visited Vienna, where they showed some of the furniture from their Mains Street flat, together with two gesso panels from Mackintosh's Ingram Street tea-rooms and some other items. They met many of the founding members of the Secession, including Josef Hoffmann, and must have been struck by the lively intellectual climate of the Viennese coffee-houses, for this was the Vienna of Freud, Wittgenstein, Mahler, Schönberg, and Musil, where every branch of philosophy, literature and the arts was under examination.

Mackintosh and Hoffmann met again at the Turin Exhibition in 1902, for which Mackintosh had designed the Scottish pavilion. He and Margaret contributed a white, silver and pink 'Rose Boudoir', based on three gesso panels by Margaret, together with Mackintosh's elegant black and white furniture. Frances and Herbert MacNair (who had left Glasgow for Liverpool, where MacNair now taught) designed a writing room, and two further rooms contained work by Jessie M. King, her future husband E. A. Taylor and George Logan. Meeting again in Turin with the banker Wärndorfer, Charles and Margaret were commissioned by him to design a music salon for his house in Vienna. Later that year Wärndorfer and Hoffmann visited Glasgow to discuss their plans for a decorative arts workshop with the couple.

The Wiener Werkstätte, with an architectural office and workshops producing metalwork, bookbinding and leatherwork, wood- and lacquerwork, was established in premises in Neustiftgasse in October 1903; the enterprise was financed by Wärndorfer,

and Hoffmann and Koloman Moser were artistic directors. They considered themselves responsible for every element of an interior, from cutlery to light fittings, and even designed individual keys. As a result of their rigorous rejection of shoddy mass production and the 'mindless imitation of old styles', everything for the new premises, including their distinctive graphics and lettering, was designed afresh by Hoffmann and Moser. In this they were wholeheartedly supported by Mackintosh, who wrote in a letter to Hoffmann: '. . . every object which you release must be most definitely marked by individuality, beauty and the utmost accuracy of execution. Your aim must above all be that every object you produce should have been made for a particular purpose and place.'

Hoffmann also insisted on the best working conditions for his craftsmen. In their 'Working Programme' of 1905, Moser and Hoffmann wrote: 'We neither can nor will compete for the lowest prices – that is chiefly done at the worker's expense. We, on the contrary, regard it as our highest duty to return him to a position in which he can take pleasure in his labour and lead a life in keeping with human dignity.'

The style of the early years of the Wiener Werkstätte was largely non-representational, relying on colourless, geometric grids offset by the opulent silverware designed by Hoffmann or Carl Otto Czeschka, the smart black and white ceramics produced by Bertold Löffler and Michael Powolny at the Wiener Keramik, and the cabinets designed by Moser with elaborate veneers and inlays. In their contrast between a spare, geometric formality and touches of luxury, the Wiener Werkstätte interiors were similar in conception to the collaboration between Mackintosh, with his often stark furniture, and his wife, who contributed rich, figurative gesso or embroidered panels to his early interiors. But while Mackintosh moved towards greater coherence and apparent simplicity, the Wiener Werkstätte thrived on sales of its more frivolous luxury goods.

Their most exotic commission was for the Palais Stoclet, a mansion built in Brussels for the great Belgian collector and railway 'king', Adolphe Stoclet, and described by his granddaughter as 'a house for angels'. Begun in 1905, it took eight years of planning and construction, and almost bankrupted the workshops. Precious materials such as polychrome marbles, malachite, onyx and bronze were used throughout: the mosaic friezes, *Expectation* and *Fulfilment*, designed by Gustav Klimt for the dining-room, contained coral, semi-precious stones and gold.

Yet despite the increasing success of the Wiener Werkstätte's jewellery, lace, bead bags, toys, postcards (some designed by Oskar Kokoschka) or Christmas decorations, Hoffmann's concern for the improved organization of the workshops continued. In 1909 the Vienna Kunstgewerbeschule had been reformed according to Arts and Crafts principles, with greater emphasis on practical workshop experience. In 1913 Hoffmann extended this practice and established the Kunstlerwerkstätte, where artists, many of whom were Hoffmann's former students from the Kunstgewerbeschule, could come and experiment with a wide range of media under

Left: Painted terracotta head by Gudrun Baudisch for the Wiener Werkstätte, c.1927

the guidance of experienced master-craftsmen. This saved young artists the expense of setting up their own workshops, and the Wiener Werkstätte, who reserved the right to buy any of the designs produced in the Kunstlerwerkstätte, was provided with a steady source of fresh ideas.

After the decimation of the First World War, followed by the influenza epidemic of 1918 in which Otto Wagner, Kolo Moser, Gustav Klimt and Egon Schiele all died, the Kunstlerwerkstätte was dominated by women. Mathilde Flögl, who became Hoffmann's chief collaborator, Maria Likarz, Fritzi Löw and Hilda Jesser designed wallpapers and textiles for the Wiener Werkstätte, while a new generation of potters – Vally Wieselthier, Susie Singer and Gudrun

Opposite: Photograph of Margaret Macdonald Mackintosh in 1900, sitting beside a cabinet designed by her husband

Baudisch – produced boldly coloured, expressionistic, figurative ceramics.

In Germany, encouraged by the powerful figure of Hermann Muthesius, the guilds, or Werkstätten, were encouraged to find commercial success not through luxury goods but through mass production. In 1905 Bruno Paul at the Munich Vereinigte Werkstätten had begun experimenting with 'Typenmöbel', unit furniture which used laminated timber sheets and standardized components, but the success of the workshops – by 1907 they employed six hundred workers and had branch offices in Hamburg, Bremen and Berlin – still depended on the huge variety of products they offered which, although often made using machines, were not mass produced. In Dresden, Richard Riemerschmid was studying the feasibility of 'Maschinenmöbel'. Peter Behrens, who had become dissatisfied with the artists' colony in Darmstadt, had been appointed by Muthesius as director of the Düsseldorf School of Applied Arts in 1903. He became a leading spokesman for the idea of *Typesierung*, standardization for mass production. In 1906 he began his association with AEG, the Allgemeine Elektrizitäts Gesellschaft (General Electric Company) in Berlin, where he was to persuade the company to furnish their workers' houses with 'Typenmöbel'.

Ideas about mass production were very much in the air when the Deutsche Werkbund was founded in 1907. The Werkbund, the brainchild of Muthesius, was an association of individual craftsmen, designers, architects and workshops – including the Werkstätten in Munich, Dresden and elsewhere – and other commercial and industrial concerns. The Werkbund's aim was to put an end to poor quality mass-produced goods by encouraging the creation of individually-designed objects through exhibitions, lectures and other forms of publicity. Behrens, Riemerschmid and van de Velde in Germany and Olbrich and the Wiener Werkstätte from Vienna were among the founding members.

There was no coherent Werkbund style, as the Werkbund *Yearbook*s show: illustrations of aeroplanes or railway stations appear next to hand-crafted objects. But its influence grew steadily, especially through the art schools (Behrens was in Düsseldorf, Riemerschmid in Munich and Bruno Paul in Berlin) and it attracted many new members. At the Werkbund exhibition held in Cologne in 1914, there was work by van de Velde and, in the Austrian pavilion, designed by Hoffmann in classical style, the essentially decorative artist, Dagobert Peche, had a room to himself; yet there was also work by Behrens, Bruno Taut and Walter Gropius, who exhibited a prototype factory with a glass façade revealing the machinery inside. At the exhibition, however, van de Velde, supported by Walter Gropius, clashed with Muthesius on the sore issue of artistic individuality versus total standardization. Although van de Velde welcomed modern materials and machine production, he declared that: 'The artist is essentially and intimately a passionate individualist, a spontaneous creator. Never will he, of his own free will, submit to a discipline forcing upon him a norm, a canon.' The argument raged on in one form or another throughout the 1920s and 1930s, and has yet to be resolved.

Stained and painted wood dresser designed by Peter Behrens for the Deutsche Werkbund, c. 1902

CHARLES RENNIE MACKINTOSH

Leaded glass panel by the Scottish designer George Walton, after a
design of stylized roses by C.R. Mackintosh

Charles Rennie Mackintosh (1868–1928), the son of a superintendent of police, trained as an architect in Glasgow in the offices of Honeyman and Keppie, where he met Herbert MacNair. Together they attended evening classes at the Glasgow School of Art, which had recently been reorganized on Arts and Crafts principles by its new head, Francis Newbery. There they met Margaret and Frances Macdonald, and the 'Glasgow Four', as they became known, began to collaborate on decorative schemes.

They exhibited posters and metalwork at the Arts and Crafts Exhibition Society in London in 1896, but their work was heavily criticized for being distorted and unnatural. The new Scottish style was dubbed the 'Spook School'; nevertheless, they found a champion in Gleeson White, editor of *The Studio*, who visited Glasgow and wrote admiringly of their work.

In 1897 Mackintosh won the competition to design the new Glasgow School of Art, which was completed in 1909. The overall scheme had an integrity and vitality which marked a radical departure from existing vernacular styles, using metalwork especially to reinforce the thematic elements. Mackintosh frequently echoed the massive outlines and vivid history of Scottish castles in his own buildings, combining a protective monumentality, enhanced by energized ornamental details, with an imaginative conception of interior space.

In 1899 he began to collaborate with Margaret Macdonald, whom he married the following year. Their flat at 120 Mains Street, Glasgow, demonstrated his concerns for interior decoration. No pattern was allowed except occasional stylized motifs embroidered by Margaret or contained in leaded-glass or metalwork panels inset into his furniture – though Mackintosh's distinctive arrangements of woven twigs formed one other permitted element. The colour scheme was in grey, black and white, and the harmony of the room lay in its proportions. Some of the furniture from the flat was shown in 1900 at the eighth Secession Exhibition in Vienna, where the couple's work was warmly received by Josef Hoffmann and other members of the Secession.

During the next few years, Mackintosh received several major commissions: for Miss Cranston's tea-rooms in Ingram Street and Willow Street, Glasgow, for Miss Cranston's own house, Hous'hill (also in Glasgow), and for two other private houses – Windyridge at Kilmacolm, and Hill House, Helensburgh, for the publisher William Blackie. In these two houses, he began to curtail his use of Margaret's stylized images, whether in gesso panels or embroidery, and to rely entirely on proportion and geometry for his effects.

In 1904 he became a partner in Honeyman and Keppie, but little new work came his way, and in 1913 he resigned from the firm. Cut off from his friends in Vienna by the war, he left Glasgow and in 1915 settled in Chelsea, where he received a few minor architectural commissions and he and Margaret designed some abstract and stylized textiles. In 1920 the couple moved to the south of France, where he painted watercolours. He died of cancer in London in 1928.

Top: Charles Rennie Mackintosh

Above: Watercolour study of polyanthus flowers, painted by C.R. Mackintosh in 1915

Right: The main bedroom at Hill House, Helensburgh, by C.R. Mackintosh

JOSEF HOFFMANN AND THE WIENER WERKSTÄTTE

Josef Hoffmann (1870–1956) studied architecture in Munich and in Otto Wagner's office in Vienna, where he met J. M. Olbrich. In 1897 he joined the Secession, where, with Koloman Moser, an illustrator who had studied at the Vienna Kunstgewerbeschule, he was responsible for exhibiting decorative arts – especially those by British Arts and Crafts movement designers. When the Secessionist painter Felician von Myerbach became principal of the Kunstgewerbeschule in 1899, Hoffmann and Moser were appointed to the staff. Hoffmann's influence on generations of students was immense.

Both Hoffmann and Moser considered Biedermeier to have been the last true 'style', and they argued for greater simplicity and restraint in the design of furniture and everyday objects. In 1903, after a visit by Hoffmann and the banker Fritz Wärndorfer to England, the Wiener Werkstätte (the Vienna Workshop) was established, inspired by the example of Ashbee's Guild of Handicraft and by the work of the 'Glasgow Four'.

Hoffmann's architectural commissions – such as a sanatorium at Puckersdorf, near Vienna, the black-and-white-tiled Cabarett Fledermaus in Vienna's Kärntnerstrasse, and the Palais Stoclet in Brussels – were now handled by the Wiener Werkstätte, for whom he designed furniture, jewellery, glass, metalwork and textiles until 1931.

By 1905 the Wiener Werkstätte employed one hundred craftworkers to execute designs by thirty-seven masters and could produce everything for the complete artistic interior. The workshops even offered garden designs, undertaken by Hoffmann's pupil, Franz Lebisch. There were separate departments for metalwork, ceramics, glass, enamelwork, leatherwork, bookbinding, graphics (they produced postcards, posters and theatre programmes), wallpapers, textiles and furniture. The luxury goods, especially the gold tablewares and jewellery or millinery, hand-printed textiles and bead bags, were the height of fashion, and clients included leading actresses, couturiers and artists.

Wiener Werkstätte postcard of the Cabarett Fledermaus, decorated by the workshops in 1907

Moser, tired of dealing with difficult clients, resigned as artistic director in 1907 after financial troubles, and devoted himself to painting and stage design.

In 1914 the workshops were reorganized when Wärndorfer withdrew and left for America. The industrialist Otto Primavesi then took over as financial backer, and outlets were opened in Zurich, Marienbad, Breslau and, briefly, in New York. In the 1920s the Wiener Werkstätte reflected the mood of the post-war years, and the various workshops' style came to be dominated by the more exotic and piquant work of designers such as Carl Otto Czeschka, Vally Wieselthier, Edouard Wimmer, the head of the fashion department which had been set up 1910, and Dagobert Peche, who introduced 'spiky Baroque' – a style inspired by folk-art, and using flowers, animals and human figures as decorative motifs.

In 1928 the Wiener Werkstätte celebrated its twenty-fifth anniversary, but in 1927 there had been political riots in Vienna, and in 1929 the ceramic workshop had to be closed down following the Wall Street Crash. The workshops went into final liquidation in 1931.

Above: Electroplated silver basket designed by Josef Hoffmann, *c.*1905

Right: Gold cigarette case set with opals, lapis, turquoises, mother-of-pearl, agate and semi-precious stones, designed by Josef Hoffmann for the Wiener Werkstätte in 1912

RICHARD RIEMERSCHMID

Richard Riemerschmid (1868–1957) trained as a painter in Munich. His first designs for furniture, in a neo-Gothic style, were produced in 1895 when he married the actress Ida Hofmann and was furnishing their new apartment. In 1897, when the Vereinigte Werkstätten were established, he started designing metalwork, in wrought iron and bronze, copper and brass, in an unadorned yet sinuous form of Art Nouveau. He also began to contribute designs to both the Vereinigte Werkstätten and other commercial firms for porcelain, glass, cutlery, lighting fixtures, carpets and, from 1905, furnishing textiles with small geometric motifs. His designs were elegant and coherent, with a powerful abstract, sculptural sense of form. His simple, often daring designs, such as the chair exhibited in his 'Music Room' in Dresden in 1899, led the way within the 'functionalist' wing of the Munich *Jugendstil* movement.

Riemerschmid also worked with the Vereinigte Werkstätten für Kunst in Handwerk founded in Dresden by his brother-in-law Karl Schmidt in 1898. In 1906 he designed his 'Maschinenmöbel', reasonably priced suites of machine-made furniture inspired by 'the spirit of the machine', for the Dresdener Werkstätten. The following year the workshops began to concentrate on serial, or mass, production, and Riemerschmid himself became a founding member of the Deutsche Werkbund.

Also in 1907 the Dresden and Munich Werkstätten amalgamated, and together worked on plans for Germany's first garden city at Hellerau near Dresden. Apart from houses, the plans included laundries, a theatre, a training school and the Werkstätten's own workshops. Le Corbusier, who was working in Peter Behrens's office, spent some time at Hellerau, and the arguments he later put forward in *L'Esprit nouveau* have much in common with Riemerschmid's ideas. Riemerschmid believed that design must grow out of modern life, and that it was artefacts such as liners, locomotives or machinery that were truly expressive of the age. 'Life, not art, creates style. It is not made, it grows.'

In 1913 he was appointed director of the Munich Kunstgewerbeschule, where he remained until 1924.

Above: Wine glasses from the 'Menzel' service designed by Richard Riemerschmid in 1903 and made by Benedikt von Poschinger, Oberzwieselau, using a revival of an old glass-making technique

Opposite left: Oak chair designed by Richard Riemerschmid and made by the Vereinigte Werkstätten für Kunst in Handwerk, Munich; exhibited in the Music Room at the Dresden Deutsche Kunst-Ausstellung in 1899

Opposite right: One of a pair of gilt cast brass candlesticks designed by Richard Riemerschmid and made by the Vereinigte Werkstätten für Kunst in Handwerk, Munich in 1897

TEXTILES

The 1890s were a period of great sophistication in textile design, and British fabrics were sold all over world, influencing designers in Europe and America. William Morris championed the use of natural dyes, flat patterning and romantic English flowers. Interest in the 'old English garden', as well as the popular botany taught by Dr Christopher Dresser, greatly influenced textile design. G. P. Baker, for example, of the Kent textile firm G. P. and J. Baker, collected alpine plants and experimented with hybrid irises, and designers such as Lindsay P. Butterfield, George C. Haité and C. F. A. Voysey all used naturalistic flowers in their pattern designs, as did Candace Wheeler in America.

Morris had also studied historical textiles, including medieval French, Italian, English and also Persian examples. His associate Thomas Wardle was interested in Indian chintzes, while the Baker brothers, who had been brought up in Turkey, based their early designs on Isnik patterns.

Although Morris and Co. produced ornate tapestry and embroidered hangings, the greatest demand was for the printed furnishing cottons known as cretonnes. Washable patterned cottons were especially popular in smoky cities for curtains (often with matching window-seat cushions) and for upholstery. Warner and Sons, a former Spitalfields silk-weaving firm which moved to Essex in 1895, produced conventionalized designs by Owen Jones, Japanese-inspired designs by Bruce Talbert and the flowing, proto-Art Nouveau patterns by A. H. Mackmurdo; the Lancashire firm of Turnbull and Stockdale, where Lewis F. Day was artistic director from 1881, was another major supplier of furnishing fabrics.

In Europe, it became common for architects and artists to design textiles. However, the Art Nouveau stylization of Henri van de Velde or Alphonse Mucha, and the geometric patterning of Richard Riemerschmid or Josef Hoffmann gave way to abstract patterning, and by 1914 the heyday of the 'artist-designed' textile was over.

Top: 'King Cup', ink and watercolour design for a printed linen by Jessie M. King, *c.*1925. Printed by Thomas Wardle for Liberty and Co.
Above: Lace panel designed for the Wiener Werkstätte by Dagobert Peche
Opposite: Woven silk, wool and cotton double cloth designed by Lindsay P. Butterfield for Alexander Morton and Co. in 1898

RESIDENCE
FOR
MR. E. W. LITTLE

FRANK LLOYD WRIGHT
ARCHITECT

A Second Generation Interprets the Style

The first years of the new century saw the development of a harmonious form of ornament based on natural geometry, an 'organic' form of design which could be reflected in all aspects of a house, from its relationship to the surrounding landscape to its furnishings and decorative motifs. The importance of using local materials and of binding a house to its landscape resulted in the emergence of distinctive regional styles of architecture and design.

The most famous of all such styles was that of the Prairie School, developed in Chicago by Louis Sullivan and the younger architects – Frank Lloyd Wright, George Grant Elmslie and George Washington Maher – who trained in his office. The great Chicago fire of 1871 had destroyed nearly 20,000 buildings, yet the city managed to rebuild itself with astonishing speed. As the British novelist Wilkie Collins observed on a visit in 1874: '. . . everybody I meet uses the same form of greeting. "Two years ago, Mr Collins, this place was a heap of ruins – are you not astonished when you see it now?"' Louis Sullivan had studied and worked in Boston, Philadelphia and Paris before settling in Chicago in 1881 and joining Dankmar Adler in a partnership that lasted until 1895. He designed numerous public buildings and offices in Chicago, including the Stock Exchange and the Carson Pirie Scott department store. He wanted his buildings to be completely free of historicism, and created broad, simple forms, based on the low flat skylines of the prairie, enlivened by rich and complex ornament abstracted from local grasses, seeds and plants.

The Scots-born George Grant Elmslie, who worked for twenty years from 1889 as Sullivan's chief draughtsman, and executed most of his ornamental designs, was possibly responsible for much of his domestic work. Elmslie designed furniture that combined geometric forms with stylized carving, as well as metalwork, leaded glass, rugs and even, for his own house, embroidered table-covers. Like Sullivan, he believed in an 'organic' use of decorative motifs, applying a theme as simply or elaborately as required throughout a building. In 1909, when Frank Lloyd Wright left for Europe, Elmslie set up his own practice, Purcell, Feick and Elmslie, and designed many houses in the Prairie style.

George Washington Maher was equally interested in the complete interior and designed many of the furnishings for the houses he built. Beginning to work on his

Interior of the Edna Purcell residence, Minneapolis, Minnesota, designed in 1913 by George Grant Elmslie

bined the selected stylized form, which might be a lion or floral motif such as the hollyhock, honeysuckle or lotus, with a specific geometric shape. The motif – perhaps a thistle combined with an octagon, or a poppy with a straight line – was then repeated 'rhythmically' inside and out to create a sense of visual unity.

Frank Lloyd Wright, however, went beyond Sullivan or Maher's ornament abstracted from nature to make the very structure of his houses organic, to make 'aesthetic and structure completely one'. Architectural beauty, Wright believed, was the product of simple and harmonious elements clearly stated, and was derived from the economy which results from following natural laws. 'Bring out the nature of the materials,' he wrote, 'let this nature intimately into your scheme.' Style could not be imposed on a building, but grew out of the basic plan and the choice of building materials, as well as the building's position within the landscape.

Wright's interest in the relationship between nature and geometry went back to his childhood, when he had played with the Froebel blocks he later gave to his own children, and was reinforced by his interest in Japanese design, which, he felt, evoked the universal principle without losing the power of individuality. In his autobiography, Wright wrote in 1932 that 'pure design is abstraction of nature-elements in purely geometric terms', and went on to say that architecture was akin to music, that creating a building was like writing a symphony. 'When I build I often hear Beethoven's music and, yes, when Beethoven made his music I am sure he sometimes saw buildings

own account in 1888, he visited Europe twice during the 1890s, and his later work shows the influence of Voysey. Maher developed his own method of unifying the exterior and interior of a house with its furnishings through decorative details, which he called his 'motif rhythm theory'. The choice of motif should, he felt, be derived principally from the needs and temperament of the client, but he then com-

like mine in character, whatever form that may have taken then.'

In California, too, the Arts and Crafts movement provided the inspiration for the development of a distinctive local style. The 'golden state' contained not only a generous climate and a varied and beautiful landscape, from the arroyo canyons to the orange groves, but a rich and romantic mix of cultures. The American immigrant population searching for a fresh architectural and decorative style could draw not only upon their own backgrounds but also upon the adobe buildings of Mexico, the Franciscan missions from the Spanish colonial past, and the artefacts of the indigenous Indian culture.

In San Francisco, after the earthquake and fire of 1906, Arthur F. Mathews and his wife Lucia founded the Philopolis Press and the Furniture Shop with the ideal of rebuilding the city afresh. Mathews, an architect and painter who had been director of the California School of Design, had trained as a painter in Paris, and his work combined figures from the classical traditions of Europe with landscapes that were purely Californian. In the furniture and complete interiors, both private and public, that he and his wife created for the Furniture Shop, the colours, landscape and flowers of California dominate. Lucia Mathews's two great interests were horticulture and painting, and the carved, incised, inlaid, gilded and painted furniture she designed, ranging from candlesticks and picture frames to large cupboards and screens, could not be more different from the plain, backwoods style of the eastern seaboard.

Bernard Maybeck was born in New York, the son of an immigrant German wood-carver. The simple wooden chalets and bungalows he built in the Berkeley Hills and the Bay area inspired his friend and patron Charles Keeler to dedicate his book *The Simple Home* to him. To Keeler, who believed in a mystical communion with the landscape, Maybeck's homes upheld the ideal of a simple and hospitable home-life promulgated by Stickley and others, and were admirably suited to their locality.

Further south, Irving John Gill, who worked in San Diego and later in Los Angeles, built houses with the massive walls and shady arcades of the Mission style. As became an architect who had worked in Sullivan's office in Chicago in the early 1890s, he used modern materials – concrete instead of adobe – as well as natural local materials such as river boulders or redwood.

It was in Pasadena, however, that the most deeply Arts-and-Crafts-inspired houses were built – the airy wooden houses of the brothers Charles Sumner and Henry Mather Greene. Ashbee met Greene and Greene in 1909 and wrote of Charles: 'Like Lloyd Wright the spell of Japan is upon him, he feels the beauty and makes magic out of the horizontal line, but there is in his work more tenderness, more subtlety, more self-effacement than in Wright's work. It is more refined and has more repose . . . perhaps it is California that speaks rather than Illinois. . . .'

Like Wright, Greene and Greene were interested in the relationship of their houses to their settings, and this interest was expressed in their choice of local materials such as arroyo stone for foundations, paths, steps and retaining walls and wood for the houses themselves – in the Gamble House (1907–9), for example, wooden porches and stone terraces link the exterior and interior. Greene and Greene's best-known houses are low-built, with dominant gabled roofs and widely overhanging eaves that seem to secure the buildings to the ground, and the brothers combined a wide variety of influences in their style of building, ranging from Maybeck's shingled Swiss chalet houses, or Craftsman bungalows, to ornamental details and surface treatments adapted from Japanese temples and palaces. In the garden of the Cordelia A. Culbertson House, built in Pasadena in 1911, for example, a loggia, a vine-covered pergola and an Italianate water garden inspired by Edith Wharton's *Italian Villas and Their Gardens* are combined with the Japanese motif of a curving path of stepping-stones leading to a gabled oriental gate.

Despite the huge differences between the newly-settled hills of Pasadena, or the vast plains of Illinois, and leafy, rural England, architects in Britain and America were aware of one another's work and felt that they shared common concerns and interests – in materials, gardens, and the expression of harmony within the local landscape. The English climate was suited to neither the horizontal forms of the Prairie School nor the shady bungalows of California, yet there are many points of contact between Wright, Greene and Greene, Webb and Lutyens. The partnership which produced the most quintessentially English country houses was that between the young Edwin Lutyens and the middle-aged Gertrude Jekyll. As a boy, 'Ned' Lutyens had been kept at home because of his delicate health, but the illustrator Randolph Caldecott, a neighbour, had encouraged him to draw, and he went to Kensington School of Art before spending a year as a paying apprentice in the architectural office of Ernest George and Peto. A commission from a family friend in 1889 enabled him to set up in practice for himself, aged only twenty. That year, he met Miss Jekyll, introduced by a friend in the hope that she would commission him to design the house she was planning to set amidst her garden at Munstead Wood. She did, and it marked the beginning of a long and fruitful collaboration.

Lutyens absorbed much from Miss Jekyll's collection of old English furniture, and his early designs for furniture are based on Stuart and William and Mary originals. He also learnt from the photographs she took to record local life and vernacular achitecture; this record (subsequently published in 1904 as *Old West Surrey*) undoubtedly reinforced the influence of Philip Webb and Norman Shaw in the evolution of Lutyens's early 'Surrey' style. And Miss Jekyll won him several vital early commissions at the turn of the century, such as that from Edward Hudson, proprietor of *Country Life*, to build Deanery Gardens for him in Berkshire. *Country Life* went on to feature much of Lutyens's work as well as that of Miss Jekyll.

Among the other masterpieces created by Lutyens and Jekyll are Folly Farm in Berkshire, Ammerdown and Hestercombe in Somerset, and Marsh Court in Hampshire. Lutyens's 'Surrey' style combined local building techniques and materials, such as half-timbering and decorative brick- and tile-work, with picturesque silhouettes of gables and ornate, seventeenth-century-style chimneys which arise out of the gardens designed and planted by Miss Jekyll. Lutyens built balconies, buttresses and walkways which, as at Folly Farm, join the gardens to the house. Gertrude Jekyll taught Lutyens not only how to make garden and house seem almost to intermingle, but also how to use the garden to link a house to its site.

Although Lutyens designed a great deal of furniture, he seldom undertook complete interiors: he had a strong sense of the way houses are naturally altered over time, and his notion of the 'organic' interior contained a powerful awareness of history. He probably felt that the furnishings best suited to his houses were antiques.

Despite his success as a country house architect, and as a creator of modern castles, such as the massive, granite Castle Drogo overlooking Dartmoor in Devon, his tastes

Above: Presentation drawing by Bernard Maybeck for a townhouse for a San Francisco department store owner, 1909

Overleaf: The entrance front of Gertrude Jekyll's house Munstead Wood, Munstead, Surrey, designed for her by Edwin Lutyens and completed in 1897

BEDROOM · FURNISHERS · ESTABLISHED · 1810 · HEAL & SON Nos 195·196·197·198 TOTTENHAM · COURT · RD

"THE NEWLYN" A SET OF PLAIN OAK FURNITURE WITH DULL STEEL HINGES & HANDLES . SOUND CONSTRUCTION : INEXPENSIVE

The Newlyn Suite, one of Ambrose Heal's earliest sets of oak furniture, illustrated in a woodcut by C.H.B. Quennell in 1898

began to veer more towards the Palladian. In 1912 he was appointed architect to the new city of Delhi, confirming his classical leanings. Later commissions included the Roman Catholic cathedral in Liverpool.

For those who could not afford to commission an architect-designed interior, there was a successor to Liberty and Co. that provided the complete English rural vernacular look: Heal and Sons. Heal's was a long-established supplier of beds and bedding, which had opened a new department for sitting-room furniture in the 1880s. Ambrose Heal, the great-grandson of the shop's founder, began to design furniture in the 'Cotswold' style established by Gimson and the Barnsleys, and his first pieces appeared in the windows of the Tottenham Court Road store in 1896. Two years later he published a catalogue of his own designs entitled *Plain Oak Furniture*, which was praised by Gleeson White in *The Studio*. The following year he published *Simple Bedroom Furniture*, a

collection of plain, homely bedroom suites that were cheap and stylish. They were exhibited in 1899 at the Arts and Crafts Exhibition Society, which Ambrose Heal joined himself in 1906, and were to prove a great commercial success.

The simple 'Newlyn' bedroom suite (all his ranges were named after such English seaside towns as Newlyn or St Ives), in fumed oak with steel handles and hinges, was illustrated in the catalogue by a distinctive woodcut of an imaginary room with low rafters, quaint leaded bay windows and an Arts and Crafts frieze around the cornice. Some of his early designs incorporated mottoes and quotations inlaid in pewter and ebony; for instance, the 'Fine Feathers' suite, in his *Plain Oak Furniture* catalogue, had inset on the wardrobe 'Fine feathers make fine birds' and on the dressing-table 'If this be vanity who'd be wise'. In 1900 Ambrose Heal took over the direction of all of Heal's advertising, using his distinctive

Oak dressing table designed
by Ambrose Heal

Arts and Crafts typography and calligraphy:
by 1905, when he became managing director, he had stamped his personality on the
entire store.

From 1905 Heal's sold a wide range of
reasonably priced plain oak 'cottage furniture' for 'Metro-Land' dwellers, as well as
cheaper, machine-made furnishings which
were considered 'excellent for servants'
bedrooms', and also fabrics from all the
leading designers and manufacturers. Later
Heal's introduced other English woods,
including walnut, elm, cherry and chest-
nut, using light staining to enhance the
grain. Dressers and dining suites were
enlived with ebonized banding and with the
distinctive ebony and pewter check inlay
that Heal used from around 1900. In the
early 1920s they introduced their 'weathered' oak finish: the grain was opened with a
wire brush and the wood coated with plaster
of Paris, then sanded so as to leave some
plaster in the grain. The oak was finished
with wax and button polish to make it easy
to maintain. Heal's retained its reputation
as the stylish furniture store for the middle-
class intelligentsia until the 1960s, and no
doubt furnished many a suburban villa in
the 'mild Home County acres' celebrated so
nostalgically in the poetry of the late Poet
Laureate, John Betjeman, and reached by
the Metropolitan Line, the first steam
underground in the world:

> Lured by the lush brochure,
> Down by-ways beckoned,
> To build at last
> The cottage of our dreams.
> City clerk turns countryman again,
> And linked to the metropolis by train.
> Metro-Land.

FRANK LLOYD WRIGHT

Frank Lloyd Wright (1867-1959) was born in Wisconsin, where he studied engineering. He worked briefly for the Chicago architect J. L. Silsbee, in whose offices he met Elmslie and Maher, and in 1888 entered the offices of Adler and Sullivan, where he quickly became chief draughtsman, responsible for many of the practice's smaller domestic commissions. In 1893 he established his own practice in Oak Park, to which many young architects came to work and study, and by 1900 he had designed over fifty houses.

Wright collected Japanese prints, and was strongly influenced by Japanese arts: he visited Japan in 1905. In 1897 he was a founding member of the Chicago Society of Arts and Crafts at Hull House, and in 1900 met C. R. Ashbee, who was at that time visiting Chicago. They remained friends for years, despite their fierce arguments over the role of the machine. While Ashbee passionately supported hand-craftsmanship, with the result that only the wealthy could afford his products, Wright strongly supported the use of new technology, realizing that the use of the machine would make it possible that 'the poor as well as the rich may enjoy today beautiful surface treatments of clean strong forms'.

His early work was also influenced by Norman Shaw's revivalist style, interpreted in America by H. H. Richardson in Boston, and by the New England Shingle style, but the house which he built for himself in Oak Park in 1899 began to show his architectural philosophy, and also contained his first designs for furniture.

Between 1901 and 1909 he developed a geometric abstraction of nature, reflecting the open, quiet skylines of the prairie in low, flat houses with overhanging roofs and prominent chimneys that conveyed a traditional image of shelter. His belief in the total integration of site, structure and furnishings was manifested, for example, in the Susan Lawrence Dana House of 1902–4, for which he designed leaded glass, lighting fixtures, furniture and even fountains, or the Frederick C. Robie House of 1908 which he completely furnished.

Oak extending dining table designed by Frank Lloyd Wright in 1896 for the William C. Fricke House, Chicago. Victoria & Albert Museum, London

Influenced by the ideas of Otto Wagner in Vienna, Wright believed that the building begins with the interior space. He created open living-spaces, often with simple, built-in furniture which was a natural extension of the structure. The furnishings had also to accentuate the symbolic meaning of the house. The fireplace, the heart of the house, was often made a focal point – not just by Wright, but by many Arts and Crafts designers – as was the dining-room, where the family and guests gathered to break bread. Wright believed that 'the horizontal line is the line of domesticity', and in the Robie House the strong horizontal and vertical rhythm of the dining table and chairs is reinforced by the low ceiling and its horizontal beams.

In 1909 Wright left Chicago for Europe with the wife of a former client. On his return to America two years later, he built a new house and studio, Taliesin, in Wisconsin, but his architecture, in Chicago, California and Japan, remained somewhat static until the 1930s, when he began to work in a more Modernist style. His later buildings, such as Fallingwater, in Pennsylvania, or the Guggenheim Museum in New York, built in the late 1950s, are as coherent and strong as his early Prairie School houses.

Oak spindle chair by
Frank Lloyd Wright,
c. 1908, one of several
variations of high-backed
dining chairs that he
designed

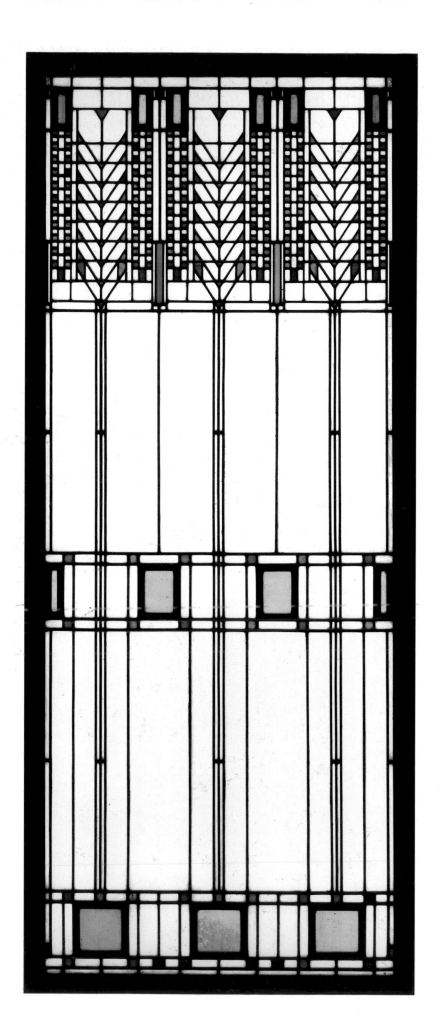

Leaded and stained glass
'Tree of Life' window
designed by Frank Lloyd
Wright for the Darwin D.
Martin House, Buffalo,
New York in 1904

Opposite: Inlaid walnut and
ebony armchair, designed
by Charles and Henry
Greene for the Blacker
House, Pasadena, *c.*1907

GREENE AND GREENE

The Gamble House, Pasadena, designed by Charles and Henry Greene, 1907–8, for one of the partners in the soap firm Proctor and Gamble and (*opposite*) a wall sconce of Honduras mahogany, ebony and leaded glass

Charles Sumner (1868–1957) and Henry Mather (1870–1954) Greene were born in Cincinnati. Charles wanted to be a painter, but both brothers studied at the Massachusetts Institute of Technology and then worked in Boston for different architectural firms. They moved to Pasadena, where their parents had just settled, in 1894.

During the 1890s they worked in a variety of styles, including Mission, New England Shingle, and colonial Queen Anne and Dutch revival. They began to be interested in Japanese design after seeing examples of Japanese architecture at the World's Columbian Exposition in Chicago in 1893, and four years later were able to enlarge their understanding of Japanese arts after meeting John Bentz, an importer of oriental antiquities and books.

In 1901 Charles Greene visited England on his honeymoon, and on his return, when *The Craftsman* began publication, he took to studying Arts and Crafts ideas, in particular the Craftsman plans for inexpensive bungalows, which had much in harmony with the Japanese architecture that he and Henry admired. In 1902 the Greenes used Stickley furniture in the James Culbertson House. Their own work was later regularly featured in *The Craftsman*.

The Robert R. Blacker House of 1907, a large, asymmetrical wooden structure set in a six-acre Japanese-style garden, was built in Pasadena for a retired lumberman. Both the house and the furniture they designed for it were influenced by Japanese design. In the David B. Gamble House in Pasadena and the Charles M. Pratt House in the Ojai Valley, they were given a free hand by the clients, both of whom were friends of the Blackers. The two houses were winter retreats, and Greene and Greene were able to oversee every detail, from the gardens to fireplace tools, abstract rugs, leaded glass and lighting fixtures such as wooden lanterns. The furniture, some of it inlaid with stylized motifs in fruitwoods, ebony or precious stones, showed great simplicity of line and form and made decorative use of pegging and dowelling or mortise-and-tenon joinery. It was Charles Greene who designed most of the furniture, which was made by two Swedish craftsmen, John and Peter Hall.

In 1916 Charles moved north to Carmel, California, where he undertook little new work. The brothers' last collaboration was in 1923.

GARDEN DESIGN

In his influential books, *The Wild Garden*, 1871, and *The English Flower Garden*, 1883, William Robinson put into words the new feeling for natural gardens. Rejecting the mid-Victorian practice of the seasonal bedding-out of annuals in strict geometric patterns, he passionately advocated wild, romantic gardens, with sweeping lawns, wide herbaceous borders and walls covered with trailing flowers that would reflect the changing seasons.

Interest in 'old-fashioned' gardens and particularly in the propagation of 'those dear old flowers', as Mrs M. J. Loftie described them – hollyhock, tiger-lily, poppy, sunflower, roses, lavender, lupin, pinks, phlox, iris, delphinium – had been growing for some time. All the Pre-Raphaelite painters had old-fashioned gardens and, at Morris's Red House, there were topiary hedges, grass walks, wattled trellises for roses and carefully preserved orchard trees. Such a style was also perfect for small suburban gardens: in 1883 the Natural History and Gardening Society at Bedford Park, for example, declared its interest in the 'cultivation of simple and old-fashioned flowers'.

Painters, architects, writers, all turned their attention to the garden, especially to the more formal topiary, clipped hedges, trellises and box edging of Italian or so-called 'Queen Anne' gardens. In 1880 E. W. Godwin and Maurice Adams published *Artistic Conservatories*, with designs for floral porches, aviaries and verandahs. In 1891 J. D. Sedding brought out *Garden Crafts Old and New*; this was followed the next year by Reginald Blomfield's *The Formal Garden in England*; in America in 1904 the novelist Edith Wharton contributed *Italian Villas and Their Gardens*; and in 1907 George Samuel Elgood, an English watercolourist who specialized in painting gardens, and who had illustrated *Some English Gardens* in 1904 for Gertrude Jekyll, published *Italian Gardens*.

Helen Allingham, an artist famous for her watercolours of cottage gardens, added *Happy England* to the genre in 1903. She was married to the Irish poet, William Allingham, and was a friend of Ruskin, Browning and Tennyson, whose garden she painted.

William Robinson, however, disagreed violently and publicly with Blomfield's ideas, most specifically over the proper use of terraces to link house and garden, and it was left to the formidable partnership of Gertrude Jekyll and Edwin Lutyens to reconcile the two approaches.

When they met in May 1889 at the house of a rhododendron collector, Miss Jekyll was forty-five and Ned Lutyens just twenty. She was being forced by increasing myopia to abandon her embroidery, silver repoussé work and wood-carving, and was increasingly concerned with the garden she was creating on her fifteen-acre plot of land next door to her mother's house in Munstead, Surrey.

She had developed an interest in gardens after reading Robinson's book and subscribing to his journal, *The Garden*, and they had met and become friends in 1875. With Lutyens, she now put her skills to professional use and by 1910 they had collaborated on nearly sixty gardens.

Getrude Jekyll was a practical gardener, supplying plants and deciding on colour harmonies, for she believed in a creative relationship with nature, using flowers and plants as an artist does the colours on his palette. She was also responsible for introducing many Japanese plants and shrubs, such as azaleas, lilies and flowering cherries, to English gardens. While she contributed the detailed planting and inspired the rose-covered pergolas, pools, steps, clipped yew, and colourful drifts of flowers that became the trademarks of their style, Lutyens decided on the formal geometry, creating paths, vistas and juxtapositions of brick, stone, water and greenery, and also designed garden seats, fountains and other features.

After 1910, Getrude Jekyll worked alone on hundreds of garden schemes while Lutyens was occupied with his more grandiose architectural plans, although they collaborated on the design of war cemeteries after the First World War. She was a regular contributor to *Country Life* and wrote many books, of which her best loved were *Wood and Garden*, 1899, and *Home and Garden*, 1900. Her influence on English gardens is almost as strong now as it was ninety years ago.

Above: Illustration from Reginald Blomfield's *The Formal Garden in England*, 1892

Left: A Mediterranean Garden by George Samuel Elgood, *c.*1900. Christopher Wood Gallery, London

Previous page: The garden at Hestercombe, Somerset, designed by Edwin Lutyens in 1903 and planted by Gertrude Jekyll

Part Five

THE
CONTINUING
INFLUENCE
OF THE
MOVEMENT

The Modern Movement is Born

As Europe moved closer and closer to the First World War, the debate about the true nature of good design was extended not only by new art movements, such as Cubism, De Stijl or Futurism, but by the emotive power of technological advance. By 1919 the emotional imperative to build for peace, to transform the tanks, guns and aircraft developed during the war into a technology to be used for the good of the working men who had fought alongside the artists, architects and designers in the trenches had become an urgent desire to create a new and better society. All over Europe, the arguments about the use of the machine, the role of the artist or the relevance of ornament were picked up where they had been left off in 1914.

In Italy, the Futurists, and in Holland, the founders of *De Stijl* magazine – Piet Mondrian, J. J. P. Oud and its editor Theo van Doesburg – had already demanded a style dictated by modern materials and based on the technological 'spirit of the times'. Already in pre-war Vienna, the radical architect, designer and writer Adolf Loos had condemned the decorative products of the Wiener Werkstätte as degenerate and pretentious, insisting that beauty lay not in ornament but in form. His own

post-war furniture designs were plain and functional, showing an understanding of the relationship between materials and form, and his buildings were totally devoid of ornament. Although Loos admired the work of English Arts and Crafts designers, he had also responded to the methods of mass-production he had seen in America, where he had studied architecture, and he advocated mass-produced and inexpensive designs such as Thonet's bentwood chairs. The simplicity of Morris's 'Sussex' chair had triumphed, but the championship of the way of life of the craft workshop no longer seemed relevant.

In post-revolutionary Russia, the artists who had embraced abstraction joined the Vkhutemas, the reorganized Moscow art schools, and went on to develop Constructivism, which supported an exploration of form as dictated by the properties of specific materials. In 1921 they announced their alliegance to Productivism, a doctrine that held that art should be practised as a trade and that the production of well-designed articles for everyday use was of far greater value than individual expression.

In France, the Swiss architect who styled himself Le Corbusier was evolving the idea that furnishings should, like fountain pens,

The dining room in a house designed by Alvar Aalto in 1938. The evolution of such spacious and practical 'open-plan' living set the style for the 'Contemporary' look of the 1950s

telephones or office furniture, be designed as 'equipment' that would work well and fulfil the demands put upon it with the same precision that we expect from such other modern 'tools' as cars or locomotives. In Berlin in 1922, Peter Behrens, in whose studio had worked Le Corbusier, Walter Gropius and Mies van der Rohe, became artistic director of AEG. This was the first industrial company to appoint a designer to oversee the creation of a coherent corporate image, and Behrens designed not only their products – including fans, kettles, telephones and street lights – but also their buildings and their advertising and other graphics.

The designer, said these diverse founders of the Modern Movement, should become as anonymous as the engineer: the individual expression of the artist had become an irrelevance; even, said some, easel-painting itself should be reduced to a 'science' of form and colour. Mass production was the means by which a greater number of people could be supplied with good, inexpensive furnishings and everyday utensils. Architecture and design were, at last, freed totally from historicism by their relationship to such new materials as concrete, plate glass and tubular steel.

The Bauhaus has always been held up as the creative hub of Modernism, and it is true that many of the various European movements fed directly into the school, yet when the thirty-six-year-old architect Walter Gropius was appointed director of Henri van de Velde's former Kunstgewerbeschule in Weimar in 1919, his initial aims were still rooted in the English Arts and Crafts movement. Gropius's appointment as director

had been suggested by van de Velde himself, and the Bauhaus – Gropius's new name for the school – was housed in the buildings the Belgian had designed for the school that he had established with the aim of providing designs for industrial manufacture as well as to teach manual craft skills.

In his 1919 *Manifesto* Gropius wrote: 'Let us together desire, conceive and create the new building of the future, which will combine everything – architecture *and* sculpture *and* painting – in a *single form* which will one day rise towards the heavens from the hands of a million workers as the crystalline symbol of a new and coming faith.' The whole basis of the Bauhaus training was to lie in direct workshop experience in the crafts; painting and sculpture were to be regarded in the same light as woodwork, metalwork, typography or weaving. The Bauhaus was to be a community of skilled artists committed to a collaborative effort. But Gropius, it must be remembered, had opposed Muthesius in the Deutsche Werkbund in 1914 over the issue of standardization for mass production, and had supported van de Velde who had argued for the importance of individual creative expression. 'The manner of teaching [at the Bauhaus],' explained Gropius in 1919, 'arises from the character of the workshop: organic forms developed from manual skills. Avoidance of all rigidity; priority of creativity; freedom of individuality, but strict study discipline.' Ruskin's belief in individual expression remained.

Each workshop had two 'masters', as the teaching staff were now known: the students also became 'apprentices' or 'journeymen'. One of the staff-members was the technical master who was in charge of the workshop, the other, the *Formmeister*, an artist who was responsible for *Form*, or design. Early *Formmeistern* included the painters Georg Muche and Paul Klee. All students followed the same course during their first year, gaining firsthand experience of the different workshops, before choosing the medium in which they would then specialize. This preliminary course was taught initially by the Swiss painter Johannes Itten, who, as something of a guru, combined lectures on form or colour with meditative breathing exercises and other mystical ideas.

During the first couple of years, the Bauhaus attracted many Expressionist painters as teachers, including Gerhard Marcks, Georg Muche, Paul Klee and Wassily Kandinsky, who had also taught at the Moscow Vkhutemas. The items produced in the pottery or the weaving workshop were, as Gunta Stölzl, the future head of the weaving workshop, wrote in 1931, 'poems heavy with ideas, flowery embellishment, and individual experience!' But by 1923 a change had occurred; Johannes Itten was persuaded to leave and was replaced by the self-taught Hungarian artist Lazlo Moholy-Nagy, who had participated in the 'Constructivist and Dadaist Congress' organized in Weimar the previous year by Theo van Doesburg, the editor of *De Stijl*. Van Doesburg had arrived in Weimar in 1921 and began to publish the magazine from there and to offer his own course, which, although highly critical of the Bauhaus for what he considered its self-indulgent romanticism, was attended by many Bauhaus students. 'Gradually there was a shift,' recalled Gunta Stölzl. 'We no-

'Wassily Chair', the first tubular steel chair, designed by Marcel Breuer at the Dessau Bauhaus in 1925

ticed how pretentious these independent, single pieces were . . . the richness of colour and form . . . did not integrate, it did not subordinate itself to the home. We made an effort to become simpler, to discipline our means and to achieve a greater unity between material and function. . . . The slogan of this new era: prototypes for industry!'

It was this shift which marked the final end of the influence of the Arts and Crafts movement, and the true beginnings of Modernism. Gropius responded ably to his students' support of the new ideas expressed by van Doesburg or by Le Corbusier in *L'Esprit nouveau*, and he encouraged the *Neues Sachlichkeit* (the 'New Objectivity') backed by the new masters such as Moholy-Nagy who brought with them the Russian Constructivist doctrine – a doctrine that rejected subjective responses to art and held that it was the idea behind a work of art that mattered, that it was irrelevant whether it was executed by the hand of an artist or by a machine. In addition to his teaching of the preliminary course, Moholy-Nagy also became *Formmeister* in the metalwork shop, where students turned from jewellery and handmade silverware to the design of modern lighting or retractable shaving mirrors. From architecture to graphics, the Bauhaus championed the anonymous designer who subordinated personal expression to practical need, and who evolved, through workshop experience, prototypes for industrial mass production. Such design would contribute to the 'cathedral of socialism', hastening equality of ownership through 'worker-housing' designed and furnished by these Modernist artists. The value of the craft workshop lay not in the way of life it offered the craftsman but – as at Hoffmann's Kunstlerwerkstätte in Vienna also – in the craftsman's experience of a vital artistic

laboratory where new design solutions could be evolved and tested.

But the Bauhaus dream was short-lived. The defeat of the local Socialist government forced the Weimar Bauhaus to close in April 1925, and Gropius moved the school to newly-designed buildings in the industrial town of Dessau. The Dessau Bauhaus was poorly financed, and outside orders from industrial firms became a vital source of income; many of the domestic innovations we now take for granted – push-button light switches, stacking kitchen bowls or reflectors for indirect lighting – emanated from the Dessau Bauhaus.

In 1928 Gropius resigned as director of the Bauhaus and was replaced by Hannes Meyer, the former head of the architecture department. In 1930 Meyer was succeeded by Mies van der Rohe, whose tubular steel furniture had already caused a sensation at the Werkbund exhibition in Stuttgart in 1927. But in 1933 the Nazis forced the Bauhaus to close. Masters and students spread all over the world, particularly to America, where they greatly influenced generations of post-war architects and designers.

The industrial aesthetic developed at the Dessau Bauhaus, at the Moscow Vkhutemas or by Le Corbusier in Paris was by no means the only solution to the debate about the future of Arts and Crafts ideals. In Scandinavia, too, artists were encouraged to become involved with industrial production, as at the famous Swedish Orrefors glass factory, but they produced designs which remained rooted in a Ruskinian appreciation of the natural world. The Svenska Slöjdföreningen, the Swedish Society of Industrial Design, had been founded

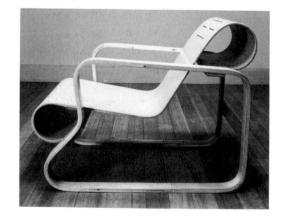

Laminated birch cantilevered armchair originally designed by Alvar Aalto for the Paimio Sanatorium, 1931–2

A room in the architecture department at the Dessau Bauhaus, c.1928, with counterweighted hanging lamps designed by Marianne Brandt and Hans Przyrembel

in 1845 and in 1917 organized the Home Exhibition in Stockholm, which included twenty-three interiors, inexpensively furnished with industrially produced designs. Designers such as Carl Malmsten, who first made his name with the furniture he produced in 1916 for the new Stockholm City Hall, continued to work within the tradition of the individual workshop, using craft skills to create simplified versions of Gustavian forms, though he also produced prototypes for industrial manufacture. Bruno Mathsson, who followed him, made simple bentwood furniture of laminated beech. And in Denmark, Kaare Klint not only made furniture in the craftsman tradition, but also designed built-in storage furniture.

But it was the Finnish architect Alvar Aalto who most fully synthesized the beliefs of the Arts and Crafts movement with the needs of the machine. In 1929, when he won a competition to build a new tuber-culosis sanatorium at Paimio, near Turku in Finland, he began to design cantilevered laminated birchwood furniture. Although at this time he met Le Corbusier in Paris, and Gropius and the De Stijl designer Gerrit Rietveld in Berlin, and did experiment with tubular metal furniture, Aalto believed that the human body should come into contact only with natural materials. His designs for chairs, tables, stools, tea trolleys and desks, which are remarkable for his attention to detail, were made from laminated birch plywood, and, where necessary, moulded to fit the human form. He set up his own firm, Artek, which also produced light fittings and textiles; when his furniture was shown in London at Fortnum and Mason's in 1933, the exhibition was visited not only by Gropius and Moholy-Nagy, but also by Voysey, who apparently praised his work. Aalto's designs thus bridged the gap between the nineteenth and the twentieth centuries.

A Continuing Legacy

By the 1920s the legacy of the Arts and Crafts movement seemed to many in England to be a joke, supported only by vegetarians wearing sandals who spent their holidays in spartan holiday camps or even 'naturist' resorts. The gabled suburban houses, with tile-hung bay windows and stained-glass panels in their front doors, that sprawled along the new arterial roads, or well-meaning church halls and municipal libraries built by architects in what passed for a decent, democratic style, seemed all that was left of William Morris's Utopian dreams of beauty and equality. But this was far from the case. The visual style of the movement may have degenerated, but many of its aims were still current and active.

From Morris's 'Anti-Scrape' to the widespread concern for the rediscovery of 'lost' craft skills, the Arts and Crafts movement was essentially preservationist. The National Footpaths Preservation Society, founded in 1887, the National Trust, founded in 1895, and the Council for the Protection of Rural England, founded in 1926, were all established by supporters of the Arts and Crafts movement. And the wider concern for the visual and social environment, the acceptance that good or bad design affects both individuals and the quality of social life, were brought more sharply into focus by the writings and agitation of architects and designers influenced by Morris and his followers.

The last organizational outpost of the Arts and Crafts movement in Britain was the Design and Industries Association, founded in 1915 following a visit by Ambrose Heal, Harry Peach and others to the 1914 Werkbund exhibition in Cologne. The DIA, which organized exhibitions, lectures and discussions, acknowledged that it was inevitable that the future of design lay with industrial mass production, and sought to convince British designers that they must learn to coexist with the needs and limitations of the machine. But although, in ceramics or textiles, designers such as Susie Cooper or the London-based Marion Dorn, did evolve a modern British style during the 1930s, in furniture and architecture, on the other hand – apart from the steel-frame furniture produced by PEL or the laminated plywood designs made by Jack Pritchard's firm Isokon – the British never really came to appreciate the potential of a 'machine aesthetic', and, in the art schools, preparation for the needs of industry remained largely ignored. Indeed, such an eminent

Armchair with leather
seating by Gordon Russell,
1927–8

founder-member of the DIA as W. R. Lethaby, principal of the Central School of Arts and Crafts, considered that industrial design, while it could be shapely, strong and useful, was basically characterless and inferior to craftsmanship. 'Although a machine-made thing can never be a work of art in the proper sense,' wrote Lethaby, 'there is no reason why it should not be good in a secondary order. . . .' In 1927, when Harry Peach, maker of cane furniture and founder of Dryad Handicrafts, organized the DIA display for an exhibition in Leipzig, he created a show of country crafts. However, by the early 1930s, the somewhat genteel morality that the Arts and Crafts style had come to represent was clearly seen to be hugely out of step with European advances in design.

Nevertheless, Peach was one of those who got the DIA involved in wider issues. A champion of many causes, he was secretary of the Leicestershire Footpaths Association, a prominent member of the Folk Dancing Society, and, as a personal friend of Ramsay MacDonald, a staunch supporter of the Labour Party. In the mid-1920s he started a 'Save the Countryside' campaign, and from his work developed the Council for the Protection of Rural England. He battled against litter and also involved the DIA in setting standards for shop signs and street advertisements, making people aware of the ways in which they could passively allow their towns and villages to be polluted by bad and thoughtless design.

Ambrose Heal, who had succeeded his father as chairman of Heal's in 1913, was another early member of the DIA. From 1917 Heal's organized influential exhibitions of modern European work (in particular French and Scandinavian), and of English pottery, textiles and graphics at their Mansard Gallery. In the 1930s the store sold a wide range of modern work, from Gordon Russell's 'Cotswold' furniture to Mies van der Rohe's cantilevered tubular steel chairs.

Gordon Russell, who joined the DIA in 1920, was in many ways typical of the British compromise in attitudes to craftsmanship and the machine. He had begun designing furniture in the antique furniture repair shop set up by his father to serve the needs of the Lygon Arms Hotel, which his father owned, in the small Worcestershire town of Broadway. After the First World War, he set up independently as a designer, producing traditional turned, rush-seated chairs and plain oak furniture inspired by Gimson and the Barnsleys, as well as other pieces which could be made largely by machine. In 1929 he opened his own shop in London, but was badly affected by the Wall Street Crash. During the 1930s he regained financial security by producing the cabinets designed for Murphy radios by his brother, the architect R. D. Russell. Gordon Russell had enormous admiration for all forms of craftsmanship, from stonewalling to lettering, but, despite his clear acceptance of the machine, he always insisted on quality (whether an item was produced by hand or machine), and the style of his work remained essentially rooted in the simple, 'honest' traditions of earlier Arts and Crafts designers. The English designers were never able to convey any sense of celebration of the benefits of the machine in their work.

One of the DIA's most influential

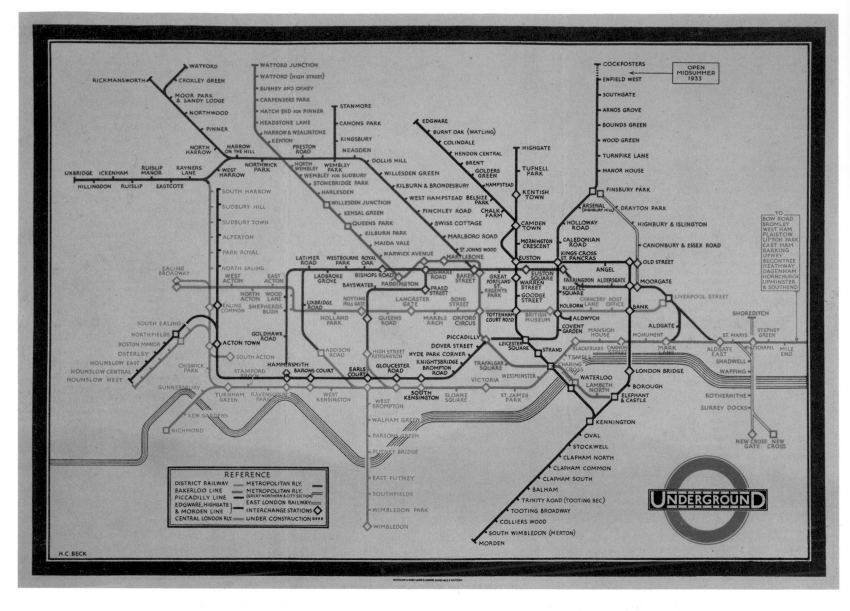

The first simplified 'Tube' map, designed for London Underground by Harry Beck in 1933. London Transport Museum

members was not a designer but an administrator, Frank Pick, who worked for the London Underground, later London Transport, and put the DIA ideals into practice, bringing art and good design to the widest possible audience. He commissioned new buildings, upholstery fabrics for trains and buses, posters, maps – the revolutionary London 'Tube' map of 1933 was the work of Harry Beck – and even a new typeface, designed in 1916 by the calligrapher Edward Johnston, who had taught illuminating and lettering at the Central School since 1899. The London Underground posters – by a wide variety of artists – were accurately described by the Vorticist painter Wyndham Lewis as 'a people's picture gallery'.

In 1943 the aims of the DIA were further realized when Gordon Russell was made head of the Utility Design Panel, set up by the Board of Trade to specify design restrictions and create prototypes for manufacture under war-time conditions. The Utility restrictions were not entirely revoked until 1953, when it was recognized that the Utility Panel had helped to spread awareness of good mass-produced design: indeed, some Labour supporters believed that the restrictions should have been kept in force as part of a socialist plan for greater equality.

But, on the whole, the years from 1910 to 1939 were idiosyncratic and eclectic. In 1913 the art critic and painter Roger Fry had founded the Omega Workshops, with Vanessa Bell and Duncan Grant as co-directors. The purpose of the Omega, which was partly inspired by Paul Poiret's Atelier Martine in Paris, was to publicize Post-Impressionism and to give those English painters whose work was unpopular some small dependable income. The Omega barely survived the war, but it did introduce abstraction and a new, vibrant sense of colour to textiles and wall coverings. A bolder use of colour also appeared in the paintings, furniture and rugs by Frank Brangwyn, a Belgian-born painter who had worked briefly for Morris and Co. in the 1880s before setting out on adventures as a seafarer. The Indonesian textile-printing art of batik enjoyed a revival in Europe and America: the Glasgow artist Jessie M. King learnt batik in Paris before the war, and later taught the craft in Scotland, while, in America, Lydia Bush-Brown made batik popular for clothes and wallhangings.

In 1919 Robert Thompson began his career as the 'Mouseman' of Kilburn, the Yorkshire village where he was born. Thompson worked with his father, the village joiner, carpenter and wheelwright, but, inspired by the medieval carving in

Page from the 1943 Utility Furniture catalogue, illustrating a bedroom

nearby Ripon Cathedral, began carving in wood. In 1919 he received his first commission from Ampleforth, a Catholic boys' school, and went on to work for many other colleges and churches, including York Minster, and also hotels; by the 1930s he employed thirty men. He worked only in English oak, and his furniture is distinguished not only by the small carved mouse that always appears somewhere on each piece, but also by the characteristic rippled surface achieved by the use of an adze, an ancient tool the use of which he revived. Thompson died in 1955, but his Kilburn workshop continues to produce his designs, and several of those who worked for him have set up their own workshops locally, 'signing' their pieces with a carved squirrel, eagle, fox or beaver.

The one aspect of the Arts and Crafts movement which found distinctive

abcdefghjkmopqrstuvx
abcdefghjkmopqrstuvxyz
ABDEGHJKMNQRSTV

The *Gill Sans* typeface designed by Eric Gill for the Monotype Corporation, 1927–8

expression in the inter-war years in England was the ideal of the 'Simple Life' which had already been formulated in different ways by William Morris, Edward Carpenter and C. R. Ashbee. It was not only a return to the land, but a search for a simpler, more harmonious relationship with nature, with work and with other people. Those who espoused the Simple Life, for instance Eric Gill or Ethel Mairet, supported a return to humanity's intimate association with the artefacts which surround daily life, and a notion of human value acquired and practised through workshop experience. Most of the new generation of craftspeople worked independently, but they met to discuss their philosophies and to share notes on ways of selling their work. A network of guilds and galleries emerged, virtually all founded and run by women, including the Red Rose Guild in Manchester, the Three Shields Gallery and the Little Gallery in London, the Sussex-based Guild of Weavers, Spinners and Dyers, and the short-lived New Handworkers' Gallery, founded in London in 1928. The new look relied upon attention to detail, texture, a subtle colour sense and, most of all, a kind of inner integrity

which expressed the almost spiritual values of the Simple Life.

The weaver Ethel Mairet spanned both generations of Arts and Crafts practitioners. She married in 1902 and accompanied her husband, Ananda Coomaraswamy, to Ceylon, where they made a study of local arts and handicrafts. On their return in 1907 they settled near Chipping Campden, where Ethel's brother, the jeweller Fred Partridge, had worked for Ashbee's Guild of Handicraft. Ashbee renovated their ancient house, Norman Chapel, and Coomaraswamy took over Ashbee's Essex House Press. But Ethel's marriage failed in 1911, she left Gloucestershire, and began to study the arts of vegetable dyeing, and weaving. In 1913 she married Philip Mairet, a young draughtsman from Ashbee's architectural office, celebrating with lunch at a vegetarian restaurant. During a troubled war (when Philip, who opposed the hostilities, first worked for the Red Cross then, when conscripted, was imprisoned for refusing to obey orders) Ethel settled in the Sussex village of Ditchling, where she set up a weaving workshop named Gospels.

Ditchling already housed a number of

craftspeople. Eric Gill had moved there in 1907 and was joined by Edward Johnston, his former tutor at the Central School, together with his family, and by Douglas Pepler, a friend from Hammersmith, who founded the Ditchling Press which published Ethel Mairet's pioneering book *Vegetable Dyes* in 1916. Gill was inspired by both medieval European and ancient Indian art, and produced typography, engraving and sculpture. In 1913 he and Pepler had founded the Guild of St Joseph and St Dominic, hoping to create a Catholic community of craftsmen and their families – a 'cell of good living' – but, as was typical of the man, Gill left the community in 1924 to start afresh in a remote Welsh valley. Nevertheless, the Ditchling community – not just the Catholic Guild of SS Joseph and Dominic but also the Johnstons, Mairets and Partridges – agreed on a rough philosophical basis founded on friendship and the feeling of common purpose that bound them together. The independent craftspeople of Ditchling, sculptor, printer, calligrapher, weaver and jeweller, provided the new generation of craftworkers with a vivid example of the Simple Life in action.

In the early 1920s a Slade School graduate, Phyllis Barron, who had begun to experiment with the difficult and largely forgotten art of discharge-printing – printing with wooden blocks on indigo-dyed cotton, then using nitric acid to discharge the colour and leave a white pattern on a blue ground – wrote to Ethel Mairet after reading *Vegetable Dyes*, and was invited to stay at Gospels for a few weeks to perfect her dyeing techniques. From 1923 Barron, as she was always known, worked in partnership with

Quomodo cantabimus canticum Domini in terra aliena?
How shall we sing the Lord's song in a strange land?

THESE WORDS OCCUR IN THE ONE HUNDRED AND THIRTY-SIXTH PSALM (*Vulgate*). WE ARE NOT CONCERNED WITH the circumstances in which the Psalm was written or which are described in it. We are only concerned with the possible application of the words to us now and here. To sing and to sing the Lord's song—even if we have some acquaintance with singing we may easily wonder what song is the Lord's. The Lord's Prayer we know; but what is the Lord's song? And what is wrong with our native land that we should call it strange? ¶ Maybe, darlings and most dear fellow-countrymen, if we knew the Lord we should know his song. *Operatio sequitur esse*, as one is one does, and if you are a singer you sing. The Lord then is a singer and first of all his song is a love song. This is what they mean when they say that the act of creation is a gratuitous act—that it is a song more pure and purposeless than even the songs of children and nightingales. For

5

Dorothy Larcher, who had studied textile-printing in India; the two printed their extremely sophisticated, semi-abstract designs with wooden blocks on cotton, linen, silk and wool, either by discharge indigo printing or by direct printing with natural vegetable dyes such as quercitron or madder and mineral colours such as iron and chrome. In 1930 they moved their workshop from London to Gloucestershire. Barron and Larcher remained friends with Ethel Mairet, and they frequently exhibited together at the specialist craft galleries.

Page from *The Lord's Song* by Eric Gill, 1934. Bodleian Library, Oxford

Ethel Mairet's workshop,
Gospels, in Sussex

In 1925 Barron and Larcher had been joined by a young graduate from the Royal College of Art, Enid Marx, who learned their techniques and went on to found her own fabric-printing workshop in London. Marx is an extremely versatile artist, who also specialized in wood engravings and designed book jackets, patterned papers and stamps. During the Second World War, Gordon Russell made her responsible for the design of Utility furnishing textiles. After the war, with Margery Lambert, she wrote two illustrated books on English popular and folk art.

Ethel Mairet also knew the pioneering potter Bernard Leach, who greatly admired her work. In 1928 Philip Mairet set up the New Handworkers' Gallery in London, which showed work by Leach, Michael Cardew, Barron and Larcher, Ethel Mairet and the furniture maker A. Romney Green. The Gallery also sold a series of pamphlets written by Philip Mairet, Leach, Gill and Romney Green, which expressed their beliefs in the spiritual values of their work. The pamphlets were printed at St Dominic's Press by Pepler (formerly Douglas but now, following his conversion to Catholicism, known as Hilary). The new craft ethic began with the same first principles advocated by Pugin, Webb and Morris: the architect or designer must have a thorough understanding of his or her materials. 'To make a perfect scarf,' as Ethel Mairet wrote, 'one must begin with the sheep.'

At Gospels, Ethel Mairet took paying students at her Ditchling School of Weaving: Gill's daughter Petra learned weaving there, and by the 1930s students were coming from Europe to benefit from her skills as a dyer.

During the 1930s Ethel Mairet also travelled extensively throughout Europe. In 1936 she met Alvar Aalto in Helsinki, and two years later visited Gunta Stölzl (or Frau Sharon, as the former head of the Bauhaus weaving workshop had now become) in Zurich and saw several Deutsche Werkstätten exhibitions in Germany. In 1939 she published *Hand-Weaving Today: Traditions and Changes*, in which she praised the work of the Bauhaus weaving workshop for producing prototypes for industry: 'weaving', she wrote, 'has set itself up on a pedestal as "art" . . . it must be part of a building . . . or associated with the necessities of life'. She believed that, on the model of the Bauhaus, independent craft workshops such as

Gospels could influence industrialists and so ultimately supply the consumer with better designs. Unlike her old friend Ashbee, who had seen his Guild as being in direct competition with manufacturers, Ethel Mairet saw that her own work (firmly rooted as it was in the values of the Simple Life) and the craft workshop's ability to produce work of excellent quality and technical innovation could perfectly complement the needs of the industrial manufacturer. The craft workshop was thus of both spiritual and practical relevance to the commercial world, and some of those who studied with Ethel Mairet, such as Marianne Straub, went on to apply their experience successfully within the context of industry, as did craftworkers also in Europe and America.

The work of this inter-war generation of craftspeople freed itself totally from historical borrowings (which were seen as providing only a 'false unity'), yet it retained and strengthened the essential Arts and Crafts belief in the supremacy of the materials, in the vital importance of personal expression through hand-work, and in the role of such work within the life of the individual and society. Ethel Mairet, Bernard Leach, Enid Marx and the numerous other potters, printers, puppet-makers, weavers or calligraphers who were their friends and associates, influenced those craftspeople who sought their own form of the Simple Life during the 1960s and who went on to found the Crafts Council to champion both the preservation of traditional craft skills and the work of the artist-craftsman. Many people who do not themselves practise craft skills continue to fight today to support the ideals of the Simple Life through environmentalism, animal welfare and other 'green' issues. The challenge that the original adherents of the Arts and Crafts movement posed to the blanket of industrialization that threatened to swamp the values they held dear remains as valid as ever.

'Butterfly', positive block-prints in iron on coarse cotton by Phyllis Barron and Dorothy Larcher

BRITISH ARTIST-POTTERS

From left to right: Stoneware cup with ashglaze made in Ajuba, Nigeria, in the late 1950s, and an earthenware bowl, slipware, made in Winchcombe, Gloucestershire *c.*1928–9, both by Michael Cardew; a stoneware vase with ash-glaze made by Katharine Pleydell Bouverie at Kilmington in 1960; a stoneware vase with Hakeme glaze with iron brushwork by Shoji Hamada, 1930; and a stoneware pot with ash-glaze made by Bernard Leach at St Ives, 1960

Bernard Leach (1887–1979), who made his first pots at a *raku* party in Japan in 1911, not only revitalized lost traditions of English pottery but also, through his writings and teaching, put forward a vastly influential new philosophy of craftsmanship. Born in Hong Kong, he spent several years of his childhood in Japan and Singapore, before moving to London where he studied at the Slade School. On his return to Japan, he spent nine years studying early Japanese, Korean and Chinese pottery and learning the techniques used by traditional Japanese potters. In 1922 he returned to England accompanied by Shoji Hamada, a young Japanese potter, who helped him to build a kiln in St Ives, Cornwall, where he began to research traditional English techniques of earthenware, stoneware and slipware pottery.

Hamada returned to Japan in 1923, but during the 1920s several other potters joined Leach in St Ives – Michael Cardew, Katharine Pleydell Bouverie and Norah Braden – fulfilling his ideal of a loose community of artist-potters. Pleydell Bouverie devoted her life to researching the different wood- and vegetable-ash glazes, setting up her own kiln at her parental home, Coleshill, where she was joined by Norah Braden. She later moved to Kilmington Manor, Wiltshire, where she continued to pot until her death. She said that she never learned to handle a brush, and her pots relied on the exquisite range of colour in her ash glazes – rich cream, black, smoky blue or green, or dove grey.

Michael Cardew, who was primarily interested in earthenware and slip-glaze decoration, left St Ives in 1926 and set up his own pottery in Devon; in the 1930s he began to work in tin-glazed stoneware. The three years from 1942 were spent in Ghana, and in 1950 he returned to Africa, this time to Nigeria, where he remained for fifteen years and founded a Pottery Training Centre. In Africa, he discovered a more flamboyant sense of form and decoration, often using rich dark browns and black glazes decorated with free, vigorous brushwork.

Hamada, although he frequently visited England, continued to work in Japan, where his meditative approach to ceramics influenced a whole generation of potters.

Leach never tried to achieve uniform perfection, believing passionately that a good pot was created intuitively and should reflect the harmony between the potter and his materials, as well as his skill and artistic judgement. He expressed his views in 1940 in *A Potter's Book:* '. . . it seems reasonable to expect that beauty will emerge from a fusion of the individual character and culture of the potter with the nature of his materials – clay, pigment, glaze – and his management of the fire, and that consequently we may hope to find in good pots those innate qualities which we most admire in people. It is for this reason that I consider the mood, or nature, of a pot to be of first importance. . . . No process of reasoning can be a substitute for or widen the range of our intuitive knowledge. . . .' Leach continued to make pots until his eyesight failed in the 1970s.

Bibliography

AGIUS, PAULINE, *British Furniture 1880–1915*, Wood-bridge, Suffolk, The Antique Collectors' Club, 1978

ANSCOMBE, ISABELLE, *A Woman's Touch: Women in Design from 1860 to the Present Day*, London, Virago, 1984

—— and GERE, CHARLOTTE, *Arts and Crafts in Britain and America*, London, Academy Editions, 1978

Arts and Crafts Essays, by members of the Arts and Crafts Exhibition Society, London, Longmans Green & Co, 1893

ASHBEE, C. R., *Craftsmanship in Competitive Industry*, Campden, Gloucestershire, Essex House Press, 1908

—— *Modern English Silverwork*, Campden, Gloucestershire, Essex House Press, 1909

ASLIN, ELIZABETH, *E. W. Godwin: Furniture and Interior Decoration*, London, John Murray, 1986

BARRETT, HELENA and PHILLIPS, JOHN, *Suburban Style: The British Home 1840–1960*, London, Macdonald Orbis, 1987

BILLCLIFFE, ROGER, *Charles Rennie Mackintosh: The Complete Furniture, Furniture Drawings and Interior Designs*, Guildford and London, John Murray, 1979

BORISOVA, HÉLÈNE and STERNINE, GREGORY, *Art Nouveau Russe*, Paris, Editions de Regard, 1987.

BROWN, JANE, *Gardens of a Golden Afternoon, the Story of a Partnership: Edwin Lutyens and Gertrude Jekyll*, London, Allen Lane, 1982

CATHER, DAVID M., *Furniture of the American Arts and Crafts Movement*, New York, New American Library, 1981

CLARK, GARTH and HUGHTO, MARGIE, *A Century of Ceramics in the United States, 1878–1978*, New York, E. P. Dutton, 1979

COOK, E. T. and WEDDERBURN, A. (ed.) *The Complete Works of John Ruskin*, 39 vols., London, George Allan, 1903–12.

COMINO, MARY, *Gimson and the Barnsleys*, London, Evans Brothers, 1980

COOPER, JEREMY, *Victorian and Edwardian Furniture and Interiors: from the Gothic Revival to Art Nouveau*, London, Thames & Hudson, 1987

CRANE, WALTER, *An Artist's Reminiscences*, London, Methuen, 1907

CRAWFORD, ALAN, *C. R. Ashbee: Architect, Designer and Romantic Socialist*, New Haven and London, Yale University Press, 1985

CROOK, J. MORDAUNT, *William Burges and the High Victorian Dream*, New Haven and London, John Murray, 1981

DUNCAN, ALASTAIR, *Art Nouveau and Art Deco Lighting*, London, Thames & Hudson, 1978

GAUNT, WILLIAM and CLAYTON-STAMM, M.D.E., *William de Morgan*, London, Studio Vista, 1971

GERE, CHARLOTTE and MUNN, GEOFFREY C., *Artists' Jewellery: Pre-Raphaelite to Arts and Crafts*, Wood-bridge, Suffolk, Antique Collectors' Club, 1989

GIROUARD, MARK, *Sweetness and Light: the 'Queen Anne' Movement 1860–1900*, Oxford, Oxford University Press, 1977

GODDEN, SUSANNA, *At The Sign of The Four Poster: A History of Heal's*, London, Heal & Son Ltd, 1984

HANKS, DAVID A., *The Decorative Designs of Frank Lloyd Wright*, New York, E. P. Dutton, 1979

HARRISON, MARTIN, *Victorian Stained Glass*, London, Barrie & Jenkins, 1980

HASLAM, MALCOLM, *English Art Pottery 1865–1915*, Woodbridge, Suffolk, Antique Collectors' Club, 1975

—— *The Martin Brothers, Potters*, London, Richard Dennis, 1978.

HAWEIS, Mrs H. R. (MARY ELIZA), *The Art of Decoration*, London, Chatto & Windus, 1881

—— *Beautiful Houses*, London, Sampson Low & Co, 1882

HENDERSON, PHILIP, *William Morris, his Life, Work and Friends*, London, Thames & Hudson, 1967

HESKETT, JOHN, *Design in Germany 1870–1918*, London, Trefoil Design Library, 1986

HOWARTH, THOMAS, *Charles Rennie Mackintosh and the Modern Movement*, London, Routledge & Kegan Paul, 1977

IRVINE, LOUISE, *Doulton in the Nursery*, Vol. 3 in Royal Doulton Series Ware, London, Richard Dennis, 1986

JEKYLL, FRANCIS, *Gertrude Jekyll: A Memoir*, London, Jonathan Cape, 1934

JEWSON, NORMAN, *By Chance I Did Rove*, Cirencester, Earle & Ludlow, 1951; reprinted Warwickshire, Roundwood Press, 1973

KIRKHAM, PAT, *Harry Peach*, London, The Design Council, 1979

KOCH, ROBERT, *Louis C. Tiffany: Rebel in Glass*, New York, Crown Publishers Inc., 1964

KORNWOLF, JAMES D., *M.H. Baillie Scott and the Arts and Crafts Movement*, Baltimore and London, The Johns Hopkins Press, 1972

LARNER, GERALD and CELIA, *The Glasgow Style*, Edinburgh, Paul Harris Publishing, 1979

LETHABY, W.R., *Philip Webb and his Work*, Oxford, Oxford University Press, 1935; reprinted London, Raven Oak Press, 1979

MACCARTHY, FIONA, *The Simple Life: C.R. Ashbee in the Cotswolds*, London, Lund Humphries, 1981

—— *Eric Gill: A Lover's Quest for Art and God*, London, E.P. Dutton, 1989

MACKAIL, J.W., *The Life of William Morris*, 2 vols., London, Longmans Green & Co, 1899

MACKMURDO, A.H., 'The History of the Arts and Crafts Movement', and 'Autobiographical Notes', unpublished typescripts, William Morris Gallery, Walthamstow, London

MORRIS, MAY (ed.), *The Collected Works of William Morris*, 24 vols., London, Longmans Green & Co, 1910–15

MUTHESIUS, HERMANN, *Das Englische Haus*, Berlin, Wasmuth, 1904–5

NAYLOR, GILLIAN, *The Arts and Crafts Movement*, London, Studio Vista, 1971

ORMOND, SUZANNE and IRVINE, MAY G., *Louisiana's Art Nouveau: The Crafts of the Newcomb Style*, Louisiana, Pelican Publishing Company, 1976

OTTEWILL, DAVID, *The Edwardian Garden*, New Haven and London, Yale University Press, 1989

PARRY, LINDA, *Textiles of the Arts and Crafts Movement*, London, Thames & Hudson, 1988

—— *Morris and Company Textiles*, London, Thames & Hudson, 1983

PECK, HERBERT, *The Book of Rookwood Pottery*, New York, Crown Publishers Inc., 1968

PEVSNER, NIKOLAUS, *Pioneers of The Modern Movement from William Morris to Walter Gropius*, London, Faber & Faber, 1936 (revised edition published as *Pioneers of Modern Design*, London, Penguin Books, 1960)

RUSSELL, GORDON, *Designer's Trade*, London, George Allen & Unwin, 1968

SCHILDT, GÖRAN, *Alvar Aalto: The Decisive Years*, New York, Rizzoli, 1986

SCHWEIGER, WERNER J., *Wiener Werkstätte: Design in Vienna 1903–1932*, London, Thames & Hudson, 1984

TILBROOK, A.J., *The Designs of Archibald Knox for Liberty and Co.*, London, Ornament Press, 1976

VAN LEMMEN, HANS, *Victorian Tiles*, Aylesbury, Bucks, Shire Publications Ltd, 1981

VOLPE, TOD M. and CATHERS, BETH, *Treasures of the American Arts and Crafts Movement 1890–1920*, London, Thames & Hudson, 1988

WEDGWOOD, A., *A.W.N. Pugin and the Pugin Family*, London, Victoria & Albert Museum, 1985

WHEELER, CANDACE, *Yesterdays in a Busy Life*, New York, Harper and Bros, 1918

WINDSOR, ALAN, *Peter Behrens, Architect and Designer*, London, The Architectural Press, 1981

WINGLER, HANS M., *The Bauhaus*, Cambridge, Mass, MIT Press, 1976

EXHIBITION CATALOGUES

Victorian Church Art, Victoria & Albert Museum, London, 1971

Christopher Dresser 1834–1904, Richard Dennis and John Jesse, The Fine Art Society, London, 1972

Mathews: Masterpieces of the California Decorative Style, Oakland Museum, California, 1972

The Arts and Crafts Movement in America 1876–1916, edited by Robert Judson Clark, Princeton University, Princeton University Press, 1972

California Design, 1910, Anderson, Moore and Winter, Pasadena Center, California, 1974

C. F. A. Voysey, Architect and Designer 1857–1941, Lund Humphries, London, 1978

A London Design Studio 1880–1963: The Silver Studio Collection, Lund Humphries, London, 1980

W. A. S. Benson 1854–1924, Haslam & Whiteway, London, 1981

Lutyens, The Work of the English Architect Sir Edwin Lutyens, 1896–1944, Arts Council of Great Britain, Hayward Gallery, London, 1981

Scandinavian Modern Design 1880–1980, edited by David R. McFadden, Cooper-Hewitt Museum, Harry N. Abrams Inc., New York 1982

Italy 1900–1945, The Mitchell Wolfson Jr. Collection of Decorative & Propaganda Arts, Miami-Dade Community College, Miami, Florida, 1984

A Decorative Art: Nineteenth-century Wallpapers, Whitworth Art Gallery, Manchester, 1985

In Pursuit of Beauty: Americans and the Aesthetic Movement, Metropolitan Museum of Art, New York, Rizzoli, 1986

'The Art that is Life': The Arts & Crafts Movement in America, 1875–1920, Wendy Caplan, Museum of Fine Arts, Boston, Mass., 1987

Art Nouveau in Munich: Masters of Jugendstil, Philadelphia Museum of Art, Philadelphia Museum of Art and Prestel Verlag, Munich, 1988

Walter Crane: Artist, Designer and Socialist, Whitworth Art Gallery, Manchester, 1989

Acknowledgements

178 **upper left**, 173 Annan Collection, Glasgow; 166 Arcaid/Richard Bryant; 61 **left** The Art Institute of Chicago. All rights reserved. Photo © 1990. Gift of Raymond W. Sheets; 59 Photo from L'Art Décoratif des Ateliers de la princesse Tenichef. Edition 'Sodrougestivo' St Petersburg 1906; 71 **lower left, 75 right** Courtesy Felicity Ashbee; 63, 183 **left**, 183 **right** K. Barlow Ltd., London; 2 Bateman's, Sussex. National Trust; 213 Bauhaus Archiv, Berlin. Photo Walter Peterhaus; 180 Bildarchiv des Österreichisches Nationalbibliothek; 20, 25, 31, 33, 80, 94, 113, 117, 118, 141, 204–5 Bridgeman Art Library; 48, 112, 123 © British Architectural Library/ RIBA; 115 **lower left**, 115 **upper** Cheltenham Art Gallery and Museums; 6, 34, 35, 45, 77 **lower left**, 81, 86, 90, 115 **lower right**, 119, 121, 129, 156, 175, 177, 181 **left**, 184 **lower**, 186, 195, 197, 198, 200, 211 Christie's, London; 46, 49, 77 **right**, 89, 133, 136, 137, 159, 199 Christie's, New York; 191 College of Environmental Design, Documents Collection, University of California; 82 Cooper-Hewitt Museum, New York Art Resource; 192–3 © Country Life; 222, 223 Courtesy Crafts Study Centre, Bath; 145 Richard Dennis; 194 Design Museum, London, 42, 44, 72, 143 Mary Evans Picture Library; 26, 41, 71 **lower right**, 85 **right**, 152, 178 **lower left** The Fine Art Society Ltd; 146 Fogg Art Museum, Harvard University, Cambridge, Mass. Bequest Greville L. Winthrop; 208 Fritz von Schulenberg Photography Ltd; 219 Geffrye Museum, London; 68–9, 71 **upper**, 73 **upper**, 83 **right**, 92–3, 134, 138–9, 225 Lark Gilmer; 154 **lower left**, 154 **right** Collection: Glasgow School of Art; 168, 214, 216 Photo © Howard Grey; 17, 30, 103, 205 **right** Guildhall Library; 39 Hammersmith and Fulham Archives. © Hammersmith and Fulham Public Libraries; 8 **left**, 52, 83 **right**, 144 **lower**, 150 **left**, 212 Courtesy of Haslam and Whiteway Ltd; 12, 140 Ian Jones, London. Photo courtesy of Haslam and Whiteway Ltd; 47, 85 **left** The Jordan-Volpe Gallery, New York; 77 **upper left**, The Jordan-Volpe Gallery, New York, Photo Rita McMahon, New York; 203 Andrew Lawson; 126 Courtesy Liberty, London. Photo Westminster City Archives; 218 London Transport Museum; 73 **lower** Manchester City Art Gallery; **part openers** Manx Museum and National Trust. Fabrics available from Alexander Beauchamp, Griffin Mill, Thrupp, Glos. GL5 2AZ and Christopher Hyland Inc., Suite 1714, D&D Building, 979 Third Avenue, New York, N.Y. 10022, USA; 83 **left** Metropolitan Museum of Art, New York. Gift of Kenneth O. Smith, 1969. Photo David Allison; 116 Metropolitan Museum of Art, New York. Gift of Sunworthy Wall Coverings, a Borden Company 1987; 61 **right**, 182 Munich, Stadtmuseum; 109 Museum of Finnish Architecture. Photo Granath; 111 National Museum, Stockholm. Photo Statens Konstmuseer; 106 Courtesy National Park Service, Frederick Law Olmsted National Historic Site; 98 National Trust Photographic Library; 170, 178–9 National Trust for Scotland; 95 Courtesy New York Historical Society; 15 Courtesy Friends of Olana, Inc. Photo Michael Frederick; 189 The Oakland Museum, gift of the Art Guild. Photo Joe Samberg; 8 **right** Phillips; 29 Philadelphia Museum of Art. Gift of Charles T. Shenkle, in memory of his mother, Mrs Edna H. Shenkle; 150 **right** The Principal and Fellows of Newnham College, Cambridge; 172, 181 **right** Sotheby's, London; 67 © 1990 Sotheby's Inc; 188 University Art Museum, Santa Barbara, California; 8, 9, 25, 28, 37, 40–41, 78, 80, 100–101, 117, 118, 124, 127, 144 **upper**, 184–5, 185, 196 Courtesy of the Victoria and Albert Museum; 128, 132, 135 Virginia Museum of Fine Arts. Gift of Sydney and Francis Lewis; 157 **left**, 157 **right** Photo courtesy Tod Volpe, Los Angeles, California; 163 **upper** Wartski Ltd, London; 161, 163 **lower left**, 163 **lower right** John Jesse, London/Wartski; 57 Whitworth Art Gallery, Manchester; 36, 55, 74, 120, 154 **upper left** The William Morris Gallery, Walthamstow, London.

Index

Globalization and the Race to the Bottom in Developing Countries

The advance of economic globalization has led many academics, policy-makers, and activists to warn that it leads to a "race to the bottom." In a world increasingly free of restrictions on trade and capital flows, developing nations that cut public services are risking detrimental effects to the populace. Conventional wisdom suggests that it is the poorer members of these societies who stand to lose the most from these pressures on welfare protections, but this new study argues for a more complex conceptualization of the subject. Nita Rudra demonstrates how and why domestic institutions in developing nations have historically ignored the social needs of the poor; globalization neither takes away nor advances what never existed in the first place. It has been the lower- and upper-middle classes who have benefited the most fr welfare systems and, consequently, it is they who are most vulnera' globalization's race to the bottom.

Nita Rudra is an Assistant Professor of Internation
Graduate School of Public and International Aff
of Pittsburgh.

Globalization and the Race to the Bottom in Developing Countries

Who Really Gets Hurt?

Nita Rudra

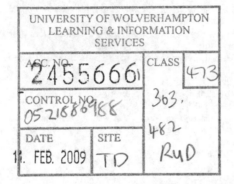

CAMBRIDGE
UNIVERSITY PRESS

CAMBRIDGE UNIVERSITY PRESS
Cambridge, New York, Melbourne, Madrid, Cape Town, Singapore,
São Paulo, Delhi

Cambridge University Press
The Edinburgh Building, Cambridge CB2 8RU, UK

Published in the United States of America
by Cambridge University Press, New York

www.cambridge.org
Information on this title: www.cambridge.org/9780521715034

First published 2008

Printed in the United Kingdom at the University Press, Cambridge

A catalogue record for this publication is available from the British Library

Library of Congress Cataloguing in Publication data
Rudra, Nita.
Globalization and the race to the bottom in developing countries: who really gets
hurt? / Nita Rudra.
p. cm.
Includes bibliographical references.
ISBN 978-0-521-88698-7
1. Globalization – Economic aspects – Developing countries.   2. Globalization –
Social aspects – Developing countries.   3. Developing countries – Social policy.
I. Title.
HC59.7.R763   2008
303.48'2–dc22
2008019384

ISBN 978-0-521-88698-7 hardback
ISBN 978-0-521-71503-4 paperback

For my parents, Sujit and Lina Rudra

Contents

x   Contents

Figures

Tables

Preface

My interest in politics and globalization emerged in my adolescence during frequent visits to India. Time after time I saw that the immense scale of poverty and destitution remained the same. Life at home in the United States, on the other hand, seemingly held the promise of endless choices and opportunities for advancement. I was particularly struck by the stark contrast between the health care and resources available to my grandfather, a village doctor in one of the most remote and poorest "gramas" (villages) in West Bengal, and my father, an FRCS (Fellow of the Royal College of Surgeons) surgeon practicing in Florida. I was astounded that two such diametrically opposed economies coexisted in the same world. From here, eventually, questions of distribution, international economics, politics, government choices, and policy design emerged. In my early years of graduate school I became particularly intrigued by the extent to which domestic policy choices seemed constrained by the global economy, and thus fascinated with issues in international political economy. It took some further study and field experience to begin to grasp the true complexity of the situation.

This book is my attempt to scratch the surface of how and why developing and developed countries face such different challenges in (and responses to) the current era of globalization. It is a product of my struggles with understanding the distributional consequences of globalization, and questions of if and how developing country governments can respond to it. The pages that follow illustrate just one view of the dynamic interactions between domestic politics and globalization in emerging nations, and their implications. With this primary purpose in mind, I set out to observe the interplay between economic openness, domestic politics, and social welfare policies in developing nations. I contend that, in emerging economies, it is, in fact, the middle class, rather than the poor, who are the ones most directly affected by changes in government welfare policies occurring as a result of economic globalization. This outcome is fundamentally not, as most people think, the product of contemporary globalization but, rather, of particular domestic institutions that have existed at least since the post-war era. Based on these findings, I surmise that the less well off in developing countries do not have the same opportunities to protect themselves from the risks associated with the expansion of global markets (or domestic markets, for that matter) as they do in the advanced industrialized countries, *but* that this is contingent upon particular domestic institutions that pre-date the current era of market expansion. We therefore need not worry about how potential reductions in welfare state policies in response to globalization hurt the poor, because the poor were never the main beneficiaries of such policies in the first place.

My interest in international political economy and the politics of developing countries has been influenced by several people. My greatest academic debts go to John Odell, James Robinson, Benjamin Cohen, and Renu Khator. John Odell has been my mentor since graduate school. His high standards of excellence, his deep intellectual curiosity, and his emphasis on good research design, together with the generous flow of his professional and intellectual advice, have had a profound influence on me. He has since given insightful comments and feedback on everything that I have written. This book might not have been completed without his influence and guidance through the years. I am deeply indebted to James Robinson. The book would never have begun without him; with boundless patience, over endless cups of coffee, he vetoed every book project I suggested – except this one. It was Jim who had the foresight to encourage me to pursue research on international economics and domestic politics with a focus on the developing world. Since then he has been a constant source of support and inspiration. He frequently challenges me to think about my argument more carefully, and little is more satisfying than his approval of my work. He has been a steady source of academic guidance and kind friendship over the years. I also sincerely thank Benjamin Cohen, who always provides such thoughtful comments and responses to my work, no matter how busy he might be. Particularly when I was struggling with the direction of the book project during its initial phases, I benefited immensely from his willingness to engage in random conversations related to this research project. Finally, I am grateful to Renu Khator, my mentor through my Masters, who is now the chancellor and president of the University of Houston. Renu encouraged and inspired me to continue with political science, despite my perceived limitations at the time.

I also greatly benefited from a wider intellectual community, which I would like to thank. My colleague and friend Simon Reich has influenced me greatly by pushing me to work even harder, never wavering in his confidence in me, and never tiring of giving me excellent career advice. I would especially like to thank him for insisting that I write this book, and for helping me craft the title. Dan Thomas deserves very special thanks for helping me kick-start the book process. It was through conversations with him that I finally found a clear direction for the analysis. He was always willing to help in any way that he could – and he did, on many different levels. My good friend and colleague Sebastian Saiegh willingly read and discussed everything I asked of him. I appreciate his critical comments and suggestions of broader literatures to consult. I am also grateful to David Bearce, who has been a great colleague and read through my chapters, patiently responding to any and all IPE-related questions. Irfan Nooruddin has been particularly helpful by graciously volunteering to read my chapters and providing valuable feedback. Sarah Brooks was very generous with her time, providing me with pages of comments on my Brazil chapter and helping me discipline my thoughts. I do not know if I was able to address all her queries and concerns successfully, but I do feel that my work is better for attempting to do so. Very special thanks go to Joseph Wong, who helped tremendously with the South Korea chapter, and who provided such insightful and thoughtful points. Ashutosh Varshney provided careful and critical comments on the Indian case study. Stephen Haggard and Robert Kaufman continuously encouraged me to pursue this topic and emphasized the important contribution it could make to the wider literature. Amy Wakeland challenged me to ask the critical questions: why is it important, and who cares? She carefully read and discussed my argument and encouraged me to think more broadly about political science. I would also like to thank Hayward Alker, Barry Ames, Michael Goodhart, William Keech, Layna Mosley, Peter Rosendorff, Samira Salem, Martin Staniland, and James Vreeland, who helped on various parts of the book and/or gave me constructive comments and suggestions.

Throughout the book-writing process I benefited from the research assistance of several students. June Park provided excellent research assistance with South Korea. Kate Floros was extremely helpful in editing and overall organization; it was good to know I could always depend on her. Ana Carolina Garriga provided assistance with Brazil. Chris Belasco and Burge Hayran played an important role in data-gathering.

I would also like to extend my sincere gratitude to all those individuals who facilitated my fieldwork in India, Brazil, and South Korea by setting up interviews, translating, data gathering, and providing critical local insights: Joao and Christiani Barroso, Cidalia Ferreira, David Fleischer, Sandeep Jha, Saurabh Gupta, Shruti, Shveta Mahajan, Sonia, Vani Arora, Yuvika Bahri, Vani Bahri, Manas Mahajan, Neha Gupta, Neha Sharma, Nidhi Chawla, Nidhi Maurya, Nupur Bansal Agarwal, Rashi Agarwal, Abhishek Upadhyay, Anshu Kalra, Deepika Sharma, Divya Bhasin,

Gaurav Aggarwal, Jaya Nagpal, and Sharad Nagpal. I need to give special thanks for the extra hard work and efforts by Jae-Jin Yang in Seoul and my aunt, Pushpa Bhowmik, in Mumbai. Without her amazing calm, diligence, and fortitude, I could not have met and interviewed some of the highest-ranking governing officials in the Indian administration at that time.

Friends and family provided a rich source of support while I worked on the book. I was extremely fortunate to have Cassandra Thomas diligently read (and reread) and edit every single chapter in this book. Her keen sense of logic and her insightful comments were instrumental in pushing me to sharpen the primary arguments in the book. She listened patiently as I struggled with my ideas, then provided me with her impressively well-thought-out feedback. It was Cassandra who provided invaluable advice on how best to organize my case studies. Vikram Mangalmurti never hesitated to dialogue with me about the project and was absolutely instrumental in making certain that the book could appeal to a wide audience. Lisa Snead has always been a solid source of support and unfailingly reminded me not to give up. I could always count on Anna Ruth Worten-Fritz to offer good sisterly advice and, most of all, emphasize the importance of having a good attitude. Pierre Laporte has been good-naturedly demanding the completion of the manuscript for years and was extremely helpful during my fieldwork in Brazil. Both through example and good advice, Eric Garcetti, Carmen Sardinas, Isabel Garcia, Kaarina Roberto, and Nupur Dashottar constantly reminded me of the importance of keeping things in perspective. I must give my brother, Krish Sundaram, the deepest thanks for having the wherewithal to withstand my book stress. He has been utterly unfailing in his support through all the trials and tribulations, as well as the sweet moments of breakthrough. Finally, I would like to recognize the important contribution of my second dad, John Ford, who passed away during the final stages of this book project. Days before his passing, the news that I had finished the book was one of the few things that brought a smile to his face. His amazing courage and attitude towards life, along with his enthusiasm for my project, filled me with the spirit I needed to finally finish.

The Graduate School of Public and International Affairs at the University of Pittsburgh provided me with a very supportive environment in which to write this book. For financial support, I would like to thank the University of Pittsburgh's Asian Studies Program, the Center for Latin American Studies, the University Center for International Studies, and the Department of Political Science.

Above all, Ravi Sundaram deserves the most credit for the completion of this book. He placed his career and needs second so that I could do whatever was needed to research this topic. He never tired from encouraging me and pushing me forward, and I was internally motivated not only by his faith in me but by his commitment to the project itself. Alongside his own work, he spent endless hours perfecting the numerous figures and tables in this book. But, most importantly, he has given me the stamina to pursue my goals without hesitation.

Finally, my parents, Lina and Sujit Rudra, to whom this book is dedicated, deserve recognition. It is my father's deep passion and yearning for higher knowledge that has served as an endless source of motivation for me. It will always be my father's dream of social justice that I hope to fulfill. I will also be eternally grateful for the unwavering support from my second set of parents, Siva and Vasantha Sundaram, in Bangalore. Ultimately, this journey would not have been possible without my parents' unshakable love and faith in me. I can never thank them enough for that.

1   Introduction

> The [Anganwadi] workers are paid only Rs. 1,000 [$21] a month and their helpers Rs. 500 [$11]. There is no dearness allowance,[1] no paid leave, and they also do not have social security.[2]

Such is the plight of India's Anganwadi workers, a low-caste disadvantaged group of workers that assists poor mothers and children with health and nutrition needs.[3] After working more than eight hours a day, total earned wages keep them well below the international poverty line of $1 per day. Their persistent demands for higher wages, job security, and social security have yet to be met by the Indian government. The key to obtaining these protections, the workers argue, is to be recognized as government employees instead of part-time workers.

India's Anganwadi are not alone. In the current era of globalization[4] disadvantaged groups of workers receive minimal or no protection against market risk. Examples from around the world attest to the near-universal tenuous position of marginal workers. The *Korea Herald* reports that approximately 70 percent of non-standard South Korean workers receive no social insurance, as compared to 1.7 percent for standard workers.[5] Brazilian legislation that provides social insurance and job dismissal protection exempts at least 40 million informal workers, including domestic workers, shoemakers, garment workers, and slum dwellers. These workers have begun clamoring for the same rights to unemployment insurance,

---

[1] Dearness allowance is a cash payment to employees that takes inflation into account and is part of the total wage cost.

[2] Protestors from the Joint Platform of Action, as quoted in "Recognize Us as Government Staff: Anganwadi Workers," *The Hindu* (Madras), July 26, 2006.

[3] More specifically, workers in "Anganwadi" centers are affiliated with the government's Integrated Child Development Services and play a crucial role in providing childcare to the poor. They tend to the health and pre-school education needs of children up to age six, as well as assisting pregnant women, nursing mothers, and adolescent girls with various aspects of health and nutrition.

[4] "Globalization" is defined in this book as the expanding international economic integration of markets in goods, services, and capital.

[5] "Bipolarization in Labor Market – How to Solve It?" *Korea Herald*, August 27, 2004.

maternity leave, paid holidays, and other benefits long afforded other working Brazilians.[6] Half a world away, thousands of Bangladeshi textile workers have taken to the streets with similar demands. Ugandan textile, leather, garment, and allied workers have recently filed grievances with the International Textile, Garment and Leather Workers Federation (ITGLWF) complaining that the Ugandan government ignores both internationally known workers' rights and the benefits required by Ugandan legislation.[7] In Thailand, the Kasikorn Research Center (KRC) expresses concern that workers in the agricultural sector and those with independent jobs, such as barbers and hawkers, will suffer as economic growth slows, since they have no access to social insurance or job security.[8]

Globalization skeptics react predictably to these scenarios; they respond with the following mantra: globalization hurts the poor. Their reasoning is fairly simple. Less developed countries (LDCs) participate in highly competitive global markets. Governments must cater to domestic and international capital interests by cutting wages and benefits. This could lead to a "race to the bottom" (RTB). According to this hypothesis, a world increasingly free of restrictions on trade and capital flows allows investors to scour the globe in pursuit of the highest rate of returns. Nations that harbor public policies that raise production costs or inhibit sound macroeconomic fundamentals risk lower profit margins and capital flight. Fearing such reprisals, governments are constrained from initiating (or maintaining) policies that guarantee a higher quality of life for their citizens, such as safety nets, environmental standards, and acceptable labor costs and protections. The anticipated result is that domestic politics loses its vigor and the forces of global commerce trump efforts to pursue all other things important to society.

China's growing presence in the global economy raises the stakes in this race to the bottom for developing nations. Greider (2001), a journalist, encapsulates these fears:

Globalization is entering a fateful new stage, in which the competitive perils intensify for the low-wage developing countries ... In the "race to the bottom," China is defining the new bottom. But the killer question asked by critics, myself included, is whether China can fulfill its vast ambitions without smashing the dreams of other striving nations ... Too many producers, too few consumers in a global system where too many workers cannot afford to buy the things they make – that's the central contradiction. The destructive qualities and repeated crises are sure to continue, critics would argue, so long as the system advances by this roving

---

[6] "Maids Fight for Wages, Security," *Gazette* (Montreal), April 24, 2000.
[7] "Can Ugandans Finally Afford to Smile?" *The Monitor* (Africa News), April 4, 2006.
[8] "Unemployment to Rise due to Economic Slowdown in Thailand," *Xinhua General News Service* (China), May 7, 2006.

exploitation of labor and prevents developing countries from pursuing more balanced, albeit more gradual, strategies.

According to this logic, the rapid race to the bottom is what hurts disadvantaged groups such as India's Anganwadi, South Korea's non-standard workers, Brazil's domestic laborers, Bangladeshi garment workers, and others. The race to the bottom hypothesis anticipates that international market pressures determine domestic social policy, and that the downward institutional convergence of policies and practices, which precludes adequate welfare protections for the poor, is inevitable.

In light of these concerns, it is surprising that the great bulk of existing scholarly research on the globalization–welfare nexus has focused on the advanced industrialized nations, not the developing world. After all, if the race to the bottom hypothesis is true, citizens of developing countries would be particularly vulnerable, given these countries' intense need for capital and, thereby, far greater susceptibility to global market pressures. And yet we have very little knowledge of if, how, and to what extent these pressures are really affecting poorer countries.[9]

This book provides the first comprehensive study of the interactions between globalization and the race to the bottom, domestic politics, and welfare strategies in the developing world. *The central focus of this book is on the observable implications of international market expansion on LDC welfare state policies.* To what extent are governments in developing countries vulnerable to RTB pressures on welfare state policies? If such pressures exist, what, if anything, can governments do about it? Is globalization simply making it impossible to protect the most disadvantaged citizens from the risks and uncertainties of globalization? Are domestic institutions and politics increasingly irrelevant in the LDCs as institutional convergence (purportedly) commences?

This book challenges the conventional wisdoms surrounding the race to the bottom hypothesis. I argue that, unlike in the advanced industrialized countries, globalization does indeed trigger a race to the bottom in developing countries. The broader implications of this defy traditional expectations, however. Previous analyses of globalization and its consequences have generally failed to examine the impact of the character and content of long-standing LDC domestic institutional arrangements. This book contends that it is not globalization per se that ultimately determines the plight of the poor but, rather, the interplay between globalization and a nation's domestic institutions. More precisely, fragmented

[9] Murillo (2000, 2002) and Brooks (2005) are important exceptions who explore the interaction between international market integration, domestic politics, and social policies in Latin America. They do not, however, focus on the effects of RTB per se.

labor movements, the government–labor relationship, and pre-existing national social policy configurations are structuring responses to the challenges of globalization. The central thesis in this book is that these domestic institutions have long deprived the poor of social protections *and* that these institutions continue to persist in twenty-first-century globalization. In other words, where social institutions have historically failed to protect the very poor in developing countries, the advent of globalization has not altered national institutional dynamics.

In fact, the statistical analyses and case studies presented in this book demonstrate that, though the poor may be most in need of services, the actual consumers of welfare state services in developing nations tend to be somewhat wealthier citizens. Hence, the key paradox is that the RTB pressures hurt mainly the middle classes in developing countries, not the poor.[10] The damage to the middle class is not colossal, however; members of the former fight vigorously to defend the status quo, thus preventing major institutional change and thwarting predictions of convergence towards the "neoliberal bottom."[11] To be absolutely precise, the nature of ongoing welfare retrenchment in LDCs does not represent the race to the actual *bottom*; rather, *the retrenchment reflects the general downward pressure from globalization on middle-class benefits.* Preventing the uniform freefall of social welfare benefits to the bottom are the distinct institutional configurations of each respective nation. These institutions generate systematically different reactions stemming from their prevailing ethos, development legacies, and political constituencies. In fact, defying the predictions of globalization skeptics, none of the existing distribution regimes show signs of advancing towards a welfare state based on neoliberalism *or*, for that matter, the principles of universalism.[12] Even when select welfare regimes adopt, for example, comprehensive social insurance coverage, the exclusion of marginalized groups persists on a de facto basis.

---

[10] Note that this book is not investigating whether the middle class in developing countries are overall winners or losers with globalization. The focus is on who gets hurt specifically by welfare retrenchment in the current era.

[11] Mishra (1999) presents the conventional view of the "neoliberal bottom." He argues that international organizations such as the World Bank and the International Monetary Fund (IMF) have been selling policies associated with the neoliberal bottom to developing countries by focusing on limiting government expenditures, deregulation, selective social services, and the private provision of welfare. Extensive reliance on means-tested welfare programs (i.e. strict eligibility criteria apply: property or wealth cannot exceed a certain amount) is also commonly associated with the neoliberal bottom.

[12] A welfare state based on the principles of universalism allows every citizen access to welfare services; social welfare schemes involve the entire population and are not limited to a particular income group.

As a result, the current predicament of India's poor Anganwadi workers and similar groups across the globe cannot be blamed simply on the race to the bottom. The distribution regimes in each of these nations never actually provided them with safeguards from market risks, either before or after economic openness policies were adopted. Also impeding any movement towards a universal welfare state is the absence of a cohesive labor movement and, in many LDCs, a government–labor relationship that is supported by clientelism. These domestic institutions or absence thereof collectively hinder substantive pro-poor welfare policies.

India's Anganwadi workers are fighting for recognition as government employees precisely because government employees are among the core of workers entitled to the most generous welfare protections. Anganwadi workers have been denied access to the much-coveted benefits ever since their positions were created in 1975. Their current demands are thus as valid today as they were several decades ago, before India's turn towards open markets. The quintessential problem now is that, as Keohane and Milner (1996: 256) put it, the "pressure of constraints and the lure of opportunities" associated with globalization make it that much more challenging for their demands to be fulfilled.

1.1   Globalization and the race to the bottom debate: the fundamental concern

A distinct and recent rise in poverty and inequality in many developing countries coincides with the adoption of economic liberalization policies and heightened anxieties about the race to the bottom. The United Nations (UN, 2005) estimates that over 58.7 percent of workers in the developing world still live on less than the $2 a day poverty threshold, and 23.3 percent live in absolute poverty, or less than $1 a day. What is worse is that the numbers of those living in absolute poverty rose during the 1990s in all regions, with the exception of select countries in the Middle East and north Africa, and east Asia (World Bank, 2000b). Studies have shown that income inequality has also increased since the early 1980s (see, for example, Cornia, Addison, and Kiiski, 2004). These statistics reveal a dismal reality for developing nations, a reality that engenders grave disappointment after scores of economists and policy-makers promised a world of boundless prosperity and consumer satisfaction as the result of globalization policies.[13] It is no surprise, then, that high-level international gatherings aimed at promoting global market expansion,

---

[13] See Guillen (2001) for a discussion on this perspective.

such as the biannual World Bank/IMF meetings, the World Trade Organization (WTO) ministerial meetings, Group of Eight summits, the World Economic Forum, and the Free Trade Area of the Americas (FTAA) summits, have drawn swarms of protestors in recent times. Demonstrators are commonly seen holding placards reflecting their alarm about the race to the bottom: "Globalization hurts the poor."

Some concerns about globalization are warranted. Many scholars have observed a positive correlation between globalization and worsening conditions for the lower strata of society, both in an absolute and a relative sense. Trade and foreign direct investment (FDI) have been found to exacerbate inequality by changing the skill composition of labor demand and thereby fueling the wage gap between skilled and less skilled workers (Hanson and Harrison, 1999; Wood, 1997). In a related point, developing countries that liberalized their capital accounts have been susceptible to financial crises and, in turn, have experienced increases in poverty and inequality (Baldacci, de Mello, and Inchauste, 2002). It is evident, even to the most ardent globalization enthusiasts, that international market integration can have negative consequences on distribution.

The current debates, however, are not about the successful functioning or necessity of markets per se. Scholars and policy-makers across the ideological spectrum have come to accept markets as the preferred mode of resource allocation, and, with this, a truism: markets create both winners and losers.[14] Certainly, developing countries that have steadfastly embraced open markets have seen improvements in economic growth (see Edwards, 1998, and Sachs and Warner, 1995).[15] Growth is not necessarily synonymous with improvements in equity, however. International economic theories, such as the Stolper–Samuelson theorem and the Ricardo–Viner model, help us predict which factors or sectors are likely to gain or lose with globalization. Tensions rise as various interests, such as marginalized groups, skilled and unskilled workers, tradable and non-tradable sectors, mobile and fixed asset holders, private foreign creditors and foreign financial intermediaries, benefit unevenly from international market policies. Globalization pessimists do not want to replace the market system; they simply want governments to do something about the negative consequences it can yield.

[14] A recent survey by international polling firm GlobeScan, analyzed in conjunction with the Program on International Policy Attitudes (PIPA) (2006) of the University of Maryland, revealed a strong global consensus for free enterprise systems and free market economies as "the best system." Citizens of both developed and developing nations were polled, and, on average, 61 percent agreed, while 28 percent disagreed.

[15] For a dissenting view, see Rodrik and Rodriguez (2000), who argue that the link between openness and growth is still an open question.

The goal of governments, then, has been to manage these distributional conflicts to ensure social stability and domestic peace. Polanyi (1944) long ago stressed that social stability depends on the coordination of redistribution with market exchange. A long line of scholars since then have noted the vital importance of maintaining welfare states alongside global market integration. The occasion for welfare state policies in LDCs is particularly acute in the present era. Early twenty-first-century globalization is unique in the way that market expansion has involved the developing world. As Garrett (2000: 942) indicates, "Large-scale portfolio lending to banks in developing countries for purposes other than raw material extraction, two-way manufacturing trade between the north and the south, and complex multinational production regimes were simply unheard of a century ago." The inference here is that, as LDCs have become more and more integrated in global markets, welfare state development has become the key means to a "fair" distribution of wealth and social stability. Take, for instance, Chilean President Michele Bachelet's statement during a recent visit to the United States:

The logic of the market does not resolve all problems ... as I see it, you need strong and powerful social policies by the state to resolve the problems of income and equality of opportunity.[16]

Herein lies the root of anxieties about current globalization. A sizable body of scholarship in the 1980s and 1990s maintained that governments could no longer manage distributional conflicts via social welfare policies. If international market expansion leads to a race to the bottom and erodes the welfare state, the implication is that government autonomy and domestic policies are being sacrificed at the altar of international markets and laissez-faire. Governments simply cannot act contrary to market forces and protect the poor as deemed necessary, given limited policy-making flexibility. The RTB model thus makes the teleological inference that competition to attract mobile factors of production leads governments to deregulate competitively until, eventually, welfare policies throughout the world would converge on the "lowest common denominator." In short, RTB scholars scrutinize the loss of state sovereignty concomitant with globalization. Ohmae's (1995: 11–12) oft-cited work summarizes it best:

[N]ation-states have *already* lost their role as meaningful units of participation in the global economy of today's borderless world ... Reflexive twinges of sovereignty make the desired economic success impossible, because the global economy

---

[16] Larry Rohter, "Visit to US Isn't a First for Chile's First Female President," *New York Times*, June 8, 2006, Section A, Late edition.

punishes twinging countries by diverting investment and information elsewhere ... [A]s the downward ratcheting logic of electoral politics has placed a death grip on their economies, they become – first and foremost – remarkably inefficient engines of wealth distribution ... the nation state is increasingly a nostalgic fiction.

Such doomsday scenarios and fast-growing anti-globalization movements drew more and more academics into the discussion. Turning to sophisticated methodological tools, positivist approaches, and systematic data collection and analysis, scholars began to dissect critically the links between global market expansion and the welfare state. If the evidence reveals that welfare states are withstanding the forces of globalization, then national governments are still the core actors and domestic politics remain vibrant. If the findings reveal otherwise, however, Ohmae's predictions ring true.

The majority of investigations to date have focused on the political economies of the advanced capitalist countries. Within the last few years a distinct and well-respected group of scholars in international political economy (IPE) and comparative political economy (CPE) have successfully challenged the race to the bottom hypothesis in the nations of the Organisation for Economic Co-operation and Development (OECD) (e.g. Bearce, 2007; Iversen, 2005; Basinger and Hallerberg, 2004; Mosley, 2003; Pierson, 2001, 1994; Huber and Stephens, 2001; Swank, 2001; Hall and Soskice, 2001; Garrett, 1998).[17] The common finding is that, in the OECD countries, a race to the bottom is not leading to cross-country harmonization of policies and practices at the lowest regulatory standard, or institutional *convergence*. Rather, domestic politics and institutions mediate the pressures of globalization, and national *divergence* prevails. Thus, by the new millennium, a new consensus has emerged among scholars in political science and economics that fears of a race to the bottom and waning welfare states have been overblown; national differences, particularly with respect to welfare (or distribution) regimes, remain more or less intact. The important message for the globalization pessimists is that the poor in OECD countries need not fear that social protections will decrease simply because of globalization.[18]

Despite these robust findings, anxieties about a race to the bottom persist among activists, journalists, and academics outside the political

---

[17] See chapter 2 for a discussion of the small number of scholars who challenge this hypothesis.

[18] Many argue that the critical pressures for change in OECD welfare states come from forces other than economic integration, such as demographics (Garrett, 1998), deindustrialization (Iversen and Cusack, 2001; Iverson, 2001), the post-industrial shift to low-productivity-improving jobs, and the welfare state's maturation (Pierson, 2001, 1996).

science field and North America.[19] The apparent disconnect between the select group of scholars who dismiss these fears and the rest of the world is striking. One important reason for this ongoing "dialogue of the deaf" is that existing empirical investigations of the globalization–welfare nexus have excluded the great majority of countries – i.e. the developing world. It is constructive to underscore that this (relatively) new consensus has been achieved absent parallel analyses in LDCs. We are, heretofore, left with little knowledge of how (and if) "domestic politics" still matters in developing nations and whether these states can similarly defy RTB pressures in welfare policies.

Less developed countries have not been entirely absent from the academic literature on globalization and the race to the bottom.[20] Studies exploring the race to the bottom in environmental standards (e.g. Chau and Kanbur, 2006; Porter, 1999), labor standards and protections (e.g. Mosley and Uno, 2007; Haouas and Yagoubi, 2004; Harrison and Hanson, 1999; Beyer, Rojas, and Vergara, 1999; Wood, 1997; Singh and Zammit, 2004; Chan and Ross, 2003; Mehmet and Tavakoli, 2003), total government spending (e.g. Rodrik, 1997a, 1998; Garrett, 2000), and, more recently, government welfare spending (e.g. Wibbels, 2006; Avelino, Brown, and Hunter, 2005; Kaufman and Segura-Ubiergo, 2001) include some developing countries. The problem is that these analyses have important limitations. First, many are largely based on conjecture and fail to present empirical data to increase confidence in their arguments. Second, studies that do conduct empirical tests are limited in the range of countries covered.[21] The tendency is to focus on single countries or regions, concentrating mostly on select countries in Latin America or east Asia. More recently, Haggard and Kaufman (forthcoming) have done a thorough analysis on welfare policies in these regions, and added the eastern European countries to the mix. The studies by Rodrik (1997a, 1998) and Garrett (2000) are also exceptions, but their measure of "total government spending" (or Rodrik's "total government consumption") is all-inclusive and does not capture the specific variables that protect

---

[19] The majority of these assertions have not involved an empirical test of RTB propositions. Examples of well-known journalists advocating the RTB thesis are Friedman (2000) and Greider (1998). Examples of major international contributors to the anti-globalization movement from the perspective of RTB are Canadian journalist Klein (2002) and Indian activist Shiva (2005). For examples of prominent RTB scholars outside the United States, see the works of Sakamoto (1994) and Cox (1996). Parenthetically, in the United States and outside the discipline of political science, sociologists appear to be more divided about RTB than IPE or CPE: see, for example, Guillen (2001) versus Ross (2004).

[20] Here I am referring to the literature in which globalization is taken as more or less exogenous, and the analysis focuses on RTB pressures on (fiscal) policy.

[21] The study by Mosley and Uno (2007) is an exception.

citizens from the risks and uncertainties of globalization. Finally, all the studies would benefit from a more detailed explanation of causal mechanisms. The linkages between globalization and LDC social policies and the processes by which the race to the bottom impresses (or not) changes in social welfare strategies have yet to be unraveled.

It is important to emphasize that a focus on welfare schemes is only one vantage point from which to assess RTB dynamics. Other policy domains are relevant, but researching them is less feasible. Exploring the race to the bottom with respect to LDC environmental standards is problematic because, although legal constraints exist, enforcement is and was extremely ineffective, even long before globalization pressures hit.[22] Popular discussions about the race to the bottom in labor costs and standards are also commonplace. This variable is included in the second part of the book as a form of welfare policy; focusing specifically on this variable is impossible, however, because time-series cross-national data are extremely sparse.[23] Finally, tax competition has been a common way to assess (and reject) race to the bottom effects in OECD nations. According to RTB hypotheses, countries will abandon capital income taxation and rely on labor and consumption taxes (Zodrow, 2003; Rodrik, 1997a). Here again, little systematic data on tax incentive policies for capital is publicly available.[24] This book incorporates the effects of tax competition in an indirect way. Since spending is commonly a function of taxes, if globalization is associated with declining social outlays then the effects of increased tax competition can be implied.[25]

The overall paucity of empirical scholarship on globalization's effects in less developed countries is not entirely surprising. First, the race to the bottom is often thought to be more relevant for the advanced industrialized countries. This is because, from the perspective of citizens in the OECD countries, developing world standards represent the "bottom" that is luring corporations away. What is not so well recognized, however,

---

[22] See Porter (1999) for a more complete discussion on this issue.

[23] See Richards and Sacko (2001) for a recent analysis using existing empirical data. See also Mosley and Uno (2007).

[24] Common incentives are value added tax, social security tax, corporate income tax, property tax, licensing fees, import duties, and sales tax. See Li (2006) for the most recent analysis on this subject. In addition, although evasion is a problem in all countries, in LDCs there exists a plethora of non-transparent ways that taxes can be reduced (Alm, Bahl, and Murray 1991).

[25] As Rodrik (1997a: 6) argues, "The increasing mobility of capital has rendered an important segment of the tax base footloose, leaving governments with the unappetizing option of increasing tax rates disproportionately on labor income. Yet the need for social insurance for the vast majority of the population that remains internationally immobile has not diminished." See also Wibbels and Arce (2003).

is that developing countries are also competing with one another for export markets and mobile capital. These pressures have intensified with the entrance of large markets such as India and China on the global stage (see Wood, 1997). The second reason for the lack of analyses on developing countries is the inherent difficulty involved in conducting this type of investigation. Data in poor countries tend to be limited and, given the vast heterogeneity characterizing LDCs, making systematic cross-regional comparisons – particularly in the realm of domestic politics – is enormously complicated. Here again, however, the reasoning is short-sighted. With respect to the data, there exist ways, albeit time-consuming ones, to get around the problem.[26] Developing countries are also not impossible to compare across regions because they share some fundamental characteristics – i.e. late industrialization, underdeveloped markets, large informal sectors, struggling labor movements, high levels of poverty, and a somewhat stronger need for state intervention. In fact, this distinctiveness of LDCs as a group is the precise reason for an analysis such as this one, which seeks to parse out the differential impacts of globalization on the two sets of countries (developed and less developed) and, in the process, advance welfare theories beyond the Anglo-European context.

1.2   The focus and plan of the book

This book attempts to illuminate how governments in the developing world are responding to race to the bottom pressures by focusing specif-ically on how the interplay of globalization and domestic politics affects social welfare policies. The primary dependent variable of concern is welfare policy, broadly defined as the aspects of public policy designed to exercise government "responsibility for the injury and dependency of its citizens."[27] Analyzing LDC welfare strategies over time provides an important way to illuminate the complex and interdependent processes of globalization and RTB pressures, domestic politics, and (social) policy reactions. The few existing studies on globalization and welfare policy in

---

[26] LDC data are indeed sparse, and generally not as readily available as they are in the OECD countries. For example, much of the data used in this book were manually coded and standardized for comparisons across countries. I also used proxies to get at data that do not exist (e.g. labor's capacity to organize). Finally, I have supplemented the quanti-tative analysis with case studies. This can provide a second check on data measures.

[27] This definition of welfare builds on Lowi (1986). Typically, "dependency" suggests state policies that alleviate the extent of worker reliance on the market (see Esping-Andersen, 1990). I argue later, however, that "dependency" in the LDC context can also suggest state efforts to promote reliance (dependency) on the market.

developing countries are conceptually vague on two counts: what "race to the bottom" and "convergence" actually represent, and the processes through which each occurs. This problem can be addressed by systematically analyzing the domestic effects of globalization within and across nations and regions over time, making it easier to recognize the presence (or absence) of convergence, trace the causal paths, and more decisively evaluate the RTB hypothesis. I argue that three domestic institutional factors ultimately structure responses to the challenges of globalization: fragmented labor movements; institutional constraints arising from government–labor interactions; and national social policy configurations.

The book, in chapter 2, opens with the driving question: is there a race to the bottom in developing countries? I hypothesize that, in direct contrast to the developed nations, governments in the developing world are indeed succumbing to race to the bottom pressures. Building on Rudra (2002), I test this proposition by exploring the effects of trade and capital flows on three conventional mainstays of public welfare schemes: social security, education, and health spending. I focus on these particular sectors because they are fundamental for social well-being (see Dreze and Sen, 1989), and because they possess the most comprehensive set of cross-national welfare data available. My results indicate that, of these, it is social security programs that are the most sensitive to international market pressures. This finding is consistent with the RTB hypothesis that increased economic integration encourages governments towards market-friendly policies. Social security programs are often negatively targeted for acting contrary to market forces by pushing up labor costs and creating dampening effects on worker productivity. Accordingly, it is easy to see why these programs might be the first to be compromised in the face of RTB pressures.

Because we want to understand *why* race to the bottom outcomes in developing countries and OECD nations differ, identifying the causal mechanisms driving this outcome is critical. I find that, ultimately, it is the fragmented character of LDC labor market institutions that helps advance the race to the bottom in the social security sector. In contrast, economic and political conditions are more conducive for labor to overcome collective action problems in the OECD countries, making it easier to balance globalization pressures with sustained social outlays. This focus on labor's organizing capabilities is critical: in the first phase of the analysis, we want to know whether labor has the capacity to negotiate at par with capital and government negotiators. Existing research reveals that policy compromises between the three groups are particularly vital in the globalizing environment, ensuring that government interventionism (for labor, in this case) will be offset with positive macroeconomic consequences (Garrett, 1998). Indeed, it is unlikely that labor groups acting alone can successfully promote such policies; rather, they must form alliances with leftist parties, and even business groups (Swensen, 2002; Robertson, 2004; Remmer, 2002; Esping-Andersen, 1990). What is less emphasized is that a strong, encompassing labor movement is a fundamental prerequisite for this to occur (Garrett, 1998; Katzenstein, 1985).[28] I demonstrate that, since labor groups are less coordinated in LDCs, policy compromises that promote a win-win situation for capital *and* labor are unlikely, and governments are driven to cut back on select interventionist social policies that are purported to have harmful macroeconomic effects.

The conclusion in chapter 2 is that the effects of globalization are mediated by domestic institutions, especially labor market institutions, and, as a consequence, the same degree of resilience to race to the bottom pressures cannot be expected in the industrializing nations. This chapter thus confirms prevailing fears that RTB pressures are indeed leading governments to implement some form of welfare retrenchment in LDCs. As the subsequent chapters make increasingly clear, however, this observation by itself does not tell us who really gets hurt by these cutbacks and what "the bottom" of welfare policies actually entails in less developed countries.

Exactly who is being hurt by race to the bottom policy reactions? Chapter 3 takes a careful look at the nature of policy interactions between government and labor market institutions, and reveals a seeming paradox: contrary to popular wisdom, RTB pressures for cutbacks in social spending are *not* directly linked to worsening conditions for the poor in LDCs.[29] It is commonly the case that, in government attempts to build a political support base (particularly in the absence of sustained economic growth), social security, health, and education benefits have often been distributed to strengthen and manipulate interactions between government, business, and privileged labor groups in the organized economy.

Welfare schemes have thus been biased towards the protection of white-collar, salaried, and some blue-collar workers. Those large segments of the population with poor mobilization skills and sustained involvement in informal, non-wage work have long been excluded. The government–labor relationship gives rise to institutional constraints (i.e. privileged access to benefits, clientelism) that reinforce the divisions within LDC labor movements and buttress middle-class welfare policies.

---

[28] "Encompassing" is a term used by Olson (1971) in reference to labor unions. It refers to a centralized labor organization that includes a wide range of labor participants.

[29] This is certainly not to suggest that the poor do not get hurt from secondary effects as a result of this exclusion. For example, without social protections in the face of any economic crisis stemming from globalization, the poor will get poorer.

I argue that, while all three categories of social spending help improve income distribution in richer countries, the impact of social spending in the developing world is much less favorable. In effect, chapter 3 presents empirical support of the theoretical argument that LDC welfare policies generally focus on the non-poor.

The relationship between openness, government social expenditures (i.e. education, health, and social security and welfare), and income distribution is evaluated through a time-series cross-sectional panel data set for thirty-five less developed countries from 1972 to 1996. Significantly, only spending on education in LDCs encourages a more favorable distribution of income in the face of globalization. I argue that the pressures deriving from a more competitive global economy increase incentives for more equity-enhancing reforms in education, whereas publicly sponsored health programs and, particularly, social security and welfare programs confront greater political lobbying and clientelism. These insights, taken together with the findings in chapter 2, reveal that the race to the bottom in social security spending primarily affects the middle class and is not of immediate consequence to the absolute poor. Even more significantly, the findings present the important implication that LDC governments *can* do something in the face of RTB cutbacks: improve the efficiency of education spending by redirecting existing resources towards the poor.

Chapter 4 delves further into domestic institutional arrangements and reveals that the question of who wins or loses from globalization – or more specifically, the race to the bottom – is ultimately dependent upon national social policy configurations. The main contribution of this chapter is to broaden the analysis of convergence to evaluate the race to the bottom. I do this by moving away from the sole focus on expenditure cutbacks to a multifaceted examination of the institutional structures of LDC welfare schemes.[30] Esping-Andersen (1990: 19) has long emphasized that "[e]xpenditures are epiphenomenal to the theoretical substance of the welfare state." The identification and persistence of set constellations of distribution regimes in the developed world has more or less put to rest expectations of a race to the bottom in that sector of the world; but the question as it is applied to developing countries is still left wide open. As a consequence, it is left unresolved as to how or why less social spending in LDCs is necessarily associated with policy convergence, or a race to the bottom towards neoliberal welfare institutions. It is certainly possible that leaders might engage in low (or decreasing) social spending while promoting "illiberal" welfare measures, such as

---

[30] See Green-Pedersen (2004) for an excellent discussion of problems with existing theoretical conceptualizations of retrenchment, or, as referred to in this book, RTB.

public employment or labor market protections.[31] In other words, while developing countries may be universally affected by the race to the bottom, it does not mean that they are moving towards neoliberal policy convergence.

Chapter 4 sets out to identify the logic and existence of set patterns of distribution regimes in the developing world. The discovery of a distinct number of distribution regimes in the developing world well into the twentieth century, as presented in chapter 4, ultimately leads this book to predict that convergence towards the "neoliberal bottom" is not expected among developing countries. Using cluster analysis, I illustrate that welfare efforts in LDCs are either directed towards promoting market development (a *productive* welfare state), protecting individuals from the market (a *protective* welfare state), or both (a *dual* welfare state).[32] Placing the analysis of welfare states squarely within the context of their political economies makes it evident that these distribution regimes are part of complex historical configurations. I argue that initial development strategies are the basis of LDC welfare state divergence. Productive welfare states evolved in nations that pursued export-oriented development, while protective welfare states emerged in more closed economies.

The analysis of the logic and character of the different distribution regimes provides further insights on "who really gets hurt." Following Esping-Andersen (1990), I show that distribution regimes play an important role in aggregating interests and structuring access to the political arena. It was the middle classes who first benefited from these welfare schemes and, as a result, developed a vested interest in upholding the status quo. As they fight to preserve their benefits, regimes ultimately vary on the extent of welfare cutbacks, where they occur, and which programs are still vigorously protected from the forces of globalization. The reason why the race to the bottom is largely affecting the middle class and bypassing the poor becomes increasingly clear: *none of the classic LDC welfare regime types were originally geared towards helping "protect" the bottom strata of the population.*

To summarize, the government–labor relationship and the discovery of distinct patterns of welfare regimes in less developed countries expose the complex relationship between the pressures of early twenty-first-century globalization, domestic politics and social policies. As it turns out, the

---

[31] Note that reductions in public employment and labor market deregulation are basic components of the structural adjustment programs (i.e. neoliberal reforms) advocated by the IMF and World Bank.

[32] Indeed, this classification excludes personalistic dictatorships, although, arguably, they are more likely to implement welfare strategies that would protect select individuals or groups from the market.

race to the bottom story is far more involved than originally asserted by proponents of this hypothesis. Developing countries are indeed experiencing the effects of a race to the bottom. Two major caveats apply, however: first, what constitutes "the bottom" differs across the three welfare regimes; and, second, "the bottom" never included protections for the poor in the first place.

Chapters 5, 6, and 7 explore three case studies: India, Brazil, and South Korea. These cases illustrate the findings from the quantitative chapters and take a more in-depth look at the RTB relationship in developing nations. Qualitative analysis allows us to get a richer and more nuanced sense of how globalization affects institutional changes in welfare regimes, particularly since the 1997 financial crises, after which the availability of quantitative data is extremely limited.[33] India, South Korea, and Brazil have been selected as three regionally important countries that represent the protective, productive, and dual welfare state, respectively. The three case studies illustrate in great detail the primary findings of this book: despite evidence of the race to the bottom in developing countries, existing institutional arrangements resist convergence towards a neoliberal welfare state, and they ensure that the lower and middle classes are the ones most directly impacted (for better or for worse).

The pressures of globalization force some cutbacks in all three welfare regimes, but, alongside a few select signs of change, each retains important elements of institutional continuity. In the protective welfare states, globalization encourages a greater emphasis on commodification efforts,[34] although much of the remaining central welfare schemes remain more or less intact. Reform in the productive welfare states focuses more on cost containment and the implementation of some protective type policies (i.e. means-tested safety nets and social insurance programs). A concerted effort continues to be made, however, to preserve a considerable amount of state control. Finally, in the dual welfare state, the reform emphasis is on cost containment and improving access to primary education. Existing programs tend to clash most intensely with reform efforts in this particular welfare regime type. It is, therefore, the dual welfare state that is likely to experience the greatest degree of institutional change in LDCs. Significantly, however, the extent of institutional continuity indicates that pro-poor policies in all three welfare regimes remain relatively limited both before and after openness policies are adopted.

---

[33] World Bank and IMF data on LDC variables relevant to this book are sporadic after 1997.
[34] Commodification efforts, explained in more detail in chapter 4, refer to government attempts to encourage market participation on the part of workers, particularly through investment in human capital.

1.3   Contributions

The broader contributions of this book are threefold. First, the analysis directs its focus on the mediating effects of developing world domestic institutional arrangements in a large-N sample of regionally and economically diverse developing nations. Drawing from Weiss's (2003) depiction of "domestic institutions" as both normative orientations and organizational arrangements, this book exposes three institutional factors that play a primary role in explaining policy responses to globalization: the fragmented character of labor organizations (chapter 2); the nature of the policy interactions between government and labor (chapter 3); and distribution regimes that reflect "the organization of the political economy which aggregates interests and structures access to the political arena" (chapter 4) (see Weiss, 2003: 22).

Second, this book attempts to overcome vague assessments of the race to the bottom and policy convergence that make falsification difficult. I analyze RTB in terms of cutbacks *and* institutional changes.[35] More specifically, through a combination of quantitative and qualitative analysis, I assess cutbacks as reductions in welfare entitlements. This is operationalized by the lowering of benefit levels, stricter eligibility criteria for, and decreased durability of benefits (see Green-Pedersen, 2004: 7). In the second part of the book, I evaluate RTB as indicated by institutional change.[36] I rely primarily on Pierson (1996: 157) and determine if institutional changes comply with the following criteria: (1) significant increases in the reliance on means testing; (2) major transfers of responsibility to the private sector; and (3) dramatic changes in benefit and eligibility rules. Because Pierson focuses mainly on social-insurance-type policies, however, I add a fourth, and more general, criterion: the discontinuity of ("illiberal") institutional legacies. In essence, Esping-Andersen's liberal welfare state represents the lowest common denominator of existing welfare regimes, frequently referred to in this book as the "neoliberal bottom." The central tenets are limited public responsibilities for market failures, the encouragement of private welfare coverage as the norm (to help minimize public budgets and encourage work productivity),

---

[35] On this point, see Green-Pedersen (2004) for an excellent critique of the RTB literature.

[36] On the issue of assessing radical institutional change, I concur with Pierson (1996: footnote 39). He notes: "Establishing what constitutes 'radical' reform is no easy task. For instance, it is impossible to say definitively when a series of quantitative cutbacks amounts to a qualitative shift in the nature of programs. Roughly though, that point is reached when because of policy reform a program can no longer play its traditional role (e.g., when pension benefits designed to provide a rough continuation of the retiree's earlier standard of living are clearly unable to do so)."

and the targeting of welfare benefits and programs to only the demonstrably needy.[37]

Finally, this book reveals that protection (or the lack of it) for the absolute poor in less developed countries is an outcome of both international economic integration and domestic institutions. The disappointing but true reality is that, in the effort to "catch up" with the developed economies, the bottom strata have long been neglected by LDC governments. In no way does this analysis suggest that globalization affects only the middle class and is having *no* effects on the poor. It also leaves open the question of whether, overall, poverty and inequality are increasing in connection to market expansion. The bottom line is that, to the extent that globalization is impacting the poor, it is not through its effects on the welfare state (i.e. through a race to the bottom). Globalization might be making it harder to implement radical structural changes favoring the poor by constraining domestic fiscal policy resources, but the direction of change is being guided by domestic institutions and politics. Unfortunately, since institutions focusing on redistribution towards the poor did not exist before the rapid advancement of globalization, creating such institutions in the contemporary era is a formidable challenge. It is no wonder that studies have found poverty and inequality to be increasing with globalization. This book might not make it politically easier for national policy-makers to pursue strategies for the poor in this era of globalization. It is hoped, however, that this book will reveal the underlying sources of policy change and the causes for both institutional and political resistance to equity-enhancing redistribution policies.

---

[37] As Pierson (2000: 798) notes, "The liberal welfare states are associated with a host of social problems such as mounting poverty and inequality, and large gaps in the support of human capital development." Chapter 4 presents a more detailed description of Esping-Andersen's liberal welfare state.

2   The race to the bottom in developing countries

As pointed out in the introduction, scores of sophisticated analyses reveal that the race to the bottom is not a concern in developed countries. Does this imply that fears of a race to the bottom in the developing world are also misplaced? A full answer to this question must begin with an account of why globalization might affect rich and poor countries differently. That is, are there compelling reasons to expect a different outcome in developing countries from what has occurred in their more developed counterparts?

I argue that it is domestic institutional differences between developed and developing countries, especially those involving labor, that give rise to different policy reactions to international market expansion. In the current economic environment, the ability of labor market institutions in the developing nations to negotiate compromises effectively (or not) between government, labor, and business is the chief factor creating these differences. Unlike the advanced industrialized nations, where labor tends to be more organized and institutions more broad-based, the fragmented character of LDC labor organizations makes it near-impossible for them to negotiate with one voice, and the differing agendas give governments under pressure from international markets the leeway to reduce benefits. Thus, without mobilized and coordinated labor market institutions, RTB pressures prevail, and retrenchment in social spending will take place.

This chapter attempts to unravel how and why the effects of globalization in the developing world are mediated by domestic institutions linked to labor. It establishes both the causal mechanisms and empirical evidence in support of the race to the bottom in developing countries, and concludes that some anxieties about the domestic effects of globalization are indeed justified. Unlike in developed countries, LDC labor market institutions have been unable to facilitate collective action among the majority of workers, and, as a result, governments are able to follow through with reform in certain social sectors.[1]

---

[1] In this chapter, labor market institutions refer to collective bargaining arrangements for labor. This includes both normative orientations and formal rules and procedures on mobilization, as well as the extent of formal organizational arrangements involving government, labor, and business.

Section 2.1 initiates the analysis by reviewing the broader literature on globalization and welfare states, and identifies the conditions under which the race to the bottom is likely to occur. The principal insight of this section is that nations without labor market institutions that can adequately coordinate negotiations between government, labor, and business are likely to succumb to RTB pressures.

Section 2.2 builds on this theoretical foundation and presents an argument as to why labor market institutions in the developing world are insufficiently equipped for such coordination in the globalizing environment; labor is unlikely to overcome its collective action problems in LDCs to discourage governments successfully from reducing welfare spending. Drawing on Olson's (1971) *Logic of Collective Action*, I argue that mobilization problems are particularly acute in less developed countries because both low-skilled and surplus labor are abundant. The pressures of international market competition and the increasing demand for low-skilled labor during the process of globalization can aggravate these difficulties, making it even more challenging to form stable alliances.

Section 2.3 presents empirical evidence in support of this argument by first constructing a globalization–welfare model specific to developing countries, then testing it with unbalanced panel data and the fixed-effects method. I disaggregate globalization in terms of trade, portfolio investment, and foreign direct investment flows and assess their effect on the "welfare state," commonly operationalized in the literature as the extent of government spending on income transfer programs (e.g. public pensions), education, and health (see Kaufman and Segura-Ubiergo, 2001, and Avelino, Brown, and Hunter, 2005). As summarized in section 2.4, my findings substantiate the race to the bottom hypothesis in the sense that globalization does lead to cutbacks in social security spending. In contrast, however, education and health expenditures are not as sensitive to RTB pressures.

2.1   Existing literature on the globalization–welfare state nexus

Proponents of the race to the bottom hypothesis expect that expanding international markets and the prioritization of efficiency and competitiveness concerns will undermine welfare spending. Garrett and several other theorists have provided empirical evidence to refute such claims in the OECD countries, however (Garrett, 1998; Quinn, 1997; Huber and Stephens, 2001).[2]

---

[2] For exceptions, see the analyses of retrenchment in the OECD countries in Allan and Scruggs (2004), Hicks and Zorn (2005), and Korpi and Palme (2003). Burgoon (2001) discusses how different types of openness spur retrenchment in some types of welfare programs, but not in others.

The general consensus is that these nations have labor market institutions that can dampen the negative effects of globalization. Although some scholars have recently begun to investigate the ability of LDC governments to resist RTB pressures and maintain or increase existing levels of social spending in developing countries, the extant literature does not sufficiently explain why, in a globalizing economy, the politico-economic conditions affecting welfare spending might differ from developed countries and, as a result, render such nations more susceptible to RTB pressures.[3]

The race to the bottom hypothesis suggests that, due to the pressures of globalization, all states, regardless of their partisan compositions and national institutional differences, will embrace free market, laissez-faire policies in order to promote competitiveness (Mishra, 1999; Drunberg, 1998; Stryker, 1998; Strange, 1997; Gray, 1998; Greider, 1998; Cerny, 1995; Evans, 1997; Gill, 1995; Wibbels, 2006). Welfare spending is expected to be adversely affected for two reasons. First, social benefits are not regarded as efficient market-disciplining devices. Both the resulting upward pressures on labor costs and the possible negative effects on work incentives are claimed to depress export competitiveness. Second, governments are increasingly constrained from raising the revenues necessary to maintain social welfare programs. "Footloose capital," or the capacity to withdraw and shift productive and financial capital with greater ease, has made it increasingly difficult for governments to generate revenues through taxation (see Wibbels and Arce, 2003).[4] As international markets expand, governments reduce taxes on capital in order to compete with other states for foreign investment and prevent capital flight. Government borrowing becomes an unattractive option, since this can lead to higher debt and interest rates, and thereby deter investment. The last two decades have thus become witness to the reification of Lindblom's "markets as prisons" idea.[5] With increasing global competition, governments find it more difficult to protect citizens from the risks and uncertainties associated with market expansion.

By analyzing fourteen OECD countries, Garrett (1998) presents one of the most convincing challenges to the RTB hypothesis as applied to social welfare spending. Garrett's analysis extends the globalization–welfare

---

[3] See Wibbels (2006) for a discussion on particular economic conditions that encourage the race to the bottom in LDCs.
[4] For a critique of this idea, see Swank (1998).
[5] See Maxfield (1998) for reference to this idea.

debate initiated by Polanyi (1944), Katzenstein (1985), and Ruggie (1994).[6] Key to Garrett's analysis is the ability of labor market institutions to negotiate compromises effectively between government, labor, and business. He convincingly argues that, if the workforce is highly mobilized and coordinated (i.e. "encompassing"), the economic demands of globalization can be effectively balanced with redistribution policies. In other words, labor can strike policy compromises, such as keeping wage growth in accordance with productivity improvements, so that the highest possible level of disposable income (wages and work-related benefits) can be maintained (see Garrett, 1998: 9). Business and government are satisfied because interventionist social policies do not encumber macroeconomic performance. Garrett concludes that globalization has, in fact, strengthened left–labor movements and, consequently, cross-national partisan differences in the developed world have been sustained.

This position is not without its critics, however. Several theorists provide alternative institutional explanations for the resilience (or contraction) of social spending in developed countries. Iversen and Cusack (2001), for example, argue that deindustrialization, and not globalization, is responsible for the expansion of the welfare state. Pierson (1996) maintains that supportive interest groups and voters have resisted the dismantling of the contemporary welfare state.[7] He rebukes analysts of the RTB hypothesis for overlooking the crucial importance of the well-developed interest group environment in industrialized nations. Consumers of welfare benefits (e.g. the elderly and the disabled), he argues, have successfully mobilized to prevent a sharp deceleration of social spending (Pierson, 1996, 1994). Other studies show that well-organized labor groups acting alone cannot be the critical factor; they have to form alliances. In other words, to negotiate policies effectively, they must coordinate with other middle-class groups (e.g. Rueschemeyer, Stephens, and Stephens, 1992; Esping-Andersen, 1990), leftist, social democratic or Christian democratic parties (e.g. Robertson, 2004; Remmer, 2002; Huber and

---

[6] The theoretical basis for this debate was laid by the seminal work of Polanyi (1944), and advanced by Ruggie (1982) with his concept of "embedded liberalism." These authors separately conjecture that the state must make a broader commitment to social welfare in order to temper the "pernicious effects" of international markets. See also Cameron (1978), Rodrik (1997a, b, 1998), and Katzenstein (1985), who demonstrate the existence of a positive relationship between trade exposure and government social spending throughout much of the twentieth century.

[7] See Clayton and Pontusson (1998), who challenge some of the tenets of this thesis and move forward with a critique of Pierson (1996).

Stephens, 2001; Hicks, 1999; Western, 1999), or certain entrepreneurs (e.g. Mares, 2005).

This second set of research de-emphasizes the role that well-organized labor groups might currently play in preventing social spending cutbacks in mature welfare states.[8] Yet none of the aforementioned studies deny that labor groups were critical before welfare states reached this advanced stage, and that they can still be a primary pressure group behind policies intended to distribute societal resources more equitably (Boix, 2006; Korpi and Palme, 2003). What is most often overlooked is that the key to preventing retrenchment *in the global era* is labor market institutions encompassing enough to ensure that "economywide wage growth does not undermine the competitiveness of the exposed sector" (Garrett, 1998: 41).[9] Under such conditions, even business leaders will support social policies for the positive externalities they are likely to bring: social stability, a containment of labor militancy, skill investment, and, for some business groups, the socialization of risk (see Mares, 2003b). If labor groups are atomized, however, building alliances with other groups (business associations and political parties in particular) and forcing government to take current labor demands seriously will be extremely difficult. It is therefore imperative in the critical evaluation of the RTB hypothesis to get some sense of the organizing capacity of labor.

Unfortunately, recent explorations of RTB effects on social spending in developing countries have failed to take into account this key variable (Mares, 2005; Kaufman and Segura Ubiergo, 2001; Adsera and Boix, 2002; Wibbels, 2006). Mares (2005), for instance, predicts that workers in high-risk sectors will receive more generous welfare schemes than workers in lower-risk sectors. Yet a fundamental assumption in her analysis – that labor in less developed countries will or can be organized sufficiently to demand such compensations – remains untested.

Thus, the effect of globalization on social spending trends in developing countries, where labor remains an important pressure group, is in need of exploration. An LDC model that effectively captures the globalization–welfare nexus must account for the role of labor market institutions in the existence and maintenance of social welfare schemes.[10] The question of

---

[8] Although never precisely defined in the extant literature, the term "mature welfare state" generally pertains to two conditions: (1) government social budget allocations constitute a significant portion of gross domestic product (GDP); and (2) social welfare services and benefits extend to the majority of the population.

[9] This is arguably true of "coordinated market economies," which show institutional resilience in the global era (see Hall and Soskice, 2001, and Kitschelt *et al.*, 1999).

[10] Unless specified otherwise, "labor" refers to both low-skilled and skilled workers.

interest is how such institutions mediate the effects of globalization in developing countries, as compared to Garrett's sample of fourteen OECD countries.

2.2   Globalization, labor and the race to the bottom in developing countries

In a globalizing economy, RTB pressures in social spending are likely to be the most intense in nations highly endowed with low-skilled labor. Quite unlike many of the developed countries, labor groups in LDCs have limited institutional power. Their bargaining position is weak because the sizable population of low-skilled laborers is faced with collective action problems exacerbated by large pools of surplus labor. Labor market institutions in the developing world are characterized by decentralized labor groups that have only tenuous ties with each other, as well as with political parties and particular entrepreneurs. Therefore, globalization will lead to less, not more, social welfare spending.

Labor market institutions in developing countries are fragmented and weak, in large part because of collective action problems. The population of low-skilled laborers in LDCs is large, and scores of studies show that it is expanding with globalization. Not only are these workers difficult to mobilize, due to their low education levels and erratic work hours, but, according to Olson (1971), the higher the numbers in a group the greater the propensity for the free rider problem to occur and the less likely that the collective good (in this instance, welfare benefits) will be supplied.[11] The problem is intensified by the existence of a large surplus labor population in most LDCs.[12] This alters the cost–benefit ratio of organizing and reduces the incentives for low-skilled labor to mobilize for two reasons. First, in an era of heightened global competition, large enterprises profit from the existence of surplus labor pools because they help minimize labor costs, are unprotected, and increase flexibility. Unionization in this environment is improbable at best. Second, the presence of surplus labor makes it impossible to offer "selective incentives," as Olson (1971) suggests, to help overcome collective action problems. For example, competition from surplus laborers makes it extremely difficult for union organizers to offer secure employment for

---

[11] For more detailed hypotheses on why low-skilled labor groups in LDCs are difficult to organize, see Deyo (1989: chap. 6), Gereffi (1995), Lok (1993), and Ingerson (1984).

[12] The term "surplus labor" refers to the extent of "hidden" unemployment prevalent in the economy, and suggests that the supply of labor to industry is unlimited (see Rudra, 2005, for details).

union members.[13] Because so many low-skilled laborers are without work, they focus on employment and are unlikely to lobby for social welfare benefits.

Skilled labor groups in developing nations, in contrast, have greater capabilities to surmount collective action problems. These groups are generally smaller in size, less threatened by a surplus labor population, and more likely to lobby for welfare benefits.[14] In fact, the recruiting grounds for labor organizations in most LDCs have historically occurred in the skilled industries (e.g. heavy industries, white-collar companies). It is therefore no surprise that skilled labor groups tend to comprise the bulk of welfare beneficiaries in developing countries.[15]

Given this logic, the growth of skilled relative to low-skilled labor would help workers as a whole to overcome their collective action problems and advance their political interests, provided that the level of surplus labor is not too high. The higher the ratio of skilled to low-skilled labor and the lower the surplus in a country, the greater the likelihood that workers will form coalitions and be able to defend welfare spending.

The barrier to progress in this case is that globalization is likely to exacerbate existing collective action problems for workers in developing countries, even if their economic situation is improving. The importance of factor endowments in determining who gains and who loses with globalization stems from the Hecksher–Ohlin and the related Stolper–Samuelson theorems. These theorems suggest that low-skilled labor in LDCs should gain with increased exposure to international markets, while, in the more developed countries, the situation of high-skilled labor and capital will improve. It can be argued that this logic also applies to capital flows. Both productive and financial capital flows will increase in nations that are utilizing their most abundant factor more efficiently. Thus, in countries rich in low-skilled labor and poor in capital and high-skilled labor, globalization should improve the economic conditions (i.e. wages and/or employment) of low-skilled labor.

More powerful and encompassing labor institutions do not necessarily follow, however. According to Rogowski (1989), owners of locally abundant factors expand their political influence when openness occurs. His analysis suggests that low-skilled labor in LDCs will have a stronger bargaining position because of the greater wealth that accompanies

---

[13] Note that, while LDCs with state-corporatist systems might offer some of these incentives, the objective is generally to control and weaken labor. Thus, the reference here is to independent unions.

[14] On this point, see Manning (1998), Shafer (1994), and Deyo (1989, 1984).

[15] For examples, see Mesa-Lago (1994, 1991), Midgley (1984), and Esping-Andersen (1996).

openness.[16] Conversely, capitalists and skilled laborers will be better able to influence government policies in the more developed countries. The implicit assumption in Rogowski's model, that the organizing potential of labor will be strong in an open economy, is inappropriate for developing nations, however. If globalization is encouraging the growth of low-skilled labor relative to skilled, as predicted by the Stolper–Samuelson theorem, and surplus pools remain large, mobilization problems will be even more difficult to overcome. Workers in LDCs, therefore, will find it difficult to advance their common political interests, despite any economic gains they may reap from globalization.

In sum, globalization leads to lower social welfare expenditures in labor-rich developing countries because fragmented, decentralized labor market institutions have limited political leverage. In developed countries, labor groups have the institutional clout to ensure that they do not lose political power with globalization, and can successfully demand compensation in the form of social welfare expenditures. The pattern of political bargaining power and interest of labor in LDCs is quite different, however. It is, in fact, the reverse of what has been predicted by existing political and economic theory.

2.3   The evidence

To evaluate this argument, I first provide comparative data on globalization and social spending trends. Then, to get a sense of the character of their labor market institutions, I compare data on "potential labor power" (PLP) in both developed and developing nations. Next, after presenting a developing world model of the globalization–welfare nexus, a more thorough empirical test of the RTB hypothesis is conducted by way of multivariate panel regressions. Lastly, the developing country model is compared to results from the OECD countries.

2.3.1   Contrasting trends in globalization and welfare: rich versus poor nations

The most sophisticated empirical works on globalization and welfare state expansionism tend to operationalize globalization by both capital and trade flows.[17] This analysis moves beyond existing studies, however, by

---

[16] Note that Rogowski does not make the distinction between skilled and low-skilled labor with respect to factor endowments.

[17] Garrett (1998). See Rodrik (1997a, 1998), for example, who argues that capital mobility and trade have differential effects on social policies.

investigating the differential effects that productive and financial capital, in addition to trade flows, can have on contemporary social policies.[18] The two can have quite distinct effects, particularly since they have different degrees of mobility.[19] Portfolio flows tend to be more volatile and thus pose a stronger "exit" threat, since they are based on speculation of stock yield differences and interest and exchange rate movements. In contrast, foreign direct investment is more stable and less sensitive to changes in other types of capital flows (e.g. short-term investment, long-term investment).[20] It is reasonable to expect, then, that, if RTB pressures are real, financial capital flows will have a stronger negative effect on welfare spending because of the (somewhat) greater risks and uncertainties associated with this type of market integration.

Trade is measured here as imports plus exports as a percentage of GDP, and capital mobility is represented by net portfolio flows and FDI as a percentage of GDP. The figures on social spending pertain to central government expenditures on education, health, and social security (SS) and welfare services (as a percentage of GDP).

Within the last two decades countries as diverse as India, South Korea, Mexico, Brazil, the Philippines, Ghana, and Kenya have begun liberalizing their economies. This turn towards openness began in the late 1970s and early 1980s. Countries in the developing world are slowly integrating into the global economy (see figure 2.1).[21]

Trends in government spending for social welfare have diverged during this period, however – expanding in the richer OECD countries and remaining relatively constant or declining slightly in the poorer developing countries (see appendix A for detailed social spending data). The total average government social budget allocations (social security, education, and health) in the developing economies have barely increased by 1 percent over the last three decades. This is striking given that social welfare programs are not a new phenomenon in LDCs. They were implemented as early as 1924, beginning with Chile, and have since spread to more than seventy other developing countries.

---

[18] Note that portfolio investment for the developing countries includes liabilities constituting foreign authorities' reserves, and covers transactions in equity securities and debt securities. This measure of portfolio flows has the largest number of observations for the developing world.

[19] Schwartz (1998) discusses the different implications of productive versus financial capital flows on welfare states.

[20] See Chuhan, Claessens, and Mamingi (1993) for empirical support for the notion that FDI is not "hot money."

[21] World Bank (1999); Yusuf (1999); Otsubo (1996); Little et al. (1993).

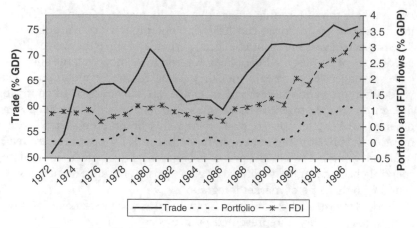

Figure 2.1 Globalization trends in developing countries, 1972–97

Note: Data for developing countries drawn from study sample of fifty-nine countries.
Sources: IMF, *Government Finance Statistics* (various years); IMF, *Balance of Payments Statistics* (various years); World Bank (2002b).

Developed countries expanded their combined social spending (SS and welfare, education, and health) from an average of 25 percent of their total GDP in the 1970s to 31 percent in the 1990s. Meanwhile, the lower-income countries spent an average of 6 percent in the 1970s and only 7 percent in the 1990s. The upper middle-income countries fared slightly better, with their total social budget expanding from 9 percent of GDP to 11 percent in the 1990s. It is notable that the social security and welfare sector experienced the most impressive increase in the OECD countries over the last few decades (3.8 percent), while SS and welfare spending in all LDCs combined improved by barely 1 percent. Tables 2.1–2.3 illustrate the striking contrast between the developing and developed countries.

The developing country sample and time frame used in this study include all those for which comparable data on welfare spending could be obtained.[22] The fifty-nine less developed countries are low-, middle- and high-income non-OECD counties.[23] This data set is regionally diverse,

[22] The time series stops at 1998 since standardized cross-country social spending data for most developing countries are scarce after this year. Furthermore, the expenditure data available post-2000 are not comparable with previous data because of a fundamental change in the IMF's accounting method (see IMF, 2001).

[23] Although Greece, Turkey, Mexico, and South Korea are currently OECD members, they are included in the LDC sample as upper middle-income countries because of the lower income levels that characterized them at the beginning of this study (the 1970s). To check

Table 2.1 *Low- and lower middle-income LDCs*

Social spending (% GDP)	1970s	1980s	1990s	Change 1970s–1990s
SS and welfare	1.47	1.58	2.07	0.47
Education	3.29	3.37	3.50	0.30
Health	1.32	1.46	1.62	0.39

Table 2.2 *Upper middle- and upper-income LDCs*

Social spending (% GDP)	1970s	1980s	1990s	Change 1970s–1990s
SS and welfare	3.86	4.27	5.40	0.49
Education	3.75	3.80	4.02	0.26
Health	1.59	1.81	2.00	0.45

Note: I include Singapore, South Korea, Greece, Cyprus, and Kuwait in the upper middle-income category since they were classified as middle-income countries throughout the 1970s and 1980s.

Table 2.3 *High-income OECD countries*

Social spending (% GDP)	1970s	1980s	1990s	Change 1970s–1990s
SS and welfare	11.68	13.69	14.23	3.4
Education	3.08	3.10	2.63	−0.19
Health	2.94	3.48	3.61	0.64
Decentralized SS and welfare	3.20	3.02	3.60	0. 40
Decentralized education	3.10	3.86	3.86	0.76
Decentralized health	1.90	2.95	3.14	1.2
Total SS and welfare	14.88	16.71	17.83	3.8
Total education	6.18	6.96	6.49	0.57
Total health	4.84	6.42	6.75	1.9

covering twenty Latin American and Caribbean countries, twelve African countries, eight Middle Eastern countries, ten Asian countries, and three European countries. Of these, the majority are low- and lower middle-income countries. This sample is biased, in the sense that it excludes eastern

if they are, in fact, outliers, regressions have been run with each country alternatively excluded individually, and then with them all excluded as a group. The estimates are not affected by their exclusion.

European countries[24] and several newly industrialized countries (NICs). For example, rapidly emerging international market participants such as China and Taiwan are among those excluded due to the lack of data.

One problem with the welfare data is that provincial and municipal expenditures are not captured and, thus, total social spending data for countries with decentralized disbursal have been underestimated.[25] This is particularly problematic for a small handful of high- and middle-income countries that have federal systems and high revenue-generating capacity at the local levels. The data used in this analysis should be viewed with this caution in mind. Nonetheless, it is reasonable to expect that trends in central government spending on social welfare reflect broader trends in developing country economies. For the OECD countries, fortunately, more decentralized data are available.[26]

2.3.2   LDC labor in a globalizing economy

Why might labor find it increasingly difficult to overcome collective action problems in a globalizing economy? The data presented in this section suggest that globalization indeed generates international demand for low-skilled labor in poor countries, and thereby encourages greater competition among countries with similar factor endowments. In several empirical studies, Wood shows how nations with high levels of low-skilled labor follow the principles of comparative advantage and place more emphasis on labor-intensive manufactured goods.[27] Table 2.4 clearly

---

[24] Eastern European countries are intentionally excluded from this data set, because their historical circumstances (particularly regarding state social spending) are distinct from the majority of non-OECD developing countries. These countries are not readily comparable to other LDCs, because they are undergoing a unique historical experience with respect to their market transitions, have comparatively different functions for the state and welfare, and, on average, maintain much higher levels of spending on welfare relative to GDP. (On the final account, the World Bank's third Policy Research Report (World Bank, 1994) places them in the same category as OECD countries.)

[25] The reason for this is that such cross-country data simply are not available. The IMF's *Government Financial Statistics* reports such figures sporadically, and it is difficult to know how much of state and local expenditures on social spending is drawn from federal subsidies, and thereby already accounted for in the data.

[26] Note that the spending data used for the OECD countries in this chapter still have some missing values for state and local government.

[27] Wood (1997, 1995, 1994) emphasizes the importance of this distinction between low-skilled and skilled labor. He claims that trade is based on the availability of skills, not capital. Wood defines skilled workers as those with more than a basic general education – e.g. professional and technical workers, managers, and craftsmen (Wood, 1994: 6). Thus, skilled workers are generally employed in high-skill intensive manufacturing. "Low-skilled labor" refers to workers who have limited or no education (referring to both Wood's BAS-EDs and NO-EDs, respectively).

Table 2.4 *The growth and share of labor-intensive manufacturing exports*

	Growth 1992–6	Share of exports 1996
Low-income countries		
Primary products	12.7	60.1
Natural-intensive manufacturing	12.6	13.4
Labor-intensive manufacturing	18.9	14.6
Technology-intensive manufacturing	13.2	3.6
Human-capital-intensive manufacturing	14.7	2.8
Lower middle-income countries		
Primary products	9.4	56.6
Natural-intensive manufacturing	7.6	4.6
Labor-intensive manufacturing	14.8	20.8
Technology-intensive manufacturing	21.2	11.3
Human-capital-intensive manufacturing	11.6	6.0
Upper middle-income countries		
Primary products	9.0	49.23
Natural-intensive manufacturing	18.8	7.23
Labor-intensive manufacturing	10.5	13.46
Technology-intensive manufacturing	13.3	15.54
Human-capital-intensive manufacturing	9.8	12.00
High-income OECD countries		
Primary products	8.07	23.86
Natural-intensive manufacturing	10.21	4.79
Labor-intensive manufacturing	8.57	9.07
Technology-intensive manufacturing	12.14	35.47
Human-capital-intensive manufacturing	9.50	23.43

Source: UN ITC Infobase, "National Trade Performances by Country 1999."

demonstrates, in line with the Stolper–Samuelson theorem, the growth of labor-intensive exports relative to other exports in countries known to have large pools of low-skilled labor.

The most important point confirmed by the data in table 2.4 is that the poorer the country the greater the likelihood that participation in international markets will be led by exports of low-skilled manufactured goods. The lowest-income countries have clearly experienced the highest growth rates in labor-intensive manufacturing. Increasing international demand for low-skilled workers might make it more difficult to overcome collective action problems. The high-income OECD countries, in contrast, have both the smallest rate of growth and the smallest share of labor-intensive exports. It is no surprise, then, that employment in high-skilled relative to low-skilled jobs shows minimal growth in low-income countries. Figure 2.2 illustrates the striking contrast between developed and developing countries in this regard.

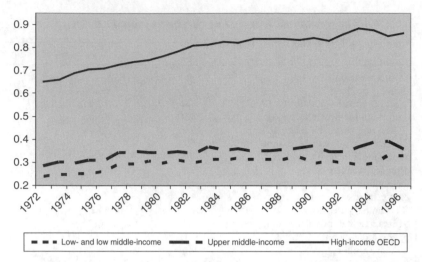

Figure 2.2 Ratio of high-skill employment relative to low-skill employment, 1972–97

According to the argument in this chapter, whether the accompanying increase in the number of low-skilled relative to skilled laborers employed in developing countries implies greater organizing capability for labor depends on the size of the surplus labor pool. Given the increasing trend in skilled labor in the middle-income countries, we can expect this capacity to increase *if* the surplus labor pool is shrinking. Figure 2.3 shows that there was indeed a slight decline in surplus labor in LDCs between 1972 and 1997, suggesting the possibility that labor power has improved. It cannot be overlooked, however, that, by the late 1990s, the level of surplus labor in LDCs was, on average, 24 percent of the working-age population, while in the OECD countries the average level was 7 percent of the working-age population. Moreover, the drop in less developed countries has only been an average of six percentage points. In sharp contrast, the level of surplus labor in Garrett's sample of OECD nations is less than a half what it was in the early 1970s. Several recent studies confirm that employment growth has failed to significantly reduce the vast amount of surplus labor that exists in the developing world (Schneider and Enste, 2002; Portes and Schauffler, 1993; UNIDO [United Nations Industrial Development Organization], 1992).

Given that the number of low-skilled laborers has been steadily increasing (since the mid-1980s) and that the developing world's surplus labor

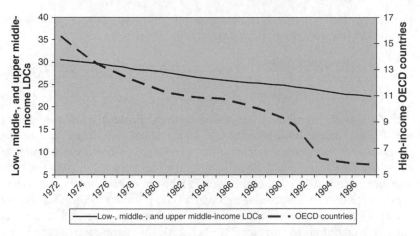

Figure 2.3 Surplus labor in LDCs and developed countries, 1972–97

Note: Surplus labor is calculated as [(working-age population – students enrolled in secondary education – students enrolled in tertiary education) – (labor force)]/working-age population.
Sources: World Bank, *World Development Indicators* (various years); ILO (2001).

population is still relatively high, the logic of Olson's theory suggests that labor market institutions will be unable to overcome their collective action problems in the current globalizing environment. To incorporate this idea, I have constructed an index of potential labor power. This is an indirect measure of labor power, used to capture the capacity of labor to form centralized, powerful labor organizations that are able, in turn, to form alliances with other interest groups, as well as more effectively negotiate with government and business representatives. The logic behind the index lies in the observation that the bargaining power of labor institutions is likely to improve with an increasing ratio of skilled to unskilled workers, given the greater capacity of the former for collective action, and decrease with the size of "surplus" labor, measured as the working-age population minus the economically active population and students in secondary and tertiary schools.[28]

In order to create the index, I divided each country's score by the highest value in the larger data sample (i.e. Sweden = 87) and multiplied by 100.

---

[28] This assessment of labor power is limited to the manufacturing sector, since data are not available for most countries outside this sector and, in any case, most labor organization takes place there.

Assuming that there is always some surplus labor and some low-skilled laborers, the PLP measure is:

$$PLP = \left[\frac{\left(\frac{\text{Number of skilled workers}}{\text{Number of low-skilled workers}} \right) \times \left(\frac{1}{\text{Surplus labor as percentage of working-age population}} \right)}{87} \right] \times 100$$

PLP falls as the number of low-skilled workers increases relative to skilled workers, and as surplus labor expands. To the extent that the surplus shrinks and labor markets become tighter, PLP increasingly depends on the ratio of skilled to low-skilled workers. Significantly, the logic of applying these direct measures of the structural conditions in labor markets as a way of assessing the extent of PLP is similar to Silver's (2003) "marketplace bargaining power" of labor. This type of bargaining power is the influence that "results directly from tight labor markets" (Silver, 2003). See appendix B for a more detailed explanation of the PLP variable.

Admittedly, PLP is an unconventional measure of labor's bargaining capacity. Garrett and other scholars capture the key features of OECD labor market institutions using existing measures of labor's negotiating and political power.[29] Unfortunately, such detailed data do not exist in the developing world. The most common method of assessing labor's potential political power in these countries is by unionization rates (Madrid, 2002; Devarajan, Ghanem, and Thierfelder, 1997; Galenson, 1994, 1962). A fundamental problem with this indicator, however, is that union density (the percentage of the working population that is unionized) is not comparable across countries in the developing world. Many LDC governments mandate compulsory membership in corporatist unions and impose constraints on labor's demand-making, leadership and internal governance (Collier and Collier, 1991). China, for example, has the highest union density in the developing world, yet labor has very little bargaining power (Chan and Senser, 1997). In general, unionization rates exaggerate labor's political strength in LDCs, and do not give any sense of the extent of "labor encompassment."[30] Moreover, no standardized cross-country time-series measures exist yet for a large number of developing countries. The next step is to employ an econometric test to

[29] Garrett (1998), for instance, captures labor market institutions in the OECD nations by operationalizing labor encompassment as union density and confederation share, and a political power measure that sums standardized scores for legislative and Cabinet-level government indicators. These two measures are aggregated to represent left–labor power.
[30] See, for example, Valenzuela (1989: 449) and Banuri and Amadeo (1991: 175). McGuire (1997) adds that unreliability in union data can result in huge discrepancies in existing cross-country compilations of union density estimates.

analyze more precisely labor's ability to mediate between the forces of globalization and pressures for welfare retrenchment.

2.3.3   Model specification

The argument that the character of labor market institutions moderates different (RTB) outcomes in poorer and richer countries is assessed in two stages. First, an LDC model examines the influence of both domestic- and international-level variables on government welfare expenditures to test the RTB hypothesis (see equation (1)). To check the robustness of the findings, each set of results is re-evaluated using an alternative measure of social spending. Second, equation (1) is reapplied to developed countries using Garrett's (1998) model to confirm whether or not the labor variable drives the differential welfare state outcomes in developing and developed countries.

I use both country and decade dummy variables to control for country-specific and time-specific fixed effects. Following Kaufman and Segura-Ubiergo (2001), I use decade rather than year dummies to account for the important differences in international conditions over the course of our time period. The years 1972 to 1979 cover the period prior to the debt crisis, while 1980 to 1989 were years generally marked by economic recession and painful structural adjustments. The final eight-year span (1990–7) covers the period of economic recovery that took place.

Based on econometric techniques advocated by Beck and Katz (1995), I correct for both panel heteroskedasticity and spatial contemporaneous autocorrelation. In addition, problems of potential serial autocorrelation within each panel are addressed by estimating and adjusting for a panel-specific AR(1) (first-order autoregressive) process. This model follows Achen's (2000) recommendation against applying the standard practice of simply using a lagged dependent to correct for serial autocorrelation. These results provide Prais–Winsten coefficients with panel-corrected standard errors (PSCEs).

2.3.3.1   The LDC model

$$(1) \; \Sigma \text{welf}_{it} = b_1 \text{PLP}_{it} + (b_2 \text{trade}_{it-1} \times \text{PLP}_{it}) + (b_3 \text{portfolio}_{it-1} \times \text{PLP}_{it}) +$$
$$(b_4 \text{fdi}_{it-1} \times \text{PLP}_{it}) + b_5 \text{trade}_{it-1} + b_6 \text{portfolio}_{it-1} + b_7 \text{fdi}_{it-1} +$$
$$\Sigma(b_j \text{X}_{jit-1}) + \Sigma(b_k \text{country}_{ki}) + \Sigma(b_l \text{decade}_{lt}) + \mu_{it}$$

Three different dependent variables are included in "welf": public expenditures on social security and welfare; spending on education; and spending on health. The *b*s are parameter estimates in this equation, while the subscripts *i* and *t* represent the country and year of the observations, respectively; ΣX represents the vector of control variables. The globalization variables ("trade," "portfolio" [portfolio flows], and "fdi") are lagged in order to take the period of "adjustments" into account.[31] Consistent with Garrett (1998), this model uses pooled cross-section and time-series data to estimate the results.[32] This estimation procedure has two benefits. First, the use of the fixed-effects model makes it possible to control for unobservable country-specific differences, eliminating much of the omitted variable bias of cross-section data.[33] Second, important changes that have occurred over time in the same country can be assessed. Using panel data ultimately combines the benefits of an increased number of observations with the ability to account for country-specific fixed effects.

The developing country model is estimated in three ways, and the results are reported in table 2.5 and appendix C. Model 1 reflects equation (1), using all three globalization indicators as causal variables. Model 2 drops FDI and re-estimates the model, since studies have shown that trade and FDI are correlated (Albuquerque, Loayza, and Servén, 2005; Aizenman and Noy, 2006). Finally, model 3 applies the two-stage least squares (2SLS) method to adjust for measurement error in the labor variable.

2.3.4   The variables

2.3.4.1   Dependent variable: social spending on education, health, and social security and welfare [WELF] The selection of social security and welfare, education, and health as the primary categories to assess welfare effort in developing countries follows the standard approach in the current literature (see, for example, Kaufman and Segura-Ubiergo, 2001, and Avelino, Brown, and Hunter, 2005). The social security and welfare variable captures traditional transfers and particularly pensions, and education and health represent spending on human capital investments. Each

---

[31] Theoretically, it is more sensible to anticipate a lagged effect, because international market occurrences take time to affect policy outcomes. See, for example, Rodrik (1997a), who uses lagged measures of openness.

[32] Note that, as emphasized earlier, this is an unbalanced data set for LDCs.

[33] For example, informal systems of old age support (i.e. extended families) are common methods of providing social security in many parts of Africa and Asia (see World Bank, 1994). Such variables are more significant in some countries than others. The fixed-effects model allows us to control for the influence of such idiosyncratic differences between countries without having to model them explicitly.

of these measures incorporates somewhat different welfare functions. The proportion of the budget devoted to social security and welfare captures what are sometimes called "uncompetitive" types of spending and transfers, a category that should be in greatest jeopardy given the "efficiency" pressures of globalization. Spending on education and health, by contrast, reflects the priority that governments give to human capital development, and could well be complementary to the demands of globalization. For example, increasing levels of FDI and trade might generate efforts to improve efficiency and, thereby, stimulate demand for better education and health systems. I examine each of these categories of spending as a share of GDP and on a per capita basis.

2.3.4.2 Primary causal variables: the interaction of economic globalization and labor power (PLP) in LDCs [TRADE × PLP, PORTFOLIO × PLP and FDI × PLP][34] At the heart of this study is the idea that globalization's effect on social spending depends on the character of labor market institutions in developing countries. The conventional measure of trade openness, exports plus imports relative to GDP, is incorporated in this model. The primary explanatory variables are the interactive effects of globalization and labor power. These interactive variables, by design, replicate Garrett's (1998) model of the globalization–spending relationship in the developed economies. Trade, net FDI flows, and portfolio flows as a percentage of GDP are combined with PLP in order to assess the extent to which existing labor market conditions can help moderate the globalization–welfare spending relationship. If the interactive effects of globalization and PLP are negative then it can be determined that the combined effects of low levels of PLP with increased exposure to higher levels of trade and capital flows result in lower government welfare commitments.

One particular caveat should be kept in mind: surplus labor may be over- or underestimated, depending on the actual age of the working population. The World Bank's metric of the "working-age population" is based on OECD standards. The value will be underestimated in countries where workers in the informal sector begin to engage in money-making activities well before the standard working age of fifteen

---

[34] Note that, following Braumoeller (2004), I run model 2.2 including triple interactions, since the inclusion of PLP in both interaction terms creates a "tacit interaction" between trade and the capital flows variable. The primary findings are not affected; the conditional coefficients are significant at the ninety-fifth percentile confidence level (see footnote 42 for details on calculation). For ease of presentation, the triple interaction results are not included here.

(to sixty-four) – i.e. child labor. Conversely, in developing countries where the retirement age is commonly under sixty-four, surplus labor may be overestimated. To address this measurement error, I apply the Lewbel (1997) method and re-estimate equation (1) using 2SLS (see model 2.3).[35]

2.3.4.3 Control variables: age dependency, youth population (population zero to fourteen years of age), elderly population (sixty-five and older), urbanization, debt, GDP per capita, growth, democracy, ethnic fragmentation and region dummies Several control variables help isolate this main relationship and check for other influences on welfare. Given that most nations in this sample are considerably underdeveloped, supplementary political and economic variables are included in order to tailor the model to these cases. Previous studies of developing country welfare spending have found that it increases with the number of young and aged dependents (World Bank, 1994; Esping-Andersen, 1990; Tang, 1996; Schmidt, 1995); the level of urbanization (Tang, 1996); both GDP per capita and growth (Brown and Hunter, 1999; Usui, 1994; Rodrik, 1997a, 1998; Tang, 1996); low debt (Schwartz, 1998); and democracy (Rudra and Haggard, 2005, Brown and Hunter, 1999; Atkinson and Hills, 1991; Eichengreen, 1996; Hicks and Swank, 1992). Unemployment figures, frequently linked to higher welfare expenditures in developed countries, are excluded because of the unreliability of such figures in developing nations (see Agenor and Montiel, 1996). I drop urbanization because of its high correlation with GDP. The percentage of the population aged over sixty-five (the elderly) is included in the model for human capital because care for the elderly is said to account for the greatest percentage of health expenditures. By the same logic, I control for the size of the youth population (ages zero to fourteen) in the education model.

---

[35] The conventional method for coping with this measurement error and mitigating the bias of the regression estimates is to use the instrumental variable approach. The difficulty, however, lies in finding outside data or instruments that are uncorrelated with the error of the equation but at the same time highly correlated with the explanatory variables. Therefore, as a solution to the insufficient instruments problem, Lewbel (1997) proposes using second and third moments of variables as instruments. For example, following Lewbel, if x_i is an element of the X matrix, then $q_i = (X_i - mean(X))^2$ is a legitimate instrument in addition to the x_i variables, and the instrumental variables estimator is consistent. Note that the Lewbel method has also recently been applied to solve problems of endogeneity (see Cheng et al., 2006, and Ebbes, 2004; personal communication with Cheng Hsiao). The following variables also serve to construct the instrument: manufactured exports, service exports, portfolio flows, urbanization, debt, democracy, and economic growth.

Ethnic fragmentation and regional diversity could also play a role. Spending on public goods such as education tends to be low in countries where ethnic groups are polarized (Alesina, Baqir, and Easterly, 1999).[36] Since, technically, everyone has access to public goods, this research suggests that, in ethnically fragmented societies, one ethnic group will resist tax revenues that will provide public goods shared by other ethnic groups. Scholars such as Haggard and Kaufman (forthcoming) argue that regional factors (e.g. international political developments after World War II that weakened labor and the left in east Asia) can affect the level of spending.[37] To test the effects of ethnic fragmentation (which, according to the data, tends to be static), I first include it as a fixed effect. These results are difficult to interpret, however, since country fixed effects cannot be included at the same time.[38] I also test the impacts of regional dummies. In the end, however, after confirming that the exclusion of neither of these two variables drives the primary results, I opt to drop them from the final model and include only the country fixed effects; the latter absorb much of the explanatory power of ethnic fragmentation and region.

2.3.5   Results

Model 2.1 is re-estimated using different dependent variables to check for robustness: welfare as a percentage of GDP and per capita welfare spending. Equation (1) is estimated for fifty-nine developing countries, from the years 1972 through 1997, using the fixed-effects procedure (see table 2.5). Ultimately, in support of the race to the bottom hypothesis, social security and welfare is the variable that is the most sensitive to variations in international level variables, particularly trade openness. The combined effect of PLP and openness, as predicted, is negative and highly significant across the models for social security and welfare. The impact of the globalization

---

[36] Fragmentation (or *fractionalization*) is defined as "the probability that two individuals selected at random from a country will be from different ethnic groups" (Fearon, 2002: 21). ETHFRAC was compiled by Soviet ethnographers in 1964 and published in the *Atlas Narodov Mira*. The Soviets considered language to be the main way to distinguish ethnicities; accordingly, ETHFRAC captures ethnolinguistic fractionalization. Fearon (2002) codes EF with a slightly different coding scheme; he argues that different ethnic groups may speak the same language, but are ethnically very different. The two measures are highly correlated, but capture slightly different conceptualizations of fractionalization.
[37] Note that the inclusion of both country and regional dummies does not affect the results. In model 2.2, the east Asian dummy is negative and significant, and the Latin American dummy is positive and significant (compared with the Middle East, the omitted category).
[38] Linear dependency problems occur when both country fixed effects and ethnic fragmentation variables are included.

variables on education and health, in contrast, is not as robust. When all relevant domestic variables are controlled for, the results reveal that labor market institutions in the developing world are unable to prevent a race to the bottom in social security and welfare.

2.3.5.1 The LDC globalization–welfare model Table 2.5 illustrates how trade openness combined with PLP displays the strongest effect on social security and welfare spending. Interestingly, although PLP has a positive and independent effect on social spending (hypothetically, when trade equals zero), it is less effective when faced with international market pressures, particularly trade openness. The pattern of coefficients for the trade openness–PLP interactive variable is fairly consistent across the different models, suggesting that these findings are quite robust. In contrast, based on the conditional coefficients, neither of the FDI and portfolio interactive terms have consistent effects on SS and welfare spending. The portfolio–PLP coefficient is negative and significant, and the FDI–PLP coefficient is positive and significant in model 2.3 only, providing cautious support for the effects of these globalization variables.[39] Nevertheless, the negative coefficients of the trade openness interactive terms across the different models provide strong confidence in the finding that SS and welfare expenditures are indeed a function of high levels of exposure to global market activity and relatively weak labor power. These results cast doubt on previous analyses of welfare spending that have focused only upon domestic variables and downplayed the importance of international level variables in their analyses.[40]

In contrast, the effects of the globalization variables on health and education expenditures are ambiguous (see appendix C for the results tables on education and health spending in LDCs). The portfolio–PLP interaction variable appears to have a positive effect on education spending; we cannot be confident about this result, however, since it does not hold up to tests of robustness. The same holds true for the health spending models. None of the globalization variables had a consistent effect on government health expenditures as seen in the social security and welfare models. The trade–PLP coefficients flip signs within models 2.1, 2.2, and 2.3. These findings, taken together, suggest that international-level

---

[39] Testing significance levels (model 2.1) reveals that conditional coefficients on portfolio flows are insignificant when the levels of trade and FDI flows are high. Similarly, FDI is also insignificant when trade and portfolio flows are high.

[40] See, for example, Schmidt (1995), Tang (1996), Midgley (1984), Wahl (1994), and Atkinson and Hills (1991).

Table 2.5 *Social security and welfare spending in LDCs*

	Model 2.1		Model 2.2		Model 2.3	
	SS and welfare (% GDP)	SS and welfare per capita	SS and welfare (% GDP)	SS and welfare per capita	SS and welfare (% GDP)	SS and welfare per capita
PLP	0.20**	12.53***	0.19**	12.21***	0.48***	11.88***
	(0.09)	(3.97)	(0.08)	(3.85)	(0.12)	(3.99)
Trade$_{t-1}$ × PLP	−0.002*	−0.10***	−0.002*	−0.11***	−0.005***	−0.15***
	(0.001)	(0.04)	(0.001)	(0.04)	(0.002)	(0.04)
Portfolio$_{t-1}$ × PLP	−0.016	−0.28	−0.016	−0.22	−0.05***	−1.14*
	(0.016)	(0.74)	(0.015)	(0.70)	(0.02)	(0.60)
FDI$_{t-1}$ × PLP	0.005	−0.55***	—	—	0.17***	2.42***
	(0.004)	(0.21)			(0.04)	(0.94)
Trade$_{t-1}$	0.004	−0.10	0.004	−0.08	−0.001	−0.27**
	(0.004)	(0.12)	(0.005)	(0.12)	(0.005)	(0.12)
Portfolio$_{t-1}$	0.12	5.03	0.12	4.84	0.18**	6.65**
	(0.08)	(3.97)	(0.08)	(3.89)	(0.07)	(3.34)
FDI$_{t-1}$	0.002	1.24*	—	—	0.02	0.19
	(0.021)	(0.70)			(0.04)	(1.06)
GDP per capita	−0.73*	67.43***	−0.69*	65.02***	−1.26***	0.04***
	(0.39)	(12.05)	(0.39)	(11.75)	(0.43)	(0.01)
Growth	−0.007	−0.23	−0.008	−0.21	−0.004	−0.30
	(0.006)	(0.19)	(0.006)	(0.19)	(0.007)	(0.26)
Democracy	0.20	11.42	0.19	11.54	0.04	3.91
	(0.16)	(7.38)	(0.16)	(7.36)	(0.19)	(8.35)
Dependents	−1.52	9.44	−1.48	11.62	−0.45	68.07
	(1.06)	(39.35)	(1.04)	(39.94)	(1.25)	(42.62)
Debt$_{t-1}$	−0.005***	−0.14**	−0.006***	−0.15***	−0.004	−0.07
	(0.002)	(0.06)	(0.002)	(0.06)	(0.003)	(0.08)
R^2	0.71	0.69	0.70	0.68	0.74	0.78
N	750	750	754	754	591	591

Notes: *** = p < 0.01; ** = p < 0.05; * = p < 0.10. Fixed-effects regression estimates. Figures in parenthesis are standard errors.

variables have inconclusive effects on the level of public resources allocated towards health and education spending.[41]

It is intriguing that globalization leads to a race to the bottom in social security and welfare, but not education and health. Why might international economic factors have a more constraining effect on the former? Arguably, assessing SS and welfare spending alone in response to globalization is a more precise test of the RTB hypothesis. This type of expenditure has a direct impact on firms' bottom line, since this program is most often funded by payroll taxes, and, as stressed by many, it can have a negative effect on the productivity of workers (see World Bank, 1994). On the other hand, while supporting high levels of health and education expenditures can affect interest rates and tax rates and thereby encourage a race to the bottom, this type of spending has less impact on total wage costs. Disentangling the pressures of globalization on health is more complicated, however, since funding for health care can be provided by payroll taxes as well as by the government. Regardless, the findings suggest that the politics of social security and welfare differ markedly from the politics of health and education spending. This relationship is investigated in greater detail in chapter 3.

The best way to make sense of these results and understand the impact of PLP on welfare at various levels of globalization is to refer back to equation 1 and estimate the effects of the conditional coefficients.[42] Figure 2.4 graphs the effects of PLP on SS and welfare spending at different levels of openness.

The overall impact of labor power on social spending, contingent upon the level of globalization, exhibits diminishing returns. As revealed in figure 2.4, the ability of PLP to defend SS and welfare spending is mitigated as openness increases. In fact, calculating the effects of openness in another way – contingent upon levels of PLP – reveals that, overall, PLP levels in developing countries are too low to have an effect on welfare spending *as globalization occurs.*[43] The data thus support the existence of a relationship between globalization and cutbacks in welfare spending in developing economies.

---

[41] When the health and education models are re-estimated without the globalization variables, the GDP per capita, demographic, and debt variables have more consistent effects.

[42] Basing the estimations on model 2.1, the effect of increasing PLP on social security and welfare spending conditional on trade, portfolio, and FDI has the form: ∂welf/∂PLP $= 0.20 - 0.002 \times$ trade$_{it-1} - 0.016 \times$ port$_{it-1} + 0.005 \times$ FDI$_{it-1}$. Note that portfolio and FDI values are held constant at their means in order to estimate the impact of changes in trade.

[43] As an example, again using model 2.1, the estimated effect of PLP on SS and welfare spending conditional on trade has the form: ∂welf/∂trade $= 0.004 - 0.002 \times$ PLP$_{it-1}$ and shows no significant effect.

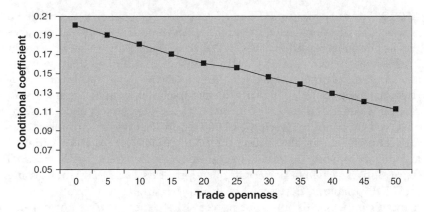

Figure 2.4 Conditional effect of PLP on social security contingent upon levels of openness

Notes: Portfolio flows and FDI are held constant at their means. The conditional coefficients are significant at the ninety-fifth percentile confidence level.

The findings with respect to the impact of some of the control variables, particularly the debt variable, reveal the importance of alternative political and economic influences on social spending, while controlling for international effects. It is surprising that democracy has no noticeable effect, particularly in light of recent analyses that emphasize its importance to social spending (Brown and Hunter, 1999; Rudra and Haggard, 2005). One difference is that the current model incorporates the insights of the welfare state literature and emphasizes the responsibility of labor market institutions in mediating the effects of globalization. Nonetheless, the extent of empirical evidence in support of the democracy–social spending relationship casts doubt on the conclusion that democracy has *no* effect on government social spending commitments. I return to this issue in the case studies in an attempt to make sense of these results.

In summary, the developing country data support the race to the bottom hypothesis with respect to social security and welfare. The weak power of labor market institutions in LDCs is unable to mitigate RTB pressures as globalization, particularly in terms of trade openness, advances. As predicted, their product terms are mostly negative and significant in developing economies. Is the character of labor market institutions in the developing world, represented here by PLP, the key mediating domestic variable that determines the different RTB outcomes in developing nations?

2.3.5.2 The comparison of RTB in LDCs and OECD countries Estimating a similar globalization–welfare model for developed countries emphasizes the importance of differences in the overall strength of labor market institutions. Findings in this section confirm that, unlike their counterparts in the developing world, institutions in the more developed countries are strong enough politically to encourage welfare state expansionism alongside globalization. This contrast between the two sets of countries is observed by adopting Garrett's (1998) globalization–welfare model for OECD nations and substituting the PLP variable for his labor variable, and then comparing the results with the developing countries. These final regressions have two important implications. First, since the results using the PLP variable in developed countries are similar to Garrett's results using his indicator of left–labor power (LLP), these regressions considerably increase confidence in the reliability of the PLP variable.[44] Second, a positive coefficient for the globalization–labor interactive variables corroborates the disparity in centralized bargaining power in the two sets of countries. These findings verify that the contrasting effects of globalization on welfare states in developed and developing countries are rooted in overall differences in labor market institutions.

The interactive globalization–PLP variable is expected to be positive in developed countries. Not only do richer nations face rather less severe collective action problems, but they also have institutions in place to help surmount them. Surplus labor problems are simply not as acute in the more developed countries. Labor markets in these countries tend to be much tighter. In addition, the pool of low-skilled laborers relative to the more skilled laborers in OECD countries has been steadily declining, suggesting that their collective action problems may be more easily overcome. It is no surprise that the average PLP in the advanced industrialized countries is eight times higher than the developing country average of PLP.[45] Finally, these are nations with long-standing liberal democratic traditions. Other welfare beneficiaries (e.g. the aged and the disabled) are also able to form strong interest groups and thus make it increasingly difficult for the government to roll back welfare spending.

Table 2.6 applies Garrett's welfare model to the high-income countries, but substitutes the PLP variable for his measure of LLP (for the corresponding education and health spending regression results, see appendix C). Additional control variables used in Garrett's (1998) analysis are GDP growth, the proportion of the population over sixty-five years

---

[44] See Campbell's (1988) tests for evaluating the validity of variables measuring a concept.
[45] Average PLP in the OECD countries is 9.8. The LDCs' average PLP is 1.2.

Table 2.6 *Social security and welfare spending in OECD countries*

	Model 2.4		Model 2.5	
	SS and welfare (% GDP)	Welfare per capita	SS and welfare (% GDP)	SS and welfare per capita
PLP	0.03	−0.81	0.008***	2.33***
	(0.02)	(5.09)	(0.002)	(0.67)
Trade$_{t-1}$ × PLP	−0.0003	0.05	–	–
		(0.08)		
Portfolio$_{t-1}$ × PLP	0.09*	33.62**	0.10*	31.36**
	(0.05)	(15.51)	(0.05)	(15.04)
FDI$_{t-1}$ × PLP	0.007***	2.00***	0.007***	1.87***
	(0.002)	(0.65)	(0.002)	(0.62)
Trade$_{t-1}$	−0.05**	−20.57***	–	–
	(0.02)	(5.06)		
Portfolio$_{t-1}$	−6.07	−2339.20	−5.60	−2031.83
	(5.69)	(1579.51)	(5.61)	(1534.37)
FDI$_{t-1}$	−0.44**	−49.07	−0.55***	−62.31
	(0.21)	(62.58)	(0.20)	(58.18)
Growth	−0.08***	−1.87	−0.10***	−3.51
	(0.03)	(9.64)	(0.03)	(8.83)
Elderly population	0.74***	384.07***	0.78***	420.74***
	(0.19)	(63.91)	(0.21)	(74.17)
Unemployment	0.41***	62.95***	0.43***	66.74***
	(0.06)	(14.55)	(0.06)	(14.52)
R2	.93	.90	.88	.86
N	348	348	348	348

Notes: *** = $p < 0.01$; ** = $p < 0.05$; * = $p < 0.10$. Fixed-effects regression estimates. Figures in parenthesis are standard errors.

old (POP65), and unemployment. Model 2.3 is not included here since PLP is subject to less measurement error in the developed countries.[46]

This final set of regressions closely replicates Garrett's results and appreciably strengthens the conclusions of this chapter. Comparing the results from the LDCs suggests that the developed countries have more effective labor market institutions and therefore the requisite political muscle to protect citizens from the adverse impacts of globalization. In nations exporting rather more skill-intensive goods, the product terms of the capital flow variables and PLP tend to be positive (see table 2.6 and

[46] The working-age population reported by the World Bank more or less corresponds to the working-age population in OECD countries.

tables C.1 and C.2).[47] In addition, in agreement with Pierson (1996), the significance of the aged population and unemployment variables indicate that labor is only one of several welfare beneficiaries that can successfully resist government penchants for welfare state retrenchment. Interestingly, in a manner similar to the results for the developing countries, globalization had less consistent effects on health and education spending (see tables C.3 and C.4).

The coefficient of trade interacted with PLP is anticipated to be insignificant in more developed nations. According to Schwartz (1998) and Huber and Stephens (1998), trade openness has a much weaker effect on social democracies than the internationalization of productive and financial capital. Increases in trade dependence have been modest in comparison to their rapid integration into financial markets over the last two decades. To account for the special characteristics of globalization in OECD countries, and because FDI and trade tend to be correlated, model 2.5 excludes trade instead of FDI. In direct contrast with developing countries, the social security and welfare model confirms expectations that RTB anxieties are not justified in the developed countries.

These findings more fully expose the explanatory power of the mediating variable, PLP. The appropriateness of applying this measure of the strength of labor market institutions to assess changes in government welfare expenditures in this era of globalization is confirmed. The results are consistent with Garrett's fully specified model, which demonstrates the positive effects of globalization in countries that do not enjoy a comparative advantage in labor. Thus, the statistical evidence presented in this chapter supports the argument that domestic institutional differences between rich and poor countries, especially those involving labor, drive contrasting race to the bottom outcomes in the current era of globalization.

2.4   Summary

This chapter demonstrates that, in direct contrast to the developed countries, developing nations are more vulnerable to race to the bottom pressures. Specifically, the investigation of fifty-nine developing countries from 1972 through 1997 indicates that social security and welfare spending is more responsive to openness than it is to increases in productive and financial capital flows. These findings challenge the emerging consensus

---

[47] Note that both the globalization variables (trade × left–labor power and capital mobility × left–labor power) are positive and significant in Garrett's central model of total government spending.

that fears of a race to the bottom are overblown. Rather, globalization affects welfare spending in the developed and developing nations differently because of the contrasting characteristics of their domestic institutions, most particularly labor market institutions. In the OECD countries, the organizing capacity of labor is relatively strong, and existing institutions can help workers overcome their collective action problems. In LDCs, however, the general trend has been a growing number of low-skilled workers relative to skilled workers. This factor, coupled with large surplus labor populations, exacerbates the collective action problems of labor, and makes it increasingly difficult for workers to mobilize systematically. Consequently, when confronted with the pressures of globalization, labor institutions in the developing world are less capable of defending their welfare benefits.

The findings in this chapter suggest that the difference in welfare state outcomes is due to a wide disparity in the encompassing nature of labor market institutions in developed and developing countries. Developing states appear to have some leeway in directing health and education expenditures, while the same cannot be said of social security and welfare. The exact reasons for this are not yet clear and warrant further investigation in the following chapters. Ultimately, in a globalizing economy, workers' prospective political gains from expanded trade and investment are outweighed by their inability to pressure the government collectively or cooperatively for social programs in their favor.

This chapter clearly demonstrates that LDCs lack encompassing labor organizations and, hence, their labor market institutions are unsuccessful at advancing policy compromises between government, business, and labor in the globalizing environment. One question remains unanswered, however: can select labor groups exert influence on particular social policies? If possible, how might particular pockets of labor groups exert such influence in developing countries? Leaders of decentralized labor groups clearly have fewer incentives and less institutional backing to care about the welfare of the whole labor force. Narrow groups of organized and skilled (and even low-skilled) workers in the formal sector can take advantage of their bargaining position and prevent the marginalized labor groups from obtaining any benefits. The ramifications of this insider–outsider problem receive closer attention in the following chapter.

3   Who really gets hurt?

Chapter 2 has established that the fragmented character of labor market institutions in developing countries makes it more likely that the governments of these nations will respond to race to the bottom pressures. Based on this evidence alone, globalization pessimists might claim that their fears are validated, and it is the end of domestic politics in the developing world; the zero-sum dichotomy between states and markets has been confirmed. But the analysis cannot stop here. What is really driving anxieties about globalization amongst academics, activists, and policy-makers is the concern that the race to the bottom hurts the poor. The fight in this case is not for (or against) domestic politics per se, but for the benefit of the less privileged.

This chapter goes a step beyond analyzing the capacity of labor to overcome collective action problems and negotiate policy compromises under globalizing conditions, and observes the effects of domestic institutional arrangements supporting government–labor relations. This approach reveals that the effects of international free-market competition are much more complex than is commonly assumed. While globalization is certainly increasing RTB pressure on less developed countries, the long-time policy interactions between government and *select* labor groups have engendered a set of social policies that were never designed to help the poor in the first place. Rather, the more privileged classes traditionally receive these benefits, and are therefore the immediate victims of any cutbacks. The findings in this chapter thus challenge the widespread perceptions that the poor are the primary targets of the unbridled race to the bottom in developing countries.

Simply observing whether the level of social spending is decreasing or increasing does not reveal the complete picture about who is being affected, either adversely or positively. Analysts who specialize in the comparative politics of developing countries provide important reasons to be skeptical of the effects of LDC welfare programs (Mesa-Lago, 1994; Weyland, 1995, 1996a, 1996b; Huber, 1996; McGuire, 1999). According to these scholars, such schemes disproportionately benefit economically and politically privileged labor groups in developing nations, such as higher-skilled blue-collar and salaried workers, and do not serve the goals of poverty alleviation. The maldistribution of benefits reinforces the divisions in the labor movement discussed in chapter 2. Nevertheless, it is still commonplace for scholars to extol the virtues of greater social spending. Resources devoted to this type of safety net purportedly protect citizens from the adverse effects of globalization, such as increasing economic uncertainty, poverty, and inequality.

There is clear reason to be cautious about the effectiveness of social spending, since a majority of relatively open developing countries continue to have high levels of inequality, in spite of the fact that most have attempted to implement some form of redistribution policies. This is particularly puzzling given that, over time, LDCs that have spent the highest amount on these welfare programs are the ones that, according to some measures, continue to be the most unequal (e.g. Brazil, Chile, Botswana).[1] The next step, then, is analyzing the distributional consequences of social spending to determine if government social commitments do in fact protect the disadvantaged from the risks and uncertainties associated with international market integration.[2]

In comparison, the efficacy of social spending in the countries of the OECD is a rather less contentious question. Esping-Andersen (1990) illustrates that, within the OECD nations, the social democratic welfare states in particular do quite well in balancing market-oriented, social welfare policies and a more equitable distribution of income. Social policies are strongly embedded in their domestic structure, institutions, and politics (Katzenstein, 1985; Pierson, 1996; Garrett, 1998).[3] The challenge ahead is to determine whether LDC social spending, which has typically favored more privileged labor groups, can be affected by the race to the bottom and yet still be reconstructed in ways that will improve the lives of all citizens. The objective of this chapter is thus twofold: (1) to resolve whether social spending helps improve conditions

---

[1] These countries have the highest Gini coefficients in the sample used in this analysis.

[2] By the "disadvantaged," I refer mostly to the poorest segments of the population, such as low-skilled and informal-sector workers. Since these groups have little economic security in LDCs (reliable employment, transferable skills, insurance mechanisms, assets, etc.), they are arguably the most affected by the risks imposed by globalization.

[3] The terms "embeddedness" and "disembeddedness" are derived primarily from Polanyi's (1944) *The Great Transformation*. In embedded economies, the market (and the institutions associated with it) is seen as integrated with all aspects of human life (political and social). In other words, developing *free* markets does not systematically dominate the policy agenda, and state-led social development (e.g. quality of life issues) assumes an equally important political priority. The policy agenda in a disembedded economy, on the other hand, tends consistently to favor either state intervention or the free market.

for the poor or is being directed towards the better off in developing countries; and (2) to determine if international market pressures push governments to engage in equity-enhancing reforms.

To address the issue of the redistributive nature of developing country social policies in this era of globalization, this chapter is divided into four sections. Section 3.1 establishes why evaluating the redistributive impact of social spending is essential to evaluate the merits and concerns of the RTB debate. Section 3.2 analyzes the relationship between globalization, welfare spending, and income distribution in the more developed economies, and then compares the results to developing countries. The primary questions are: (1) whether international market expansion has had a negative effect on income distribution in developing countries, as is so often proclaimed by globalization critics; and (2), if so, whether social spending is an effective tool to tackle it. This section reinforces an important theme from chapter 2: that citizens of developing nations face different prospects and challenges from those of richer countries as markets expand. In section 3.3, I question if any of the categories of social spending (education, health, and/or SS and welfare) are undergoing equity-enhancing reforms alongside globalization. To uncover answers to these questions, I employ two-stage least squares time-series cross-sectional estimations on thirty-five developing countries and eleven high-income OECD nations, covering data from 1972 to 1996.[4] To interpret the results in section 3.3, section 3.4 draws on the insights of the rational choice literature and illustrates how institutional constraints stemming from the historical government–labor relationship can help explain the effects of social spending on income distribution in a globalizing economy.

The findings in this chapter reveal several interesting patterns. To begin with, income distribution tends to be much more sensitive to trade flows in developing countries than it is in the more industrialized nations. The results indicate that increasing amounts of trade worsen income distribution in the developing world *if* the government does not engage in certain types of social spending to alleviate it. Capital flows, in contrast to trade flows, have a minimal effect on inequality in both sets of countries. Finally, while it is heartening that *all* three categories of social spending help improve income distribution in OECD countries, the effects of social

---

[4] Note that this is an unbalanced data set. Continuous inequality data for LDCs are sparse. I use yearly data in order to make use of every observation and to capture (when possible) the effects of annual changes that averages can miss. The LDC and OECD samples in this analysis both include all countries for which it is possible to obtain comparable data on income distribution and social spending.

spending are much less favorable in globalizing LDCs. Only spending on education encourages a more favorable distribution of income as the market expands, while health spending shows a weaker effect on improving equality in the globalizing environment, and SS and welfare expenditures in developing countries actually worsen income distribution. The results in this chapter are at odds with much of the World Bank literature, which argues that most types of government social spending are regressive or, at best, inefficient in developing countries.

Ultimately, this chapter emphasizes how the constraints and inducements of globalization affect the redistributive impact of certain types of social spending. Redistributive education policies are encouraged as economies open up, because their benefits are well known and are consistent with the normally divergent policy preferences of different social actors (e.g. capitalists, workers) striving to cope with the competitive pressures of globalization. Investments in programs that are typically financed through payroll costs, however, such as health and SS and welfare, are subject to greater political lobbying and clientelism. These latter benefits have typically been used by governments to manipulate and bolster their relationship with particular labor groups and thereby help reinforce the fragmented nature of labor market institutions in developing nations. Cross-class alliances are thus more likely to form in favor of education reform, over and above progressive changes in other social welfare programs.

3.1   Importance of the distributive effects of social spending in developing nations

The question of whether social spending helps improve the incomes of the poor in an era of rapidly expanding markets is vital for race to the bottom analyses. The RTB theory suggests that globalization severely constrains the ability of nations to pursue policies that protect the most disadvantaged groups. Chapter 2 clearly demonstrates that globalization curtails the expansion of some categories of social welfare. Is it also the case, however, that these welfare programs protect the poorer sectors of society as is commonly assumed? More specifically, do domestic institutions in developing countries support SS and welfare, education, and health programs that promote pro-poor redistribution?

Two important repercussions arise if social spending in developing countries is primarily directed towards more privileged groups rather than improving the lives of the poor. First, many of the anxieties about globalization and the race to the bottom have been misdirected towards only international-level variables; we have to take a much closer look at domestic politics and institutions to explain actual social welfare outcomes (e.g. worsening income inequality). Second, simply expanding the social budget will not help resolve distributional problems.

In the developed world, maintaining welfare states is both a preferred and viable strategy as these nations move towards greater market integration. Scholars argue that a race to the bottom must be avoided since social spending that protects the disadvantaged can be an asset to the economy (i.e. it provides greater social stability and political support for globalization policies) as openness occurs. Additionally, since research shows that the polities of the more advanced nations are relatively insulated from international political and economic pressures, the politics of social spending is less likely to be affected by globalization.

Welfare politics appears to be somewhat more vulnerable to international market conditions in the developing world, however. Scholars have argued not only that welfare spending in developing nations tends to be regressive (Malloy, 1979, 1993; Huber, 1996), but, as suggested in chapter 2, collective action problems inhibit the capacity of labor market institutions to demand more redistributive-type spending, particularly under conditions of globalization. It is therefore important, when analyzing the full extent and consequences of the race to the bottom, to investigate the possibility that LDC welfare programs actually protect the better off from the risks associated with an open economy. If this is the case, fears of declining social spending must be put into proper perspective. By the same logic, both globalization pessimists and optimists should be cautious about drawing the conclusion that countries with increasing levels of social spending are necessarily doing well for their poorest citizens.

3.1.1   Links between globalization, welfare spending, and inequality in OECD countries

For over two decades scholars have explored the dynamics behind the globalization–welfare relationship in more developed countries. Until recently the conventional wisdom has been that international market pressures would force the ultimate demise of the welfare state, because this type of government is costly and obstructs growth and efficiency efforts. Globalization scholars have now rejected this hypothesis in developed economies, however, and find that welfare spending can, in fact, *benefit* markets by increasing productivity and attracting capital.[5] For this

---

[5] Garrett (1998) shows that the macroeconomic consequences of redistribution policies in social democracies are not negative. He surmises that "these economic 'goods'

to hold true, however, globalization must be accompanied by a welfare state that is successfully redistributive and thereby promotes social stability.

Recent work has suggested that welfare spending in the developed economies not only protects the disadvantaged from the economic dislocations associated with globalization, but is increasingly part of the competitive formula (Scheve and Slaughter, 2006; Katzenstein, 1985; Garrett, 1998; Rieger and Leibfried, 1998). Welfare policies are an important outcome of the bargained consensus between business, government, and labor, particularly in the social democratic countries. As discussed in chapter 2, when labor market institutions are encompassing, labor can act collectively and negotiate certain trade-offs (e.g. lower wages for employment security) for two mutually beneficial outcomes: (1) social benefits not undermined by openness; and (2) flows of trade and capital undeterred by the level of social benefits. Welfare states in OECD nations have thus been constructed from both "bottom-up" and "top-down" pressures and, by design, protect market "losers."

All three types of spending explored in chapter 2 are expected to affect income distribution in OECD countries positively. As Marshall (1950) long ago argued, increases in social security spending can produce less inequality, particularly in Western countries that promote means-tested pensions,[6] although some disagreement persists on the precise type of social insurance scheme that most effectively helps the destitute.[7] Education spending can improve income distribution by providing the poor with the skills to earn higher incomes. Finally, health spending may help close inequality gaps by improving the health of the poor, reducing the incidence of illness, and thereby improving productivity and job security. These arguments assume, however, that social spending enables the poor to increase their incomes more rapidly than the rich.

If spending is indeed redistributive in developed countries then greater public expenditures on social programs and macroeconomic performance can be justified. The flow of neither trade nor capital will necessarily be disrupted when governments devote more resources to equity-enhancing

---

[predictable patterns of wage setting, in accordance with productivity and competitiveness, high-skilled and productive workers, low levels of social strife, etc.] are attractive even to mobile asset holders in the volatile global economy, offsetting the disincentives to investment generated by big government and high labor costs highlighted in neoliberal economics" (Garrett, 1998: 5). Also see Burgoon (2001).

[6] Means testing or targeting suggests that individuals earning below a specified amount (of wealth or property) are entitled to the benefit, or will receive the benefit at a reduced rate.

[7] Controversy persists as to whether means-tested social insurance programs or universalism contribute to inequality and if flat-rate systems or earnings-related benefit levels have the most redistributive effect. See Korpi and Palme (1998).

social programs. Mobile asset-holders can view government redistribution policies as productive, because redistributive welfare states can lead to lower social strife and encourage business–labor cooperation (Garrett, 1998). Put simply, one condition for maintaining high levels of social spending under conditions of globalization is that the welfare state has a positive effect on income distribution.

3.1.2   The link between globalization, welfare spending, and inequality in LDCs

As indicated in the introduction of the book, analyses of the globalization–welfare relationship in the developing world have begun only recently. Significantly, these attempts to assess LDCs' capacities to cope with the negative effects of globalization have overlooked one critical issue: many of the social welfare programs in these countries were not originally designed to protect marginalized groups. Several studies report that, from their inception, government social policies, particularly those pertaining to income transfers, have been implemented in a "top-down" fashion and used for purposes of political control and patronage instead of redistribution (Mesa-Lago, 1994; Huber, 1996; Weyland, 1996a, 1996b; McGuire, 1999).

If the findings in these studies are generalizable, we can expect that the rich are gaining relative to the poor from increases in government welfare spending. Social security might exacerbate inequality if richer groups enjoy more generous benefits packages (relative to contributions) than the poor. One consequence is that, in the face of ongoing market risks and uncertainties, wealthier beneficiaries maintain income stability as the unprotected poor experience greater economic hardships. Education spending can exacerbate income distribution if the poor have minimal opportunity to gain skills that will help them earn higher incomes. Finally, health spending may increase the gap between income groups if existing spending is directed mostly towards specialized care and providing health subsidies for the rich; without access to affordable health care, the poor will have little safeguard against illness and hence productivity, job security, and, ultimately, income will suffer.

In many developing countries, an urban formal-sector coalition that includes unions, civil servants, managers, and government officials has long benefited disproportionately from the social welfare system. Even in states where clientelism may be less pervasive, welfare provisions are limited to the formal sector, which is as low as 10 percent of the workforce in many developing countries (ILO [International Labour Organization], 2001). These conditions serve as a disincentive to forming more encompassing labor market institutions that could result in a redistribution of benefits from the richer labor groups to the poorer ones.

The implication of these studies is that, if social welfare systems do little to decrease the gap between the rich and poor, it will be particularly challenging for governments to maintain stability in the era of globalization. As argued in the previous chapter, a bargained consensus between labor, business, and capital is difficult to achieve in the developing world, and becomes even harder when confronted with international political and economic pressures. Since workers in LDCs do not have the same types of encompassing organizations as they do in many advanced economies, the growing duality between surplus and formal-sector workers creates a more competitive environment and makes it increasingly difficult for different subgroups of workers to forge coalitions and pursue equity-enhancing social policies.

Those engaging in the race to the bottom debate must take pause if indeed social spending in developing countries is not redistributive. The findings in chapter 2 would then demand further interpretation. If greater social spending is not reaching the poor then a race to the bottom is of immediate consequence to less vulnerable groups. Are decreases (or increases) in social security and welfare spending, in particular, directly affecting the income security of the poor? Ultimately, the distributional impact of social spending must be considered in order to determine whether encouraging states to spend more on existing welfare programs during globalization is in fact sound policy.

The critical question, then, is whether increasing welfare spending is to be greeted as progress. Existing studies in the comparative politics and globalization literatures have not empirically determined whether welfare spending, alongside international economic factors, affects income distribution positively or negatively. Even if, as some studies claim, privileged groups receive a disproportional amount of the benefits, government interventions may still improve the situation of the poor to some degree.[8] If welfare spending is regressive, however, increasing social spending could theoretically have the same destabilizing effects as lowering social spending in more progressive countries.[9] Do empirical data support the claim that governments of developing countries are

---

[8] For instance, although Brazil's corporatist state created the National Confederation of Workers in Agriculture (CONTAG) in 1963, the rural workers mobilized under this organization were eventually able to achieve some success in establishing progressive social policies in the 1990s (Weyland, 1996a, 1996b).

[9] According to Huber (1996), Costa Rica would be an example of a progressive LDC, because it has developed according to social democratic principles of universality and equity.

unlikely to redistribute resources *to the poor* in an era of globalization? Or does globalization provide certain incentives that encourage redistributive reform? Are certain types of social spending more redistributive than others? The model presented in the next section assesses whether the different types of social spending have a positive or negative impact on income distribution in globalizing economies.

3.2   The base model: the effects of globalization and social spending on income distribution

This model tests the determinants of income distribution in thirty-five developing countries and eleven high-income OECD nations. All cases for which data (on income distribution and social spending) are available are considered in this analysis. The sample represents fourteen low- and low middle-income non-OECD countries, eighteen upper middle- and high-income non-OECD countries, and eleven high-income OECD countries. The data form a time-series cross-section unbalanced panel covering annual information from 1972 to 1996. I apply the fixed-effects method using country and decadal dummies. This method controls for idiosyncratic differences across countries with regard to inequality.

Recall from chapter 2 that social spending is subject to measurement error due to decentralized spending in some developing countries. Fortunately, in this particular model, a new statistical procedure allows us to correct for this problem. In order to disentangle the links between globalization, social spending, and income distribution, the statistical analysis relies on the application of the 2SLS estimation procedure. The Lewbel (1997) procedure of using higher moments of the spending variables as instruments is applied in this model.[10]

The baseline equation is as follows:

$$\text{Gini}_{it} = \Sigma(\text{welfare}^{\#}_{it-1}) + \Sigma(\text{globalization}_{it-1}) + \Sigma(X_{it-1}) + \Sigma(\text{country}) + \Sigma(\text{decade}) + \mu_{it}$$

This equation tests the direct effects of openness and welfare spending on inequality. *Gini*$_{it}$ is the dependent variable, with larger Ginis suggesting greater income inequality. The Gini coefficient is a number between zero and 100, where zero means perfect equality (everyone has the same

---

[10]   Refer to footnote 35 in chapter 2. The first stage includes higher moments of the welfare variable, the globalization variables, PLP, external debt, democracy, and the appropriate demographic controls.

income) and 100 means perfect inequality (one person has all the income, everyone else earns nothing). Higher Ginis thus represent higher levels of inequality in household- and individual-based distribution of incomes.[11] *Welfare*$^{\#}_{it-1}$ represents the same vector of welfare variables observed in chapter 2: education, health, and SS and welfare. It is the predicted value ($^{\#}$) estimated in the first stage. The subscripts i and t represent the country and decade of the observations, respectively.[12] *Globalization* represents the vector of international market variables: trade and capital flows. X_{it-1} is the vector of control variables: democracy, population, and GDP per capita.[13] Finally, decade dummies are included to account for the effects of regional and international conditions. All the variables are lagged to ensure that the direction of causality occurs from the exogenous variables to the dependent variable. See appendix D for detailed explanations of each of the variables.

One problem with pooled models is that countries with structural differences may exhibit identical coefficients. The determinants of inequality arguably differ in the OECD countries from the non-OECD countries. For example, democracy and urbanization can affect the distribution of government resources. The upper-income OECD nations were democratic, industrialized economies before the time frame of this study, however. Both these causal variables, particularly *democracy*, show little variation in the high-income industrialized countries and thus cannot be expected to have a major impact on current income distribution. Rather, *GDP growth* is more likely to have distributive effects in the OECD economies.[14] Regressions on the high-income OECDs and developing countries are therefore run separately.

3.2.1   *The dependent variable: income distribution*

Deninger and Squire's (1996) data on Gini coefficients are used to measure inequality in this analysis. This World Bank compilation of statistics on household income inequality is the most widely used in

---

[11] Deninger and Squire (1996: 580) state, "Given that the difference is not too large, we conclude that there is no reason to expect a large systematic bias in empirical work as a result of using both household-based and individual-based Gini coefficients."

[12] Decade dummies are particularly important to check the effects of the 1980s crisis on the model, particularly since social spending plummeted during that decade.

[13] Once again, as explained in chapter 2, country dummies are used to absorb much of the explanatory power of ethnic fragmentation and region.

[14] The logic of Kuznets' (1950) theory does not apply to this set of countries, since they are already "mature" economies.

current development research.[15] The benefit of using the Deninger and Squire data set derives from their painstaking efforts to satisfy particular standards of quality.[16] Ultimately, they accept only 682 out of their 2,600 observations as their "high-quality" set. See appendix E for technical details on the values used in this study.

The Gini coefficient is an appropriate dependent variable for this analysis, for two reasons: (1) gauging inequality is a commonly accepted method for determining whether the poor are gaining over time; and (2) large Ginis suggest the presence of instability (Alesina and Perotti, 1996), which many globalization analysts argue is also a possible outcome of globalization (Rodrik, 1997a).[17] Only data from the "high quality" sample are applied. Appendix F displays summary statistics for Gini coefficients in the developed and developing countries.

One possible objection to the use of this proxy is that worsening income inequality might not have an effect on poverty. To address this, I re-estimate the model using the concentration of income in the lowest quintile as the dependent variable. Significantly, measuring the dependent variable in these two ways affords a view of globalization and social spending effects on both relative and absolute poverty. These results are shown in appendix G.

---

[15] See, for example, the influential works of Sala-i-Martin (2002), Forbes (2000), and Birdsall, Ross, and Sabot (1995). There are, of course, scholars who take issue with the sparse data coverage and its methodology (see Atkinson and Brandolini, 2001, and Galbraith and Kum, 2003).

[16] These standards are: (1) data must be based on household surveys; (2) the population covered must be representative of the entire country; and (3) the measure of income (or expenditure) must be comprehensive, including income from self-employment, non-wage earnings, and non-monetary income.

[17] A possible alternative dependent variable is instability. It would be useful to know if welfare spending is effective in maintaining social stability as globalization occurs. The problem, however, is that instability is an empirically and conceptually difficult variable to construct (Linehan, 1980). Aggregate statistics of instability, such as the degree of political violence, civil strife, and labor strikes, do not quite capture the link between openness, welfare spending, and its domestic consequences. Political violence is hard to disassociate from regime type, while numerical data on civil strife and labor strikes are not informative. As Murillo (2001) convincingly argues, the latter reflect institutional opportunities, cultural legacies, and political resources. Consequently, if we find through aggregate statistics that instability is rising alongside increased welfare spending, it is impossible to differentiate instability due to the effectiveness of redistribution policies (because governments have been required to take benefits away from the rich to make concessions to the poor) from that due to their ineffectiveness (because the poor are not receiving enough benefits). In addition, examining inequality is a more direct way of assessing whether the poor are gaining relative to the rich. As Alesina and Perotti (1996) indicate, increasing inequality leads to instability, and so the motivating factor in this analysis is to assess whether the preceding condition leading to social unrest is actually occurring with globalization.

3.2.2   Independent variables

3.2.2.1 Welfare spending For the purposes of this analysis, welfare in developing countries is best captured by per capita spending on health, education, and SS and welfare as reported in the IMF's *Government Finance Statistics* (GFS). This measure is used instead of welfare spending as a percentage of GDP, since per capita spending provides a more direct estimate of the *absolute* level of resources committed. As in chapter 2, "welfare" includes spending on social security and welfare, which captures primarily traditional transfers and pensions, as well as education and health. If welfare spending is redistributive then the coefficients of the three public expenditure variables will be negative and significant.

There are limitations with using the GFS data, however. Total social spending data do not reveal how expenditures for the different categories are disaggregated. For instance, data on education spending do not indicate if resources are distributed towards primary and secondary levels or university education, the former usually being associated with more redistributive-type spending. Similarly, it cannot be determined whether health expenditures are devoted to basic preventative care or costly curative programs. Since macroeconomic cross-country data do not provide this detailed information, we are forced to assess if *overall* spending is favorable for the poor. The results should be interpreted with this limitation in mind.

3.2.2.2 Globalization In order to incorporate the two primary international forces said to affect domestic politics, I once again measure the extent of globalization by both capital and trade flows. The conventional measure of openness, exports plus imports relative to GDP, is incorporated in this developing country model. I test the effect of capital flow by disaggregating it into portfolio and foreign direct investment flows. It is of interest to see whether various indicators of globalization have a direct impact on inequality, as suggested by the literature. If the globalization critics are correct then we can expect the openness coefficients to be positive and significant. Note that FDI tends to be statistically insignificant, and, since it is correlated with trade (and trade, not FDI, has the more significant impact in the race to the bottom model in chapter 2), it is dropped from the model.

3.2.2.3 Democracy Democratic nations should exhibit a more favorable distribution of income. Several studies argue that more authoritarian regimes cause income distribution to be skewed, because income will be concentrated in the hands of the few elites who hold political power

(Weede, 1982; Muller, 1988; Burkhart, 1997).[18] The Polity IV data set (2000), produced by the University of Maryland's Center for International Development and Conflict Management (CIDCM), is used here to derive this measure. Democracy is scored on a scale of zero to ten (ten being the highest), and rated by: (1) regulation, competitiveness, and openness of executive recruitment; (2) executive constraints; and (3) the regulation and competitiveness of political competition. Following Brown and Hunter (1999) and Kaufman and Segura-Ubiergo (2001), I also estimate the model using a dichotomous measure of democracy. Any country scoring at least seven is coded democratic, the rest as authoritarian. I use this approach since non-democracies should perform differently from democracies with respect to income distribution.

3.2.2.4 Economic development, urbanization, and population growth
Economic development, urbanization, and population growth are generally considered important determinants of inequality. According to Kuznets (1955), development has an inverse U-shaped relationship with inequality such that inequality increases in a nascent economy and then begins to decline as the country gets richer (Ahluwalia, 1976; Weede and Tiefenbach, 1981; Bollen and Jackman, 1985; Crenshaw, 1992; Burkhart, 1997). In the early stages of development, wealth is concentrated in the hands of the few who possess entrepreneurial and productive capabilities. A wealthier economy accelerates the urbanization process, dissipates rents by offering wider access to investment opportunities, and provides more revenue and infrastructure for redistribution. The per capita GDP variable is a quadratic estimation (GDP and GDP^2), and thus a negative and significant coefficient would confirm Kuznets' hypothesis.

Population growth is generally expected to have a negative impact on inequality. Rapid population growth can put stress on a country's resources and make it more difficult to improve labor productivity (Sheahan and Iglesias, 1998).[19] Population pressures automatically reduce the size of the share of personal incomes and lessen the probability that there will be an equaling out of income. Scholars argue that the effects of population growth on inequality are more directly measured through the age structure, however (Hargens and Felmlee, 1984; Sheehey, 1996). For

---

[18] Burkhart (1997) also argues that moderate levels of democracy have skewed income distribution, because economic benefits favor the urban middle class.

[19] Sheahan and Iglesias (1998) point out that population growth tends to increase the absolute size of the agricultural labor force, decreasing the ratio of land per laborer, and thus affecting labor productivity and incomes.

example, the POP65 variable should have a positive coefficient, because a larger elderly population suggests lower productivity, lower savings rates, and smaller intergenerational transfer of income (Deaton and Paxson, 1997). The POP65 percentage thus "unpacks" the effects of population growth.

Urbanization can also affect income distribution. The growth of the urban population contributes to a larger middle class, more employment, and a modern workforce (Boschi, 1987). As the labor force shifts from agriculture to the urban sector, low-paid rural jobs become less important and inequality is expected to decrease. Moreover, urban-based development sets the foundation for the expansion of a high-wage modern sector as well as better education and health facilities. Vanhanen (1997) predicts a negative relationship between urbanization and inequality, since the former leads to greater school enrollment and higher literacy rates. Because of the high correlation with GDP per capita, however, I drop urbanization and rerun each of the models as a check on the initial findings. The results do not change.

3.2.3   Results

The regression results reveal an interesting pattern. The developed nations fare much better than their less developed counterparts in utilizing social spending to maintain a favorable distribution of income, particularly under conditions of globalization. Portfolio flows have no effect on income distribution in either developed or developing countries, while trade flows exacerbate inequality problems only in the LDCs. As expected, the different components of social spending (education, health, and SS and welfare) help reduce the gap between rich and poor in developed countries. Perhaps more importantly, however, after all the relevant domestic variables are controlled for, most types of social spending in developing countries are not redistributive during globalization, *apart from* education spending.

The base model is first applied to the OECD countries to assess whether inequality models of richer nations need to consider the effects of international market integration. How valid are the concerns of globalization critics who warn that moving jobs offshore to low-wage economies worsens income distribution in the developed world (Nader, 1993; Greider, 1998; Atwood, 1993; Phillips, 1993; Gill, 1995; Daly, 1996; Scholte, 1997)? If their predictions are correct then the coefficients for both portfolio flows and the trade variable should be positive and significant. The results reported in table 3.1 challenge these claims and suggest that greater exposure to international markets has *no* effect on inequality.

Table 3.1 *Determinants of income distribution in OECD countries*

Variable	Model 3.1	Model 3.2	Model 3.3
Trade	0.01 (0.02)	−0.01 (0.02)	0.01 (0.02)
Portfolio flows	1.56 (6.24)	2.54 (6.13)	1.86 (6.26)
SS and welfare	−0.00102[†] (0.00064)		
Education		−0.013* (0.007)	
Health			−0.004 (0.004)
Growth	0.15** (0.07)	0.13* (0.07)	0.16** (0.07)
POP65	0.23 (0.36)	0.47 (0.44)	0.27 (0.50)
1970s	−0.34 (0.76)	−0.42 (0.76)	−0.15 (0.77)
1980s	−1.14* (0.61)	−0.95[†] (0.62)	−0.92[†] (0.63)
N	84	84	84
R^2	0.99	0.99	0.99

Notes: ** $= p < 0.05$; * $= p < 0.10$; † $= p < 0.15$. Fixed-effects regression estimates. Figures in parentheses are standard errors.

These results corroborate the findings of Mahler, Jesuit, and Roscoe (1999), who also discover few significant relationships between trade and capital flows and income distribution in developed countries.

What happens if the international economic variables are dropped from the model? Given that little empirical evidence exists here or elsewhere to show that globalization is a critical factor in explaining inequality trends in the industrialized world, I re-estimate the model without them. Although the results do not radically change in the absence of globalization variables, table 3.2 reveals stronger impacts from the social spending variables. The coefficients for both education and SS and welfare are now negative and significant, suggesting that these types of government social spending improve income inequality. Health spending appears to be the least effective social spending category. Inequality shows little sensitivity to the demographic variables. It is possible that the percentage of the population that is aged (POP65) does not have a direct effect on income distribution. Scholars have recently argued that the long-run stability and continuity of the welfare state in developed economies depends on well-entrenched interest groups (e.g. retirees, labor, the disabled) (Pierson, 1996). According to this logic, the impact of social spending would out-weigh the effects of the demographic variables in countries that have reached advanced stages of political and economic development. Country-specific factors (dummy variables in the regression equation) also play a major role in determining levels of inequality (results not shown here). Altogether, these results suggest that the spending inequality profiles of the more

Table 3.2 *Determinants of income distribution in OECD countries – revised*

Variable	Model 3.4	Model 3.5	Model 3.6
SS and welfare	−0.0012* (0.00062)		
Education		−0.015** (0.007)	
Health			−0.005[†] (0.003)
Growth	0.16** (0.07)	0.127* (0.067)	0.16** (0.07)
POP65	0.26 (0.34)	0.53 (0.45)	0.31 (0.45)
1970s	−0.31 (0.74)	−0.37 (0.75)	−0.11 (0.75)
1980s	−1.13* (0.62)	−0.95[†] (0.63)	−0.84 (0.64)
N	84	84	84
R^2	0.99	0.99	0.99

Notes: ** = $p < 0.05$; * = $p < 0.10$; † = $p < 0.15$. Fixed-effects regression estimates. Figures in parentheses are standard errors.

globalized developed economies are more or less the same as the less globalized ones.

The next step is to compare how trade and capital flows affect income distribution in developing countries. Should openness have similar effects on inequality in developed and developing economies? Garrett (2000) and Rodrik (1998) combine their sample of rich and poor countries and thus do not consider structural differences between the two sets. Nevertheless, weak political and regulatory institutions, ineffective labor movements, histories of political repression and clientelism, and (relatively) late integration into the global economy are common characteristics for most LDCs, and give ample reason to suspect that openness might affect this set of countries differently. Table 3.3 reports the results for the less developed countries.

In direct contrast to the OECD countries, these results indicate that trade exacerbates inequality in poorer countries. The effects of trade are small, but significant. These findings give greater voice to globalization critics who focus on the developing world (Heredia, 1997; Cornia, 1999; Gopalkrishnan, 2001; Rao, 2001). It is also telling that each of the social spending variables is positive and significant. This finding, that government social expenditures exacerbate inequality in developing countries, supports recent World Bank reports that argue that the rich benefit relative to the poor under existing public education and health programs (World Bank, 2001b). The findings on SS and welfare also provide statistical support for studies of developing country social policies in the comparative politics literature discussed earlier.

Table 3.3 *The dependent variable: income distribution in non-OECD countries*

Variable	Model 3.7	Model 3.8	Model 3.9
Trade	0.06** (0.03)	0.05** (0.03)	0.05** (0.02)
Portfolio flows	−0.41 (0.80)	−0.10 (0.72)	−0.23 (0.77)
SS and welfare	0.11*** (0.04)		
Education		0.11** (0.05)	
Health			0.37*** (0.11)
Democracy	−4.07*** (1.47)	−2.96** (1.24)	−2.96** (1.20)
GDPcap	30.92** (12.57)	4.65 (13.97)	14.39 (12.89)
GDPcap^2	−2.62*** (0.91)	−0.78 (0.96)	−1.57* (0.91)
POP65	0.89 (1.51)	1.53 (1.61)	1.07 (1.66)
Urban	−0.37*** (0.13)	−0.27** (0.13)	−0.29** (0.13)
1970s	−1.77† (1.14)	−1.97† (1.23)	−1.83* (1.07)
1980s	−0.73 (1.00)	−0.66 (0.86)	−0.46 (0.87)
N	97	107	107
R^2	0.98	0.99	0.99

Notes: ***= $p < 0.01$; **= $p < 0.05$; *= $p < 0.10$; †= $p < 0.15$. Fixed-effects regression estimates. Figures in parentheses are standard errors.

It is interesting that the GDP variables are not significant in the presence of education and health spending. Much scholarly research has focused on the curvilinear relationship of wealth to inequality, establishing the Kuznets curve as both a stylized fact and economic law (Weede and Tiefenbach, 1981; Simpson, 1990; Crenshaw, 1992; Nielsen and Alderson, 1995). Since these studies do not control for social spending, however, it is possible that institutionalized welfare programs in the developing world offset the effects of the pressures described in Kuznets' theory. Recall that economic forces (i.e. investment opportunities) drive the logic of the Kuznets curve, while political variables (e.g. government intervention) are excluded from his model (Kuznets, 1955).

Capital flows, unsurprisingly, show no effect on inequality. None of the models in this analysis thus far have found capital flows to have a significant effect on social indicators. One possible explanation is that many developing countries have only recently begun to liberalize their capital accounts, and portfolio flows, on average, remain at a very low level relative to GDP (0.28 percent). Of course, some developing countries have experienced higher capital flows (e.g. Argentina, Brazil, South Korea, Mexico, Thailand, Indonesia), but these are clearly the exceptions. I therefore drop the capital flows variable in subsequent regressions. It should be emphasized, however, that including portfolio flows in any of the regressions does not affect the basic substantive findings of this chapter.

3.3   Globalization and prospects for equity-enhancing reform

If, as indicated in the results, openness exacerbates inequality, is it also possible that globalization provides incentives for social reform? As argued earlier, a redistributive welfare state helps maintain stability in the face of globalization, and it can spur competitiveness and discourage "exit." The question, then, is whether there are enough incentives to reform social spending so that it can mediate the adverse affects of globalization in LDCs. To test this possibility, the following model assesses the impact of government-directed social programs when states and domestic markets are subject to the pressures of foreign competition:

$$\text{Gini}_{it} = \Sigma(\text{welfare}^{\#}_{it-1}) + \Sigma(\text{globalization}_{it-1})$$
$$+ \Sigma(\text{globalization}_{it-1} \times \text{welfare}^{\#}_{it-1}) + \Sigma(X_{it-1})$$
$$+ \Sigma(\text{country}) + \Sigma(\text{decade}) + \mu_{it}$$

In this equation, the coefficient for the interactive term between *globalization* and *welfare* indicates whether increases in different types of social spending help cushion the adverse effects of openness. If social spending is indeed more redistributive as markets expand then the coefficient on the interaction terms will be negative and significant.

Table 3.4 provides some empirical support for this speculation. It appears that the negative effects of openness on inequality are mitigated primarily by education spending. Public health spending has a significant but weaker effect on improving income distribution as trade expands. In the case of social security expenditures, however, increasing government budget allocations to this category clearly worsens income distribution. For a clearer illustration of these interaction effects, see appendix H.

These results for education are now at odds with emerging literature from the World Bank, which posits that public spending on education does not help the poor (see World Bank, 2002b, Hanushek, 1995, Nelson, 1999, and Mingat and Tan, 1992, 1998). Two possible reasons account for the discrepancy in results. Most importantly, the models differ by the inclusion of specific explanatory variables in this analysis (i.e. globalization), which are often excluded from the World Bank models. This is the first study to assess whether incentives for social reform increase in the face of globalization. Second, the World Bank analyses apply different dependent variables to assess the effects of education spending, such as

Table 3.4 *Determinants of income distribution in LDCs*

Variable	Model 3.10	Model 3.11	Model 3.12
Trade × SS and welfare	0.0008** (0.0004)		
Trade × education		−0.0009** (0.0004)	
Trade × health			−0.0019[†] (0.0012)
SS and welfare	0.06 (0.04)		
Education		0.15*** (0.05)	
Health			0.42*** (0.12)
Trade	0.02 (0.03)	0.10*** (0.03)	0.10*** (0.04)
Democracy	−3.72** (1.50)	−3.17** (1.24)	−2.88** (1.24)
GDPcap	36.73*** (12.02)	−4.64 (13.29)	3.85 (13.96)
GDPcap^2	−3.12*** (0.86)	−0.03 (0.96)	−0.78 (1.02)
POP65	−0.19 (1.38)	1.78 (1.47)	1.90 (1.51)
Urban	−0.26* (0.13)	−0.29*** (0.11)	−0.34*** (0.12)
1970s	−1.24 (1.25)	−1.92* (1.13)	−1.80* (0.98)
1980s	−0.16 (0.92)	−0.56 (0.65)	−0.33 (0.65)
N	97	107	107
R^2	0.99	0.99	0.99

Notes: *** = $p < 0.01$; ** = $p < 0.05$; * = $p < 0.10$; † = $p < 0.15$. Fixed-effects regression estimates. Figures in parenthesis are standard errors.

enrollment and drop-out rates. The dependent variable in this study (inequality) is designed to capture more aggregate and long-term effects of spending.

The findings for health spending and its positive impact on income distribution (i.e. a negative coefficient) are not as strong as for education, but they still differ from the conclusions of Filmer and Pritchett (1999) and other World Bank studies that find government-directed health spending to be ineffective (Gwatkin and Guillot, 1999; Gwatkin, 2000; Musgrove, 1996). Again, these researchers are analyzing alternative dependent variables (e.g. infant mortality), and they do not necessarily consider the effects of globalization. Openness is thus an important variable to include in models for both health and education outcomes.

The results for SS and welfare spending are not comparable with other studies, however, since this is the first attempt to test their effects on inequality. The finding that SS and welfare spending exacerbates inequality in the face of rising trade flows is new, and supports many of the arguments posited, but not tested, by scholars mentioned earlier. These results imply that not only is this type of spending ineffective for the poor during globalization, it actually worsens the distribution of income.

The coefficients of the interacted variables are significant even when alternative explanatory variables are used as controls. As discussed earlier, the country dummies should account for much of the variance, given the large importance of country-specific effects such as history, cultural differences, etc. in explaining inequality. Tables 3.3 and 3.4 both reveal that urbanization, GDP per capita, democracy, and country dummies have strong effects on inequality in this model. Despite the strong effects of the control variables, however, government social spending still shows a negative impact on income distribution in developing countries, albeit small.

3.4   Robustness checks

To check the stability of these results, I re-estimate the model using the income share of the bottom quintile of the population as the dependent variable. Quintile data provide a second test of whether social spending benefits the poor during globalization. I also substitute the democracy dummy with the second-order polynomial function of democracy used in Burkhart (1997). These results are reported in appendix G. The primary (and secondary) findings are, significantly, not affected by these two changes and thus provide greater confidence in the validity of the statistical pattern revealed in table 3.4.

As a final check on the results, I rerun the models by using data averaged first by five years and then by decades to minimize potential problems relating to missing data.[20] I also run the models dropping those countries with the most missing data. The results are minimally affected.

In sum, globalization affects income distribution in developing economies more than it does in the developed countries. The negative and significant results for the various categories of OECD social spending lend support to the claim that the mature welfare states of Europe are redistributive and relatively immune to the effects of globalization. The findings for less developed countries, in contrast, reveal that, first, trade has an adverse effect on income distribution and, second, many of the existing welfare programs are not redistributive during globalization. The implication is that *the race to the bottom in social security and welfare is most directly hurting the middle class in developing countries*. Under conditions of globalization, only education spending encourages the reduction of income inequality. The significant coefficients on democracy, GDP per capita, and urbanization support the existing literature in its claims that domestic variables are also important determinants of developing country welfare spending.

---

[20] Note that I also interpolate missing data using Stata's *ipolate* command.

3.5   Interpretation of results: the role of government–labor relations, information, and interests

The statistical estimates in the last section reveal that education spending is more redistributive in the face of globalization than either health or social security and welfare. How can this pattern be explained? This finding is particularly interesting, given that development agencies such as the World Bank and the United Nations Development Programme (UNDP) often report that public spending in LDCs has been skewed towards the rich.[21] With deeper international market integration, however, education spending appears to have a positive effect on redistribution. A closer look at the government–labor relationship in an era of expanding markets sheds some light on these results. Drawing from the insights of the rational choice literature, I argue that the combination of institutions, information, and the preferences of politicians and interest groups affects social policy outcomes.[22]

Institutional constraints that evolved from government–labor interactions can contribute to the regressive nature of social security, education, and health programs. Under conditions of globalization, however, if there is a spread of information, and the interests of politicians and interest groups are affected, these institutional constraints can be overcome. The combination of institutional constraints, interests, and information thus offer a plausible explanation for the variations found in the equity-enhancing performance of education, health, and social security in the current era of globalization.

First, (formal-sector) labor's interactions with government and politics has contributed to the formal and informal constraints that discourage the poor and disadvantaged from mobilizing and demanding more equitable social reforms. The fragmented nature of labor organizations and, as Weyland (1995, 1996b) argues, the clientelist machinations and internal state fragmentation that can arise from government–labor relations underscore the basic difficulties in realizing social reform for the masses of poor people. Nonetheless, the spread of information can provide a means to overcome these institutional constraints (see Milner, 1997).[23] For example, increased scholarship, as well as political and media attention to the importance of education in a globalizing environment, can have a positive effect on the policy choices of various social groups. On the other hand, information asymmetry regarding the benefits of social investments, such as in social security, may create political disadvantages. Finally, the role of

---

[21] See, for example, the *World Development Report 2002* (World Bank, 2001b) and the *Human Development Report 2002* (UNDP, 2002).

[22] This emphasis on institutions, interests, and information draws on Milner's (1997) analysis.

[23] As Milner (1997: 18) summarizes, institutions are "socially accepted constraints or rules that shape human interactions."

preferences must also be considered (Milner, 1997). Redistributive reform will occur when the new policies improve politicians' ability to retain office, and when social actors enhance their net income. It is conceivable that, in a competitive global economy, progressive changes in education are increasingly consistent with the policy preferences of rival social actors (e.g. business and labor), while health and social security and welfare reform in developing countries are less so.

Elaborating on the first point, despite great variations within and between developing countries, some generalizations about government–labor relations can be applied. An emphasis upon rapid industrialization alongside the overall absence of transparent and accountable governance has created opportunities for a particularistic relationship between government and a relatively small portion of the larger workforce. Starting in the early twentieth century, LDC governments began reorganizing their economies towards manufacturing. In a world already industrialized and technologically advanced, the challenge was to do this as quickly as possible. Governments thus solicited cooperation from a small segment of workers in the key sectors at the neglect of the much larger workforce in the urban informal and agricultural sectors, with the primary aims of containing labor militancy and promoting industrial peace. Legislation and public policy that once included only civil servants, the military, and other professionals eventually expanded to incorporate salaried, skilled, and some low-skilled workers in key sectors. Generous welfare benefits commonly became a part of the package of "inducements and constraints" to control labor (Collier and Collier, 1979).

In the absence of a vibrant democratic environment with accountable administrative structures, however, welfare constituents demanded special favors and privileges, and politicians began to use these systems for patronage purposes. Education, health, and SS and welfare programs often served as vehicles of clientelism (Mesa-Lago, 1994; Weyland, 1995, 1996a, 1996b; Huber, 1996; Nelson, 1999). For example, in addition to distributing benefits to narrow groups of privileged workers, politicians appointed teachers, health personnel, and social workers in exchange for political support. Such practices served to contain labor militancy, reinforce divisions between labor groups (between insiders and outsiders), and promote political cooperation (amongst insiders). It is no surprise that these groups of privileged workers often lobby against social welfare reforms (Nelson, 1999). Weyland (1996b) further argues that patronage ties with different public agencies and officials can erode the central control of the state, making it even more difficult to reach consensus on redistributive reform. As a consequence, large numbers of rural poor and informal-sector workers continue to receive minimal social protections, even in countries that have been aiming for universal social coverage (Huber, 1996).

These institutional constraints (clientelism, state fragmentation) maintain the government–labor relationship that creates formidable obstacles to more equitable social welfare reform in the current era (see Kaufman and Nelson, 2004). Politicians who deliver social benefits continue to be influenced by narrow organized interests, regardless of the recent wave of democratization. Not only are the poor difficult to mobilize, their political difficulties are particularly severe unless their concerns overlap with the somewhat better off (Nelson, 1989). Several studies have shown, however, that disadvantaged groups face great difficulty finding allies to support their demands for fairer redistribution policies (Weyland, 1995, 1996a, 1996b; McGuire, 1999).

The results in this chapter, however, suggest that, as developing countries integrate into the global economy, these types of institutional constraints can be overcome in the area of government-sponsored education programs. How do the disadvantaged overcome such institutional obstacles, particularly to education reform, in an era of globalization? The interests of the poor and non-poor may converge *in the case of equity-enhancing education programs* for two primary reasons: (1) the increased distribution of information on education; and (2) the growing compatibility of policy preferences of rival social actors.[24] These conditions may well explain why the poor have been successful at obtaining a mass base of support for education reforms, while finding less in the health sector and none at all in social security and welfare.

Awareness of the benefits of greater education investment has increased dramatically. Intense media and scholarly attention is focused on this issue. Information is distributed through abundant scholarly research, the activities of international financial institutions (IFIs), and widespread publicity concerning the east Asian model. Neither health nor SS and welfare sectors have experienced the *same level* of endorsement from these three sources, particularly with respect to their importance in a globalizing economy.

More studies in economics and international political economy suggest that improving the skill base of the economy in developing countries mitigates the potentially harmful impact of globalization on inequality (Thompson, 1995; Davis, 1996; Feenstra and Hanson, 1996, 1997; Robbins, 1996; Wood, 1997; Bourguignon and Verdier, 2000; Chan

---

[24] See Mares (2003a, 2003b) for an excellent discussion of the role of cross-class alliances in the development of social policy in the OECD countries.

and Mok, 2001; Mazumdar and Quispe-Agnoli, 2002).[25] The adoption of skill-based technologies, transferred by transactions between developed and developing economies, increases the relative demand for skilled labor in both sets of countries (although the skill level of labor demanded in general in LDCs is still less than in the industrialized OECD nations). Easterly (2002: 82) argues that "the quality of education will be different in an economy with incentives to invest in the future." In contrast, studies pertaining to the economic effects of investments in health argue that overall productivity will increase, but do not necessarily show its direct relationship with international markets (Knowles and Owen, 1995; Rivera and Currais, 1999; Arora, 2001; Bloom, Canning, and Sevilla, 2001).

In addition to scholars, IFIs and developing nation policy-makers have underscored the merits of education in a global economy. Developing nations have been searching to draw lessons from the east Asian experience since the late 1980s and early 1990s. They focus specifically on building human capital vis-à-vis education (Nogami, 1999; Tilak, 2001). Moreover, although the World Bank emphasizes the importance of investing in *both* education and health in scores of its publications, working papers, reports, etc., it is the leading provider of finance for education projects in the developing world. In the fiscal year 2002, for example, a year of global economic slowdown, the bank's education lending went up by 26 percent to $1.4 billion, while loans to the health sector remained steady at $1.2 billion (World Bank, 2003a). Conceivably, other aspects of the social budget have not been subject to the same opportunities of information dissemination. As a result, social actors are, arguably, less exposed to complete information about the benefits of health and social security and welfare, relative to education.

Finally, the spread of information on education and its benefits can facilitate the formation of alliances between the poor and non-poor in a global economy. Compatible preferences of politicians and interest groups are the missing link explaining the statistical patterns that emerged in the previous section. Put simply, politicians and social actors from different classes are more likely to support education reform over health and social security reform. Policy-makers prefer more equitable education

---

[25] Note that several of these studies (e.g. Robbins, 1996; Feenstra and Hanson, 1997) argue that inequality will worsen if the demand for skilled labor is increasing relative to unskilled labor. This argument holds only in the short run, however. Governments must eventually carry out steps to improve the quality of nations' primary and secondary education if it is to be the foundation of successful tertiary education (see Chatterji, 1998). In addition, basic manufacturing jobs in LDCs require a minimal level of education (Wood, 1994). With the exception of countries with extraordinarily high levels of surplus labor, officials must take an interest in all levels of education to ensure long-term competitiveness.

spending, since it is known to help growth in a knowledge-based global economy (Bourguignon and Verdier, 2000). A more highly skilled labor force will increase returns to capital, draw in greater foreign investment, and court a more robust economy. Political support for the government in power will subsequently increase.[26]

Politically active interest groups (e.g. business and formal-sector workers) also favor education reform, because increasing the skill premium of the workforce ultimately promotes income maximization. Forward-looking business owners, in particular, are beginning to favor more equitable education systems (Nelson, 1999). Not only does improving the education system have substantial pay-offs as human capital investment but, more attractively, it is also a fixed cost incurred by the government and not capitalists concerned with the "bottom line." Globalization and growing demands for a more educated labor force ultimately mitigate business reluctance to support policies in favor of education reform (e.g. more progressive taxes, higher interest rates). Accordingly, both the poor and the non-poor have an incentive to overcome institutional constraints by forming broad coalitions in favor of redistributive education reforms.

Equity-enhancing policy reforms in health and SS and welfare, on the other hand, do not necessarily meet the policy preferences of *both* business and labor. Certainly, it would seem that government health spending would also count as a fixed cost that business should be happy to roll over to the government. In direct contrast to education, however, a large percentage of health costs (i.e. health insurance) are financed by payroll taxes. As such, health expenditures can make up a substantial component of the wage bill and have a direct impact on labor costs. Therefore, even if health reform may have pay-offs as human capital investments, it is less likely to be favored by business interests because of the direct effect on their income. Additionally, profit-maximizing firms have less incentive to support publicly funded health programs in developing countries where labor is abundant and easily substitutable, *ceteris paribus*.

Social security, or pensions, is generally the most regressive component of the social budget. Results from this study reveal that SS spending becomes even more regressive with globalization. It is easy to see why

---

[26] One possible objection is that, if the country is a democracy, then investment in education may not have immediate political pay-offs, and politicians will have less incentive to implement education reform. Although this may be true, the tenure of most popularly elected governments is, on average, three to five years, which is sufficient for at least some of the benefits of education to be realized. Second, because of the spread of information, making education an explicit government priority (e.g. President George W. Bush's policy on education in fiscal year 2002) has mass appeal.

obstacles to SS reform would mount, since both businesses and privileged labor groups have a vested interest in maintaining the existing system. Businesses are likely to be the first to resist reform in this sector because of the impact it would have on their competitiveness through higher wage costs. Formal-sector workers, the current beneficiaries of the existing welfare system, are also likely to resist demands for more redistributive pension funds because of the risks they face with globalization. Recall that chapter 2's results suggest that states can no longer provide these groups with the same level of protections that they once did under the long phases of import substitution industrialization (ISI). Increasingly, they are affected by economic uncertainties (i.e. unemployment, falling wages, etc.). Recent strikes and protests over such issues as job security, wages, benefits, etc. in countries as diverse as Bolivia, India, Brazil, Colombia, South Africa, and South Korea illustrate this point. In addition, governments may be particularly sensitive to the demands of these interest groups since they have the highest voter concentration.

To form cross-class alliances to overcome the institutional constraints against more universal social security coverage is more difficult than doing so for education. Information on its benefits is not as well known, and it is not as much in the interests of the non-poor already receiving benefits. Even reform-oriented governments may ultimately find it politically advantageous to maintain the existing regressive pension system and sustain their long-standing ties with privileged labor groups.

3.6   Summary

Is social spending redistributive in an era of globalization? Are existing discussions of the race to the bottom missing the mark, given that they operate under the assumption that social spending has a positive impact on the social welfare of the disadvantaged? It is clear from the findings in this chapter that social spending is redistributive in OECD countries irrespective of globalization, but this is not the case in developing countries. This analysis suggests that openness has a much more severe impact on inequality in developing nations. Only education spending helps mitigate these adverse effects, while health and social security and welfare spending do not. So, from this particular angle, the poor do gain something directly from globalization.

In an effort to make sense of these outcomes, I rely on rational choice theories and the importance of institutions, information, and interests. Institutional constraints come from a pervasive clientelism that has evolved from government tendencies to allocate benefits disproportionately to privileged labor groups in exchange for political support. Since the current beneficiaries have a vested interest in maintaining the existing system, it becomes difficult for the marginalized population to mobilize and form cross-class coalitions. I argue in this chapter, however, that globalization creates incentives for the creation of cross-class alliances in favor of reforms in education. Incentives increase because information about the benefits of improving the skill premium of (both low-skilled and high-skilled) labor in a technologically driven global economy is spreading, and businesses and labor both prefer that the government pay for this type of human capital investment. More equitable reforms in SS and welfare and health, on the other hand, would be costly for the middle and upper classes, and there are no (perceived) pay-offs in terms of improving their positions in a globalizing economy. In sum, influenced by a more competitive global environment, LDCs are finding it less challenging to implement equity-enhancing reforms in education, but more difficult to redirect existing social security and health programs towards the poor.

Having established that welfare retrenchment is most directly hurting the middle classes in developing countries, one unanswered question remains: does the race to the bottom hypothesis suggest that these nations are experiencing "convergence"? In the next chapter I assess if all LDCs are advancing towards the "neoliberal bottom." To do this, I move beyond a sole focus on the *levels* of social spending and look more closely at the content and structure of welfare states in developing countries. More details about why LDC social policies are geared towards the more privileged and not towards protecting the poor remain to be revealed.

4 LDC welfare states: convergence? What are the implications?

Chapters 2 and 3 have presented three important findings thus far. First, in direct contrast with the nations of the OECD, governments of developing countries are sensitive to globalization and race to the bottom pressures in social security and welfare. Nevertheless, the findings in chapter 2 suggest that, paradoxically, those that comprise the bottom quintile of income distribution are not the ones directly harmed by a race to the bottom; this is mostly because social security, education, and health spending in LDCs tends to be regressive, helping mostly the middle class. The third major finding is that, while levels of health and education may not be increasing in response to globalization, public education spending is becoming more equitable. These findings overall are instrumental in illustrating the complex relationship between states and markets in the current era of globalization; domestic institutions (i.e. labor market institutions, the government–labor relationship) mediate and influence policy outcomes in a decisive and meaningful way.

Are the broader implications of these findings that the race to the bottom is leading towards convergence in lower-income economies? In other words, are all developing nations advancing towards the adoption of the "lowest common denominator" – the "neoliberal bottom" – in welfare provisions for their citizens, emphasizing minimal social welfare protections and deregulation, and investing only in those social policies that complement markets (e.g. education)?[1] In fact, have all the key elements of welfare provision in developing countries been captured by just the three commonly emphasized programs in the broader welfare literature: social security, education, and health? Finally, is it fair to say that, as markets expand, the poor continue to be neglected in *all* developing countries?

Until this point, we have forced broad generalizations, perpetuating a common assumption in the literature that the political economies of

[1] See Mishra (1999) for further descriptions of the neoliberal welfare policies currently encouraged in developing countries.

developing countries are more or less homogeneous. This chapter seeks to evaluate this assumption critically and answer the above questions by initiating a more detailed analysis of developing countries' distribution regimes. It will do this through a multifaceted examination of the content or institutional structures of the LDC "welfare states," moving away from evaluating the race to the bottom solely in terms of expenditures and cutbacks. Identifying welfare states (which I also refer to as "distribution" or "welfare regimes") is important to highlight the range of social policies, schemes, and distribution-related institutions that are systematically linked to the state's larger role in "organizing and managing the economy" (Esping-Anderson, 1990: 2). Esping-Andersen argues that conceptualizing welfare states solely in terms of their expenditures can misrepresent their salient characteristics and how these fit into the broader workings of a country's political economy.

Surprisingly, existing scholarship overlooks the prospect of varieties of welfare regimes in the developing world. In direct contrast, over the last decade and a half the identification of set constellations of distribution regimes in the OECD countries has become key to the abandonment of the RTB hypothesis and concerns about convergence in favor of *systematic divergence* (Esping-Andersen, 1990; Huber and Stephens, 2001; Kitschelt *et al.*, 1999).[2] This same possibility – systematic divergence in distribution regimes – has never been explored in developing countries however. Whereas it is now commonplace in the OECD literature to refer to the theoretical and institutional content of welfare states rather than focusing on spending alone, the limited number of studies on LDC welfare schemes have focused mostly on the level of social spending, and have altogether neglected any consideration of nationally negotiated social pacts. Significantly, the persistence of systematic divergence (i.e. distinct distribution regimes) in less developed nations well into twenty-first-century globalization would suggest that the domestic structures and institutions of developing nations are not likely to erode easily in the near future, as is hinted by proponents of the race to the bottom hypothesis.

---

[2] As explained later, I derive three hypotheses from the existing literature. "Systematic divergence" suggests that differences between welfare states in the universe of cases are characterized by a particular order and logic, and not random. "Extreme divergence" implies that each country has a welfare state that responds only to local needs and shares little similarities with other nations. "Convergence" lies at the other extreme, describing a situation in which all welfare states are similar to one another. Recall that the RTB hypothesis predicts that welfare states will tend towards convergence, or institutional and policy changes akin to the (neo)liberal welfare model.

Building on Esping-Andersen (1990), this chapter identifies systematic divergence, or the existence of two ideal types of welfare states, in the developing world. Efforts are primarily directed either towards promoting the market dependence of citizens (a *productive* welfare state) or protecting select individuals from the market (a *protective* welfare state). Cluster analysis reveals a third group with elements of both: the weak dual welfare state. One of the most striking discoveries is that none of the classic LDC welfare regimes has been geared towards protecting the most vulnerable strata of the population, shedding greater light on the findings in chapter 3. Existing welfare states in the developing world tend to favor the middle class, or those who are capable of participating in markets (productive welfare state) and the relatively small percentage of the population employed in the formal sector (protective welfare state).

This chapter evaluates institutional convergence by using other developing countries as a comparative reference point. Data limitations prohibit the observation of convergence over time.[3] This task is left to the case studies. In the following chapters, case studies allow a more detailed investigation into the questions if and how distribution regimes are changing in response to globalization. The evidence thus far suggests, despite evidence of a race to the bottom in the developing country welfare regimes, that these nations are *not* moving towards the universal adoption of neoliberal welfare institutions, and the situation of welfare protections for the poor remains more or less as it was before globalization.

The structure of this chapter is as follows. In the next section, I discuss the shortcomings of the existing comparative political economy and international political economy literatures in recognizing the prospects for systematic divergence in developing countries. Section 4.2 lays out the logic supporting systematic variations in welfare regimes. Section 4.3 uses cluster analysis to provide a statistical test of the proposed typology of welfare regimes. Section 4.4 suggests a causal story behind the cluster results. The final section discusses the implications, caveats, and next steps.

4.1   Welfare states in developing countries? The existing literature

Discussions of the race to the bottom and its consequences are hollow if we do not know what social welfare arrangements have existed to protect

---

[3] Indeed, this is how studies questioning convergence and systematic divergence in the industrialized nations were initiated, and critical similarities and differences between developed countries unveiled (Brickman, Jasanoff, and Ilgen, 1985; Esping-Andersen, 1990; Hall and Soskice, 2001).

the most vulnerable in the first place. Surprisingly, scholars have paid very little attention to the question of the "LDC welfare state" and its institutional contents.[4] IPE scholars imply that a race to the bottom in a globalizing economy ensures significant similarities between the political economies of the many developing nations, and the existence of some sort of "LDC welfare state" is implicitly assumed (Avelino, Brown, and Hunter, 2005; Cerny, 1995; Rudra, 2002; Garrett, 2001; Wibbels, 2006). Since developing countries face similar economic challenges (e.g. demand for capital, large pools of surplus labor), they are expected to converge on neoliberal welfare policies for the purposes of attracting capital and promoting exports.

The negative correlation between expanding markets and social spending in less developed countries confirms this hypothesis (Wibbels, 2006; Rudra, 2002; Garrett, 2000). By focusing on social spending per se, however, IPE scholars presuppose the existence of the developing country welfare state without investigating its particulars. With little sense of the salient characteristics, it is unclear how or why less social spending is necessarily associated with an embrace of market-friendly neoliberal policies. Leaders may very well engage in low (or decreasing) social spending while promoting "illiberal" welfare measures, such as public employment or labor market protections.[5] The convergence question thus remains unresolved.

The gross lack of efforts to investigate institutional commonalities among the LDCs may, perhaps, have its roots in CPE convergence debates that for decades focused only on developed nations. Convergence is defined as "the tendency of societies to grow more alike, to develop similarities in structures, processes and performances" (Kerr, 1983: 3). From the 1960s until the early 1990s scholars believed that only post-industrial societies could experience convergence, since (successful) industrialization requires a particular arrangement of social and economic forces.[6] The inference was that developing countries were marked by "extreme divergence." In other words, developing nations had to be vastly

---

[4] The book by Gough et al. (2004) is one important exception in the discussion of LDC welfare regimes. They do not focus on locating their typology within the traditional political economy debates discussed in this analysis, however, and they introduce an impressive list of descriptive factors that are difficult to operationalize across all cases (e.g. insecurity). Additionally, Kurtz (2002) presents a very interesting analysis of welfare regimes in Chile and Mexico.

[5] Note that reductions in public employment and labor market deregulation are basic components of the structural adjustment programs (i.e. neoliberal reforms) advocated by the IMF and World Bank.

[6] These analyses follow from stagist or modernization theories of the 1960s.

different from one another because they were still in the early stages of economic development.[7]

Consequently, in contradistinction to the IPE literature, the early CPE discussions of convergence in OECD nations advanced two impressions of developing political economies: (1) the types are endless; and (2) welfare states are precluded because of low economic development. The leveling forces of industrialization are hypothesized to produce convergence in OECD social structures and policies – e.g. pluralistic decision-making, the ability of the state to extract resources, a preponderance of committed industrial workers, etc. (for examples, see Form and Bae, 1988, and Kerr et al., 1964). The logic implies that, if nations with high standards of living exist in a homogeneous world, then countries with low standards of living must live in a vastly heterogeneous one. The existence of welfare states is also seen as one of the by-products of industrialization. Only nations at high levels of economic development can form a welfare regime (Wilensky, 1975; Cutright, 1965). Plausible as these arguments may be, CPE scholars have not tested them as they apply to the developing world, and IPE scholars take an opposing position.

Ultimately, the problem in both camps is that the systematic divergence hypothesis has simply not been explored in developing countries. The discovery of distinct patterns of distribution regimes has more or less put to rest expectations of convergence in the developed nations but left open the question as applied to developing countries. Nonetheless, these advancements in the OECD literature hold important lessons for the developing world, as is often the case. First, studies indicating systematic divergence in the developed nations suggest that the level of development does not necessarily predetermine the configuration of national political economies. Both Esping-Andersen (1990) and Hall and Soskice (2001) reveal that national political economies are what determine economic performance and social well-being, and not the reverse. Second, the detection of either distinct patterns of distribution regimes *or* production regimes can confirm the systematic divergence hypothesis. Finally, as Esping-Andersen (1990) demonstrates, the theoretical substance of welfare states is of import to political economy, along with the level of expenditures.

---

[7] The literature on strong and developmental states serves as an exception to the assumption of extreme divergence among developing countries. The problem, however, is that this literature effectively depicts the political economies of a select few northeastern Asian countries; by default, the rest of the developing world falls into a single residual category defined by the absence of some basic characteristics essential for growth. In other words, in this literature, the majority of LDCs are identified on the basis of what political institutions they do *not* have rather than those they do have.

Resolving the convergence debate in developing countries has significant implications for policy and politics, particularly given trends in market integration. If early CPE views are indeed correct, and extreme divergence prevails, the policy decisions of developing world governments are without any (extraterritorial) bounds.[8] This would impose strong limitations on researchers and policy-makers committed to encouraging development in lower-income countries. Exemplars of history, the missions of IFIs, and generalized policy prescriptions lose persuasion in favor of "wait and see." The opposite occurs if IPE scholars are correct about RTB effects and convergence does exist, suggesting that domestic structures and processes are meaningless, and policy responds primarily to international economics. If systematic divergence characterizes the developing world, however, policy-makers are responsive to local needs and politics, as well as some transnational forces, such as survival in a global economy.

4.2   Contemplating systematic divergence in LDCs: patterns of welfare regimes

4.2.1   Questioning CPE convergence: why LDCs are likely to have welfare states

The analysis in this chapter challenges the contention of comparative political economy convergence scholars that welfare states are necessarily a post-industrial phenomenon. The historical experience of the OECD nations coupled with the specific challenges of contemporary globalization have made it impossible for governments in the developing world to ignore *embedded liberalism*, or calls to maintain social stability alongside market expansion (see Ruggie, 1982, 1994). The repercussions of nineteenth-century globalization, which focused on using state intervention to maintain "market-driven equilibria" instead of social protections, are well known: domestic unrest, economic breakdown, and inter-state rivalries, leading ultimately to World War I (Polanyi, 1944).[9] Largely in reaction to this experience, governments of OECD nations in

---

[8] Recall that proponents of the convergence hypothesis in the CPE literature suggest that high levels of economic development provide the primary context to which policy-makers respond. This is "extraterritorial" in the sense that decision-making in the OECD countries is being driven by similar forces and thereby transcends national boundaries. By inference, then, low levels of economic development provide no specific context for policy-makers to respond to.

[9] Examples of nineteenth-century state intervention are tariffs, access to capital, and encouragement of large-scale industries (Gerschenkron, 1962; Bairoch, 1993).

the period after World War II formalized their welfare regimes for the purposes of social welfare and stability (i.e. twentieth-century globalization).[10] It is therefore plausible, as Collier and Messick (1975) show, that the successful workings of welfare systems in advanced economies provide important precedents for modern developing countries.[11] In contrast, when today's advanced economies first embarked on the journey to industrialization, no real precedents for a welfare state existed.

Globalization since World War II has been accompanied by new challenges, particularly for late entrants to the international market, rendering the economic and political costs of ignoring embedded liberalism very high. First, the "magnitude, complexity, and speed" of today's global financial, commodity, and service market operations carry risks and uncertainties to citizens of *all* nations.[12] Compared to the advanced economies, LDCs are in a position of "maximum uncertainty," since only a few of them can actually influence the markets in which they trade and invest (Waterbury, 1999). Second, social reactions to the market are a common thread in both developed and developing countries. This is evidenced in developing countries by the large number of labor and capital strikes in response to the adoption of neoliberal policies. Third, although labor as a class is not strong and suffers from collective action problems, as the findings in chapter 2 indicate, pockets of labor groups can and do affect social policies. Fourth, the relatively recent spread of democracy and its link to embedded liberalism should not be underestimated. The expansion of the right to vote puts all those negatively affected by globalization in a better position to insist that international market expansion be moderated by the pursuit of other objectives.

To summarize, nineteenth-century-style state interventionism in the current era is just as unlikely in the developing world as it is in the developed nations. The contention that embedded liberalism is common practice among developing economies casts doubt on CPE predictions regarding (the lack of) LDC welfare states and extreme divergence. The first part of the IPE convergence argument seems plausible, however: challenges to growth in a global economy are likely to affect domestic social policy decisions. How convincing, though, is their reasoning that international

---

[10] Despite the growing mobility of capital and the collapse of the Bretton Woods arrangements in the early 1970s, which led to pressures on governments to revert to nineteenth-century-style state interventionism, embedded liberalism has been maintained. See Pitruzzello, 2004, for an interesting discussion of the differences between nineteenth- and twentieth-century globalization.

[11] I am grateful to Benjamin Cohen for emphasizing this point.

[12] See Keohane and Nye's (2000) discussion of what is (and is not) new about contemporary globalization.

market pressures ultimately force the universal acceptance of market-friendly social policies? While some combination of markets and domestic interventionism for social welfare has been common to all countries since World War II, the different historical, economic, and political realities of developing countries suggest not only that their national social systems will differ from the developed countries, but also that they will systematically vary from one another as well. This investigation rests on the premise that LDCs maintain some form of capitalist market economy. In all the countries in the sample, private enterprise exists, and the market remains the principal means of distribution.

4.2.2   Questioning IPE convergence: twentieth-century globalization and different LDC welfare regimes

4.2.2.1 Emphasis on commodification The capacity to "commodify" is likely to be the key factor differentiating developing country welfare states. This refers to the degree to which government-backed social policies ensure that the majority of people depend on wage labor, with wage levels largely determined by market forces (see Esping-Andersen, 1990). Commodification in this sense does *not* apply to the developed world, since the workforce is already "proletarianized."[13] Advanced welfare states in the post-war era have instead focused on counterbalancing proletarianization with "decommodification," or permitting people to make their living independent of pure market forces (Esping-Andersen, 1990).

Esping-Andersen (1990: 2) argues that the first step in conceptualizing the welfare state involves locating the primary source of tension that gave rise to its particular political economy, or to the "state's larger role in managing and organizing the economy." In the early European experience, proletarianization was the major source of conflict (Esping-Andersen, 1990; Koo, 1990). Concerns about the *absence* of proletarianization, however, particularly in the post-war era, have been the focus of LDC political economies (Koo, 1990).[14] This is chiefly because the progressive shift of the labor force from primary agricultural activities to secondary manufacture and tertiary commerce and services has not

---

[13] The difference between commodification and proletarianization is that the former refers to the process while the latter refers to the *successful* dependence of the majority of the workforce on (formal) wage labor for survival. OECD welfare states do not focus on commodification, since these economies have shifted emphasis from industrial production to services.

[14] As noted in the introduction, this assumption tends not to apply to personalistic dictatorships.

occurred as it did in Europe.[15] At issue, then, is not the elimination of *internal* "class, inequality, and privilege," as it has been in the OECD nations (Esping-Andersen, 1990), but, rather, minimizing *external* divisions between the rich and poor economies by expanding wage labor and "catching up" with the industrialized nations.

Significantly, business as well as labor is dependent upon welfare states that focus on commodification. Proletarianization in the current era arguably requires somewhat greater state intervention. The demand for skilled labor has increased, and a minimal level of education is often a prerequisite for entering today's markets (Blunch and Verner, 2000; Tendler, 2003). Wood (1994) and Wood and Ridao-Cano (1996), for example, find that, even in basic manufacturing sectors, workers in LDCs are generally low-skilled (not unskilled). This is in direct contrast to the experiences of early industrializers, where private entrepreneurs needed much less state intervention to begin production (Gerschenkron, 1962). In Europe, an actual "deskilling" of the workforce occurred during early industrialization, and literacy rates declined (Stone, 1969; Nicholas and Nicholas, 1992; Sanderson, 1972).[16] Households, churches, and Sunday schools, rather than the state, provided primary education (Nicholas and Nicholas, 1992).[17] According to the evidence presented by Goldin and Katz (1998), the complementarity between skill and technology did not begin until as late as the twentieth century.[18]

4.2.2.2 Point of divergence Despite the intense need for governments in the developing world to focus on expanding wage labor, some countries in the post-war era have placed substantially greater priority on decommodification *prior to* full-scale commodification efforts. First, the latter is politically much more difficult to achieve in some countries because of the mistrust that emerged towards international markets in the 1930s.

---

[15] See the data presented by Erickson and Peppe (1976), which confirm this trend in OECD countries. See Browning and Roberts (1990) for an alternative argument. In most LDCs, secondary-sector employment remains limited, while the tertiary sector, distinguished by large numbers of informal-sector workers, has been forced to absorb much of the rural surplus (Koo, 1990; Evans and Timberlake, 1980; Erickson and Peppe, 1976).

[16] The term "deskilling" refers to the replacement of skilled workers by a large class of unskilled, sub-literate factory operatives. See Nicholas and Nicholas (1992).

[17] Some argue that, because of the laissez-faire tradition, states hesitated to intervene in education. Initiatives to do so began in the late nineteenth century (Kiesling, 1983). To give one important example, the first real non-private school in England was introduced as late as 1944 with the 1944 Education Act. This permitted local authorities to establish and maintain both primary and secondary schools (Morrish, 1970: 83).

[18] Goldin and Katz (1998: 694) describe technology–skill complementarity as when "skilled or more educated labor is more complementary with new technology or physical capital than is unskilled or less educated labor."

Colonial interference and declining terms of trade for agricultural exports in that decade hampered the complementarity (real or perceived) between international market participation and the rapid expansion of formal wage labor, at least in the early stages. Second, recall that precedents set by the experiences of the OECD nations matter (Collier and Messick, 1975); pressures on all governments to provide some degree of decommodification intensified in the post-war period. Finally, LDC labor is more dependent on a "decommodifying" welfare state than its early European counterparts. The former relies on the state to represent its needs, because workers suffer from both persistent collective action problems (see Bellin, 2000) and the prolonged absence of a guaranteed minimum income.[19] Developing states are inclined to intervene to provide this minimum income (through public works projects, public employment, labor market protections, etc.), since the transformation of surplus labor into formal wage labor has been occurring through the market process at an extremely slow rate.[20]

In sum, it is feasible that some developing countries prioritize independence from the market even *before* full-scale proletarianization has been achieved (i.e. a protective welfare state). If this is the case, not all nations will have "productive welfare states" that direct welfare efforts primarily towards encouraging wage labor. The implication is that the relationship between commodification and decommodification in developing countries may not be linear, as it has been in the post-industrial economies (see figure 4.1).

4.2.3   Delineating different welfare regimes in developing countries

It is important to emphasize that a blueprint for a developing world welfare state that promotes either commodification or decommodification per se never existed. In the post-war era, referring back to the "primary tension that drives political economies," LDC welfare states took qualitatively different forms depending on *how* governments chose

---

[19] For many of the early industrializers, agriculture played a strong role in industrialization, while in the LDCs, as Bates (1981) argues, the popular strategy of rapid industrialization often came at a cost to the efficiency of the agricultural sector. The end result is a large surplus labor economy in which the absorption rate of labor is persistently low. This is not to deny that much of Europe had a large surplus (rural) population when welfare policies were first adopted. As Pandit and Casetti (1989) have shown, however, the level and rate of absorption of labor into the manufacturing sector was considerably slower in the developing world than in the now developed countries. This was further exacerbated by trends in the twentieth century towards greater mechanization, whereas the early industrialization experience was more labor-intensive (Baer and Herve, 1966).

[20] These government efforts are decommodifying in the sense that workers become less dependent on the market.

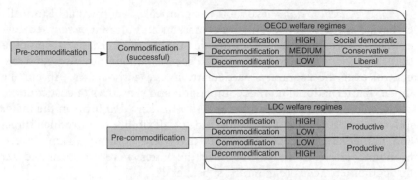

Figure 4.1 The era of embedded liberalism: welfare states in developed and developing countries

Source: The OECD decommodification rankings (low, medium, high) are from Esping-Andersen (1990: 52).

to address the lack of proletarianization and pursue their primary objective of creating a modern industrial order. Government intervention in the economy was guided by one of two goals: making firms internationally competitive, or insulating firms from international competition.[21] Why political leaders pursued one strategy over another is based on a whole host of factors, and is explored elsewhere (see Waterbury, 1999).[22] Central to this investigation is the fact that ruling elites pursued social benefits compatible with the chosen development strategy, and key to this compatibility was the co-optation of potentially powerful groups.[23] None of the elements of welfare state regimes were designed with poverty alleviation in mind.

[21] While state intervention could be directed towards both goals, historically LDCs have tended to advance in one area while retreating in the other. See statist literature for further arguments that government representatives are not simply a passive registrar of interests, implementing goals for what they perceive as the beneficial interests of society (e.g. Evans, Rusechemeyer, and Skocpol, 1985). It could be argued that governments had more policy-making autonomy during the initial stages of industrialization, given the disproportional reliance of capital and labor on the state.

[22] One possible objection is that the causal arrows could be reversed, and high levels of human capital (commodification) influenced LDCs to be more accepting of international market participation. While there might be some merit to this claim, a relatively highly educated workforce was no guarantee that LDCs would pursue outward-oriented strategy. Argentina and Uruguay, for example, had the highest rates of literacy (91 percent) in the developing world in the 1960s; they pursued the alternative strategy, however, and rejected an emphasis upon international market participation.

[23] This was feasible as the planned nature of industrialization meant that governments more or less knew who would be the winners. Even in the export-oriented countries (e.g. Taiwan, South Korea), governments "led" the markets and "picked" the winners (see, for example, Wade, 1990).

Protective welfare states have roots in a political economy that historically eschewed emphasis on international markets and ultimately focused government efforts on insulating domestic firms from international competition. This focus allowed politicians to exercise maximum discretion and control over the economy, particularly in the early stages. Absent the threat of international market competition and pressures of cost containment, rulers could provide allowances to workers *and* firms in the major industrializing sectors. Politicians had the flexibility to introduce direct and immediate benefits to workers that were contrary to employers' economic interests, mostly because the latter were compensated for through other means (e.g. tariffs, subsidies).

As a consequence, protective welfare states are a curious fusion of elements of socialism and conservatism. Like the OECD social democratic model, protective welfare states have a strong distrust of markets. Both regime types claim to detest the dehumanizing effects of unfettered capitalism. Commonalities with the statist variant of the conservative model also exist, particularly with its emphasis on the preservation of authority (see Huber, 1996). The conservative forces in protective welfare states fear that international markets can destroy their power and privilege.[24] Leaders thus prefer social rights that simultaneously promote loyalty to the state and create divisions among social groups (labor and business).[25] Full-scale commodification would certainly make it difficult for the state to be *the* most dominant factor in the expanding international economy.

At the same time, protective welfare states in developing countries are distinct from both the social democratic and conservative welfare models in that policies and strategies directed specifically towards reducing poverty are negligible. The pivotal factor is that emphasis on decommodification occurs prior to proletarianization and, consequently, social rights are directed towards a small clientele. Welfare policies may not be redistributive and beneficent, even though they are often thought of in this way. Titmuss (1965: 27) long ago stated that "when we use the term social policy we must not [...] automatically react by investing it with a halo of altruism, concern for others, concern about equality and so on." Before proletarianization occurs, making rights conditional upon labor market

---

[24] See, for example, Diamond's (1987) discussion on class formation in post-colonial states. See also Esping-Andersen's (1990: 41) discussion of statism and how it was feared that capitalism would destroy power and privileges.

[25] Schneider (2004: 37) argues that, in late-industrializing nations, state intervention in labor markets, wages, unions, and strikes actually hinders the development of lasting employer organizations. Rather than organizing to deal directly with labor, businesses focus more on influencing state policies concerning labor.

attachment, some work performance and actuarialism results in welfare benefits for only a small, privileged stratum.[26] This is a sharp departure from the OECD social democratic and conservative welfare states, in which emphasis on universalism and earnings-related contributions, respectively, has guaranteed the relatively poor access to government-supported social protections (see Korpi and Palme, 1998).[27]

Productive welfare states, in contrast to protective welfare states, prioritize commodification, and evolved initially from systems that actively encouraged participation in export markets. The goal of encouraging the international competitiveness of domestic firms creates an emphasis on cost containment and requires governments to surrender some control over the economy.[28] The range of social policies is then much more limited, as rulers are constrained from pursuing worker benefits that are independent of employer interests. In other words, the policies that prevail are those that can successfully serve the interests of workers and capital simultaneously.

In this respect, productive welfare states share certain elements with the liberal model. In contrast to its counterpart, this regime type embraces some of the nineteenth-century liberal enthusiasm for the market and self-reliance. The particular property of the liberal paradigm that ultimately comes to distinguish the productive welfare state is the emphasis upon strengthening the commodity status of labor in a globalizing economy. At the same time, the fundamental point of departure from the liberal model is that the state–market relationship is complementary rather than adversarial. Considerable public intervention aims to enhance international market participation. Social policies are circumscribed by this goal and promote worker loyalty without hindering business activity.

---

[26] See Esping-Andersen's (1990: 48) discussion on conditions for entitlements. "Actuarialism" refers to "the idea that the individual has a personal entitlement of a contractual nature."

[27] In an analysis of eighteen OECD countries, Korpi and Palme (1998) find that earnings-related benefits and "encompassing" social insurance institutions most effectively reduce inequality and poverty. Encompassing institutions constitute universal programs covering all citizens and are combined with earnings-related benefits for the economically active population. According to Korpi and Palme, the encompassing model is found primarily in the social democratic welfare states. These countries have the lowest poverty and inequality rates. The corporatist model ranks second (between social democratic welfare states and liberal welfare states) in the alleviation of poverty and inequality. Social programs in the corporatist model are directed towards the economically active population. Because these nations are successfully commodified, however, unlike the LDCs, most individuals with low incomes are part of the (formal) economically active population and, thereby, are eligible for benefits and protections.

[28] For example, even if governments intervene in the setting of prices and wages, their decisions will be constrained by considerations of international market performance.

In contrast, the OECD nations were never driven to be "productive welfare states" per se, because the commodification process was much more gradual, spanning over two centuries, and required rather less state intervention.[29]

The tension in this model lies in reconciling the push for dependence on wage labor with demands for emancipation from the market. As argued earlier, an excessive focus on commodification puts system survival at stake (Polanyi, 1944). Furthermore, although labor market dualism will be less prominent given government measures to provide capital with an abundance of productive workers, a clear class hierarchy still exists. Efforts to keep pace with an already industrialized international economy result in the rapid, simultaneous expansion of white-collar and blue-collar work (see Koo, 1990). The ongoing controversy then is the extent to which decommodification can be selectively employed to ensure system longevity. Governments of productive welfare states can attempt to address this problem through repression or by offering some minimum level of social benefits, usually for white-collar workers. While it is feasible that a protective welfare state could eventually evolve into a productive welfare state, *the reverse is unlikely to occur.*[30]

The productive welfare state shares one common element with the protective welfare state: policies that eschew the poor. Government efforts in productive welfare states are geared towards those who can participate in the market. As a consequence, non-participants, such as the chronically unemployed, disabled, or sick, receive somewhat fewer state resources. In a manner similar to that of the liberal welfare state, work ethic norms are encouraged rather than welfare, which is frequently stigmatized. The provision of welfare for the poor is even more inadequate in productive welfare states, since the targeted or means-tested programs that are the primary poverty alleviation strategies in liberal welfare states are much less available.[31] Targeting options in developing countries are expensive, because of the administration costs of identifying, reaching, and monitoring the target population (see Grosh, 1994).

---

[29] Recall that proletarianization was supported initially by private and non-governmental institutions. Much of the OECD welfare states literature takes commodificaton as a given, and focuses instead on government attention to developing a *highly* skilled workforce and training systems. See, for example, Hall and Soskice (2001).

[30] In other words, if productive welfare states are successful, they cannot become "protective," since the latter emphasize decommodification *before* commodification.

[31] Targeted or means-tested programs are aimed at recipients who fall below a nationally mandated income level or property limit. Korpi and Palme (1998) reveal that liberal welfare states that apply targeting as the means to reduce poverty are the least successful at reducing poverty. The social democratic and corporatist welfare states place less priority on means-tested programs.

4.2.4   Cluster analysis: testing contrasting hypotheses

Do developing countries display convergence or extreme divergence? Or, as this chapter posits, are they characterized by systematic divergence? Is it possible to discern a distinct statistical pattern that lends support to the idea that different welfare models in the developing world do exist and that they correspond to the protective/productive typology outlined above?

Cluster analysis is a quantitative method that can help discriminate between the above hypotheses. By facilitating the classification of objects into relatively homogeneous groups, this method can determine the number of LDC distribution regimes, if any. Each group identified by cluster analysis is as internally homogeneous as possible, but as distinct as possible from all other groups. The technique is applied to find similarities between units under classification, rather than interrelationships between variables (factor analysis). The objective is to group n units into r clusters, where r is much smaller than n (Lewis-Beck, Bryman, and Liao, 2004). Cluster analysis is one of the most popular means of constructing a typology.[32] Although it originated in psychology and anthropology, it has now become a valuable tool in biology, geography, political science, sociology, economics, and mathematics.[33]

To begin the search for natural groupings in the data, a clustering method must be selected. Partitioning, or non-hierarchical, methods do not apply here, since the number of clusters is not known a priori. Instead, I apply the hierarchical agglomerative linkage method, which considers each observation as a separate group. Next, the agglomerative algorithm considers $N(N-1)/2$ possible fusions of observations to find and combine the closest two groups. This process repeats itself until all observations belong to a single group, and a hierarchy of clusters is created. To begin this procedure, however, computation of a similarity or distance matrix between the entities is required. I apply the most common representation of distance, the Euclidean distance (Aldenderfer and Blashfield, 1984; Everitt, 1974) to calculate the distance between the units. To give a simple

---

[32] In addition to cluster analysis, the Q-sort technique is used by social scientists to develop classification schemes. This technique is unworkable, however, if the number of cases that need to be classified (thirty-two) exceeds the number of variables (ten) used for the analysis. Furthermore, the main purpose of Q-methodology is to provide the researcher quantitative means for examining *human subjectivity* (McKeown and Thomas, 1988). If accounting for self-reference is important to the researcher then the Q-method is best applied in place of cluster analysis (see Thomas and Watson, 2002).

[33] For example, cluster analysis has been used to refine diagnostic categories in psychiatry, detect similarities in artifacts by archaeologists, identify models of development in political science, and establish religiosity scales in sociology.

example, if two cases are identical, then the Euclidean distance between them will be zero. The final product is a tree-like representation of the data, or dendrogram, which illustrates the successful fusion of countries. It is completed only when all the countries are in one group.

Several agglomerative linkage methods exist in cluster analysis. The most common are single linkage, complete linkage, average linkage and Ward's method. These represent different mathematical procedures to calculate the distance between clusters. Following standard practice in the social sciences, and given the disadvantages of single and complete linkage (see Panel on Discriminant Analysis, Classification, and Clustering, 1989), Ward's method is used here and the weighted average linkage method is then applied as a robustness check.[34] Ward's method is designed to optimize the minimum variance within clusters, and works by joining groups that result in the lowest increase in the error sum of squares (Ward, 1963; Aldenderfer and Blashfield, 1984). At each stage, after the union of every possible pair of clusters is considered, the method fuses the two clusters whose increase in the total within-cluster error sum of squares is minimal. Several studies have observed that, in comparison to the above-mentioned alternatives, Ward's method ranks first in the recovery of true clusters (Blashfield, 1976; Tidmore and Turner, 1983).

Cluster analysis will confirm the systematic divergence hypothesis if it reveals a distinct number of welfare regimes corresponding to the productive/protective dichotomy. If early comparative political economy speculations of extreme divergence are correct, however, then cluster analysis will demonstrate no identifiable pattern. The number of clusters will be large, far outnumbering the two patterns predicted in this analysis. Finally, the third possibility, international political economy's predictions of convergence, will be confirmed if all developing nations fall into one cluster.

At this point, however, the IPE literature lends itself to significant ambiguity. Are less developed countries likely to converge upon productive or protective welfare states? Recall that the central process underlying convergence tendencies is the challenge of growth in a global economy. On the one hand, most IPE scholars implicitly assume that international market pressures will drive developing nations towards embracing social policies most similar to OECD liberal welfare states, which would result in LDC productive welfare states.[35] At the same time, however, as this

---

[34] I use the weighted average linkage method so that, if some of the clusters are small, the results will not be biased. This method gives equal weight to groups with small numbers of observations.

[35] Proponents of neoliberalism have long been encouraging LDCs to redirect public expenditure priorities towards fields offering high economic returns *and* the potential to improve income distribution, such as primary health care, and primary education.

analysis points out, since the 1930s many developing countries have found that insulating themselves from international markets has been the best way to respond to the challenges of growth in the post-war era. Consequently, it is feasible that many less developed countries may instead have evolved into protective welfare states.

4.2.4.1 Operationalizing concepts The primary goal is to assess welfare priorities in the developing world and see whether they follow the predicted pattern of privileging commodification or decommodificaton.[36] Simply applying the most common method – examining government budget priorities – is insufficient here, for three reasons. First, as Esping-Andersen (1990: 19) explains, "Expenditures are epiphenomenal to the theoretical substance of welfare states." Second, as the World Bank (1990) and the ILO (see Figueiredo and Shaheed, 1995) have pointed out, governments of developing countries often employ less resource-intensive means to protect their workers, such as labor market policies and public employment.[37] Third, it is impossible to know whether spending serves the desired goals or clientelistic needs (see Nelson, 1999; World Bank, 2003b). This issue is particularly salient in evaluating goals for commodification. If government spending is high, but the allocated resources are being misused and have little effect on improving the health and education of (potential) workers, then the country in question cannot be a productive welfare state.

The difficulty here is the dearth and questionable reliability of data that can capture such occurrences across the developing world. One solution, albeit imperfect, is to include a combination of policy, spending, and outcome variables.[38] The other alternative is to wait for more effective institutions to evolve or, relatedly, for more reliable data to become available. In such a case, the hazard is that policy-makers and citizens of LDCs are likely to face the consequences of a vicious cycle involving insufficient data, the neglect of important research, and the persistence of weak, ineffective institutions. Put simply, more effective welfare institutions may be dependent upon analyses such as this one, which attempt to make use of available data.

---

[36] Significantly, the concept of decommodification applied in this analysis is necessarily broader than Esping-Andersen's (1990) interpretation. For critiques of Esping-Andersen, see Lewis (1997), Gal (2004), and Room (2000).

[37] Arguably, while these policies command fewer government resources, they may ultimately be more expensive for the larger society in LDCs.

[38] How the inclusion of outcome variables helps the data problem is explained in more detail below.

Exercising the first option, I build on the insights of the most renowned experts of welfare in both developed and developing countries – Esping-Andersen (1990) and Dreze and Sen (1989), respectively – to determine the most appropriate indicators of developing world welfare states.[39] Spending and outcome variables are used to capture extensive public efforts aimed directly at expanding the basic capabilities of the population to suit wage labor markets. An emphasis on decommodification is detected by pervasive policies and government spending geared towards protecting individuals from the risks and uncertainties of the market. Protective welfare policies are then more commonly associated with (but not limited to) social-insurance-type variables. According to Esping-Andersen (1990: 22), decommodification ultimately "strengthens the worker and weakens the absolute authority of the employer." While it is reasonable to expect some overlap between "productive" and "protective" variables in practice, the division is driven by two very different logics and produces distinct socio-political outcomes (Dreze and Sen, 1989; Esping-Andersen, 1990).[40] See appendix I for more detailed explanations of the data sources and variables discussed below.

4.2.4.2 Variables representing productive welfare efforts Degrees of commodification are determined by the level of public investment in primary and secondary education, and basic health care, as well as literacy rates, rates of infant mortality, and the percentage of infants vaccinated against diphtheria, pertussis, and tetanus (DPT).[41] In the cluster analysis, I observe government expenditures on education and health as a proportion of the total public budget, since the aim here is to capture the extent of *government commitment* (see Rudra and Haggard, 2005). To put this in perspective, if education spending, for example, is measured instead as a percentage of GDP, countries such as South Korea and Singapore fall in the same percentile range as developing countries such as Mali, Malawi, and Liberia. All the same,

---

[39] The productive/protective dichotomy builds on Dreze and Sen's (1989: 16) distinction between "promotion" and "protection." In particular, Dreze and Sen's choice of promotion variables, or resources devoted to improving primary education and health, are used to determine "commodifying" or productive welfare states. The "decommodification" concept is drawn mainly from Esping-Andersen (1990). His argument that decommodification ultimately ensures that human fate is not directed by the laws of the market is central to the selection of "protective" variables in LDCs.

[40] For example, some scholars may argue that protective welfare benefits (e.g. pensions, labor protections) make workers more productive in the marketplace. The productive/protective dichotomy deals with ideal types and, in reality, we should expect some overlap, or modal tendencies of population distributions, between the polar alternatives.

[41] Note that immunization against measles is also included and does not affect the cluster groupings (not shown here).

measuring spending relative to the total budget more clearly reveals qualitative differences between LDC welfare states, and unveils a considerable variance between countries. As a compromise, I apply spending as a percentage of GDP and per capita spending as robustness checks.

The outcome variables (literacy, mortality, and immunization rates) help the analysis for two reasons. First, outcome variables reflect past policies. Nations with a legacy of responsiveness to international markets are likely to have pursued market-promoting social policies at an early date. In other words, if developing countries have high "outcomes," it suggests that previous leaders have emphasized commodification. This is particularly relevant since, as previously explained, once an economy has successfully achieved commodification the country cannot thereafter become a protective welfare state. Second, outcome variables can help see beyond the numbers. Public officials might be engaging in high levels of clientelism, using resources for patronage purposes rather than effecting positive outcomes. From this perspective, high levels of spending alongside low outcomes are telling, indicating weak government commitment towards a productive welfare state. Nevertheless, since other factors might determine outcomes in addition to government spending (efforts of non-governmental institutions and organizations, GDP, etc.), I drop all the outcome variables and run the model again as a check. The cluster groupings are almost identical, although, as predicted, the differences between clusters are less obvious *but still statistically significant* (see appendix J).

4.2.4.3 Variables representing protective welfare efforts Five variables capture the extent to which developing country governments aim to decommodify, or protect workers from market risks and uncertainties: the extent of public employment, spending on social security and welfare (pensions, family allowances, unemployment, old age, sickness and disability), housing subsidies, labor market protections, and investment in tertiary education. As a final point, while means-tested poor relief should also be included as a protective welfare mechanism, cross-country comparable data are virtually non-existent.

Public employment is one of the most pervasive methods of market protection in the developing world (see Rodrik, 1997c). In some cases, it provides short-term security in earnings, such as hiring for public work projects, but in the larger number of instances the public sector provides "secure" jobs (Rodrik, 1997c; Gelb, Knight, and Sabot, 1991). As Robinson states:

The permanent status that many, in some cases the majority of, civil service employees enjoy means that apart from dismissal for grave disciplinary reasons they are assured of employment until retirement, providing a degree of protection and privilege not found in the private sector. (Robinson, as quoted in Rodrik, 1997c)

Given that cross-country comparable data on public employment are extremely sparse, the percentage of the government budget that is spent on employee wages and salaries is used to estimate this variable.

Analyzing spending on social security and housing as a means to guard against income risks is common in the broader welfare literature. In developing countries, pensions tend to be the largest component of this spending. They ensure a steady flow of income over a lifetime, regardless of market shocks and uncertainties. Unemployment, family allowances, and sickness protections, though less common in developing countries, provide security in the face of short-term absence from the market. Housing subsidies also help stabilize incomes (Chapman and Austin, 2002; Renaud, 1984). Higher-skilled workers, and especially civil servants, often receive housing as part of their wage package.

Labor market protections are common welfare measures in the developing world that help "guarantee" incomes by placing institutionalized restrictions on firms' hiring and firing decisions (Betcherman, Luinstra, and Ogawa, 2001). Data for such protections, however, are beset with problems (Rama and Artecona, 2002). One reliable, albeit crude, indicator is the ratification of ILO conventions by nations. Enforcement standards are effectively nil, and ratifications do not necessarily translate into policy innovations. Recent research has shown that ratification has a significant effect on labor costs (Rodrik, 1996), however, and can reflect internal political factors such as government preferences or the power of left-wing parties (Brookmann, 2001). It is fair to assume, then, that labor market protections will be relatively low in countries that have ratified a very low number of ILO conventions (e.g. the United States, South Korea, Singapore).[42]

Lastly, the provision of free or heavily subsidized tertiary education when primary- or secondary-level education access is less than universal awards a strong promise of future income security to those who have access to the former (see World Bank, 2002b).[43] Particularly

---

[42] As a robustness check, I also run "labor regulation data" constructed by Botero et al. (2004). The drawback in using this data set is that it focuses on one year, and data are missing for three LDCs from the sample. Excluding the major outliers, the correlation between the ILO data in the sample and Botero et al. is 0.65. The final results differ in that Panama, Paraguay, Greece, Colombia and Thailand fall from cluster 1 (productive) to cluster 2 (dual).

[43] Demographics play an important role in determining levels of public spending on education and social security. Note that, in addition to assessing the different levels of education spending (primary, tertiary) as a percentage of total government expenditures, they are also measured as a percentage of GDP, and spending per student relative to GDP per capita. Although the final cluster results are minimally affected by the alternative

Table 4.1 *Determining the number of clusters by the Duda and Hart (1973) procedure*

	Duda/Hart	
Number of clusters	Je(2)/Je(1)	pseudo-T-squared
1	0.6329	17.4
2	0.5907	12.47
3	0.6622	5.1
4	0.5848	9.94
5	0.4350	7.79
6	0.4675	2.28
7	0.3835	3.21
8	0.6985	3.45
9	0.5853	4.25
10	0.3488	5.6

since high-skilled labor is in relatively high demand yet scarce supply in the majority of developing countries, such workers can secure great advantages in the bargaining process.

4.3   Analysis results

The results of the cluster analysis are shown in tables 4.1–4.3. Because cluster analysis has a low tolerance for missing data, the final sample size is thirty-two countries. This sample is still marked by regional and economic diversity, and thus remains fairly representative of the developing world. Each variable represents data averages for 1990 through 1997 (the latest date for which cross-national data are available for a large number of

specifications, the latter is emphasized since it is the only measure that takes demographics into account. Several countries in Africa and south Asia, for instance, show average levels of spending on primary education. Because these LDCs have the highest growth rates of school-age population, however, the number of children actually benefiting from state assistance is quite small, and the lack of funds is creating an education crisis. Evaluating LDCs on the basis of spending per student provides a more accurate assessment of commitment to primary education. Zambia, Bangladesh, and Malawi are excellent examples. This measure also effectively captures disproportionate spending on small populations of students enrolled in tertiary education. For SS and welfare, however, controlling for number of beneficiaries is more complex, since the data do not tell us the number of aged persons receiving these benefits. In addition, this category is not limited to pensions. Nonetheless, to get a general sense of the impact of elderly demographics, a variable is created by dividing the social security and welfare data by the proportion of persons aged over sixty-five. The results are very similar, with only Panama dropping from cluster 1 to cluster 2.

Table 4.2 *Cluster groupings*

Country	Cluster
Chile	1
Colombia	1
Costa Rica	1
Cyprus	1
Greece	1
Israel	1
Kuwait	1
Malaysia	1
Mauritius	1
Panama	1
Paraguay	1
Singapore	1
South Korea	1
Sri Lanka	1
Thailand	1
Trinidad and Tobago	1
Argentina	2
Brazil	2
Mexico	2
Uruguay	2
Bolivia	3
Dominican Republic	3
Egypt	3
El Salvador	3
India	3
Iran	3
Lesotho	3
Morocco	3
Tunisia	3
Turkey	3
Zambia	3
Zimbabwe	3

Notes: South Korea is included because it did not become a member of the OECD until 1996. Turkey is included because, although a member of the OECD since 1961, it is not a high-income country. Greece is included because it has only recently been classified as a high-income country by the World Bank.

developing countries). Results are analyzed in the following three steps: (1) assessing how many cluster groups exist; (2) determining which countries fall into each cluster; and (3) evaluating the characteristics of each cluster and its member countries to assess whether or not they confirm systematic divergence.

Country	Commodification						Decommodification					
	Immunization	Infant mortality	Literacy	Primary and secondary education spending	Health spending	Country average	Housing spending	ILO conventions	Wages and salaries spending	SS and welfare spending	Tertiary education spending	Country average
Cluster 1 (productive)												
Chile	9	8	8	2	10	7	7	7	3	10	2	6
Colombia	2	6	6	7	9	6	5	8	2	4	3	4
Costa Rica	7	8	8	5	10	8	1	7	10	8	5	6
Cyprus	10	9	9	9	5	8	6	7	6	9	1	6
Greece	4	9	9	3	7	6	3	9	4	8	2	5
Israel	10	10	7	9	6	8	8	6	1	9	4	6
Kuwait	7	9	3	8	3	6	6	3	4	5	9	5
Malaysia	8	8	5	8	4	7	9	3	5	3	8	6
Mauritius	6	7	5	7	8	7	7	4	9	7	9	7
Panama	5	6	7	4	10	6	6	9	9	9	4	7
Paraguay	1	5	7	2	4	4	5	5	9	6	7	6
Singapore	8	10	6	5	5	7	9	5	6	1	5	5
South Korea	5	10	10	6	1	6	4	1	1	5	1	2
Sri Lanka	7	7	6	7	3	6	3	4	3	7	8	5
Thailand	8	5	8	6	8	7	6	2	7	1	3	4
Trinidad and Tobago	6	7	10	3	8	7	10	2	9	7	7	7
Cluster average	*6*	*6*	*8*	*6*	*6*	*7*	*6*	*5*	*5*	*6*	*5*	*5*
Cluster 2 (dual)												
Argentina	3	6	9	6	1	5	3	9	4	10	2	6
Brazil	2	4	5	2	5	4	1	10	1	9	5	5
Mexico	5	5	6	1	2	4	4	10	4	8	3	6
Uruguay	9	7	10	4	4	7	1	10	2	10	3	5
Cluster average	*5*	*6*	*8*	*3*	*3*	*5*	*2*	*10*	*3*	*9*	*3*	*5*
Cluster 3 (protective)												
Bolivia	1	1	4	1	3	2	2	6	7	8	6	6
Dominican Republic	1	3	4	9	9	4	10	4	5	2	1	4
Egypt	4	2	1	8	2	3	8	8	4	4	6	6
El Salvador	3	4	2	1	9	2	5	1	10	3	1	4
India	1	2	1	4	1	2	8	5	1	2	8	5
Iran	10	4	2	3	7	5	9	1	10	5	7	6
Lesotho	3	1	3	10	9	5	5	1	7	1	10	5
Morocco	6	2	1	10	2	4	5	6	8	4	8	6
Tunisia	9	5	1	9	6	4	7	8	8	6	9	7
Turkey	2	3	4	5	3	3	3	5	9	6	5	5
Zambia	4	1	2	2	6	3	2	6	2	1	10	4
Zimbabwe	6	3	5	10	6	6	10	1	8	5	10	7
Cluster average	*4*	*3*	*3*	*5*	*5*	*4*	*6*	*4*	*7*	*4*	*7*	*6*

Notes: The cluster analysis results have been calculated using *wardslinkage* command in Intercooled Stata 8. The stopping rule is Duda and Hart (1973). Averages are rounded to the nearest integer to facilitate comparability. Housing, health, and social security and welfare are ranked according to percentage of total government spending. Education variables are ranked as spending per student (refer to footnote 43). Note that, as explained later in the text, the membership of Panama, Paraguay, and Greece in cluster 1 is not robust.

The first critical step is to determine the number of clusters present in the data. The appropriate number is a question of particular interest, since it can provide support for the ideas of either comparative or international political economy, or for systematic divergence. If, as implied by CPE scholars, no cluster structure is shown then efforts to identify a few broad categories of welfare states among developing countries are meaningless. The distinctions between countries are greater than the similarities between them. At the other extreme, a single cluster would imply that developing countries as a whole are a relatively homogeneous group. The IPE view then prevails, and state intervention to "create a modern industrial order" has had more or less the same welfare consequences in all developing countries.

Over thirty "stopping rules" (procedures to determine the number of clusters in a data set) are applicable in cluster analysis. Fortunately, Milligan and Cooper (1985) have conducted a well-known study to distinguish between them and assess which criteria provide the most valid test for the existence of a cluster. Their experiment suggests that the Duda and Hart (1973) procedure is one of the best stopping rules. The ratio criterion for this procedure is Je(2), which is the sum of squared errors within a cluster when the data are broken into two clusters. Je(1) provides the squared errors when one cluster exists. The three-group solution is most distinct here, since the sum of squared errors (Je(1)) increases substantially in the four-group solution. Duda and Hart Je(2)/Je(1) estimates are presented in table 4.1. The conventional rule for deciding the number of groups is to determine the largest Je(2)/Je(1) value (0.6622) that corresponds to a low pseudo-T-squared value (5.1) that has a higher T-squared value above and below it. The results from this method, surprisingly, indicate that a *three*-group solution is most distinct in this hierarchical cluster analysis, contrary to the expected two ideal regime types.

The next step is to determine which countries are in each cluster. Table 4.2 presents the country members of the three clusters. This pattern reveals that, although region plays a role, it is not a predominant factor in the welfare groupings. While only Latin American countries comprise cluster 2, the members of clusters 1 and 3 represent Africa, the Middle East, east Asia,[44] Latin America, and south Asia. Income effects appear to play a somewhat larger role, although, again, not a decisive one. Cluster 3 contains only low-income and lower middle-income countries. Cluster 1 reveals a more economically diverse set of countries, however, ranging from lower middle-income to high-income LDCs. This finding shows that poorer

---

[44] Indonesia, originally included in cluster 3, has to be dropped from the analysis because the data necessary for robustness checks are missing.

nations can also successfully promote commodification. Similarly, cluster 2 contains both low middle- and high middle-income countries.

The existence of three clusters fundamentally challenges both the extreme divergence and convergence hypotheses. The next logical question is whether the statistical analysis supports systematic divergence. To assess this, the clusters are ranked according to their levels of welfare efforts towards protection and production. Decile data are computed for each welfare variable, and then each cluster (and country) is ranked from one to ten. For example, the first decile is the point with 10 percent of the data below it and 90 percent above it. It is given the lowest score of one. The ninth decile is the point with 90 percent of the data below it, while the score given to values within the top 10 percent is ten. Table 4.3 displays these values. The greatest weight is placed on the cluster averages, since the statistical procedure uses algorithms to differentiate the most homogeneous *groups*. It is noteworthy that differences between deciles tend be quite significant.[45] The average for each country within the cluster is important, but each welfare category contains information that should not be overlooked. See appendix K for a graphical representation of the results (dendrogram).

Focusing on the cluster averages, several patterns emerge. Clusters 1 and 3 appear to favor the productive and protective components of welfare, respectively. Cluster 2, in contrast, favors neither welfare state category. This discovery reveals that some LDC welfare states take dual roles in the post-war economy, raising questions about whether dual welfare state status is transitory. A detailed breakdown of the clusters is given below.

Cluster 1 clearly privileges commodification over decommodification. As would be expected, several of the east Asian economies, as well as some Latin American countries noted for their emphasis on education (e.g. Costa Rica), fall into this category. The average scores for commodification are higher than the average scores for decommodification in most of the member countries. Panama and Paraguay appear to be anomalies, since their scores do not appear to reflect the prioritizing of productive welfare activities. This turns out not to be too surprising, however, for, as we shall see, further robustness checks reveal that these two countries (along with Greece) appear to be sensitive to model specification and fluctuate between clusters 1 and 2.

In cluster 3, empirical evidence for the developing world welfare paradox is highly suggestive: poorer countries, which arguably need

---

[45] For example, LDCs falling in the sixth decile for primary education spend almost 30 percent more per student per capita than do those in the fifth decile.

productive welfare states the most, appear to be expending the least effort towards this goal. Attention to housing and tertiary education seems to feature most prominently in the protective welfare states. The outcome variables are telling. For several developing countries (e.g. Egypt, Lesotho, Morocco), despite their high spending on primary education, literacy rates remain low. This suggests that funds either are being used for clientelistic purposes or are simply incommensurate with the level of need. Health spending also appears to be regressive in relation to outcome variables. On the other hand, several LDCs in this category rank in the top percentiles for protective categories such as wages and salaries and tertiary education.

The smallest group, cluster 2, appears to place emphasis on productive and protective activities, yet average scores for both welfare categories are moderate (i.e. five). This cluster is more appropriately labeled a *weak* dual welfare state, since these countries place more emphasis on the proletarianization process than the protective welfare states, but significantly less than the productive welfare states. In terms of commodification, the difference between cluster 2 and cluster 1 is that health and education are *both* stressed in the latter.[46] Uruguay is an exception; its level of health spending is low relative to cluster 1, however. Brazil's profile is also distinct, in that, although education spending is low and outcome variables are not as high as other members of cluster 2, its literacy rates outrank similar middle-income countries in cluster 3. Most striking is that, on the protective side, cluster 2 ranks in the highest percentile for labor protections (ILOCNV) and social security and welfare. On the other hand, average scores for housing, wages and salaries, and tertiary education spending are considerably lower than in clusters 1 and 3.

The existence of cluster 2 is an important revelation. Based on the theoretical discussion, we can assume that governments of weak dual welfare states in the early post-war period were not completely hostile to international markets. It is certainly possible to be primarily inward-oriented but, at the same time, encourage some export competitiveness. Cluster 2, then, represents a combination of the two ideal regime types: social policies that respond to the demands of capital *and* the needs of labor groups. Consequently, relative to the other two clusters, we might expect heightened political competition for scarce public resources. Partisan politics, for example, may be vibrant in these countries. One optimistic scenario, if partisan politics can successfully steer greater productive welfare efforts, is that they can then offset the tendency towards

---

[46] Notice that, in cluster 1, the spending or outcome variables (or both) in health and education are high.

Table 4.4 *Effects of current welfare regimes on poverty (percent undernourished)*

Independent variable	Coefficient estimates
LDC welfare regime	0.57
(commodification/decommodification)	(0.87)
Democracy	0.18
	(0.70)
GDP per capita	−8.33***
	(2.88)

Notes: *** = p < 0.01. N = 28, R^2 = 0.37. Robust standard errors in parentheses. Data for "percent undernourished" from the UNDP's *Human Development Reports*: http://hdr.undp.org/statistics/data, accessed May 3, 2006. Note that "welfare regime" remains insignificant when "GDP per capita" (and "democracy") is dropped from the model because of potential multicollinearity issues (with "welfare regime").

elitism engendered by early decommodification policies. This raises questions about the transitory nature of this cluster; weak dual welfare states could get mired in partisan politics that ultimately perpetuate the status quo (if capital and/or protected labor wins), or they could move incrementally towards productive welfare status (if structurally unemployed labor groups win).

Confirmation of the protective/productive welfare typology supports the contention that welfare regimes in developing countries have been geared towards privileging higher-income groups. Put another way, very low-income individuals excluded from the market receive the lowest priority for social protections in all three regime types. The primary beneficiaries in protective welfare states are a small group of formal-sector workers, while, in the productive welfare state, only income-earners (actual and potential) enjoy some guarantee of a steady stream of income through education opportunities. The poverty tables in appendix L suggest that regime types are uncorrelated with levels of poverty; countries in all three categories maintain extremely high poverty rates. This does not, however, rule out the possibility that certain developing world welfare models might have *indirect* effects on poverty, simply through encouraging greater economic growth.

Table 4.4 takes a more systematic look at whether developing country welfare regimes focus on protecting the poor. The multiple regression technique assesses whether developing country welfare regimes have any *direct* effect on poverty alleviation. To operationalize regime types, I subtract each country's decommodification score from its commodification score in table 4.3; higher values are thus associated with productive welfare states.[47] A negative and significant coefficient would suggest that, as the score increases (regimes are more productive), poverty is reduced, and, when the score decreases (regimes are more protective), poverty increases. Conversely, a positive coefficient means that, as the measure is increased (regimes are more productive), poverty is increased, and, when the measure is decreased (regimes are more protective), poverty is decreased. The percentage of the population that is undernourished is used as a proxy for poverty, since alternative poverty data are sporadic at best for these countries.[48] As expected, the coefficient for welfare regime type is insignificant, suggesting that LDC welfare regimes are *not* directed towards protecting the poor. Since small sample size can be a problem, I also re-estimate the results using a bootstrapping technique.[49] The findings are unaffected.

4.3.1   Robustness checks

Do the cluster results hold up to changes in the conditioning information? The results for the cluster groupings and member countries are highly robust to three important changes. First, I run the analysis using an alternative to Ward's method. One common problem associated with Ward is that it tends to be heavily influenced by outliers (Ketchen and Shook, 1996). To check this, I use instead the weighted average method, which gives groups equal weighting in determining the combined group, regardless of the number of observations in each group. Given that differing clustering methods most often produce different results, Lorr (1983) suggests that similar results from two distinct methods provide great confidence that the underlying structure is being recovered. As second and third robustness checks, I substitute the welfare variables measured relative to GDP and GDP per capita in place of those measured as a proportion of total public expenditures. With the exceptions of Greece, Paraguay, and Panama, which fall into cluster 2 (instead of cluster 1), the results are identical in both models.

[47] I also estimate the model substituting the cluster variables (1= productive, 2 = dual, 3 = protective) with commodification/decommodification scores, and the results are the same.

[48] Data on numbers of undernourished people are still unavailable for four countries, however: Cyprus, Greece, Israel, and Singapore.

[49] Small sample size can influence the ratio of the coefficient to standard error upon which the statistical inferences are based. The bootstrapping technique uses the small sample as a good approximation of the unobserved population, and then draws samples with replacement over a given number of replications, in this case 1,000. The large number of replications increases confidence in the sampling distribution.

4.4   Initial interpretation of the results

The cluster results suggest that developing countries tend to favor either productive or protective welfare states. Scholars from a variety of disciplines have long recognized the intrinsic and instrumental values of *both* productive and protective types of social legislation (see, in particular, Dreze and Sen, 1989). So why, then, the ultimate trade-off between commmodification or decommodification efforts in LDCs? Close attention to how historical legacies of managing state–international market tensions have affected welfare states sheds some insights on these results. Building on the neoclassical political economy (NPE) and historical institutionalist literatures, it can be understood that the initial choice of development strategy and complementary welfare policies create distributional coalitions, which thereafter have a vested interest in maintaining existing institutions and reinforcing them.[50] This analysis therefore presents the possibility that institutional continuity is linked to the role of positive feedback effects from the original distribution regimes.

The NPE literature maintains that state intervention encourages the formation of narrow interest groups that engage in rent-seeking behavior.[51] Government intervention in protective welfare states initially creates social policies that cater to the groups empowered (directly or indirectly) by minimal international market exposure (i.e. workers in the civil services, the military, urban formal-sector and salaried workers). These distributional coalitions make it increasingly difficult for the government to engage in the significant amount of redistribution required to promote commodification. Productive welfare states, on the other hand, introduce benefits acceptable to employers struggling to compete in the international economy. Demands for greater labor benefits are subsequently met with stiff political resistance. Leaders are ultimately loath to pursue policies that alienate their traditional support groups and increase social instability. As a consequence, this self-reinforcing process suggests that, once welfare regimes are institutionalized, actors and interests may undergird their existence.[52]

Testing the precise causal relationship linking industrialization strategies, welfare regime types, distributional coalitions, and path

---

[50] This proposition derives from arguments that state intervention creates distributional coalitions (see Colander, 1984, and Srinivisan, 1985), and also builds on the institutionalist theories of path dependence (see Thelen, 1999, 2004).

[51] The term "rent-seeking" refers to lobbying activities triggered by different licensing practices of governments. The increased income gains of the beneficiary occur at a loss to the greater society. For examples, see Srinivisan (1985) and Collander (1984).

[52] This path dependence can be disrupted by significant events such as repressive dictatorships or economic crises. See, for example, Collier and Collier (1991).

dependence is beyond the reach of this analysis on account of the data problems involved.[53] Nonetheless, one way to assess if there is some link between countries' initial decisions regarding the extent of their participation in international markets and the welfare regimes that evolve (and persist) is to compare early development strategies with the recent (1990s) cluster groupings. Signs of such a connection can be taken as a preliminary indication that social actors who benefit from the original welfare arrangements make reversals increasingly unlikely.

To get some sense of initial post-war development strategies, I examine the level of manufactured exports (as a percentage of GDP) in each country at the earliest dates available and compare this to their 1990s commodification/decommodification scores.[54] After crises erupted in many developing countries following their initial experimentation with import substitution, most had settled upon their distinct industrialization strategies by the late 1960s and early 1970s. Unfortunately, the earliest available export data for most developing countries date from the 1970s. Economies that focused on orienting firms towards international markets are expected to reflect high levels of manufactured exports. Figure 4.2 lends support to the assertion that more inward-oriented LDCs (low manufactured exports) in the earlier decades tend towards protective welfare regimes (low commodification scores) in the present. These data thus provide the first indications of a connection between early development strategies, the implementation of (initially) compatible social policies, and the distributional coalitions that evolve to defend it.[55]

To evaluate the relationship between initial development strategies and developing country welfare regimes further, I perform a multiple regression test on the thirty-two cases using robust standard errors to correct for heteroskedasticity. I control for two common variables said to affect government investment in commodification: GDP per capita and democracy (for examples, see Brown and Hunter, 1999, and Kaufman and Segura-Ubiergo, 2001). The regression results, summarized in table 4.5, suggest that the initial development strategy has a significant effect on current welfare regimes and thus provides greater support for "lock-in."

[53] Operationalizing distributional coalitions across countries, for example, is extremely difficult in this type of analysis.
[54] I focus on manufactured export ratios instead of trade ratios in order to obtain a more precise indicator of industrialization strategy. For instance, LDCs that export abundant primary products but were focused on inward-oriented industrialization strategies have high trade ratios that would make them appear outward-oriented. The commodification/decommodification scores are calculated by subtracting each country's decommodification score from its commodification score in table 4.3.
[55] Note that, as the previous section details, the categorization of Paraguay and Panama in cluster 1 is not robust.

Table 4.5 *Effects of early development strategies on current welfare regimes*

Independent variable	Coefficient estimates
Manufactured exports (1970s)	0.70**
	(0.34)
Democracy	0.14*
	(0.076)
GDP per capita	0.77**
	(0.29)

Notes: ** = p < 0.05; * = p < 0.10. N = 32, R^2 = 0.41. Robust standard errors in parentheses.

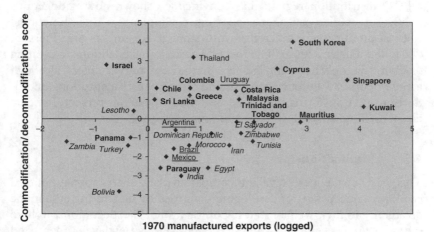

1970 manufactured exports (logged)

Figure 4.2 Welfare regimes and early development strategies

Notes: Productive welfare states are represented in bold, dual welfare states are underlined, and protective welfare states are italicized.

"Manufactured exports" is intended to represent a political variable, since it serves as a proxy for enduring distributional coalitions formed in the early stage of development.

The sample size is admittedly small and, as stated earlier, can be problematic. To increase confidence in the results, I apply the bootstrap technique once more, and again get similar results.[56] The persistent

---

[56] I also run ordered probit models using the 1990 cluster category (1 = productive welfare, 2 = (weak) dual welfare state, 3 = protective) as the dependent variable and find similar results. I do not present these results because reporting the coefficients of an ordered probit model is quite involved, and the consequence of small sample size in probit models is greater than it is for least squares estimation (Hart and Clark, 1999).

effects of early development strategies should still be viewed with caution, however, since country-specific variables (e.g. initial factor endowments, history, culture) and data for important political controls (e.g. partisanship) are unavailable. These results nonetheless bolster the argument for a relationship between early development strategies and current developing world welfare regimes.

This exposition does not allow any analysis of institutional change. Clearly, some countries have experienced changes in their welfare regimes such that they no longer correspond to their early development strategies. For example, nations such as Colombia and Costa Rica pursued mostly inward-oriented development strategies in the early post-war era, and yet they are productive welfare states.[57] Already steps ahead, research on OECD distribution regimes has convincingly shown how endogenous political dynamics can alter supporting coalitions and their functional roles to produce very different institutional arrangements (see Pierson, 2004, and Thelen, 2004). The role of distributional coalitions in creating "lock-in" has only been implied here. In the case study chapters, although a more rigorous theoretical analysis and testing of *both* institutional reproduction and transformation are beyond the scope of this project, I undertake a preliminary analysis of institutional change.

4.5   Implications

This study challenges prevailing comparative and international political economy conceptions of developing countries by illustrating systematic divergence in their welfare states. Contrary to CPE expectations, welfare states are not necessarily by-products of post-industrial development, and they cluster into three distinct welfare regime types. Most importantly for this analysis, the findings from this chapter question IPE convergence predictions by examining the institutional content of the developing world welfare state and demonstrating that these nations maintain qualitatively different kinds of distribution regimes in the current era of globalization. As suggested by IPE analysts, the pressures of international market competition impose important constraints on policy-makers in terms of the choices made as to how best to strengthen their position in the global economy. At the same time, however, the persistent variation among the types of welfare states implies that local needs and politics continue to serve as important sources of diversity. The LDC welfare state thus

---

[57] Significantly, these countries contrast with LDCs that remained protective welfare states in the 1990s, even after switching to outward orientation strategies as early as the 1980s (e.g. Turkey, Morocco, India).

remains a key institution to manage the tensions and dilemmas that emerge from exposure to the international economy. The important paradox, however, one that is critical to the race to the bottom debate, is that none of these distribution regimes were originally designed to address issues of poverty. The existence of three clusters of welfare regimes well into the twentieth century intimates that developing countries, similarly to developed nations, demonstrate a sustained capacity to formulate systematically different social policies that aim to align economy and society.

Before stressing the broader implications, however, it is important to be clear about the theoretical and empirical limitations of the analysis applied in this chapter. The proposed causal explanation linking LDC policy-makers, development strategies, distributional coalitions and welfare regime type is tentative and begs further exploration. Empirically, the findings from this study can only be suggestive. The unavailability of data impresses strong limitations on the number of observations included and, consequently, the kinds of econometric tests employed. Future research would greatly benefit from more extensive and reliable time-series data.

Nonetheless, this first attempt to uncover "varieties of welfare capitalism" in the developing world based on existing data is provocative. To the extent that the analysis hits upon key differences in welfare regimes, important policy and research implications emerge. This chapter suggests the importance of going beyond simply analyzing the level of government expenditures in globalizing countries. Rather, recognizing the different domestic arrangements related to welfare in LDCs underscores the concentration of institutional protections for the middle class rather than the poor, and it provides a more precise way to assess whether the historic choices of these nations (productive, protective, dual) will endure in the face of rising international market competition. As such, a race to the bottom neither mandates convergence nor means that the poor are worse off as a consequence.

The cross-sectional nature of this analysis provides important insights on developing political economies, but it prohibits a more complete test of IPE convergence theories. One of the fundamental questions ahead, then, is whether or not developing countries are maintaining their welfare institutions *into the twenty-first century*, particularly as international market pressures intensify with the entrance into the market of such potential powerhouse countries as China and India. I now turn to the case studies to answer this question, and to explore in more detail the main findings in the quantitative analyses.

5   Globalization and the protective welfare
        state: case study of India

The following three chapters illustrate the findings from the previous portion of the book by selecting one representative from each cluster: a protective welfare state (India); a productive welfare state (South Korea); and a weak dual welfare state (Brazil). These case studies are intended as heuristic devices, rather than another hard test of the hypotheses in this book. The purpose of the case illustrations is to provide a more nuanced and detailed look at the primary research finding: as international market demands systematically affect government policy decisions in developing countries, distinct institutional arrangements governing the distribution of welfare persist and, as a consequence, middle-class labor groups are the ones most directly hurt by race to the bottom pressures. The country overviews essentially provide greater in-depth analysis of how national social policy configurations are structuring responses to globalization. The addition of the case study analysis allows a more applied understanding of the consequences of globalization in terms of cutbacks (RTB) *and* institutional changes. In addition, they permit consideration of the role of other factors not emphasized in the quantitative analysis, such as democracy.

One caveat should be kept in mind as the case studies unfold in the following chapters. Because the causal linkages have been empirically verified in the earlier chapters, I take on the broad panorama of each country's political economy and related social welfare strategies in a swift, bold, and unrestrained manner. In other words, the quantitative analysis serves as the primary guide to this schematic interpretation of the seemingly unrelated, chaotic, and complex events related to a race to the bottom. I dare say that, if these chapters were to be viewed in isolation from the previous discussion, some readers would find the interpretation of events capricious, and it would certainly not win the plaudits of experts and practitioners specializing in specific areas of welfare reform in these countries. My primary goal, however, is to provide a broad, contextual understanding of the relationship between the race to the bottom, domestic politics, and welfare policies in developing countries.

Beginning with the case of India, this chapter confirms that RTB pressures are quite real. Total government expenditures have decreased by almost 6 percent since India adopted liberalization policies in 1991.[1] Even more alarmingly, government social security, health, *and* education expenditures have concomitantly declined since 1991, suggesting that the resources devoted to this particular sector are being targeted as efforts to impose fiscal discipline and prepare for international competition intensify.[2] Manmohan Singh, the minister of finance from 1991 to 1996 and the current prime minister, made a telling statement in 1992 about how globalization and race to the bottom pressures in social welfare funding were constraining the Indian government's room to maneuver:

Some people have criticized the stabilization program as being anti-poor. I admit that in an economy which has been living beyond its means, stabilization does hurt... It is true that the fiscal compulsions have forced us to restrain the growth of all expenditure, including social expenditure. But considering that interest payments are a fixed contractual obligation, that defense expenditure cannot be cut beyond a certain point because of the security environment confronting us, that expenditure on government cannot be drastically reduced without a wage and DA[3] freeze or a sharp reduction in employment, that various subsidies cannot be removed overnight, we had very little option but to do what I did. *Those who criticize the cuts in social spending should tell us what other expenditure could be cut to make room for increased spending on social sectors.* (Singh as quoted in Mooij and Dev, 2004: 112; emphasis added)

The globalization–welfare state nexus in developing countries is far more complex than is anticipated by the race to the bottom debate, however, and India proves no exception. In spite of cutbacks in several social policy areas, India maintains a protective welfare regime. India's key modes of welfare protection – generous labor market protections and high levels of public employment – have experienced minimal changes, and commodification strategies still lag far behind nationally set goals and international standards. Furthermore, it is not just social spending that tends to serve the better off in India, as India's distribution regime more generally has historically concentrated protections on the non-poor. It thus becomes apparent why, in the final analysis, the current race to the bottom is more directly hurting the middle class and not India's poor; the

---

[1] This estimate is calculated as a percentage of GDP from the IMF's *Government Finance Statistics*, for various years from 1972 to 2003. Note that, prior to globalization, India's total government spending increased at an annual average of 3 percent. A declining trend, at an annual average of 0.04 percent, began after globalization.

[2] These sectors show a decline in spending when measured both as a percentage of GDP and as a proportion of total government expenditures.

[3] DA represents "dearness allowance," or cash payments to employees that take inflation into account and are part of the total wage cost.

fate of the latter continues to be determined by pre-existing domestic institutional arrangements that never protected them in the first place.

This chapter is divided into six sections. Section 5.1 describes the key features of India's protective welfare state. This section takes its cue from chapter 4, staying away from the sole focus on social spending, and undertakes a multifaceted examination of the content or institutional structure of India's welfare regime. The following section (5.2) exposes the effects of globalization on India's protective welfare state. More specifically, I illustrate the extent of the race to the bottom, exploring the Indian case in connection to the findings of chapter 2.

Section 5.3 is divided into two parts. The first puts the extent of welfare cutbacks into broader perspective. I reveal the high degree of institutional continuity in India's welfare regime despite the retrenchment of some social sectors. This section goes beyond the findings of the cluster analysis in chapter 4 to reveal the ways in which globalization does or does not affect *institutional changes* in welfare schemes. This reconceptualization reveals that the race to the bottom does not necessarily lead to institutional convergence towards the minimal neoliberal welfare state, and, aside from some noted education reforms, India's protective welfare state still concentrates on middle-class benefits.

The second part of section 5.3 makes clear *why* institutional continuity persists in India, by focusing on the mediating effects of domestic institutions. I illustrate, in turn, how the three institutional factors outlined in the previous chapters determine policy responses to globalization in India: the organization of the political economy, which aggregates interests and structures access to the political arena (chapter 4); the nature of the policy interactions between government and labor (chapter 3); and the fragmented character of labor organizations (chapter 2). I should emphasize here that, in all the case studies, I discuss more generally the expression of fragmented labor movements (or PLP) rather than focus on the structural characteristics of the labor market.[4] Section 5.4 asks the key question: who really gets hurt? This section delves into how a race to the bottom in India's social sectors hurts the middle class as a consequence of its historically protectionist welfare regime. Section 5.5 examines other factors not considered in the quantitative analysis. Finally, section 5.6

---

[4] In exploring the character of LDC national labor market institutions in the following chapters, low PLP (or the structural constraints of the labor market – large numbers of low-skilled labor, surplus labor – that inhibit labor mobilization in LDCs) is already assumed. More detailed data on PLP for India, Brazil, and South Korea are available in chapter 2. The focus here is more generally on the implications of fragmented labor movements.

draws some general conclusions about protective welfare states in the current era of globalization.

5.1   India's protective welfare state

As revealed in the previous chapter, India's distribution regime is classified as protective. The Indian government has long focused on decommodification efforts in two particular ways: labor market protections, and employment creation in the public sector. Not only does India rank among the highest in the developing world in terms of the percentage of workers employed in the public sector, it also maintains some of the most labor-friendly rules and norms governing working conditions and industrial relations. These two pillars represent the core of India's protective welfare state.

At the same time as these protective measures became enshrined in the constitution, Jawarhalal Nehru, the independence leader and India's first prime minister, envisioned a strategy of promoting national security by building a relatively autarkic economy (Nayar, 2001). He adopted an economic model that was guided by Mahatma Gandhi's emphasis on *swadeshi*, or self-reliance.[5] Import substitution industrialization policies were soon implemented in an effort to eschew international market influences and thereby promote India's strategic independence. India's development approach was characterized as "export pessimism," and, eventually, the sluggish growth of exports was linked to India's dawdling "Hindu rate of growth." By successfully "delinking" its economy, India essentially participated in world markets far less than any other large developing country in the first few decades after independence (Rudolph and Rudolph, 1987).

As a consequence, the extensive tax and tariff structures, as well as stiff regulations in connection with trade and foreign investment, succeeded in cutting India off from the global economy, and thereby simultaneously reduced government and employer resistance to costly welfare measures. Not having to compete in international markets, less efficient public-sector firms began to dominate the organized economy, and the size of the public bureaucracy (including the government's key administrative service, the Indian Administrative Services [IAS]) expanded (Rudolph and Rudolph, 1987). Employment in state enterprises and the number of civil servants rapidly increased. By the same logic, both public and private employers could pass on the costs of high labor market protections by raising domestic prices and offering often substandard goods and services.

[5] The first *Swadeshi* movement, from 1905 to 1908, called for a total boycott of foreign goods, particularly imports (Encarnation, 1989).

Taking a closer look at India's decommodification bias, recall from chapter 4 that labor market protections are restrictions on the ability of economic agents to enter or exit contractual, formal employment relationships (Gitterman, 2002). This includes not only the formal ILO core codes, such as freedom of association and collective bargaining, but also legislation that promotes labor market rigidities (e.g. costly layoffs, inflexible wages). India's strong pro-labor bias is reflected in several constitutional enactments upon independence in 1947 and more than 200 labor laws guaranteeing labor some of the most generous freedoms in the developing world. Of these, the most important are the Trade Unions Act, Industrial Disputes Act (IDA), and Contract Labor Act (CLA), which govern labor's freedom to organize, the terms and conditions of employment, and prohibitions against hiring contract labor, respectively. For example, since India's independence, firms with more than 100 workers have had to apply for formal government permission to lay off workers, and this permission is rarely forthcoming (Sen Gupta and Sett, 2000; Basu, Fields, and Debgupta, 1996). It is no surprise that India ranks in the top percentile of developing countries in several indices of labor market regulations (i.e. mandatory severance pay, statutory duration of maternity leave, number of strikes and lock-outs per year), as documented by Rama and Artecona (2002).

Paradoxically, however, by making it more difficult for firms to dismiss and hire workers, India's extensive labor laws are a direct affront to its second decommodification strategy of employment creation. The emphasis upon employment provision as a tool to address poverty has its roots in Kautilya's *Arthastra* Sanskrit writings on politics and statecraft in the fourth century BC (Dev, 1995).[6] Since independence this policy priority has taken two tracks. The first is the continuation of pre-independence strategies that provided public relief work, particularly during famines. The Employment Guarantee Scheme (EGS) in the state of Maharashtra and, nationally, the Jawahar Rojgar Yojna (JRY), for example, guarantee unskilled manual work for those willing to work at very low wages. In general, however, no more than five days per family per month are offered by JRY, and at its highest level of enrollment no more than 1.2 percent of the workforce is employed (Subbarao, 1997).[7] While the EGS has

---

[6] Note that an emphasis on the merits of education also has its roots in ancient Indian texts (see Scharfe, 2002). What is interesting for this analysis is that, even though emphasis on both protective and productive welfare strategies can be traced back to ancient India, it is only a commitment to the former that is maintained at present.

[7] This percentage was calculated by dividing Subbarao's (1997) statistic that approximately 55 million people gained employment during the agricultural off-peak season by the size of the labor force listed in the World Bank's *World Development Indicators* for 1997.

provided an important source of relief (and empowerment) for the rural poor, it has also been widely critiqued for corruption and the more affluent gaining a larger share of EGS earnings (Gaiha, 1996; Echeverri-Gent, 1994; Ravallion, 1991). The second and more far-reaching track guarantees secure employment in the public sector, benefiting mostly the middle class (civil servants, employees of state-owned enterprises). India ranks fourth highest in the developing world after Benin, Zambia, and Ghana, with public-sector employees comprising 72 percent of total employment in the organized sector (Heller and Tait, 1984; ILO's LABORSTA database).

Alternative welfare strategies, as discussed in chapter 4, have not received the same resources or policy attention in India. According to data from the IMF's *Government Finance Statistics*, total central spending in education, health, *and* social security reaches just 1 percent of GDP, which is far below the developing world average of 7 percent.[8] Consistent with India's emphasis on protective welfare policies, however, total government spending on social security has been higher than its investment in education. Spending on housing is also, on average, less than 1 percent of GDP, and has received extremely low priority on India's public policy agenda (Sivam and Karuppannan, 2002).

With the bulk of the benefits and privileges associated with India's welfare policies directed towards labor market protections and public employment, the resources allocated to means-tested, or targeted, anti-poverty schemes are comparatively meager.[9] The lack of investment in poverty programs is actually quite surprising, given India's history of socialism and extensive public commitments to help the poor, particularly after independence. Analyses of some of India's major pro-poor schemes, such as rural public works (RPW) and the Integrated Rural Development Programme (IRDP), reveal that the outlays have been misdirected, either failing to attract the poor or enabling "leakages" to the (relatively) well off (Gaiha, 2000). The Public Distributions System (PDS) is the earliest publicly funded safety net and, according to Radhakrishna and Subbarao's (1997) World Bank study, India's most "far reaching in terms

[8] It is difficult to find consistent data on social spending in India. Recent data from the government of India suggest that total central government spending on education, health, and social security averages approximately 5 percent of GDP (see appendix M).

[9] For a broader overview of existing poverty alleviation schemes in India, see Ministry of Finance (2005: chap. 10). It is difficult to obtain data on the total amount spent on means-tested poverty alleviation programs in India. One estimate suggests that, on average, 0.3 percent of GDP is spent on programs focused on lower-caste members (see Mooij and Dev, 2002, 2004). These tend to be the largest of India's targeted programs, but others do exist.

of coverage as well as public expenditure (on subsidy)."[10] Yet Radhakrishna and Subbarao's (1997) findings reveal that overall PDS welfare gains in terms of income and nutritional status have been "very meager."

India has also maintained a "reservation policy" under which specific quotas are reserved for the scheduled caste and scheduled tribe (i.e. members at the bottom of India's caste hierarchy, formerly known as the untouchables) in government jobs, education institutions, public housing, and several political institutions, such as parliament, state assemblies, and panchayats (village councils). Consistent with the institutional norms of India's protective welfare state, employment (i.e. quotas or "reservations") in the public sector has been a primary means for assisting the lowest caste. While this program has had some success, scholars argue that the majority continue to remain in a situation of poverty (see Deshpande, 2005).

To summarize, India's distribution regime maintains an imbalance between select protective welfare policies and an extremely low commitment towards human capital investment. The next section introduces the globalization question: what is the effect of international market integration on India's protective welfare state?

5.2   Race to the bottom?

India's embrace of globalization began in the mid-1980s with Rajiv Gandhi's trade and industry reforms, but did not gain momentum until after the balance of payments crisis of the early 1990s.[11] Gandhi's halting efforts were India's second major attempt at liberalization, and illustrate the difficulties in transitioning from such a tightly controlled domestic economy to an internationally oriented market economy. Both scholars and policy-makers generally agree, however, that India's long-lived inward-oriented socialist regime, inspired by Nehru, finally experienced a decisive break in 1991 when the then prime minister, Narasimha Rao, eliminated import licensing for most goods, cut import duty rates, actively promoted foreign direct investment, allowed the exchange rate to depreciate, and made attempts to deregulate financial markets.

---

[10] PDS provides selected food commodities, such as rice, wheat, sugar, and kerosene oil, at subsidized prices.

[11] Rising inflation, the Bofors scandal, and the defeat of Rajiv Gandhi's Congress (I) party in 1989 by the leftist National Front coalition significantly deterred the liberalization process (Denoon, 1998). India's first attempts at liberalization (1966–8) during the premiership of Indira Gandhi drew strong labor and business opposition, and hence were short-lived.

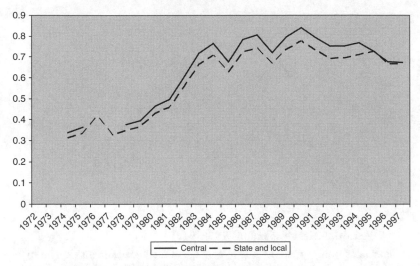

Figure 5.1 Social security and welfare, 1972–97

Notes: Social spending as a percentage of total government expenditures shows a similar trend, with spending levels tapering off in the mid-1980s. Per capita social security spending peaked in 1990 (graphs not shown here).

State and local spending data should be viewed with caution, since states' total expenditures include central government transfers.

Source: IMF, *Government Finance Statistics* (various years).

Policy reactions to globalization pressures are most evident in India's social security, education, and health sectors. In contrast, as will be seen in the next section, the race to the bottom has made less of an imprint on the core of India's welfare strategies (labor market protections and public employment). Cutbacks in education, health, and social security expenditures began shortly after Gandhi's attempts at liberalization and have not since been restored. Figures 5.1–5.3 illustrate these trends. These findings for education and health expenditures are not completely consistent with the predictions in chapter 2 that only social security would be sensitive to the impact of RTB pressures. See appendix M for more recent data on these trends collected from national sources.

In all three sectors, spending peaks around the mid-1980s and declines steadily after 1991, alongside increases in trade and capital flows. Important post-liberalization national policy rulings on India's social security and health sectors provide additional evidence of the race to the bottom. The reductions in education spending, however, are the most surprising, given India's publicly declared intentions in 1986 and 1991 to invest more heavily in education. The Planning Commission's

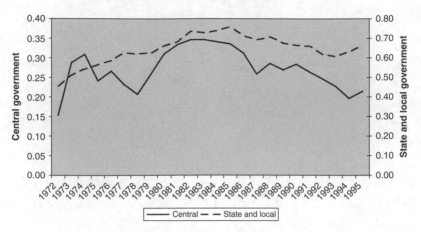

Figure 5.2 Health spending, 1972–97

Note: Health spending as a percentage of total government expenditures shows a clearer peak, and then declines after 1983. Health spending per capita begins to level off and shows only a slight decline starting in 1985 (graphs not shown here).

State and local spending data should be viewed with caution, since states' total expenditures include central government transfers.

Source: IMF, *Government Finance Statistics* (various years).

subsequent reduction of budgetary resources directed towards this sector suggest that the pressures of globalization are indeed very real.[12]

5.2.1   Social security

While there is much heterogeneity among Indian states in terms of their social sector spending and achievements, this analysis focuses on the budget and priorities at the central level. The latter has strong influence and direct control over the direction of social spending in the states (Rao and Singh, 2005), and India's constitution reveals a clear predisposition towards the central government in the distribution of fiscal powers. Even though such items as social planning and services, the welfare of labor, social security, and unemployment are included on the Concurrent List, the actual delegation of responsibilities reveals an inherent "centripetal" bias (Rao and Singh, 2005: 136).[13] The almost parallel trends between the

[12] India's Planning Commission is the government institution responsible for formulating five-year plans that determine the priorities and effective allocation of India's resources.

[13] The Concurrent List refers to those categories in which the state and central governments have joint jurisdiction.

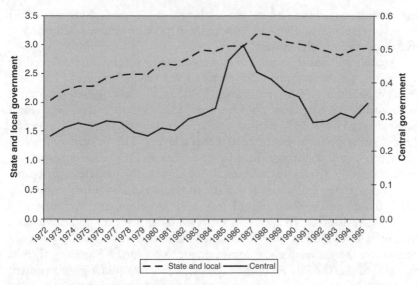

Figure 5.3 Education spending, 1972–97

Notes: Education spending as a percentage of total government expenditures and education spending per capita show similar trends, with spending levels peaking in the late 1980s (graphs not shown here).

State and local spending data should be viewed with caution, since states' total expenditures include central government transfers.

Source: IMF, *Government Finance Statistics* (various years).

central and state and local governments in social spending suggest that this is indeed so, although it should be noted that substantial heterogeneity among states' social performance does exist. Nonetheless, inter-state variations in both social commitment and performance – Kerala, for example, does exceptionally well – should be kept in mind.

As figure 5.1 indicates, since India's turn towards globalization the country has had to pull back the reins on its rising social security expenditures. Two major policy initiatives suggest that this trend will continue in the long run. In 1998 India imposed stricter eligibility criteria by raising the retirement age from fifty-eight to sixty. This change was one of the less politically controversial moves towards social security reform, raising only minor protests by youth associations.[14] As a result, India's dependency ratio (the proportion of dependents to working-age population) immediately decreased. This was a significant attempt to reduce the state social security budget, particularly since the

[14] "Youth Front against Raising Retirement Age," *The Hindu* (Madras), October 6, 2001, Southern States section.

implementation of the pay-as-you-go Employee Pension Scheme (EPS) for private-sector workers in 1995 called for a continued 1.6 percent contribution from the state.[15]

A second and much more controversial policy reform that reflects the race to the bottom is pension privatization for state employees. The New Pension Scheme (NPS), passed in 2004, is a market-based guarantee mechanism that requires contributions from union, state, and local employees to be placed in individual pension accounts, ostensibly lowering the extent of publicly guaranteed benefit levels. The reform unleashed major protests and outrage from leftist parties and trade unions, and has since been called back to parliament for review. Nonetheless, first-time institutional developments, such as the formation of a statutory regulatory body, the Pension Fund Regulatory and Development Authority, to undertake revisions in the pension sector, and the first ever comprehensive examination of policy questions connected with the OASIS program underscore the government's commitment to reform.[16] Significantly, the majority of the OASIS recommendations towards reducing government pension commitments have since been placed on the policy agenda. The recent advancements, overall, have given Indian social security experts confidence that the reform process is inevitable.

5.2.2   Health care and education

Evidence of a race to the bottom in India's public health sector is revealed in the National Health Policy, passed in 2002. First, not only does the proposal (to raise total health expenditure from a mere 0.9 percent of GDP to 2.0 percent) fall far below the 5 percent recommended by the World Health Organization, but expenditures have since declined (Ministry of Finance,

[15] Note that the state was already making a similar contribution to the Family Pension Scheme, which was replaced by the more comprehensive EPS in 1995 (Goswami, 2002). Initially, private sector workers were only covered by the Employee Provident Fund (EPF). This is a fully funded program that provides a lump sum benefit at retirement. Reformers have long been concerned that EPF does not adequately provide protection from longevity and inflation. The implementation of EPS did not satisfy reformers, however, as workers' contribution rates increased by two percentage points, and factors such as ceilings on pensions and the lack of indexation suggest that returns from EPS will be lower and will further disadvantage the private sector (Goswami, 2002: 104). This is disconcerting, since private-sector workers have long received low levels of old age protection under India's social security system, and India's worker contribution rates were already "amongst the highest in the world" (Ministry of Social Justice and Empowerment, 1999). Note that the Old Age and Social Income Security (OASIS) report on social security calls for (and parliament is considering) the withdrawal of the 1.6 percent state contribution to EPS.
[16] India is one of the few countries to have set up an independent regulatory agency for its social security system.

2005: table 210). Second, the plan drew national criticism for encouraging a greater role for private care, and shirking government responsibilities at the primary level.[17] Generally, 83 percent of all health care expenditure is borne "out of pocket," making India one of the most privatized systems in the world (Ministry of Health and Family Welfare, 2002: 10). This is a concern, since government has failed to increase its regulation of the private sector to ensure that there are common standards of performance.[18] The impact of globalization has also been felt in the reduction of central grants to the states for public health and disease control programs (Purohit, 2001).

Finally, after several concerted and very public efforts to prioritize education after liberalization efforts had begun in 1985, the first official government document to declare that globalization was still putting pressure on education resources made headlines.[19] Recent government documents declare that economic liberalization and the accompanying structural adjustment policies constitute one of the biggest challenges in funding education.[20] Declining education expenditures, in the absence of any specific policy initiatives designed to curb education spending, suggest that budgetary allocations to this sector are among those targeted in the globalizing environment.

5.2.3   Summary

Since the adoption of economic liberalization policies in India, reduced public spending and select policy changes indicate retrenchment in social security schemes and health care. More specifically, raising the retirement age and establishing the NPS were policies aimed at reducing overall non-wage costs linked to social security. Retrenchment pressures in the health sector are revealed by cutbacks in central grants to the states for public health and disease control programs, a decline in overall spending, and a continued role for private care and deregulation despite the fledgling nature of India's health care system. The most unexpected finding is

---

[17] See "National Health Policy is Slammed," *Times of India* (Delhi), November 5, 2001.

[18] "Health for All: A Goal Too Far?" *Financial Express* (Mumbai), May 31, 2003.

[19] See "Social Reforms to Boost Productivity," *The Hindu* (Madras), August 24, 2000. For example, the National Policy of Education in 1986 first introduced the idea that education is a fundamental right for all children up to age fourteen. The United Front government presented this Bill in 1997. Finally, the United Progressive Alliance (UPA) made universal access to quality basic education a fundamental pillar of its Common Minimum Programme in 2004 – a continuation of the United Front's Basic Minimum Services program initiated in the late 1990s.

[20] For the details, see Ministry of Human Resource Development (2000: Part II – Analytic Section, cont. 3), prepared by the ministry in conjunction with the National Institute of Educational Planning and Administration.

that public spending on education has been decreasing since liberalization in spite of the fact that education has been declared a national policy priority by the last two administrations.

5.3   Institutional change

In light of the race to the bottom cutbacks discussed above, is globalization causing regime change? Is India's protective welfare state headed towards the neoliberal bottom? Or is India transitioning to a productive welfare state? With the onset of globalization, the minimal changes in official labor policies and public employment rates reveal that a paradigm shift in India's welfare philosophy has not yet occurred. Nonetheless, India has implemented some *incremental* changes, guided by the institutional norms and organizations of its protective welfare state. The first subsection below discusses the degree of persistence of India's welfare state, and the next presents a brief illustration of how and why domestic institutional arrangements in India have prevented radical regime change.

5.3.1   Welfare regime change?

Overall, India's current state of affairs suggests that regime change has been minimal. In the details to follow, I illustrate this on the basis of four criteria discussed in the introduction: significant increases in the reliance on means testing; major transfers of responsibility to the private sector; dramatic changes in benefit and eligibility rules; and the discontinuity of "illiberal" institutional legacies.

In terms of the first criterion for institutional change, increases in means testing, there has been minimal change. India's targeted poverty policies have not seen much improvement in recent decades, and, as such, are consistent with previous practices. Expenditures on means-tested anti-poverty programs that aim to help the disadvantaged directly have actually fallen since 1990. For example, 1990–2001 government data estimates presented by Mooij and Dev (2002, 2004) show a significant decline in welfare programs devoted to the scheduled tribes and castes, and targeted programs such as the Drought Prone Areas Programme, Integrated Rural Development Programme, and rural wage employment programs. This certainly does not bode well for the poor, given that these programs have long registered far less than 1 percent of GDP (see figure 5.4). While the current administration's recent launch of the ambitious National Rural Employment Guarantee Programme (NREGP), which guarantees rural households 100 days of employment per year, may turn out to

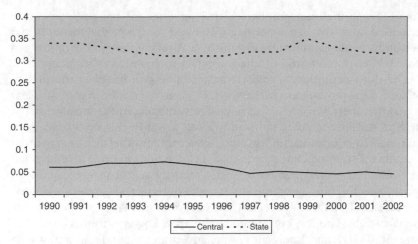

Figure 5.4 Expenditure on scheduled castes, scheduled tribes, and backward castes, 1990–2002

Source: Ministry of Finance (2003, 2004).

be an exception, it has been widely criticized.[21] The overall trend in means-tested programs remains one of minimal change.

The second criterion, dramatic changes in benefit and eligibility rules, has also shown little evidence of being met. While some incremental changes have been made to social security, such as an increase in the retirement age and a contribution by civil servants of 10 percent of their salaries, when placed in an international context these changes can be seen to be relatively minor. India's mandated retirement age is still below the international average of sixty-two, and the dualism between social insurance benefits for the private and public sectors remains.[22] In addition, civil service pension spending has risen rapidly since the early 1990s, and remained relatively stable from 2000 to 2004 (Palacios and Whitehouse,

---

[21] Launched in February 2006, the first phase of the program will take place in 200 of India's most impoverished districts. It is scheduled to be expanded nationwide. The prime minister, Manmohan Singh, has described the initiative as "historic" (Amelia Gentleman, "India's War on Poverty: Easy Victory Unlikely," *International Herald Tribune*, February 28, 2006). Nonetheless, based on India's past experience with employment guarantee programs, both activists and scholars remain extremely skeptical about the viability of the current plan. They question the government's (under)estimations of the cost of the program, the extent of its long-term commitment, and the spread of corruption (see Sharad Joshi, "National Employment Guarantee Scheme – Well-intentioned, but Poorly Designed," *Hindu Business Line*, August 24, 2005, and Amelia Gentleman, February 28, 2006).

[22] See the retirement age data reported by Bonturi (2002).

2006). Since the total number of civil servants has not simultaneously increased over the same period, this trend suggests that benefits per person have not significantly diminished. A recent newspaper report put it well: "Pension reform in India is moving at a painfully slow pace."[23]

The third condition, a major transfer of responsibility to the private sector (in the provision of social services), has also not been met. While it is true that there is some discussion of privatization in the social security, health, and education sectors, advances towards this end have been minimal. In education, for example, government officials have reported recently that they will not accede to WTO demands to open up education services.[24] The privatization of social security is still in the discussion phase, and the final outcome is yet to be determined. Privatization has increased in India's health sector, but this is a trend that began long before globalization. The level of public health spending is extremely low (0.6 percent of GDP and 1 percent of total government spending), and was so long before India's turn to global markets.[25]

The final mode of assessment of regime change is whether major policy or funding changes have been directed towards the mainstays of India's welfare state. In other words, we need to look at the extent of institutional continuity. The continuation of labor market protections and state responsibility for securing employment are the most convincing signs of institutional continuity, and deflect concerns of convergence towards the liberal welfare state. In terms of India's extensive labor market protections, there have been surprisingly few official policy changes. Amendments to the IDA and CLA that allow more flexibility for employees to hire and fire, as well as permit the hiring of contract labor, face stiff resistance from unions.[26] Intense pressure for reform began during Rao's administration in the early 1990s. A tripartite body of business, government, and labor, the second National Commission on Labor (NCL), was formed, and the most wide-ranging reforms were proposed *for the first time* in the 2000–2 budget (Roychowdhury, 2003). These reforms are still being debated in parliament, however, and, even more significantly, the current administration has shown a greater reluctance to pursue any

---

[23] "Reform Pensions," *Financial Express* (Mumbai), August 8, 2006.
[24] "India May Remove Education from WTO Wishlist," *Indian Express* (Delhi), February 3, 2006.
[25] Systematic data on private health expenditures are not available for the early years after independence.
[26] Currently, the IDA requires firms employing more than 100 workers to seek prior government permission for layoffs and any changes in job specifications, while the CLA prohibits contract workers in certain situations at the discretion of the government.

drastic changes, announcing in May 2004 that it would "refrain from uncritical endorsement of the hire and fire approach."[27]

Nevertheless, it cannot be said that RTB pressures are completely absent in terms of labor market reform. As several Indian labor scholars, and even the media, document, labor reforms still occur informally and – as Jenkins (2004) puts it well – "by stealth." First, to bypass laws against retrenchment, employers have stopped paying salaries or simply abandoned operations (Kaur and Maheshwari, 2005; Sen Gupta and Sett, 2000).[28] Second, while the federal laws might still be intact, some individual states have adopted more liberal labor policies (e.g. amendments to the CLA in Andhra Pradesh), creating less resistance to reform among neighboring states (Jenkins, 2004).[29]

Public employment has been more resistant to change, however, both de jure and de facto, particularly in terms of India's overstaffed bureaucracy. In fact, from the mid-1970s to the mid-1990s, most of the increase in "organized" employment has been absorbed by the public sector. Raw public-sector employment figures from 1985 to 2003 reveal an increase of over 1 million persons. Pressure for restructuring has occurred mostly in public-sector manufacturing enterprises rather than the public sector as a whole (Roychowdhury, 2003). One of the few policies designed to reduce the public sector workforce, the Voluntary Retirement Scheme (VRS), has not been that successful. This policy has eliminated fewer than 2 percent of "potentially redundant employees," according to recent estimates (Agarwala and Khan, 2002).[30] The fundamental problem is that the thousands of officially declared "sick" industries, or those enterprises (particularly public) that operate at chronic losses, are notoriously difficult to shut down. Figure 5.5 illustrates the "stickiness" of jobs in the public sector. Total numbers employed in the public sector have steadily increased, but, as a percentage of the total, public employment has remained relatively constant since economic liberalization policies began to be adopted in the mid-1980s.

In sum, the legacy of India's protective welfare state appears to be conditioning the direction of social welfare change in the current era of

[27] Andy Mukhergee, "India's Harsh Labour Laws May Change, Quietly," *International Herald Tribune*, February 2, 2005.

[28] Of course, while employers have long attempted to bypass these laws, the pressures of globalization and the growing informalization of the workforce, as well as the increasing number of "sick" industries, have accelerated this practice (Sinha, 2004; Jenkins, 2004).

[29] See also Andy Mukherjee, "India's Harsh Labour Laws May Change, Quietly," *International Herald Tribune*, February 2, 2005.

[30] Datta (2001) reports data from the Ministry of Heavy Industries and Public Enterprise to the effect that, from 1991 to 2002, a total of 138,472 workers (or approximately 0.7 percent of the total employed in the public sector) accepted VRS.

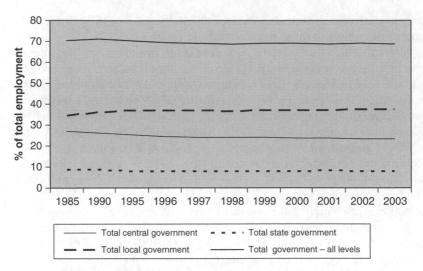

Figure 5.5 Total public employment in India, 1985–2003

Note: "Total public employment" covers all employment of the general government sector plus employment by publicly owned enterprises.
Source: ILO's LABORSTA database (accessed September 2005).

globalization. Relatively marginal changes to the core elements of its protective welfare state signal a particular pattern of policy responses. In contrast to public employment, the most visible effects of RTB pressures occur in the traditionally neglected welfare sectors – health and education, and even social security. Relative to India's key protective welfare schemes that have been encouraged since independence, social security programs are relatively new. Recall that the EPS was introduced as late as 1995. Social reforms in India thus appear to vary according to both the pressures of globalization *and* the prevailing normative orientations and organizational structures of India's distribution regime.

5.3.2   Mediating role of domestic institutions

This section draws on the Indian case to demonstrate the causal mechanisms that underlie institutional continuity, as discussed in chapters 2, 3, and 4. First, I investigate how India's protective welfare state aggregates interests and structures access to the political arena. Next, I look at how India's government–labor relationship enables only select labor groups to have privileged access to politicians and welfare benefits. This ultimately reduces the incentives for workers to overcome their collective action problems, over and above the existing structural constraints discussed in chapter 2. Finally, I describe India's fragmented labor movements in detail to illustrate how non-encompassing labor groups are able neither to encourage a transition to a more universalistic welfare state nor to block race to the bottom reforms.

How is it that decommodification policies continue to prevail over commodification policies at the expense of the majority of the population? India's early industrial strategy helped provide three groups in particular privileged access to politicians and the policy agenda: the industrial capitalist class, the landed elite, and the professionals (civilian and military), including white-collar workers in the public sector (Bardhan, 1984).[31] Some sections of unionized workers eventually became part of this dominant coalition (Bardhan, 1984: 67). This is not to suggest that these groups act cohesively in the form of strong business associations or labor unions. Rather, they remain individually strong, but collectively weak. Welfare policies that were implemented in tandem with this industrial strategy had, at a minimum, the tacit consent of one of these broader groups.

While India's constitution recognized the importance of both productive and protective welfare policies, it was the protective welfare policies favored by the dominant coalition that received political commitment and material support from governing elites. Organized labor and white-collar professionals, particularly in the public sector, were the primary pressure groups. Domestic industrialists and the landed elite, while initially opposed to many of the protective benefits, were too divided to offer resistance. In the insulated economic environment, however, the IAS, Members of Parliament, and members of India's Legislative Assembly found alternative ways of compensating them with licenses, subsidies, cheap credit, and protectionism.

In the meantime, it was not the case that the importance of commodification-type policies, particularly education, went unrecognized by the political elite. Political rhetoric in support of universal primary education in India has always been strong. For at least the first five decades after independence, however, the Indian government grossly failed to meet its education targets and progressively allocated fewer and fewer budgetary resources to this sector (Tilak, 1999). The fundamental problem is that elites have consistently managed to direct education investment away from the poor and promote what best supports their interest: tertiary education.

---

[31] As Weiner (1986) explains, the government's ISI policies, industrial licensing system, policy of taking over sick firms, and restrictions on foreign investment all benefited the industrialists. The subsidized credit, governmental price support program, and subsidized inputs (water, power, fertilizers, diesel fuel) benefited rich farmers. Finally, the bureaucrats gained power and income through their control over the elaborate system of patronage, particularly in the distribution of state subsidies.

India's early industrial strategy gave priority to industries producing capital goods, which translated into a high demand for skilled labor. Members of India's privileged groups put pressure on the state to invest in tertiary education in order to have continued access to these coveted jobs.

The lack of investment in mass education also helps the elite groups maintain their position and reinforce their assets (Tilak, 1990; Weiner, 1991). In private interviews with this author, one of India's highest governing officials in the previous government, led by the Bharatiya Janata Party (BJP), was glib, saying: "Politicians do not want the poor to be educated." Reform advocates have been repeatedly frustrated with the lack of a clear motivation to make education a budgetary priority (see Shariff and Ghosh, 2000: 1405).[32] This is not surprising, as, for decades, none of the members of the dominant coalition demonstrated an interest in promoting education, and those who would benefit directly from the expansion of primary and secondary education have not had the same privileged access to politicians.

Similar dynamics underlie the fate of primary health care in India. On the eve of independence the Indian government's Bhore Committee initiated a program for the national provision of medical and health services to citizens. It was one of the "most rational and far-sighted documents of its kind" (Deodhar, 1982: 78). The plan included guidelines for effective rural health services, integrated preventative, promotive, and curative services with the full participation of the population, and health care provision to the neediest. Again, however, India's efforts at promoting universal health care never won the support of any of the members of India's dominant coalition. The Bhore Committee's plan ultimately gave way to super-speciality and diagnostic care, serving the interests of domestic and foreign investors such as those associated with the high-tech, medical, and electronic equipment industries (Purohit, 2001).

Essentially, the core elements of India's protective welfare state have persisted because the system put in place by early state elites is now sustained by the bureaucracy, sections of the governing party, and portions of the labor community. Any radical attempts at reform that require significant redistribution and create more universalistic welfare policies

---

[32] In the early years after independence it was strikingly apparent that political debates lacked a clear motivation for making education a priority (Weiner, 1991). A review of the activities of the Central Advisory Board of Education (CABE), which is the principal forum for formulating and reviewing national education policy, highlights the lack of direction underlying India's educational policies. It is not until the late 1960s, two decades after independence, that any link between education and national economic development was emphasized. Various rationales for the importance of primary education have been given, such as nationalism, religious and cultural development, and "educational progress." CABE documents are referenced from Biswas and Agrawal (1986).

have been met with weak political support. As a consequence, despite the current economic reforms and growing disenchantment with the state, it has proved difficult to dismantle institutionalized welfare policies. In fact, many observers comment that globalization and local beliefs in its negative consequences have incited greater protests amongst existing welfare beneficiaries in India and made them even more determined to hold on to their benefits as far as possible.

The government–labor relationship and how it evolved presents a second reason why it is difficult to dismantle India's protective welfare state. Rudolph and Rudolph (1987) characterize this relationship as one of state dominance. They observe, "It serves the interests of the state to keep labor fragmented and prevent it from concentrating its force along oligopolistic lines, hence weakening its voice in policymaking and minimizing its political role" (269). Labor leaders in India are far more focused on promoting their own political interests and the concerns of their affiliated groups than on welfare policies that serve the interests of the entire labor force.

Institutional constraints in the form of clientelism and patronage have arisen to support this relationship. India's "steel frame of administration" is led by a single dominating elite civil service, the Indian Administrative Services (formerly the Indian Civil Service). The IAS is the principal "face" of the government to the public and is responsible for implementing government programs. It is, in theory, at the helm of ensuring a sound business environment, curbing corruption, and providing public services (World Bank, 2000a). Instead, India's administrative system has become highly permeable to the appropriation of public resources for private ends (Jain, 2001; Bardhan, 1984). Civil servants and ministers are known to use the social policy agenda for patronage; welfare benefits and appointments encourage the cooperation of formal labor, "buy" political support, and reward friends. For example, governing elites have long distributed subsidies towards higher education to gain political favors from public servants, teachers, and high-income elite groups (Tilak, 1999). The Indian government's cooperation with the General Insurance Corporation to insure those segments of the population with the greatest ability to pay serves as another example. This has led to the unregulated growth of the private health sector, which excludes more than 90 percent of the Indian population (Ellis, Alam, and Gupta, 2000).

Ultimately, unless governing elites and political parties sever their close ties with formal labor, welfare benefits in India will continue to be protective towards a very small (privileged) segment of the population.[33] The

[33] Each political party in India sponsors its own labor union. As a result, each enterprise hosts multiple unions affiliated to various political parties (Lansing and Kuruvilla, 1987).

government–labor relationship has consequently provided various unions political influence that is grossly disproportionate to their membership. The power of such unions has, furthermore, allowed excess employment in the public sector to continue (see Kuruvilla, 1996: 650).

India's highly fragmented labor movement suggests a third reason why institutional continuity persists, and it explains in particular how and why this can occur at the same time that the government succumbs to (some) RTB pressures. Based on the success of European labor movements (discussed in chapter 2), it can be surmised that, if India's labor movement overcomes its collective action problems and develops more encompassing organizations, two related scenarios preventing a race to the bottom and, possibly, institutional change are feasible: (1) it could prevent RTB cutbacks by backing policies that balance efficiency and compensation concerns; and/or (2) India could advance towards a more universalistic welfare state. Instead, India's labor movement is unable to foster a transition to a welfare state that serves a broader clientele or to encourage increases in spending that would benefit more labor groups. The fragmented structure and composition of India's formal labor organizations undermines the political power of labor as a group.[34] Labor unions in India, in consequence, do not represent the collective interests of workers. Rudolph and Rudolph (1987: 268) summarize it best:

Disproportionate organization and mobilization of white-collar professional and skilled labor reveals that organized labor has elected to follow the path of least resistance, to work with the conscious and accessible rather than with vulnerable and dependent unskilled laborers in industry and agriculture.

At best, labor in India can help push for the status quo.

Rules and norms governing collective action and industrial relations exacerbate the extent of fragmentation. For example, the Trade Union Act (1926) requires only seven persons to form a union, and it permits an unlimited number of unions in each factory. Unions tend to view this Act as an indication of their freedoms, particularly their right to organize. Analysts argue, however, that the multiplicity of unions in India has exacerbated inter-union rivalries and created a conflict-ridden industrial relations climate (Lansing and Kuruvilla, 1987; Mathur, 1996; Papola, 1994; Ratnam, 1996; Sinha, 1994). In just one decade, from 1980 to 1990, the number of unions doubled from 4,435 to 8,828, whereas union density increased only slightly over one percentage

---

[34] Unlike many developing countries, union membership has always been voluntary in India.

Table 5.1 *Employment in unionized and non-unionized sectors (millions),* *selected years 1972-99*

	Unionized	Non-unionized	Total	% unionized
1972	18.8	217.5	236.3	8.0
1978	21.2	249.5	270.7	7.8
1983	24.0	278.7	302.7	7.9
1988	25.7	296.3	322.0	8.0
1991	26.7	342.1	368.8	7.2
1994	27.4	365.4	392.7	7.0
1996	29.9	381.6	409.5	7.3
1999	28.1	408.0	436.1	6.4

Sources: 1972–88: Sinha (2004); 1991–9: Tata Services (2002).

point.[35] India has about ten major confederations that have more than 500,000 members.

The prospects for improving fragmented labor movements in the globalizing environment are not encouraging. First and foremost, unions are losing standing. The pervasive belief is that unions nowadays do not have the scope to negotiate on behalf of labor relative to the past. Every union member and leader interviewed for this study vocalized the opinion that international market pressures for low wages and the growing demand for informal labor have transferred greater bargaining power to employers. Second, studies show that inter-union rivalries have intensified and left–labor party ties have weakened with globalization (Roychowdhury, 2003). Neither is labor receiving much party support, as parties traditionally sympathetic to labor issues have taken "pro-market" positions since reform began in earnest in 1991 (Sarangi, 2005). It is no surprise, then, that the percentage of trade union membership has been declining, although it is critical to emphasize that this change has not been dramatic (see table 5.1). Labor groups in India are not likely to form a unified front anytime soon, and will, by default, continue to support policies that favor the middle class.

Without effective resistance from India's fragmented labor movement, the government instituted some RTB-type social reforms – albeit incremental ones – in response to the pressures of globalization. These did not

[35] Union density represents union membership as a percentage of total paid (formal) employees (and not the larger workforce). Union density increased from 25.5 percent in 1980 to 27 percent in 1990. Contrast these numbers with Sweden, for instance, where there are only sixty-four unions, and union density is 84 percent.

occur completely without opposition from labor groups, however. For instance, the great majority of India's major trade unions have been opposed to social security reforms that facilitate the transition to the defined-contribution plan. Similarly, union demands regarding pension funds, including resisting foreign investment, maintaining current state deposit rates, continuing access to the Provident Fund, and increasing the rate of return for the country's largest state-run pension fund scheme, have all gone unheeded. Interestingly, active union support for the "social security for the unorganized sector" Bill has been subdued in comparison.

In terms of protesting cuts in the health and education budgets, labor has yet to provide unified support. Some central labor union representatives have participated in select "education for all" campaigns. Various teachers' unions staged several protests over reforms in higher education (e.g. state and central budget cuts, increases in working hours, attempts to emphasize meritocracy in recruitment and promotions), but these reactions were reportedly "too late."[36] The privatization of the health sector marches onward despite occasional protests, and, as analysts observe, the private health care industry in India is "quietly facilitating a revolution."[37]

Despite some incremental changes in spending and welfare policies, India's welfare state remains largely consistent. There have been no significant increases in means-tested programs, no major transfer of responsibility to the private sector, no dramatic changes in benefit and eligibility rules, nor any discontinuity of "illiberal" institutional legacies. According to these criteria for regime change, therefore, it has not taken place. This institutional continuity is a result of several factors, including the following: the interests and privileged access to political power of certain groups; a government–labor relationship that grants only select groups access to benefits; and a fragmented labor movement that is unable to unify for the sake of protecting its wider interests or prevent some welfare retrenchment (in middle-class benefits).

5.4   Who really gets hurt?

Who is impacted most by the race to the bottom in India? Does it hurt the poor, as proponents of the race to the bottom hypothesis assert, or has this type of spending missed the poor from the start? Against this backdrop, is globalization providing any incentives for reforms that would benefit subordinate groups? In all cases, the majority of India's protective welfare

---

[36] A. Jayaram, "Teachers' Stir: A Fight that Came Late," *The Hindu* (Madras), February 19, 2001.
[37] "India Questions UNESCO Report," *The Hindu* (Madras), November 10, 2005.

schemes have been directed towards the relatively better-off urban, formal sector, which constitutes only 10 percent of India's working population. Cutbacks in existing social schemes then suggest that the middle and lower-middle classes feel the immediate effects of welfare reform, rather than the bulk of India's poor: small farmers and agricultural laborers, artisans and self-employed in household enterprises, petty traders, and casual non-agricultural workers (Bardhan, 1984). These sectors constitute the underprivileged "casual laborforce" in India.[38] The Indian case study reveals that, overall, the situation for the disadvantaged is not significantly improving (*in terms of welfare benefits*), and the pre-globalization tradition of neglecting the poor is being maintained. The one exception is that some resources in the education sector are being redirected towards promoting universal education. This finding is consistent with the predictions in chapter 3. In this section, I focus on the impacts of social security, education, and health reforms, since this is where race to the bottom effects in India have been the greatest.

5.4.1   Social security

Social security programs in India are the most regressive in comparison to the other sectors. This is primarily because less than 10 percent of the working population is covered by formal provisions for old-age income security (Ministry of Social Justice and Empowerment, 1999), and, furthermore, civil servants, followed by public enterprise employees, maintain the highest level of pension provisions. In other words, some estimates indicate that almost one-third of the pension budget is directed towards civil servants, and up to 70 percent is spent on all subcategories of public-sector employees,[39] who for decades did not have to make any pension contributions during the tenure of their employment.[40]

The extent of social insurance coverage for the elite white-collar workers (senior public-sector officials and the managerial class) is striking. Agarwala and Khan (2002) estimate that labor elites account for approximately 1 percent of the workforce, or 3 million workers. Their compensation packages, which include top medical care, housing, old-age

---

[38] This term is commonly used in India to refer to those working outside the formal sector, or informal labor force.

[39] This percentage is derived from official estimates of the proportion of workers in the public sector relative to total employment (see Tata Services, 2002).

[40] In addition to their pension benefits, public employees also have access to the General Provident Fund (GPF), to which workers may contribute a minimum of 6 percent of their monthly salary (Goswami, 2002). This is in contrast to the private sector, where employees must contribute 12 percent to their provident funds.

benefits, survivor benefits, and employment injury and benefits, parallel the highest international standards. As Guhan (1992: 285; emphasis added) puts it:

The fundamental problem is that coverage tends to be highly skewed towards the public services and workers in the organized factory to the almost complete neglect of the self-employed, workers in the urban informal sector, and, most important, the large mass of rural laborers. Typically, the categories which are covered benefit directly from budgetary funds (as in the case of public employees) or through social insurance, to which there is a sizable contribution from the exchequer, while the element of social assistance available for workers in the unorganized sector is relatively insignificant. Consequently, *the social security system taken as a whole is highly regressive.*

The direct impact of the current SS reforms thus falls primarily upon public employees. Of course, while some types of government employees are more privileged than others, the latter's wages and benefits are still substantially higher than their counterparts in the unorganized economy.[41] It is no wonder that public employees have shown stiff resistance to the new pension scheme, in which the state no longer guarantees their high benefits. For instance, one of the most contentious issues of reform is that government employees will no longer be guaranteed a fixed pension, and they will now have to contribute to their own pension benefits, at a rate of 10 percent of their salary every month.

The race to the bottom in social security thus primarily hurts the middle class. It neither hurts nor helps the poor directly. The latest attempts to provide coverage for the informal sector have yet to be successful. Most recently, Atal Vajpayee, the former prime minister, launched a proposal, the Social Security Scheme for Unorganized Workers, in 2004 as part of the Common Minimum Programme (CMP).[42] The scheme would provide unorganized workers with old-age pensions, and accident and medical insurance. At the time of writing, however, the Bill still awaits parliamentary clearance, and has been criticized for its vague definitions of "unorganized workers," for inadequate penal provisions for violators, for demanding unreasonable enrollment fees and stable employment,

---

[41] Public-sector employees have traditionally enjoyed higher wages and salaries than their counterparts in the private sector (Rudolph and Rudolph, 1987: 263–5).

[42] Also referred to as basic minimum services, the United Front government in 1997 passed the CMP, which presented specific guidelines aimed at empowering the disadvantaged. The CMP was subsequently extended by the current UPA coalition government. One of its basic principles is "[t]o enhance the welfare and well-being of farmers, farm labor and workers, particularly those in the unorganised sector, and assure a secure future for their families in every respect" (Common Minimum Programme, as quoted in "UPA Government to Adhere to Six Basic Principles of Governance," *The Hindu* [Madras], June 28, 2004).

and for having minimal legislative backing.[43] At present, the majority of Indian workers engaged in unorganized and informal work do have access to a few voluntary pension schemes, but these are not well publicized (Ministry of Social Justice and Empowerment, 1999).[44] It is, therefore, the middle classes who are most greatly affected by the post-liberalization retrenchment in social security benefits.

5.4.2   Health care

In the arena of health reforms the effects of globalization do have some direct impact on the poor, but, again, the group most hurt by changes is the middle class. Recent studies have found that public health subsidies in India disproportionately favor the richer groups. First, only one-third of government health expenditure is on preventive and curative care, and, of this, nearly 75 percent is spent on secondary- (specialized care) and tertiary-sector hospitals (specialized, capital-intensive care) (Sankar and Kathuria, 2003). Rural areas are often overlooked, as only 33 percent of government health expenditures are distributed to such areas even though they account for 73 percent of the population (Garg, 1998). Second, upper-income groups go to private hospitals for superior treatment, *and* they are the largest consumers of public health facilities. Contrary to common practice in OECD countries, access to public facilities is not universal in many developing nations, and India is an exemplar case. The poor can ill afford even basic public health services. Although treatment in public hospitals is subsidized, richer groups receive privileged access to public subsidies.[45] Finally, only 26 percent of the miniscule portion that the government spends on public health is allocated to preventative care (e.g. disease prevention, maternity, and child health), which tends to give higher benefits to the poor (Garg, 1998). Furthermore, chronic

---

[43] The legislation has been criticized harshly by the left. See, for example, W. R. Varada Rajan, "Expose This Cruel Fraud on Unorganised Workers," *People's Democracy*, March 7, 2004, and M. K. Pandhe, "Mobilise Workers to Modify Unorganised Workers Bill," *People's Democracy*, January 20, 2008. In addition, Chandrasekhar and Ghosh (2006) conclude that "the amount of coverage is so low that it would still leave most families with need to look elsewhere to finance the total costs of these contingencies."

[44] The most well known is the Public Provident Fund (PPF), which, according to some official estimates, still provides coverage for less than 1 percent of the working population more than three decades after its implementation (Gillingham and Kanda, 2001). Under PPF, individuals receive rates of return that are administratively determined. Benefits are normally paid out in lump sum upon retirement, although early withdrawals are permitted after five years.

[45] See discussion by Mahal (2003). Significantly, Mahal finds that, even if private health care increases in India (as the government is attempting to accomplish), the redistributive effect will be small when richer groups have privileged access to public facilities.

medicine shortages in public health facilities require households to bear a substantial share of the costs (Ramesh and Nishant, 2004).

Unlike reductions in the social security sector and government health spending since liberalization, however, the growing participation of private industry and multinationals in the health care sector is of immediate consequence to the poor. Purohit (2001) argues cogently that allowing greater private-sector participation detracts from the Indian government's commitment to basic health facilities. Private companies focus on high profit margins, super-speciality, and diagnostic care, making it increasingly unlikely that the basic needs of the majority who are part of the unorganized economy will be met.

Nonetheless, the point to be emphasized in this analysis is that the conditions exacerbating India's health performance and care for the poor existed long before globalization. The World Bank's Operations and Evaluation Department has confirmed that, in the 1970s and 1980s, the tenuous quality of public health assistance in India was affected by the limited resources devoted to health care (which did not in any case effectively target the most vulnerable groups), inadequate management and personnel policies, poor maintenance and equipment, and inter-district disparities in fertility, health, and cultural and institutional characteristics (World Bank, 1999a). The World Bank has invested more in India's health sector than in any other country, but still reports that, "over the *past three decades*, progress, particularly for the poor, has been slow and uneven" (World Bank, 1999a: 1; emphasis added). Globalization might exacerbate this situation of deteriorating public health services for the poor but, clearly, India has long been struggling with providing high-quality health care for the majority of its population.

5.4.3   Education

Education spending in India is also widely critiqued for its bias towards the privileged. A comprehensive review in 1985 by the Ministry of Education reported that expenditure on elementary education had fallen by 35 percent since the First Five-year Plan (in the mid-1950s), while the share for university education had risen by 78 percent. Not surprisingly, then, enrollment in higher education grew five times as rapidly as it did in primary education during this same period (Tilak, 1990). One of India's experts on education, Jandhyala Tilak (1990, 1999) has repeatedly labeled the country's lack of educational achievement its "most conspicuous failure." In light of India's constitutional mandate (article 46) that "the State shall promote with special care the educational and economic interest of the weaker sections of the people," rhetoric has far surpassed reality.

A comparison of the percentage of children reaching grade five in 2000/1 (59 percent) with similar countries is telling: Cameroon (85 percent); China (99 percent); Zambia (77 percent); Indonesia (89 percent) (UNDP, 2004).

In striking contrast to the social security and health sectors, however, declining total education expenditures since globalization have occurred alongside a redistribution of existing resources towards education programs that benefit the poor. Within the last decade, and for the first time since independence, there have been unmistakable signs that India is slowly shifting its priorities towards elementary education. India's accomplishments have won the plaudits of external agencies such as the IMF, which recently declared India's recent achievements in universal elementary education a "quiet revolution" (Wu, Kaul, and Sankar, 2005).

Three important legislative changes indicate this commitment. First, efforts to address the elitist bias in India's educational system began immediately after liberalization's tentative beginnings in 1986 with the second National Policy on Education.[46] The policy aimed to achieve universal enrollment and the retention of children in school up to age fourteen by 1995. Two relatively successful and expanding schemes that came out of this policy focus on improving basic amenities in village schools and universalizing primary education by emphasizing decentralized management, participatory processes, and capacity-building at all levels of government.

Second, after decades of effort, the ninety-third constitutional amendment was passed in 2001, recognizing elementary education as a fundamental right and making it compulsory. This is quite an accomplishment, given that Weiner's (1991) historical analysis observes in detail how India has repeatedly failed to make education compulsory since independence.[47] The national program that came out of the recent amendment, *Sarva Shiksha Abhiyan*, stipulates that all children will have completed primary school by 2007 and upper primary education by 2010. *Sarva Shiksha Abhiyan* focuses on increasing participation (particularly of the traditionally disadvantaged, such as the handicapped, girls, and those

---

[46] Tilak (1990) laments the fact that India has taken an average of eighteen years to formulate new education policies. The first National Policy on Education was adopted eighteen years after independence, and next, eighteen years later, the second (1986) policy was developed.

[47] Weiner (1991) argues that the central government's shortfall has been that India's laws permit but do not require central and local governments to make education compulsory. It is important to emphasize here, however, that Weiner's analysis ends in the early 1990s, just as globalization policies were being adopted on a large scale.

living in less populated rural areas), transparency, and public account-ability. It also takes measures to ensure states' commitment.

Finally, in 2004 the government imposed an education tax of 2 percent on all central direct and indirect taxes. These revenues have been ear-marked specifically for primary education. Indeed, the Tenth Five-year Plan (2002–7) directly reveals that revenues for the primary sectors will come at the cost of subsidies to university education, as opposed to raising total spending altogether.

How, then, has India managed to overcome political resistance to redis-tributive reforms in education, but not other social sectors? Increasing awareness of the importance of education in a globalizing economy has helped mobilize an informal coalition of policy-makers, domestic business, and the poor. As predicted in chapter 2, the spread of information on the benefits of education has contributed to a cross-class interest convergence. India's governing elites are playing a leading role in spreading information about the benefits of education in an increasingly competitive international market environment.

At the same time, the poor *and* business groups in India have displayed unprecedented support for universal education. On November 28, 2001, almost 50,000 people from poor villages and towns had mobilized during the deliberation of the Education for All (93rd Amendment) Bill in parlia-ment. Sadgopal called it a "historical event":

It was probably the first time in the history of independent India that people had gathered to demand the right to education. These peasants, landless laborers and slum dwellers, both men and women, demolished the myth promoted by the state and the educated civil society that the poor are interested only in roti, kapda and makaan (food, clothing and shelter) and not in educating their children. They understood that ... today, without a Class 12 certificate, a young person stands little chance of obtaining either employment or admission to professional courses. For the Scheduled Caste and Scheduled Tribes, too, the benefits of reservation become available only after Class 10 or 12 as the case may be. Hence the demand for right to education for all children up to 18 years.[48]

Business support for primary education is even more striking, given that there has been a long history of apprehension among India's corporate sector to take upon itself "social responsibilities" such as education. At a recent convention on "Corporate Sector Participation in Elementary Education" organized by the Confederation of Indian Industry (CII), the minister for human resource development, Arjun Singh, appealed to

---

[48] Anil Sadgopal, "A Convenient Consensus," *Frontline* (Madras), December 22, 2001. Note that this group was concerned that the Bill applied "Education for All" to the age group of six to fourteen, rather than all children from birth to eighteen years.

industry "to look at supporting elementary education not as an act of charity but a decision, which would lead to reform in education, and economic upliftment thereafter."[49] Most tellingly, despite contention within the industry, CII, India's largest and strongest business association, has come out in support of the 2 percent tax earmarked for primary education.[50]

The high levels of spending on tertiary education per student confirm the long history of bias towards this sector. The data also confirm, however, that the 1990s trend in primary education spending shows some improvement, while tertiary-level spending is on the decline. Although inter-state variances still exist, these trends nonetheless suggest that India is gradually redirecting its priorities.[51] The 7 percent growth in literacy rates (for adults above fifteen years of age) in 2000–1 (from 57 to 61 percent), the highest ever annual increase in India, is a good indication that India's growing commitment to universal education is taking effect (*World Bank*, 2005b; see also Dev and Mooij, 2002).

Nevertheless, these developments in education, while positive, must be kept in broader perspective. India's recent achievements have thus far failed to have a major impact. The recent UNESCO (2005) *EFA Global Monitoring Report* did not include India on its list of countries that stood a chance of attaining the goal of universal primary education by 2015. Instead, India ranked among the thirty countries least likely to meet literacy targets because their "very low literacy rates are not increasing fast enough" (UNESCO, 2005: 70). This report was received with great disappointment among India's governing officials.[52]

5.4.4   Summary

It appears that education is one social sector that is experiencing equity-enhancing reform as globalization advances. The trends shown in figure 5.6 suggest that, while the education budget as a whole may be declining, India is redistributing resources away from tertiary and towards primary education. Although the decline in expenditures on tertiary

---

[49] "Arjun Singh Calls upon Industry to Support Elementary Education," CII Online, August 26, 2004. Available at www.ciionline.org/news/newsMaina4ce.html?news_id= 826200423418PM (accessed July 9, 2007).

[50] CII Online, August 26, 2004.

[51] In no way has India made a dramatic shift away from higher education. Note that Dev and Mooij (2002) argue that university and higher education recorded a record rise in the late 1990s (in terms of central expenditures). Rather, the emphasis here is that there were some earnest and effective attempts at redistribution by the Indian government in the 1990s.

[52] "India Questions UNESCO Report," *The Hindu* (Madras), November 10, 2005.

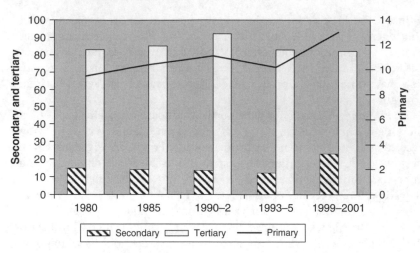

Figure 5.6 Spending on primary, secondary, and tertiary education, selected years 1980–2001

Notes: Years chosen are based on data availability.
Data represent spending at all levels of government.
Source: UN's: Global Educational database.

education is undeniably small, it is particularly striking that resources devoted to this sector began to shift soon after India's financial crisis in 1991. While the changes may not be fast enough or sufficient to solve the existing problems, it is nonetheless encouraging that reforms are being implemented in such a way as to include the least privileged groups.

The health and social security sectors in India have long neglected the disadvantaged, and so the recent cutbacks have the greatest impact on the non-poor and show little evidence of (successful) equity-enhancing improvements. The education sector is unique in its efforts to include the least advantaged segments of the population. Most social programs remain biased in favor of the privileged, however, and the overall impact of globalization on social spending seems to result in harm to the middle classes, with minimal direct effects on the poor.

5.5   Other factors: democracy, ethnic fragmentation, and culture

Given India's long-standing democracy, it is virtually impossible to ignore the prospective role of political freedoms in influencing some changes to India's distribution regime. This warrants a full investigation elsewhere, but, to get a sense, it is worthwhile to consider the following puzzles: why did education reforms become a campaign priority in 2004, although efforts to mobilize the poor began more than a decade earlier, in 1988? Why was the ambitious NREGP (National Rural Employment Guarantee Programme) launched only recently when rural poverty has been a perennial issue? Even more strikingly, the Social Security for Unorganised Workers Bill, which aims to provide benefits for India's 400 million informal-sector workers, has recently been drafted. Exploring these issues may provide some evidence that democracy can affect institutional changes.

There has been a widespread perception that the surprise defeat of the BJP-led National Democratic Alliance in the 2004 general election was a signal that democracies must respond to the poor under conditions of globalization. The former deputy prime minister, L. K. Advani, later admitted that the "India Shining" and "Feel Good" catchphrases widely used by the BJP in its campaign in reference to India's economic accomplishments since liberalization failed to impress the poor.[53] Analysts argue that the urban and rural poor found this particularly offensive. The poverty-stricken residents of one entire village (Harkishan Pura) decided to boycott the elections in response to the increasingly difficult economic conditions they had faced since liberalization. One villager commented: "India may be shining for them [politicians] but our life is without any sheen and shine."[54] It is telling, then, that the newly elected leadership (United Progressive Alliance) immediately presented education as its highest priority, after years of struggling in parliament, as part of its wider campaign to reach out to the poor.[55] Analysts skeptical about the NREGP's long-term prospects attribute its recent adoption to the fact that "the government needed to pass this legislation to fulfill its election promise," but anticipate that "it would soon die a natural death."[56]

Why, then, did the econometric tests in chapter 2 fail to produce consistent results on democracy? The electoral connection, while important, may also be evident in some authoritarian and semi-democratic systems (see Kaufman and Nelson, 2004: 484). Another possibility is that democracy matters, but the time lag for institutions related to democracy to impact on social welfare strategies is difficult to determine except on a case-by-case basis. In the case of the Education for All legislation, the poor began mobilizing and pressuring government officials in the late 1980s, but the Bill did not come into effect until more than one decade later. It may also be

---

[53] Vinay Kumar, "Advani Admits 'India Shining' Campaign Failed to Click," *The Hindu* (Madras), May 28, 2004.
[54] "Village Decides to Boycott Elections," *Times of India* (Delhi), March 8, 2004.
[55] Access to primary education was a central theme of the Common Minimum Programme.
[56] Amelia Gentleman, "India's War on Poverty: Easy Victory Unlikely," *International Herald Tribune*, February 28, 2006.

the case that democracies do not spend more (i.e. increase the *level* of spending) with globalization, as was observed in chapter 2, but encourage more efficient distribution of different welfare resources (see Rudra and Haggard, 2005).

Other socio-political factors, such as ethnic divisions and culture, arguably contribute to the continuity and change (i.e. RTB pressures in certain non-core sectors) of India's protective welfare state. Ethnic diversity helps explain why establishing encompassing labor organizations in India might be exceptionally challenging. As Varshney (2002) has argued, many of the divisions in India's civil society and related political rivalry occur along pre-existing ethnic rather than class lines. Indeed, social divisions in India are extremely complex (religion, linguistic, caste, class, regional) (Manor, 1996), making it all the more challenging for workers to establish common interests in the globalizing environment; sensitivity to race to the bottom pressures and the continuity in particularistic welfare policies are underscored. Finally, the hierarchical caste system and value of group status deeply embedded in India's culture cannot be completely ignored in analyzing its patterns of public good provision. Weiner (1991) links the culture factor to the persistent adoption of elitist social policies, such as the long-time neglect of mass education. Neither culture, democracy, nor ethnic fragmentation can fully explain the post-liberalization changes in India's welfare state, however, since these are relatively stable variables; the recent equity-enhancing reforms in education are an example.

5.6　Implications

Ultimately, the details of the Indian case study reveal that, even in the face of some RTB cutbacks, overall many of the protective welfare schemes remain more or less intact. Signs of institutional continuity are threefold. First, the key elements of India's protective welfare state – labor market protections and public employment – have been relatively resistant to globalization pressures. Second, although India has experienced one important equity-enhancing change that does benefit the poor (i.e. a greater commitment to universal education), government support of protective measures still strongly prevails over productive measures. For instance, health outcomes in India remain extremely dismal and political elites are doing little to change this. Finally, the poor have long been neglected by India's protective welfare state, and this continues to be the case as India expands its reach in international markets. Existing welfare schemes continue India's historical tradition of disproportionately protecting a very small portion of India's larger workforce.

This chapter has also demonstrated how and why protective welfare states such as India have not experienced radical regime change in the current globalizing environment. The pressures of globalization moderated by well-entrenched interest groups, the government–labor relationship, and fragmented labor organizations in India produced two repercussions: (1) they inhibited a coordinated response to globalization that could avoid the trade-off between efficiency and welfare; and (2) they reinforced a welfare state that protects the better off. Greater information about the benefits of education and cross-class interest convergence contributed to the one exception in pro-poor reform: slight improvements in primary education. In addition, India's democratic environment is also one of the intervening variables that contributed to pro-poor reform. Democracy may not have emerged as significant in the quantitative chapters (see particularly chapter 2), because the effects of democracy are more complex than is commonly understood.

At the same time, these findings raise several questions. What are the long-term implications? Will the incremental changes towards labor market flexibility (de facto) and improvements in education lead to a paradigmatic shift to a productive welfare state? For now, it is too early to tell, but the resilience of welfare policies (e.g. public employment) that continue to buttress powerful interest groups does not bode well for this transition. Nevertheless, although India's education reform efforts have not been groundbreaking, particularly given the much larger changes required to improve the living conditions of the majority of the population, they are a promising development in light of the country's history of poverty and its neglect of elementary education. Another question worth investigating in future analysis is why some protective welfare states emphasize some decommodification policies (e.g. public employment) over others (e.g. social security). This case study suggests that country-specific historical circumstances may be the culprit.

6 Globalization and the productive welfare state: case study of South Korea

What are the effects of globalization on productive welfare states? In contrast to protective welfare states, such as India's, are they advancing towards the neoliberal bottom?[1] Who gets hurt from changes in welfare policies as markets expand in productive welfare states? Using details from the case of South Korea, this chapter seeks to answer these questions by illustrating how the interplay of international markets and domestic institutions shapes social policies in a productive welfare state. Just as in protective welfare states (e.g. India), globalization pressures are real and have prompted cutbacks in several of South Korea's welfare programs. At the same time, the South Korean government has also explored ways to make the productive welfare state more "protective." The introduction of universal pensions and health insurance constitutes two examples. This is very distinct from India, a protective welfare state, where the (relatively) major path-breaking reforms have been in the "productive" welfare category (e.g. education). Despite succumbing to some race to the bottom pressures, however, the main features of South Korea's productive welfare state remain intact: promoting citizens' market reliance through extensive state intervention and a concentration of public resources on commodification, particularly education. As a result, the situation of better-off groups in society is similar for both regime types: long-standing domestic institutions essentially guarantee that the more privileged sectors will have access to protections from the risks and uncertainties associated with the globalizing environment. This chapter reveals how international market pressures have led to some welfare retrenchment, yet institutional continuity characterizes South Korea's productive welfare state in the current era of globalization.

---

[1] For productive welfare states, which, by definition, invest disproportionately more than other LDCs on human capital and less on protective welfare schemes, signs of neoliberal changes might include less state involvement (spending and regulation) in the provision of social safety nets for its citizens (except perhaps means-tested programs) and more private provisioning of productive welfare schemes.

The first section describes the key elements of South Korea's distribution regime, outlining how and why it is a productive welfare state. Section 6.2 demonstrates the effects of RTB pressures on South Korea's welfare state. Next, by illuminating the interplay between globalization and domestic institutions, section 6.3 reveals the extent of institutional continuity in South Korea's productive welfare regime and how and why these long-lived institutions tend to guide policy choices even in the current era. Section 6.4 looks into who is most hurt by the race to the bottom in South Korea, and section 6.5 considers the effects of "other factors" affecting the degree of regime persistence. Section 6.6, in conclusion, reflects on the overall implications for productive welfare states in an expanding global economy.

6.1   South Korea's productive welfare state

South Korea's welfare state has applied extensive state intervention to encourage citizens to be dependent on the market.[2] Particularly since the administration of President Park Chung Hee (1961–79) adopted an export-oriented development strategy in the early 1960s, welfare policy has centered on the promotion of wage labor by simultaneously increasing public support for education services and minimizing protectivist welfare policies that increase reliance on the state. This is not to suggest that South Korea's early approach to industrialization is the primary reason why investment in education is so high and protectionist policies so low. History, culture, factor endowments, and security concerns, as well as the American and, particularly, the Japanese occupations, are also linked to the South Korean prioritization of education. The relevant point is that the government's emphasis on the linear advancement of education (from first concentrating resources on primary-level education and then moving on to secondary-level education) is also associated with the 1960s development strategy and the consequent emphasis on linking benefits to the expansion of wage labor.

Efforts towards an expanding secondary education started in the 1960s *after* primary education had been universalized and the export-oriented growth strategy adopted. Education development and economic planning were not systematically coordinated before the 1960s. Despite

---

[2] See Holliday (2000) for a related discussion of South Korea's "productive welfare state." Holliday defines the east Asian productive welfare state as one that places social policies as secondary to economic policies, but he does not empirically distinguish between the two. The analysis in this book, however, is unique in its attempts to differentiate social policies in the developing world.

President Syngman Rhee's (1948–60) attempts, the administration lacked "a well thought out economic development plan that could guide educational need" (Seth, 2002: 116). It was not until after President Park Chung Hee's administration adopted the export-oriented strategy that the Five-year Plan for Educational Reconstruction was linked to the first Five-year Economic Development Plan (Lee, 1974). One of Park's primary objectives was to increase the primary enrollment figure to 100 percent and gradually shift education planning and development towards the secondary level (Seth, 2002). This linear expansion of investment in education stands in contrast to the policy adopted in many developing countries, such as India, which began investing heavily in tertiary education *before* primary or secondary education even approached universal coverage. It is no coincidence that policy-makers in South Korea began to view education development on a par with economic planning, while India, for decades, subordinated education goals to the needs associated with its chosen development strategy.

Cultivating a workforce commensurate with the needs of its early industrialization strategy has been a priority of successive South Korean governments since the 1950s. In the 1960s, even though a primary-level education was mostly sufficient since South Korea was focused on low-skill, labor-intensive exports, the president organized the first Council for Long-range Comprehensive Educational Planning. Policy-makers quickly came to recognize the importance of "the human factor" in achieving the mission of export-oriented economic growth (Lee, 1974: 16–17).[3] During his inaugural address, Park Chung Hee noted:

Self-reliant economy and self-defense are the basis of national independency, peace and prosperity. We will make greater efforts to educate for brains, who are needed to build a highly industrialized society based on heavy-chemical industries and to upgrade our science and technology to the world class.[4]

Education has been the centerpiece of South Korea's productive welfare state, rather than "protective measures" such as social security, labor market protections, public employment, and housing. South Korea's welfare state has emphasized individual responsibility and encouraging citizens to become more dependent on the market. Take, for example, the

---

[3] As Amsden (1989) puts it, however, it is important not to deify South Korea's education system. South Korea's long-term education planning was not always completely successful, although it did consistently maintain some important features.

[4] President Park Chung-Hee's Inauguration Address, December 27, 1978 (in Korean). The Korean text can be downloaded from the website of the National Archives and Records Service: www.archives.go.kr/president/index.html.

revolutionary words of President Park after a widely supported military coup had brought him to power:

You, a young girl sitting in the second class compartment, your white hand holding a book of French poetry. Your white hands I abhor. We must work. One cannot survive with clean hands. Clean hands have been responsible for our present misery... I believe the slogans of "Economy comes first," "Priority goes to construction" and "Labor's supreme." (Park, 1963: 177, 179)

Public officials clearly embraced the view that providing all citizens with a formal education complies with the "Economy comes first" philosophy and is key to promoting individual self-reliance. Park emphasized in the early 1960s:

Reorganization of the school system and rationalization of its management, reform of education taxes providing for free and compulsory education...and an administrative posture giving priority to field education should be established... *I stress the indispensable importance of education for training in the productive capabilities vitally essential to industrial modernization and economic reconstruction.* (Park, 1962: 232–3; emphasis added.)

Ever since then the South Korean government has played a central role in education, both through provision and intervention. Successive governments have spent, as a proportion of the total budget, much larger sums on education than on other social sectors. On average, South Korea spends almost three times more on education than on health and social security combined. The extent of education spending as a percentage of total government spending (i.e. 24 percent) at the dawn of the twenty-first century is an indication of the government's commitment to education relative to other social welfare services. South Korea falls in the top quintile of the full sample for its expenditures as a proportion of total government spending.[5] In stark contrast to India, the great majority of this spending is devoted to primary and secondary education, and most of the elementary schools and two-thirds of the secondary schools are public (Kim and Lee, 2002).

Compared to the size of its economy, however, the South Korean government spends an average amount on education relative to other LDCs.[6] This is still consistent with the institutional norms of South Korea's productive welfare state, as, without necessarily increasing the *level* of expenditures, the government is heavily involved in regulating

---

[5] This calculation is based on the sample of developed and developing countries used in this analysis.
[6] This has been the case from the early 1980s until the present. During the 1970s South Korea spent slightly less than the LDC average on education.

education and ensuring that the expansion of lower education has occurred in an orderly (and equitable) fashion, and it has made concerted efforts to improve the efficiency of spending (see McGinn *et al.*, 1980). For example, the government has ensured universal access to primary and secondary education by centralizing control in the Ministry of Education (MOE), controlling tuition rates, regulating the entry process to primary, secondary, and tertiary education, and randomly assigning students by computer to attend both private and public schools (Lee, 2002; Kim, 2001; Seth, 2002).

In contrast, the South Korean government has played a minor role in both the provision and regulation of health care. Similarly to India, the government has invested little in health delivery, and since the 1960s it has taken a laissez-faire approach to the supply side of health services by the private sector. In 1966 only 7 percent of total health care services were provided by public institutions (see McGuire, 2006: 11), and currently, four decades later, it has risen slightly, by three percentage points, to 10 percent (Lee, 2003). Public outlays on disease prevention and health promotion continue to be extremely low (OECD, 2004). Unlike India, however, the poor quality of public-sector provision of services (qualifications, service at public health care facilities, updated equipment) has not been the fundamental issue and is at par with international standards (Jo and Choi, 2002; OECD, 2004). How, then, has South Korea achieved such dramatic improvements in life expectancy and infant mortality rates over the last few decades? McGuire (2006) argues convincingly that it is South Korea's rapid income growth that is responsible for this achievement, not public intervention.

At the same time as it has been promoting productive policies such as education, the South Korean government has long prevented the expansion of protective welfare schemes such as social security, housing, public employment, labor market protections, and direct poverty alleviation programs. In terms of social insurance protections, both coverage and the level of benefits have been very low. Despite President Park's public promise to introduce a National Pension Scheme in 1972, and the formation of several task committees to introduce the program, he postponed the program just four days after it was officially launched (Kim, 2006). Only civil servants, military personnel, private school teachers, and workers in large establishments enjoyed some pension coverage.[7] It is remarkable that, even today, government expenditures on social security

---

[7] For example, large South Korean firms maintained a severance pay system that granted employees a lump-sum amount paid on retirement or separation from the firm (Yang, 2001a).

barely exceed 1 percent of GDP, despite the recent reforms in the NPS designed to support universal social security coverage (discussed in more detail later). This is far below even the most liberal welfare states, such as the United States, which spends 21 percent of its GDP on SS and welfare.[8]

Housing needs have been largely ignored by the South Korean government (Park, B.-G., 1998; World Bank, 1979), even in the face of a chronic housing shortage. It was not until the 1980s that President Roh Tae-woo's (1988–1993) regime pursued the "Two Million Housing Units Construction Plan" to address the housing shortage (Doling, 1999). These houses were to be built in four years, and the role of the public sector in housing provision was to increase. President Kim Young Sam (1993–7) stopped supporting the construction of public housing rental units soon afterwards however, in 1994. Park (1998) reports that, after 1993, government expenditure on housing decreased by over 10 percent annually.[9]

In stark contrast to India and many other developing countries, South Korea has also avoided public employment as an effective or desirable social welfare protection strategy. Even when public enterprises accounted for a proportionately high percentage of total investment in the early 1970s, public enterprise contribution to jobs created was extremely modest (Jones, 1975). Jones (123) argues that South Korea's public enterprises were "a most inefficient means of employment creation." Civil servant employment similarly constitutes a low percentage of total employment relative to other developing countries, and has been steadily decreasing since the turn of the century. Data indicate that South Korea's total public employment (as a percentage of the labor force) places the country in the bottom quintile of developing nations. Its ratio of public employment to total employment is twenty percentage points less than the global average in developing economies.[10] South Korea's public works programs did not start until the late 1980s and, even then, employed a very small percentage of the poor. Indeed, South Korea's low unemployment levels even during times of economic crisis have contributed to the overall lack of demand for public employment as a welfare strategy.

---

[8] These values are based on data from the IMF's *Government Financial Statistics*, various years.

[9] Note that the proportion of government expenditure on housing decreased from 2.3 percent in 1989 to 0.6 percent in 1995.

[10] Data from the ILO report total public employment, including those employed in state-owned enterprises. Estimating a sample of non-OECD countries that include east European nations reveals a public employment average of 31 percent. Data from South Korea reveal that total average public employment has been 9.7 percent since the late 1970s, placing the country in the bottom quintile of the data set.

Similarly, for most of South Korea's modern history, governments have played a minimal role in providing labor market protections. Some legislative protections against dismissals did exist; because of the implicit practice of lifetime employment, however, governments did not face great pressures to enforce them. The issue was that lifetime employment contracts were limited to a very small percentage of workers affiliated with chaebols.[11] These large industries could manage the costs of doing so because of the many years of sustained economic expansion. At the same time, until the late 1980s labor repression was standard practice, as were heavy restrictions on organizing and protesting.[12] The absence of such labor market protections has long ensured that employers maintained a clear advantage in the bargaining process.

Finally, South Korea's productive welfare state has been averse to providing monetary assistance to working individuals who live at or below the poverty level. South Korea maintained a Poor Law tradition for over thirty-five years after independence in 1945. Although article 19 of the first constitution in 1948 stipulated that "those individuals incapable of working due to the old age, illness, or other reasons shall be protected under law by the state," no institutional support was put into place until the 1960s (Kim, J.-S., 2004). Korea's primary poverty alleviation strategy, the Livelihood Protection System (LPS), was implemented in 1961 and involved six kinds of aid: livelihood, medical, educational, maternity, funeral, and self-support. The problem was that these protections had very low coverage because of extremely stringent conditions for eligibility. By 1974 only one out of four persons in absolute poverty was receiving benefits (Kim, J.-S., 2004). Cash benefits were estimated to reach fewer than a half of those under the official poverty line (Kwon, 2002). The fundamental philosophy, as indicated by article 3 of the 1963 Social Security Act, was "not to hamper the spirit of self-support of the people" and cash assistance was to be issued "gradually as provided for by law in light of the economic circumstances of the state" (Kim, J.-S., 2004: 150). The means test provision thus applied only to non-able-bodied persons, disqualifying the large number of working poor between the ages of eighteen and sixty-five. Even today, South Korea's means-tested programs, though expanded, are still described as "strict" by policy experts and cover only 3 percent of the population (see Kwon and Holliday, 2007).

[11] Chaebols are large business conglomerates in South Korea, most often family-owned and usually clustered around one parent company.

[12] In particular, labor repression was practiced using three mechanisms: restrictions on union organization, controls on the incidence and manner of strikes, and limits on wage increases in private firms.

In sum, in direct contrast to India, the South Korean government has long placed proportionately greater weight on human-capital-type welfare programs, specifically education, than on more protective social schemes that increase dependence on the state as opposed to the market. The contrasting characteristics of the two regime types reinforce the findings in chapter 4 that most LDCs face a trade-off between human capital investment and protective welfare policies. The next section explores the pressures of globalization and the extent of cutbacks in South Korea's welfare state.

6.2   Race to the bottom

Advances towards more open markets in South Korea began in the early 1980s. In 1980 South Korea implemented the first major programs for liberalizing import protections, followed by a five-year tariff reduction plan beginning in 1984. After significant pressure from the United States, capital account liberalization was also initiated in the early 1990s (Lukauskas and Minushkin, 2000; Crotty and Lee, 2002). The 1997–8 financial crisis and subsequent IMF-mandated policy changes resulted in even more substantial trade reforms and the further dismantling of controls on international capital flows (e.g. additional reductions in tariff barriers, the elimination of quantitative restrictions and a number of subsidy programs, lower barriers to FDI, the complete opening of the bond market to non-residents, and the removal of all restrictions on foreign borrowing by South Korean firms). The pressures of globalization thus began to intensify in the early 1980s, followed by more extensive reforms after the financial crisis of 1997–8 (Yang and Hwang, 2001; Choi, 2002; Kim, 1994). The following sections focus on the effect of globalization on South Korea's welfare regime beginning in the early 1980s, with particular focus on the aftermath of the crisis.

Did these advances towards globalization lead to a race to the bottom? In a manner similar to what happened in India, the major welfare cutbacks linked to globalization pressures have occurred in the sectors that are not key features of South Korea's welfare regime: social security and labor market protections. The trend in both sectors was an initial improvement in benefits after globalization policies were first adopted in 1980, followed gradually by retrenchment, most predominantly after the financial crisis. The cutbacks in South Korea's social security sector are particularly startling, given that, in both domestic and external academic and policy-making circles, South Korea is commonly referred to as a "welfare laggard." This label has been earned primarily because of the consistently low levels of public spending allocated to social-insurance-type functions.

Indeed, as discussed earlier, the level of social security spending (relative to both GDP and total government expenditures) is exceptionally low in comparison to other countries, both in its own and in contiguous income brackets.[13] South Korea has been similarly criticized for labor management relations that have grossly favored the latter. Deyo's (1989) analysis has made a lasting impression by attributing South Korea's phenomenal economic growth to a "dark underside": the extreme political subordination and exclusion of workers. Signs of a race to the bottom emerge in both social security and labor protections, however, despite the already existing low commitments relative to international standards.

6.2.1   Social security

Cutbacks in the social security sector subsequent to economic liberalization are consistent with the predictions of chapter 2. Before the crisis, however, and not long after the initiation of globalization policies in the early 1980s, the government adopted two important reforms in the social insurance sector that suggested resistance to race to the bottom pressures. Both these reforms involved higher costs for the government and employers, accounting for some of the rise in SS expenditures after the late 1980s (see figure 6.1). First, South Korea implemented a partially funded National Pension Service (NPS) in 1988.[14] Second, unemployment insurance was instituted in 1992 for firms with thirty or more employees, and later expanded to firms with five or more employees after the financial crisis resulted in high numbers of unemployed workers.[15]

Of the two reforms, South Korea's newly implemented NPS calls for greater focus, since unemployment benefits have been extremely modest overall and cover only a small fraction of the unemployed. This is not to underplay the significance of the adoption of an unemployment scheme in South Korea, since very few developing countries have done so. Analysts are skeptical that the new program is part of a "genuine insurance scheme creating entitlement to benefits," however. As Bidet (2004: 11) pointedly

---

[13] Argentina and Greece, for example, spend an average of 5.3 and 7.6 percent on social security (as a percentage of GDP), respectively, while South Korea allocates only 1.2 percent on average. These averages are calculated from the IMF's *Government Finance Statistics* over the 1972–97 time period.

[14] The NPS is labeled as "partially funded" because it has elements of both a fully funded and a pay-as-you-go scheme. As a fully funded system, it has a substantial amount of reserved funds, and plan sponsors must contribute to equal actuarial liabilities. It also has elements of pay-as-you-go, since payment of annuities is not guaranteed by the reserves and contribution rates are not based on actuarial estimates (see Yang, 2000).

[15] "Will the Unemployed's Right to Live Be Secured?" *Hankyorhe* (Seoul), February 3, 1998, 23.

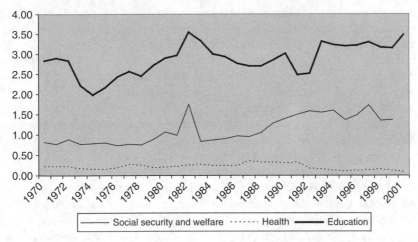

Figure 6.1 Government social expenditures as a percentage of GDP, 1970–2001

Source: IMF, *Government Finance Statistics* (various years).

summarizes the situation, "The new and radical possibility of joining a genuine unemployment insurance scheme may now exist on the statute book, but it has so far made little impression on popular thinking. The idea of registering as a jobseeker and being paid an allowance remains alien to many Koreans..." He further documents that the employment budget was cut by 60 percent between 1999 and 2000.

The National Pension Service, on the other hand, appears to be a marked departure from South Korea's past. For decades after independence, the majority of industrial laborers and the self-employed did not have pensions (Yang, 2000). From 1960 to 1988 only civil servants, military personnel, private school teachers, and workers in large establishments enjoyed coverage. In 1988 pensions became mandatory in workplaces with ten or more employees, and then in establishments with five or more employees in 1992. President Kim Young Sam made the expansion of pension coverage one of his main electoral pledges the following year. Honoring his commitment, in 1995 coverage was extended to include the rural self-employed and fishermen, and four years later the urban self-employed were included as well. The NPS is funded by employers and employees only.

Soon after the financial crisis, however, and in the face of mounting criticism from business representatives (e.g. the Korea Chamber of Commerce and Industry), the government began revising the pension law. Concerns about the sustainability of South Korea's social programs were particularly intense after the financial crisis of the late 1990s. The primary issue was that, in the current environment, the level of benefits was considered too generous relative to the low level of mandated contributions.[16] These contentious reform Bills were adopted even before the NPS had started to pay out full pensions.[17] Labor's reaction to these reforms is well represented by the following statement from an official of one of South Korea's leading labor confederations: "The government's estimates [of the expected draining of funds] have been made by blowing the financial crisis totally out of proportion."[18]

Three major reforms initiated in 1998 suggest welfare retrenchment. First, the average income replacement rate was reduced from 70 percent to 60 percent.[19] A current reform Bill, proposed in 2003, focuses on even more substantial curtailment of the benefit level. The Ministry of Health and Welfare explained that contributors will ultimately "pay more but get less."[20] Second, the eligible age was to be raised from sixty to sixty-five. And, third, it was agreed that the contribution rate would be re-evaluated every five years starting in 2013.[21]

While South Korea's aging population and government mismanagement have certainly contributed to the urgent push for reform, signs of globalization pressures are also evident. From the RTB perspective, it is revealing that the South Korean government has had to avoid two fiscal tools for stabilizing the fund: increasing taxes and introducing higher government contribution rates. Applying general revenues to maintain pension benefits is off the bargaining table because of the effect it would have on tax rates.[22] Social insurance schemes are based solely on employer and employee contributions. Labor union officials have argued, rather futilely, that the government should consider supporting low-income subscribers "with state funds like in advanced countries,

---

[16] In 2000 the World Bank reported that the NPS will incur deficits by 2037 and the fund will be completely depleted by 2049 ("World Bank Recommends Systemic Reform of Korea's Pension Scheme," *Korea Herald* (Seoul), January 17, 2000).

[17] There are recipients, however, of survivor pensions, invalidity pensions, and lump-sum benefits (Kwon, 1999). The payment of full pensions is scheduled for 2008.

[18] "Pay More, Get Less under New Pension Plan," *Korea Times* (Seoul), August 22, 2003.

[19] South Korea's replacement rate is the monthly pension at retirement age (on average sixty-one), divided by the wage of the last month at work.

[20] "Pay More, Get Less," August 22, 2003.

[21] "KDI Proposes Pension Reform to Cope with Aging Population," *Korea Times* (Seoul), May 28, 2002.

[22] As one official from South Korea's Employer Federation commented regarding pressures for a retrenchment of pension benefits, not only are they against the government increasing taxes to raise the requisite resources, it is known that the government simply will not agree to it.

instead of trying to increase the burden on citizens."[23] A 2004 proposal requesting a basic pension plan financed by general taxes has been adamantly opposed by the government (Kim, 2006). Palley (1992: 801) concludes that currently "the political-economic drive of low income taxes and low taxes on equity transactions...leaves few resources available for necessary services for the disabled and the elderly."

South Korea's contribution rate is very low by international standards, and advocates of the race to the bottom hypothesis could feasibly argue it currently represents the "lowest common denominator" in government spending on social insurance benefits.[24] Increasing the contribution rate above the current 9 percent is hotly contested by the business community, primarily because of the effect this would have on payroll costs.[25] While the government has agreed to consider recalculating the benefit every five years, a gradual increase in the contribution rate was not legislated (Phang and Shin, 2002), and analysts of pension reform express great skepticism (Yang, 2001a; Moon, 2002). What has been agreed is that the maximum limit of the contribution rate will stay intact until 2009.

To summarize, the implementation of unemployment insurance and, in particular, the National Pension Service suggests resistance to RTB pressures. Major reforms have been made to these programs, however, including a reduction in the average income replacement rate, an increase in the eligible age of recipients, and a regular re-evaluation of the contribution rate starting in 2013. These changes impact South Korea's existing social insurance scheme and suggest that welfare retrenchment eventually occurs after economic openness policies have been adopted.

6.2.2 Labor market protections

Race to the bottom effects also emerge in South Korea's system of labor market protections. As in social security, these cutbacks came after an initial period of expansion following the economic liberalization. Not long after

---

[23] "Pay More, Get Less," August 22, 2003.

[24] For example, (employer and employee) contribution rates in the United States are 12.4 percent, 13 percent in Japan, up to 28 percent in Brazil, and 9.5 percent in India – a low-income country that requires no pension contribution from the wage-earners (*Social Security Programs throughout the World*, available at www.ssa.gov/policy/docs/progdesc/ ssptw). Note that, for many nations with low contribution rates by wage-earners, the contribution rates of either the government or the employer, or both, are high (e.g. Sweden, Australia, Brazil). The South Korean government does not make any financial contributions to the social insurance scheme aside from administration costs and a small portion of the pensions for those on low income.

[25] Moon (2002); "Firms, Labor Question Pension Plan," *Korea Times* (Seoul), August 8, 2004.

economic liberalization was initiated, in 1988, labor gained important political freedoms, such as the right to organize, union pluralism at the national and industrial level, and pledges of limited government interference in dispute resolution and arbitration. Since these gains, however, labor has faced a difficult battle. Primary issues included official recognition of the Korean Confederation of Trade Unions (KCTU), which was delayed until as late as 2001; the recognition of teachers' unions, which, after a long and protracted fight, was accepted in 1999; and the recognition of multiple unions at the enterprise level, which has been postponed three times and is now set to be implemented in 2009. The slow pace of these reforms post-globalization suggests that RTB pressures contribute to the government's reluctance to provide labor with the full set of basic standards adjudicated by the ILO. Since the financial crisis, labor's situation seems only to have worsened. The ILO has consistently ruled that the South Korean government continues to violate freedom of association principles (US Department of Labor, 2003; Cho, 2002; Jang, 2004; Buchanan and Nicholls, 2003). Concerns include the arrest and detention of trade unionists, the government's refusal to register new labor unions, and the adoption of labor legislation contrary to freedom of association.

Race to the bottom pressures also appear to have affected legislation related to employment protections. These reforms, on balance, favor employers. The first major indication of RTB effects is the formal dismantling of the system of lifetime employment. This is an arrangement whereby an employer guarantees lifetime employment to workers, who, in turn, remain committed to that firm (Lindauer, 1984). A Supreme Court ruling on the Labor Standards Act (LSA) in 1989 marked the end of this regime by codifying South Korea's labor laws and legislating limitations on worker dismissals (Kitt, 2003). While employers view the LSA as a concession to labor since "urgent managerial need" now has to be established before lay-offs are permitted, workers view any regulations permitting lay-offs as a direct affront to their rights. The fundamental problem is that the LSA conditions for dismissal are sufficiently vague to render management and labor alike unsure of their rights (Kitt, 2003). In practice, however, employers have gained the advantage; Kim Soh-Young (2004: 545) observes that, by 1991, the Supreme Court had legally expanded the scope of employers' managerial need and clearly gave more consideration to the employers' interests than the concerns of employees. In addition, the 1998 amendments to the LSA were an attempt to make lay-offs easier for employers by eliminating the need for court orders to effect dismissals.

Changes in the laws were not the only way for employers to gain advantages over employees. Employers who still found the requirement for "managerial urgency" too onerous resorted to other means to forgo the rigors of dismissal. First, they avoided the LSA by the use of "honorable retirement." In 1998 35 percent of firms utilized honorable retirement to encourage the "voluntary" dismissal of workers (Kitt, 2003). Second, and with more profound effect, employers increasingly began to recruit temporary, or "non-standard," workers, who are not statutorily protected from "unjust" dismissals (Lee and Lee, 2003; Kim and Cheon, 2004; Kitt, 2003).

6.2.3   Summary

In sum, after the turn towards globalization and the 1997 financial crisis, labor market protections have declined because of frequent violations of freedom of association, the dismantling of the lifetime employment regime, the legalization of redundancy dismissals, recommended early retirements, and the increased hiring of non-standard workers. This, in addition to the retrenchments in social insurance policies, suggests the effects of a race to the bottom on South Korea's welfare state.

6.3   Institutional change

Despite the cutbacks just discussed, the South Korean welfare state is characterized by institutional continuity. Recall that Pierson (1996) uses three criteria to determine institutional change versus continuity: (1) significant increases in the reliance on means testing; (2) dramatic reductions in benefit and eligibility rules; and (3) major transfers of responsibility to the private sector. I add a fourth: the persistence of institutional legacies. The fact that South Korea has not experienced the first three, while long-standing institutions persist, suggests that, despite some retrenchment, the country is not racing to the neoliberal bottom. It is evident that the institutional norms associated with South Korea's productive welfare state continue to guide the direction and character of reforms under the conditions of globalization. All the new protectionist schemes introduced after economic liberalization are employment-based and thereby encourage market dependency, including the revised poverty alleviation schemes. Furthermore, the sustained emphasis on equity in (lower) education ensures that a strong, interventionist role for the government will persist well into the twenty-first century. South Korea also maintains government investment in education to a much greater extent than protective welfare schemes.

The first part of this section therefore focuses on the ways in which institutional continuity manifests itself in South Korea's welfare state, despite the effects of RTB pressures. The second subsection deals with the question of *why* paradigmatic welfare regime change has been difficult in South Korea.

6.3.1   Welfare regime change?

This section explores the four criteria for institutional change in turn. The incremental changes to South Korea's protective welfare schemes are worth noting. Important elements of its productive welfare state remain intact, however.

First, despite some changes, South Korea has not moved towards a major expansion of means testing. The National Basic Livelihood Security (NBLS) system was adopted in 2000 to replace the 1961 Livelihood Protection System. The key difference in the two programs is that the program now includes working persons who fall below the poverty line. While this appears to be a promising development, the OECD (2000: 138) reports that the eligibility criteria are still very stringent and, ultimately, not much better than NBLS (see also Kwon and Holliday, 2007). Interestingly, consistent with the institutional norms of South Korea's welfare state that encourage market dependence, cash benefits are conditional upon voluntary participation in cooperatives or vocational training. Benefits are denied to those who are able to work and refuse to comply with benefit rules, such as a refusal to accept training placements offered by authorities (OECD, 2000). Jung (2005: 18) concludes:

> The Korean government...has hardly had experience in their implementation for social assistance recipients. Accordingly, whether the NBLS system would turn out to be an epoch-making social assistance program, elevating the level of the Korean social welfare remains to be seen.

Second, there have been no radical changes in benefits. The cutbacks in social security discussed in the previous section can hardly be considered dramatic. It is difficult to represent the increase in the retirement age by five years or the reduction of the replacement rate by ten percentage points (from 70 to 60 percent) as a paradigm shift to a liberal welfare state. The average replacement rate in a liberal welfare state such as the United States is 46 percent, which is substantially lower than it is in South Korea (Congress of the United States, 2005).[26] In addition, South Korea's mandated retirement age for receiving benefits is now about

---

[26] The difference in the rates should be regarded as a rough evaluation. Replacement rates in various countries are not always directly comparable and must be viewed with caution.

average. It is the same as in most liberal welfare states and even some social democratic welfare states.

In terms of eligibility, both health insurance and pension coverage have become universal, but only de jure: 40 percent of South Korean wage-earners still remain without any coverage (see Kang, 2005). From this perspective, then, benefits in the aggregate have not experienced much increase.

The third condition, of "major transfer of responsibilities to the private sector," does not hold in the South Korean case. Private-sector participation has increased only in those social sectors that have always been market-oriented. In social security, the government resisted World Bank pressures to integrate retirement allowance in a funded and privately managed defined-contribution plan (Yang, 2004). In education, the bulk of post-secondary institutions were private long before globalization policies were implemented, and this continues to be the case. Recent efforts to increase the number of independent private schools at the secondary level have met with significant resistance.[27] A similar situation exists for South Korea's health sector, although the private sector has long dominated health care at all levels (primary, secondary, and tertiary). As noted earlier, the government has always played a minor role in South Korea's health delivery system. The private-sector, fee-for-service system prevailed even before the 1988 introduction of insurance plans, and has expanded since then. For example, 34.5 percent of all hospitals were public in 1975, and this share had dropped to 4.9 percent by 1994 (Yang, 2001b). While this is a large percentage change, in terms of absolute numbers the extent of public involvement has always been minimal. In 1975 approximately sixty-three hospitals were public, and this number had fallen to thirty-two by 1994. Moreover, the government continues to maintain minimal regulations regarding location, quality, and the type of service the private sector provides, as well as the level and nature of competition between them (Ramesh, 2004). The long-standing trend of private-sector dominance in the health sector thus continues into the twenty-first century.

Finally, continued state intervention in education services ensures that "market dependency" is consistent with past institutional norms. The South Korean government still intervenes heavily in education and maintains strong centralized control over this process, despite the rising concerns of reform advocates that excessive state intervention has compromised the quality of education and poses an obstacle for continued economic development in the globalizing era.

---

[27] "Roh Opposes Elite Private Schools," *Korea Herald* (Seoul), March 24, 2006.

Recent governments have been keenly aware of the need to improve the quality of South Korean education in the current era of globalization. A speech made by the minister of education soon after education reform was first initiated in 1995 (i.e. the Commission for Education Reform) encapsulates this sentiment:

We are about to step into a new era of unprecedented changes as national boundaries disappear and globalization proceeds. A new paradigm of economy is formulated as intellectual capital such as knowledge, technology and information replaces tangible and physical assets. In the light of rapid changes, we are all confronted with new challenges, and we must prepare ourselves to survive through the new era. The future jobs will require more diverse vocational abilities and knowledge, calling for educational reform and a guaranteed system of lifelong education for all.[28]

Demands for greater school autonomy and less state regulation by all sectors of society (teachers, labor groups, civil society groups, business) have met with only limited success, however. The education system has remained highly centralized and uniform in standard, content, and method, with the exception of only some minor reforms (Seth, 2002; Kim, 2005). Specifically, the main areas of concern about centralized command and its compromising of educational quality – the system of student quotas, the tendency towards uniformity of curriculum and a state entrance exam – remain more or less intact. The Presidential Commission for Education Reform, appointed in the early 1990s, resulted in minimal reforms and actually reinforced the status quo, leaving "structural problems unaddressed" (Kim, 2005; Seth, 2002). The South Korean Assembly has passed a Bill that is a modified version of the current system without many of the elements of reform (Park, 2000). As Kim (2005: 13, 14; emphasis added) puts it:

In spite of such a favorable environment, however, the reform measures which the civilian governments employed did not bring significant changes to the existing educational system... [I]nternal conditions shifted the themes of education reform debate from liberalization, decentralization, and so on, to a reform that would enhance educational performances – in particular, "quality, excellence and the nation's competitiveness" – within the existing arrangement but *with enhanced state intervention* and financial commitment.

The Private Schools Law, aiming for both deregulation and decentralization, represents the latest contentious political battle. This law will encourage more private high schools to become "self-reliant" and attract

---

[28] "Educational Reform Must Cope with Social Diversification," *Korea Times* (Seoul), April 30, 1999.

top-quality students. In response, the conservative Grand National Party boycotted parliamentary sessions and caused a legislative impasse.[29] Plans to implement more autonomy and transparency in state universities by increasing stakeholder participation are also stalled.[30]

This is not to suggest that absolute institutional stasis characterizes the South Korean productive welfare regime. The codification of labor market protections and the attempt at universal coverage of both social and health insurance that started in the late 1980s (discussed in greater detail in section 6.4) are indeed significant developments, given the virtual absence of formal protectionist policies since independence. These reforms do not constitute paradigmatic institutional change, however, for three specific reasons. First, these schemes are employment-based, and thereby reinforce the productive welfare state's emphasis on market reliance. Second, the South Korean government's attention to education still far surpasses its investment in protective policies. For example, in 2001 public spending on education exceeded social security by a ratio of two to one. Finally, as was the case in India, the working poor continue to have limited access to protections from market risks (as is explained in greater detail in section 6.4).

In sum, since the current reforms are being guided by the South Korean principle of market reliance, it is more accurate to interpret recent welfare reforms in the country as following a "productive" path. These findings are consistent with Kwon and Holliday (2007: 242; emphasis added). They argue:

The extent of the reforms undertaken since [the 1997–8 Asian financial crisis] has been exaggerated by many observers and analysts. In fact, when the reality of Korean social policy is separated from the rhetoric that surrounded it..., the extensions that took place in the late 1990s turn out to have been rather modest. *Crucially, they did not alter the fundamental character of the Korean welfare state in this era of globalization.*

6.3.2   Mediating role of domestic institutions

In this section I explore the mediating role of institutions in response to globalization pressures and investigate why key elements of the productive state have remained intact in spite of some retrenchment. First, the strategy of export-oriented development and the prioritization of

---

[29] "Schooling the Brightest," *Yonhap* (Seoul), December 29, 2005.
[30] "Education Marked by Disputes over Reform," *Korea Times* (Seoul), December 29, 2005. According to the plan, universities would be governed by a board consisting of a president, regional community members, and alumni representatives. The goal is to allow ordinary workers to have influence on the university governance committee.

commodification policies have structured access to the political arena for particular distributional coalitions (i.e. the chaebols). These groups support the key features of South Korea's productive welfare state. Second, given that labor is not among the privileged interest groups, the government–labor relationship does not depend on protective welfare benefits to maintain labor's political support and social peace. Instead, the government–labor relationship evolved on a basis of open conflict and confrontation. This antagonistic relationship makes it exceptionally difficult for government and labor to reach mutually beneficial agreements that could be advantageous for all categories of South Korean workers in the globalizing environment. Adding to this, labor groups are fragmented. Ideological divisions abound, making it virtually impossible to for them to lobby *with one voice* against race to the bottom pressures or ensure unified support for pro-poor social policies.

Elaborating on the first point, in the attempt to pursue a successful export-oriented development strategy, a symbiotic relationship between government and big business evolved (Kim, 1997; Evans, 1998). From the early 1960s onward President Park preferred to deal with a small number of entrepreneurs, and persuaded them by expanding their licenses in industries and protecting them from foreign inputs. The critical differentiating factor from the Indian approach was that this support was contingent upon firms' increasing their exports and outward foreign investment.

Government prioritization of commodification was beneficial to the chaebols, guaranteeing a readily available, trained, and productive workforce even in the initial phases of development. As Amsden (1989: 235) notes, education was one of the primary reasons the chaebols "reoriented their activities away from rent seeking and toward profit maximizing." She continues:

Once the entrepreneurs saw the managers were capable of managing, that the engineers were capable of producing products that worked, capital investment became a viable option.

This economic weight that the chaebols have generated has provided them with privileged access to the policy-making environment, *relative to other interest groups* (see, for example, Park, 1987). By the late 1970s, for instance, it was common practice for large firms to demand favorable treatment in exchange for financial contributions to the ruling party (Haggard and Moon, 1990; Nam, 1995).[31] South Korean governments

---

[31] Note that, while government manipulation does not guarantee that business associations will always be effective, entrepreneurs may still exploit their personal linkages to gain benefits (Park, 1987). The relevant point is that other interest groups in South Korea cannot resort to either of these options.

are therefore sensitive to political counter-attacks by the large business representatives, such as the Federation of Korean Industries (FKI) (see Haggard and Moon, 1990, for examples). Given these structural constraints, the government has been far from immune to the chaebols' resistance to the implementation of more protective welfare measures.

South Korea's major business leaders concur that such protective welfare policies and programs would interfere with the "economy first" approach and reduce worker productivity. Big business leaders have actively protested against the current slate of protective reforms (e.g. labor market reform, pensions, NBLS), and are concerned that they will exacerbate labor–management relations by emboldening labor. At a relatively recent meeting with the government, one of the heads of the nation's five largest economic organizations was quoted as saying, "Accommodating such demands basically goes against the basic principle of 'no work, no pay' and can have dangerous implications. Such demands simply cannot be met."[32] Another participant argued, "It is our hope that the government consult with businesses before implementing these changes since they can have a strong impact on their financial conditions."[33] Although chaebol resistance is not always successful, reformers face an uphill battle in confronting the largest interest group in the country.

The nature of the government–labor relationship has also contributed to the institutional bias towards education and against the protective welfare benefits that South Koreans generally view as promoting state dependency. In contrast to India, South Korea's government–labor relationship has evolved on the basis of repression and confrontation. Until recently, successive governments unabashedly pursued a pro-business stance and overtly excluded labor. No attempt was made to harmonize the interests of labor and capital in South Korea, other than the emphasis on education. Rather than attempting to incorporate the labor movement and mobilize workers as a base of support, as in India, labor policy in South Korea for decades involved extensive repression of workers' rights. The government was "quick and ruthless" in reacting to any signs of labor unrest (Koo, 2001; Deyo, 1989). Factory and working conditions constituted "virtual prisons," and scholars have often compared labor's plight to slavery (Lie, 1998). Demands for government protection for labor long went unheeded. Put simply, in the first four decades after independence the government's economic and political

---

[32] "Business Leaders Ask Gov't Not to Interfere in Labor Issues," *Korea Times* (Seoul), February 12, 1999.
[33] "Business Leaders Ask," February 12, 1999.

strategy did not require protective welfare benefits to "buy" labor's political support. As Koo (2000: 19) explains:

Although the South Korean labor regime is usually described as a corporatist system, its actual operation was based on a crude repressive form of control rather than a sophisticated corporatist system. Unlike the situation of most corporatist labor regimes, in which officially sanctioned unions are allowed to channel worker representation, the South Korean government was primarily interested in keeping workers unorganized and controlling them through security forces rather than though labor branches of the government... [T]he South Korean government relied primarily on threats and punishment, using security ideology to control labor agitation... This exclusionary approach produced a cadre of hard-core unionists by driving them out of the industrial arena – many union activists were fired and blacklisted from future employment – and by pushing them, inadvertently, to develop close ties with political activists and student radicals.

This government–labor relationship and the resulting effects on policy stand in stark contrast with India, in that welfare benefits have not served as a great source of clientelistic support and patronage. Rather, the government's past disregard of worker needs and demands has created an extremely adversarial industrial relations environment. Employer–employee relations tend to be hostile, and independent labor groups maintain a deep-seated distrust of the government. As Lie (1998: 114) describes it, after decades of harsh labor repression "[T]he accumulation of human tragedies – physical and spiritual anguish – [has] manifested itself in the cultural expression of *han*, which can be loosely translated as *ressentiment* [resentment]." The consequence is that current social policy negotiations are characterized by long-running disagreements between government, employers, and labor, making it particularly difficult to change the welfare status quo. Policy compromises that might allow the government to balance social interventionism with macroeconomic stability are unlikely in this environment.

The most telling example of this contentious government–labor relationship is the malfunctioning of the Tripartite Council, which was set up to facilitate dialogue and compromise between government, business, and labor representatives on issues related to globalization and social reform. It was hailed both nationally and overseas as a promising development for labor relations. Labor's disaffection with the forum rapidly escalated, however, and not much more than one year later one of labor's leading confederations, the KCTU, withdrew from the council. The KCTU president, Lee Kap Yong, remarked that "[i]t is not a genuine mechanism of social cooperation but a capitalist tool of control to prevent labor resistance and to carry out their own plan of structural restructuring effectively" (Koo, 2000: 246). The council has failed to live up to its potential as an effective tool for engaging labor's cooperation (Henderson *et al.*, 2002; Lee and Lee, 2003; Koo, 2000; Song, 1999).

Divisions within South Korea's labor movement add to this institutional paralysis. The country's national labor market institutions are not sufficiently encompassing to overcome labor's collective action problems. Although PLP in South Korea has increased over the decades it has not approached the levels of European countries, and workers are unable to promote policies that mitigate the negative effects of globalization. The distrustful government–labor relationship also reinforces the divisions within South Korea's labor movement. Early attempts to depoliticize labor gave rise to ideological rifts and the formation of radical labor movements. The Federation of Korean Trade Unions (FKTU) was originally formed in 1946 by right-wing groups backed by the US military forces, only to be taken over in 1961 by General Park's Plan for the Reorganization of Labor Groups. Park took control of the FKTU leadership to "establish a system of unified industrial unionism to overcome organizational disorder and to prevent undisciplined labor disputes" (Guillen, 2001: 141). Park's efforts to control labor through the FKTU backfired, however, and increased labor dissidence. Because the dominant union confederation was a puppet organization, defections to more radical, combative, but illegal unions ultimately culminated in more militant labor organizations, such as the KCTU.

The KCTU is perceived as being militant and progressive, while the FKTU, which for many years was the only official union recognized by the government, is generally more conservative and viewed as being sympathetic to the government. Union rivalries increased in the late 1990s as the FKTU began to compete with the now legally recognized KCTU for membership and loyalties. In interviews conducted for this analysis, both FKTU and KCTU officials made it clear that cooperation is not likely in the near future. Henderson *et al.* (2002: 25–6) draw a similar conclusion:

[T]he historical and ideological and political differences between the FKTU and KCTU remain and the experiences of economic crisis seem to have done little to alter the situation. While particular issues sometime result in a "common front", for the most part mutual distrust prevents the coherent response to business and government policy that might otherwise have been anticipated.

The fragmented nature of the labor movement is exacerbated by the high percentage of unions representing workers from big companies (chaebols), while the large numbers of non-standard workers tend to avoid unionization. Furthermore, the status differentials between the two groups are deeply rooted in institutional practices and will not disappear easily.[34] Finally, their cohesion is further undermined by not having viable leftist or class-based parties around which to rally (Buchanan and Nicholls, 2003).

One prominent example of this labor rivalry is the long and heated pension debate that persisted throughout the 1990s. The KCTU supported a single-pillar pension plan, which would unite wage-earners and the self-employed in an effort to pool risks and contribute to social integration (Kim, 2006; Yang, 2004). The FKTU, on the other hand, threw its weight behind a plan that would adopt separate management systems and avoid income transfers between the two groups. Such ideological divisions inhibit workers from presenting themselves to the government as a coherent political group. Even in the rare circumstances when labor has been more unified, it has lost. Both labor organizations fought in vain against the reduction of social security and labor benefits.[35]

A similar scenario of union conflict characterizes the health reform debate. The KCTU strongly supported centralization of the 350 medical insurance societies as a means to reduce inequality between the rich and poor. The FKTU, on the opposite side of the issue, preferred decentralization without government regulation (Lee, 2003; Joo, 1999). Its members feared that centralization would result in industrial employers and employees bearing a greater burden than the self-employed, because the latter had premiums that were inadequate to cover their expenses (Lee, 2003). Overall, organized labor played a small part in pushing for a greater government involvement in providing health care, as well as in the introduction and extension of national health insurance (Kwon, 2003).

Taken together, the three intervening domestic institutions (national social policy configurations that privilege political access to select groups, an uncooperative government–labor relationship, and fragmented labor institutions) have helped to fortify a productive welfare regime that continues to direct state welfare efforts towards education and maintains minimum government investment in protective welfare schemes. South Korea's development strategy created interest groups (i.e. chaebols) that supported this type of welfare state, while subordinate groups remained divided and left without the same privileged access to the political process. The government–labor relationship as it evolved in the early decades after independence has made it particularly difficult today to adopt policy compromises between labor and capital. South Korea's fragmented labor movements add to this environment, because they lack the

---

[34] See also Koo (2001), who makes a similar point.
[35] "Pension Reform Faces Challenges," *Korea Herald* (Seoul), February 17, 2004.

institutional clout to prevent a race to the bottom and to ensure that social policies in the globalizing environment are beneficial for all labor groups.

6.4   Who really gets hurt?

The crowning question is: who has been hurt by the retrenchment reforms since globalization? I demonstrate that it is not the poor, as anticipated by RTB analysts, but the middle class, as argued earlier in this book. To begin, I identify which groups constitute "the disadvantaged," since the international approach to the definition of poverty (e.g. the population living on less than $1 per day) poses problems in the South Korean case: with the rapid income growth since the 1960s, groups living below the international absolute poverty line have been extremely small. Next, I explore the various categories of reforms, and show that it is, in fact, not these groups that are losing benefits alongside globalization, but their more privileged counterparts.

The numbers of absolute poor in South Korea are low in comparison to other developing countries, representing approximately 8.5 percent of the population by official government estimates (Lee and Kim, 2003). This group generally consists of "non-standard workers," who are part-time employees, short-term, or temporary workers, "dispatch employment," and the self-employed (Betcherman, Luinstra, and Ogawa, 2001).[36] Labor groups add to this category workers in informal enterprises (i.e. micro and/or unregistered) who anticipate lasting employment relations but whose working conditions are poor. Certainly, not all non-standard workers are destitute, and far more in South Korea fall into the indigent category, which the government regards as better off than the extremely poor, but whose income still falls below a specified standard.[37] Betcherman, Luinstra, and Ogawa (2001) point out that, when compared to OECD countries, South Korea has a relatively large share of self-employed and those in unpaid family work. Standard workers, or full-time wage-earners, are estimated to comprise only 30 percent of the working population (OECD, 2004).

To determine, then, whether it is the poor or the more privileged who are most affected by social policy reform, it is necessary to look at the effects on the absolute poor, the gains or losses for non-standard workers, and any improvement or worsening in the conditions for standard

---

[36] Note that it appears that each country has different terms for part-time, contract, and informal-sector workers. India refers to this group as "casual workers."

[37] Non-standard workers may also include lawyers, entrepreneurs, and other self-employed professionals. The data are not available.

workers. Since detailed data on the absolute poor are both limited and difficult to access, however, I focus on changes in protections for non-standard workers. Moreover, in the South Korean case it is reasonable to assume that better conditions for non-standard workers bode well for the destitute, who are a subcomponent of this group.[38]

6.4.1 Labor market protections

The RTB effects in labor market protections involve formal dismantling of the lifetime employment regime and the Labor Standards Act, which provided formal codification of lay-offs. These cutbacks have mostly affected the standard workers, not South Korea's more disadvantaged sectors. They have had a minimal effect on the country's non-standard workers for one simple reason: only management and highly skilled workers ever qualified for permanent employment. In an extensive study of labor market behavior in South Korea, Lindauer (1984) shows that the bulk of employees, production workers, and unskilled operatives did not have lifetime employment protections. Obviously, then, the formal dismantling of the lifetime employment system has the most direct effect on South Korea's more privileged labor groups. By the same logic, since non-standard workers are "subject to pre-negotiated termination dates and can be replaced at the whim of management without prohibitive costs like union interference or severance obligations," the few protections that the LSA provides against lay-offs to permanent workers do not apply to them (Kitt, 2003: 560).[39]

Furthermore, preferences for hiring non-standard workers are increasing as employers avoid compliance with the LSA. To help reduce costs and compete better in the globalizing economy, large firms increasingly subcontract production to small firms (Abe and Kawakame, 1997). This affects the coverage of a very small percentage of workers, since small business owners are reluctant to enroll workers in welfare programs, and the workers themselves in these firms tend not to be covered by collective contracts (Yang, 2006).

---

[38] Determining the exact percentage of non-standard workers in South Korea is problematic. Scholars, government officials, and labor groups disagree upon the definition, and, as a consequence, produce different estimates of non-standard workers. For example, in August 2005 the Ministry of Labor reported the share of non-standard workers to be 36.6 percent of total wage-earners, while labor groups claimed it to be 57.1 percent (nodong jaryo [Labor Data] 2005). Consequently, references to non-standard workers in the following sections should be interpreted with this caveat in mind.

[39] Kitt (2003) notes that temporary workers with certain longer-term contracts have some protections under the LSA. Also, see Kitt (2003) for a discussion of employers' frustrations with the LSA.

Labor market protections have always excluded non-standard workers, and thus their erosion under the influences of race to the bottom pressures has minimal effect on this group. Instead, it is the more privileged workers who are harmed by the cutbacks. The same trend can be observed in social security, health, and labor market reforms.

6.4.2 Social security (and social assistance)

Since 1988 social insurance has slowly moved towards universal coverage de jure. The implementation of the National Pension Service and unemployment and health insurance have clearly made remarkable advancements towards protecting greater numbers of standard workers (see table 6.1). The percentage of non-standard workers covered in all these sectors is still small, however and, to make matters worse, coverage has decreased in recent years (see table 6.1). The poor amongst the elderly have also failed to benefit from the recent social security reforms (see Kwon, 2001).

Kim (2006: 22) observes that the NPS is experiencing great difficulty in "maintaining the institutional characteristic of an occupationally inclusive system due to increasing coverage gaps." Despite the broadening of statutory rights and access to such programs, the attractiveness of hiring (unprotected) non-standard workers is increasing under the conditions of globalization, as government and employers alike are facing pressures to keep total wage costs down (Kim and Kim, 2003; You and Lee, 2000; Kim, Bae, and Lee 2000). A recent report provides a comprehensive assessment on the state of non-standard workers in South Korea. The authors demonstrate the limitation of the legal approach to expand social

Table 6.1 *Comparison of social insurance coverage: standard versus non-standard workers*

Welfare programs	Employment types	2002	2003	2004	2005
National Pension Service	Total wage-earners	52.7	57.7	59.5	61.4
	Standard workers	62.9	70.8	72.5	75.7
	Non-standard workers	25.7	30.5	37.5	36.6
National Health Insurance	Total wage-earners	55.5	59.5	61.3	61.9
	Standard workers	66.6	72.5	73.8	75.9
	Non-standard workers	28.8	32.6	40.1	37.7
National Unemployment Insurance	Total wage-earners	48.0	49.8	52.1	53.1
	Standard workers	56.2	59.7	61.5	63.8
	Non-standard workers	26.2	29.2	36.1	34.5

Source: Kang (2005: 61).

security coverage for non-standard workers by pointing out pervasive non-compliant behaviors by both employers and low-income employees (Sohn, Koh, and Kang, *et al.*, 2004).[40] The problem is exacerbated by the fact that governments fail to enforce penalties for employers who neglect their legal obligation (Sung, 2006).

The newly implemented unemployment insurance has problems not only because of low benefits and the low duration of pay (OECD, 2000), but the poor are excluded, since temporary workers, the self-employed, and unpaid family workers are not covered. The OECD reports (2000: 83) that over a half of those unemployed do not receive benefits because they were not previously covered by the Employment Insurance Scheme. Table 6.1 confirms that the percentage of non-standard workers covered has declined under this scheme as well. It is no surprise that Lee, Hur, and Kim (2001) and Bidet (2004) conclude that unemployment benefits cannot be considered a primary safety net against unemployment.

Turning to South Korea's poverty alleviation programs, how have recent reforms helped the poor? As discussed earlier, the Livelihood Protection System formed the basis of public assistance from the 1960s until the Temporary Livelihood Protection System and NBLS were introduced in the late 1990s.[41] Figure 6.2 reveals that the number of beneficiaries always was small, however, and shrank even further in the 1990s. This is striking, as the percentage of poor people in South Korea increased by almost 80 percent following the financial crisis (Kakwani, Khandker, and Son, 2003). The OECD (2000) concludes that the number of beneficiaries has declined because of strict eligibility criteria, the low levels of benefits, and administration problems. For example, the income capacity of the entire extended family is taken into account when assessing entitlement to the NBLS. Only 3 percent of the population is covered by the new public assistance program (see Kwon and Holliday, 2007). According to the OECD (2000: 19):

It is important to stress that many low-income individuals will remain unprotected under NBLS… [B]enefit criteria [are] subject to unusually strict income criteria, based on the income capacity (and not actual income) of the extended family. This particular provision of the law will have to be revised if the official target of providing benefits of last resort to those in need is to be reached. Also, despite the increase, benefits remain very modest. The authorities should consider raising them, perhaps in stages, so that they at least reach the poverty line.

---

[40] Non-standard workers are intentionally neglecting to enroll to meet immediate living expenses (Sohn, Koh, and Kang, *et al.*, 2004: 298).

[41] The Temporary Livelihood Protection System was similar to the Livelihood Protection System but had a higher property level for eligibility.

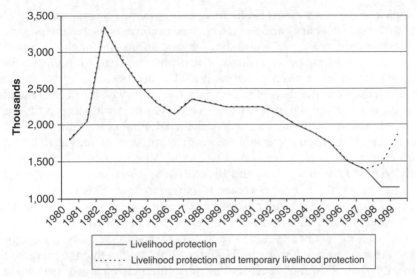

Figure 6.2 Beneficiaries of livelihood protection benefits, 1980–99

Source: OECD (2000).

In addition, Lee and Kim (2003) find that the total income benefits for households with small incomes have decreased compared with the former system. Households with special needs, such as those with a disabled member, are at the greatest disadvantage under the current system.

The retrenchments made in the late 1980s did not directly affect non-standard workers. It is South Korea's standard workers who bear the brunt of the recent cutbacks in social security, while the implementation of unemployment benefits has been of little benefit to subordinate groups.

6.4.3   Health care

The expansion of health insurance has actually worsened the situation of the poor, on account of the growing cost. As has been noted in the Indian case as well, however, this trend existed before economic liberalization. The health sector has witnessed two major reforms. The first is the transition from private voluntary health insurance (initiated in 1977) to the 1989 legislation requiring mandatory coverage in an employer-based plan for all workers. In December 1999 the second major reform required all South Korea's 350 health insurance societies to merge into a single insurer in a national health insurance system. The rationale behind both the social security and health insurance reforms was that the pooling of risks would make pensions and health care affordable for all. These are certainly significant developments. The problem is that, while costs have increased, coverage has not been universal in practice.

Both the small numbers of non-standard workers who are now included in the scheme and the majority of those who remain without protections are grappling with the increasing financial pressures. Out-of-pocket expenses have risen alongside the implementation of universal health insurance, for several reasons (Flynn and Chung, 1990; Kim, 2005; Kwon, 2003; Peabody, Lee, and Bickel, 1995). First, in addition to high co-payments, the benefit coverage is extremely low. This is an issue in South Korea, because the cost of health care tends to be exceptionally high and is now rising further.[42] With low benefits, private health insurance is ultimately providing the bulk of coverage for services at unregulated market prices. Kwon and Holliday (2007) argue that the merger of social health insurance societies has not ultimately changed the benefit package previously offered.

Second, government attempts to control skyrocketing expenditures by limiting doctors' fees have had adverse consequences. In an effort to avoid the effects of fee regulation, physicians began increasing the volume of uninsured medical services that were not regulated (OECD, 2004; Peabody, Lee, and Bickel, 1995; Kwon, 2003). Finally, the government still allowed physician charges to increase by 45 percent in 2000, as a means to dampen their overwhelming protests against the mandated separation of drug prescription and dispensation.

In addition to the low coverage of non-standard workers, health insurance protections targeted to the absolute poor are minimal. The Medical Assistance Program, funded by government subsidies to cover the fees of the indigent, reaches only 3 percent of the population (see Jo and Choi, 2002: 7, and OECD, 2004: 63). This is far from sufficient, given that it is estimated that more than 8 percent of the population live below the poverty line.

6.4.4   Education

Finally, unlike India, the recent education reform efforts have also failed to alter the conditions affecting the poor. While the South Korean

---

[42] Two primary reasons why prices are high are the overuse of advanced medical technology and the promotion of expensive antibiotics and other drugs (Lee, 2003; You and Lee, 2000).

government has consistently made improvements towards greater access to lower education institutions, the poor still face the same constraints to pursuing university education that they did throughout the 1960s and 1970s. Overall, even though recent presidents have recognized the urgent need for reform in this area, education opportunities for the poor have remained unchanged. Changing the quality of educational instruction to meet the demands of a globalizing environment ultimately took greater priority on the policy agenda than promoting more equitable access to higher education.

Government efforts to ensure universal access to primary and secondary education, and to promote equity between schools, have had the unintended effect of creating unequal opportunities for college-level education.[43] The university-level quota system and pressure to perform well on college entrance exams have generated an extremely high demand for out-of-school private tutoring. Given that, as a result of South Korea's government intervention, all students are receiving the same level and type of education, private tuition becomes the only means for individuals to gain a competitive edge. This allows the students who can afford extensive extra-curricular learning to earn higher marks on the entrance examination and gain an advantage in finding employment in competitive jobs. This particular aspect of the South Korean education system has a regressive effect, since the poor are spending a disproportionate share of their income on private tutoring, and the rich still outspend them.[44] Sorenson (1994: 34) reports, "Poor parents resent the advantages of tutoring and other extracurricular help affluent parents are able to provide their children." A 1980 ban on private tutoring has been largely ineffective.

To address this financial pressure on the poor, reform advocates have insisted that the government significantly increase education spending and invest in improving the quality of educational institutions so that demand for private tutoring decreases concomitantly.[45] Other proposed measures included further expanding student quotas, reforming the state entrance exam, and granting greater autonomy to private schools and universities. As discussed earlier, however, reforms in these areas were

---

[43] The government has ensured equal access to primary and secondary education, and maintained uniform academic standards across schools, by such policies as minimizing differences in tuition rates, randomly assigning students by computer to attend private and public schools, setting the curriculum in both types of institutions, and attempting to limit competition between higher education institutions by putting quotas on the total number of new admissions (Lee, 2002; Kim, 2001).

[44] Note that private tutoring is not limited to the wealthy population in South Korea.

[45] "People's Coalition for Education Reform," *Hankyoreh* (Seoul), May 7, 1995.

relatively minor and did not effect a major change in the government's approach to education.

The objective of decreasing private spending on education has been embraced by the government. It was an important part of former President Kim Young Sam's education reform initiative, launched in 1995. This reform effort, however, was eventually put on the back-burner (Seth, 2002) and took second place to making educational instruction more compatible with the demands of globalization. The Presidential Commission on Education Reform 1995 began its final document with the words: "A nation's economic survival and prosperity would depend on its global competitiveness" (Kim, S.K., 2004: 524). Reforms have since focused on achieving greater effectiveness in local education systems and preparing students for an information-oriented global economy. One example is the Brain Korea 21 program, introduced in 1999.[46] Equity reform advocates have criticized these programs for fostering greater elitism (Seth, 2002).

As a result, private education expenditures (as a percentage of GDP) have steadily increased alongside globalization, almost doubling between 1993 and 2001.[47] Private expenditure on education in South Korea is now among the highest in the world, reaching 3.4 percent of GDP in 2001 (World Bank, 2006).[48] Ultimately, the South Korean government has neither improved the quality of public education nor contained private education expenditures.[49]

Consistent with the past, however, the government has continued to maintain its focus on equality in the lower levels of schooling. For example, in 1985 the government introduced free middle-school education for students living in remote areas, and by 2004 the plan was for completely free education.[50] Although elementary school had been free and compulsory since 1959, compulsory middle-school education had been delayed for decades. Other examples are the extension of low-interest college loans and the 1999 plan to exempt large numbers of students from low-income families from fees (Seth, 2002). President Park Chung Hee's vision has thus been sustained into the present for primary and secondary education, but not for the higher levels.

---

[46] Brain Korea 21 involved increasing investment in engineering, science, and technical programs at select universities.

[47] See World Bank's EdStats (Education Statistics) database: Thematic Data, table 1.1, Private education expenditures as a percentage of GDP. Available at http://data.worldbank.org/edstats/td7.asp (accessed June 21, 2006).

[48] World Bank's EdStats database: Thematic Data, table 1.1.

[49] "Government Urged to Shift Focus," *Korea Herald* (Seoul), June 8, 2006.

[50] "Education Reforms Needed," *Korea Herald* (Seoul), January 20, 2001.

We must build up society where no privilege in education is tolerated in the education field. Education privilege for the rich and the strong alone should be entirely eliminated. The door of education should be wide open to all talents regardless of wealth, background or family lineage. (Park, 1962: 209)

This outcome is surprising, since the analysis in chapter 3 predicts that pro-poor reforms are most likely to occur in education under conditions of globalization, because of greater information about its benefits and cross-class cooperation towards this end. Why did this not happen in the case of access to upper-level education in South Korea? Information was certainly widespread for the need for education reform in general. As President Kim Young Sam emphasized, "Education reform is the top priority in globalization policy and the type of education needed in the new era is to depart from the existing system."[51] Civil society groups and representatives of labor and business are in complete agreement that the quality of South Korea's current education system is a problem and cannot meet the demands of creating a competitive workforce in the globalizing environment; the prevailing sense is that the need for reform is urgent. An FKI poll shows that companies distrust university educa-tion.[52] In recent elections the three major presidential candidates criticized the quality of South Korea's education, and were unanimous in stressing "the importance of creative and talented manpower to better cope with a rapidly changing world at the dawn of the 21st century."[53] Reforms in higher education are currently *the* most important concern of the entire nation (Han, 2003).

Problems have emerged, however, because the need to improve *equity* in South Korea's higher education system lacked cross-class consensus. Only teachers' unions and labor and civil groups demand that the govern-ment increase the amount of resources spent on education *and* limit the expansion of private schools in order to promote equity. They argue that the expansion of such elite "self-reliant" schools will impair the central tenet of the South Korean education system: the guarantee of equal opportunities for education.[54] More generous state subsidies, on the other hand, could increase the number of public universities as well as

---

[51] "President Kim Ordered Education Reform Programs in the First Half of the Year," *Daily Donga* (Seoul), January 17, 1995.
[52] "Firms Want *Education* Market Opening," *Korea Times* (Seoul), August 20, 2004.
[53] "Nominees Pledge Reform of College Admission System," *Korea Times* (Seoul), November 25, 1997.
[54] "Schooling the Brightest," *Yonhap* (Seoul), December 29, 2005. Note that the Korean Teachers and Education Workers' Union supports greater school autonomy; see, for example, the views of its new hard-line leader in the following: "Hard-line Woman Leads Teachers' Union," *Korea Times* (Seoul), April 1, 2006.

hasten the development of innovative and high-quality programs. This would have the effect of improving public university education without having to charge more for tuition. It would also subdue the fierce competition amongst students to enter the relatively few but prestigious public universities, and thus deflate the need for households to spend extra finances on private tutoring costs. The Federation of Korean Industries, however, protests that the government should enhance competition between schools rather than increase government expenditures (Park, J.-C., 1998). Thus, in the absence of cross-class interest convergence, equity-enhancing reform in South Korea's higher education system has not been realized.

6.4.5   Summary

The more privileged standard workers in South Korea are the ones getting hurt by RTB pressures, since non-standard workers never enjoyed many benefits in the first place. In the late 1980s the government made concerted efforts to provide some labor market protections and further develop public assistance programs (NBLS), as well as create a more redistributive social and health insurance system. These attempts at redistribution were more far-reaching than any made by the Indian government under the conditions of globalization. The great majority of non-standard workers in South Korea remain with minimal protections after economic liberalization, however. In education, reforms have granted the poor even greater access to lower education, but they continue to find it difficult to obtain high-quality university education. This pattern has been a long-standing problem in South Korea's education sector.

Only education at the lower levels has provided and continues to provide benefits to South Korea's disadvantaged sectors. Recent reforms in social insurance schemes, however, have had a minimal effect, as the non-standard workers were never really included in them to start with. Rather, the middle-class standard workers are the ones most affected by welfare retrenchment (and expansions) in labor market protections, social security, and health care. This is a common trend in both productive and protective welfare states.

6.5   Other factors: democracy, civil society groups, and Japanese influences

Do other factors help explain why the primary elements of South Korea's productive welfare state persist and why important protective elements (e.g. social insurance policies and labor freedoms in 1988) were also introduced? Here, again, democracy plays an intervening role. First, South Korea's turn to democracy in the late 1980s increased the pressures on the government for greater accountability to a diverse electorate (Wong, 2004).[55] With growing public discontent over the close government–business relationship, recent presidents have sought to distance themselves from the chaebols and create alliances with other civic groups (Nam, 1995). The second major impact of democracy is the expanding influence of major civic groups that have allied with labor in endorsing progressive welfare programs such as the NBLS (see Jung, 2005, and Kwon, 2003). It is not a coincidence that many of these protective reforms were implemented soon after the inception of democracy in 1987. Democracy, however, cannot fully explain why labor benefits increased initially after democratization, but then experienced cutbacks much later, in the late 1990s.

The influence of Japan also plays a large role in the development of South Korea's productive welfare state. Many of the social insurance programs adopted were shaped by Japanese models, particularly in health. Japan appears to maintain similar principles of a productive welfare state, such as generalized attempts to discourage state dependence. White and Goodman's (1998) analysis, however, suggests that South Korea does maintain a distinct national form of welfare, and cautions that "it is misleading to think in terms of one homogeneous, overarching 'East Asian welfare model'" (14).

6.6   Implications

The South Korean case provides important insights into the interplay of globalization and domestic institutions and the effects that this has on social policies. Market expansion brings race to the bottom pressures even in productive welfare states. In the case of South Korea, these effects have been most evident in social security and labor market protections. Nonetheless, this case study once again confirms that retrenchment in these sectors is not a sign that South Korea is advancing towards the neoliberal bottom. Two factors support the contention that the core elements of the country's productive welfare state remain more or less intact: (1) the government still encourages market dependency by actively prioritizing and intervening in (lower) education, and by implementing new protection schemes that are primarily employment-based; and (2) South Korea's disadvantaged sectors continue to receive minimum

[55] Wong (2004) presents an excellent account of the role of democracy in South Korea's welfare reforms.

protections from market adversities. Similarly to the Indian case, welfare cutbacks have been concentrated in South Korea's comparatively new social programs.

What is the future of the productive welfare state in twenty-first-century globalization? The South Korean case makes it clear that, even in light of recent cutbacks, government dedication to the productive welfare state continues; at the same time, attention to more protective welfare schemes has increased since the turn towards open markets. It can be argued, then, that South Korea is experiencing some incremental changes, but along a productivist path. At the same time, though, the evidence thus far suggests that the likelihood that these new changes will be more universalistic de facto is relatively low. Demands for non-standard workers, who come to employers free of onerous costs and protections, are increasing steadily. The mediating role of domestic institutions may be the primary reason why the race to the bottom is not hurting (or helping) the poor, but globalization is certainly making it more difficult for new programs to include them. If the European social democratic states serve as a guide, *both* encompassing labor organizations and government investment in universalistic welfare programs are fundamental prerequisites for paradigmatic change in this era of globalization. South Korea falls short on both counts.

7   Globalization and the dual welfare state: case study of Brazil

Analyzing details from the case of Brazil, this chapter explores the impacts of globalization on weak dual welfare states. Specifically, the Brazilian case responds to the three core questions of this book as they apply to dual welfare states. How and why do globalization and race to the bottom pressures lead to welfare retrenchment in dual welfare states? Do cutbacks mean that dual welfare states are undergoing institutional transformation towards a neoliberal welfare state (i.e. convergence)? In dual welfare states, who really gets hurt by welfare reforms in the current era of globalization?

This type of welfare regime, as discussed in chapter 4, pursues a mixed strategy of protective and productive social policies.[1] On the productive side, Brazil emphasizes (near-)universal primary enrollment; the quality of education is poor and gets worse at the secondary level, however. Brazil's protective schemes are focused on the provision of social security and labor market protections. As with India and South Korea, RTB pressures have resulted in cutbacks in some of its welfare programs. In contrast to the other welfare regime types, however, Brazil's welfare regime appears to be the most dynamic, in that retrenchment has occurred in some of its long-standing welfare programs with the intent of improving equity. In fact, significant changes to *both* the protective and productive components have occurred. While these advancements are promising, several elements of institutional continuity remain: (1) Brazil's recent advancements in education – both in terms of quality and quantity – have still not progressed beyond the primary level; (2) the reforms in Brazil's protective welfare schemes have been parametric and not structural; and (3) the middle class continue to receive the bulk of the benefits while the urban poor, long neglected by Brazil's welfare state,

---

[1] Based on the logic in chapter 4, I label Brazil a weak, rather than strong, dual welfare state, since the latter implies that governments emphasize both productive and protective welfare strategies to a greater degree than governments of either productive or protective regimes. Outputs in strong dual welfare states would theoretically favor universalistic redistribution programs (both productive and protective).

persist with limited access to these protections. Thus, similarly to India and South Korea, ongoing cutbacks in welfare are really hurting the more privileged sectors of Brazilian society.

Given Brazil's dual welfare status, each section discusses both productive and protective strategies. Section 7.1 discusses the primary features of Brazil's weak dual welfare state. Section 7.2 explores the impact of RTB pressures, while section 7.3 illustrates the extent to which these cutbacks amount to institutional continuity and change. The subsequent section (7.4) asks, "Who really gets hurt?" Section 7.5 explores other factors (particularly democracy), and section 7.6 draws some conclusions about the status of dual welfare states in this era of globalization.

7.1   Brazil's weak dual welfare state

Brazil's "weak dual welfare state" status is a result of the prioritization of decommodification policies alongside concerted government efforts towards creating a productive wage labor force. Like India, Brazil has a history of emphasizing protective welfare strategies to increase the dependence of particular citizens on the state. At the same time, Brazil has invested in commodification policies to a far greater extent than India, creating some degree of overlap with productive welfare regimes such as South Korea. Brazil falls into a distinct welfare category, however, precisely because commodification policies still take "second place" to protective welfare schemes. The stratification effects are unique. Rather more citizens receive social insurance protections; the welfare schemes vary by occupation, however, and preserve old status distinctions and hierarchy. Ultimately, the Brazilian welfare state falls between the two extremes of India's disproportional neglect of productive welfare policies and South Korea's long history of nurturing individual self-reliance and discouraging protective social schemes.

Brazil's social policy emphasis on decommodification coincided with policy-makers' turn away from free trade and the adoption of an import substitution strategy in the 1930s. The Getulio Vargas administrations (1930–45 and 1950–4) set the precedent for using labor policies and social insurance to encourage social peace by establishing the Ministry of Labor in 1930 and passing the Consolidation of Labor Act in 1943.[2] To maintain control of society, the state corporatist structure set up during that time offered decommodification-type benefits in exchange for labor

---

[2] Note that the 1923 *Lei Eloi Chaves* initiated the first labor laws governing dismissals and pensions for senior employees. It focused primarily on railway workers, however; the expansion of these laws occurred under the Vargas administration.

acquiescence and political passivity.[3] From their inception, benefits were aimed at the favored labor syndicates. The Ministry of Labor under Vargas in 1945 unified benefits into a single social insurance institution, the Instituto de Servicos Sociasis do Brasil (ISSB), although civil servants and the armed services retained separate and far superior pension schemes. While the social protection system emerged in part as a result of labor pressures, Brazil's welfare system was initiated in top-down paternalistic fashion to ensure social control (Malloy, 1979). The result is a system of elite-led social security and labor policies that maintains support from the groups they were originally designed to benefit.

Emphasis on a coordinated education strategy followed close behind, however, as Brazil became more export-oriented. To begin with, Brazil's development strategy was not as "closed" as that of protective welfare states such as India. Concomitant with the focus of protecting domestic firms from international market competition, the textile industry was still expanding its exports in the 1940s, and policies towards transnational firms were far more permissive than in either India or South Korea (Kaufman, 1990; Nayyar, 1978).[4] Ultimately, by the middle of the 1960s, although the development strategy was still primarily inward-oriented, full-fledged export-led growth strategies had also been adopted.[5] During this time, policy-makers began placing an emphasis on "human capital," and major innovations towards universal education were conceived (Haussman and Haar, 1978; Haar, 1977). In contrast, earlier attempts to establish a long-term comprehensive plan – during Brazil's more inward-oriented period – were grossly unsuccessful. As Haussman and Haar (1978: 37) put it, national education laws before the late 1960s were

---

[3] Schmitter (1974: 85) defines state corporatism as "a system of interest representation in which the constituent units are organized into a limited number of singular, compulsory, noncompetitive, hierarchically ordered and functionally differentiated categories, recognized or licensed (if not created) by the state and granted a deliberate representational monopoly in exchange for observing certain controls on their selection of leaders and articulation of demands and supports."

[4] Nayyar (1978) estimates that, by 1969, the share of transnational manufacturing firms in the export of manufactures in Brazil was 43 percent. In comparison, transnational firms' share of exports was only 5 percent in India, and in South Korea it was 15 percent.

[5] The central government of Brazil began promoting foreign investment and export-oriented growth as early as the late 1940s, and this became a central pillar of the economic policies of both President Juscelino Kubitschek in the late 1950s and Arthur da Costa e Silva in the late 1960s (Armijo and Ness, 2002; Baer, 1989; Alarcon and Mckinley, 1992). Armijo and Ness (2002) observe that, from the late 1960s through the 1970s, Brazil was one of the largest recipients of foreign direct investment and commercial loans among the developing nations. The focus of this case study commences in the late 1980s, since that was the first time that the leadership made significant efforts towards lifting import barriers and capital controls.

"both ambiguous and contradictory, watered down by numerous compromises and excessive revisions."[6]

Since the late 1960s, then, Brazil's welfare state has maintained very generous social protections towards elite members of the workforce and established a public education system that provides universal access to *primary* education. Suboptimal investments in terms of improving education, however, have resulted in poor-quality provision and instructional services. A large number of those eligible do not make use of the system because of its shortcomings, and those that do still lack basic skills. A significant unprotected informal sector still exists, and protective welfare policies maintain status distinctions alongside (slow) advancements in commodification.

7.1.1   Decommodification policies

Brazil's emphasis upon decommodification has its roots in the "revolution of 1930," brought about by Getulio Vargas. From the outset, Vargas's campaign invoked the "social question":

One cannot negate the existence of a social question in Brazil as one of the problems that will have to be dealt with seriously by public authorities... We need to coordinate activities between the states and the federal government to study and adopt measures to create a national Labor Code... These measures include instruction, education, hygiene, diet, housing, protection of women and children, of invalids and old people, credit, salary relief...and so forth. (from the platform of the Liberal Alliance, 1930, as quoted in Levine, 1997: 146)[7]

Ultimately, Vargas's strategy for dealing with the social question led to a fundamental restructuring of the relationship between state and society that has left its mark on social policies today. Central to this restructuring process was the labor legislation (Consolidacao das Leis do Trabalho [Consolidation of Labor Laws] – CLT) and social security policies. These two welfare schemes set the foundation for excessive state intervention in labor–management relations. Brazilians welcomed the initiatives because they promised better working and living conditions, despite the trade-offs. Succeeding administrations have continued to focus on these two aspects of welfare policy to manage social peace. Housing subsidies and access to public employment have also served as important

---

[6] The primary debate was between those who supported public schooling versus the proponents of private education (Gadotti, 1997). The 1961 law presented an ambiguous document reconciling these two positions.

[7] Vargas was the presidential candidate for the Liberal Alliance in 1930.

welfare tools to "buy" labor support, but have not been central to Brazil's welfare strategy.

Using the model of Italian corporatism, policy-makers aim to bind workers to the system by providing job security and social insurance benefits in exchange for strict regulations on freedom of association. The strategy is supported by an elaborate body of regulations governing and controlling labor mobilization and overall employment relations (by the CLT). The institutionalization of the Labor Courts by the CLT, as well as the generous provision of benefits and entitlements to protect select groups of workers from "employers' exploitation," were trade-offs with restrictions on trade union freedoms (Amadeo and Camargo, 1993).[8] The goal of this paternalistic effort was to win workers' allegiance and remove them as a source of opposition.[9] With the state supporting, defining, and regulating the form and content of employment relations, the state and different components of civil society established a "forced harmony" (Levine, 1997; Malloy, 1979; French, 1998).

Pensions and job security are, therefore, central to Brazil's welfare system. Social security benefits have long comprised the bulk of welfare expenditures in Brazil. Federal government spending on social security, both as a percentage of GDP and total budget, ranks in the ninetieth percentile for developing countries. Over the last few decades Brazil has spent, on average, 7 percent of its GDP on social security, which is more than three times the average of LDCs.[10] On average, 31 percent of total government spending is allocated to this sector, which is four times the mean of developing countries. In 2002 Brazil spent more on social security as a percentage of GDP than the OECD average (OECD, 2005).

Job security is the second pillar that has roots in the Vargas regime. The CLT's labor code has often been categorized as one of the "world's most advanced [pieces of] labor legislation," given the breadth of matters covered with respect to hiring, firing, and guaranteed job tenure, among other aspects

---

[8] Labor courts decide any matter in the realm of labor law, and their primary goal is to protect the employee when resolving labor disputes.

[9] The CLT required strikes to be authorized by the Labor Court. Note that the 1964 military government reformed the CLT to reduce labor protections and increase control over collective bargaining, strikes, and wage determination.

[10] This average (1972–97) is based on the IMF's *Government Finance Statistics* data. Note that scholars concur that Brazil's spending data should be interpreted with caution (Lloyd-Sherlock, 1998; da Silva, Estache, and Jarvela, 2004). For various reasons, calculating the precise amount of investment in social sectors in Brazil is problematic. First, with data through 1995, any calculation of real expenditures is challenging, because Brazil has experienced such extreme rates of inflation. Second, it is extremely difficult to get a sense of total spending (at all levels of government), since Brazil has about 5,600 autonomous municipalities and twenty-seven state systems.

(see Levine, 1997). Until 1966 the termination of employee contracts after ten years was forbidden by law, except for "serious fault," and the employer had to bear the burden of proof (French, 1998). After 1966 the Ten-year Protection rule fell into disuse and was replaced by the FGTS (Fundo de Garantia do Tempo de Servico), which provided a severance fund for discharged workers. Since 1988 the penalty for dismissal has increased threefold. It is telling that, unlike in South Korea, economic reasons do not constitute "just cause" for dismissal (Vause and Palhano, 1995).

Firms do not have to seek permission to lay off workers, as is the case in India; Brazilian employers face the additional burden of the Labor Court system, however. Labor Courts tend to have a pro-labor bias and the burden of proof is, essentially, on the employer (Amadeo, Gill, and Neri, 2000). The number of cases received by the Labor Courts is extraordinary: Filho (2005) estimates that, over the last sixty-three years, they have received almost 49.1 million cases, and the complaints have been rising. Labor courts have significant policy-setting power, given that they legislate where labor laws (in the Labor Code or constitution) are ambiguous (Amadeo, Gill, and Neri, 2000). It is no surprise that Brazil maintains some of the highest labor market protections by international standards. Djankov *et al.* (2003) and Heckman and Pages (2003) rank Brazil among the highest in Latin America and the developing world, based on the low degree of flexibility of working conditions and conditions for termination of employment.

Housing, public employment, and means-tested benefits are less central to the Brazilian dual welfare state. Even though housing subsidies were part of the benefit package for organized workers during the Vargas administration, they became one of the expendable policy programs. Brazil's housing policy-making institution, the National Housing Bank, was abolished by the mid-1980s and clearly revealed "the government's lack of determination in facing the housing problem" (Valenca, 1992: 54). In terms of public employment, Brazil has a tradition of granting state employees job security and advancement without merit (Lambert, 1969). In overall terms, however, the percentage employed in the public sector is small (11 percent of the working population), far below the LDC average of 31 percent and India's high average of 70 percent. Consequently, when viewed in a comparative context, jobs in the public sector have not been the predominant means of garnering political support. Finally, although Brazil has made some important advancements in means-tested programs, such as Bolsa Escola,[11] it accounts for only roughly 1 percent of GDP (OECD, 2005), a

[11] Bolsa Escola, implemented in 1997, involves a cash transfer to poor households on the condition that the children are sent to school.

small amount, especially when compared to the social security budget. Nonetheless, it is telling that, relative to the other welfare regime types represented by India and South Korea, the dual welfare state spends relatively more on means-tested programs.

7.1.2   Commodification policies

Vargas's commitment to education was articulated in various speeches, the Liberal Alliance platform, and the National Education Plan that was part of the 1934 constitution.[12] The first general education law was proposed in 1948, but did not pass until 1961.[13] Nevertheless, Brazil has experienced an "extraordinary rate of growth in education provision" since the 1950s (Araújo e Oliveira, 2004). By 1965 Birdsall, Bruns, and Sabot (1996) estimate that, in comparison to other countries at its income level, Brazil had very high primary enrollment rates. Radical innovations to Brazil's Basic Education Law in the early 1970s prescribed some type of education training for all. The years between 1967, when the government founded MOBRAL (the Brazilian Literacy Movement), and 1971, with the overhauling of basic education, were the so-called years of "economic miracle" and of "educational inertia" (Gadotti, 1997: 127). The central government in Brazil retains responsibility for establishing policy guidance, monitoring, and providing financial support for education.

Brazil spends an average amount (both centrally and locally) on education compared to other developing countries. What is distinct is that a fair portion of this is allocated towards primary education. With approximately 40 percent of its total education expenditures on pre-primary and primary education in 1999–2002, Brazil ranks at par with the LDC average and surpasses India's average of 38 percent.[14] More telling, however, is the fact that Brazil's net primary enrollment rate of 80 percent in 1995 was higher than the global average and just below the average of high-income non-OECD countries.[15]

---

[12] The National Education Plan called for free and "semi-mandatory" education (Levine, 1997).

[13] The 1961 law formed the Federal Education Council Law and decentralized the education system.

[14] See USAID's Global Education Database, available at http://qesdb.usaid.gov/ged/index.html; accessed July 27, 2007. Note that South Korea's average proportion of education spending allocated towards primary education was 65 percent in the early 1970s, falling to 45 percent by 1995. After universal access to primary education had been achieved, South Korea shifted resources to the expansion of secondary education.

[15] Note that these figures were calculated using the USAID Global Education Database for non-OECD countries where 1990s data were available.

Despite these efforts at improving primary education, however, Brazil's education system suffers from significant shortcomings. First, despite the commitment to primary education, Brazil spends proportionately more per student on tertiary education. Like India, Brazil is notorious for this elitist bias in education and spending resources at the expense of more progressive policies. Second, the *quality* of primary education in Brazil is very poor; and, third, the government lacks a commitment towards improving both the access to and quality of secondary education. Repetition, absenteeism, and high dropout rates are the main problems that plague Brazil's schools. To give an idea of the extent of repetition rates in secondary education, over a half of those enrolled are above the appropriate school age (Araújo e Oliveira, 2004). Dropout rates then become a particular problem once students reach this level. A recent World Bank study estimates that only one out of three students who join the ninth grade will successfully complete higher secondary education (Herran and Rodriguez, 2000). Only 66 percent of students currently in first grade are expected to complete lower secondary education. The consequence of these staggering dropout rates is that a large percentage of Brazilian workers are functionally illiterate, with the average worker having only about five years of education (de Castro, 2000). In 1997 a national assessment test for the system for Evaluation of Basic Education (SAEB) revealed that only 26 percent of students enrolled in (upper) secondary education are achieving at the expected level for their grade (Herran and Rodriguez, 2000). With only 20 percent of its public expenditure devoted to secondary education, Brazil falls fifteen percentage points below the global average and ten percentage points less than the average for LDCs in its income categories.[16] Brazilian scholars regard the current rise in enrollments as the natural consequence of increasing primary enrollment rates.

In terms of health provision, as with South Korea and India, policy-makers have taken minimal responsibility in providing preventative care and have let private industry play the dominant role. The Ministry of Health, established in the 1950s, develops and coordinates national health policy, and has primary responsibility for preventative care. Access to health services until the late 1980s was reserved for those enrolled in the social security program, however. Brazil's public health spending ranks below the LDC average and has decreased in recent years.[17] Barreto de

---

[16] See USAID's Global Education Database. This refers to 1995 data, or 1996 data if 1995 data were missing. Countries have been included based on data availability.

[17] The LDC average spending on health in 1998 was 1.5 percent of GDP and 6 percent of total government expenditures. Brazil's 1998 total health spending as a percentage of GDP and total government spending was 1.2 and 3 percent, respectively. These estimates are based

Oliveira, Beltrão, and Medici (1994) estimate that health care spending would have to increase by at least 25 percent in order for Brazilians to have a minimal resource base to pay the costs of minimum health care.[18] Health care today is still a neglected issue, which is reflected by indicators in which Brazil lags behind countries in its income group. Infant mortality, for instance, is considerably higher than in Paraguay, Colombia, the Philippines and the Dominican Republic. One-third of the population still lacked basic health care services by the mid-1990s (Nelson, 2004).

To summarize, Brazil's weak dual welfare state, correlated with its mixed development strategy, is associated with an emphasis on social security, labor market protections, and universal access to primary education *in comparison to other developing countries*. Primarily because the quality of its education system is still below par, Brazil ranks below South Korea's productive welfare status. The next section investigates the impact of race to the bottom pressures on Brazil's weak dual welfare state.

7.2   Race to the bottom

Brazil began adopting policies aimed at both trade and capital liberalization in 1988, but the pace of reforms did not accelerate until the Fernando Collor de Melo administration (1990–2). After a period of failed stabilization plans and high inflation during the 1980s, the 1990s has been recognized as "the decade of market-oriented reforms" (Campos and Pinheiro, 2002: 3). The beginnings of this period were marked by the elimination of the majority of non-tariff barriers from the ISI period, a greater than 50 percent reduction in tariff rates, the abolition of special import regimes, a floating exchange rate, and a fairly substantial easing of inward capital controls (Campos and Pinheiro, 2002; Armijo and Ness, 2002).[19]

7.2.1   Social security

In consonance with RTB predictions, social security and labor market protections experienced cutbacks after an initial expansion in the 1980s. Reforms in both these sectors have dominated debates in Congress since globalization reforms began to be implemented. Of these two sectors,

---

on the IMF's *Government Finance Statistics* data. Data from the Human Development Indicators, United Nations, and the Economic Commission for Latin America and the Caribbean (ECLAC) similarly indicate that Brazil's health spending is below the average.

[18] Barreto de Oliveira, Beltrão, and Medici (1994) base this prediction on 1989 data. According to the IMF's *Government Finance Statistics*, however, public spending on health in 1989 and in 1998 is roughly equivalent.

[19] Note that tariffs on capital goods are still above those in east Asia (Moreira, 2004).

social security has experienced the greatest pressures for reform. Analysts predict that recent reforms in social security will cause government expenditures in this sector to decline soon. Indeed, globalization pressures were not the only – and perhaps not even the primary – impetus for reform. Two big domestic-level motives for social security reform were to address financial problems created by the expansions stipulated in the 1988 constitution and to correct gross inequities in the social security system. The key point here is that the rising pressures of globalization (e.g. the late 1990s financial crisis and rising private-sector demands) added to this list stronger demands for fiscal discipline, and ultimately became pivotal to the success of long-stalled social security reforms.

As stated earlier, allocations to the social security sector have comprised the lion's share (almost 50 percent) of the total government budget and equal almost the entire budget of education and health taken together. The level of social security spending doubled after the 1988 constitution initiated policies aimed at universalizing social security benefits. The constitution called for a substantial increase in rural workers' benefits, established the minimum wage as the minimum pension level, recalculated pensions to compensate for the value eroded by inflation, and instituted lax eligibility criteria for both private and public workers (Barreto de Oliviera and Beltrão, 2001). After 1988 Brazil also became one of the few countries in the developing world to offer unemployment insurance.

Not surprisingly, as a consequence, Brazil has one of the highest payroll taxes in the world, and, since the 1990s, high levels of public and pension debts (World Bank, 2001a). Indeed, as RTB hypotheses would predict, international market expansion placed additional pressure on Brazil to reduce its social security spending and curb its pension debt. Reforms aimed at cutting back social security expenditures were finally passed in 1998, 1999, and 2003, and are estimated to reduce pensions over the next several decades (World Bank, 2005a).

Passing the first set of reforms in 1998 and 1999 involved a long, protracted political battle. Congress had voted down the reform measures proposed by President Fernando Henrique Cardoso (1995–2002) four times in the previous four years. The recent cutbacks have been aimed at decreasing the cost of social security, although the final outcome was significantly watered down from the original proposal. Reforms included measures to discourage early retirement, an increase in mandated contributions collected from all public servants, a tax on higher-level civil service pensions, a new benefit formula to calculate benefits based on actual lifetime contributions, benefit ceilings, stricter eligibility requirements, and a minimum vesting period of ten years for civil servants to receive pension benefits (World Bank, 2005a, 2001a; Kay, 2001).[20] The changes also paved the way for the easier passage of future reforms by removing from the Constitution much of the detailed provisions regarding the social security system.[21]

The 2003 reforms pushed through by President Luiz Inácio Lula da Silva marked a milestone, because they aimed at reducing the gross inequities between the pensions received by the private sector and the civil servants at the national and sub-national levels (Pension Regime for Government Workers, or RJU). Stricter rules and conditions for pension eligibility, contribution and benefit levels were applied to the RJU. More specifically, the major changes revolved around discouraging early retirement and leveling the public- and private-sector pension systems by implementing such measures as overall wage and benefit caps, a reduction in survivor pensions, a benefit/contribution ceiling equal to that received by private-sector workers (2,400 reals), and a new benefit formula that changed the pension base from the last wage to the average of 80 percent of the highest real wages after 1994 (Medici, 2004; World Bank, 2005a). The most controversial reform required an 11 percent tax on all current pensioners receiving more than 1,058 reals ($360) a month in benefits.[22]

Globalization's influence on social security reform in the 1990s was evident in several ways. First, crises have been positively linked with financial liberalization (Tornell, Westermann, and Martinez, 2004; Radelet and Sachs, 1999). President Cardoso was able to use the urgency of the late 1990s financial crisis to push the 1999 reforms through Congress (Huber, 2005; Souza, 1999). Second, the Brazilian government has been increasingly concerned about the reactions of international investors to the ongoing social security negotiations. Wary of his strong leftist credentials, international investors watched Brazilian President Lula's efforts to push through reforms particularly closely.[23] Markets plunged several times as investors panicked in response to setbacks in

---

[20] The reforms based benefits on actual levels instead of the last thirty-six months of work. This was significant, given that the previous system encouraged workers retiring early, particularly the self-employed, to declare a higher salary amount just before retirement and declare a lower income prior to the last thirty-six months of their career (Kay, 2001).

[21] Pension reform between 1988 and 1998 was particularly difficult because a three-fifths majority in Congress was required to make changes. Note that the increase in total social security expenditures immediately after the reforms were implemented was primarily due to increases in disability-related pension expenditures, as well as a race to early retirement from a number of Brazil's civil servants, who were goaded by the threat of pension reform (see World Bank, 2005a).

[22] "Editorial Assesses Obstacles to Lula's Social Security Reform," *World News Connection*, April 18, 2003.

[23] "Pensions Cause Investor Caution," *Gazeta Mercantil Invest News* (São Paulo), January 15, 2003.

the reform negotiation process, which were viewed as reflective of Brazil's inability to bring the budget deficit under control.[24] Investors anticipated that successful reforms would reduce interest rates and bring down the deficits. Despite (or perhaps because of) his leftist base of support, President Lula has focused on mollifying investor demands. He spent the first part of his administration courting international investors by pushing through neoliberal reforms and encouraging fiscal constraint.[25] Both during the campaign and after the elections, Lula and leaders of his party, the Partido dos Trabalhadores (PT), promised "ad nauseum" to please markets by implementing a responsible fiscal policy, honoring all debt contracts, and pushing through social security and tax reform.[26]

7.2.2   Labor market protections

As with South Korea, Brazil's labor market reforms occurred in two stages, initially moving in a pro-labor direction, but eventually leading to some retrenchment. With the onset of democracy in 1985, and before market reforms were consolidated, several pro-labor reforms and workers' rights were adopted into labor law. The most significant changes related to the right to strike (including for public-sector workers), the freedom to register unions, and prohibitions on state intervention in union affairs and conflicts (Amadeo and Camargo, 1993). With respect to job security, the employer contribution to the FGTS (the severance fund) was increased from 8 percent to 40 percent, the maximum working week reduced to forty-four hours, and the maximum length of daily work was reduced to eight hours (Amadeo et al., 1995).

Once economic openness policy reforms had been implemented, however, followed by an economic crisis in 1994, President Cardoso began to push for labor flexibility between 1995 and 1999. He began by denouncing Brazil's ratification of ILO convention 158 on the termination of employment, arguing that labor market flexibility was needed (Cook, 2002). Congress also permitted part-time contracts and the temporary suspension of employees for up to six months. The temporary worker contracts were particularly controversial, as labor organizations argued that it would increase dualism between "those who have rights and those

---

[24] "Market Uneasy on Pension Reform Discussions," *Gazeta Mercantil Invest News* (São Paulo), July 14, 2003, and "Pensions Cause Investor Caution," January 15, 2003.

[25] "Brazil Returns Successfully to Bond Markets," *Financial Times* (London), April 29, 2003.

[26] "Delicate Balancing Act Still Required," *Latin America Regional Report* (London), November 19, 2002.

who do not" in the Brazilian labor market.[27] Brazil's business sector's response was that they wanted "the country's labor laws to be made 'flexible' in order to strengthen international competition and attract international investments."[28] Interestingly, based on interviews conducted for this study, workers and union leaders of Brazil's major labor confederations stated that their greatest concern was not the risk of losing social security benefits, but the pressure that international market competition was putting on them to give up their job protections. As a former deputy, Marcio Moreira Alves explained to a local newspaper, "There is a sort of liturgy imposed by the economic globalization of the developing countries." He continued, "Firstly, the opening of borders to foreign trade and capital, followed by the increase of industrial production, the privatization of state companies and, finally, the reduction of the social cost of jobs."[29]

7.2.3   Health care

In direct contrast to reforms in social security and labor, policies and expenditures related to health and education show minimal signs of RTB effects. Since the adoption of globalization policies, the 1988 constitution includes a declaration of the right to health care for all persons regardless of occupation and income, and the right to education (which could be claimed in court). Policies to fulfill the constitutional mandate in health care took two (albeit related) tracks, both of which defied RTB expectations. First, significant government interventions and institutional changes aimed directly at increasing access to health care were initiated. Second, linked to access, was the establishment of the Unified Health System (SUS), which was a reform aimed at decentralizing health care. Decentralization reforms have shifted some of the financial burden of the central government to states and municipalities. Importantly, both efforts ensure the government's (central or local) rising involvement in the financing, distribution, and provision of health care in Brazil.

Prior to 1988 access to high-quality health care was limited to those enrolled in compulsory health insurance (social security) schemes administered by a federal agency, the Instituto Nacional de Assistencia Medica da Previdencia Social (INAMPS). Those not paying social security

---

[27] "Temporary Job Contract Demonstration Ends without Incident," *Gazeta Mercantil Invest News* (São Paulo), January 21, 1998.

[28] "Job Security Threatened, Unions Say," *Inter Press Service* (Rome), November 19, 1996.

[29] "Brazil: Labor Deregulation Crosses the Border," *Inter Press Service* (Rome), January 13, 1998.

contributions, such as many in the rural and informal sectors, as well as the (lower-income) self-employed, had to rely on the overburdened and underequipped public health care system. The private sector's role in the provision of health care grew progressively more important, as the INAMPS would contract its services to help care for the insured clientele.

After the constitutional change, access was encouraged by emphasizing the public sector and preventative care, making private-sector services complementary. First, the institutional autonomy of the INAMPS was curtailed by absorbing it into the Health Ministry (Arretche, 2004).[30] Second, government revenues, rather than the social security budget, were responsible for financing health care through social security arrangements (Elias and Cohn, 2003).[31] Finally, a 2001 amendment required the federal government to spend an amount equal to the previous year's budget, while state and municipal governments were required to spend 12 and 15 percent of their budgets, respectively (Elias and Cohn, 2003).

The decentralization of health care has been another goal of the recent reforms. The SUS involves integrating a regionalized and decentralized system of health care, with coordinated management at each level of government (Almeida et al., 2000). As a result of the decentralization measures, state and local provision of primary health care increased, while federal health expenditures decreased. Elias and Cohn (2003) report that, by 1996, although the federal share of health spending witnessed a 53.7 percent drop, municipal financing increased approximately 12 percent per capita. Importantly, the federal government retains significant responsibility over financing and coordination, even though the municipalities are in charge of the management of the health care systems, and even surpassed 15 percent of their budgets in some cases (Arretche, 2004; Almeida et al., 2000).

7.2.4   Education

In addition to health reforms, major reforms aimed at improving Brazil's investment in the education sector have also been adopted since liberalization. To begin with, Brazil's average spending on education as a percentage of GDP before liberalization (5 percent) was higher than the regional Latin America average (3 percent), and even above the average

---

[30] The Ministry of Health had been responsible for developing and coordinating national health policy, and for public health and preventative medicine. It was financed by government revenues.

[31] From 1996–2001, in order to fund this constitutional change, the Ministry of Health relied on a tax on all financial transactions (Elias and Cohn, 2003).

of the European Union. Since 1988 significant reforms have been accompanied by a marked increase in education expenditures. First, the constitution mandated minimum spending levels at all levels of government. The federal government must spend 18 percent of its resources on education, and the state and local governments are required to spend 25 percent. Second, in the mid-1990s the government instituted a wide-ranging set of reforms aimed at improving the resources for and quality of education, focusing for the most part on the primary level. The federal government took the lead role in national education policy formulation, guaranteeing equity and quality assurance, and ensuring that the specific responsibilities of various levels of government were clearly specified, particularly with the *Lei de Diretrizes e Bases da Educacao Nacional* (LDB), approved in 1996 (World Bank, 2002a).

7.2.5 Summary

In conclusion, pensions and labor market protections appear to be more affected by RTB pressures than health and education sectors. The next area of inquiry is twofold. First, are these current reforms (cutbacks or otherwise) an indication of institutional change? In other words, do the cutbacks in social security suggest that Brazil is moving towards convergence in policies akin to the liberal welfare state? Or is it the case that improvements in commodifying policies (education and health) indicate that Brazil is advancing towards a productive welfare state?

7.3 Institutional change

This section illustrates how the dual welfare state exhibits a greater dynamism than either the productive or protective welfare regimes analyzed in this book. Landmark policy reforms in some of its long-standing institutions (e.g. social security) as well as expansions in select means-tested programs represent important changes to Brazil's status quo. Nevertheless, despite the reforms in social security, labor markets protections, and health and education, social policy changes during globalization still reflect important elements of institutional continuity. Cutbacks are not leading to a liberal welfare state, nor do expansions indicate a significant step towards a productive welfare state or universalism in benefits (a social democratic welfare state).

The first part of this section thus focuses on institutional continuity in Brazil's welfare state, and the ways in which it is manifested. Next, in the second subsection, I explore reasons *why* institutional continuity persists. I demonstrate how and why the impact of globalization on welfare schemes is contingent upon the mediating effects of Brazil's long-standing domestic institutions.

7.3.1   Welfare regime change?

As discussed in previous chapters, I use four main criteria to determine institutional change: (1) significant increases in the reliance on means testing; (2) dramatic reductions in benefit and eligibility rules; (3) major transfers of responsibility to the private sector; and (4) the persistence of institutional legacies. This section looks at these criteria as applied to Brazil's particular experience. The Brazilian welfare state is marked by both institutional continuity and change. The cutbacks (and expansion) of welfare benefits in the globalizing environment do not suggest convergence towards "the bottom," however, or the liberal welfare state.

While Brazil's welfare policies have changed to increase the reliance on means testing, these changes have not been so radical in practice. Brazil's most effective means-testing strategy since globalization policies were adopted is rural pensions (OECD, 2005). These are considered social assistance because of the weak link between contribution and benefits. The new provisions aimed directly at redistribution by expanding coverage and relaxing eligibility requirements for the rural poor as follows: a doubling of all social assistance and rural benefit values; a reduction of five years in age limits for benefits (to sixty for men, fifty-five for women); equalization of the benefit for the entire rural population (men and women receive equal access); and setting values of the minimum social insurance and social assistance benefits equal to the minimum wage.[32]

Other programs that expanded the reliance on means testing include benefits to the elderly and disabled, as well as income support programs, such as Bolsa Familia (BF), implemented in 2003. Bolsa Familia, which builds on President Cardoso's earlier Bolsa Escola program, targets the poor and provides incentives to improve their health and education status, contributing to both the productive and protective elements of Brazil's dual welfare state status.[33] Despite these important advances, means-tested programs still constituted only 0.9 percent of GDP in 2002. This amount is in stark contrast with the 10.7 percent that Brazil spends on pensions. More recently, President Lula's most dramatic

---

[32] Pension benefits are disbursed to rural workers on the condition that they can indicate a minimum of ten years of rural activities, regardless of whether they have contributed to the system previously (Bonturi, 2002).

[33] Bolsa Escola provides cash (45 reals per month) to poor families that send their children to school.

initiative, the "Zero Hunger" anti-poverty initiative, has been hampered by poor management and disagreements over the distribution of benefits.[34]

The second criterion involves decreases in benefit and eligibility rules. Benefits and eligibility in labor market protections have experienced minimal change. While cuts have been made, such as the changes in means-tested programs, they have not been radical in practice. If anything, benefits have been reduced for the labor force as a whole by default. Existing labor laws apply to formal-sector workers only, excluding the large informal-sector population of the Brazilian economy. As the Brazilian informal labor force expands, then, labor market protections apply overall to an increasingly small percentage of workers.

Benefit and eligibility rules for social security have altered in Brazil since globalization, however. Eligibility and benefits have been reduced for the upper income levels, while expanding at the lower income levels, particularly for the rural poor. Rather than necessarily symbolizing regime change, however, recent reforms reflect the first efforts towards reining in the excesses of the Brazilian dual welfare state. Both benefit and eligibility rules have been excessively generous for certain groups of Brazilian workers, particularly those in the public sector. First, prior to reform, the average retirement age in Brazil was very low. President Cardoso provoked strong reactions when he criticized those who retire under fifty as "layabouts who take advantage of a country of poor and destitute people."[35] Cardoso argued that the average age of retirement was forty-nine, and many retire as early as thirty-four.[36] Second, the benefits of public-sector workers have been touted as "the most generous in the world."[37] The average pension benefit for civil servant retirees was twenty-six times higher than that of their counterparts in the private sector (World Bank, 2001a). Furthermore, it was not uncommon for the pensions of high-ranking government officials to be equivalent to four or five times their salaries.

While the new reforms provide somewhat more stringent eligibility conditions and benefit formulae for these upper-income groups, they represent only a first step (albeit an important one) towards mitigating the excesses of Brazil's social insurance scheme; the stratifying effects remain. No doubt the reforms have a redistributive effect upon the

---

[34] "Zero Hunger Runs into Problems," *Latinnews Daily* (London), June 9, 2003.
[35] "Social Security Reform Advances," *Latin American Weekly Report* (London), May 19, 1998.
[36] "Brazil Chamber of Deputies Approves Social Security Reforms," Associated Press, February 13, 1998.
[37] "Lula's Great Pension Battle," *The Economist* (US edition), April 5, 2003.

existing beneficiaries of the system, particularly the rural sector, which has received an expansion of benefits since 1988. Social insurance remains predominantly contribution-financed and reserved for formal-sector workers, however (OECD, 2005). Different social security systems continue to coexist, and the constitution maintains generous rules for specific categories of workers (Pinheiro, 2005). Workers in several sectors (e.g. education, health care, and social assistance institutions) continue to enjoy exemptions and lower contribution rates, and civil servants continue to benefit from more generous pension entitlements than their counterparts in the private sector (OECD, 2005). It must be emphasized that pre-reform benefits for public-sector workers were exceptionally high.

The recent developments, then, are radical by Brazilian standards, but not when placed in a comparative context. The major advances are to require workers to work longer for benefits and to bring replacement ratios more in line with the more generous OECD standards. By the same token, although recent reforms boost the retirement age, Brazil still has a long way to go to reach the international average (see Bonturi, 2002).[38] It is for reasons such as these that capital market analysts claim that Brazil's pension reforms have simply not been enough.[39] As Velloso, a public-finance specialist in Brasilia recently lamented, "Under Lula, nothing has changed."[40]

Thus, under the new rules, the upper-income groups that have long been covered by social security are indeed now more vulnerable to the risks and uncertainties of globalization. Nonetheless, benefits for current workers (civil servants, and even new entrants to the public sector) are still extremely high by both Brazilian and international standards. Recent social security reforms can be viewed as an important first step in the very long process towards promoting a more equitable pension system.

The third criterion, that of major transfers of responsibility to the private sector, certainly does not hold. As in South Korea's case, a significant *change* in the responsibilities of the private sector has not occurred since globalization. The recent reforms in social security have been parametric (Kay, 2001; Medici, 2004). It is telling that, like South Korea, Brazil resisted World Bank pressure and opted to maintain

---

[38] Bonturi (2002) reports that the average retirement age in Brazil in 2000 was fifty-six.
[39] "Pension Bill Seen Only Resolving Immediate Problems," *Gazeta Mercantil* (São Paulo), April 23, 2003.
[40] Raul Velloso, "Bloated, Wasteful, Rigid and Unfair," *The Economist* (US edition), September 2, 2004.

its pay-as-you-go public pension system rather than embracing individual accounts, despite efforts by both the Collor (1990–2) and Cardoso administrations (1995–2002).[41] Instead, as a way to increase the pension value above the ceiling, a complementary pension fund was created for public employees. In 2003 social security minister Ricardo Berzoini was quick to stress that the complementary pension funds for civil servants are not related to the privatization issue.[42]

The private sector played an important role in both education and health decades before globalization policies were adopted. Public policies have long favored private schools in Brazil (Plank, 1996). In contrast to South Korea, the private sector has been a major provider of educational services in lower education levels as well as higher. Until 1964 schools at the secondary level had been predominantly (over 58 percent) private. The long-run trend in Brazil has actually been towards limiting rather than expanding the role of the private sector (Haussman and Haar, 1978; James, King, and Suryadi, 1996), although high-income families continue to maintain a strong demand for high-quality private primary and secondary education (Plank, 1996; James, King, and Suryadi, 1996: 493).

Reforms in health provision ultimately perpetuated the dual system of private and public health care, resulting in an increased role for the former, while the Brazilian government continues its practice of minimum spending on preventative care. The large role for the private sector has its roots in the early 1960s, when access to health care was linked to social security contributions. The INAMPS contracted with the private sector to provide its clientele with health services (Lobato and Burlandy, 2001). In addition, privileged income groups dissatisfied with the public health care system increasingly turned to private insurance, leading to a growing supply (Arretche, 2004). Almeida et al. (2000) estimate that private health insurance coverage increased by 73 percent from 1987 to 1996. Despite growing demands by reform advocates to curtail the role of the private sector in health care, the 1988 constitution permitted private institutions to continue to play a complementary role to SUS with limited government regulation.[43] On average, private spending on health is 43 percent greater than public spending (UN, 2004). Total private spending on health, as a

---

[41] Matijascic and Kay, 2006; "World Bank Will Not Interfere in Brazil's Reform," *Gazeta Mercantil Invest News* (São Paulo), May 27, 2003.

[42] "Pension Reforms Are Not Related to Privatization," *Gazeta Mercantil Invest News* (São Paulo), July 1, 2003.

[43] Article 199 included the private sector in reform as follows: "Private practice of medicine was permitted, and private institutions could play a complementary role in the SUS, with priority going to philanthropic and not-for-profit organizations" (Elias and Cohn, 2003: 45).

percentage of GDP, is roughly equal to that of India, although the ratio of public to private spending is far lower in India.

In terms of the fourth criterion, the persistence of institutional legacies, Brazil continues to pursue the weak dual welfare strategy: commodification efforts still focus on primary education and lag behind Brazil's generous protective (decommodification) welfare schemes. Overall, reforms during the globalizing era have not changed the structure of Brazil's welfare system. To begin with, social security spending still constitutes the largest percentage of general government social spending. Spending on pensions still greatly exceeds spending on health and education combined (see figure 7.1), and the proportions are not expected to change

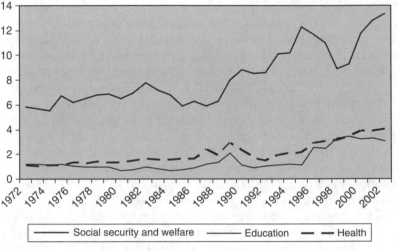

Figure 7.1 Government social spending as a percentage of GDP, 1972–2003

Note: Spending as a percentage of total government expenditures and per capita spending show parallel trends.

Sources: IMF, *Government Finance Statistics* (various years).

Central-level data: Ministerio da Fazenda, "Estatística – Contabilidade Governamental: Despesa da Uniao por Grupo de Natureza," available at www.stn.fazenda.gov.br/estatistica/est_contabil.asp (accessed August 28, 2005).

State-level data: Ministerio da Fazenda, "Estatística – Estados e Municipios: Financas do Brasil – Receita e Despesa dos Municipios" (various years), available at www.stn.fazenda.gov.br/estatistica/est_estados.asp (accessed August 28, 2005).

I would also like to thank George Avelino, David Brown, and Wendy Hunter for access to their ECLAC database, 2001, used in Avelino, Brown, and Hunter (2005).

much in the near future (see also OECD, 2005). Total government education expenditures have hovered around 4 percent of GDP, and even experienced a short-term decline in the early 1990s.

By the same token, labor market reforms on the whole have been relatively minor. Cook (2002: 45) concludes that, despite the erosion of union bargaining power, "while organized labor could not halt many of the changes, it managed to conserve core interests." The most far-reaching policy proposals aimed at expanding labor market flexibility have yet to be implemented. Brazilian businessmen still await a major overhaul of the CLT, which they see as the biggest obstacle towards improving international competitiveness.[44] Proposed changes are modifications to union structure, collective bargaining, union finances, and the power of the Labor Courts. All these reforms, it is hoped, will make it easier for companies to hire workers.[45]

Second, reforms in education have produced important changes on the primary level, but the secondary level still lags behind. Many studies indicate that recently implemented programs, such as the Development of Elementary Schooling and Valuing of Teachers (FUNDEF) and Bolsa Escola, have successfully improved the quality of and access to primary education. Similar programs focusing on secondary education have yet to be implemented, however. One of these, the Basic Education Maintenance and Development Fund (FUNDEB), is still in the negotiation phase. In addition, the president of the National Council of State Secretaries of Education, Gabriel Chalita, recently called the FUNDEB proposal "disrespectful," since the funds per child were so meager.[46]

Not surprisingly, a recent World Bank report (2000a) concludes that Brazil still faces "substantial challenges" in secondary education. The report finds that the continued problem of repetition leads to high rates of dropout, an overwhelmingly urban bias (25.9 percent of primary total enrollments are rural, while lower secondary enrollment in rural areas is only 5.2 percent), and poor instructional quality (World Bank, 2000a). Moreover, public financing continues to be skewed towards tertiary education. While higher education enrollments represent only 2 percent of total enrollment, it captured 22 percent of total expenditures (UN, 2005; World Bank, 2000a).

---

[44] "Brazilian Businessmen to Influence Construction of Union, Labor and Tax Reforms," *Gazeta Mercantil Invest News* (São Paulo), March 14, 2005.
[45] "Labor Unions," *LatinFinance* (Coral Gables, FL) March 2004.
[46] "Brazil's Finance Minister Announces Release of R$200 Million for Basic Education; Palocci Opens the Coffer for Education," *Gazeta Mercantil* (São Paulo), November 30, 2005. He stated that R$766.90 per child per year was minimal when compared to the R$200 million that the São Paulo state government spends in bonuses for teachers.

In conclusion, while changes have occurred, Brazil's welfare state has shown a great degree of institutional continuity. Although there have been increases in the reliance on means testing and decreases in benefit and eligibility rules, these changes have not been dramatic. Major transfers of responsibility to the private sector have not taken place. Finally, the institutional legacies associated with Brazil's dual welfare state continue to guide the direction and character of reforms under conditions of globalization.

7.3.2   Mediating role of domestic institutions

This section explores how and why long-standing domestic institutions make regime change difficult, even under the pressures of globalization. First, as predicted in the quantitative analyses, social policies instituted alongside early development efforts benefited certain interest groups and provided them privileged access to the political arena. These groups blocked the access of subordinate groups to policy-making and the rights of citizenship. Second, intent on both co-opting and controlling the labor movement, the government–labor relationship that evolved was one based on clientelism. Third, in an environment in which PLP is low and an environment of particularism prevails, it has been difficult for workers to form encompassing institutions that can negotiate on a par with business and government to block welfare reforms; neither can they ensure that reforms benefit the larger group of workers.

Brazil's protective welfare policies were implemented alongside the ISI strategy in the 1930s. The primary beneficiaries were large-scale industrial capitalists, organized labor, civil servants, and governing elites. Despite the fact that social legislative programs were costly, industrialists ultimately accepted them as a carrot-and-stick approach to manipulate the actions of emerging labor groups. In return, they were promised a more cooperative, stable workforce and other economic benefits. As Levine (1997: 11) explains, "Business leaders accepted this formula gratefully, because it assured that the state would play a mediating role between employers and their workers, and it promised to assure protection and a steady supply of capital." Not having to face pressures to compete for export markets, as was required of South Korean firms, public and private Brazilian firms could recoup the high labor costs by raising prices in domestic markets (Birdsall, Bruns, and Sabot, 1996).[47]

---

[47] As Leff (1968) notes, the Brazilian government operated under an implicit "export surplus" theory of trade. Accordingly, firms had to turn to international markets only after domestic industry had been "adequately" supplied.

Organized labor, civil servants, and governing officials benefited most directly from the social welfare legislation, while the urban poor and rural workers were excluded originally. Civil servants had the advantage of policies designed to protect their job and income security. Organized labor gained from official government recognition of its legitimate status as well as social policies that provided concrete benefits (Malloy, 1979: 55). Finally, by the mid-1940s, responsibility over social welfare and labor activity helped increased federal power, and governing elites began to gain advantage by using these resources as a means of mobilizing public support (Kaufman, 1990; Skidmore, 1967; see also Weyland, 1996a, 1996b). Rural workers were the last to be included, in 1963, when CONTAG (the Confederação Nacional dos Trabalhadores na Agricultura – or National Confederation of Agricultural Workers) came into being, and the rural sector was incorporated into the scope of social security legislation (Beltrão, Pinheiro, and Barreto de Oliveria, 2004).[48] The urban poor did not have a similar organization, however, and were never included in the umbrella of social protections.

Of these groups, civil servants, governing elites, and some organized labor groups have the greatest interest in preserving the status quo. This is because benefits are unequally distributed both within and between occupational categories, reflecting the bargaining power of various groups (Malloy, 1979). The rural sector, for instance, receives meager benefits compared to urban wage-earners (Huber, 1996; Weyland, 1996a). The servants of the state, on the other hand, have traditionally received extremely generous protections (Kay, 2001). Party politicians have also been strong defenders of the status quo, since they rely on their control over the distribution of benefits (and jobs in these sectors) to maintain support (Weyland, 1996b).

These narrow coalitions have lobbied against reforms of Brazil's social welfare scheme initiated in the 1970s, and consequently prevented marginalized groups from securing access to modern social policies and citizenship (see Weyland, 1996b). Civil servants launched fierce protests against the recent social security reforms, succeeding in delaying their implementation during the Cardoso administration and watering down many of the final proposals. Public officials have tried to maintain the extent of their

---

[48] Consistent with its objective to be in command of emerging groups, the state promoted CONTAG in order to control the rural population (Weyland, 1996a). Beltrão, Pinheiro, and Barreto de Oliveria (2004) note that the first efforts to include the rural sector began in 1955, with the creation of the Rural Social Service. The aim of this agency was to provide social assistance to the rural sector. The Rural Workers' Edict created the Fund for Social Security and Asssitance of Rural Workers (FUNRURAL) in 1963 (Beltrão, Pinheiro, and Barreto de Oliveria 2004).

control over benefits by defending traditional operating procedures. For example, the Ministries of Finance and Planning opposed social security reform proposals, as did many bureaucrats, who specifically resisted the plan to delink social insurance from labor registration and questioned the net benefits of the social security taxes (Weyland, 1996b). Similarly, government agencies such as the INAMPS and the private health sector succeeded in maintaining many of the elements of the existing system (Weyland, 1995; Arretche, 2004). They lobbied against extensive decentralization of the health care system and for maintaining a continued role for the private sector. In the end, decentralization reforms did occur, but the role of the private sector was preserved. President Cardoso encapsulated the political constraints well in his reference to social security reforms:

[P]ension reform is a thorny issue. It is not easy to say: do it as in such and such country because each country has its peculiarities and there is a problem here which is the transition. Even if we imagined a different system from the current one, it is necessary to see what is going to be done about those who have already contributed, those with expectations of rights, those that organized their lives around such and such pension benefits. (President Cardoso, quoted in Melo, 2004: 334)

Ultimately, then, efforts to cooperate and compromise with these vested interest groups have guided the direction of reforms, resulting in mostly incremental changes to the status quo.

The historical nature of the government–labor relationship in Brazil presents a second reason why institutional change is difficult. The institutional constraints posed by the relationship impede the implementation of more universal benefits. Unlike South Korea, but like India, political leaders opted to incorporate the labor movement during the early ISI period, aiming to mobilize workers as a major political constituency (Collier and Collier, 1991). For example, at a Labor Day 1951 event, President Vargas stated:

The Labor Day celebration has a symbolic importance both for me and for you: it represents a new coming together of workers and the government. It is with deep emotion that we restore this relationship… I can repeat today from my heart what I said once before: that the workers never disappointed me. They never came to me seeking selfish or private favors. They always spoke in the name of the collectivity to which they belong, for the recognition of their rights, for improvement in their living conditions, for redress of grievances of members of their class, and for the well-being of those sharing these difficulties… I need you, workers of Brazil, my friends, my companion in our long journey, as much as you need me. (President Vargas, quoted in Levine, 1997: 150)

The important distinction with Brazil's form of labor incorporation, in comparison to India, is that the principal goal is to control and prevent the emergence of autonomous labor groups (i.e. depoliticization), thereby keeping society weak and divided to ensure greater state control and power.[49]

Recall that it was fundamental to President Vargas's welfare strategy to reward or win the allegiance of servants of the state and actively employed labor (Levine, 1997; Mesa Lago, 1985). From the onset, the expansion of benefits was exclusionary and tailored according to occupational status. This co-optation strategy introduced the logic of clientelism into the formerly rational legal state structures (Malloy, 1993). In other words, the state corporatist system encouraged the advancement of narrow interest through direct links with the state, instead of class action. Only specific groups could enter into direct negotiations with the ministry to demand protection and bargain for better schemes of social protection (Malloy, 1979: 69). Elites were thus able to guarantee the obedience and support of workers in exchange for particularistic benefits (Weyland, 1996b).

The character of the government–labor relationship in Brazil is also linked to explanations as to why productive welfare policies (education) implemented during the turn towards a more export-oriented strategy did not advance much beyond achieving universal primary enrollment. First, as Schneider (2004) suggests, state intervention on behalf of labor reinforces barriers to lasting business coalitions. Firms are forced to dispute state power individually rather than act collectively to counterbalance labor. Indeed, business associations in Brazil are weak and fragmented (Schneider, 2004; Weyland, 1996a).[50] As Leff (1968) puts it, "The relatively poorly organized business leaders compete and advance incompatible proposals," and their response to education policies was no exception. For instance, the *salario-educacão*, introduced in 1964, was a tax on firms to fund primary education. The fact that such financing was legislated and enforced was certainly a marked distinction from India, which never had clear financing policies on education until the 1990s. Brazil's school finance system fared poorly, however, because it was open to political manipulation and firms would seek special loopholes from the government to avoid the tax (Plank, 1996).

---

[49] It could be argued that, in contrast to Brazil, a weak and fragmented society was not a *deliberate* consequence of the incorporation approach in India. Candland (1995) argues that the term "party incorporation" best describes India's form of labor mobilization. Each of India's ten large labor unions is affiliated with a different party. Depoliticization of labor, then, has not been a goal in India as it has been in Brazil. At the same time, it is possible that, because of state corporatism, benefits in Brazil are more generous and have wider coverage than is the case in India.

[50] This is certainly not to suggest that state intervention on behalf of workers is the only reason why business is weak in Brazil (see Schneider, 2004).

The turn towards an emphasis upon commodification-type policies thus occurred under conditions very different from those in South Korea. Many of the jobs in education were based on patronage ties. As Birdsall, Bruns, and Sabot (1996: 14) explain:

The education system, the largest employer in Brazil and a rich source of jobs, has been hampered by the political system: teaching, administrative and maintenance appointments have been treated as political spoils. This clientelistic system perpetuates incontestable patronage, with those outside denied access to power and the benefits of economic growth.

Under such conditions, Brazil's advancements in education more or less stagnated at the primary level. The government–labor relationship overall continues to reinforce the status quo and make it difficult for marginalized groups to be primary beneficiaries of Brazil's distribution regime.

Finally, divisions among labor movements, reinforced by Brazil's government–labor relations, undermine emerging efforts at class solidarity and present an explanation for some successful retrenchment efforts as well as institutional continuity. Fragmented labor is unable to form encompassing institutions capable of negotiating on behalf of workers' wider interests. Consistent with the other cases, they are able neither to present a united front, nor to prevent RTB reforms as workers in some European social democracies do by balancing efficiency and equity concerns. Weyland (1996b: 5) explains:

To promote rapid industrialization, the Brazilian state imposed in the 1930s and 1940s a segmented state-corporatist system which forced urban workers into a welter of different unions and thus kept them divided and weak. Since the state and business sought to limit labor militancy and since many union leaders had a stake in the established system, crucial features of this fragmented pattern of organization have survived even in new democracy. For instance, several union peak associations compete with each other… Remnants of corporatism and persistent clientelism have greatly intensified problems in organizing collective action. They have impeded the emergence of encompassing associations and social movements through which the poor could press their interest in redistributive reform.

Certainly, labor groups in Brazil have been adamantly opposed to social security reform proposals, and were particularly disappointed by President Lula's determination to implement them. The issue is that Brazil's largest labor confederations have not cooperated on these issues and the character of reforms. With respect to labor flexibility, leftist confederations such as the Central Unica dos Trabalhadores (CUT) and Confederação General dos Trabalhadores (CGT) have remained opposed to the reforms. But the CUT's main conservative rival, Forca Sindical (FS), has supported more flexible contracts and was viewed as more consonant with the changes that the government and employers wanted in labor reform. As Cook (2002: 14) notes, "Forca's actions undermined the CUT's position and curried favor with the Cardoso administration. Indeed, Forca Sindical's allies in Congress were instrumental in backing labor legislation during this period." In interviews conducted for this study, high-ranking officials of the CUT stated clearly that FS cooperation with the government on flexible contracts solidified the rift between the two rival confederations.

Labor groups were similarly divided over the debate on pension reform. The CUT, which represents public-sector workers, advocated maintenance of the existing social security rules for public servants. For example, they submitted proposals for expanding state-managed social security, making eligibility conditions more flexible, and increasing the value of benefits (Pinheiro, 2005). FS, on the other hand, representing mostly private-sector workers, advocated the unification of social welfare schemes for private- and public-sector workers. They mobilized public opinion against public servants by painting them as a privileged few and stated, "It was not fair that only private sector employees pay the price of economic adjustment and face unemployment, wage restraint and other sacrifices" (Cardoso, 2002). Parenthetically, while labor leaders have agreed upon the need for social security reform in general,[51] they have angrily protested the introduction of such measures that make it easier for employers to dismiss workers.[52] Regardless, in both cases the institutional fragmentation of Brazil's labor unions undermined organized labor's ability to present a united front against retrenchment. In the unusual cases where unions were more encompassing, such as CONTAG, the rural workers' union, retrenchment has been averted *and* equity-enhancing reforms have been more successful.

To summarize, Brazil's dual welfare strategy is supported and reinforced by the well-entrenched interest groups formed during the implementation of the country's early industrialization. Organized labor, civil servants, and governing officials were the traditional beneficiaries, and soon afterwards, in large part due to CONTAG, the rural sector gained some access. This distribution pattern has been reinforced by the clientelistic government–labor relationship encouraged by the Vargas administration, and has prevented the implementation of more universalistic welfare benefits. Division within Brazil's labor movement was a deliberate outcome that still exists today, and, as a result, some retrenchment

[51] "Brazilian Labor Unions Reject Government Social Security Reform Proposal," *World News Connection* (Washington, DC), April 16, 2003.
[52] "Job Security Threatened, Unions Say," *Inter Press Service* (Rome), November 19, 1996.

policies have been successful, but not to the extent that they have challenged the fundamental structures of the dual welfare state.

7.4   Who really gets hurt?

At this point, it is clear that civil servants have been the primary beneficiaries of welfare benefits, followed by organized labor in the formal sector, and, lastly, in terms of social security, the rural sector. Labor market protections apply to formal-sector workers only, excluding over 50 percent of the population that belongs to Brazil's informal sector. It is obvious, then, that the most privileged groups, the servants of the state, are the ones the most "hurt" by globalization pressures on social security, while formal-sector workers are vulnerable to the effects of reforms in labor market policies. Recent social security changes, in fact, were designed precisely to curtail the benefits of the most privileged strata and bring them more in line with the rest of those covered by insurance.

Poor rural workers, on the other hand, clearly gained from increases in non-contributory pensions (i.e. social assistance) in the late 1980s.[53] It should be stressed, however, that some social security provisions for this sector date back as far as 1963. The poor *urban* informal workers have been the least affected by the reforms, excluded from both the cutbacks and expansions in line with globalization.[54] The exclusion of the urban informal sector has been the case for decades in Brazil, however, and cannot be regarded as an outcome of globalization. One important exception has been improvements in primary education (the BF program), which is consistent with the findings from chapter 3. This section thus pays particular attention to how welfare reforms accompanying globalization have affected a subset of Brazil's poor, the urban informal-sector workers.

7.4.1   Social security and labor market protections (and social assistance)

While it is not difficult to establish that race to the bottom pressures have affected civil servants by reducing the extent of their privileges and benefits relative to pre-globalization levels, did the reforms directly hurt or help the poor? The Lula government argued that the 2003 reforms would redress broad inequalities and free up money for pro-poor social

---

[53] Recall that non-contributory pensions are classified as social assistance in Brazil because of the weak link between benefits and contributions.

[54] Unfortunately, no reliable data on the size of the urban informal sector in Brazil are available.

programs. The clearest answer at this point is that the benefits are far from immediate. The World Bank (2005a) estimates that it will take almost fifty years for the first set of social security reforms to halve the pension deficit of the social security system for private workers (RGPS) from 12 to about 6 percent. The 2003 reforms will reduce the projected RGPS pension deficit by approximately one-third in the first fifty years (World Bank, 2005: 13). The long-run deficit of the RJU is to be reduced by an even smaller amount. A recent OECD (2005) report concludes that, despite improvements in social security, the long-term pressures on the budget have not been eliminated. Significantly, however, the rural poor have experienced important gains with the late 1980s reforms. The social security policies that followed were designed cautiously to ensure that the poorest beneficiaries – predominantly the rural poor – were protected from the cutbacks (World Bank, 2005a).

The problem is that, so far, the benefits for the urban informal-sector workers have remained largely unaffected, despite the series of reforms. They have long operated without either social security or labor market protections. Since Brazil maintains one of the largest non-contributory pension schemes in the developing world, it is particularly striking that the principles of rural social security have not been applied to the urban informal sector. According to one report, 54.3 percent of the working-age population does not pay into the social security system, and many of them are still unable to collect a pension.[55] Weyland (1996a, 1996b) also argues that, while social security reform has helped the rural poor, the means-tested element for the urban population is too stringent, and thereby excludes a large percentage of urban informal-sector workers. A recent comparative analysis of non-contributory pensions in Brazil and South Africa finds that the conditions for entitlement are much tougher for the 1993 social security scheme (the Beneficio de Prestacao Continuada) that applies to the Brazilian urban informal sector than it is for the rural sector scheme, the Prevedencia Rural (HelpAge International, 2003). In sum, increasing openness has failed to improve social security protections significantly for the urban working poor. The situation is made worse by the fact that the number of workers in the unprotected informal sector has been increasing (Carneiro and Arbache, 2003; Portes and Hoffman, 2003). Brazil's urban poor have yet to gain (or lose) from the current social security and labor market reforms in this era of globalization.

[55] "Pensions: An Impossible Dream for Most Workers," *Inter Press Service* (Rome), June 23, 2003.

7.4.2   Health care

Health reforms under the conditions of globalization have not hurt the poor, but have not really helped them either. The middle and upper classes have long demanded, and have had access to, superior private health care, and this has not changed since the reforms. The poor, on the other hand, continue to receive low-quality health services. This is a trend that began in the late 1960s, however, with the rapid development of the private sector, which was the focus at that time. Health care reforms under globalization have served only to continue this trend.

The fight against Brazil's unequal health care system began in the mid-1970s. Brazil's military regime (1964–85) installed a model that emphasized curative care and provided sophisticated, high-quality health services accessible only to the middle and upper classes. Reformers belonging to the "sanitary movement" (Movimento Sanitarista), formed in the 1970s by medical professionals, local health authorities, and experts from academia and research institutes, argued that the root of the problem was the rapid development of the social-insurance-based system of health care, which favored the private health care providers. With the population's growing reliance on the private sector, the publicly provided systems became outmoded, and had low standards, long queues and inefficient facilities (see Baer, 2001). As a result, the middle and upper classes preferred to buy into private health care. The reform movement thus demanded changes that would serve the needs of the urban and rural poor by strengthening the public sector and shifting the emphasis to primary and preventative health care, such as vaccinations and sanitation (Weyland, 1996a; Arretche, 2004).

Yet, as Weyland's (1996a) thorough analysis of Brazil's health reform movements indicate, efforts in the 1970s met with limited success. Policy changes to improve efficiency and coverage were limited to some administrative reforms that put one institution in charge of both rural and urban health care.[56] Consequently, Weyland (1995) argues that the relationship between the public and private health sectors remained intact and continued to sustain Brazil's inequitable dual health care system.[57]

The 1988 constitution thus represented a landmark opportunity for the Sanitarista movement to push forward their proposals for improved equity

---

[56] FUNRURAL was abolished as an independent agency, the National Institute of Social Insurance (INPS), was placed in charge of health insurance, and INAMPS was put in charge of administering health care (Weyland, 1996a, 1995).

[57] The most successful redistributive reform was the Programa de Interiorizacao das Acoes de Saude e Saneamento (PIASS), which brought sanitary and basic medical facilities to rural poor in the northeast.

and efficiency in Brazil's health system. The constitution declared free and universal entitlement to all levels of health care, increased spending at all levels of government, and encouraged the formation of participatory councils. The Sanitaristas also supported decentralization, since Brazil's centralized, social-insurance-based system of health care was perceived to favor private, large, and well-organized health care providers and perpetuate the dual system (Arretche, 2004).

An overwhelming number of studies reveal that the recent reforms, however, have been unsuccessful in either changing the inegalitarian nature of health provision or improving access to health services (see, for example, Medici, 2003, Alves and Timmins, 2001, Almeida et al., 2000, and Elias and Cohn, 2003). The primary problem was that, ultimately, the constitution ensured institutional continuity; private institutions continue to play a complementary role to the Unified Health System, subject to limited regulation. This perpetuated the dual system, for two important reasons. First, the upper and middle classes, previously covered by INAMPS, remained unsatisfied with the quality of public health care provided by the SUS, and increasingly sought private health care plans (Collins, Araujo, and Barbosa, 2000).[58] This effectively continued the mandate of granting the poor low-quality public health care facilities (Almeida et al., 2000; Carneir and Arbache, 2003). Elias and Cohn (2003: 46) conclude, "Both the provision of and access to health services operate according to a logic of private practice and market principles, to the detriment of a logic that aims to fulfill the needs of the population."

The second reason that health reforms have had a limited impact on equity involves problems related to decentralization (see Arretche, 2004). Decentralization has favored the well-off areas that have greater revenue-generating capacity, predominantly located in the southeast (Collins, Araujo, and Barbosa, 2000). Local government was given greater responsibility, but did not have the resources or capabilities to target the poor (Alves and Timmins, 2001). In the first four years, for example, much of the construction boom for public clinics was incomplete due to insufficient funds (Baer, 2001). Finally, the constitution was vague about the exact responsibility of each level of government (Baer,

---

[58] Article 198 helped maintain the dual system by establishing a Unified Health System and a Complementary Medical Care System (SPAM). While the SUS provides health services primarily to the higher-risk population of poor, the SPAM is similar to its social security predecessor (INAMPS) and provides health services to a limited segment of the population (Elias and Cohn, 2003).

2001). There was no guarantee that the local system would provide health care based on equity.[59]

Why didn't globalization increase the incentives for successful health care reform? As predicted in chapter 3, the health sector faced much lobbying and clientelism, which ultimately prevented reform. And, as was discussed earlier, bureaucrats and the private sector had a particular interest in maintaining the status quo. Weyland concludes that these vested interests ultimately "made a drastic reorientation of Brazil's health care system impossible. Conservative forces celebrated their victory, while the health reform movement lamented its defeat" (Weyland, 1995: 1708).

7.4.3   Education

In contrast, the incremental expansion of primary education has been directly beneficial to the poor. Reforms in this sector have been implemented relatively successfully over the last two decades. Two of the programs mentioned earlier were groundbreaking: the Development of Elementary Schooling and Valuing of Teachers and Bolsa Escola, which evolved into Bolsa Familia. To promote equity directly, FUNDEF contained special measures to address within-state spending inequalities (i.e. revenues were distributed to states and municipalities based on enrollments). It also guaranteed a minimum per-pupil expenditure in primary schools, and built in incentives for teachers (increased wages) (Gordon and Vegas, 2005).[60] Studies have since documented the positive effects on enrollment, especially in poor regions, and positive trends in repetition and dropout rates (World Bank, 2002a; de Mello and Hoppe, 2005). Bolsa Escola, which provided low-income families with children with a small stipend, also had an effect on reducing poverty for the families that it reached (Lavinas et al., 2000). While there is still much room for improvement in terms of targeting and policy design (Schwartzman, 2005; Rawlings and Rubio, 2005), most scholars and international organizations view Bolsa Escola as an important step towards improvement in

---

[59] This is not to suggest that there were no successes for the reform movement. For example, Elias and Cohn (2003) point out that, even though universality is far from being achieved, decentralization has improved the capability of basic health care programs, such as the Family Health Program. Almeida et al. (2000) point out that the basic health services network has undergone a marked expansion since the early 1980s. What is significant for this analysis, however, is that the salient features of the pre-reform health system (e.g. dualism between public and private health care), which prevent access for the majority of the poor, remain, despite increased spending.

[60] Importantly, FUNDEF resources could not be used to pay pensions (World Bank, 2002a).

education for the poor (Araujo and do Nascimento, 2001; Criança, 2001; Aguiar and Araujo, 2002).

Did globalization play a role in increasing the incentives for equity-enhancing education reform, as predicted in chapter 3? Indeed, a significant amount of information on the benefits of education in a globalizing environment has become available. Kaufman and Nelson (2004: 252–3) discuss how "conclaves, conferences, and studies" led to increasing prioritization of education throughout Latin America. Not surprisingly, then, the Latinobarometro public survey recently revealed that the broader public has recognized the importance of education in the current environment (Kaufman and Nelson, 2004). Contrary to the general pattern of increasing cross-class interest convergence on education reform, however, there is little evidence that support for education reforms came from the business sector (Tendler, 2002).[61] Rather, education reforms were more of a top-down initiative from technocrats and bureaucrats in Brazil. How, then, were administrators able to overcome the institutional constraints of clientelism to make reform such as FUNDEF and Bolsa Escola possible? It is worth emphasizing that business did not resist the reforms, as was the case in South Korea, where business actively protested proposals to increase the *level* of education spending.

7.4.4   Summary

In conclusion, who has been most affected by globalization-driven reforms in Brazil? The poorest segments of the population – the informal workers, the unemployed, and the underemployed – have historically been excluded from any sort of welfare protections, and thus rollbacks of those protections can have little effect on these groups. It is, in fact, the more privileged groups, the formal-sector workers and the servants of the state, who have been the most hurt by RTB pressures to reform social security and labor market policies. In the case of education, on the other hand, globalization has provided incentives for some expansion, which has had a directly beneficial effect on the poor.

7.5   Other factors: democracy and partisanship

The end of military rule in 1985 clearly played a role in explaining recent welfare reforms, particularly in social insurance schemes, labor market protections, and education. Unlike the case of South Korea, however,

---

[61] As Kaufman and Nelson (2004: 503) point out, however, recent business support for public education campaigns suggests that their interest may be growing.

scholars are more cautious about the effects of democracy on these reforms. While some have observed a correlation between democracy and redistribution of resources, such as in education (Brown, 2002), several others have emphasized the complex relationship between democracy and equity-enhancing reform in Brazil (Grindle, 2000; Kaufman and Nelson, 2004; Weyland, 1996b). Certainly, progressive reforms to labor market protections, health, and social security were passed in the drafting of the 1988 constitution. Scholars have surmised that the interplay between reform-minded bureaucrats and democratization brought many of these issues to the agenda (see Weyland, 1996a, and Grindle, 2000). Significant education reforms did not take effect until more than a decade later (see Draibe, 2004), though, and the race to the bottom effects discussed earlier also took place more than a decade after democracy was introduced. One possibility perhaps worth investigating in future research is that it is not democracy per se that mediates the effects of globalization on welfare policies, but "new democracy."

Perhaps other factors must be observed, in addition to the broad category of democracy. Remmer's (2002) intriguing analysis, for instance, suggests that, contrary to conventional expectations, leftist partisanship might be a factor in implementing conservative fiscal policies. The implementation of the 2003 reforms in social security by a leftist president, Lula, was indeed impressive, particularly since his more conservative predecessors had not been so successful. Lula was also responsible for "Fome Zero" (Zero Hunger) and greater Bolsa Escola/Bolsa Familia initiatives.

7.6   Implications

As in the other cases, market integration brings some RTB-type reforms in dual welfare states. Contrary to the examples of the protective and productive welfare states represented by India and South Korea, respectively, however, Brazil's dual welfare state is somewhat more dynamic; a significant portion of the welfare cutbacks in Brazil occurred in some of its most well-entrenched programs, such as social security. Thus, in comparison, the dual welfare state appears to maintain rather greater promise for path-breaking reforms in the current era of globalization. Notable changes in both productive and protective welfare sectors have indeed occurred. Some advancements in means-tested programs have occurred concomitant with the advent of globalization, and Lula has managed to introduce equity-enhancing reforms in the historically regressive social security system, as well as important reforms in primary education, since economic liberalization.

Nonetheless, important elements of institutional continuity remain, in terms of the failure to improve higher education and the continued prioritization of protective welfare schemes that have significant stratifying effects. Thus, the primary issues of concern are the following: (1) commodification schemes still need considerable improvement; and (2) domestic institutions in Brazil still do not provide the urban informal sector with adequate social security, health, and labor market protections.

8   Conclusions

The governments of the South...are in any case deprived of the resources required for the financing of social policies or for redistribution. They are in effect victims of...the *unbridled race to reduce taxation and social expenditures*. [B]y constraining the governments of the South to respond to the market and the international financial institutions rather than to the aspirations of the peoples, the present globalization...has built a world where persons and people are put to the service of economic growth, productivity and financial profitability.

> (Global Call to Action against Poverty [GCAP], March 2005, emphasis added)[1]

Globalization wrecks...communities, impoverishes our people and fosters exclusion and individualism.

> (Donald Kasongi of Tanzania World Social Forum, 2004, Agency for Co-operation and Research in Development [ACORD])

Along with optimism for progress, the ascendance of global capitalism has given rise to fears of decreased welfare protections and benefits, as well as a loss of sovereign power for individual nations. Academics, journalists, policy-makers, and activists around the world caution that globalization will inevitably lead to a race to the bottom. According to the RTB hypothesis, in a world unhindered by restrictions on trade and capital flows, investors will pursue the highest rate of return, wherever that may be found. Nations that go counter to the market by protecting their citizens from the worst of its effects could lose out in the competition for global business and funds. Safety nets, environmental standards, and acceptable labor costs and protections could all raise production costs or risk lower profit margins. Governments therefore cannot initiate, or even maintain, policies that promote a higher quality of life for their people. Domestic politics becomes irrelevant in the face of global commerce.

The high demand for capital in developing countries increases concerns that citizens of these nations are at particular risk in the face of global

---

[1] The GCAP is a worldwide alliance of almost 1,000 non-profit organizations, activists, and non-governmental organizations.

market pressures. Even though a considerable number of scholars ultimately reject the RTB hypothesis, based on data from the developed
world, which shows significant *divergence* in the ways that these nations
provide for various levels of social welfare alongside market expansion
(Esping-Anderson, 1990; Hall and Soskice, 2001; Huber and Stephens,
2001; Kitschelt *et al.*, 1999; Iversen, 2005; Garrett, 1998), this book shows
that there is some validity to these fears for the less developed nations.

In this study, I have challenged prevailing conceptions about the
impacts of globalization on citizens of developing countries. It is the
poor who have been widely perceived as the victims of the "unbridled
race to reduce taxation and social expenditures." Fundamentally, the race
to the bottom debate in LDCs has been set up as a zero-sum game
between states and markets. Reality is much more complex. While globalization does indeed lead to a race to the bottom in developing economies,
institutions are *not* undergoing radical transformation and it is *not* the poor
who are worse off. In fact, it is the more privileged lower to upper middle
classes who take the brunt of the direct effects of the race to the bottom.

It is, therefore, the middle class and not the poor who are directly
impacted by welfare reforms, and the reason can be found in distinct
and persistent institutional arrangements. Essentially, LDC welfare states
have long been geared towards the middle and upper classes, and, in fact,
were never originally designed to protect the poor. Globalization *by itself*
does not determine policies that help (or hurt) the poor in the developing
world; it is domestic institutions that structure responses to the challenges
of economic openness. As the current consumers of welfare state services
fight to defend the status quo, distinct institutional configurations generate systematically different reactions. The end result is that developing
countries experience cutbacks in some areas of welfare, while retaining
continued protection in others. Defying zero-sum predictions, the race to
the bottom does not signify the end of domestic politics, and national
differences are far from extinct. Current LDC welfare policies therefore
reflect *both* external market pressures *and* domestic institutional arrangements. As a consequence of this interaction, in the final analysis, globalization is not leading to institutional convergence at the "neoliberal
bottom," and the effects of any RTB cuts in welfare policies are primarily
impacting the middle classes and largely bypassing the poor.

8.1 The case studies in perspective: globalization, domestic institutions, and social policies

This book demonstrates three important findings. First, the race to the
bottom has important effects on social policies in developing countries.

The clearest impact has been to pressure governments to cut back on social programs that can directly affect the bottom line of firms. This has largely been a result of trade, and not capital liberalization. Chapter 2 and the case study illustrations indicate that social security and labor market protections are the programs most susceptible to change. Race to the bottom pressures result in some degree of retrenchment in these two categories in all three welfare regimes (productive, protective, and dual). The Indian case study, however, suggests a differential impact from RTB pressures in other welfare states. Rather than official policy changes, the retrenchment of labor market protections occurs "by stealth" (or de facto). Additionally, expenditures on health and education may also experience cutbacks. This is not surprising, since protective welfare states tend to place less priority on commodification-type policies. The case studies thus present the added insight that cutbacks in human-capital-type programs in response to globalization pressures are more likely in protective welfare states, where they are not as well supported by entrenched interest groups.

The reason why RTB pressures have affected social policies in developing countries is the relatively decentralized condition of their labor movements. The experiences of the OECD countries have shown us that the effects of globalization on the welfare state are either absent or positive when labor movements are encompassing. In this scenario, labor groups coordinate policies with government and capital representatives (e.g. wage restraint in accordance with productivity, labor peace) so that they can enjoy the benefits of generous social policies without compromising efficiency. By contrast, since labor movements tend towards disunity in LDCs, policies are not coordinated, and welfare schemes yield adverse political and economic consequences. Narrow groups of workers from the formal sector fight to maintain their comparatively generous labor protections and benefits, pushing up labor costs and effectively feeding the demand for non-standard and informal-sector workers. This creates a classic insider–outsider problem that also serves to cement labor's political differences. Labor demands thus remain unfulfilled, as governments face mounting pressure for fiscal discipline. To avoid punishment from mobile asset-holders, and to help promote export markets, the government implements welfare reform. These cutbacks are generally not colossal and yet still, as in the example of President Lula's 2003 reforms in Brazil, they can serve to mollify investors. Clearly, even if isolated groups of workers are important government allies, their collective weakness (i.e. low PLP) eventually translates into some degree of welfare retrenchment.

The second major finding exposes the big paradox: the race to the bottom is not impacting the poor. Chapter 3 reveals that the nature of the (historical) government–labor relationship gives rise to institutional constraints that prevent the implementation of pro-poor social policies. Often used as vehicles of clientelism, political elites distribute social benefits to co-opt the more powerful labor groups. Thus, social benefits are used on a discretionary basis in exchange for political favors and labor quiescence. These findings suggest that, in addition to the problem of low PLP discussed in chapter 2, the government–labor relationship is also a factor reinforcing the insider–outsider problem. Both the Indian and Brazilian case studies illustrate these trends.

The South Korean case study, however, suggests an alternative to this type of government–labor relationship. Rather than using welfare benefits to pacify labor groups and foster clientelistic relations, the government–labor relationship may evolve solely on the basis of harassment and repression, thus limiting the extent of labor-friendly benefits.[2] This form of government–labor arrangement also results in weaker institutional support for welfare policies that protect the poor. Whether the nature of this government–labor relationship is subject to generalization across all productive welfare regimes is a future research topic worthy of investigation.

Chapter 4 delves deeper into the race to the bottom paradox and reveals that, in fact, none of the distribution regimes in developing countries were originally designed to protect the poor in the first place. Productive welfare states, such as South Korea, emphasize market reliance and promote commodification policies, focusing on education. Given that this regime type supports policies that discourage citizens' dependence on the state, programs designed to protect the poor are discouraged.

Protective welfare states, such as India, attempt to minimize citizen dependence on the market and prioritize decommodification-type policies. One might logically predict that regime types with these ideological foundations would prioritize policies that protect the poor. The Indian government has certainly sustained strong rhetoric in support of a pro-poor welfare regime, particularly after independence. Because decommodification-type policies were pursued before successful commodification took place (i.e. the majority of workers are dependent upon wage labor), however, only welfare protections for a very small, relatively privileged subset of the larger workforce, such as civil servants, the military, and organized labor, have found political and institutional backing.

---

[2] The government–labor relationship in Brazil involved harassment and repression as well (see Collier and Collier, 1991), but, at the same time, labor was "bought off" with a somewhat broader range of welfare protections.

The third regime type, the weak dual welfare state, which is a blend of both regime types, also tends to neglect the poor. Nevertheless, it is very interesting that the dual welfare state investigated in this analysis, Brazil, revealed greater pro-poor protective benefits when analyzed alongside India and South Korea. Important examples are Brazil's social insurance program, which includes the rural population, and the rather greater resources devoted to improving education for the poor, such as Bolsa Escola.

The one situation in which the poor were directly affected by race to the bottom pressures had positive redistributive consequences: improvements in primary education. In the cases in which either access to or the quality of primary education was pitiful, pro-poor redistributive policies have been adopted. Chapter 3 establishes that globalization provides incentives for overcoming institutional constraints to equity-enhancing reforms in education through the spread of information and cross-class interest convergence. These predictions hold true in India's protective welfare case, and mostly true in Brazil's dual welfare state. The difference is that, in Brazil's dual welfare state, business did not actively support redistributive reform in primary education. Nonetheless, it was equally critical that business did not actively lobby against reform, as was the case in South Korea's productive welfare state.

The South Korean case thus suggests that the politics of education reform under globalizing conditions is quite different in productive welfare states. The goal of business interests in this scenario is to improve the quality of education rather than to promote redistribution; both access to and the quality of lower levels of education in South Korea are, and have been, quite high by international standards. For example, South Korea's business associations did not support policy proposals that would help decrease the demand for private tutoring and thereby improve the access of lower income groups to tertiary-level education. In essence, the goal of current education reform seems to be one of ensuring access to a prescribed minimum level of education as a means to satisfy business needs for an educated labor force rather than from any inherent interest in promoting educational equality.

The third major finding is that RTB pressures do not lead to institutional convergence. In fact, none of the regime types reflected advances towards the neoliberal bottom; institutional diversity prevails in the developing world. Chapter 4 first supports this discovery using cluster analysis to verify that three distinct clusters of LDC welfare states persist well into twenty-first-century globalization. The nature of these welfare regimes is linked to the different ways in which their governments chose to respond to the earlier challenges of growth in the global economy – aiming either to expose domestic industries to or to protect them from international markets. Developing countries implemented welfare policies compatible with their particular development strategies, making welfare states endogenous to initial development models. Those who benefited from these programs became part of the dominant coalition and developed a vested interest in upholding some degree of institutional continuity.[3]

This book does not suggest, however, that the fate of LDC distribution regimes is one of overdetermined path dependence. The case illustrations reveal that globalization has indeed resulted in some movement away from both the productive and protective baselines, although the primary structural features of all three regime types remain intact. By adopting some education reforms, the Indian case suggests that protective welfare states are making incremental changes in the productive direction. In interesting contrast, South Korea's adoption of universal health and social insurance schemes shows that the productive welfare states appear to have adopted more protective welfare schemes.[4] The dual welfare state reveals some advancement on both fronts. Brazil has adopted important education reforms and made significant efforts towards improving the redistributive impact of the existing social insurance schemes.

Nonetheless, important elements of institutional continuity remain in all three regimes. In India, the core protective welfare schemes remain intact, as evidenced by the safeguarding of desirable public-sector jobs in its overstaffed bureaucracy. The government in South Korea maintains education as its top budgetary priority, and the state's extensive regulatory role in the education sector continues unabated. Brazil has experienced the greatest amount of change, with significant reforms to its social security program. With a disproportionate amount of state resources still budgeted to the social security sector, however, and lackluster improvements to secondary education, Brazil maintains its status as a weak dual welfare state.

Finally, all the welfare regimes reveal institutional continuity in terms of weak safety nets for the disadvantaged. Groups in India, South Korea, and

---

[3] In the case studies, I point out that the government–labor relationship may also be influenced by the early development strategy. In protective welfare states, for instance, the government is more likely to incorporate labor into the dominant coalition, because its closed development strategy created the political and economic space to do so.

[4] This is not to suggest that South Korea is advancing towards a protective welfare state. Recall from chapter 4 that productive welfare regimes, if successful, cannot become protective, since the latter uphold decommodification policies *before* the workforce has become dependent upon wage labor. Since South Korea is at or past the stage of commodification, the direction of welfare change is an open question. Advancement towards the liberal welfare state is unlikely, given the highly interventionist role of the state and the still weak means-tested programs. A social democratic welfare state is also unlikely in the country, since labor movements are not encompassing and protective welfare programs are still primarily employment-based.

Brazil that were left without protections in the earlier stages of development remain with limited protections today. These are primarily the groups that comprise casual labor in India, non-standard workers in South Korea, and the urban informal sector in Brazil. Globalization has not changed matters in this regard.

8.2   Questioning prevailing assumptions and future research

The analysis in this book both draws upon and contributes to various debates in the social sciences related to globalization, domestic politics, welfare, and poverty. It represents a concerted effort to bring the great majority of the countries in the world into the study of welfare states, a research tradition long focused upon the experiences of a small number of advanced industrialized nations. In the process, by observing the unique experience of developing country welfare regimes and how they have been coping with the pressures of globalization, the limitations of conventional views have been exposed. This book has only just begun to unveil the complex relationships surrounding globalization, domestic institutions, and social policy in developing nations, however. A rich research agenda lies ahead for those interested in exploring and advocating social protections for the poor in twenty-first-century globalization.

8.2.1   Rethinking the trade-off between states and markets
in developing economies

Many of the recent debates have centered on whether international markets or the state are the key drivers of policy under the conditions of globalization. The real concern is whether globalization has eroded the authority of the state to maintain and promote policies that respond to local needs and interests. Any welfare-policy-related changes that appear to please foreign investors have led scholars and activists alike to conclude that the balance of power between capital and labor has shifted and that state control over domestic policies has been compromised.

This book challenges this zero-sum dichotomy, however. The analysis in this book reveals that developing nations are clearly more sensitive to international economic pressures than the OECD countries. Some policy outcomes from international market pressures are indeed deterministic, in the sense that divided labor movements in LDCs cannot successfully negotiate win-win outcomes for capital and labor as globalization advances. At the same time, political reactions are indeterminate, because globalization pressures are also mediated by other types of domestic institutions, such as the type of distribution regime. Regimes represent an "interdependent web of an institutional matrix" that induces complementary organization forms and institutions that tend to be self-sustaining (see North, 1990: 95, and Hall and Soskice, 2001).[5] As a result, different distribution regimes guide the direction of policy in different ways as markets expand. Thus, while globalization does indeed impact domestic policies, local needs and politics do still matter.

A third complicating factor challenging the simple states-versus-markets view of developing countries is that domestic institutions can also change under the pressures of international market expansion. For example, we have seen that the institutional constraints posed by the government–labor relationship in many LDCs were to some extent transformed in the education sector and resulted in equity-enhancing reforms. Hence, the big picture that emerges from this analysis is that developing nations are moving along well-trodden, country-specific paths, invoking elements of both continuity and (guided) change.

8.2.2 Rethinking the political economies of developing countries

The existing literature has (implicitly) assumed that developing countries either maintain similar political economies, or that they are so vastly different from one another that general policy prescriptions are of little use. Both views scoff at the idea of a "welfare state" in countries at such low levels of economic, social, and political development, and the possibility of distinct distribution regimes has similarly been overlooked. With little recourse, then, we have been focusing on social policies that have been the mainstay of welfare regimes in OECD nations and ignoring the spectrum of welfare policies pursued by LDC governments.

The broader consequence has been that, for developing countries, we have had no real starting point to analyze either existing or potentially politically viable social policies. This analysis underscores the importance of removing this black box surrounding redistribution policies in developing countries. It takes seriously the literature indicating that distribution (and production) regimes are what affect economic performance and social well-being, not vice versa. By asking if, how, and why the principle of embedded liberalism has been just as much a reality for developing countries as it has been for the advanced industrialized nations, this book makes two important policy-relevant discoveries about the uniqueness of LDC political economies.

---

[5] The adoption of costly welfare benefits and a development strategy that tends to be less (economically) open is an example of a complementary organization form.

First, unlike the OECD countries, most developing countries face a trade-off between pursuing policies that encourage human capital investment and adopting welfare schemes that protect isolated groups from market risks. Even more fundamentally, this choice among welfare strategies turns out to be systematic. I argue in chapter 4 that there was a "founding moment of institutional formation" which sent countries along different welfare paths, and that this moment is critical to understanding the nature of regime diversity today.[6] Linking the choice of early development strategies with differing welfare regimes sheds some light on why a certain set of welfare policies is consistently favored in some developing countries but not in others. This is why the promotion of human capital investment has been more difficult in some countries (e.g. India) than in others (e.g. South Korea).

Second, the particular institutions and structures created in the formative period have narrowed the possible range of outcomes *for the poor* in the contemporary period. Welfare regimes empowered certain groups at the expense of others and helped reinforce the power structure within society. The important feedback mechanism identified in this book is thus the "power-distributional effect," wherein those who benefit from the existing system have a vested interest in sustaining it (see Weiss, 2003: 23).[7] Marginalized groups continue to be excluded, not only because they lack class mobilization, but because the existing structure actively reinforces their subordinate position by facilitating the organization and empowerment of other "insider" groups.

Nonetheless, institutions do not necessarily completely lock policymakers into a particular set of choices (see Pierson, 2000, and Thelen, 2004). The incremental changes in welfare strategies discussed earlier are a clear illustration of this point. This analysis, however, can only pique scholarly interest in the exact mechanisms of welfare regime change. A productive inquiry for the successful implementation of pro-poor policies would benefit immensely from developing more sophisticated tools for understanding institutional change. For instance, more detailed historical work exploring the cohesiveness and strategic skill of the dominant coalitions in upholding particular welfare strategies would significantly further discourse in this area. Finding weak points or sources of divisions in the elite group can be an important source of institutional change (Mahoney, 2000).

---

[6] See Thelen's (1999: 387) discussion of critical junctures.
[7] See Pierson (2000) and Mahoney (2000) for informative discussions on different institutional feedback mechanisms.

8.2.3   Rethinking the capital–labor dichotomy

The welfare literature has long relied upon power resource theories to explain the emergence and expansion of welfare states based on the power of labor and the left. As scholars such as Swensen (2002), Mares (2003a, 2003b, 2005), and Thelen (2004) have recently pointed out, however, studies that assume that capitalist and labor interests are always at odds are incorrect. The findings in this book ultimately attune to the recent literature that questions this tenet of power resource theory by positing that capitalists may not be opposed to social policies and that their preferences can vary in different countries. To begin with, the findings in chapter 2 hint that labor in developing countries is too weak to be responsible for the existing social policies and programs of these nations.[8] They simply could not have acted alone, however skewed social legislation might be in terms or redistribution.

As it turns out, in each of the three welfare regime types, capitalist preferences are compatible with the welfare policies employed. In the protective welfare states, capitalists are amenable to social-insurance-type policies because of the benefits they gain in return – more labor peace. They can also afford to do so, since governments can compensate them in other ways in the closed economic environment. In productive welfare states, capitalists support welfare arrangements that eschew protectionist welfare policies and keep labor costs to a minimum. Additionally, this book highlights the critical importance of cross-class alliances in effecting equity-enhancing policy changes in the current phase of globalization, particularly in education. To be sure, policy-makers also play an important role, as entrepreneurs that facilitate these alliances in the various circumstances.

Further investigating whether and how the role and interests of capitalists change with globalization would thus be instrumental to developing a better understanding of the dynamics of institutional change. Given the role played by business interests in social welfare legislation, it is worthwhile to explore if and how globalization has affected their support for social policies other than just education. For example, while capitalists and organized labor might have once settled on social policies adopted in the protective welfare regimes, if and how has this agreement changed since the adoption of economic openness policies? Chapter 2 highlights indications that, absent encompassing labor movements, it has become more and more difficult for capital and labor to agree on social policies. The case studies

---

[8] Note that chapter 2 focuses on the role of labor in welfare retrenchment, and not welfare expansion. Nonetheless, the low PLP findings raise questions about the independent role of labor in welfare expansion.

further present instances where capitalist support for protective social policies such as social security appear to be waning (e.g. Brazil). It would be meaningful to focus more specifically on how the impact of such changes in business support might affect specific welfare regimes.

8.2.4   Broader questions for future research

This book leaves open three broader research questions for further analysis. First, the arguments refer to "developing countries" as a group, which includes the least developed. Because of data limitations, however, several of them are excluded. A future research task is to choose a case study from this group and assess if, how, and to what extent the typology of welfare states fits even the world's poorest countries, such as the Central African Republic. Second, it was noted in the case studies that, within the broader category of "productive" and "protective" welfare states, countries vary in the specific types of welfare programs they pursue. It would be worthwhile to assess whether there are systematic reasons (e.g. related to economic development, democracy) for choosing certain types of protective (or productive) strategies over another.

Finally, the case studies also revealed that democracy and democratization play a more complex role in the development and expansion of welfare regimes than predicted by existing analyses. Is it the broad category of regime type, or is it actually "new democracy," or simultaneous transitions (democratization and globalization) that provide the impetus for welfare reforms? Being able to predict the ways in which democracy systematically affects distributive politics and policies will be particularly important as democracy matures (or fails to do so) and globalization advances in the twenty-first century.

8.3   Prospects for the future?

Polanyi (1944: 3) warned that balancing the institutionalization of the self-regulating market with social protectionism is no easy task:

Our thesis is the idea that a self-adjusting market implied a stark utopia. Such an institution could not exist for any length of time without annihilating the human and natural substance of society; it would have physically destroyed man and transformed his surroundings into a wilderness. Inevitably, society took measures to protect itself, but whatever measures it took impaired the self-regulation of the market, disorganized industrial life and thus endangered society in yet another way.

Developing countries have certainly struggled to find this balance, and now face a double bind in the face of twenty-first-century globalization.

On the one hand, the measures that society took "to protect itself" in developing countries have been limited to the more privileged sectors of society. These measures, according to Polanyi's logic, disorganize industrial life and endanger society. Now, under globalization, not only are demands rising for a self-regulating market and an investment-friendly environment, but these pressures are also impacting the middle class and making it even harder for welfare regimes to shift in a pro-poor direction. If the final goal is the market–society balance to which Polanyi refers, it is imperative that current reforms favor the poor, who tend to be the absolute majority in most LDCs.

Are prospects for the future so dim? Perhaps not. Positive developments have emerged from this analysis, which ought not to be lost in the process of untangling the complex relationship between globalization, domestic politics, and LDC welfare strategies. Certainly, advancement in education reform is one encouraging sign of progress for the poor. Evidence that cross-class alliances in favor of progressive change can be facilitated when subordinate groups mobilize is also encouraging. For example, in addition to unqualified endorsement from business, India's poor also mobilized en masse in favor of the 2001 Education for All legislation. Additionally, democracy can provide an environment more conducive to promoting reforms. As discussed above, some of the case studies, specifically Brazil and South Korea, highlighted the potential positive impact of "new democracy," particularly when accompanied by the efforts of reform-minded bureaucrats. Finally, scholars, activists, and policy-makers alike should not lose sight of the power that they hold by virtue of their ability to disseminate information. Educating the populace about the importance of education and, in the case of Brazil, providing information about the benefits of social security reform affected the introduction of equity-enhancing change. The resonance of this type of information lies in its ability to persuade a broad range of groups of the potential benefits. This is a powerful tool, and one that can be used by all those invested in ensuring, as Rodrik (1997a: 2) puts it, that "international economic integration does not contribute to domestic social *dis*integration."

Appendix A: LDC social spending[1]

Table A.1 *Social security and welfare spending*

SS and welfare (% GDP)	1970s	1980s	1990s	Change 1970s–1990s	Income classification
Bangladesh	0.495	0.497	–	–	Low-income
Cameroon	1.084	1.005	0.596	−0.488	Low-income
Ghana	1.530	0.715	1.034	−0.497	Low-income
India	0.368	0.682	0.746	0.378	Low-income
Kenya	0.210	0.036	0.020	−0.190	Low-income
Lesotho	0.067	0.781	0.785	0.717	Low-income
Liberia	0.370	0.319	–	–	Low-income
Malawi	0.640	0.258	–	–	Low-income
Mali	0.996	1.106	–	–	Low-income
Mozambique	–	–	–	–	Low-income
Nepal	0.068	0.102	0.260	0.192	Low-income
Nicaragua	2.253	1.284	4.672	2.419	Low-income
Nigeria	–	–	–	–	Low-income
Pakistan	0.334	0.948	–	–	Low-income
Panama	3.208	3.823	5.518	2.310	Low-income
Tanzania	0.205	0.179	–	–	Low-income
Zambia	0.558	0.629	0.442	−0.116	Low-income
Zimbabwe	1.881	1.685	3.345	1.464	Low-income
Bolivia	0.343	1.388	3.683	3.340	Lower middle-income
Brazil	6.291	6.765	9.546	3.255	Lower middle-income
China	–	–	0.008	–	Lower middle-income
Colombia	–	2.842	1.266	–	Lower middle-income
Dominican Republic	0.984	0.928	0.620	−0.364	Lower middle-income
Ecuador	0.120	0.197	0.280	0.161	Lower middle-income
Egypt	4.490	5.054	2.980	−1.511	Lower middle-income
El Salvador	0.575	0.529	0.668	0.093	Lower middle-income
Fiji	0.796	1.446	1.267	0.471	Lower middle-income
Guatemala	0.675	0.391	0.458	−0.217	Lower middle-income

[1] Note that income categories in the appendix tables are based on the 2006 classification by the World Bank. In tables 2.2 and 2.4, and figures 2.2 and 2.3, the high-income countries are included as upper middle-income countries.

Table A.1 (*cont.*)

SS and welfare (% GDP)	1970s	1980s	1990s	Change 1970s–1990s	Income classification
Guyana	2.073	2.612	–	–	Lower middle-income
Honduras	0.980	–	–	–	Lower middle-income
Indonesia	–	–	0.972	–	Lower middle-income
Iran	1.638	2.790	2.996	1.358	Lower middle-income
Jordan	3.978	3.898	5.261	1.283	Lower middle-income
Morocco	1.903	1.799	1.925	0.022	Lower middle-income
Paraguay	1.951	2.497	1.779	−0.172	Lower middle-income
Peru	0.042	0.027	–	–	Lower middle-income
Philippines	0.340	0.215	0.447	0.108	Lower middle-income
Sri Lanka	6.093	3.496	4.354	−1.738	Lower middle-income
Syria	1.613	1.878	0.531	−1.082	Lower middle-income
Thailand	0.595	0.561	0.577	−0.018	Lower middle-income
Tunisia	3.269	3.604	4.994	1.725	Lower middle-income
Argentina	4.663	4.724	6.674	2.011	Upper middle-income
Botswana	0.167	0.805	0.714	0.547	Upper middle-income
Chile	8.208	10.663	7.041	−1.168	Upper middle-income
Costa Rica	4.094	2.997	4.357	0.263	Upper middle-income
Malaysia	0.768	1.203	1.458	0.690	Upper middle-income
Mauritius	5.181	4.161	3.717	−1.464	Upper middle-income
Mexico	3.417	2.431	3.002	−0.415	Upper middle-income
South Africa	–	1.600	–	–	Upper middle-income
Trinidad and Tobago	1.777	1.767	4.350	2.572	Upper middle-income
Turkey	0.473	0.255	0.971	0.499	Upper middle-income
Uruguay	10.654	12.932	17.970	7.316	Upper middle-income
Venezuela	1.496	1.645	–	–	Upper middle-income
Cyprus	4.691	5.429	7.526	0.028	High-income
Greece	8.091	11.260	6.017	−2.074	High-income
Israel	9.505	9.076	11.311	1.806	High-income
Kuwait	1.379	4.457	8.917	7.538	High-income
Singapore	0.200	0.366	0.714	0.514	High-income
South Korea	0.815	1.130	1.722	0.907	High-income

Table A.2 *Education spending*

Education (% GDP)	1970s	1980s	1990s	Change 1970s–1990s	Income classification
Bangladesh	1.134	1.138	–	–	Low-income
Cameroon	2.639	2.582	2.958	0.319	Low-income
Ghana	3.506	2.681	3.884	0.378	Low-income
India	0.272	0.336	0.333	0.061	Low-income
Kenya	4.690	5.457	5.475	0.785	Low-income
Lesotho	6.596	8.156	10.215	3.618	Low-income

Table A.2 (*cont.*)

Education (% GDP)	1970s	1980s	1990s	Change 1970s–1990s	Income classification
Liberia	3.706	4.153	–	–	Low-income
Malawi	2.913	3.599	–	–	Low-income
Mali	3.766	2.840	–	–	Low-income
Mozambique	–	–	–	–	Low-income
Nepal	1.112	1.871	2.219	1.106	Low-income
Nicaragua	1.244	1.766	4.663	3.419	Low-income
Nigeria	–	–	–	–	Low-income
Pakistan	0.348	0.547	–	–	Low-income
Panama	5.388	4.497	4.560	−0.828	Low-income
Tanzania	3.675	3.239	–	–	Low-income
Zambia	5.577	4.076	2.890	−2.687	Low-income
Zimbabwe	3.925	6.778	6.312	2.387	Low-income
Bolivia	3.111	3.203	3.788	0.676	Lower middle-income
Brazil	1.083	1.027	1.091	0.008	Lower middle-income
China	–	–	0.182	–	Lower middle-income
Colombia	–	3.163	2.985	–	Lower middle-income
Dominican Republic	2.084	1.791	1.685	−0.400	Lower middle-income
Ecuador	3.131	3.874	2.669	−0.462	Lower middle-income
Egypt	4.813	4.428	4.401	−0.412	Lower middle-income
El Salvador	3.044	2.625	1.899	−1.145	Lower middle-income
Fiji	5.058	5.893	5.586	0.528	Lower middle-income
Guatemala	1.617	1.597	1.567	−0.050	Lower middle-income
Guyana	6.015	6.666	–	–	Lower middle-income
Honduras	3.257	–	–	–	Lower middle-income
Indonesia	1.689	1.918	1.543	−0.146	Lower middle-income
Iran	3.831	4.482	4.478	0.647	Lower middle-income
Jordan	4.365	4.364	4.942	0.577	Lower middle-income
Morocco	5.026	5.493	5.353	0.328	Lower middle-income
Paraguay	1.458	1.183	1.991	0.534	Lower middle-income
Peru	3.576	2.656	–	–	Lower middle-income
Philippines	1.877	2.347	3.194	1.317	Lower middle-income
Sri Lanka	2.881	2.663	2.781	−0.100	Lower middle-income
Syria	3.393	2.659	2.183	−1.210	Lower middle-income
Thailand	3.203	3.617	3.344	0.141	Lower middle-income
Tunisia	6.560	5.433	5.805	−0.755	Lower middle-income
Argentina	1.756	1.041	0.810	−0.947	Upper middle-income
Botswana	5.906	7.003	8.542	2.636	Upper middle-income
Chile	4.501	3.678	2.951	−1.550	Upper middle-income
Costa Rica	5.611	4.741	5.307	−0.304	Upper middle-income
Malaysia	5.601	5.787	5.174	−0.427	Upper middle-income
Mauritius	3.578	3.776	3.582	0.004	Upper middle-income
Mexico	2.620	2.885	3.501	0.881	Upper middle-income
South Africa	–	1.835	–	–	Upper middle-income
Trinidad and Tobago	4.108	3.516	3.737	−0.371	Upper middle-income

Table A.2 (*cont.*)

Education (% GDP)	1970s	1980s	1990s	Change 1970s–1990s	Income classification
Turkey	3.717	2.440	3.400	−0.317	Upper middle-income
Uruguay	2.463	1.874	2.078	−0.385	Upper middle-income
Venezuela	3.809	4.414	–	–	Upper middle-income
Cyprus	3.062	3.303	3.656	0.594	High-income
Greece	2.844	3.696	2.967	0.123	High-income
Israel	5.455	5.627	5.712	0.257	High-income
Kuwait	3.319	5.137	5.778	2.459	High-income
Singapore	3.002	4.619	3.760	0.758	High-income
South Korea	2.459	3.043	3.353	0.894	High-income

Table A.3 *Health spending*

Health (% GDP)	1970s	1980s	1990s	Change 1970s–1990s	Income classification
Bangladesh	0.485	0.617	–	–	Low-income
Cameroon	0.813	0.806	0.786	−0.027	Low-income
Ghana	1.365	1.015	1.348	−0.016	Low-income
India	0.248	0.305	0.248	0.000	Low-income
Kenya	1.666	1.767	1.533	−0.133	Low-income
Lesotho	1.915	3.979	5.382	3.468	Low-income
Liberia	2.123	1.800	–	–	Low-income
Malawi	1.414	2.000	–	–	Low-income
Mali	0.995	0.696	–	–	Low-income
Mozambique	–	–	–	–	Low-income
Nepal	0.586	0.777	0.688	0.102	Low-income
Nicaragua	0.718	2.223	4.161	3.443	Low-income
Nigeria	–	–	–	–	Low-income
Pakistan	0.244	0.225	–	–	Low-income
Panama	4.386	4.703	5.004	0.618	Low-income
Tanzania	1.834	1.483	–	–	Low-income
Zambia	2.191	2.176	1.793	−0.398	Low-income
Zimbabwe	1.821	2.148	2.411	0.590	Low-income
Bolivia	0.961	0.830	1.104	0.143	Lower middle-income
Brazil	1.227	1.809	1.916	0.689	Lower middle-income
China	–	–	0.027	–	Lower middle-income
Colombia	–	0.651	1.143	–	Lower middle-income
Dominican Republic	1.586	1.549	1.662	0.076	Lower middle-income
Ecuador	0.848	1.264	1.621	0.773	Lower middle-income
Egypt	1.509	1.037	0.875	−0.634	Lower middle-income
El Salvador	1.293	1.184	1.100	−0.193	Lower middle-income
Fiji	2.284	2.240	2.386	0.102	Lower middle-income

Table A.3 (*cont.*)

Health (% GDP)	1970s	1980s	1990s	Change 1970s–1990s	Income classification
Guatemala	0.846	0.886	0.945	0.100	Lower middle-income
Guyana	2.327	3.954	–	–	Lower middle-income
Honduras	1.821	–	–	–	Lower middle-income
Indonesia	0.410	0.462	0.433	0.023	Lower middle-income
Iran	1.301	1.661	1.744	0.442	Lower middle-income
Jordan	1.792	1.522	2.393	0.600	Lower middle-income
Morocco	1.151	0.942	0.945	−0.205	Lower middle-income
Paraguay	0.339	0.422	0.705	0.366	Lower middle-income
Peru	1.018	0.956	–	–	Lower middle-income
Philippines	0.572	0.678	0.629	0.057	Lower middle-income
Sri Lanka	1.608	1.514	1.503	−0.105	Lower middle-income
Syria	0.363	0.398	0.634	0.272	Lower middle-income
Thailand	0.637	0.985	1.223	0.585	Lower middle-income
Tunisia	1.985	2.319	2.191	0.205	Lower middle-income
Argentina	0.499	0.236	0.309	−0.190	Upper middle-income
Botswana	1.867	2.029	1.967	0.100	Upper middle-income
Chile	2.407	1.901	2.418	0.012	Upper middle-income
Costa Rica	2.087	5.906	6.664	4.577	Upper middle-income
Malaysia	1.674	1.495	1.426	−0.249	Upper middle-income
Mauritius	2.109	1.952	1.941	−0.168	Upper middle-income
Mexico	0.620	0.353	0.463	−0.157	Upper middle-income
South Africa	–	0.538	–	–	Upper middle-income
Trinidad and Tobago	2.018	1.803	2.258	0.241	Upper middle-income
Turkey	0.506	0.431	0.716	0.210	Upper middle-income
Uruguay	0.961	1.053	1.666	0.705	Upper middle-income
Venezuela	2.124	2.003	–	–	Upper middle-income
Cyprus	1.532	1.946	2.045	0.513	High-income
Greece	2.630	3.949	2.461	−0.169	High-income
Israel	2.711	2.481	3.404	0.693	High-income
Kuwait	1.568	2.893	2.984	1.416	High-income
Singapore	1.452	1.401	1.128	−0.324	High-income
South Korea	0.197	0.266	0.188	−0.009	High-income

Appendix B: Assessing potential labor power

Few efforts have been made to measure and compare labor power across developing countries and over time. Union density is the most commonly used cross-national indicator of labor power. As noted earlier, however, union density is more appropriately applied in the developed world than in the LDCs. Most LDCs are still far from attaining strong and independent unions. Even in LDCs with (relatively) high union density, labor is rife with collective action problems and often subject to a broad range of government controls. For more details on PLP – its connection with marketplace bargaining power, the different country rankings on PLP, its strengths and weaknesses – see Rudra (2005).

Given the unreliability of direct organizational measures, as Encarnation's (1989) analysis suggests, alternative assessments of labor's bargaining power tend to be tautological. According to Encarnation (1989), bargaining power is generally defined by the outcome, and so it is difficult to tell which party had more bargaining power if negotiations are "won by those who win." This approach makes it virtually impossible to differentiate between power and negotiated outcomes. Consequently, Encarnation (1989: 20) concludes that bargaining power must refer to the ability of laborers to "improve the range of plausible outcomes available to each [negotiator], and to improve the probability of securing the outcome that each prefers."

Importantly, the measure of PLP used in this analysis avoids the tautology problem. It does so by getting some sense of labor's *propensity* for collective action rather than collective action per se. After all, since labor discontent can be costly for political leaders (and workers), governments often respond to labor demands before strikes or other militant actions occur. Offe and Wiesenthal (1985: 216) argue that in such circumstances "the organization then has become strong enough to derive some power (i.e. control over its environment) from its recognized *potential* of power. In other words, concessions are likely to be made not because members have struck, but in order to avoid a strike."

To assess whether PLP serves as an indirect measure of workers' political power, additional steps must be taken. Comparing PLP to other non-tautological assessments of labor's bargaining power is the most precise way to accomplish this. McGuire's (1999) creation of the Labor Strength Index (LSI) represents the only other effort to assess the "real" magnitude of labor's bargaining power in LDCs and compare it across countries. Because of data limitations, however, it represents only one period of time (the 1990s). LSI is based on four dimensions: (1) union membership as a percentage of the non-agricultural labor force; (2) the proportion of formal-sector workers covered by collective contracts; (3) the level of collective bargaining power (national/sectoral, enterprise, or both); and (4) the number of major ILO conventions ratified.[1] This is a multifaceted attempt to capture several important dimensions of labor strength that are not directly measured by PLP.

The comparison of PLP and LSI in table B1 significantly increases confidence in the reliability of PLP as an indicator of labor's bargaining power. The correlation coefficient, excluding the outliers, is 0.61 (see figure B1). The correlation is actually higher than expected, since LSI includes unionization data (and its inherent weaknesses), and because PLP captures some important non-traditional sources of labor's bargaining power.[2]

For the great majority of cases, the PLP rankings are similar to LSI. Interestingly, it is mostly the east Asian cases – e.g. Singapore, South Korea, Malaysia, and Thailand – that show the most contrast.[3] Their PLP score is "high," which is certainly contrary to conventional wisdom on labor in these nations. The PLP scores are consistent with more recent analyses by Yap (2003) and Brown (2004), though, who bring important new insights on labor in the east Asian countries and explain why labor's political influence in these authoritarian nations has commonly been misinterpreted.

According to both Yap (2003) and Brown (2004), workers in these nations have been in a very unusual position in the developing world because of the central economic role they have played in the countries'

---

[1] The number of ILO ratifications is, arguably, the weakest component of LSI, since ratification does not necessarily ensure enforcement. A detailed evaluation of the strengths and weaknesses of LSI is a subject for a future study, however.

[2] Interestingly, LSI closely resembles Silver's (2003: 13) reference to "associational power" (most importantly, trade unions and political parties). The comparisons in table B1 and figure B1 suggest that marketplace bargaining power and associational power are closely related.

[3] LSI and PLP also differ in some of the African cases, where LSI tends to be higher than PLP (Ghana, Mali). This is most probably because data availability for all four components of LSI is apt to be limited in these countries, and so these scores may be biased upward (see McGuire, 1999: 12).

Table B.1 *Comparing potential labor power and labor strength index*

Countries	PLP	LSI (McGuire)
Argentina	high	high
Bangladesh	low	low
Bolivia	med–low	low
Botswana	low	low
Brazil	high	high
Cameroon	low	med–high
Chile	med–high	low
China	high	med–high
Colombia	med–high	med–low
Costa Rica	med–high	med–high
Cyprus	med–high	high
Ecuador	med–low	med–low
Egypt	med–high	med–high
El Salvador	low	low
Ghana	med–high	med–low
Greece	med–high	high
Guatemala	med–high	med–low
Honduras	low	low
India	med–low	med–low
Indonesia	med–low	low
Israel	high	med–high
Kenya	med–high	med–high
Malaysia	high	low
Mali	med–low	high
Mauritius	low	med–low
Mexico	med–high	med–high
Morocco	low	low
Nicaragua	med–low	med–high
Nigeria	med–low	med–low
Pakistan	low	low
Panama	low	low
Paraguay	med–low	low
Peru	med–low	med–low
Philippines	high	mcd–low
Singapore	high	low
South Africa	high	med–low
South Korea	high	low
Thailand	high	med–low
Tunisia	med–low	low
Turkey	med–high	med–high
Uruguay	high	med–high
Venezuela	med–high	med–low
Zambia	med–low	med–high
Zimbabwe	med–low	med–low

Table B.1 (*cont.*)

Percentile range	Value
Below 25th	low
25th–50th	mid-low
50th–75th	med-high
Above 75th	high

Note: To facilitate direct comparison with McGuire (1999), the PLP values in the table are averages for 1990–7 only. Several LDCs had to be dropped from the comparison because they were not included in LSI data. Also, because McGuire's index additionally includes developed and eastern European nations, I eliminated these countries from the sample, recalculated the percentiles, and rechecked the comparison. The results were almost identical to those reported above.

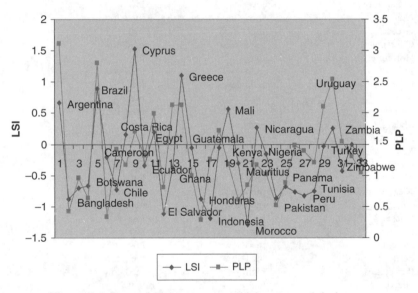

Figure B.1 Potential labor power and labor strength index

Note: Some of the countries have been dropped from the figure in order to reduce clustering.

development. Repressive labor strategies have been part and parcel of the east Asian nations' export-oriented industrialization strategy for economic development (see also Kuruvilla, (1996). Somewhat paradoxically, however, precisely because of this dependence on labor, the state has had to accommodate labor in different ways.[4] Labor's collective political consciousness has thereby evolved differently in these countries, while the more familiar signs of political power (e.g. strikes, unionization, centralization of bargaining power) have been conspicuously absent.[5] As Young (2004: 552) argues, "In studies [...] where the forms of consciousness and organization are found not to conform to these [familiar] expectations, labor is deemed to be 'weak' or 'immature', and seen to be peripheral to the development of state, society and the economy [...] The outcome may not conform to very generalized theoretical expectations, but that calls for re-evaluation and refinement of theory, rather than a dismissal of the significance of working class struggles." One important advancement of the PLP indicator, then, is that it can approximate labor movements that do not develop the familiar institutional forms.

Ultimately, the indicator applied in this study, PLP, offers three broad advantages: (1) it corresponds to conditions specific to labor in developing countries; (2) it is comparable across LDCs; and (3) it has a time-series component that can capture the dynamic aspects of bargaining power. The first advantage privileges PLP as an indicator of labor strength because its logic is based on the particular circumstances faced by labor in LDCs. The desirability of the second two characteristics is more obvious. A standardized measure available over time and across countries greatly reduces the biases that can affect empirical analyses of labor in the developing world.

---

[4] Yap (2003), for instance, discusses "credible apologies" that east Asian governments make to labor. They may dismiss, demote, or replace certain government officials deemed responsible for the policies that "hurt" labor, downsize or eliminate the relevant agency, or offer reparations. Additionally, representatives from academia, labor, or business may be invited in to review, evaluate, or oversee changes to government.

[5] For example, Yap (2003) draws from Bates (1981) and argues that labor can withdraw economic resources (e.g. alter their production mix, engage in the black market) to protest against the government's economic policies. In reference to workers in Thailand, Brown (2004) discusses the importance of taking account of industrial workers and their organization as *potential political actors*. He argues that "even when labor is invisible, in the sense of not being a public, organized actor overtly engaged in formal political processes, the politics of the working class is nonetheless there and is significant. For, behind the scenes, there has been a continual jockeying to channel and control workers and their struggles. This is to ensure that they either do not emerge as a public, organized force, or if they do, they are organized in a manner that is in keeping with the broader economic, ideological and political interests of those dominating contests for state power" (Brown, 2004: 133).

Appendix C: Additional tests for the RTB hypothesis

Table C.1 *Education spending in LDCs*

	Model C.1		Model C.2		Model C.3	
	Educ. (% GDP)	Educ. per capita	Educ. (% GDP)	Educ. per capita	Educ. (% GDP)	Educ. per capita
PLP	0.02(0.06)	1.47(2.60)	0.04(0.06)	2.24(2.31)	0.13*(0.08)	1.33(2.37)
Trade$_{t-1}$ × PLP	−0.001(0.001)	0.052*(0.027)	−0.001(0.001)	0.03(0.03)	−0.001(0.001)	0.08***(0.03)
Portfolio$_{t-1}$ × PLP	0.02*(0.01)	1.28***(0.41)	0.015(0.010)	1.05***(0.38)	0.007(0.013)	1.52***(0.43)
FDI$_{t-1}$ × PLP	−0.005(0.004)	−0.95***(0.17)		–	0.02(0.02)	−2.01*(0.98)
Trade$_{t-1}$	−0.003(0.003)	−0.19***(0.06)	−0.003(0.003)	−0.18***(0.06)	−0.003(0.002)	−0.16**(0.05)
Portfolio$_{t-1}$	−0.04(0.04)	−2.69***(1.42)	−0.03(0.04)	−2.17*(1.31)	0.01(0.05)	−3.59***(1.28)
FDI$_{t-1}$	0.01(0.02)	1.44***(0.55)		–	0.01(0.02)	−0.14(0.49)
GDP per capita	−0.07(0.20)	68.28***(6.20)	−0.08(0.20)	69.47***(6.43)	−0.53***(0.20)	82.07***(7.72)
Growth	−0.012***(0.004)	−0.19***(0.08)	−0.012***(0.004)	−0.17***(0.08)	−0.009***(0.004)	−0.24***(0.08)
Democracy	−0.04(0.07)	0.89(2.25)	−0.03(0.07)	−.41(2.22)	0.08(0.08)	6.63***(1.93)
Youth pop. (0–14)	−0.04*(0.02)	−2.02***(0.56)	−0.04*(0.02)	−2.08***(0.59)	−0.01(0.02)	−1.37*(0.60)
Debt$_{t-1}$	−0.005***(0.001)	−0.10***(0.03)	−0.005***(0.001)	−0.11***(0.03)	−0.004***(0.001)	−0.15***(0.03)
R^2	0.91	0.90	0.91	0.90	0.94	0.93
N	787	787	791	791	618	618

Notes: ★★★ = p < 0.01; ★★ = p < 0.05; ★ = p < 0.10. Fixed-effects regression estimates. Figures in parenthesis are standard errors.

Table C.2 *Health spending in LDCs*

	Model C.4		Model C.5		Model C.6	
	Health (% GDP)	Health per capita	Health (% GDP)	Health per capita	Health (% GDP)	Health per capita
PLP	0.042*(0.025)	−2.28***(0.56)	0.043(0.02)	−2.13***(0.57)	0.11***(0.03)	−0.07(0.79)
$\text{Trade}_{t-1} \times$ PLP	−0.001**(0.0003)	0.03***(0.01)	−0.001***(0.0003)	0.019***(0.006)	−0.001**(0.0004)	0.01(0.01)
$\text{Portfolio}_{t-1} \times$ PLP	0.002(0.004)	−0.03(0.12)	0.002(0.004)	−0.02(0.12)	−0.010*(0.005)	−0.30**(0.14)
$\text{FDI}_{t-1} \times$ PLP	−0.001(0.003)	−0.16***(0.06)	—	—	0.012(0.013)	0.01(0.33)
Trade_{t-1}	−0.001(0.003)	−0.069**(0.035)	−0.001(0.002)	−0.065*(0.035)	−0.001(0.002)	−0.02(0.04)
Portfolio_{t-1}	−0.007(0.020)	−0.06(0.57)	−0.01(0.02)	−0.06(0.56)	0.03(0.02)	0.99*(0.57)
FDI_{t-1}	0.003(0.011)	0.07(0.26)	—	—	0.01(0.01)	−0.12(0.28)
GDP per capita	0.12(0.11)	27.81***(2.96)	0.12(0.11)	28.05***(2.77)	−0.00(0.00)	24.20***(3.43)
Growth	−0.006***(0.002)	−0.10***(0.04)	−0.006***(0.002)	−0.10***(0.04)	−0.005***(0.002)	−0.08(0.05)
Democracy	−0.01(0.04)	1.23(1.21)	−0.01(0.04)	0.89(1.22)	−0.02(0.05)	1.52(1.20)
Elderly population	−0.06(0.05)	3.21***(1.14)	−0.07(0.05)	3.34***(1.23)	−0.02(0.05)	2.84***(1.14)
Debt_{t-1}	−0.001(0.001)	−0.04**(0.02)	−0.001(0.001)	−0.037**(0.018)	−0.001(0.001)	−0.05**(0.02)
R^2	0.92	0.93	0.92	0.93	0.94	0.94
N	786	786	790	790	617	617

Notes: *** = $p < 0.01$; ** = $p < 0.05$; * = $p < 0.10$. Fixed-effects regression estimates. Figures in parenthesis are standard errors.

Table C.3 *Education spending in OECD countries*

	Model C.7		Model C.8	
	Educ. (% GDP)	Educ. per capita	Educ. (% GDP)	Educ. per capita
PLP	0.03(0.02)	5.12(4.48)	0.005**(0.002)	1.20*(0.66)
Trade$_{t-1}$ × PLP	−0.0003(0.0003)	−0.06(0.07)	−	−
Portfolio$_{t-1}$ × PLP	0.03(0.03)	7.08(5.10)	0.03(0.03)	8.84*(5.05)
FDI$_{t-1}$ × PLP	0.003**(0.002)	0.81***(0.31)	0.004***(0.002)	0.95***(0.32)
Trade$_{t-1}$	−0.01(0.01)	−3.77(2.64)	−	−
Portfolio$_{t-1}$	−3.15(2.53)	−840.44*(467.72)	−3.21(2.53)	−889.24*(472.42)
FDI$_{t-1}$	−0.30**(0.14)	−55.22**(24.44)	−0.38***(0.13)	−71.91***(24.09)
Growth	−0.07***(0.02)	−7.73*(4.12)	−0.07***(0.02)	−8.63*(4.24)
Youth pop. (0–14)	−0.26***(0.07)	−93.97***(13.91)	−0.23***(0.07)	−84.14***(12.82)
Unemployment	0.07**(0.03)	−0.43(5.80)	0.08**(0.03)	0.87(5.94)
R2	0.81	0.91	0.83	0.91
N	348	348	348	348

Notes: ***=p < 0.01; **=p < 0.05; *=p < 0.10. Fixed-effects regression estimates. Figures in parenthesis are standard errors.

Table C.4 *Health spending in OECD countries*

	Model C.9		Model C.10	
	Health (% GDP)	Health per capita	Health (% GDP)	Health per capita
PLP	0.03*(0.01)	5.15*(2.97)	0.002(0.002)	0.74(0.70)
Trade$_{t-1}$ × PLP	−0.0004*(0.0002)	−0.07(0.05)	−	−
Portfolio$_{t-1}$ × PLP	−0.01(0.03)	10.73(7.62)	0.001(0.03)	11.81(7.73)
FDI$_{t-1}$ × PLP	0.001(0.002)	0.20(0.32)	0.002(0.002)	0.28(0.33)
Trade$_{t-1}$	−0.01(0.02)	3.67(2.73)	−	−
Portfolio$_{t-1}$	−1.13(3.64)	−1611.03*(891.33)	−0.97(3.65)	−1593.51*(895.33)
FDI$_{t-1}$	−0.08(0.15)	0.52(31.05)	−0.13(0.15)	−3.94(30.87)
Growth	−0.07***(0.02)	−3.58(4.28)	−0.07***(0.02)	−3.32(4.39)
Youth pop. (0–14)	−	−	−	−
Elderly pop.	0.59***(0.17)	157.43***(32.34)	0.58***(0.17)	164.71***(32.86)
Unemployment	0.11***(0.04)	8.70(7.67)	0.12***(0.05)	8.34(8.00)
R2	0.92	0.91	0.92	0.91
N	348	348	348	348

Notes: ***=p < 0.01; *=p < 0.10. Fixed-effects regression estimates. Figures in parenthesis are standard errors.

Appendix D: Variables in the inequality model

Variables	Description	Sources
Dependent variable:		
Inequality	Gini coefficients of household income distribution	Deninger and Squire (1996)
Quintile 1 data	Concentration of income in the lowest quintile	Deninger and Squire (1996)
Independent variables:		
Welfare spending per capita	Spending on social security and welfare, education, and health per capita	IMF, *Government Finance Statistics*, various editions
Trade	Amount of total trade (EX+IM) as percentage of GDP; trade ratios above median of 50 percent considered "open"	World Bank (2000a) and World Development Indicators CD-ROM
Portfolio flows	Amount of portfolio flows as percentage of GDP	World Bank (2000a) and World Development Indicators CD-ROM
The percentage of aged [POP65]	"Aged" = number of persons over sixty-five as percentage of total population	World Bank (2000a) and World Development Indicators CD-ROM
Growth	Annual percentage growth rate of GDP at market prices based on constant 1987 local currency	World Bank (2000a) and World Development Indicators CD-ROM
GDP per capita	GDP per capita (constant 1995 US dollar)	World Bank (2000a) and World Development Indicators CD-ROM
Democracy	Scale 0–10; 10 = strong democracy; countries rating 7 and above labeled "democracy" (indicator derived from the codings of the competitiveness of political participation, the openness and competitiveness of executive recruitment, and constraints on the chief executive)	CIDCM (2000): political regime characteristics and transitions, 1800–2000 (M. G. Marshall and K. Jaggers, principal investigators)
Urbanization	Urban population as percentage of total	World Bank (2000a) and World Development Indicators CD-ROM

Appendix E: Technical notes on Gini coefficients

Recipient unit: applies to either the household or the individual.

Given that the difference is not too large, we conclude that there is no reason to expect a large systematic bias in empirical work as a result of using both household-based and individual-based Gini coefficients (Deninger and Squire, 1996: 580)

Income: either gross or net income for developing countries; only net income for OECD countries.

Although the distinction between gross income and net income may affect the level of measured inequality in a cross-country sample, the quantitative importance of this effect will depend on the progressivity and effectiveness of the tax system and might therefore be of less relevance for developing countries to the degree that the role of redistributive taxation is smaller in these countries. (Deninger and Squire, 1996: 580)

Variable measured: either income or expenditure (with 6.6 added to the expenditure-based Ginis).

One way of avoiding the exclusion of thirty-nine countries for which Gini coefficients are based on expenditures would be to add the difference of 6.6 between expenditure-based and income-based coefficients to the 136 expenditure-based Gini coefficients in the sample. (Deninger and Squire, 1996: 582)

Coverage: comprehensive coverage of the population.

Appendix F: LDC Gini coefficient statistics

Table F.1 *Summary statistics of Gini coefficients in developing countries*

Country	Mean	Median	Standard deviation	Minimum	Maximum	Year of maximum value	Year of minimum value
Bangladesh	35.85	35.73	1.65	33.3	39.0	1981	1977
Brazil	58.09	57.78	2.74	54.2	61.9	1974	1982
Chile	55.86	56.49	2.40	53.2	57.9	1989	1980
China	32.68	33.8	3.78	25.7	37.8	1992	1984
Colombia	51.25	51.32	3.24	46.0	54.5	1978	1974
Costa Rica	45.65	46.07	2.93	42.0	50.0	1977	1982/1986
Dominican Republic	46.94	47.00	3.35	43.3	50.5	1989	1984
Egypt	41.60	41.60	4.24	38.6	44.6	1975	1991
Ghana	41.73	41.54	1.42	40.5	43.3	1989	1992
Greece	41.13	41.71	1.07	39.9	41.8	1988	1981
Guatemala	55.68	58.26	5.18	49.7	59.1	1989	1979
Honduras	53.26	54.00	1.76	50.0	54.9	1986	1991
India	37.92	38.42	1.10	35.8	39.1	1991	1973
Indonesia	40.57	40.01	2.29	38.3	45.2	1978	1993
Iran	49.19	49.19	.44	48.9	49.5	1984	1972
Jordan	45.79	47.26	2.67	42.7	47.4	1980	1987
Malaysia	50.43	51.00	2.18	48.0	53.0	1976	1984
Mauritius	45.07	45.70	1.57	43.3	46.2	1986	1991
Mexico	54.07	54.98	3.62	50.0	57.9	1975	1977
Morocco	45.80	45.80	.01	45.79	45.8	1991	1984
Nigeria	45.15	44.07	2.27	43.6	47.8	1992	1986
Pakistan	38.46	38.73	.54	37.8	39.0	1985	1991
Panama	50.90	48.76	4.87	47.5	56.5	1989	1980
Peru	50.05	49.36	1.23	49.3	51.5	1994	1981
Philippines	45.60	45.73	.55	45.0	46.1	1985	1991
Singapore	40.12	40.85	1.81	37.0	42.0	1983	1978
South Korea	36.32	35.70	2.44	33.6	39.1	1976	1988
Sri Lanka	41.58	42.75	4.63	35.3	46.7	1987	1973
Tanzania	47.65	47.65	4.17	44.7	50.6	1977	1993
Thailand	46.66	47.40	3.63	41.7	51.5	1992	1975

Table F.1 (*cont.*)

Country	Mean	Median	Standard deviation	Minimum	Maximum	Year of maximum value	Year of minimum value
Trinidad and Tobago	43.91	43.91	3.09	41.7	46.1	1976	1981
Tunisia	49.16	49.60	1.62	46.8	50.6	1975	1990
Turkey	47.55	47.55	4.89	44.1	51.0	1973	1987
Venezuela	44.01	43.23	4.38	39.4	53.8	1990	1979
Zambia	54.53	54.50	4.62	50.1	59.0	1996	1991
Average	*46.22*	*46.21*	*2.64*	*25.7*	*61.9*	–	–

Appendix G: Robustness check

Table G.1 *Dependent variable: quintile 1 income in developing countries*

Variables	Model G.1	Model G.2	Model G.3
Social security and welfare (spending per capita)	0.0001 (0.0001)		
Education (spending per capita)		−0.0001 (0.0001)★★★	
Health (spending per capita)			−0.0003★ (0.0002)
Trade	0.0002★★ (0.0001)	−0.0002★ (0.0001)	−0.0001† (0.0001)
Trade × social security and welfare	−0.000002★★★ (0.000006)		
Trade × education		0.000003★★★ (0.000001)	
Trade × health			0.000005★★ (0.000002)
Democracy	−0.0049★★ (0.002)	−0.005★★ (0.002)	−0.005★★★ (0.002)
Democracy^2	0.0005★★ (0.0002)	0.0004★ (0.0002)	0.0005★★ (0.0002)
GDPcap	−0.06★★ (0.03)	−0.02 (0.03)	−0.03 (0.03)
GDPcap^2	0.005★★ (0.002)	0.001 (0.002)	0.003 (0.002)
POP65	−0.01★★★ (0.003)	−0.01★★★ (0.003)	−0.01★★★ (0.003)
Urban	0.001★★★ (0.0004)	0.001★★★ (0.0003)	0.001★★★ (0.0003)
1970s	0.001 (0.003)	−0.003 (0.003)	−0.002 (0.003)
1980s	−0.001 (0.002)	−0.004★★ (0.002)	−0.003★ (0.002)
N	90	100	100
R^2	0.98	0.98	0.98

Notes: ★★★ = $p < 0.01$; ★★ = $p < 0.05$; ★ = $p < 0.10$; † = $p < 0.15$. Fixed-effects regression estimates. Figures in parentheses are standard errors.

The pattern of results for quintile data replicates the findings in table 3.4. Note that the expected signs for the primary and secondary results are now reversed. Under the conditions of globalization, increased government spending on education and health encourages a larger concentration of income for the poorest households, while greater social security spending lowers their income.

The primary difference with the regression results in table 3.4 is that the interaction of trade and health spending in this set of regressions is now significant (the sign is the same). On the one hand, it can be argued that the contrasting results confirm the weak effect of public health spending on the poor during globalization. This inconsistency in results warrants further investigation, however, and more data would be helpful to verify these findings. The signs for the first- and second-order polynomial functions of democracy and per capita GDP (Kuznets, 1955) are also reversed. In other words, income and democracy worsen the economic situation of the poorest households during the early stages of development. Over time, however, both democracy and higher aggregate income lead to a greater concentration of wealth in the lowest quintile.

Significantly, these democracy results corroborate with Burkhart (1997). It is also noteworthy that substituting the first- and second-order polynomial functions of democracy for the dummy democracy variable in the table 3.4 regressions does not change the (primary or secondary) results (not shown here).

Appendix H: Conditional impact of trade on inequality

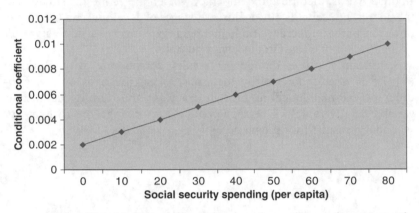

Figure H.1 Mediating effects of trade on inequality contingent upon the level of social security spending

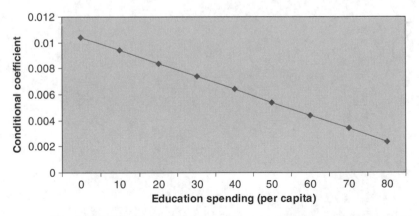

Figure H.2 Mediating effects of trade on inequality contingent upon the level of education spending

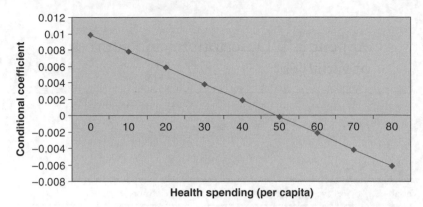

Figure H.3 Mediating effects of trade on inequality contingent upon the level of health spending

Note: These graphs have been created using the uninteracted coefficient for trade, and the interacted coefficients for trade and social spending variables. The uninteracted coefficient for trade measures the impact of trade when social spending is zero. Significance tests reveal that all conditional coefficients in figures H.1 and H.2 are significant. In figure H.3, conditional coefficients are significant until the level of trade increases beyond 40 percent.

Appendix I: Descriptions and sources of variables

Variable	Description	Source
Years	1990–7 average	
Measles, DPT	Percentage of children between twelve and twenty-three months vaccinated against measles, diphtheria, pertussis, and tetanus	World Bank World Development Indicators (CD-ROM)
Infant mortality	Infant mortality (per 1,000 live births)	World Bank World Development Indicators (CD-ROM)
Literacy rates	Adult total literacy rate (percentage of people aged fifteen and above)	World Bank World Development Indicators (CD-ROM)
Primary education spending	Government expenditures on pre-primary and primary education expenditures as percentage of total government expenditures; expenditure per student per GDP per capita also included	UNESCO *Statistical Yearbooks* (1970–99) and IMF *Government Finance Statistics* Yearbooks (1970–99)
Health spending	Government expenditure on health as percentage of total government expenditure	IMF *Government Finance Statistics*, various years
Housing spending	Government expenditure on housing as percentage of total government expenditure	IMF *Government Finance Statistics*, various years
ILOCNV	Cumulative number of ILO conventions ratified by a country	Rama and Artecona (2002) and www.national-academies.org/internationallabor
Wages and salaries spending	Government employment contributions as percentage of total government expenditure	IMF *Government Finance Statistics*
Social security and welfare spending	Government expenditure on social security and welfare as percentage of total government expenditure	IMF *Government Finance Statistics*
Tertiary education spending	Expenditures on tertiary education as percentage of GDP; tertiary expenditure per student per GDP per capita also included	World Bank World Development Indicators (CD-ROM)

Appendix J: Cluster results minus outcome variables

| | Commodification | | | Decommodification | | | | | |
Country	Primary and secondary education spending	Health spending	Country average	Housing spending	ILO conventions	Wages and salaries spending	SS and welfare spending	Tertiary education spending	Country average
Cluster 1 (productive)									
Chile	2	10	6	7	7	3	10	2	6
Colombia	7	9	8	5	8	2	4	3	4
Costa Rica	5	10	8	1	7	10	8	5	6
Cyprus	9	5	7	6	7	6	9	1	6
Israel	9	6	8	8	6	1	9	4	6
Kuwait	9	3	6	6	3	4	5	9	5
Malaysia	8	4	6	9	3	5	3	8	6
Mauritius	7	8	8	7	4	7	7	9	7
Panama	4	10	7	6	9	9	9	4	7
Paraguay	2	4	3	5	5	9	6	7	6
Singapore	5	5	5	9	3	6	1	5	5
South Korea	6	1	4	4	1	1	5	1	2
Sri Lanka	7	3	5	3	4	3	7	8	5
Thailand	6	8	7	6	2	7	1	3	4
Trinidad and Tobago	3	8	6	10	2	9	7	7	7
Cluster average	*6*	*6*	*6*	*6*	*5*	*5*	*6*	*5*	*5*
Cluster 2 (dual)									
Argentina	6	1	4	3	9	4	10	2	6
Brazil	2	5	4	1	10	1	9	5	5
Mexico	1	2	2	4	10	4	8	3	6
Uruguay	4	4	4	1	10	2	10	3	5
Greece	3	7	5	3	9	4	8	2	5
Cluster average	*3*	*4*	*4*	*2*	*10*	*3*	*9*	*3*	*5*
Cluster 3 (protective)									
Bolivia	1	3	2	2	6	7	8	6	6
Dominican Republic	8	9	5	10	4	5	2	1	4
Egypt	8	2	5	8	8	4	4	6	6
El Salvador	1	9	5	5	1	10	3	1	4
India	4	1	3	8	5	1	2	8	5
Iran	3	7	5	9	1	10	5	7	6
Lesotho	10	9	10	5	1	7	1	10	6
Morocco	10	2	6	2	6	8	4	8	5
Tunisia	9	6	8	7	8	8	6	9	7
Turkey	5	3	4	3	5	9	2	5	5
Zambia	2	6	4	2	6	2	1	5	4
Zimbabwe	10	6	8	10	1	8	5	10	7
Cluster average	*5*	*5*	*5*	*6*	*4*	*7*	*4*	*7*	*6*

Appendix K: Dendrogram for cluster analysis

Figure K.1 presents graphically the information concerning which countries are grouped together at various levels of dissimilarity. The vertical lines extend upwards for each observation, while the horizontal line connects to the lines from other observations at various dissimilarity values. The observations continue to combine until they are all grouped together at the top of the dendrogram. Significantly, the dendrogram gives visual clues about the strength of the clustering. Shorter vertical lines represent groups that are more similar to each other (e.g. Argentina and Uruguay; India and Bolivia; Morocco and Egypt), while longer lines indicate that these groups are more distinct from each other.

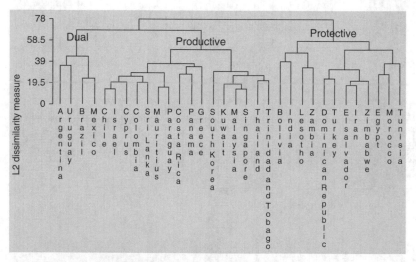

Figure K.1 Dendrogram for cluster analysis

Note: Weighted average linkage.

Appendix L: Poverty tables

Table L.1 *Poverty gap at $1 a day (PPP) (percent)*

Country	Poverty
Chile	0.5 (2000)
Colombia	3.07 (2003)
Costa Rica	0.8 (2001)
Cyprus	–
Greece	–
Israel	–
Kuwait	–
Malaysia	–
Mauritius	–
Panama	2.26 (2002)
Paraguay	7.384 (2002)
Singapore	–
South Korea	–
Sri Lanka	0.84 (2002)
Thailand	0.5 (2002)
Trinidad and Tobago	–
Argentina	–
Brazil	–
Mexico	–
Uruguay	0.5 (2004)
Bolivia	13.55 (2002)
Dominican Republic	0.77 (2003)
Egypt	0.5 (2000)
El Salvador	9.346 (2002)
India	8.2 (2000)
Iran	–
Lesotho	–
Morocco	–
Tunisia	0.5 (2000)
Turkey	0.79 (2004)
Zambia	36.398 (2002)
Zimbabwe	–

Notes: The "poverty gap" is the mean shortfall from the poverty line (counting the non-poor as having zero shortfall), expressed as a percentage of the poverty line, calculated on a purchasing power parity (PPP) basis. This measure reflects the depth of poverty as well as its incidence. Data showing as 0.5 signify a poverty gap of less than 0.5 percent. "Poverty" is defined as the population living below the national poverty line (1990–2002).
Source: World Bank, World Development Indicators.

Table L.2 *Poverty headcount ratio at $1 a day (PPP)*
(percentage of population)

Country	Poverty
Chile	2.0 (2000)
Colombia	7.03 (2003)
Costa Rica	2.22 (2001)
Cyprus	–
Greece	–
Israel	–
Kuwait	–
Malaysia	–
Mauritius	–
Panama	6.52 (2002)
Paraguay	16.37 (2002)
Singapore	–
South Korea	–
Sri Lanka	5.552 (2002)
Thailand	2.0 (2002)
Trinidad and Tobago	–
Argentina	–
Brazil	–
Mexico	–
Uruguay	2.0 (2003)
Bolivia	23.2 (2002)
Dominican Republic	2.52 (2003)
Egypt	3.08 (2000)
El Salvador	19.04 (2002)
India	34.7 (2000)
Iran	–
Lesotho	–
Morocco	–
Tunisia	2.0 (2000)
Turkey	3.412 (2002)
Zambia	75.84 (2002)
Zimbabwe	–

Notes: The "Population below $1 a day" is the percentage of the population living on less than $1.08 a day at 1993 international prices. As a result of revisions in PPP exchange rates, poverty rates cannot be compared with poverty rates reported previously for individual countries. Data showing as 2.0 signify a poverty rate of less than 2.0 percent. "Poverty" is defined as the population living below the national poverty line (1990–2002).
Source: World Bank, World Development Indicators.

Table L.3 *Population living below $1 a day (1990–2003) (percentage)*

Country	Poverty
Chile	<2
Colombia	8.2
Costa Rica	2
Cyprus	–
Greece	–
Israel	–
Kuwait	–
Malaysia	<2
Mauritius	–
Panama	–
Paraguay	16.4
Singapore	–
South Korea	<2
Sri Lanka	5.552 (2002)
Thailand	2.0 (2002)
Trinidad and Tobago	–
Argentina	3.3
Brazil	8.2
Mexico	9.9
Uruguay	<2
Bolivia	14.4
Dominican Republic	<2
Egypt	3.1
El Salvador	31.1
India	34.7
Iran	<2
Lesotho	36.4
Morocco	<2
Tunisia	<2
Turkey	<2
Zambia	63.7
Zimbabwe	56.1

Note: "Poverty" is defined as the population living below the national poverty line (1990–2002).
Source: UNDP, *Human Development Reports*, various years.

Table L.4 *Population living below the national poverty line (1990–2002)* *(percentage)*

Country	Poverty
Chile	17
Columbia	64
Costa Rica	22
Cyprus	–
Greece	–
Israel	–
Kuwait	–
Malaysia	15.5
Mauritius	10.6
Panama	–
Paraguay	21.8
Singapore	–
South Korea	–
Sri Lanka	–
Thailand	13.1
Trinidad and Tobago	–
Argentina	–
Brazil	17.4
Mexico	10.1
Uruguay	–
Bolivia	62.7
Dominican Republic	28.6
Egypt	16.7
El Salvador	48.3
India	28.6
Iran	–
Lesotho	49.2
Morocco	19
Tunisia	7.6
Turkey	–
Zambia	72.9
Zimbabwe	34.9

Source: UNDP, *Human Development Reports*, various years.

Appendix M: Social expenditures on social security, health, and education in India (percent of GDP) based on national data

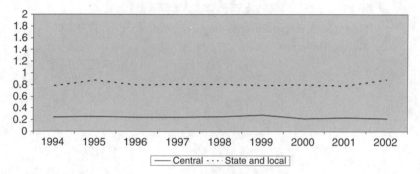

Figure M.1 Social security and welfare spending as a percentage of GDP, 1994–2002

Source: Ministry of Finance (2004).

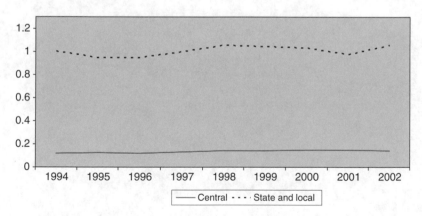

Figure M.2 Health spending as a percentage of GDP, 1994–2002

Source: Ministry of Finance (2004).

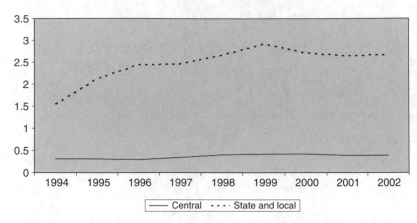

Figure M.3 Education spending as a percentage of GDP, 1994–2002
Source: Ministry of Finance (2004).

References

Abe, Makoto, and Momoko Kawakame. 1997. "A Distributive Comparison of Enterprise Size Korea and Taiwan," *The Developing Economies* **35**(4): 382–400.

Achen, Christopher H. 2000. "Why Lagged Dependent Variables Can Suppress the Explanatory Power of Other Independent Variables." Paper presented at the Annual Meeting of the Political Methodology Section of the American Political Science Association, University of California, Los Angeles, July 20–2.

Adsera, Alicia, and Carles Boix. 2002. "Trade, Democracy, and the Size of the Public Sector: The Political Underpinnings of Openness," *International Organization* **56**(2): 229–62.

Agarwala, Ramgopal, and Zafar Dad Khan. 2002. "Labor Market and Social Insurance Policy in India: A Case of Losing on Both Competitiveness and Caring," Working Paper no. 37168, World Bank Institute, Washington, DC.

Agenor, Pierre-Richard, and Peter J. Montiel. 1996. *Development Macroeconomics*. Princeton, NJ: Princeton University Press.

Aguiar, Marcelo, and Carlos Henrique Araujo. 2002. *BOLSA-ESCOLA Education to Confront Poverty*. Paris: UNESCO. Available online at http://unesdoc.unesco.org/images/0012/001294/129453m.pdf.

Ahluwalia, Montek Singh. 1976. "Income Distribution and Development: Some Stylized Facts," *American Economic Review* **66**: 128–35.

Aizenman, Joshua, and Ilan Noy. 2006. "FDI and Trade – Two Way Linkages," *Quarterly Review of Economics and Finance* **46**(3): 317–37.

Alarcon, Diana, and Terry Mckinley. 1992. "Beyond Import Substitution: The Restructuring Projects of Brazil and Mexico," *Latin American Perspectives* **73**(19): 72–87.

Albuquerque, Rui, Norman Loayza, and Luis Servén. 2005. "World Market Integration through the Lens of Foreign Direct Investors," *Journal of International Economics* **66**(2): 267–95.

Aldenderfer, Mark S., and Roger K. Blashfield. 1984. *Cluster Analysis*. Beverly Hills: Sage.

Alesina, Alberto, Reza Baqir, and William Easterly. 1999. "Public Goods and Ethnic Divisions," *Quarterly Journal of Economics* **114**(4): 1243–84.

Alesina, Alberto, and Roberto Perotti. 1996. "Income Distribution, Political Instability and Investment," *European Economic Review* **40**: 1203–28.

Allan, James P., and Lyle Scruggs. 2004. "Political Partisanship and Welfare State Reform in Advanced Industrial Societies," *American Journal of Political Science* 48(3): 496–512.

Alm, James, Roy Bahl, and Matthew N. Murray. 1991. "Tax Base Erosion in Developing Countries," *Economic Development and Cultural Change* 39(4): 849–72.

Almeida, Celia, Claudia Travassos, Silvia Porto, and Maria Eliana Labra. 2000. "Health Sector Reform in Brazil: A Case Study of Inequity," *International Journal of Health Services* 30(1): 129–62.

Alves, Denisard, and Christopher D. Timmins. 2001. "Social Exclusion and the Two-tiered Health Care System of Brazil," Working Paper no. R-436, Inter-American Development Bank, Washington, DC.

Amadeo, Edward J., and José Márcio Camargo. 1993. "Labour Legislation and Institutional Aspects of the Brazilian Labour Market," *Labour* 7: 157–80.

Amadeo, Edward J., Indermit S. Gill, and Marcelo C. Neri. 2000. "Do Labor Laws Matter? The 'Pressure Points' in Brazil's Labor Legislation," in Indermit S. Gill and Claudio E. Montenegro (eds.), *Readdressing Latin America's "Forgotten Reform": Quantifying Labor Policy Challenges in Argentina, Brazil and Chile.* Washington, DC: International Bank for Reconstruction and Development, 35–78.

Amadeo, Edward J., Ricardo Paes e Barros, José Márcio Camargo, and Rosane Mendonca. 1995. "Brazil," in Gustavo Márquez (ed.), *Reforming the Labor Market in a Liberalized Economy.* Washington, DC: Inter-American Development Bank, 35–78.

Amsden, Alice. 1989. *Asia's Next Giant: South Korea and Late Industrialization.* New York: Oxford University Press.

Araujo, Carlos Henrique, and Elimar P. do Nascimento. 2001. "Bolsa Escola: Effects and Potential." Paper presented at the twenty-fourth General Conference organized by the International Union for the Scientific Study of Population, Salvador de Bahia, Brazil, August 18–24.

Araújo e Oliveira, João Batista. 2004. "Expansion and Inequality in Brazilian Education," in Colin Brock and Simon Schwartzman (eds.), *The Challenges of Education in Brazil.* New York: Oxford University Press, 41–68.

Armijo, Leslie Elliott, and Walter L. Ness, Jr. 2002. "Modernizing Brazil's Capital Markets, 1985–2001: Pragmatism and Democratic Adjustment." Paper prepared for the Annual Meeting of the International Studies Association, New Orleans, March 25–8.

Arora, Suchit. 2001. "Health, Human Productivity, and Long-term Economic Growth," *Journal of Economic History* 61: 699–749.

Arretche, Marta. 2004. "Toward a Unified and More Equitable System: Health Reform in Brazil," in Robert B. Kaufman and Joan M. Nelson (eds.), *Crucial Needs, Weak Incentives: Social Sector Reform, Democratization, and Globalization in Latin America.* Washington, DC: Woodrow Wilson Center Press, 155–88.

Atkinson, Anthony Barnes, and Andrea Brandoloni. 2001. "Promise and Pitfalls in the Use of Secondary Datasets: Income Inequality in the OECD Countries as a Case Study," *Journal of Economic Literature* 34: 771–99.

Atkinson, Anthony Barnes, and John Hills. 1991. "Social Security in Developing Countries: Are There Lessons for Developed Countries?" in Ehtisham Ahmad, Jean Dreze, and John Hills (eds.), *Social Security in Developing Countries*. Oxford: Clarendon Press, 81–111.

Atwood, Margaret. 1993. "Blind Faith and Free Trade," in Ralph Nader (ed.), *The Case against "Free Trade": GATT, NAFTA, and the Globalization of Corporate Power*. San Francisco: North Atlantic Books, 92–6.

Avelino, George, David S. Brown, and Wendy Hunter. 2005. "The Effects of Capital Mobility, Trade Openness, and Democracy on Social Spending in Latin America, 1980–1999," *American Journal of Political Science* 49(3): 625–41.

Baer, Werner. 1989. *The Brazilian Economy: Growth and Development*, 3rd edn. Westport, CT: Praeger.

2001. *The Brazilian Economy: Growth and Development*. 5th edn. Westport, CT: Praeger.

Baer, Werner, and Michael E. A. Herve. 1966. "Employment and Industrialization in Developing Countries," *Quarterly Journal of Economics* 80(1): 88–107.

Bairoch, Paul. 1993. *Economics and World Development*. Chicago: University of Chicago Press.

Baldacci, Emanuele, Luiz de Mello, and Gabriela Inchauste. 2002. "Financial Crisis, Poverty and Income Distribution," Working Paper WP/02/04, International Monetary Fund: Washington, DC.

Banuri, Tariq, and Edward Amadeo. 1991. "Worlds within the Third World: Labour Market Institutions in Asia and Latin America," in Tariq Banuri (ed.), *Economic Liberalization: No Panacea*. Oxford: Clarendon Press, 172–227.

Bardhan, Pranab. 1984. *Land, Labor and Rural Poverty*. New York: Columbia University Press.

Barreto de Oliveira, Francisco E., and Kaizô Iwakami Beltrão. 2001. "Brazil: The Brazilian Social Security System," *International Social Security Review* 54(1): 101–12.

Barreto de Oliveira, Francisco E., Kaizô Iwakami Beltrão, and Andre Cezar Medici. 1994. "Financing Social Security in Brazil," in Francisco E. Barreto de Oliveira (ed.), *Social Security Systems in Latin America*. Washington, DC: Inter-American Development Bank, 59–108.

Basinger, Scott J., and Mark Hallerberg. 2004. "Remodeling the Competition for Capital: How Domestic Politics Erases the Race to the Bottom," *American Political Science Review* 98(2): 261–76.

Basu, Kaushik, Gary S. Fields, and Shub Debgupta. 1996. *Retrenchment, Labor Laws and Government Policy: An Analysis with Special Reference to India*. Washington, DC: World Bank.

Bates, Robert. 1981. *Markets and States in Tropical Africa*. Berkeley: University of California Press.

Bearce, David. 2007. *Monetary Divergence: Domestic Policy Autonomy in the Post-Bretton Woods Era*. Ann Arbor: University of Michigan Press.

Beck, Nathaniel, and Jonathan Katz. 1995. "What to Do (and Not to Do) with Time-series Cross-section Data," *American Political Science Review* 89(3): 634–48.

Bellin, Eva. 2000. "Contingent Democrats: Industrialists, Labor and Democratization in Late-developing Countries," *World Politics* 52: 175–205.

Beltrão, Kaizô Iwakami, Sonoe Sugahara Pinheiro, and Francisco E. Barreto de Oliveira. 2004. "Rural Population and Social Security in Brazil: An Analysis with Emphasis on Constitutional Changes," *International Social Security Review* 57(4): 19–49.

Betcherman, Gordon, Amy Luinstra, and Makoto Ogawa. 2001. "Labor Market Regulation: International Experient in Promoting Employment and Social Protection," Social Protection Discussion Paper, no. 0128, World Bank, Washington, DC.

Beyer, Harald, Patricio Rojas, and Rodrigo Vergara. 1999. "Trade Liberalization and Wage Inequality," *Journal of Development Economics* 59(1): 103–23.

Bidet, Eric. 2004. "Social Protection in the Republic of Korea: Social Insurance and Moral Hazard," *International Social Security Review* 57(1): 3–18.

Birdsall, Nancy, Barbara Bruns, and Richard H. Sabot. 1996. "Playing a Bad Hand Badly," in Nancy Birdsall and Richard H. Sabot (eds.), *Opportunity Forgone: Education in Brazil*. Washington, DC: Inter-American Development Bank, 7–48.

Birdsall, Nancy, David Ross, and Richard H. Sabot. 1995. "Inequality and Growth Reconsidered: Lessons from East Asia," *World Bank Economic Review* 9: 477–508.

Biswas, A., and S. P. Agrawal. 1986. *Development of Education in India: A Historical Survey of Educational Documents before and after Independence*. New Delhi: Concept.

Blashfield, Roger K. 1976. "Mixture Model Tests of Cluster Analysis: Accuracy of Agglomerative Hierarchical Methods," *Psychological Bulletin* 83: 337–88.

Bloom, David E., David Canning, and Jaypee Sevilla. 2001. "The Effect of Health on Economic Growth: Theory and Evidence," Working Paper no. 8587, National Bureau of Economic Research, Cambridge, MA.

Blunch, Niels-Hugo, and Dorte Verner. 2000. "Is Functional Literacy a Prerequisite for Entering the Labor Market? An Analysis of the Determinants of Adult Literacy and Earnings in Ghana," Working Paper no. 2410, World Bank, Washington, DC.

Boix, Carles. 2006. "Between Redistribution and Trade: The Political Economy of Protectionism and Domestic Compensation," in Pranab Bardhan, Samuel Bowles, and Michael Wallerstein (eds.), *Globalization and Egalitarian Redistribution*. New York: Russell Sage Foundation, 192–216.

Bollen, Kenneth A., and Robert W. Jackman. 1985. "Political Democracy and the Size Distribution of Income," *American Sociological Review* 50: 438–57.

Bonturi, Marcos. 2002. "The Brazilian Pension System: Recent Reforms and Challenges Ahead," Economics Department Working Paper no. 340, Organisation for Economic Co-operation and Development, Paris.

Boschi, Renato R. 1987. "Social Movements and the New Political Order in Brazil," in John D. Wirth, Edson de Olivereira Nunes and Thomas

E. Bogenschild (eds.), *State and Society in Brazil*. Boulder, CO: Westview Press, 178–212.

Botero, Juan C., Simeon Djankov, Rafael La Porta, Florencio Lopez-de-Silanes, and Andrei Shleifer. 2004. "The Regulation of Labor," *Quarterly Journal of Economics* 119(4): 1339–82.

Bourguignon, François, and Thierry Verdier. 2000. "The Political Economy of Education and Development in an Open Economy." Paper presented at the Poverty and Income Inequality in Developing Countries workshop organized by the Centre de Recherche sur les Dynamiques et Politiques Economiques et l'Economic des Ressources (CEDERS) and the OECD Development Centre, Marseilles, November 27–8.

Braumoeller, Bear F. 2004. "Hypothesis Testing and Multiplicative Interaction Terms," *International Organization* 58(4): 807–20.

Brickman, Ronald, Sheila Jasanoff, and Thomas Ilgen. 1985. *Controlling Chemicals: The Politics of Regulation in Europe and the United States*. Ithaca, NY: Cornell University Press.

Brookmann, Bernhard. 2001. "The Ratification of ILO Conventions: A Hazard Rate Analysis," *Economics and Politics* 13(3): 281–309.

Brooks, Sarah M. 2005. "Interdependent and Domestic Foundations of Policy Change: The Diffusion of Pension Privatization Around the World," *International Studies Quarterly* 49(2): 273–94.

Brown, Andrew. 2004. *Labour, Politics, and the State in Industrializing Thailand*. London: RoutledgeCurzon.

Brown, David S. 2002. "Democracy, Authoritarianism and Education Finance in Brazil," *Journal of Latin American Studies* 43: 115–41.

Brown, David S., and Wendy Hunter. 1999. "Democracy and Social Spending in Latin America, 1980–92," *American Political Science Review* 93(4): 779–90.

Browning, Harley, and Bryan R. Roberts. 1990. "Urbanization, Sectoral Transformation, and the Utilization of Labor in Latin America," *Comparative Urban Research* 8(1): 86–102.

Buchanan, Paul, and Kate Nicholls. 2003. "Labor Politics and Democratic Transition in South Korea and Taiwan," *Government and Opposition* 38(2): 203–37.

Burgoon, Brian. 2001. "Globalization and Welfare Compensation: Disentangling the Ties that Bind," *International Organization* 55(3): 509–51.

Burkhart, Ross E. 1997. "Comparative Democracy and Income Distribution: Shape and Direction of the Causal Arrow," *Journal of Politics* 59: 148–64.

Cameron, David. 1978. "The Expansion of the Public Sector: A Comparative Analysis," *American Political Science Review* 72(4): 1243–61.

Campbell, Donald. 1988. *Methodology and Epistemology*. Chicago: University of Chicago Press.

Campos, Nauro F., and Armando Castelar Pinheiro. 2002. "Does it Take a Lula to Go to Davos? A Brief Overview of Brazilian Reforms, 1980–2000," Working Paper no. 580, William Davidson Institute, University of Michigan, Ann Arbor.

Candland, Chris. 1995. "Trade Unionism and Industrial Restructuring in India and Pakistan," *Bulletin of Concerned Asian Scholars* 27(4): 63–78.

Cardoso, Adalberto Moreira. 2002. "Workers' Representation Insecurity in Brazil: Global Forces, Local Stress," working paper, International Labor Organization, Geneva.

Carneiro, Francisco G., and Jorge S. Arbache. 2003. "The Impacts of Trade on the Brazilian Labor Market: A CGE Model Approach," *World Development* 31: 1581–95.

Cerny, Philip. 1995. "Globalization and the Changing Logic of Collective Action," *International Organization* 49(4): 595–625.

Chan, Anita, and Robert J. S. Ross. 2003. "Racing to the Bottom: Industrial Trade without a Social Clause," *Third World Quarterly* 24(6): 1011–28.

Chan, Anita, and Robert Senser. 1997. "China's Troubled Workers," *Foreign Affairs* 76(2): 104–17.

Chan, David, and Ka-Ho Mok. 2001. "Educational Reforms and Coping Strategies under the Tidal Wave of Marketization: A Comparative Study of Hong Kong and the Mainland," *Comparative Education* 37: 21–41.

Chandrasekhar, C. P., and Jayati Ghosh. 2006. "Providing Social Security to Unorganised Workers," *Hindu Business Line* June 27. Available online at www.thehindubusinessline.com/bline/2006/06/27/stories/2006062702011100.htm.

Chapman, David, and Ann Austin. 2002. *Higher Education in the Developing World: Changing Contexts and Institutional Responses*. Westport, CT: Greenwood.

Chatterji, Monojit. 1998. "Tertiary Education and Economic Growth," *Regional Studies* 32: 349–54.

Chau, Nancy, and Ravi Kanbur. 2006. "The Race to the Bottom, from the Bottom," *Economica* 73: 193–228.

Cheng, Harrison, Cheng Hsiao, Jeffrey Nugent, Jicheng Qiu, and Shell China. 2006. "Managerial Autonomy, Contractual Incentives, and Productivity in a Transitional Economy: Some Evidence from China's TVEs," *Pacific Economic Review* 11(3): 341–61.

Cho, Yong-Man. 2002. "Protection of Fundamental Labor Rights and Improvement in Power Balance between Labor and Management." Paper prepared for the International Conference on International Labor Standards and Industrial Relations in Korea, November 29.

Choi, Nakgyoon. 2002. "Korea's Trade Policy Regime in the Development Process," Discussion Paper no. 02–06, Korea Institute for International Economic Policy, Seoul.

Chuhan, Punam, Stijn Claessens, and Nlandu Mamingi. 1993. "Equity and Bond Flows to Asia and Latin America," Policy Research Working Paper no. 1160, World Bank, Washington, DC.

CIDCM. 2000. Polity IV Dataset (computer file, version p4v2000), Center for International Development and Conflict Management, University of Maryland. Available at www.cidcm.umd.edu/inscr/polity.

Clayton, Richard, and Jonas Pontusson. 1998. "Welfare State Retrenchment Revisited," *World Politics* 51: 67–98.

Colander, David C. 1984. *Neoclassical Political Economy: The Analysis of Rent-seeking and DUP Activities*. Cambridge, MA: Ballinger.

Collier, David, and Richard E. Messick. 1975. "Prerequisites versus Diffusion: Testing Alternative Explanations of Social Security Adoption," *American Political Science Review* 69(4): 1299–315.

Collier, Ruth Berins, and David Collier. 1979. "Inducements versus Constraints: Disaggregating 'Corporatism,'" *American Political Science Review* 73(4): 967–86.

1991. *Shaping the Political Arena: Critical Junctures, the Labor Movement, and Regime Dynamics in Latin America.* Princeton, NJ: Princeton University Press.

Collins, Charles, José Araujo, and Jarbas Barbosa. 2000. "Decentralising the Health Sector: Issues in Brazil," *Health Policy* 52: 113–27.

Congress of the United States. 2005. Press release, "President's Social Security Benefit Cuts Would Hurt Middle-income Workers the Most," Washington, DC, Joint Economic Committee, Democrats, May 19.

Cook, María Lorena. 2002. "Labor Reform and Dual Transitions in Brazil and the Southern Cone," *Latin American Politics and Society* 44(1): 1–34.

Cornia, Giovanni Andrea. 1999. "Liberalization, Globalization and Income Distribution," World Institute for Development Economics Research Working Paper no. 157, United Nations University, Helsinki.

Cornia, Giovanni Andrea, Tony Addison, and Sampsa Kiiski. 2004. "Income Distribution Changes and Their Impact in the Post-Second World War Period," in Giovanni Andrea Cornia (ed.), *Inequality, Growth, and Poverty in an Era of Liberalization and Globalization.* Oxford: Oxford University Press, 26–55.

Cox, Robert W. 1996. "A Perspective on Globalization," in James H. Mittelman (ed.), *Globalization: Critical Reflections.* Boulder, CO: Lynne Rienner, 21–30.

Crenshaw, Edward. 1992. "Cross-national Determinants of Income Inequality: A Replication and Extension Using Ecological-evolutionary Theory," *Social Forces* 71(2): 339–63.

Criança. 2001. "Bolsa Escola: A Poverty Relief Project for the HIPC Countries," working paper, Missão Criança, Brasilia. Available at www.missaocrianca.org. br/index.php?option=com_docman&task=doc_view&gid=4&Itemid=28.

Crotty, James, and Kang-Kook Lee. 2002. "Is Financial Liberalization Good for Developing Nations? The Case of South Korea in the 1990s," *Review of Radical Political Economics* 34: 327–34.

Cutright, Phillips. 1965. "Political Structure, Economic Development, and National Social Security Programs," *American Journal of Sociology* 70: 537–50.

Daly, Herman E. 1996. "Free Trade: The Perils of Deregulation," in Jerry Mander and Edward Goldsmith (eds.), *The Case against the Global Economy.* San Francisco: Sierra Club Books, 229–38.

Da Silva, Luis Correia, Antonio Estache, and Sakari Jarvela. 2004. "Is Debt Replacing Equity in Regulated Privatized Infrastructure in Developing Countries?" Policy Research Working Paper no. 3374, World Bank, Washington, DC.

Datta, Ramesh C. 2001. "Economic Reforms, Redundancy, and National Renewal Fund: Human Face or Human Mask?" Paper presented at the forty-third Annual Labor Economics Conference at the Institute for Social and Economic Change, Bangalore, December 18–20.

Davis, Donald R. 1996. "Trade Liberalization and Income Distribution," Working Paper no. 5693, National Bureau of Economic Research, Cambridge, MA.

Deaton, Angus S., and Christina H. Paxson. 1997. "The Effects of Economic and Population Growth on National Saving and Inequality," *Demography* 34(1): 97–114.

De Castro, Maria H. G. 2000. *Education for All: Evaluation of the Year 2000 – National Report – Brazil*. Paris: United Nations Educational, Scientific, and Cultural Organization.

De Mello, Luiz, and Mombert Hoppe. 2005. "Education Attainment in Brazil: The Experience of Fundef," Working Paper no. 424, Organisation for Economic Co-operation and Development, Paris. Available at www.olis. oecd.org/olis/2005doc.nsf/43bb6130e5e86e5fc12569fa005d004c/a5973f617 ac5674cc1256fdc007cfb04/$FILE/JT00181600.DOC.

Deninger, Klaus, and Lyn Squire. 1996. "A New Data Set Measuring Income Inequality," *World Bank Economic Review* 10: 565–91. Available at www. worldbank.org/research/growth/dddeisqu.htm.

Denoon, David. 1998. "Cycles in Indian Economic Liberalization, 1966–1996," *Comparative Politics* 31(1): 43–60.

Deodhar, N. S. 1982. "Primary Health Care in India," *Journal of Public Health Policy* 3(1): 76–99.

Deshpande, Ashwini. 2005. "Affirmative Action in India and the United States," background paper for *World Development Report 2006*, World Bank, Washington, DC.

Dev, S. Mahendra. 1995. "India's (Maharastra) Employent Guarantee Scheme: Lessons from Long Experience," in Joachim Von Braun (ed.), *Employment for Poverty Reduction and Food Security*. Washington, DC: International Food Policy Research Institute, 108–43.

Dev, S. Mahendra, and Jos Mooij. 2002. "Social Sector Expenditure in the 1990s: Analysis of Central and State Budgets," *Economic and Political Weekly* 37: 853–66.

Devarajan, Shantayanan, Hafez Ghanem, and Karen Thierfelder. 1997. "Economic Reforms and Labor Unions: A General Equilibrium Analysis Applied to Bangladesh and Indonesia," *World Bank Economic Review* 11(1): 145–70.

Deyo, Frederic C. 1984. "Export Manufacturing and Labor: The Asian Case," in Charles Bergquist (ed.), *Labor in the Capitalist World Economy*. Beverly Hills: Sage, 267–88.

1989. *Beneath the Miracle: Labor Subordination in the New Asian Industrialism*. Berkeley: University of California Press.

Diamond, Larry. 1987. "Class Formation in the Swollen African State," *Journal of Modern African Studies* 25(4): 567–96.

Djankov, Simeon, Rafael La Porta, Florencio Lopez-de-Silane, Andrei Shleifer, and Juan Botero. 2003. "The Regulation of Labor," Working Paper no. 9756, National Bureau of Economic Research, Cambridge, MA.

Doling, John. 1999. "Housing Policies and the Little Tigers: How Do They Compare with Other Industrialised Countries?" *Housing Studies* 14(2): 229–50.

Draibe, Sonia Miriam. 2004. "Federal Leverage in a Decentralized System: Education Reform in Brazil," in Robert R. Kaufman and Joan M. Nelson (eds.), *Crucial Needs, Weak Incentives: Social Sector Reform, Democratization, and Globalization in Latin America*. Washington, DC: Woodrow Wilson Center Press, 375–406.

Dreze, Jean, and Amartya Sen. 1989. *Hunger and Public Action*. Oxford: Clarendon Press.

Drunberg, Isabelle. 1998. "Double Jeopardy, Globalization, Liberalization, and the Fiscal Squeeze," *World Development* 26(4): 591–605.

Duda, Richard O., and Peter E. Hart. 1973. *Pattern Classification and Scene Analysis*. New York: John Wiley & Sons.

Easterly, William. 2002. *The Elusive Quest for Growth*. Cambridge, MA: MIT Press.

Ebbes, Peter. 2004. "Latent Instrumental Variables: A New Approach to Solve for Endogeneity," PhD dissertation, University of Groningen.

Echeverri-Gent, John. 1994. *The State and the Poor: Public Policy and Political Development in India and the United States*. Berkeley, CA: University of California Press.

Edwards, Sebastian. 1998. "Openness, Productivity and Growth: What Do We Really Know?" *Economic Journal* 108: 383–98.

Eichengreen, Barry. 1996. *Globalizing Capital*. Princeton, NJ: Princeton University Press.

Elias, Paulo Eduardo, and Amelia Cohn. 2003. "Health Reform in Brazil: Lessons to Consider," *American Journal of Public Health* 93(1): 44–8.

Ellis, Randall P., Moneer Alam, and Indrani Gupta. 2000. "Health Insurance in India," *Economic and Political Weekly* 45(4): 207–17.

Encarnation, Dennis J. 1989. *Dislodging Multinationals: India's Strategy in Comparative Perspective*. Ithaca, NY: Cornell University Press.

Erickson, Kenneth Paul, and Patrick V. Peppe. 1976. "Dependent Capitalist Development, US Foreign Policy, and Repression of the Working Class in Chile and Brazil," *Latin American Perspectives* 3(1): 19–44.

Esping-Andersen, Gosta. 1990. *The Three Worlds of Welfare Capitalism*. Princeton, NJ: Princeton University Press.

1996. *Welfare States in Transition*. London: Sage.

Evans, Peter B. 1997. "The Eclipse of the State? Reflections on Stateness in an Era of Globalization," *World Politics* 50(1): 62–87.

1998. "Transferable Lessons? Re-examining the Institutional Prerequisites of East Asian Economic Policies," *Journal of Developmental Studies* 34(6): 66–86. [Reprinted in Yilmaz Akyüz (ed.), 1999, *East Asian Development: New Perspectives*. London: Frank Cass, 66–86.]

Evans, Peter B., Dietrich Rusechemeyer, and Theda Skocpol (eds.). 1985. *Bringing the State Back In*. Cambridge: Cambridge University Press.

Evans, Peter B., and Michael Timberlake. 1980. "Dependence, Inequality, and the Growth of the Tertiary: A Comparative Analysis of Less Developed Countries," *American Sociological Review* 45: 531–51.

Everitt, Brian. 1974. *Cluster Analysis*. New York: John Wiley & Sons.

Fearon, James D. 2002. "Ethnic Structure and Cultural Diversity around the World: A Cross-national Data Set on Ethnic Groups." Paper presented at the Annual Meeting of the American Political Science Association, Boston, August 29–September 1.

Feenstra, Robert C., and Gordon Hanson. 1996. "Globalization, Outsourcing, and Wage Inequality," *American Economic Review Papers and Proceedings* 86: 240–5.

1997. "Foreign Direct Investment and Relative Wages: Evidence from Mexico's Maquiladoras," *Journal of International Economics* 42: 371–94.

Figueiredo, José B., and Zafar Shaheed. 1995. *Reducing Poverty through Labour Market Policies*. Geneva: International Labour Organization.

Filho, Roberto F. 2005. "Celebrating Twenty-five Years and Speculating over the Future from a Brazilian Perspective," *Comparative Labor Law and Policy Journal* 25(1): 21–32.

Filmer, Deon, and Lant Pritchett. 1999. "The Impact of Public Spending on Health: Does Money Matter?" *Social Science and Medicine* 49: 1309–23.

Flynn, M. L., and Y. S. Chung. 1990. "Health Care Financing in Korea: Private Market Dilemmas for a Developing Nation," *Journal of Public Health Policy* 11 (2): 238–53.

Forbes, Kristin J. 2000. "A Reassessment of the Relationship between Inequality and Growth," *American Economic Review* 90(4): 869–87.

Form, William, and Kyu Han Bae. 1988. "Convergence Theory and the Korean Connection," *Social Forces* 66(3): 618–44.

French, John D. 1998. "Drowning in Laws but Starving (for Justice?): Brazilian Labor Law and the Workers' Quest to Realize the Imaginary," *Political Power and Social Theory* 12: 177–214.

Friedman, Thomas. 2000. *The Lexus and Olive Tree: Understanding Globalization*. New York: Anchor Books.

Gadotti, Moacir. 1997. "Contemporary Brazilian Education," in Carlos Alberto Torres and Adriana Puiggrós (eds.), *Latin American Education: Comparative Perspectives*. Boulder, CO: Westview Press, 123–48.

Gaiha, Raghav. 1996. "The Employment Guarantee Scheme in India: Is It Mistargeted?" *Asian Survey* 36(12): 1201–12.

2000. "Do Anti-poverty Programmes Reach the Rural Poor in India?" *Oxford Development Studies* 28(1): 71–95.

Gal, John. 2004. "Decommodification and Beyond: A Comparative Analysis of Work-injury Programmes," *Journal of European Social Policy* 14(1): 55–69.

Galbraith, James K., and Hyunsub Kum. 2003. "Estimating Inequality of Household Incomes: Filling Gaps and Correcting Errors in Deninger and Squire," University of Texas Inequality Project Working Paper no. 22, University of Texas, Austin.

Galenson, Walter. 1962. *Labor in Developing Economies*. Berkeley: University of California Press.

1994. *Trade Union Growth and Decline*. New York: Praeger.

Garg, Charu C. 1998. "Equity of Health Sector Financing and Delivery in India," Takemi Program Research Paper no. 145, Harvard School of Public Health, Boston.

Garrett, Geoffrey. 1998. *Partisan Politics in the Global Economy.* New York: Cambridge University Press.

2000. "The Causes of Globalization," *Comparative Political Studies* 33(6/7): 941–91.

2001. "Globalization and Government Spending around the World," *Studies in Comparative International Development* 35(4): 3–29.

Gelb, A., J. B. Knight, and R. H. Sabot. 1991. "Public Sector Employment, Rent Seeking and Economic Growth," *Economic Journal* 101: 1186–99.

Gereffi, Gary. 1995. "Global Production Systems and Third World Development," in Barbara Stallings (ed.), *Global Change, Regional Response.* New York: Cambridge University Press, 100–42.

Gerschenkron, Alexander. 1962. *Economic Backwardness in Historical Perspective.* Cambridge, MA: Belknap Press.

Gill, Stephen. 1995. "Globalization, Market Civilization, and Disciplinary Neoliberalism," *Millennium: Journal of International Studies* 24(3): 399–423.

Gillingham, Robert, and Daniel Kanda. 2001. "Pension Reform in India," Working Paper no. WP/01/125. Washington, DC: International Monetary Fund.

Gitterman, Daniel. 2002. "A Race to the Bottom, a Race to the Top or the March to a Minimum Floor? Economic Integration and Labor Standards in Comparative Perspective," in David Vogel and Robert Kagan (eds.), *Dynamics of Regulatory Change: How Globalization Affects National Regulatory Policies.* Berkeley: University of California Press, 331–70.

Goldin, Claudia, and Lawrence F. Katz. 1998. "The Origins of Technology–Skill Complementarity," *Quarterly Journal of Economics* 113(3): 693–732.

Gopalkrishnan, Narayan. 2001. "What about the Global Poor? Globalization from Above and Below," *Social Alternatives* 20: 40–4.

Gordon, Nora E., and Emiliana Vegas. 2005. "Educational Finance Equalization, Spending, Teacher Quality and Student Outcomes: The Case of Brazil's FUNDEF," in Emiliana Vegas (ed.), *Incentives to Improve Teaching: Lessons from Latin America.* Washington, DC: World Bank, 151–86.

Goswami, Ranadev. 2002. "Old Age Protection in India: Problems and Prognosis," *International Social Security Review* 55: 95–120.

Gough, Ian, Geof Wood, Armando Barrientos, Philippa Bevan, Peter Davis, and Graham Room. 2004. *Insecurity and Welfare Regimes in Asia, Africa and Latin America: Social Policy in Development Contexts.* Cambridge: Cambridge University Press.

Gray, John. 1998. *False Dawn: The Delusions of Global Capitalism.* New York: New Press.

Green-Pedersen, Christoffer. 2004. "The Dependent Variable Problem within the Study of Welfare State Retrenchment: Defining the Problem and Looking for Solution," *Journal of Comparative Policy Analysis* 6(1): 3–14.

Greider, William. 1998. *One World, Ready or Not: The Manic Logic of Global Capitalism.* New York: Simon & Schuster.

2001. "A New Giant Sucking Sound," *The Nation* 273(22): 22–4.

Grindle, Merilee. 2000. "The Social Agenda and the Politics of Reform," in Joseph S. Tulchin, and Allison M. Garland (eds.), *Social Development in Latin America: The Politics of Reform.* Boulder, CO: Lynne Reinner, 17–54.

Grosh, Margaret E. 1994. *Administering Targeted Social Programs in Latin America: From Platitudes to Practice*. Washington, DC: World Bank.

Guhan, S. 1992. "Social Security in India: Looking One Step Ahead," in B. Harriss, S. Guhan, and R. H. Cassen (eds.), *Poverty in India: Research and Policy*. Mumbai: Oxford University Press, 282–98.

Guillen, Mauro. 2001. *The Limits of Convergence: Globalization and Organizational Change in Argentina, South Korea and Spain*. Princeton, NJ: Princeton University Press.

Gwatkin, Davidson R. 2000. "Health Inequalities and the Health of the Poor: What Do We Know? What Can We Do?" *Bulletin of the World Health Organization* **78**: 3–18.

Gwatkin, Davidson R., and Michel Guillot. 1999. "The Burden of Disease among the Global Poor: Current Situation, Future Trends, and Implications for Strategy," *Health, Nutrition and Population Series*, World Bank, Washington, DC.

Haar, Jerry. 1977. *The Politics of Higher Education in Brazil*. New York: Praeger.

Haggard, Stephen, and Robert R. Kaufman. Forthcoming. *Revising Social Contracts: Welfare Reform in Latin America, East Asia and Eastern Europe*. Princeton, NJ: Princeton University Press.

Haggard, Stephen, and Chung-In Moon. 1990. "Institutions and Economic Policy: Theory and a Korean Case Study," *World Politics* **42**(2): 210–37.

Hall, Peter, and David Soskice. 2001. "An Introduction to Varieties of Capitalism," in Peter Hall and David Soskice (eds.), *Varieties of Capitalism: The Institutional Foundations of Comparative Advantage*. Oxford: Oxford University Press, 1–68.

Han, You-Kyung. 2003. "Higher Education in Korea: Context, Issues and Prospect," unpublished manuscript, Sangji University, Wonju City, South Korea.

Hanson, Gordon H., and Ann Harrison. 1999. "Trade Liberalization and Wage Inequality in Mexico," *Industrial and Labor Relations Review* **52**(2): 271–88.

Hanushek, Eric A. 1995. "Interpreting Recent Research on Schooling in Developing Countries," *World Bank Research Observer* **10**: 227–46.

Haouas, Ilham, and Mahmoud Yagoubi. 2004. "Trade Liberalization and Labor-demand Elasticities: Empirical Evidence from Tunisia," Discussion Paper no. 1084, Institute for the Study of Labor (IZA), Bonn.

Hargens, Lowell L., and Diane H. Felmlee. 1984. "Structural Determinants of Stratification in Science," *American Sociological Review* **49**: 685–97.

Harrison, Ann, and Gordon H. Hanson. 1999. "Who Gains from Trade Reform? Some Remaining Puzzles," *Journal of Development Economics* **59**(1): 125–54.

Hart, Robert, Jr., and David H. Clark. 1999. "Does Size Matter? Exploring the Small Sample Properties of Maximum Likelihood Estimation." Paper presented at the Annual Meeting of the Midwest Political Science Association, Chicago, April 15–17.

Haussman, Fay, and Jerry Haar. 1978. *Education in Brazil*. New York: Archon Books.

Heckman, James, and Carmen Pages. 2003. "Law and Employment: Lessons from Latin America and the Caribbean," Working Paper no. 10129, National Bureau of Economic Research, Cambridge, MA.

Heller, Peter S., and Alan A. Tait. 1984. "Government Employment and Pay: Some International Comparisons," Occasional Paper no. 24, International Monetary Fund, Washington, DC.

HelpAge International. 2003. *Non-contributory Pensions and Poverty Prevention: A Comparative Study of Brazil and South Africa*. London: HelpAge International.

Henderson, Jeffrey, David Hulme, Richard Phillips, and Eun Mee Kim. 2002. "Economic Governance and Poverty Reduction in South Korea," Working Paper no. 439, Manchester Business School, Manchester.

Heredia, Blanca. 1997. "Prosper or Perish? Development in the Age of Global Capital," *Current History* 96: 383–8.

Herran, Carlos A., and Alberto Rodriguez. 2000. *Secondary Education in Brazil*. Washington, DC: Inter-American Development Bank.

Hicks, Alexander. 1999. *Social Democracy and Welfare Capitalism: A Century of Income Security Politics*. Ithaca, NY: Cornell University Press.

Hicks, Alexander, and Duane Swank. 1992. "Politics, Institutions, and Welfare Spending in Industrialized Democracies, 1960–1982," *American Political Science Review* 86(3): 658–74.

Hicks, Alexander, and Christopher Zorn. 2005. "Economic Globalization, the Macro Economy, and Reversals of Welfare Expansion in Affluent Democracies, 1978–1994," *International Organization* 60(3): 631–62.

Holliday, Ian. 2000. "Productivist Welfare Capitalism: Social Policy in East Asia," *Political Studies* 48(4): 706–23.

Huber, Evelyne. 1996. "Options for Social Policy in Latin America: Neoliberal versus Social Democratic Models," in Gosta Esping-Andersen (ed.), *Welfare States in Transition: National Adaptations in Global Economies*. London: Sage, 141–91.

2005. "Inequality and the State in Latin America." Paper prepared for the conference of the American Political Science Association's Task Force "Difference and Inequality in the Developing World," Chartottesville, VA, April 22–3.

Huber, Evelyne, and John D. Stephens. 1998. "Internationalization and the Social Democratic Model," *Comparative Political Studies* 31(3): 353–98.

2001. *Development and Crisis of the Welfare State*. Chicago: University of Chicago Press.

ILO. 2001. *Key Indicators of the Labour Market 2001–2002*. New York: Routledge.

IMF. 2001. *Government Finance Statistics Manual*, 2nd edn. Washington, DC: International Monetary Fund.

Ingerson, Alice. 1984. "The Textile Industry and Working-class Culture in Labor," in Charles Bergquist (ed.), *The Capitalist World Economy*. Beverly Hills: Sage, 217–42.

Iversen, Torben. 2001. "The Dynamics of Welfare State Expansion: Trade Openness, Deindustrialization and Partisan Politics," in Paul Pierson (ed.), *The New Politics of the Welfare State*. Oxford: Oxford University Press, 45–79.

2005. *Capitalism, Democracy and Welfare*. Cambridge: Cambridge University Press.

Iversen, Torben, and Thomas Cusack. 2001. "The Causes of Welfare State Expansion: Deindustrialization or Globalization?" *World Politics* 52(3): 313–49.

Jain, Arvind. 2001. "Corruption: A Review," *Journal of Economic Surveys* 15(1): 71–122.

James, Estelle, Elizabeth M. King, and Ace Suryadi. 1996. "Finance, Management, and Costs of Public and Private Schools in Indonesia," *Economics of Education Review* 15(4): 387–98.

Jang, Sang-Hwan. 2004. "Continuing Suicide among Laborers in Korea," *Labor History* 45(3): 271–97.

Jenkins, Rob. 2004. "Introduction," *India Review* 3(4): 257–68.

Jo, Jaegoog, and Kwang Choi. 2002. "Health Policy in Korea," Institute of Economic Research Discussion Paper no. 127, Hitotsubashi University, Tokyo.

Jones, Leroy P. 1975. *Public Enterprise and Economic Development: The Korean Case.* Seoul: Korea Development Institute.

Joo, Jaehyun. 1999. "Explaining Social Policy Adoption in South Korea: the Cases of the Medical Insurance Law and the Minimum Wage Law," *Journal of Social Politics* 28(3): 387–412.

Jung, In-Young. 2005. "Social Assistance Reform in Post-economic Crisis Korea: The Policy-making Process of the National Basic Livelihood Security Act." Paper presented at the workshop "Transformation in East Asian Social Policy," University of Bath, January 13–15.

Kakwani, Nanak, Shahidur Khandker, and Hyun H. Son. 2003. "Poverty-Equivalent Growth Rate: with Applications to Korea and Thailand," mimeo, World Bank, Washington, DC.

Kang, Seungbok. 2005. "The Gap of Working Conditions between Standard and Nonstandard Workers" [in Korean], *Monthly Labor Review*, December.

Katzenstein, Peter. 1985. *Small States in World Markets: Industrial Policy in Europe.* Ithaca, NY: Cornell University Press.

Kaufman, Robert R. 1990. "How Societies Change Developmental Models or Keep Them: Reflections on the Latin American Experience in the 1930s and the Postwar World," in Gary Gereffi and Donal L. Wyman (eds.), *Manufacturing Miracles: Path of Industrialization in Latin America and East Asia.* Princeton, NJ: Princeton University Press, 110–38.

Kaufman, Robert R., and Joan M. Nelson. 2004. "Introduction: The Political Challenges of Social Sector Reform," in Robert R. Kaufman and Joan M. Nelson (eds.), *Crucial Needs, Weak Incentives: Social Sector Reform, Democratization, and Globalization in Latin America.* Washington, DC: Woodrow Wilson Center Press, 1–22.

Kaufman, Robert R., and Alex Segura-Ubiergo. 2001. "Globalization, Domestic Politics, and Social Spending in Latin America: A Time-series Cross-section Analysis, 1973–1997," *World Politics* 53(4): 553–87.

Kaur, Rupinder, and Sunil Kumar Maheshwari. 2005. "Labor Reforms: A Delicate Act of Balancing the Interests," Working Paper no. 2005–07–02, Indian Institute of Management, Ahmedabad.

Kay, Cristóbal. 2001. "Reflections on Rural Violence in Latin America," *Third World Quarterly* 22(5): 741–75.

Keohane, Robert O., and Helen Milner. 1996. *Internationalization and Domestic Politics*. Cambridge: Cambridge University Press.

Keohane, Robert O., and Joseph Nye. 2000. "Globalization: What's New? What's Not? (And So What?)," *Foreign Policy* **118**: 104–19.

Kerr, Clark. 1983. *The Future of Industrial Societies: Convergence or Continuing Diversity?* Cambridge, MA: Harvard University Press.

Kerr, Clark, John T. Dunlop, Frederick H. Harbison, and Charles A. Myers. 1964. *Industrialism and Industrial Man: The Problems of Labor and Management in Economic Growth*. New York: Oxford University Press.

Ketchen, David J., and Christopher L. Shook. 1996. "The Application of Cluster Analysis in Strategic Management Research: An Analysis and Critique," *Strategic Management Journal* **17**(6): 441–58.

Kiesling, Henry J. 1983. "Nineteenth-century Education According to West: A Comment," *Economic History Review* **36**(3): 416–25.

Kim, Dong-One, Johngseok Bae, and Changwon Lee. 2000. "Globalization and Labour Rights: The Case of Korea," *Asia Pacific Business Review* **6**(3/4): 133–53.

Kim, Dong-One, and Seongsu Kim. 2003. "Globalization, Financial Crisis, and Industrial Relations: The Case of South Korea," *Industrial Relations* **42**(3): 341–67.

Kim, Eun Mee. 1997. *Big Business, Strong State: Collusion and Conflict in South Korean Development, 1960–1990*. New York: SUNY Press.

Kim, Gwang-Jo. 2001. "Education Policies and Reform in South Korea," in World Bank (ed.), "Secondary Education in Africa: Strategies for Renewal," Africa Region Human Development Working Paper no. 25246, World Bank, Washington, DC, 29–39.

Kim, Jo-Seol. 2004. "Formation and Development of the Welfare State in the Republic of Korea: Process of Reform of the Public Assistance System," *Developing Economies* **42**(2): 146–75.

Kim, June Dong. 1994. "Incidence of Protection: The Case of Korea," *Economic Development and Cultural Change* **42**(3): 617–29.

Kim, Minah Kang. 2005. "Current Challenges in Delivering Social Security Health Insurance." Paper presented at the International Social Security Association's Meeting of Directors of Social Security Organizations in Asia and the Pacific, Seoul, November 9–11.

Kim, Soh-Young. 2004. "The Legal Regulation of Wrongful Dismissal in Korea," *Comparative Labor Law and Policy Journal* **25**(4): 535–60.

Kim, Su Ki. 2004. "Public and Private in South Korea's Education Reform Vocabulary: An Evolving Statist Culture of Education Policy," *International Education Journal* **5**(4): 521–30.

Kim, Sungteak, and Byung-You Cheon. 2004. "Labor Market Flexibility and Social Safety Net in Korea." Paper prepared for Asian Development Bank seminar on Dynamic and Sustainable Growth in Korea and Asia, Seoul, May 14.

Kim, Sunwoong, and Ju-Ho Lee. 2002. "Changing Facets of Korean Higher Education: Market Competition and the Role of the State." Paper prepared for presentation at the workshop "Upgrading Korean Education in the Age of

Knowledge Economy: Context and Issues," sponsored by the Korea Development Institute and the World Bank, Seoul, October 14–15.

Kim, Yeon-Myung. 2006. "Towards a Comprehensive Welfare State in South Korea," Asia Research Centre Working Paper no. 14, London School of Economics and Political Science, London.

Kitschelt, Herbert, Peter Lange, Gary Marks, and John D. Stephens. 1999. *Continuity and Change in Contemporary Capitalism*. Cambridge: Cambridge University Press.

Kitt, Brett. 2003. "Downsizing Korea? The Difficult Demise of Lifetime Employment and the Prospects for Further Reform," *Law and Policy in International Business* 34(2): 537–72.

Klein, Naomi. 2002. *No Logo*. New York: Harper Collins.

Knowles, Stephen, and P. Dorian Owen. 1995. "Health Capital and Cross Country Variation in Income Per Capita in the Mankiw–Romer–Weil Model," *Economic Letters* 48: 99–106.

Koo, Hagen. 1990. "From Farm to Factory: Proletarianization in Korea," *American Sociological Review* 55: 669–81.

——— 2000. "The Dilemmas of Empowered Labour in Korea: Korean Workers in the Face of Global Capitalism," *Asian Survey* 40: 227–50.

——— 2001. *Korean Workers: The Culture and Politics of Class Formation*. Ithaca, NY: Cornell University Press.

Korpi, Walter, and Joakim Palme. 1998. "The Paradox of Redistribution and Strategies of Equality: Welfare State Institutions, Inequality, and Poverty in the Western Countries," *American Sociological Review* 63(5): 661–87.

——— 2003. "New Politics and Class Politics in the Context of Austerity and Globalization: Welfare State Regress in 18 Countries, 1975–1995," *American Political Science Review* 97(3): 425–45.

Kurtz, Marcus. 2002. "Understanding the Third World Welfare State after Neoliberalism: The Politics of Social Provision in Chile and Mexico," *Comparative Politics* 34(3): 293–313.

Kuruvilla, Sarosh. 1996. "Linkages between Industrialization Strategies and Industrial Relation/Human Resource Policies: Singapore, Malaysia, the Philippines, and India," *Industrial and Labor Relations Review* 49(4): 635–57.

Kuznets, Simon. 1955. "Economic Growth and Income Inequality," *American Economic Review* 45: 1–28.

Kwon, Huck-Ju. 1999. "Inadequate Policy or Operational Failure? The Potential Crisis of the Korean National Pension Programme," *Social Policy and Administration* 33(1): 20–38.

——— 2001. "Income Transfers to the Elderly in Korea and Taiwan," *Journal of Political Science* 30(1): 81–93.

——— 2002. "Welfare Reform and Future Challenges in the Republic of Korea: Beyond the Developmental Welfare State?" *International Social Security Review* 55(4): 23–38.

Kwon, Soonman. 2003. "Pharmaceutical Reform and Physician Strikes in Korea: Separation of Drug Prescribing and Dispensing," *Social Science and Medicine* 57: 529–38.

Kwon, Soonman, and Ian Holliday. 2007. "The Korean Welfare State: A Paradox of Expansion in an Era of Globalisation and Economic Crisis," *International Journal of Social Welfare* **16** (3): 242–8.

Lambert, Francis. 1969. "Trends in Administrative Reform in Brazil," *Journal of Latin American Studies* **1**(2): 167–88.

Lansing, Paul, and Sarosh Kuruvilla. 1987. "Industrial Dispute Resolution in India: Theory and Practice," *Loyola of Los Angeles International and Comparative Law Journal* **9**(2): 345–75.

Lavinas, Lena, Maria Ligia Barbosa, Daniele Mañao, and Mariana Bittar. 2000. "Combating Poverty by Increasing School Attendance: The Case Study of Bolsa-Escola in Recife." Paper presented at conference organized by Human Development Department Latin America and Caribbean Regional Office of the World Bank, "Education and Poverty: Including the Excluded," Madrid, May 29–31.

Lee, Jisoon. 2002. "Education Policy in the Republic of Korea: Building Block or Stumbling Block?" Working Paper no. 37164, World Bank Institute, Washington, DC.

Lee, Jong-Chan. 2003. "Health Care Reform in South Korea: Success or Failure?" *American Journal of Public Health* **93**(1): 48–51.

Lee, Sunwoo, and Meegon Kim. 2003. "Poverty and Anti-poverty Measures in South Korea," in Kwong-Leung Tang and Chack-Kie Wong (eds.), *Poverty Monitoring and Alleviation in East Asia.* New York: Nova Science, chap. 5.

Lee, Won-Duck, and Byoung-Hoon Lee. 2003. "Korean Industrial Relations in the Era of Globlization," *Journal of Industrial Relations* **45**(4): 505–20.

Lee, Won-Duck, Jai-Joon Hur, and Hokyung Kim. 2001. "Assessing the Role of Korean Employment Insurance and Work Injury Insurance as a Social Safety Net." Paper prepared for the Korea Labor Institute International Symposium for Sharing Productive Welfare Experience, Seoul, September 6–7.

Lee, Yung Dug. 1974. *Educational Innovation in the Republic of Korea.* Paris: UNESCO Press.

Leff, Nathaniel. 1968. *Economic Policy-making and Development in Brazil, 1947–1964.* New York: John Wiley.

Levine, Ross. 1997. "Financial Development and Economic Growth: Views and Agenda," *Journal of Economic Literature* **35**(2): 688–726.

Lewbel, Arthur. 1997. "Constructing Instruments for Regressions with Measurement Error when no Additional Data Are Available, with an Application to Patents and R&D," *Econometrica* **65**(5): 1201–13.

Lewis, Jane. 1997. "Gender and Welfare States: Some Further Thoughts," *Social Politics* **4**(2): 160–77.

Lewis-Beck, Michael S., Alan Bryman, and Tim Futting Liao (eds.). 2004. *The Sage Encyclopedia of Social Science Research Methods,* vol. III. Thousand Oaks, CA: Sage.

Li, Quan. 2006. "Democracy, Autocracy, and Tax Incentives to Foreign Direct Investors: A Cross-national Analysis," *Journal of Politics* **68**(1): 62–74.

Lie, John. 1998. *Han Unbound: The Political Economy of South Korea.* Stanford, CA: Stanford University Press.

Lindauer, David. 1984. "Labor Market Behavior in the Republic of Korea: An Analysis of Wages and Their Impact on the Economy," Staff Working Paper no. 641, World Bank, Washington, DC.

Linehan, William J. 1980. "Political Instability and Economic Inequality: Some Conceptual Clarifications," *Journal of Peace Science* 4: 187–98.

Little, Ian M., Richard N. Cooper, W. Max Corden, and Sarath Rajapatirana. 1993. *Boom, Crisis, and Adjustment: The Macroeconomic Experience of Developing Countries.* Oxford: Oxford University Press.

Lloyd-Sherlock, P. 1998. "Inverted Targeting: Why Public Social Spending in Latin America Fails the Neediest," Working Paper no. 1998:14, Business School, University of Hertfordshire, Hatfield.

Lobato, Lenaura, and Luciene Burlandy. 2001. "The Context and Process of Health Care Reform in Brazil," in Sonia Fleury, Susana Belmartion, and Enis Baris (eds.), *Reshaping Health Care in Latin America.* Ottawa: IDRC Books, chap. 4.

Lok, Helen P. 1993. "Labour in the Garment Industry: An Employer's Perspective," in Chris Manning and Joan Hardjono (eds.), *Indonesia Assessment 1993.* Canberra: Australian National University Press, 155–72.

Lorr, Maurice. 1983. *Cluster Analysis for Social Scientists.* San Francisco: Jossey-Bass.

Lowi, Theodore. 1986. "The Welfare State: Ethical Foundations and Constitutional Remedies," *Political Science Quarterly* 101(2): 197–220.

Lukauskas, Arvid, and Susan Minushkin. 2000. "Explaining Styles of Financial Market Opening in Chile, Mexico, South Korea and Turkey," *International Studies Quarterly* 44: 695–723.

Madrid, Raul. 2002. "The Politics and Economics of Pension Privatization in Latin America," *Latin American Research Review* 37(2): 159–82.

Mahal, Ajay. 2003. "The Distribution of Public Health Subsidies in India," in Abdo Yazbeck and David H. Peters (eds.), *Health Policy Research in South Asia: Building Capacity for Reform.* Washington, DC: World Bank, 33–63.

Mahler, Vincent A., David K. Jesuit, and Douglas D. Roscoe. 1999. "Exploring the Impact of Trade and Investment on Income Inequality," *Comparative Political Studies* 32: 363–95.

Mahoney, James. 2000. "Path Dependence in Historical Sociology," *Theory and Society* 29(4): 507–48.

Malloy, James. 1979. *The Politics of Social Security in Brazil.* Pittsburgh: University of Pittsburgh Press.

——— 1993. "Statecraft, Social Policy, and Governance in Latin America," *Governance: An International Journal of Policy and Administration* 6: 220–74.

Manning, Chris. 1998. "Does Globalization Undermine Labor Standards? Lessons from East Asia," *Australian Journal of International Affairs* 52(2): 133–47.

Manor, James. 1996. "Ethnicity and Politics in India," *International Affairs* 72(3): 459–75.

Mares, Isabela. 2003a. *The Politics of Social Risk: Business and Welfare State Development.* New York: Cambridge University Press.

——— 2003b. "The Sources of Business Interest in Social Insurance: Sectoral versus National Differences," *World Politics* 55(2): 229–58.

2005. "Social Protection around the World: External Insecurity, State Capacity and Domestic Political Cleavages," *Comparative Political Studies* **38**(6): 623–51.

Marshall, T. H. 1950. *Citizenship and Social Class, and Other Essays*. Cambridge: Cambridge University Press.

Mathur, Ajeet. 1996. "The Experience of Consultation During Structural Adjustment in India (1990–92)," *International Labour Review* **132**(3): 331–45.

Matijascic, Milko, and Stephen J. Kay. 2006. "Social Security at the Crossroads: Toward Effective Pension Reform in Latin America," *International Social Security Review* **59**: 3–26.

Maxfield, Sylvia. 1998. "Understanding the Political Implications of Financial Internationalization in Emerging-market Countries," *World Development* **26**(7): 1201–19.

Mazumdar, Joy, and Myriam Quispe-Agnoli. 2002. "Trade and the Skill Premium in Developing Countries: The Role of Intermediate Goods and Some Evidence from Peru," Working Paper no. 2002–11, Federal Reserve Bank of Atlanta.

McGinn, Noel, Donald Snodgrass, Yung Bong Kim, Shi-Bok Kim, and Quee-Young Kim. 1980. *Education and Development in Korea*. Cambridge, MA: Harvard University Press.

McGuire, James. 1997. *Peronism without Peron*. Stanford, CA: Stanford University Press.

1999. "Labor Union Strength and Human Development in East Asia and Latin America," *Studies in Comparative International Development* **33**: 3–33.

2006. "Basic Health Care Provision and Under-5 Mortality: A Cross-national Study of Developing Countries," *World Development* **34**(3): 405–25.

McKeown, Bruce, and Dan Thomas. 1988. *Q Methodology*. Newbury Park, CA: Sage.

Medici, André Cezar. 2003. "Family Spending on Health in Brazil: Some Indirect Evidence of the Regressive Nature of Public Spending in Health," technical paper, Inter-American Development Bank, Washington, DC.

2004. "The Political Economy of Reform in Brazil's Civil Servant Pension Scheme," Technical Note on Pensions no. 002, Inter-American Development Bank, Washington, DC.

Mehmet, Ozay, and Akbar Tavakoli. 2003. "Does Foreign Direct Investment Cause a Race to the Bottom: Evidence from Four Asian Countries," *Journal of the Asia Pacific Economy* **8**(2): 133–56.

Melo, Marcus André. 2004. "Institutional Choice and the Diffusion of Policy Paradigms: Brazil and the Second Wave of Pension Reform," *International Political Science Review* **25**(3): 320–41.

Mesa-Lago, Carmelo (ed.). 1985. *The Crisis of Social Security and Health Care*. Pittsburgh: Center for Latin American Studies.

1991. "Latin America and the Caribbean," in Ehtisham Ahmad, Jean Dreze, and John Hills (eds.), *Social Security in Developing Countries*. Oxford: Oxford University Press, 356–94.

1994. *Changing Social Security in Latin America*. Boulder, CO: Lynne Rienner.

Midgley, James. 1984. *Social Security, Inequality and the Third World*. New York: John Wiley and Sons.

Milligan, G., and M. C. Cooper. 1985. "An Examination of Procedures for Determining the Number of Clusters in a Dataset," *Psychometrika* **50**: 159–79.

Milner, Helen. 1997. *Interests, Institutions and Information: Domestic Politics and International Relations*. Princeton, NJ: Princeton University Press.

Mingat, Alain, and Jee Peng Tan. 1992. *Education in Asia: A Comparative Study of Cost and Financing*. Washington, DC: World Bank.

1998. "The Mechanics of Progress in Education: Evidence from Cross Country Data," Policy Research Working Paper no. 2015, World Bank, Washington, DC.

Ministry of Finance. 2003. *Expenditure Budget 2003–2004*, vol. I. Delhi: Ministry of Finance. Available at http://indiabudget.nic.in/ub2003–04/eb/vol1.htm.

2004. *Indian Public Finance Statistics 2003–2004*. Delhi: Ministry of Finance.

2005. *Economic Survey 2004–2005*. Delhi: Ministry of Finance. Available at http://indiabudget.nic.in/es2004–05/chapt2005 (accessed July 27, 2005).

Ministry of Health and Family Welfare. 2002. *National Health Policy 2002*. Delhi: Ministry of Health and Family Welfare. Available at http://mohfw.nic.in/np2002.htm (accessed July 27, 2005).

Ministry of Human Resource Development. 2000. *Education for All: Year 2000 Assessment*. Delhi: Ministry of Human Resource Development. Available at www2.unesco.org/wef/countryreports/india/rapport_2_2_1.html (accessed August 3, 2005).

Ministry of Social Justice and Empowerment. 1999. *OASIS (Old Age Social and Income Security) Report 1999*. Delhi: Ministry of Social Justice and Empowerment.

Mishra, Ramesh. 1999. *Globalization and the Welfare State*. Cheltenham: Edward Elgar.

Mooij, Jos, and S. Mahendra Dev. 2002. "Social Sector Expenditures in the 1990s: Analysis of Central and State Budgets," *Economic and Political Weekly*, March 2.

2004. "Social Sector Priorities: An Analysis of Budgets and Expenditures in India in the 1990s," *Development Policy Review* **22**(1): 97–120.

Moon, Hyungpyo. 2002. "The Korean Pension System: Current State and Tasks Ahead." Paper presented at the OECD/International Network of Pension Regulators and Supervisors conference on Private Pensions in Asia, Seoul, October 24–5.

Moreira, Mauricio Mesquita. 2004. *Fear of China: Is There a Future for Manufacturing in Latin America?* Washington, DC: Inter-American Development Bank.

Morrish, Ivor. 1970. *Education Since 1800*. London: Allen & Unwin.

Mosley, Layna. 2003. *Global Capital and National Governments*. Cambridge: Cambridge University Press.

Mosley, Layna, and Saika Uno. 2007. "Racing to the Bottom or Climbing to the Top? Economic Globalization and Collective Labor Rights," *Comparative Political Studies* **40**(8): 923–48.

Muller, Edward N. 1988. "Democracy, Economic Development, and Income Inequality," *American Sociological Review* 53: 50–68.

Murillo, Maria Victoria. 2000. "From Populism to Neoliberalism: Labor Unions and Market Reforms in Latin America," *World Politics* 52(2): 135–74.

2001. *Labor Unions, Partisan Coalitions, and Market Reforms in Latin America.* New York: Cambridge University Press.

2002. "Political Bias in Policy Convergence: Privatization Choices in Latin America," *World Politics* 54(4): 462–93.

Musgrove, Philip. 1996. "Public and Private Roles in Health: Theory and Financing Patterns," Discussion Paper no. 339, World Bank, Washington, DC.

Nader, Ralph, ed. 1993. *The Case against "Free Trade": GATT, NAFTA, and the Globalization of Corporate Power.* San Francisco: North Atlantic Books.

Nam, Chang-Hee. 1995. "South Korea's Big Business Clientelism in Democratic Reform," *Asian Survey* 35(4): 357–66.

Nayar, Baldev Raj. 2001. *Globalization and Nationalism: The Changing Balance in India's Economic Policy, 1950–2000.* New Delhi: Sage.

Nayyar, Deepak. 1978. "Transnational Corporations and Manufactured Exports from Poor Countries," *Economic Journal* 88: 59–84.

Nelson, Joan M. 1989. "The Politics of Pro-poor Adjustment," in Joan M. Nelson (ed.), *Fragile Coalitions: The Politics of Economic Adjustment.* New Brunswick, NJ: Transaction Books, 95–113.

1999. *Reforming Health and Education: The World Bank, the IDB, and Complex Institutional Change.* Washington, DC: Johns Hopkins University Press.

2004. "The Politics of Health Sector Reform: Cross-national Comparisons," in Robert R. Kaufman and Joan M. Nelson (eds.), *Crucial Needs, Weak Incentives: Social Sector Reform, Democratization, and Globalization in Latin America.* Washington, DC: Woodrow Wilson Center Press, 23–64.

Nicholas, Stephen J., and Jacqueline M. Nicholas. 1992. "Male Literacy, 'Deskilling', and the Industrial Revolution," *Journal of Interdisciplinary History* 23(1): 1–18.

Nielsen, Francois, and Arthur S. Alderson. 1995. "Income Inequality, Development and Dualism: Results from an Unbalanced Cross-national Panel," *American Sociological Review* 60: 674–701.

nodong jaryo [Labor Data]. 2005. "bijonggyujik goyong siltae" [The State of Non-standard Employment]. *wolgahn nodong* [Monthly Labor].

Nogami, Takehisa. 1999. "The Relevance of the East Asian Experience to Ethiopia," *Economic Focus* 2(1). Available at: www.eeaecon.org/pubs-focus-vol2no1.htm.

North, Douglass. 1990. *Institutions, Institutional Change and Economic Performance.* Cambridge: Cambridge University Press.

OECD. 2000. *Pushing Ahead with Reform in Korea: Labour Market and Social Safety-net Policies.* Paris: Organisation for Economic Co-operation and Development.

2004. "SHA-based Health Accounts in Thirteen OECD Countries Country Studies: Korea," Health Technical Paper no. 7, Organisation for Economic Co-operation and Development, Paris.

2005. *Pensions at a Glance: Public Policies across OECD Countries*. Paris: Organisation for Economic Co-operation and Development.

Offe, Clause, and Helmut Wiesenthal. 1985. "Two Logics of Collective Actions," in John Keane (ed.), *Disorganized Capitalism*. Cambridge, MA: MIT Press, 170–220.

Ohmae, Kenichi. 1995. *The End of the Nation-state*. New York: Simon & Shuster.

Olson, Mancur. 1971. *Logic of Collective Action*. Cambridge, MA: Harvard University Press.

Otsubo, Shigeru. 1996. "Globalization: A New Role for Developing Countries in an Integrating World," Policy Research Working Paper no. 1628. World Bank, Washington, DC.

Palacios, Robert, and Edward Whitehouse. 2006. "Civil-service Pension Schemes around the World," Social Protection Discussion Paper no. 602, World Bank, Washington, DC.

Palley, Howard. 1992. "Social Policy and the Elderly in South Korea," *Asian Survey* 32(9): 787–801.

Pandit, Kavita, and Emilio Casetti. 1989. "The Shifting Patterns of Sectoral Labor Allocation during Development: Developed versus Developing Countries," *Annals of the Association of American Geographers* 79(3): 329–44.

Panel on Discriminant Analysis, Classification, and Clustering. 1989. "Discriminant Analysis and Clustering," *Statistical Science* 4(1): 34–69.

Papola, T. S. 1994. "Structural Adjustment, Labor Market Flexibility and Employment," *Indian Journal of Labor Economics* 37(1): 3–16.

Park, Bae-Gyoon. 1998. "Where Do Tigers Sleep at Night? The State's Role in Housing Policy in South Korea and Singapore," *Economic Geography* 74(3): 272–88.

Park, Chung Hee. 1962. *Our Nation's Path: Ideology of Social Reconstruction*. Seoul: Hollym.

1963. *The Country, the Revolution and I*. Seoul: Hollym.

Park, Jong-Chan. 1998. *On the Educational Budget* [in Korean]. Seoul: Center for Free Enterprise.

Park, Moonkyu. 1987. "Interest Representation in South Korea," *Asian Survey* 27 (8): 903–17.

Park, Se-Il. 2000. "Reforming Labor Management Relations: Lessons from the Korean Experience: 1996–97," Policy Study no. 2000–02, Korea Development Institute, Seoul.

Peabody, John, Sung-Woo Lee, and Stephen Bickel. 1995. "Health for All in the Republic of Korea: One Country's Experience with Implementing Universal Health Care," *Health Policy* 31: 29–42.

Phang, Hanam and Keechul Shin. 2002. "A Reform Proposal for Korean Pension System: Coordinated Development of the Public–Private Pensions." Paper presented at the OECD/INPRS/KOREA Conference on Private Pensions in Asia, Seoul, October 24–5.

Phillips, David. 1993. "Dolphins and GATT," in Ralph Nader (ed.), *The Case against "Free Trade": GATT, NAFTA, and the Globalization of Corporate Power*. San Francisco: North Atlantic Books, 133–8.

Pierson, Paul. 1994. *Dismantling the Welfare State: Reagan, Thatcher and the Politics of Retrenchment*. Cambridge: Cambridge University Press.
1996. "The New Politics of the Welfare State," *World Politics* 48(2): 143–79.
2000. "Three Worlds of Welfare State Research," *Comparative Political Studies* 33(6/7): 791–821.
2001. "Post-industrial Pressures on the Mature Welfare States," in Paul Pierson (ed.), *The New Politics of the Welfare State*. Oxford: Oxford University Press, 80–106.
Pinheiro, Vinicius C. 2005. "The Politics of Pension Reform in Brazil," in Carolin A. Crabbe (ed.), *A Quarter Century of Pension Reform in Latin America and the Caribbean: Lessons Learned and Next Steps*. Washington, DC: Inter-American Development Bank, 187–216.
Pitruzzello, Salvatore. 2004. "Trade Globalization, Economic Performance, and Social Protection: Nineteenth-century British Laissez-faire and Post-World War II US-embedded Liberalism," *International Organization*, 58(4): 705–44.
Plank, David N. 1996. *The Means of Our Salvation: Public Education in Brazil, 1930–1995*. Boulder, CO: Westview Press.
Polanyi, Karl. 1944. *The Great Transformation*. New York: Farrar and Rinehart.
Porter, Gareth. 1999. "Trade Competition and Pollution Standards: 'Race to the Bottom' or 'Stuck at the Bottom'?" *Journal of Environment and Development* 8(2): 133–51.
Portes, Alejandro, and Kelly Hoffman. 2003. "Latin American Class Structures: Their Composition and Change during the Neoliberal Era," *Latin American Research Review* 38(1): 41–82.
Portes, Alejandro, and Richard Schauffler. 1993. "Competing Perspectives on the Latin American Informal Sector," *Population and Development Review* 19(1): 33–60.
Program on International Policy Attitudes. 2006. "20 Nation Poll Finds Strong Global Consensus: Support for Free Market System, but also More Regulation of Large Companies." Available online at: www.worldpublicopinion.org/pipa/articles/btglobalizationtradera/154.php?nid=&id=&pnt=154&lb=btgl; questionnaire available at: http://65.109.167.118/pipa/pdf/jan06/FreeMarkets_Jan06_quaire.pdf.
Purohit, Brijesh. 2001. "Private Initiatives and Policy Options: Recent Health System Experience in India," *Health Policy and Planning* 16(1): 87–97.
Quinn, Dennis. 1997. "The Correlates of Change in International Financial Regulation," *American Political Science Review* 91(3): 531–51.
Radelet, Steven, and Jeffry Sachs. 1999. "What Have We Learned, So Far, from the Asian Financial Crisis?" Consulting Assistance on Economic Reform Discussion Paper no. 37, Harvard Institute for International Development, Harvard University, Cambridge, MA.
Radhakrishna, R., and Kalanidhi Subbarao. 1997. "India's Public Distribution System: A National and International Perspective," Discussion Paper no. 380, World Bank, Washington, DC.
Rama, Martín, and Raquel Artecona. 2002. "A Database of Labor Market Indicators across Countries," unpublished manuscript, World Bank, Washington, DC.

Ramesh, Bhat, and Jain Nishant. 2004. "Analysis of Public Expenditure on Health Using State Level Data," Working Paper no. 2004-06-08, India Institute of Management, Ahmedabad.

Ramesh, M. 2004. *Social Policy in East and Southeast Asia*. London: RoutledgeCurzon.

Rao, Govinda, and Nirvikar Singh. 2005. *Political Economy of Federalism in India*. New Delhi: Oxford University Press.

Rao, J. Mohan. 2001. "Globalization and the Fiscal Autonomy of the State," Political Economy Research Institute Working Paper no. 25, University of Massachusetts, Amherst.

Ratnam, Venkata C. S. 1996. "Tripartism and Structural Changes: The Case of India," *Indian Journal of Industrial Relations* 31(3): 346–78.

Ravallion, Martin. 1991. "Reaching the Rural Poor through Public Employment: Arguments, Evidence, and Lessons from South Asia," *World Bank Research Observer* 6(2): 153–75.

Rawlings, Laura, and Gloria M. Rubio. 2005. "Evaluating the Impact of Conditional Cash Transfer Programmes," *World Bank Research Observer* 20 (1): 29–55.

Remmer, Karen. 2002. "The Politics of Economic Policy and Performance in Latin America," *Journal of Public Policy* 22(1): 29–59.

Renaud, Bertrand. 1984. *Housing and Financial Institutions in Developing Countries*. Washington, DC: International Bank for Reconstruction and Development, World Bank.

Richards, David L., and David H. Sacko. 2001. "Money with a Mean Streak? Foreign Economic Penetration and Government Respect for Human Rights in Developing Countries," *International Studies Quarterly* 45(2): 219–39.

Rieger, Elmar, and Stephan Leibfried. 1998. "Welfare State Limits to Globalization," *Politics and Society* 26: 363–90.

Rivera, Berta, and Luis Currais. 1999. "Economic Growth and Health: Direct Impact or Reverse Causation?" *Applied Economics Letters* 6: 761–4.

Robbins, Donald J. 1996. "HOS Hits Facts: Facts Win; Evidence on Trade and Wages in the Developing World," Development Discussion Paper no. 557, Harvard Institute for International Development, Harvard University, Cambridge, MA.

Robertson, Graeme. 2004. "Leading Labor: Unions, Politics and Protest in New Democracies," *Comparative Politics* 36(3): 253–73.

Rodrik, Dani. 1996. "Labor Standards in International Trade: Do They Matter and What Do We Do about Them?" in Robert Z. Lawrence, Dani Rodrik, and John Whalley (eds.), *Emerging Agenda for Trade: High Stakes for Developing Countries*. Washington, DC: Overseas Development Council, 35–80.

1997a. *Has Globalization Gone Too Far?* Washington, DC: Institute for International Economics.

1997b. "Sense and Nonsense in the Globalization Debate," *Foreign Policy* 107: 19–37.

1997c. "What Drives Public Unemployment?" Working Paper no. 6141, National Bureau of Economic Research, Cambridge, MA.

1998. "Why Do More Open Economies Have Bigger Governments?" *Journal of Political Economy* **106**(5): 997–1033.

Rodrik, Dani, and Francisco Rodriguez. 2000. "Trade Policy and Economic Growth: A Skeptic's Guide to the Cross-national Evidence," in Ben Bernanke and Kenneth Rogoff (eds.), *NBER Macroeconomics Annual*, Cambridge, MA: MIT Press, 261–338.

Rogowski, Ronald. 1989. *Commerce and Coalitions*. Princeton, NJ: Princeton University Press.

Room, Graham. 2000. "Commodification and Decommodification: A Developmental Critique," *Policy and Politics* **28**(3): 331–51.

Ross, Robert S. 2004. *Slaves to Fashion*. Ann Arbor: University of Michigan Press.

Roychowdhury, Supriya. 2003. "Public Sector, Restructuring and Democracy: The State, Labour and Trade Unions in India," *Journal of Development Studies* **39**(3): 29–50.

Rudolph, Lloyd I., and Susanne Hoeber Rudolph. 1987. *In Pursuit of Lakshmi: The Political Economy of the Indian State*. Chicago: University of Chicago Press.

Rudra, Nita. 2002. "Globalization and the Decline of the Welfare State in Less Developed Countries," *International Organization* **56**(2): 411–45.

2005. "Are Workers Winners or Losers in the Current Era of Globalization?" *Studies in Comparative International Development* **40**(3): 29–64.

Rudra, Nita, and Stephen Haggard. 2005. "Globalization, Democracy, and 'Effective' Welfare Spending in the Developing World," *Comparative Political Studies* **38**(9): 1015–49.

Rueschemeyer, Dietrich, Evelyne H. Stephens, and John D. Stephens. 1992. *Capitalist Development and Democracy*. Chicago: University of Chicago Press.

Ruggie, John G. 1982. "International Regimes, Transactions and Change: Embedded Liberalism in Postwar Economic Order," *International Organization* **36**(2): 379–415.

1994. "At Home Abroad, Abroad at Home: International Liberalization and Domestic Stability in the New World Economy," *Millennium: Journal of International Studies* **24**(3): 507–26.

Sachs, Jeffrey, and Andrew Warner. 1995. "Economic Reform and the Process of Global Integration," *Brookings Papers on Economic Activity* **1**: 1–118.

Sakamoto, Yoshikazu. 1994. "A Perspective on the Changing World Order: A Conceptual Prelude," in Yoshikazu Sakamoto (ed.), *Global Transformation: Challenges to the State System*. New York: United Nations University Press, 15–54.

Sala-i-Martin, Xavier. 2002. "The World Distribution of Income," Working Paper no. 8933, National Bureau of Economic Research, Cambridge, MA.

Sanderson, Michael. 1972. "Literacy and Social Mobility in the Industrial Revolution in England," *Past and Present* **56**: 75–104.

Sankar, Deepa, and Vanish Kathuria. 2003. "Health Sector in 2003–4 Budget," *Economic and Political Weekly* 38(15): 1443–6.

Sarangi, Prakash. 2005. "Economic Reforms and Changes in the Party System," in Jos Mooij (ed.), *The Politics of Economic Reforms in India*. New Delhi: Sage, 71–97.

Scharfe, Hartmut. 2002. *Education in Ancient India*. Boston: Brill.

Scheve, Soroka, and Matthew J. Slaughter. 2006. "Public Opinion, International Economic Integration, and the Welfare State," in Parnab Bardhan, Samuel Bowles, and Michael Wallerstein (eds.), *Globalization and Egalitarian Redistribution*. New York: Russell Sage Foundation, 217–60.

Schmidt, Sonke. 1995. "Social Security in Developing Countries: Basic Tenets and Fields of State Intervention," *International Social Work* 38: 7–26.

Schmitter, Philippe C. 1974. "Still the Century of Corporatism?" in Frederick Pike and Thomas Stritch (eds.), *The New Corporatism: Social Political Structures in the Iberian World*. Notre Dame, IN: University of Notre Dame Press.

Schneider, Aaron. 2004. "Wholesale versus Within Institution Change: Pacting Governance Reform in Brazil for Fiscal Responsibility and Tax," research paper, World Bank, Washington, DC.

Schneider, Friedrich, and Dominik H. Enste. 2002. *The Shadow Economy*. Cambridge: Cambridge University Press.

Scholte, Jan A. 1997. "Global Capitalism and the State," *International Affairs* 73: 427–53.

Schwartz, Herman. 1998. "Social Democracy Going Down or Down Under," *Comparative Politics* 30(3): 253–72.

Schwartzman, Simon. 2005. "Education-oriented Social Programs in Brazil: The Impact of Bolsa Escola." Paper submitted to the Global Development Network conference on Education Research in Developing Countries (Research for Results on Education), Prague, March 31–April 2.

Sen Gupta, Anil K., and P. K. Sett. 2000. "Industrial Relations Law, Employment Security, and Collective Bargaining in India: Myths, Realities and Hopes," *Industrial Relations Journal* 31(2): 144–53.

Seth, Michael. 2002. *Education Fever: Society, Politics and the Pursuit of Schooling in South Korea*. Honolulu: University of Hawaii Press.

Shafer, D. Michael. 1994. *Winners and Losers*. Ithaca, NY: Cornell University Press.

Shariff, A., and P. K. Ghosh. 2000. "Indian Education Scene and the Public Gap," *Economic and Political Weekly* 35(16): 1396–406.

Sheahan, John, and Enrique V. Iglesias. 1998. "Kinds and Causes of Inequality in Latin America," in Nancy Birdsal, Carol Graham, and Richard Sabot (eds.), *Beyond Tradeoffs*. Washington, DC: Brookings Institution Press, 29–61.

Sheehey, Edmund J. 1996. "The Growing Gap between Rich and Poor Countries: A Proposed Explanation," *World Development* 24: 1379–84.

Shiva, Vandana. 2005. *Earth Democracy*. Cambridge, MA: South End Press.

Silver, Beverly. 2003. *Forces of Labor: Worker's Movements and Globalization since 1870*. New York: Cambridge University Press.

Simpson, Miles. 1990. "Political Rights and Income Inequality: A Cross-national Test," *American Sociological Review* **55**: 682–93.

Singh, Ajit, and Ann Zammit. 2004. "Labour Standards and the 'Race to the Bottom': Rethinking Globalization and Workers' Rights from Developmental and Solidaristic Perspectives," *Oxford Review of Economic Policy* **20**(1): 85–104.

Sinha, Pravin. 1994. "Unions in a Period of Transition," in C. S. Benkata Ratnam, Gerd Botterweck, and Pravin Sinha (eds.), *Labour and Unions in a Period of Transition*. New Delhi: Friedrich Ebert Stiftung.

——— 2004. "Representing Labour in India," *Development in Practice* **14**(1/2): 127–35.

Sivam, Alpana, and Sadasivam Karuppannan. 2002. "Role of State and Market in Housing Delivery for Low-income Groups in India," *Journal of Housing and the Built Environment* **17**: 69–88.

Skidmore, Thomas. 1967. *Politics in Brazil, 1930–1964*. New York: Oxford University Press.

Sohn, Mi Ah, Sang-Baek Koh, Yun-Ja Kang, Eun-Sook Lee, Jung-Ok Kong, Jung-Soo Kim, Han-Soo Song, Jae-Young Moon, Ji-Youn Sun, Hye-Yun Jo, Hyun-Me Kim, Jang-Won Sun, Jong-Hyuk Jung, Gil-Joo Moon, and Wook Jun. 2004. *A Survey Report on the Working and Health Conditions of Nonstandard Workers*. Seoul: National Human Rights Commission of Korea. Available at http://edu.humanrights.go.kr/know/product/46_T20051115_07.pdf.

Song, Ho-Keun. 1999. "Labour Unions in the Republic of Korea: Challenge and Choice," Labour and Society Programme, Discussion Paper no. 107/199, International Labour Organization, Geneva.

Sorenson, Clark. 1994. "Success and Education in South Korea," *Comparative Education Review* **38**(1): 10–35.

Souza, Amaury. 1999. "Cardoso and the Struggle for Reform in Brazil," *Journal of Democracy* **10**(3): 49–63.

Srinivisan, T. N. 1985. "Neoclassical Political Economy, the State and Economic Development," *Asian Development Review* **3**(2): 38–58.

Stone, Lawrence. 1969. "Literacy and Education in England 1640–1900," *Past and Present* **42**: 69–139.

Strange, Susan. 1997. "Erosion of the State," *Current History* **96**: 365–9.

Stryker, Robin. 1998. "Globalization and the Welfare State," *International Journal of Sociology and Social Policy* **18**(2–4): 1–49.

Subbarao, Kalanidhi. 1997. "Public Works as an Anti-poverty Program: An Overview of Cross-country Experience," *American Journal of Agricultural Economics* **79**(2): 678–83.

Sung, Eun Mee. 2006. "Social Insurance Enrollment of Nonstandard Workers: Conditions, Problems, and Policy Options," *Hungjang eso miraerul* 116. Available at http://kilsp.jinbo.net/maynews/readview.php?table=organ&item=&no=221.

Swank, Duane. 1998. "Funding the Welfare State: Globalization and the Taxation of Business in Advanced Market Economies," *Political Studies* **46**: 671–92.

——— 2001. "Political Institutions and Welfare State Restructuring: The Impact of Institutions on Social Policy Change in Developed Democracies," in Paul

Pierson (ed.), *The New Politics of the Welfare State*. Oxford: Oxford University Press, 197–237.

Swensen, Peter. 2002. *Capitalists against Markets: The Making of Labor Markets and Welfare States in the United States and Sweden*. New York: Oxford University Press.

Tang, Kwong-Leung. 1996. "The Determinants of Social Security in Developing Countries: A Comparative Analysis," *International Social Work* **39**: 377–93.

Tata Services (2002). "Statistical Outline of India 2001–2," Tata Services, Mumbai.

Tendler, Judith. 2002. "The Fear of Education." Background paper presented at the fiftieth anniversary meeting of the Banco do Nordeste, Fostaleza, Brazil, July 19.

———. 2003. "The Fear of Education." Background paper for the World Bank 2003 report on *Inequality and the State in Latin America*.

Thelen, Kathleen. 1999. "Historical Institutionalism in Comparative Politics," *Annual Review of Political Science* **2**: 369–404.

———. 2004. *How Institutions Evolve: The Political Economy of Skills in Germany, Britain, the United States, and Japan*. Cambridge: Cambridge University Press.

Thomas, Dominic M., and Richard Watson. 2002. "Q-sorting and MIS Research: A Primer," *Communications of the Association for Information Systems* **8**: 141–56.

Thompson, Henry. 1995. "Free Trade and Income Redistribution in Some Developing Countries and NICs," *Open Economies Review* **6**: 265–80.

Tidmore, F. Eugene, and Danny W. Turner. 1983. "On Clustering with Chernoff-type Faces," *Communications in Statistics A* **12**: 381–96.

Tilak, Jandhyala B. G. 1990. *The Political Economy of Education in India*. Buffalo: SUNY Press.

———. 1999. "Emerging Trends and Evolving Public Policies in India," in Philip G. Altbach (ed.), *Private Prometheus: Private Higher Education and Development in the 21st Century*. Westport, CT: Greenwood Press.

———. 2001. "Building Human Capital in East Asia: What Others Can Learn," Working Paper no. 37166, World Bank, Washington, DC.

Titmuss, Richard. 1965. *Social Policy*. New York: Pantheon Books.

Tornell, Aaron, Frank Westermann, and Lorenza Martinez. 2004. "The Positive Link between Financial Liberalization, Growth, and Crises," Working Paper no. 10293, National Bureau of Economic Research, Cambridge, MA.

UN. 2005. Sixtieth Session of the General Assembly. Implementation of the first United Nations Decade for the Eradication of Poverty (1997–2006). Report of the Secretary General. August 30. Available online at http://daccessdds.un.org/doc/UNDOC/GEN/N05/476/33/PDF/N0547633.pdf?OpenElement.

UNDP. 2002. *Human Development Report 2002: Deepening Democracy in a Fragmented World*. New York: Oxford University Press.

———. 2004. *Human Development Report 2004: Cultural Liberty in Today's Diverse World*. New York: Oxford University Press.

———. 2005. *Human Development Report 2005: International Cooperation at a Crossroads: Aid, Trade and Security in an Unequal World*. New York: Oxford University Press.

UNESCO. 2005. *EFA Global Monitoring Report 2006: Literacy for Life*. Paris: UNESCO. Available online at http://portal.unesco.org/education/en/ev.php-URL_ID=43009&URL_DO=DO_TOPIC&URL_SECTION=201.html.

UNIDO. 1992. *UN Industry and Development Report 1992/3*. Vienna: United Nations Industrial Development Organization.

US Department of Labor. 2003. *Foreign Labor Trends: Korea*. Washington, DC: Government Printing Office.

Usui, Chikako. 1994. "Welfare State Development in a World System Context: Event History Analysis of First Historical Social Insurance Legislation among 60 Countries, 1880–1960," in Thomas Janoski and Alexander Hicks (eds.), *The Comparative Political Economy of the Welfare State*. New York: Cambridge University Press, 254–77.

Valenca, Marcio. 1992. "The Inevitable Crisis of the Brazilian Housing Finance System," *Urban Studies* **29**(1): 39–56.

Valenzuela, J. Samuel. 1989. "Labor Movements in Transitions to Democracy," *Comparative Politics* **21**(4): 445–72.

Vanhanen, Tatu. 1997. *Prospects of Democracy: A Study of 172 Countries*. New York: Routledge.

Varshney, Ashutosh. 2002. *Ethnic Conflict and Civic Life: Hindus and Muslims in India*. New Haven, CT: Yale University Press.

Vause, W. Gary, and Dulcina de Holanda Palhano. 1995. "Labor Law in Brazil and the United States: Statism and Classical Liberalism Compared," *Colombia Journal of Transnational Law* **33**(3): 583–635.

Wade, Robert. 1990. *Governing the Market*. Princeton, NJ: Princeton University Press.

Wahl, Ana-Maria. 1994. "Economic Development and Social Security in Mexico, 1845–1985: A Time-series Analysis," *International Journal of Contemporary Sociology* **35**: 59–81.

Ward, Joe H., Jr. 1963. "Hierarchical Grouping to Optimize an Objective Function," *Journal of the American Statistical Association* **58**: 236–44.

Waterbury, John. 1999. "The Long Gestation and Brief Triumph of Import-substituting Industrialization," *World Development* **27**(2): 323–41.

Weede, Erich. 1982. "The Effects of Democracy and Socialist Strength on the Size Distribution of Income," *International Journal of Comparative Sociology* **23**: 151–65.

Weede, Erich, and Horst Tiefenbach. 1981. "Some Recent Explanations of Income Inequality," *International Studies Quarterly* **25**: 255–82.

Weiner, Myron. 1986. "The Political Economy of Industrial Growth in India," *World Politics* **38**(4): 596–610.

1991. *The Child and the State in India*. Princeton, NJ: Princeton University Press.

Weiss, Linda. 2003. "Introduction," in Linda Weiss (ed.), *States in the Global Economy: Bringing Domestic Institutions Back In*. Cambridge: Cambridge University Press, 1–36.

Western, Bruce. 1999. *Between Class and Market: Postwar Unionization in the Capitalist Democracies*. Princeton, NJ: Princeton University Press.

Weyland, Kurt. 1995. "Social Movements and the State: the Politics of Health Reform in Brazil," *World Development* 23: 1699–712.

1996a. *Democracy without Equity: Failures of Reform in Brazil*. Pittsburgh: University of Pittsburgh Press.

1996b. "Obstacles to Social Reform in Brazil," *Comparative Politics* 29: 1–22.

White, Gordon, and Roger Goodman. 1998. "Welfare Orientalism and the Search for an East Asian Welfare Model," in Roger Goodman, Gordon White, and Huck-Ju Kwon (eds.), *East Asian Welfare State: Welfare Orientalism and the State*. London: Routledge, 3–24.

Wibbels, Erik. 2006. "Dependency Revisited: International Markets, Business Cycles, and Social Spending in the Developing World," *International Organization* 60(2): 433–68.

Wibbels, Erik, and Moises Arce. 2003. "Globalization, Taxation, and Burden-shifting in Latin America," *International Organization* 57(1): 111–36.

Wilensky, Harold L. 1975. *The Welfare State and Equality: Structural and Ideological Roots of Public Expenditure*. Berkeley: University of California Press.

Wong, Joseph. 2004. *Healthy Democracies: Welfare Politics in Taiwan and South Korea*. Ithaca, NY: Cornell University Press.

Wood, Adrian. 1994. *North–South Trade, Employment, and Inequality*. New York: Oxford University Press.

1995. "How Trade Hurt Unskilled Workers," *Journal of Economic Perspectives* 9 (3): 57–80.

1997. "Openness and Wage Inequality in Developing Countries: The Latin American Challenge to East Asian Conventional Wisdom," *World Bank Economic Review* 11(1): 33–57.

Wood, Adrian, and Cristóbal Ridao-Cano. 1996. "Skill, Trade and International Inequality," Institute of Development Studies Working Paper no. 47, University of Sussex, Brighton.

World Bank 1979. *World Development Report 1979*. Washington, DC: World Bank.

1990. *World Development Report 1990*. New York: Oxford University Press.

1994. *Averting the Old Age Crisis*. New York: Oxford University Press.

1999a. "Health Care in India: Learning from Experience," Operations Evaluation Department Report no. 187, World Bank, Washington, DC.

1999b. *World Development Report 1999/2000: Entering the 21st Century*. New York: Oxford University Press.

2000a. *Reforming Public Institutions and Strengthening Governance*. Washington, DC: World Bank.

2000b. *World Development Report 2000/2001: Attacking Poverty*. Washington, DC: World Bank.

2001a. "Critical Issues in Social Security," World Bank Country Study no. 22513, International Bank for Reconstruction and Development, Washington, DC.

2001b. *World Development Report 2002: Building Institutions for Markets*. New York: Oxford University Press.

2002a. "Brazil Municipal Education: Resources, Incentives, and Results," World Bank, Washington, DC.

2002b. *World Development Indicators 2002*. Washington, DC: World Bank.

2002b. *World Development Report 2003: Sustainable Development in a Dynamic World*. Washington, DC: World Bank.

2003a. Press Release no. 2003/038/S. World Bank, Washington, DC.

2003b. *World Development Report 2004: Making Services Work for Poor People*. Washington, DC: World Bank.

2005a. "Brazil: World Bank Approves US$658.3 Million for Fiscal and Social Security Reforms," News Release no. 2005/496/LAC, World Bank, Washington, DC.

2005b. *World Development Indicators 2005*. Washington, DC: World Bank.

Wu, Kin Bing, Venita Kaul, and Deepa Sankar. 2005. "The Quiet Revolution," *Finance and Development* **42**: 2.

Yang, Bong-Min. 2001a. "The National Pension Scheme of the Republic of Korea," Working Paper no. 37162, World Bank Institute, Washington, DC.

2001b. "Health Insurance and the Growth of the Private Health Sector in the Republic of Korea," Working Paper no. 37163, World Bank Institute, Washington, DC.

Yang, Jae-Jin. 2000. "The 1999 Pension Reform and a New Social Contract in South Korea," PhD dissertation, Rutgers University, Newark, NJ.

2004. "Democratic Governance and Bureaucratic Politics: A Case of Pension Reform in Korea," *Policy and Politics* **32**(2): 193–206.

2006. "Corporate Unionism and Labor Market Flexibility in South Korea," *Journal of East Asian Studies* **6**(2): 205–31.

Yang, Yung, and Min Hwang. 2001. "The Pricing Behavior of Korean Manufactured Goods during Trade Liberalization," *Journal of Policy Modeling* **23**: 357–69.

Yap, Fiona O. 2003. "Non-electoral Responsiveness Mechanisms: Lessons from the Asian Less-democratic Newly Industrializing Countries," *British Journal of Political Science* **33**: 491–514.

You, Jong-Il, and Ju-Ho Lee. 2000. "Economic and Social Consequences of Globalization: The Case of South Korea," Center for Economic Policy Analysis Working Paper no. 17, New School University, New York.

Young, Ken. 2004. "Review of *Labour, Politics, and the State in Industrializing Thailand*," *Journal of Contemporary Asia* **34**(4): 551–2.

Yusuf, Shahid. 1999. "The Changing Development Landscape," *Finance and Development* **36**(4): 15–18.

Zodrow, George R. 2003. "Competition and Tax Coordination in the European Union," *International Tax and Public Finance* **10**(6): 651–71.

Index